CONSTITUTIONAL LAW
IN CRIMINAL JUSTICE

CONSTITUTIONAL LAW IN CRIMINAL JUSTICE

Tina M. Fielding Fryling
Mercyhurst University

Wolters Kluwer
Law & Business

Published by Wolters Kluwer Law & Business in New York.

Wolters Kluwer Law & Business serves customers worldwide with CCH, Aspen Publishers, and Kluwer Law International products. (www.wolterskluwerlb.com)

To contact Customer Service, e-mail customer.service@wolterskluwer.com, call 1-800-234-1660, fax 1-800-901-9075, or mail correspondence to:

Wolters Kluwer Law & Business
Attn: Order Department
PO Box 990
Frederick, MD 21705

Printed in the United States of America.

1 2 3 4 5 6 7 8 9 0

ISBN 978-1-4548-0304-1

Library of Congress Cataloging-in-Publication Data

Fryling, Tina M. Fielding, author.
    Constitutional law in criminal justice / Tina M. Fielding Fryling.
        pages cm
    Includes bibliographical references and index.
    ISBN 978-1-4548-0304-1 (alk. paper)
    1. Criminal procedure—United States. 2. Civil rights—United States. I. Title.
KF9619.85.F79 2014
345.73'05—dc23

2013048358

About Wolters Kluwer Law & Business

Wolters Kluwer Law & Business is a leading global provider of intelligent information and digital solutions for legal and business professionals in key specialty areas, and respected educational resources for professors and law students. Wolters Kluwer Law & Business connects legal and business professionals as well as those in the education market with timely, specialized authoritative content and information-enabled solutions to support success through productivity, accuracy and mobility.

Serving customers worldwide, Wolters Kluwer Law & Business products include those under the Aspen Publishers, CCH, Kluwer Law International, Loislaw, ftwilliam.com and MediRegs family of products.

CCH products have been a trusted resource since 1913, and are highly regarded resources for legal, securities, antitrust and trade regulation, government contracting, banking, pension, payroll, employment and labor, and healthcare reimbursement and compliance professionals.

Aspen Publishers products provide essential information to attorneys, business professionals and law students. Written by preeminent authorities, the product line offers analytical and practical information in a range of specialty practice areas from securities law and intellectual property to mergers and acquisitions and pension/benefits. Aspen's trusted legal education resources provide professors and students with high-quality, up-to-date and effective resources for successful instruction and study in all areas of the law.

Kluwer Law International products provide the global business community with reliable international legal information in English. Legal practitioners, corporate counsel and business executives around the world rely on Kluwer Law journals, looseleafs, books, and electronic products for comprehensive information in many areas of international legal practice.

Loislaw is a comprehensive online legal research product providing legal content to law firm practitioners of various specializations. Loislaw provides attorneys with the ability to quickly and efficiently find the necessary legal information they need, when and where they need it, by facilitating access to primary law as well as state-specific law, records, forms and treatises.

ftwilliam.com offers employee benefits professionals the highest quality plan documents (retirement, welfare and non-qualified) and government forms (5500/PBGC, 1099 and IRS) software at highly competitive prices.

MediRegs products provide integrated health care compliance content and software solutions for professionals in healthcare, higher education and life sciences, including professionals in accounting, law and consulting.

Wolters Kluwer Law & Business, a division of Wolters Kluwer, is headquartered in New York. Wolters Kluwer is a market-leading global information services company focused on professionals.

To Grace, Madeline, Madison, and Mason

SUMMARY OF CONTENTS

CONTENTS

2 THE FOURTH AMENDMENT: THE BASICS OF SEARCH AND SEIZURE   47

3 SEARCHES AND ARRESTS WITH A WARRANT AND PROBABLE CAUSE 113

6   THE FIFTH AMENDMENT   295

7 THE SIXTH AND EIGHTH AMENDMENTS 381

9 THE FIRST AND SECOND AMENDMENTS: FREEDOM OF SPEECH, ASSEMBLY, RELIGION, AND THE RIGHT TO BEAR ARMS 505

PREFACE

Students who aspire to work in the criminal justice or court system in any capacity need to be familiar with the provisions of the Constitution that specifically apply to criminal law and procedure. The Constitution related to American culture when it was written in 1787 and, amazingly, continues to be relevant to American culture today. The framers of the Constitution were concerned about general, unwarranted searches and seizures, while today Americans debate over terrorism, airport searches, and racial profiling by police and other government officials. While the framers did not need to consider iPods, electronic pagers, and cellular telephone records when drafting the Constitution, they did worry about protecting politically outspoken citizens from government searches. The Constitution today continues to protect Americans from government intrusion into electronic versions of soapbox declarations and broadsheet and pamphlet publications. Although Supreme Court justices have invoked various approaches to interpretation over the years, foremost among them continues to be the attempt to determine the framer's intent in devising the provisions of the Constitution. Yet, as Franklin D. Roosevelt quipped, "The United States Constitution has proved itself the most marvelously elastic compilation of rules of government ever written." As an attorney who represents criminal clients, I see every day how the Constitution continues to be integral to our court system.

Constitutional Law in Criminal Justice sets forth the provisions of the Constitution that relate most directly to criminal law. Its practical approach encourages students to consider how these provisions affect daily attitudes, capabilities, events, and responses in policing, courtrooms, and federal agencies. The Constitution guides every facet of the investigation of crime and threats to our safety and national security. To further the understanding of these processes, this book examines both the wording of the original constitutional provisions and the central developments in how those provisions have been subsequently interpreted by the Supreme Court and, in some instances, by lower courts.

This text also provides open-ended scenarios, based on actual cases, for students to consider. Through these scenarios, students will explore the actions they will need to think through and take every day as members of the criminal justice system. These actions and their motives will be scrutinized at many levels, and practitioners need to keep abreast of changes in the law as they are handed down by various courts. The law is not an exact science, but in the area of constitutional law in particular, many decisions courts make about what constitutes acceptable police action or admissible evidence are extremely fact specific.

Constitutional Law in Criminal Justice explains the concepts of incorporation and the Fourteenth Amendment in terms that are easily grasped by students, enabling them to understand the amendments applicable to the states, what those amendments were intended to achieve, and why they became such important elements in our criminal system. The Fourth, Fifth, and Sixth Amendments are emphasized, but the First and Second Amendments are included, as well, with emphasis on how they relate to crime and criminal justice.

After reading *Constitutional Law in Criminal Justice*, students should understand the expectations and requirements that will be placed on them as they endeavor to pursue their careers in compliance with the Constitution's provisions and their changing application. This effort will require constant diligence and proper documentation of their actions every day, and this text offers the tools for research and analysis they will need to achieve success. By balancing presentation of the rules handed down by the courts with questions and scenarios challenging students to assess the Constitution's impact on both criminal and everyday activities, the text integrates students' professional and personal concerns.

I especially wish to thank my mentors, Dr. Peter Benekos and Dr. Frank Hagan, both for their constant support throughout my career in teaching and this writing process and for their friendship. I would also like to thank David Herzig and Susan Boulanger at Aspen Publishing for their patience and assistance as I completed this project. I am also indebted to Christine Kern who assisted me with the supplemental materials in this text and to Christine Holden and Nicole Sloane who reviewed some of the chapters of this book. I would also like to thank my research assistants, Anthony Hugar and Mary Mancuso, who assisted me with some of the organization and ideas for this book. I wish also to thank my friend, Carolyn Washe, who has supported me in many ways through this process. I am grateful every day to my late grandmother, Grace Sieklucki, who loved me unconditionally and was always proud of me. Finally, I would like to thank Peter Octavian and my children, Grace, Madeline, Madison, and Mason, who tolerated my lessened attention to them during late nights, early mornings, and every time in between, as my attention turned to completing this book.

CONSTITUTIONAL LAW IN CRIMINAL JUSTICE

INTRODUCTION TO CONSTITUTIONAL CRIMINAL PROCEDURE

1

LEARNING OBJECTIVES: Students will

1. Understand why the Constitution and Bill of Rights were written
2. Understand the due process and crime control models of criminal procedure
3. Understand how courts interpret the Constitution
4. Understand the structure of the appellate court system

While we may hope that we will never be involved in the criminal justice system as defendants, we should consider the fact that perhaps the reason we are not defendants, even wrongfully accused ones, is due to the constitutional protections that have been put into place by the Constitution of the United States.

Consider an underage college student who might have a can of beer in his backpack as he walks across campus. Assuming that the student is not particularly loud, violent, or obnoxious as he makes his way back to his dorm room, campus police will most likely continue past him and not bother him, even if the student is known to be one of the heartier partiers on campus. When a person is pulled over by the local police department for going faster than the allotted speed limit, why is it that the officer cannot always search the car to see what the person might have in the car? Every day, we as citizens of the United States are protected by the Constitution, and specifically by the amendments that have been added to the Constitution, many of which limit the actions of the police and other government officials. The first ten amendments to the Constitution are referred to as the Bill of Rights due to the fact that they limit the conduct of the government.

Our Constitution was written by individuals who were forming a government that focused on the right of the people to be secure, not the right of the government to oppress. The Constitution sets up our government and provides it with certain powers, but the amendments to the Constitution secure and guarantee rights to the people, while limiting the government's powers in certain areas. It is important to consider why the framers of the Constitution were

CONSTITUTION OF THE UNITED STATES

www.bigstock.com.

writing this document to begin with. What provisions of the English government did they approve of and want to keep in their newly formed government? Why had they come to America—what were they hoping to escape? All of the framers' experiences with the English government shaped the document that we rely on today to assure our freedom from governmental interference.

HISTORICAL ANTECEDENTS OF THE U.S. CONSTITUTION

English Documents

While England does not have a Constitution per se, it does have many documents that provided a basis for the Constitution of the United States and other documents that provide freedoms to its citizens. The first is the **Magna Carta**, which was drafted in 1215 and is sometimes referred to as the Great Charter. The citizens of England rebelled against King John, who ruled between 1167 and 1216, and were attempting to protest heavy taxation by the government and heavy-handed rule by the king. The king was forced to sign the Magna Carta, which set forth the idea that people would be imprisoned only based on a trial by their peers or a clear violation of the law of the land. The Magna Carta was reissued as new kings took rule and has become a symbol of liberty in England. The due process clauses of the Fifth and Fourteenth Amendments of the Constitution originated from the English Magna Carta.

The second document that specifically provided a basis for our Constitution is England's Bill of Rights. This document, adopted in 1688, was passed by Parliament to declare certain rights and liberties for English subjects, and was brought about when a new monarchy, King William and Queen Mary, took the place of the overthrown King James II. The document allowed subjects to petition the king when they had concerns; allowed Protestants to bear arms; ensured freedom of speech for members of Parliament; prohibited excessive bail, fines, and cruel and unusual punishment; provided rules for jurors; and stated that Parliament should meet frequently. You will see that many of these exact rights were adopted and included in the United States Bill of Rights.

Early Documents Guiding the North American English Colonies

The United States government, while definitely unique in its structure and in the rights it provides to individuals, borrowed ideas from other countries, especially England, where the original colonists who settled our country and the framers of our Constitution hailed from. The above-referenced documents, along with other traditions that were longstanding in England, influenced our forefathers when drafting our Constitution. However, the forefathers were also influenced by traditions and types of governance that the colonists did not believe in and that were among the primary reasons the colonists left England to begin with. The Constitution was drafted in 1787, following the implementation of other documents, such as the **Declaration of Independence**.

The first formal document adopted by the American citizens was the **Mayflower Compact**, signed on November 11, 1620, by the colonists sailing to the new world via the Mayflower. The original document has been lost but versions of the original referred to the principles of Christianity and a hope to band together into a civil body with some semblance of order. Following the Mayflower Compact, various ethnic groups and other groups of colonists adopted their own rules and codes, akin to our current individual state governments, and officially formed colonies. Many of these codes, referred to as compacts, encompassed a religious purpose. A common focus of these codes was the attempt to guarantee individual rights while still establishing order and reserving some powers to the government.

Oppression by Parliament

While the colonists were establishing their own form of government, they were still officially being ruled by England. Parliament began to pass numerous acts the colonists viewed as oppressive. Other countries, such as France, began to attempt to lay claim to American soil, and Great Britain was financially responsible for funding the battles for land against both other empires and the Native Americans. Parliament attempted to make the colonists partially responsible for this cost and passed the **Stamp Act** in 1765. This act required that stamps be purchased and placed on official documents. In the same year, Parliament also passed the **Quartering Act**, which required that colonists house and feed British soldiers. The Quartering Act influenced the framers of the Constitution to include the Third Amendment, which prohibits the government from requiring such housing for soldiers. The Stamp Act was eventually repealed, but Parliament continued to pass laws that directly affected the colonists, who were especially upset about the fact that they had no voice in the passage of these various acts. Oppression by the British government led to the infamous **Boston Tea Party**, during which the colonists dressed as Native Americans and boarded three British ships in Boston Harbor, throwing tea overboard as an act of protest. This demonstration further angered the British government, and Parliament passed more laws that gave England greater power over the colonies.

The First Continental Congress

The **First Continental Congress** was held in 1774 in Philadelphia, Pennsylvania, when representatives from the established colonies met to discuss their concerns over English rule. The colonies agreed to band together to stand against England and develop a list of rights for the colonists, to present a statement regarding their complaints to the king, and to boycott the purchase of certain British goods. Much controversy ensued, similar to the controversy that exists today in terms of buying foreign or local goods. While some colonists remained loyal to England and these rules, others rebelled, and our nation became, to some extent, at war with itself, as well as with England and with Native Americans.

The Second Continental Congress

The colonists knew that they would eventually have to do more than make statements to Great Britain, and a group of men referred to as "minutemen" were "on call" to defend the colonists against Britain in the event of an attack. The first shots between the two countries ensued on April 19, 1775, and soon thereafter, representatives from the colonies again convened in Philadelphia. The **Second Continental Congress** established and discussed financial support for an organized army, and battles between the colonies and England continued. The Second Continental Congress also decided that each established colony should form its own government.

The Declaration of Independence

In July 1776, the delegates of the Second Continental Congress drafted the **Declaration of Independence** in order to formally announce the colonies' breaking off from British rule. The Declaration of Independence asserted the right to "life, liberty, and the pursuit of happiness" and declared that all men were created equal. The document also focused on why the colonists were trying to break free from England. Consider how these ideas relate to how we treat citizens who break the law, and as you become familiar with the provisions of the Constitution, notice how these themes are echoed in the Constitution.

The Articles of Confederation

The Second Continental Congress set to work trying to determine exactly how the new government should be set up, considering the tenets of the Declaration of Independence. In 1777, the **Articles of Confederation** set forth the structure for the new government. Thirteen states were already in existence, and because they had previously been told to set up their own governments, they were generally resistant to a proposal that would result in their having to answer to a higher governmental authority. Nonetheless, the Articles, approved in 1781, allowed the states to retain some power while also delegating power to what would become the federal government. This structure allowed our government to be centralized while maintaining the individual governments established in the colonies, which later became states.

The Convention of Delegates

In 1787, a convention of delegates from the original 13 colonies met in Philadelphia in the attempt to revise the Articles of Confederation because the Articles lacked a good balance between the federal and state governments and, in fact, established only a very weak federal government. At the 1787 convention, delegates decided to significantly change the provisions of the Articles, and the question for the delegates was whether to focus on encompassing tradition, both from the colonies and Britain, or to establish a completely different type of government. George Washington presided over the meetings, and the delegates eventually decided to draft a completely new document, rather than trying to salvage the previously passed Articles of Confederation. The goal was to establish a government in which no one entity would have complete power, and thus a system of "checks and balances" was established. Fifty-five delegates from every state except Rhode Island met in Philadelphia from May 25, 1787, to September 15, 1787, in what is now referred to as the **Constitutional Convention**. Each state could cast one vote to adopt or reject the Constitution.

Many resolutions were drafted, but two main resolutions were proposed at the Constitutional Convention. The first was the **Virginia Resolution**, which called for a national government with a legislature, executive branch, and judicial branch. The second, the **New Jersey Plan**, was supported by many of the smaller states, and proposed a similar governmental structure to the Articles of Confederation. An issue of representation concerned whether each state would receive votes proportionate to its size or the exact same number of votes. The agreement to allow both types of representation is known as the **Great Compromise**. As a result, in our current system the House of Representatives provides votes based on a state's population and the Senate provides the same number of two votes per state. In the House, the number of votes each state receives is adjusted periodically based on each state's current population. The delegates also agreed to adopt a system in which power was shared between the executive branch, the legislature, and the judiciary branch.

THE U.S. CONSTITUTION

Following the debate and agreement on the basic tenets of the new government, a committee was formed to actually draft the Constitution and set up the government. Some of the provisions of the Constitution and basic ideas dated back to the Magna Carta, which guaranteed that the law established by Parliament would prevail over the king's power. The Magna Carta also established some individual rights such as trial by jury, which is also guaranteed in our Constitution. Thus, the colonists' attempt to distance themselves from Great Britain and what they considered the oppressive system of English government nonetheless resulted in their adoption of some of the provisions of English law that they believed limited the power of the government in favor of individual rights. Regardless, a theme throughout the Constitution is that all of the powers delegated to the federal government are given to it by the people.

The Constitution was finally passed on September 17, 1787, in Philadelphia, Pennsylvania, our country's first capital. The provisions of the body of the Constitution are general and create three branches of government. The Constitution's provisions also permit the document to be changed as the country's needs change. It included six articles, one of which established a process by which amendments would be added to the Constitution. Interestingly, three delegates refused to sign the Constitution; one argued that it needed a Bill of Rights to provide specific rights to individuals and reduce the potential strength of the federal government. The Bill of Rights was later added in order to convince the three dissenters to ratify. Each state was required to ratify the Constitution after its passage and before it would go into effect—ratification by the states ensured that the states would indeed have a part in forming the new government.

The state delegates did have reservations about ratifying the Constitution, and to encourage ratification, three representatives wrote a series of articles supporting the Constitution in a newspaper entitled **The Federalist Papers**. These articles supported passage of the Constitution and gave reasons why a federal government was needed. The articles focused on the fact that men could not properly govern themselves without a centralized government, and maintained that the government must control itself along with the people. Other representatives, labeled **anti-federalists**, argued against a centralized government, fearing the same problems that existed with the English government against whom the colonists had rebelled. Specifically, these individuals argued that granting the federal government the right to tax citizens set a dangerous precedent, that a fair trial should be guaranteed to everyone, and that the sovereignty of the states was threatened by giving the federal government so much power.

Following much debate, the Constitution was ratified with the condition that a Bill of Rights would be added. In 1791, ten amendments were passed, and those amendments were also ratified by the states' delegates. Even though amendments have been added to the Constitution since that time and the Courts have evolved in their interpretation of the document, the document itself has stood strong since its inception, establishing what the framers hoped to be an effective, strong, and lasting government.

The Constitution establishes three branches of government. Article I develops the **legislative branch**, or Congress, which includes the House of Representatives and the Senate. These bodies draft and pass new laws and regulations, but other branches are responsible for enforcing or interpreting them. The **executive branch**, established in Article II of the Constitution, refers to the office of the president. The president is elected, not appointed or born into the office like British royalty, and the president is responsible for foreign policy, appointment of various important officials, and generally carrying out the law.

The **judicial branch** is established in Article III of the Constitution and is the branch of government you will become most familiar with as you study constitutional law as it relates to criminal procedure. Ultimate judicial power is given to the Supreme Court of the United States; there is no higher court to which an appeal may be taken. Specifically, Article III of the Constitution provides that "[t]he judicial power of the United States, shall be vested in one Supreme Court, and in such inferior courts as the Congress may from time to time ordain and establish." Congress can also create lower courts, and has created a system of federal courts, including trial level courts and appellate courts. The Supreme Court is the highest appellate court of the federal system and is a court to which state cases can also be appealed; as such, the Supreme Court is often referred to as the "Court of Last Resort." Congress has established courts to hear cases involving Native Americans on Reservations, and has also established military tribunals that oversee their own appellate courts. States have established certain types of specialty courts, including family court and juvenile court. The Constitution also establishes that Congress retains the ability to determine which types of cases courts can hear, providing yet another layer of checks and balances.

The judicial branch provides a check on the other two branches of government. The Supreme Court can declare a law unconstitutional and can interpret laws, which means that even a law properly passed by Congress and approved by the president may be invalidated by the Court, especially if the law is determined to be unconstitutional. On the flip side, a court may make a determination as to what it believes the law should be in an area where no governing laws in that area have been passed. When a court makes law in an area where the legislature has not passed a law, the court is making **common law**. Any case that is decided by a judge is considered to establish common law, as opposed to the legislature's passage of laws. Laws passed by the legislature provide us with **statutory law**.

Each time a court interprets a statute, future courts will often interpret the statute the same way in the future. Further, sometimes no statute exists that establishes a law in a particular area, and it is thus up to courts to develop that law. The new law that is developed is an example of common law. After a court determines what it believes the common law should be, the legislature might then decide that it dislikes the law as it has been developed by the court and can pass a law of its own. Also, sometimes the legislature enacts statutory law that adopts court-developed common law. The courts have to uphold and enforce that law unless it is declared to be unconstitutional by the Supreme Court. By declaring certain laws unconstitutional, the Supreme Court has been able to define the balance of powers between the state and federal government.

The Bill of Rights

The first ten amendments to the Constitution are referred to as the **Bill of Rights**. As you read this list of rights, consider how each limits the government, and consider which rights you believe are the most important to citizens of the United States. Which do you believe is most representative of the uniqueness of our rights as citizens of the United States?

> **AMENDMENT I**—Congress shall make no law respecting an establishment of religion, or prohibiting the free exercise thereof, or abridging the freedom of speech, or of the press; or the right of the people peaceably to assemble, and to petition the Government for a redress of grievances.
>
> **AMENDMENT II**—A well regulated Militia, being necessary to the security of a free State, the right of the people to keep and bear Arms, shall not be infringed.
>
> **AMENDMENT III**—No Soldier shall, in time of peace be quartered in any house, without the consent of the Owner, nor in time of war, but in a manner to be prescribed by law.
>
> **AMENDMENT IV**—The right of the people to be secure in their persons, houses, papers, and effects, against unreasonable searches and seizures, shall not be violated, and no Warrants shall issue, but upon probable cause, supported by Oath or affirmation, and particularly describing the place to be searched, and the persons or things to be seized.
>
> **AMENDMENT V**—No person shall be held to answer for a capital, or otherwise infamous crime, unless on a presentment or indictment of a Grand Jury, except in cases arising in the land or naval forces, or in the Militia, when in

actual service in time of War or public danger; nor shall any person be subject for the same offense to be twice put in jeopardy of life or limb; nor shall be compelled in any criminal case to be a witness against himself, nor be deprived of life, liberty, or property, without due process of law; nor shall private property be taken for public use, without just compensation.

AMENDMENT VI—In all criminal prosecutions, the accused shall enjoy the right to a speedy and public trial, by an impartial jury of the State and district wherein the crime shall have been committed, which district shall have been previously ascertained by law, and to be informed of the nature and cause of the accusation; to be confronted with the witnesses against him; to have compulsory process for obtaining witnesses in his favor, and to have the Assistance of Counsel for his defense.

AMENDMENT VII—In Suits at common law, where the value in controversy shall exceed twenty dollars, the right of trial by jury shall be preserved, and no fact tried by jury, shall be otherwise re-examined in any Court of the United States, than according to the rules of the common law.

AMENDMENT VIII—Excessive bail shall not be required, nor excessive fines imposed, nor cruel and unusual punishments inflicted.

AMENDMENT IX—The enumeration in the Constitution, of certain rights, shall not be construed to deny or disparage others retained by the people.

AMENDMENT X—The powers not delegated to the United States by the Constitution, nor prohibited by it to the States, are reserved to the States respectively, or to the people.

As you review these amendments, you will note that there are some that you have heard of a lot recently, and some that you rarely ever consider. For example, the issue of gun control has been litigated in the Supreme Court recently and is a common controversy in the political realm, while the issue of whether citizens are required to house soldiers in their homes is rarely discussed in general conversation. Consider the amendments that specifically regulate how the criminal justice system interacts with criminal defendants. You will note that some of those issues, such as search and seizure, are litigated on a daily basis, while some, like the issue of "cruel and unusual punishment" are rarely litigated but still are considered important when an issue pertaining to them arises. Further, while you learn about the Supreme Court's decisions regarding these amendments, you will see that the Court's interpretation of the amendments is ever changing and fluid.

The First Amendment. The First Amendment is peripherally related to the issue of the rights of criminal defendants in that it has been used to both justify and argue against the passage of certain laws that result in behavior being considered a crime. This amendment permits certain behaviors, but it has been left to the courts to determine how much protection to give those rights when they begin to affect the right of other citizens to live in a safe society. The right of individuals to speak freely, which naturally encompasses the right to protest freely, affected many of the major historical events in our country, such as the Vietnam War and, most recently, presidential elections. Consider how different our political process would be if individuals did not have the right to state their views to others. Even online social network applications such as Facebook and Twitter abound with comments focusing on political issues, including criticism of religion, the laws,

LANDMARK FIRST AMENDMENT FREEDOM OF SPEECH CASES

Gitlow v. New York, 268 U.S. 652 (1925)
State and local governments must respect the First Amendment.

West Virginia State Board of Education v. Barnette, 319 U.S. 624 (1943)
Freedom of speech guarantees a citizen's right not to have to say anything. Specifically, students do not have to recite the Pledge of Allegiance.

Cohen v. California, 403 U.S. 15 (1971)
A state cannot attempt to censor its citizens' speech in order to make society more "civil." Specifically, a man cannot be arrested for wearing a jacket that says "Fuck the draft."

R.A.V. v. City of St. Paul, 505 U.S. 377 (1992)
The First Amendment prevents the government from prohibiting speech when the government does not like the ideas within the speech. Hate speech is protected.

Wisconsin v. Mitchell, 508 U.S. 475 (1993)
A defendant's sentence can be enhanced if he intentionally selects his victim based on the victim's "race, religion, color, disability, sexual orientation, national origin or ancestry."

Milkovich v. Lorain Journal Co. et al., 497 U.S. 1 (1990)
A statement must be proved false before it can be considered defamatory.

Brandenburg v. Ohio, 395 U.S. 444 (1969)
Speech can be criminalized if it "is directed to inciting or producing imminent lawless action and is likely to incite or cause such action."

Texas v. Johnson, 491 U.S. 397 (1989)
Flag burning is protected speech and states cannot pass laws prohibiting it.

THE COURT'S CURRENT POSITION ON FREE SPEECH

The most recent case in the area of free speech is that of **Snyder v. Phelps,**[1] decided by the Court in 2011. The case involved the congregation of the Westboro Baptist Church, which for 20 years had picketed the funerals of members of the military. The purpose of the picketing was to make a statement that God hates the United States for its tolerance of homosexuality, especially in the military. The congregation was also protesting the clergy scandals that had taken place in the Catholic church. When members of the church went to Maryland to picket the funeral of a Marine who had been killed in Iraq in the line of duty, they quietly and peacefully displayed signs on public land, which was approximately 1,000 feet from the church in which the funeral took place. The signs made statements such as "Thank God for Dead Soldiers," "Fags Doom Nations," "America is Doomed," "Priests Rape Boys," and "You're Going to Hell." The protestors displayed the signs until approximately 30 minutes before the funeral began.

The Marine's father filed a diversity action against the church, the founder of the church who had traveled to Maryland, and his daughters who had also participated in the picketing. The suit included claims of intentional infliction of emotional distress, intrusion upon seclusion, and civil conspiracy. A jury found Westboro liable and entered a judgment of millions of dollars against the church. Westboro challenged the verdict, arguing that the First Amendment protected this speech. The case made its way to the Supreme Court. The Court ruled for the defendants, agreeing that their free speech had been violated. The Court stated that speech is considered to be of public concern when it can "be fairly considered as relating to any matter of political, social, or other concern to the community" or when it "is a subject of general interest and of value and concern to the public." The statement's controversial or arguable inappropriate nature should not be considered. The Court ruled that the speech in this case did relate to public, not private, matters, because it directly spoke to the morality of the United States and its citizens. Even if Westboro's speech was hurtful to Matthew Snyder and his grieving relatives, it was still protected. The jury found that the picketing was "outrageous," as required in the state tort statute defining intentional infliction of emotional distress, but the First Amendment trumps the jury's finding. The Supreme Court reiterated that it would protect even hurtful speech if it related to public issues, so as not to stifle public debate. One justice dissented, arguing that Matthew Snyder's father wanted only to bury his son in peace and that, because the picketers had chosen Matthew Snyder's funeral because he practiced the Catholic faith and because he was in the military, the picketers were in fact trying to target Matthew Snyder, a private individual.

---

1. 562 U.S. ___ (2011).

and the president. These comments can legally be posted only because of the broad right to free speech, religion, and even press that has been permitted by the Supreme Court upon interpretation of the First Amendment. The Supreme Court considered the meaning of these clauses very early on in its history and the provisions of the First Amendment were some of the first provisions to be incorporated to the states as being fundamental to the freedoms we experience in our country. The First Amendment also states that the government can neither establish a religion or forbid anyone from following a religion.

The Second Amendment. Criminal statutes can limit one's right to have a firearm, either because the type of firearm is prohibited or because the individual has committed a crime or engaged in some conduct that prevents him from possessing a firearm. Much debate exists regarding the appropriate interpretation of this amendment. Grammatically, there are three ways the Second Amendment can be interpreted. First, it can be argued that the Second Amendment consists of an opening justification phrase followed by a declarative clause. Under this interpretation, the opening phrase is essential to the main clause, and this interpretation would result in a protection of the right to bear arms if a person is serving in the militia.

The second possible interpretation views the first phrase as one non-exclusive example of one instance in which individuals have the right to bear

LANDMARK SECOND AMENDMENT CASES

Presser v. Illinois, 116 U.S. 252 (1886)
The Second Amendment does not bar the states from enacting laws that bar private militias, and the states have the authority to regulate the militia.

United States v. Miller, 307 U.S. 174 (1939)
The National Firearms Act of 1934, which requires that certain types of firearms be registered, is constitutional.

District of Columbia v. Heller, 554 U.S. 570 (2008)
Handguns cannot be banned, although certain people can be banned from possession of firearms (the mentally ill, those convicted of certain crimes).

McDonald v. Chicago, 561 U.S. 3025 (2010)
Handguns cannot be banned, except to certain groups as discussed in the **Heller** case, and firearms can be banned in certain locations, such as near public schools.

arms. Using this interpretation, the Second Amendment would protect the individual right to bear arms for more reasons than just military purposes.

The third possible interpretation views the first clause as explanatory; that militia service is the reason that we allow people to keep and bear arms, but that there are not other restrictions. Thus, the fact that the second part of the amendment guarantees the right to bear arms to "the people" means that all citizens can bear arms, not just those involved in the militia. The Supreme Court has interpreted this amendment in very few cases.

The Fourth Amendment. The Fourth Amendment is one of the best-known amendments and one of the most relevant to criminal procedure. In fact, the amendment has been interpreted by the Supreme Court in many cases, and the decisions have greatly impacted the way law enforcement officials perform their job duties daily. The amendment provides a guideline for law enforcement officials to conduct searches and seizures and also provides wording regarding the use of warrants. The focus of the Fourth Amendment is whether a search is reasonable and when a warrant is needed in order to conduct a search. The Fourth Amendment is complex despite perhaps seeming fairly simple on its face.

The Fifth Amendment. The Fifth Amendment relates directly to criminal procedure in that it provides the right of a defendant to have his case heard by a grand jury. Two well-known provisions of the Fifth Amendment are the double jeopardy clause and the clause that provides that no one shall be compelled to be a witness against himself. This concept is commonly used (and perhaps sometimes misused) when someone is asked a question and replies, "I plead the fifth!" A very important clause in the Fifth Amendment that has shaped our criminal justice system, including police conduct and the manner in which cases move through the system, is the final portion of the amendment, which states that an individual cannot be deprived of life, liberty, or property without due process of law. The idea of due process also appears in the Fourteenth Amendment to the Constitution, and you will see that both clauses are used by the Supreme Court to provide an orderly and fair system of justice.

The Sixth Amendment. The Sixth Amendment provides that trials should be speedy and public, which in effect ensures that individuals who are accused of crime are assured of finality in their case and witnesses to make sure that their rights are not being violated during court proceedings. The Sixth Amendment also provides that defendants will know what they are being charged with and be able to confront anyone who is presenting evidence to the court. Further, the Sixth Amendment sets forth the very important right of a defendant to be represented by an attorney during his criminal proceedings.

The Seventh, Ninth, and Tenth Amendments. The Seventh, Ninth, and Tenth Amendments apply only to civil proceedings and governmental power in the civil realm and are not relevant to criminal procedure.

The Eighth Amendment. The Eight Amendment limits the government's ability to impose excessive bail and fines to those accused of crimes. The more controversial issue is that of "cruel and unusual punishment." This issue has been litigated in the context of the death penalty, as well as in the context of other sentencing options and even such concerns as prison conditions.

The Fourteenth Amendment. The Fourteenth Amendment is very important in the context of criminal procedure. The Fourteenth Amendment has two components: the privileges and immunities clause and the due process clause. The privileges and immunities clause has been utilized to support the equality of all citizens in many areas of the law and is not specific to criminal law. The due process clause mirrors that of the Fifth Amendment and has been interpreted by the Supreme Court as making the provisions of the Bill of Rights applicable to the states. The due process clause has two concepts, substantive due process and procedural due process. The applicability of the amendments to the states and the concepts of substantive and procedural due process will be discussed more thoroughly later in this chapter.

CONSTITUTIONAL INTERPRETATION

Theories of Constitutional Interpretation

The Supreme Court uses three main theories to determine how to interpret, and sometimes reinterpret, the words appearing in the Constitution: (1) intent of the framers (originalism), (2) evidence of current traditions, customs, and practices, and (3) structural logic. When possible, the first consideration of any court should be to ascertain the intent of the framers and consider why an amendment was written in a specific way and why it uses that particular wording. As discussed, the founders of our country were interested in breaking free from England and what they felt was an oppressive government. The framers first established the powers of the government (through the Constitution itself) but then added the amendments to limit the government's power. Thus, when the Supreme Court attempts to interpret any provision of the Constitution, it must consider first what the framers intended to accomplish by drafting that amendment. This type of interpretation is referred to as **originalism**.

One example of this type of interpretation is the requirement that defendants be given a public trial. Although some of us might prefer that no one become aware that we are being accused of a crime, the purpose of this provision of the Sixth Amendment was really to help ensure that defendants received a trial free from error. In England, trials were often closed to the public and thus if something inappropriate happened during the proceeding, there were often no witnesses present other than the defendant and the prosecutor. The defendant could later complain that the proceedings were not fair, but seldom would he be believed. Having a public trial allowed witnesses to enter the courtroom, which in turn creates a "checks and balances" system.

In many cases, however, especially in present day society, there is no way the courts could begin to consider what the framers intended when the constitutional amendments were drafted. Certainly, when the framers drafted the amendments and they went into effect in November 1791, the framers could not have been considering whether an automobile, a cell phone, or a computer should be searched or seized. Thus, courts often have to go beyond the framers' intent to rule on an issue.

One way courts make decisions is based on current customs, traditions, and viewpoints of our society. Courts occasionally overturn their own rulings. This difference can result from a change in the makeup of the court (for example, the number of liberals versus number of conservatives on the court). A court might also make its decision based on whether society tolerates certain ideas and rules. Each time a case is heard by the Supreme Court, a number of **amicus briefs** are filed by various parties. For example, if an issue regarding gun control is brought before the court, groups which oppose or favor gun control can file briefs which support one side or the other, even if those groups were not a named party to the original court case. The Court will consider those groups' arguments, which often also cite polls, surveys, and research that have taken place regarding the topic the court is considering. The Court may be swayed by the research and evidence presented to it.

One example of an issue in which the Court changed its mind, as discussed below in the section on incorporation, is the issue of whether double jeopardy is an important, fundamental right that is central to our system of justice. The Supreme Court originally determined that it was not a fundamental right and then later changed its ruling to say that it was. The Court has also struggled with the issue of cruel and unusual punishment and specifically the issue of the death penalty. Society's views on whether our system has the right to take the life of a defendant fluctuates and, therefore, can influence the Supreme Court's decision when that issue comes before it.

Another way that courts can make a determination on what a particular provision of the Constitution means is to consider the entire document as a whole, using **structural reasoning**. In other words, if interpreting one portion of the Constitution in a certain way conflicts with how some other provision has been interpreted or conflicts with what another section clearly means, the provision would have to be interpreted otherwise. For example, two sections of the Constitution that might conflict to some extent have been the ability of a defendant to receive due process in all proceedings versus the First Amendment right of the media that allows it to publish information about the defendant's proceedings, especially in juvenile cases. As you may know, juvenile proceedings are often kept secret owing to concerns about labeling juveniles and affecting their lives negatively in the future. However, the media has the right to keep the public informed of what is happening in our courts. Courts have had some difficulty interpreting conflicting provisions of the Constitution in a way that would support the Constitution as a whole document. The concept of structural reasoning is also used to interpret potentially conflicting sections of statutory law.

Interpreting the Amendments

How does the Supreme Court interpret the constitutional amendments when a case comes before it today? This question is not easy to answer. The Court is challenged when asked to apply the provisions of the Constitution to questions in specific cases that come before it. As is obvious from the list of the first ten amendments, (the Bill of Rights), the amendments are written very succinctly, and these short statements lend themselves to various interpretations. For example, one of the most controversial amendments is the Second Amendment, which states that the "right of the people to keep and bear arms shall not be infringed." Ask your friends and family members what they believe this amendment means. No doubt, the responses you receive will be extremely diverse. Some, considering the context of the use of weapons by the colonists at the time the Constitution was written, believe that the framers of the Constitution developed this amendment in order to allow the colonists to utilize weapons in defense of themselves against British soldiers and to hunt animals for food. Others will argue that the framers were concerned that the British government was going to completely take away the colonists' right to have weapons for any reason and that the amendment was a bold attempt to allow citizens to carry any weapon they desired, at any time, for any reason. The Supreme Court, thus, has had to consider which of these views, or perhaps whether some view in between the two, is correct. Depending on the membership of the Supreme Court and the social climate during which a case interpreting the Second Amendment is decided, even the Supreme Court can change whether it is interpreting the amendment liberally or conservatively.

You will see that many of the landmark United States Supreme Court cases in the area of criminal procedure were decided during the 1960s and early 1970s. These decisions by and large give citizens numerous rights and involve an interpretation of the amendments that side on the rights of the people and limit the actions of the government. For example, the case of **Miranda v. Arizona**[2] was decided by the Supreme Court in 1966 and has resulted in the famous "you have the right to remain silent" verbiage that almost every American citizen is familiar with, due to the prevalence of the

---

2. 384 U.S. 436 (1966).

"reading of rights" by police to criminals on popular crime shows. Although we are so familiar with this verbiage that we consider it almost a formality at this point in time, when the case was decided, it was a huge victory for citizens who found themselves in a confrontation with police.

As you read the Supreme Court cases in this book, you will also find that the Court sometimes sets forth a **bright-line rule** in its decision, while other times it determines that certain rights should be considered by police agencies and the lower courts on a **case by case** basis. A bright-line rule is easy for a law enforcement agent to follow and does not require the officer's use of **discretion** (his ability to decide how to enforce the law in a given situation). Consider, for example, the rule that states that the **Miranda** rights must be read to a suspect prior to any police custodial interrogation.

However, some rules are less straightforward and more open to interpretation. For example, in the case of **Illinois v. Gates**,[3] the Supreme Court ruled that a court must consider the "totality of the circumstances" in a case when determining whether or not the facts of that case support a request for a search warrant. The Court provided lower courts a list of factors to consider in making this determination.

Some scholars favor bright-line rules so that police officers know what to do in their daily jobs without the use of excessive discretion. However, others argue that no two circumstances encountered by an officer will ever be exactly the same, that officers do best with guidelines as opposed to inflexible rules, and that it is most appropriate to let officers make their own decisions depending on the facts of each case.

Many argue that the Constitution, and especially its amendments, is a living document that requires periodic changes in interpretation. Regardless of what you learn in your constitutional law class, be aware that you will need to keep up with the law when you begin your career in the criminal justice and legal fields. The Court sometimes overturns its own decisions, and thus criminal justice professionals are required to constantly be aware of changes in the law. Lower courts can also sometimes differ with the Supreme Court's rulings and attempt to avoid the Court's rulings. For example, some lower courts have suggested that the **Miranda rights**, which might seem to some to be a cornerstone of our criminal justice system, are merely a court-created rule, do not spring from the Constitution, and could be abolished. Miranda rights were established in the case of **Miranda v. Arizona**,[4] decided by the Supreme Court in 1966. The case required that defendants be informed of certain rights, such as their right to remain silent, before law enforcement agents engage in "custodial interrogation" of that person. For example, application of the **Miranda** case to an officer's questioning of a suspect often is dependent upon the meaning of the phrase

---

3. 462 U.S. 213 (1983).
4. 384 U.S. 436 (1966).

"custodial interrogation," which must be defined in order for a law enforcement officer to know how to properly perform his job. However, the rule is not necessarily defined in the **Miranda** case and has been interpreted further depending on the specific attendant factual situation by lower courts. Thus, in addition to the substantive law that you will learn in this class, you should also be learning to read and interpret Supreme Court case law so you will always be able to know the current state of the law as it is changed and added to by the courts.

Balancing Interests

When interpreting the provisions of the Constitution, a court should balance the interests of the government with the interests of the public. As members of the public, we all certainly want the government to have enough control over our fellow citizens that crimes can be solved and people who might harm others can be incarcerated. The government represents the people and thus has those same interests. However, as citizens, we also do not want to be governed by an oppressive government that can control our every action and infringe upon our right to have privacy as we go about our daily activities. The court must consider both of these viewpoints in making decisions about constitutional amendments. Courts attempt to interpret the provisions of the Constitution so that the interests of the government in controlling crime are balanced with the right of each citizen to be free from governmental intrusion.

YOU BE THE JUDGE

You are the president of a university and are faced with being the ultimate decision maker regarding a student issue. Many university campuses have had difficulties with campus shootings. Although there has been no specific threat to your campus, many students, their parents, and employees of the university are concerned about the possibility of a mass shooting on campus. Campus security has decided to set up checkpoints going into the library and all of the dorms where students who are entering those buildings will be subject to having their backpacks and any sort of luggage searched to make sure there are no guns in their bags. Students are very upset, arguing that this practice (1) violates their right to privacy and (2) will delay their entrance into the dorm and library as they stand in a line of people waiting to be checked. Staff, faculty, administrators, and most parents are very pleased with this idea, feeling that everyone on campus will be safer. How would you balance the two different groups and what will your final decision be?

LAW AND THE CRIMINAL JUSTICE SYSTEM

Procedural and Substantive Law

The rules that courts and the legislature make fall into the categories of **procedural law** and **substantive law**. Procedural law includes any legal rules that tell courts and attorneys how to proceed with a case. Further, procedural rules require the government to give notice and, in many cases, a hearing, before it deprives a person of life, liberty, or property. Procedural rules include the **rules of evidence**, which are generally passed on both the state and federal levels. These rules control what evidence is actually presented in court and how and whether the court can consider certain types of evidence. The rules of criminal procedure and the rules of evidence strive to provide fair notice and a fair hearing, along with supporting other tenets of due process. The media often portrays trials as being full of "surprise witnesses" and the use of evidence by one side that the opposing side knows nothing about. This rarely happens in real life, as the rules of evidence require that both sides in a case exchange documents and information regarding what evidence they will present at trial. Evidence that one side will request to be excluded at trial will also be determined in advance of the trial through **pre-trial motions**. Pre-trial motions are motions that are brought prior to a person's trial in the attempt to convince the court to exclude the presentment of certain evidence at trial or to permit certain evidence to be introduced at trial. As a result, an entire case may be withdrawn by the prosecutor if the court rules that certain evidence must be excluded and the absence of that evidence leaves the prosecutor without enough evidence to prosecute the case. Even when the trial still progresses, a pre-trial argument regarding whether certain evidence will be permitted at trial avoids lengthy, interruptive arguments during the trial. This is especially important in a jury trial, in which jury members will often feel as though they are being left out of something important when the attorneys have discussions with the judge regarding information that the jurists are not allowed to hear.

Procedural Law. When a court decides which **procedures** must be followed in a certain case, they will consider the following factors: (1) the importance of the right to be safeguarded, (2) the extent to which additional safeguards would reduce the possibility of an erroneous decision, and (3) the increased burden (financially or otherwise) that would be placed on the government for the procedures to be carried out.[5]

For example, in many states, a case in which a defendant has received the death penalty must be appealed directly to the highest court of that state, rather than to an appellate court. A court cannot raise the amount of bail

---

5. **Cafeteria & Restaurant Workers Union v. McElroy**, 367 U.S. 886 (1961).

in a person's case without a hearing, and a person cannot be sentenced without receiving adequate notice of the sentencing date. All of these safeguards add cost to the criminal justice system, but are invaluable in that they provide for citizens to receive notice and a chance to be heard before a court makes a decision in their case. Procedural rules dictate situations such as whether a person must be given warnings before being terminated from her job or what appeal rights a person has if he is denied some right, such as the right to bear arms, because of having a criminal record.

Procedural laws that relate directly to the Constitution include whether police can conduct a search and seizure without a warrant (Fourth Amendment), whether a person must always be indicted by a grand jury before his case moves forward through the criminal system (Fifth Amendment), and what steps must be taken by the court system in order for a person to receive due process (Fifth and Fourteenth Amendments).

Substantive Law. In contrast, **substantive law** guarantees that citizens' liberty will be protected. Substantive law protects the liberties that are referred to in the Fourteenth Amendment. The government cannot arbitrarily deprive an individual of his or her liberty. The notion that citizens are protected from police conduct that "shocks the conscience" of the court is an example of substantive law. The term "shocks the conscience" is used often in court cases, and includes anything that would be seen as manifestly unjust by a judge. Cruel and unusual punishment could be "shocking" to a court, as could a jury verdict that seems completely out of line considering the facts that have been presented. Most recently, issues have arisen as to whether detainees in military prisons can be tortured and whether such behavior "shocks the conscience." A substantive case involving this concept is **County of Sacramento v. Lewis**.[6] In that case, sheriff's deputies engaged in a high speed chase, following two men on a motorcycle. The driver of the motorcycle, Brian Willard, lost control and the motorcycle tipped over; the officer could not stop and hit the motorcycle's passenger, Phillip Lewis. Lewis' parents sued the sheriff's department, accusing them of depriving Lewis of his Fourteenth Amendment due process right to life due to the deliberate and reckless conduct of the officers. The Supreme Court ruled in favor of the sheriff's department, stating that the court should consider whether the officers' action "shocks the conscience" and was "reckless." The Court stated that "[h]igh speed chases with no intent to harm suspects physically or to worsen their legal plight do not give rise to liability under the Fourteenth Amendment."

Other types of substantive law that relate to the Constitution include whether the government can criminalize what people say (First Amendment), whether citizens can possess and carry weapons (Second Amendment), and whether certain types of punishment, such as the death penalty or certain

---

6. 523 U.S. 833 (1998).

lengthy sentences for other types of crimes, are "cruel and unusual" (Eighth Amendment). The question of whether laws can apply to certain individuals differently than to others is also a question of substantive law (Fourteenth Amendment Equal Protection Clause). For example, a crime that applies to persons of a certain gender or socioeconomic status would violate the Equal Protection Clause. Many discriminatory laws that used to be on the books in various states, such as those that forbade black citizens from sitting in the front of a public bus or drinking from a certain water fountain, have been eliminated because they violated the Equal Protection Clause.

The main body of the Constitution includes an **ex post facto** clause, which prohibits the government from applying any substantive law retroactively. Citizens have the right to know what acts are illegal so that they have an opportunity to choose to act in accordance with the law. Thus, a new law that is passed to prohibit a certain type of criminal behavior can only apply to someone who engages in that type of behavior after the law is passed.

Due Process and Crime Control Models

Our justice system is based on the principle set forth in both the Fifth and the Fourteenth Amendments called **due process**, which gives each individual the right to be treated fairly and have a say in the judicial process. However, the Supreme Court, depending on the era and the members of the court at a given time, decides cases using two conflicting models of criminal procedure, the due process model and the crime control model. These models will be further described here. You may find that you tend to subscribe mostly to one of these models, or you may find your viewpoint involves a mix of both. As you read about specific Supreme Court cases in the remainder of this book, think about whether the Court seemed to be making its decision based on primarily principles of due process, primarily principles of crime control, or some combination of the two.

The **crime control model** is based on the premise that crime control is of the utmost importance and should be the focus of the Court in making decisions in cases in which criminal procedure is an issue. Advocates of the crime control model are concerned with moving cases efficiently and quickly through the criminal justice system. Advocates of this system also believe that persons who are brought into the system as defendants are guilty and thus their case should move through the system without particular concern about procedure and process. Advocates agree that at trial, defendants should receive the benefit of being presumed innocent, but that prior to trial, cases should not focus on procedure—rather, the police should be free to "do their job" and the defendant will receive his "day in court" at trial. Advocates also prefer an informal system with nonjudicial processes being preferred to court proceedings.

The **due process model** focuses on human freedoms and rights. Advocates of this model argue that the most important characteristic of our justice system is the right of all people to be free from governmental interference, and that this consideration should be focused on by the court system at all levels, from the time a police officer encounters an individual all the way through a person's appeal of his case to the Supreme Court of the United States. Advocates of the due process model do not focus on the efficiency of the system (although individuals do have a constitutional right to a "speedy trial," a concept that is discussed later in this text). A delay caused by a court's consideration of whether the initial contact between the defendant and the police was constitutional would be considered time well spent in the eyes of an advocate of the due process system. Further, according to a due process advocate, a criminal defendant should be considered "not guilty" at all stages of the process and should be treated accordingly. Courts play a more formal role in a due process system, providing a "check and balance" on the police and prosecutorial systems throughout all of the criminal court proceedings.

Precedent and Stare Decisis

Once the Supreme Court decides a particular issue, a **precedent** is set. For example, a supervisor in a workplace might state that he does not want to allow a certain employee to take time off from work for a minor injury because doing so would set a "dangerous precedent." The idea is that once a decision is made in a particular case, the same decision should be made for all future similar cases in order to appear "fair." The same concept is followed within the court system. Once the Supreme Court makes a decision, lower courts must follow that decision until and unless the Supreme Court decides to change its decision in the future. (The Supreme Court does have the ability to change the law that it has made, and examples will be presented throughout this book demonstrating where the Court has done so; however, the ability of the Court to state that it is following precedent helps to avoid the politicization of the Court, as discussed later in this chapter.)

However, it is preferable to practitioners within the criminal justice system that courts not change their rulings. A police officer can do his job according to the law if he believes that the Supreme Court's decision, for example, regarding the obligation to read Miranda rights to a suspect, will remain the law for the foreseeable future. If the Court did not follow its own past decisions and was constantly changing the law, it would be very difficult for attorneys to advise their clients and for government agents such as police to know how to interact with criminal suspects.

The Supreme Court can specifically rule that a decision it makes should not be considered precedential. An example of this comes from the 2000 presidential election. That election race, between George W. Bush and Al Gore, was very close and in the end rested on the results from the State of Florida. The results of the vote were so close that a recount was required under state law, and Bush was declared the winner after the recount. Gore contested the certified results, and the Florida Supreme Court ordered the recount of ballots that had previously been rejected by machine counters. The Supreme Court stepped in and ruled that the Florida Supreme Court's order to recount the ballots was unconstitutional and that the original certified amount should hold. The Supreme Court stated that its ruling was "limited to the present circumstances" and thus should not be used in the future as precedent. A future election with similar issues would result in a brand new review by the Supreme Court, not a reliance on the **Bush v. Gore**[7] decision.

A similar concept is that of **stare decisis**, which is a Latin term meaning "let the decision stand." This terminology refers to the fact that precedent that is set in one case should be followed in other similar cases so that the law is consistent. Without this doctrine, the same court could decide two cases with similar facts in two different ways. Attorneys can advise their clients as to how to follow the law based on the fact that stare decisis exists. Otherwise, it would be very difficult for those who want to conform their actions to the law to know how the law will be interpreted by the courts in any situation.

HOW THE U.S. COURTS WORK

Adversarial System

Most people understand that our criminal court system, and even our civil court system, is based on an **adversarial** process. Each side is able to present evidence to support its cause, and each side desires to "win" the argument during its day in court. Theoretically, the defense and the prosecution work toward different goals and oppose each other. A neutral judge hears each case and is responsible for determining what evidence is presented in court and what the law is. A judge or a jury will decide which of the facts that are presented to the court are true.

In the criminal court system, the prosecutor represents all of the people of the state. You will notice that in a civil action, the names of the parties are used in the caption of the case, yet the names of victims are not referred to in criminal court cases. Instead, criminal cases have names such as "Commonwealth v. Joe Jones" or "State v. Joe Jones." The "Commonwealth" or "State" name refers to the fact that all citizens of a particular state or of the United States, in a federal case, have an interest in our society being free of crime, and thus all citizens are bringing the charge or charges against the defendant. Thus, technically, the adversarial process is between all of "the people" of a state and the defendant who purportedly broke a law.

An argument rages regarding whether an adversarial system can be ultimately interested in determining the truth. Because the system is adversarial, many times pieces of evidence that would definitely show the defendant's guilt are thrown out of court. However, keep in mind that our system also requires that each defendant be presumed innocent and not guilty, and that

---

7. 531 U.S. 98 (2000).

the prosecution must prove the defendant's guilt, rather than the defendant having to prove his innocence.

Further, the court or jury would have to make the decision that the defendant is guilty **beyond a reasonable doubt**, which differs from the alternative standard used for civil cases of a **preponderance of the evidence**. The preponderance of the evidence standard is lower, with the consideration being whether it is more likely than not that the defendant in a civil case did perform a certain act. In a criminal case, "beyond a reasonable doubt" means that the fact finder must be certain, without doubt, that the defendant committed the act. The standard does not require 100 percent certainty, as that generally only results from actually watching the defendant commit a crime or seeing him commit the crime on a video, but it is a high burden of proof in which the fact finder is not supposed to doubt its ultimate determination of guilt.

The fact that there are two different standards in criminal and civil court sometimes results in a "not guilty" decision in criminal court, while the same dispute can be brought in a civil court proceeding and the individual could be found "liable." This situation was present in the O.J. Simpson trial, in which Simpson was acquitted (found "not guilty") in criminal court of the charges of murdering his ex-wife and another individual. However, Simpson was then named in a civil lawsuit brought by the family members of the deceased individuals, who claimed that Simpson caused the "wrongful death" of the two individuals. The civil jury determined that a preponderance of the evidence did exist and that Simpson was ultimately liable for civil damages to be paid to the victims' families.

Many of the cases you read in this course will involve situations in which the court's determination of whether evidence comes before a jury plays a major role in the jury's ultimate decision. Consider the following example.

> A defendant is charged with robbery in Pennsylvania. He has committed two other robberies of a similar nature in Alabama. Those robberies took place over 20 years ago, but involved the exact same method, right down to the clothing that the he wore when committing the robbery, the type of establishment being robbed, and the words that he stated to the clerks in the stores that he robbed. The defendant is brought to trial, and an evidentiary rule in Pennsylvania provides that past crimes cannot be presented to the jury to prove the defendant's bad character. Because of this, the jury is not able to consider the two prior robberies (absent some exception), even though they would most likely sway the jury in making its decision as to whether this defendant committed the crime.

Some would argue that excluding evidence such as convictions for prior robberies is deceitful and does not lead to the jury deciding what the truth really is. However, consider various reasons that the courts developed this evidentiary rule. The jury may assume that the person must be guilty in this case as well, without considering the actual facts presented to them. Someone who committed a crime 25 years ago and has not committed any crimes since should be able to present his case to a jury without the jury immediately considering him to be a "bad person" because of criminal acts that he committed many years ago. In the end, our system is not perfect and does not always result in a finding of the truth, but the overriding goal of our system is to provide fairness to individual defendants.

Structure of the Appellate Court System

After moving through the trial court in either the state or federal system, depending on whether the person has violated a state law or a federal law, a criminal case can work its way up through the secondary appeal courts of the state (or federal system). The defendant always has the right to have his case heard on appeal at this level. If the defendant loses or if the commonwealth/ government loses and either party wishes to appeal the decision, the case will move to the next level of court, where a **petition for certiorari** will be filed. This is a request for the court to agree to consider and make a ruling on the case.

In the state system, the next level will be the highest appellate court of that state. In the federal court system, the case will move to the Supreme Court. The Court can either grant the petition for certiorari, which means it will accept the case and make a decision on it, or deny the petition for certiorari, which means the Court will not hear the case, and the intermediate appellate court's decision will stand. In the state system, the case moves from the intermediate court level to the highest state court, which also has the ability to either grant or deny certiorari. If the state supreme court grants **allocatur** (the state equivalent of certiorari) and then makes a decision that one party does not agree with, that party can then appeal the case to the Supreme Court of the United States, which again can either grant certiorari or deny it. Time limits apply to each of these situations, and if a petition for certiorari is not filed within a certain amount of time following the intermediate appellate court's decision, the filing party will have waived her right to bring that issue before the court, and the court will not decide the case, no matter how important the issue may be. The Supreme Court grants certiorari in approximately 150 cases per year; thousands of cases are submitted per year.

No new evidence is submitted to the court when a case is on appeal at any level. At the trial court a record is created that includes all documents and other evidence submitted as exhibits at trial, plus a written record of all testimony that was set forth at trial. Attorneys submit briefs, a written argument to the court, summarizing the evidence and testimony, setting forth the law that applies to the case, and advocating to the court how they believe the law should apply to the facts. Attorneys then appear before the court and argue

FIGURE 1.1. STRUCTURE OF THE STATE COURT SYSTEM

State Court System

United States Supreme Court
The U.S. Supreme Court can decide which cases it will hear on appeal. There are also some cases for which the court will serve as the original trial court.

State Supreme Courts of Appeal
These courts can decide which cases to hear on appeal.

State Intermediate Courts of Appeal
Most states have this level of court, and these courts generally are required to hear cases that are appealed to them.

State Trial Courts
Almost all cases are originally heard in this court.

their case orally, with the judges being able to ask them questions about their arguments. Each attorney has a set and limited amount of time to make an argument.

Structure of the Supreme Court

The Supreme Court is the highest judicial body in the United States and consists of nine justices, all of whom are nominated by the president of the United States and confirmed by a majority vote of the Senate. One of the nine justices becomes the chief justice. Supreme Court justices hold life terms, and can be removed only by impeachment, death, or retirement. This rule is set forth in Article III of the Constitution, which states that federal judges serve "during good behavior."

All federal court judges hold life terms, which encourages judges to make decisions based on what they believe is "right," as opposed to making decisions based on political ambitions and the quest to be retained. State court judges in some states are elected by popular vote, and generally have to run for retention after a certain number of years. This arrangement can result in judges attempting to make decisions based on what they believe the public will want in order to vote them back into office when their term is up. For example, a judge who often makes decisions that are adverse to the police and upholds the rights of defendants may face

FIGURE 1.2. STRUCTURE OF THE FEDERAL COURT SYSTEM

Federal Court System

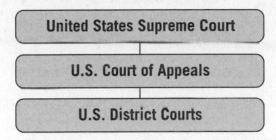

opposition from the local fraternal order of police organization when his position is up for retention. Other states have merit selection of judges, which means judges are appointed, which can be a very politically based process.

Because Supreme Court justices are nominated by whichever president happens to be in office when a seat opens on the Court, the composition of the Court will change. A president will consider the political views of a person when nominating her for a judicial position. This explains the Supreme Court's occasional overruling of its prior decisions: As new justices with different political persuasions come onto the Court, the attitude by the majority of justices might change.

HOW THE SUPREME COURT WORKS

The Supreme Court begins a new term every year on the first Monday in October, and Court sessions generally last until late June or early July. The justices hear oral arguments on cases during "sittings" and render decisions in "recesses." During oral arguments, each side receives 30 minutes to present their case and answer questions posed to them by the Court. The public can sit in on arguments when the Court is sitting. Proceedings are very formal. When the justices enter the room, the Court Marshal begins the session by saying "Oyez! Oyez! Oyez! All persons having business before the honorable, the Supreme Court of the United States, are admonished to draw near and give their attention, for the Court is now sitting. God save the United States and this Honorable Court!" Generally, the Court recesses at the end of June and the justices spend the summer preparing for October arguments.

YOU BE THE JUDGE

Go to the website for the Supreme Court of the United States, http://www.supremecourt.gov. Under the "oral arguments" tab you can listen to or review transcripts of arguments that have been made by attorneys to the Supreme Court. Select a case and listen to the oral argument or review the transcripts. If you were a Supreme Court justice, which side would you rule for? After making your decision, find the Court's decision in that case and read it. Did you rule in favor of the same part as the Supreme Court? Do you agree with the Supreme Court's ultimate ruling?

When will the Supreme Court grant certiorari in a case? The Supreme Court has a set of rules that guides it in determining whether a case is worthy of granting certiorari. Rule 10 of the Supreme Court Rules provides that the Court can use its discretion in granting certiorari and that no case has an automatic right to be granted certiorari. However, the rules indicate that a writ of certiorari should be granted only when "compelling reasons" exist. The rule further states that the Court will consider the following: (a) whether one court of appeals has reached a decision that is in direct contrast to the decision of another court of appeals determining the exact same issue, (b) whether a state court of last resort (normally a state supreme court) has rendered a decision that is in contrast to the decision of another state court of last resort in determining the exact same issue, and (c) whether a court of appeals or state court has decided an important question of law that "has not been, but should be" decided by the Supreme Court or has decided a case that conflicts with "relevant decisions" of the Supreme Court. The **rule of four** refers to the fact that four Supreme Court justices must decide that a case is worthy of consideration by the Court in order for it to be heard. Considering there are nine Supreme Court justices, fewer than half of the judges need to decide that a case is serious enough to hear. Despite this, most cases that are filed in front of the Supreme Court are not heard; in most cases, certiorari is not granted.

It is rare that a case that involves only a factual issue or the misapplication of a law that has been "properly stated" will be heard by a state supreme court or the Supreme Court of the United States. If certiorari is not granted, then the previous decision from the court below the Supreme Court stands, although the Supreme Court has not set a precedent as to how it believes the issue from that case should be decided. The Court leaves itself open to consider that issue later if it should decide to hear a case that presents that issue.

YOU BE THE JUDGE

You are a Supreme Court justice. The following case comes before you and you must determine whether to grant certiorari for that case. How would you decide whether or not to grant certiorari, given the limited guidelines provided by Rule 10? If you decide not to review the case, how does your decision affect citizens?

Smith is the individual responsible for track maintenance and construction projects for a railroad company and has been the responsible individual since one month after construction began on a project that involved realigning train tracks over a large ravine. An oil pipeline runs through the ravine and a backhoe operator working on the project hit the oil pipeline, causing a release of oil into the river. A protective platform was used to shield the oil pipeline from equipment prior to Smith's supervision of the project but had not been used once Smith started his supervision. Otherwise, Smith had no direct involvement in the accident that caused the spill. Federal criminal charges were brought against Smith based on the Clean Water Act; it was alleged that Smith "negligently" discharged oil into navigable water. Smith was sentenced to six months in federal prison, followed by six months in a halfway house and six months of supervised release.

Smith appealed his case to the United States Court of Appeals, which affirmed his conviction, finding that as long as a jury determines that a person failed to use such care as a reasonably prudent and careful person would have used under similar circumstances, that person can be found criminally liable. Smith argued that the standard should be whether a person is involved in gross negligence or willful conduct, rather than simple negligence. Smith now wishes for the Supreme Court to review his case.

APPEALS

If a defendant is unhappy with the outcome of his case at the trial court level, he can file an appeal to his state's intermediate level court, or in the case of a federal conviction, to the federal appeals court. The reviewing court will consider the record that has been made in the lower court and will base its ruling off that record. No new evidence or testimony can be presented to the appellate court. Any documents that have been filed in the case and any exhibits entered at trial can be considered, as can the **transcripts** from the lower court hearing, including the preliminary hearing, pre-trial hearings, the trial, the sentencing, and any post-sentence motions. The transcripts that are prepared in a case include a word-for-word rendition of everything that was said by anyone during a court proceeding. A court stenographer sits in on proceedings and types everything that is being said, using a machine that in effect uses shorthand codes. Technology has also advanced to the point where some jurisdictions are using transcription equipment that does not require a live stenographer but instead records the voices in the courtroom. The difference, however, between a reviewing court reading a transcript and actually being present in the courtroom during the proceeding is that a reviewing court is unable to watch the demeanor of the person speaking or hear the inflection in the person's voice. Thus, the reviewing court is unable to detect whether the person is telling the truth or not based on body language, eye contact, or the inflection of the person's voice. The court is also unable to sense things like humor or sarcasm when reading a written transcript. For these reasons and others, the reviewing court cannot determine who was telling the truth and who was lying while reading the transcripts. The jury or the judge at the trial court level act as the finders of fact, and the appellate court will not overturn those decisions unless they are determined to "shock its conscience." This would only happen if the reviewing court determined that there was absolutely no way that a rational jury or a rational judge would decide the case in the manner in which it was decided at the trial court level. This type of determination by a reviewing court is very rare. Transcripts are expensive to obtain, but the Supreme Court ruled that an indigent client has the right to have trial transcripts produced at no cost because they are so important to the reviewing court's ability to determine whether the lower court proceeding was free from error.[8]

See Figure 1.3 for an example of a page from a trial transcript.

In most jurisdictions, a defendant who does not prevail at trial has a right to appeal his case to the next level despite the Supreme Court's ruling in 1894 that a defendant does not have to be afforded the right to appeal his case, although defendants argued that it was required under the concept of due process. In **McKane v. Durston**,[9] the Supreme Court decided that this was the case regardless of how grave the defendant's offense was. The prosecution can also appeal a case, although such an appeal is generally rare. Because of the double jeopardy clause, a prosecutor can rarely appeal a case in which a defendant receives an acquittal. In fact, the Supreme Court stated that appeals by the prosecution "in criminal cases are something

---

8. **Griffin v. Illinois**, 351 U.S. 12 (1956).
9. 153 U.S. 684 (1894).

FIGURE 1.3. PAGE FROM A TRIAL TRANSCRIPT

1	Q. Where did you go that evening and who were you with?
2	A. I went to Robin's Tavern, and I went with Frank Hagan and Peter
3	Benekos.
4	Q. How did you get there?
5	A. I drove my car.
6	Q. What type of car do you have?
7	A. A 2012 MINI-Cooper.
8	Q. What time did you arrive at the tavern?
9	A. I think I was around 11:00. Approximately after 11:00, I think.
10	Q. Who was at the tavern when you got there?
11	A. Anthony Hugar, Mike Sulkowski, and Pedro Rodriguez. I didn't know
12	anyone else at the tavern that night.
13	Q. How much did you drink at the tavern?
14	A. I don't know. A few beers I think. I started drinking beer and then I
16	blacked out and fell down.
17	Q. Did you go to the hospital?
18	A. Someone called an ambulance and the ambulance took me to the
19	hospital, yes.
20	Q. When did you realize you had fallen?
21	A. I woke up and realized I was in a hospital. My wife was there and she
22	told me that I had fallen down. I don't remember anything about falling,
23	and she said that the bartender, Brian Ripley, had called her and told her
24	that I had fallen and an ambulance was on its way.
25	Q. Did your wife ever tell you whether the bartender had mentioned
26	how many beers you had that night?
27	A. No, and frankly I never asked her. It wasn't something I wanted to
28	talk about with her, because she always told me I drank too much.
29	Q. Have you ever gone to drug and alcohol counseling, participated in
30	any inpatient program for alcohol abuse, or attended any meetings such
31	as Alcoholics Anonymous?

Page 28

unusual, exceptional, not favored. The history shows resistance of the Court to the opening of an appellate route for the Government until it was plainly provided by the Congress, and after that a close restriction of its uses to those authorized by statute."[10] Thus, states and the federal government can mandate when the prosecution can file an appeal.

However, a prosecutor can appeal a defendant's sentence, arguing that it was too lenient, or a prosecutor can appeal rulings which might have excluded evidence that the prosecutor desired to present at the time of trial. The latter type of appeal might take place prior to the defendant's trial, plea, or sentencing, and is referred to as an **interlocutory appeal**. The general rule is that a case should be appealed only after it has gone through the entire process, all the way to sentencing and post-trial motions. However, certain matters require an appellate court to consider the issue before a trial can take place, as the result of the reviewing court's decision would greatly affect the trial. The Supreme Court has set forth the following three types of pre-trial decisions that would affect the trial in this manner.[11] These types of decisions are (1) whether the outcome of the case would be conclusively determined by the issue; (2) whether the matter appealed was collateral to the merits of the case; and (3) whether the matter would be unable to be reviewed by the reviewing court if the trial or other proceedings were permitted to proceed. For example, in the case of **Stack v. Boyle**[12] the Supreme Court determined that a reviewing court must immediately make a decision on the defendant's argument, rather than waiting. In that case, the defendant wanted to appeal the amount of bail set by the trial court; he argued that the amount of bail required for him was too high and thus violated the Eighth Amendment guarantee against excessive bail. If the appellate court had waited until the defendant was tried and sentenced, the issue of the bail amount would have been moot. Following trial or a plea and sentencing, the defendant would have either been (1) sentenced and thus bail would have been moot or (2) acquitted and thus bail would have been moot. However, issues involving the suppression of evidence are not considered an appealable issue. The Supreme Court considers such issues to be related to an individual's trial, so they are not appealable until after the outcome of the trial. Other issues that can be appealed following a defendant's sentence are (1) the sentence itself, (2) whether the evidence presented at trial was sufficient to convict the defendant of the crime, (3) whether the judge erred in making any ruling during the trial, (4) whether a violation of the rules regarding disclosure of evidence took place, (5) whether a trial was speedy, and (6) whether jury selection was done properly.

An appellate court could determine that an error occurred at the trial court level, but could nevertheless fail to order a new trial or other new proceedings based on the use of the **harmless error** doctrine. This doctrine dictates that an error that occurred at the trial court level will only merit a remand back to the trial court if the error clearly changed the outcome of the proceedings.

10. **Carroll v. United States**, 354 U.S. 394 (1957).

11. **Lauro Lines s.r.l. v. Chasser**, 490 U.S. 495 (1989).

12. 342 U.S. 1 (1951).

If enough evidence exists that could have, and probably would have, resulted in the defendant's conviction other than the evidence that will be excluded from trial, the court will not reverse or remand the case. Consider the following scenario and decide whether the trial court's decision would or could have been different if the evidence the defendant wants excluded actually was.

YOU BE THE JUDGE

Defendant Larry Green was charged with arson; specifically, the government accuses him of setting fire to his own car in order to file for and receive insurance proceeds for the car. The prosecution presents several credible witnesses who do not know Larry but saw him setting fire to the carpeted trunk of his car as it was parked in a desolate field. One of the witnesses even videotaped Larry as he set his car on fire. A forensic expert testified that he found evidence of accelerants in the back of the car. A similar accelerant was found in Larry's house, along with a manual on how to set carpeting on fire. Larry did not testify at his own trial, and the jury rendered a verdict of "guilty."

During the course of the trial, the prosecutor pointed at Larry and referred to him as "Sparky" whenever he spoke to the jury about Larry or asked a witness a question about Larry. Larry has appealed his case and argues that the prosecutor's act of referring to him as "Sparky" caused the jury to find him guilty. Assume that it is inappropriate for the prosecutor to refer to the defendant in this manner. Would the trial have resulted in a not guilty verdict if the prosecutor had not acted this way?

THE SUPREME COURT

Supreme Court Jurisdiction

The Supreme Court is the highest appellate court of the land and, in this capacity, it exercises appellate jurisdiction over cases. However, the Court also has **original jurisdiction** over a few types of cases, primarily those that involve dignitaries from other countries or disputes between states. **Jurisdiction** is a court's ability, by law, to hear a particular case or controversy. The premise behind the Supreme Court's original jurisdiction in the case of a dispute against two states is that no state court could arrive at a neutral decision when another state is suing the state in which the deciding court sits. The Supreme Court's ability to hear cases involving foreign dignitaries also "depoliticizes" such decisions.

The Supreme Court's use of judicial power was established in the case of **Marbury v. Madison**.[13] William Marbury had been appointed as a justice of the peace by President John Adams, but Marbury's commission was not delivered in accordance with the requirements of the law. Marbury petitioned the Supreme Court, requesting that it force the Secretary of State (James Madison) to deliver the commission. Marbury based his request on the Judiciary Act of 1789, which required such a deliverance. The Supreme Court ruled against Marbury, stating that the Judiciary Act was unconstitutional. This case established the concept of judicial review by the Supreme Court and clarified the role of the three branches of the government (executive, judicial, and legislative). This system is referred to as a system of "checks and balances."

Similarly, the ability of the Supreme Court to rule on whether a state court has properly interpreted the federal Constitution was established in the case of **Martin v. Hunter's Lessee**.[14] The case involved a tract of land that the Colony of Virginia had confiscated for itself during the Revolutionary War. A treaty was signed with England following the war and permitted the original owners to receive the land. Virginia refused to cooperate and individuals tried to appeal the case from the Virginia courts to the Supreme Court of the United States. The Virginia Supreme Court refused to allow the case to go to the Supreme Court, arguing that the provision of the federal Judiciary Act of 1789, which authorized appeals from state courts to the Supreme Court, was unconstitutional. Virginia argued that the United States was a compact of states and not a national government and that the United States could not make a law that controlled the states. The Court rejected this argument and stated that the **Supremacy Clause** of the Constitution specifically makes the United States sovereign and the United States the final arbiter of all cases that arise under the Constitution. The Supremacy Clause is Clause 2 of Article VI of the Constitution and states:

> This Constitution, and the Laws of the United States which shall be made in pursuance thereof; and all treaties made, or which shall be made, under the authority of the United states, shall be the supreme law of the land; and the judges in every state shall be bound thereby, anything in the constitution or laws of any state to the contrary notwithstanding.

The Supremacy Clause mandates that all state laws must follow federal law if a conflict arises between federal law and either the state constitution or state law of any state.

Another case, **Cohens v. Virginia**,[15] also established the Supreme Court's power and the supremacy of the federal government. The United States

---

13. 5 U.S. 137 (1803).
14. 11 U.S. 603 (1813).
15. 19 U.S. 264 (1821).

Congress had authorized the operation of a lottery in the District of Columbia. The Cohens sold D.C. lottery tickets in the Commonwealth of Virginia, and their action violated the criminal code of Virginia. The Cohens were tried and convicted in Virginia, and the Virginia court then declared itself the final body that could determine a dispute between a state and the national government, stating that its criminal law prohibiting the sale of lottery tickets trumped the federal law allowing it. The Supreme Court upheld the convictions but also stated that the Supreme Court had full appellate jurisdiction over any case that was tried before a state court. The state of Virginia, as defendant, was concerned that the ruling limited state's rights. The Supreme Court's final ruling, however, stands: the Supreme Court has jurisdiction to determine whether a statute is in conflict with federal law and is unconstitutional.

Eras of the Supreme Court

The eras of the Supreme Court are referred to by the name of the justice who held the position of chief justice when certain rulings or types of rulings were made. The Court's earliest beginnings, until about 1801, did not render many decisions and the Supreme Court had little power at that point. The Marshall era, from 1801 to 1835, was an important time in the Court's history, and it was under Justice Marshall that the Court established the principle of judicial review and gave itself the final determination on constitutional issues. Prior to the Marshall era, each justice always drafted his own opinion; the Marshall era developed the practice of one majority opinion.

The years 1836 to 1864 were the Taney era and the Court was remembered for cases that influenced the Civil War. During the years 1864 to 1910, the Reconstruction Era following the Civil War, the Court interpreted the new Civil War amendments to the Constitution and developed the concept of substantive due process. From 1910 to 1930, the Court considered the incorporation of the Bill of Rights to the states. From 1930 to 1953, the Court gave a broad reading to the powers of the federal government and many of its decisions focused on giving the federal government more power. Justice Earl Warren held the position of chief justice from 1953 to 1969, and it was during this time that the Court decided many cases relating to criminal procedure, including the determination that many of the rights affecting those accused of crimes were incorporated to the states, the right of a defendant to have evidence seized unconstitutionally excluded from court, and the right of a defendant to be appointed an attorney to represent him in court. The Burger Court sat from 1969 to 1986 and handed down decisions regarding affirmative action, abortion, and the death penalty. Chief Justice Rehnquist served from 1986 to 2005, an era when the Court focused on federalism. The Court is currently under the leadership of Chief Justice Roberts, and constitutional scholars categorize the Court's decisions as being more conservative than those of the Rehnquist Court. Each era has its own personality, depending on the judges sitting on the Court and the majority views of the American public during that period.

Court Decisions

The nine Supreme Court justices do not always agree on the result in a particular case. The Court issues a written decision that sets forth its decision, the reasoning behind its decision, and the facts it utilized in order to make that decision. The Court's written decision is called the Court's **opinion**. At least a majority of the justices (five of nine) have to agree on the result, and their written decision is referred to as the **majority opinion**. Although it is possible that all nine judges will agree on the final result, as many as four judges can believe that a different result should be reached. These judges can also issue a written opinion, referred to as a **dissenting opinion**. Even though a dissenting opinion encompasses the "losing" argument, language from dissenting opinions sometimes is picked up later by the Supreme Court to justify a decision in a different case or to overrule its previous decision.

Further, sometimes a majority of justices agree on what the ultimate result of a case should be but do not agree on the reasoning behind the result, or a justice wishes to emphasize a particular analysis of the case. This type of opinion is referred to as a **concurring opinion**. An opinion in which the rationale clearly differs but the justice reaches the same result can also be called a **plurality opinion**. For example, in the case of **Katz v. United States**,[16] the issue before the Court was whether a man who was transmitting illegal wagering information from a phone booth had an expectation of privacy in the conversations he was having in the phone booth. The government had placed a listening device in the phone booth. The majority opinion determined that an expectation of privacy did exist and that the "search" of the phone booth by placing the listening device on it was unreasonable and thus unconstitutional. Justice Harlan agreed with the majority opinion but wrote his own opinion, setting forth a two-part test that he believed should be used when courts are attempting to determine whether a person possesses an expectation of privacy in a place. The test set forth in Harlan's opinion has been utilized by courts since that time to determine the extent of a constitutional right to privacy. Often, more than one concurring or dissenting opinion is published.

When the Supreme Court agrees to accept a case and then makes a final ruling on it, the Court's first option is to **affirm** the decision of the court below it. This means that the Court will agree with the lower court, and that court's decision will stand. In other words, if the defendant was convicted in the lower court and is now appealing his case, the Supreme Court would affirm the case if it held that there was no legal error in the defendant's conviction.

However, if the lower court ruled in favor of one party and the Supreme Court wishes to rule in favor of the opposing party, the Supreme Court will **reverse** the lower court's decision. This means the Court decides that

---

16. 389 U.S. 347 (1967).

prejudicial error took place at the lower court level in terms of the way the lower court interpreted the law. Often, a reversal will also result in the case being **remanded**, or sent back, to the lowest court (the trial court or the federal district court). A remand can have various outcomes, depending on the issue that was being appealed. If the Supreme Court decided to suppress a major piece of evidence in a case, it is possible that the case will be dropped by the prosecutor when the case is remanded, if there is not sufficient evidence otherwise to continue with the case. Alternatively, the case could continue to a new trial without that evidence being included. Finally, a court might need to hold an evidentiary hearing to obtain testimony and then follow the Supreme Court's guidelines on a particular issue. A case of **first impression** is one in which the Supreme Court has never made a determination regarding that issue. The Supreme Court might also **distinguish** one case from another, indicating that a different rule of law will apply to one case or the other because the facts of the cases differ. If the facts that differ between the two cases are important enough, the court can limit the holding in its decision in the first case to facts that are similar to the first case and make a new rule for cases that have facts of the second type.

Following its movement through the trial court and appellate system, a case could also involve other post-trial remedies, including motions whereby a defendant argues, for example, that his attorney was ineffective in his representation or that newly acquired evidence would change the outcome of his case.

Retroactivity. When the Supreme Court hands down a decision, it often regards an issue that relates to many cases that have gone through the court system previously and, in the realm of criminal law, many defendants who are incarcerated at the time the decision is made. However, the Court may or may not state whether its decision is **retroactive**, that is, whether it applies to cases that have been finally adjudicated previously or whether it applies only to cases that will be forthcoming. One example of a case in which the Court determined that its ruling should be retroactive was that of **Gideon v. Wainwright**, discussed previously, which granted defendants the right to the assistance of counsel in certain cases. The Court did not state in its opinion whether or not the case was retroactive to defendants who had already been convicted, so each state had to make its own determination as to whether new proceedings would be granted to defendants who did not have counsel at their trials or other proceedings. A similar issue arose in the area of juvenile murder defendants receiving life in prison without the possibility of parole. Each state has had to determine whether to apply the decision to those who are already in prison because of a life without parole statute. Certainly, making a decision retroactive can overload the court system because each and every defendant who is already in prison would find themselves back in court for new proceedings. The Supreme Court has given states some guidance to determine when the ruling in a particular case should be retroactive.

In **Griffith v. Kentucky**,[17] the Supreme Court ruled that any new rule it announces should be considered to be retroactive to any cases that are pending at the time the Court issues its decision. That way all similarly situated defendants are treated the same way. Even when a new rule represents a "clear break" from the law of the past, any cases that are pending should be reviewed in accordance with the new, not the old, rule.

Habeas Corpus Petitions. Occasionally a constitutional error takes place in a case but is not discovered until it is too late to follow the normal court process in filing on appeal. In such a case, a **habeas corpus** petition will be filed in federal court. The term "habeas corpus" literally translates to "that you have the body"; in other words, the state has a person imprisoned wrongfully. These petitions are often filed in federal court, and a defendant has an absolute right to file one, according to Article I, Section 9, of the United States Constitution. A state prisoner can file a habeas corpus petition in federal court if he or she can assert a constitutional violation, where otherwise a state prisoner might have no ability to file claims in federal court. If a habeas corpus petition is denied, the prisoner may then have a route to the Supreme Court when he may not have had one based on his state case. Because a habeas corpus petition can involve a federal court reviewing a case that was originally brought in state court, such a petition is called a "collateral attack" on the state court judgment.

The Supreme Court has placed restrictions on the ability of inmates to file these petitions, including time limitations for filing and certain types of issues that cannot be raised in a habeas corpus petition. Habeas corpus proceedings cannot be used to request that the court create a new law and the request must be related to a federal constitutional issue, unless for some reason the claim relates to fair procedure. Further, a defendant must exhaust all state remedies before filing a habeas corpus petition. Finally, a defendant cannot file more than one habeas corpus petition if he has forgotten to raise an issue in his first petition. If he files a petition and believes that he has not received fair consideration for the issues raised in that petition, he might be able to bring a subsequent petition, but he cannot bring a second or subsequent petition raising issues he forgot to include in his first petition. Although occasionally a court entertaining a habeas corpus petition can consider new evidence, generally the court is restricted to the records of the original case, as in a direct and subsequent appeal. No right to counsel exists for habeas corpus petitions because filing a habeas corpus is not an appeal of right; however, a state cannot prohibit inmates from helping each other prepare habeas corpus motions.

The statute governing habeas corpus petitions is Section 2241 of Title 28 of the United States Code (28 U.S.C. §2241). Because so many habeas corpus petitions were being filed in federal court, in 1996 this statute was

---

17. 479 U.S. 314 (1987).

amended by Congress to restrict the number of petitions a prisoner can file (generally second petitions are banned), and with a few exceptions, prisoners were also barred from bringing up claims that had already been raised and reviewed in state court.[18] Many states also have their own habeas corpus proceedings.

SPECIAL CONSTITUTIONAL CONCERNS

Judicial Restraint and Judicial Activism

The theory of **judicial restraint** is the theory that judges should limit the exercise of their power and limit their decision in each case to the facts and issues brought in that case. In other words, a court should not try to strike down laws unless they are clearly unconstitutional and should consider only the words of the Constitution and the framers' intent, not other outside influences. A Supreme Court justice acting with judicial restraint will avoid striking down prior decisions of the Court and will defer to the legislature, more often than not presuming that statutes are constitutional. Justice Felix Frankfurter is considered a judge who practiced judicial restraint.

The first case in which the Supreme Court engaged in judicial restraint was the case of **Luther v. Bordon**.[19] The **Luther** case involved Martin Luther, who was part of a group that was attempting to overthrow the charter government of Rhode Island. Martin Luther was arrested by state official Luther M. Borden, who searched Martin Luther's home and, in so doing, damaged Martin Luther's property. Martin Luther requested that the Court determine that Luther Borden acted without proper authority in conducting the search and further urged that the Court find that the charter government was not the lawful government of Rhode Island. Martin Luther based his argument on the fact that Article IV of the Constitution states that the United States "shall guarantee to every State in this Union a Republican Form of Government." The Supreme Court stated that the president and Congress should enforce that clause and that, as it was a politically charged question, it should be left out of the purview of the Supreme Court.

Alternatively, **judicial activism** is the opposite theory that a judge's role should be to hand down decisions that have implications for the future. A judge engaging in judicial activism should hand down decisions that make new law, rather than just interpreting history. Judges who use judicial activism allow their personal views about the issues that come before them to

---

18. These provisions are found in 28 U.S.C. §§2254, 2255.
19. 48 U.S. 1 (1849).

sway their decisions. An example of prominent Supreme Court cases that involve judicial activism include **Brown v. Board of Education of Topeka**[20] and **Roe v. Wade**.[21] In the **Brown** case, the Supreme Court ordered that public schools be desegregated. Racial segregation was common at the time the **Brown** case was decided, and in fact, the segregation of schools was actually based on state laws establishing separate public schools for black and white students. In its unanimous decision, which declared that these laws were unconstitutional, the Supreme Court stated that the act of segregating students was harmful, particularly to black students, even if the separate facilities were "equal" in their quality. The Court cited in its decision research that indicated that black children are harmed psychologically by being forced to attend a different school than white students. As you can see, the Court based its decision on much more than the simple issue of whether the language of the Constitution permits "separate but equal" laws.

You are probably familiar with **Roe v. Wade**, in which the Supreme Court held that the constitutional right to privacy extends to a woman's ability to decide whether or not to have an abortion. The Court's decision in the **Roe** case continues to be controversial, as the Court did put some limitations on abortion, determining that states do have an interest in protecting prenatal life and the health of a mother. The Supreme Court held that the idea of the right of privacy should be interpreted broadly, while pro-life supporters who oppose the Court's decision argue that the Court's decision is not based on a constitutional foundation but is based too much on the justices' personal attitudes. In this case, the Supreme Court clearly considered more than just the four corners of the Constitution and the framers' intent, focusing on the more overreaching issue of how much citizens of the United States expect the government to be permitted to infringe on personal decisions that affect us. Both the **Brown v. Board of Education** and **Roe v. Wade** cases are good examples of instances where the Supreme Court considered difficult, politically charged issues and went outside the four corners of the Constitution to make its decision.

Wrongful Convictions

As you move through this book and read all of the Supreme Court cases that involve granting constitutional rights to defendants, consider how horrifying it would be if these rights were violated, and as a result, an innocent person was imprisoned for a crime she did not commit. While considering the possibility that this has happened to others, consider also how you would feel if this happened to you. Unfortunately, our system is not perfect and at times, mistakes are made or, worse, an unethical person intentionally misrepresents the truth in a court case. The most appalling example of this

---

20. 347 U.S. 483 (1954).
21. 410 U.S. 113 (1973).

occurs when someone is placed on death row after conviction for something he did not do and the truth of his innocence is not discovered until after his execution.

The issue of wrongful convictions came to the forefront of the American justice system in the 1980s with the use of **DNA** evidence. DNA, or deoxyribonucleic acid, is a nucleic acid that contains all of the genetic instructions in living organisms. DNA is unique in humans and is found in body substances that are commonly left behind at crime scenes, including blood, skin, semen, saliva, and hair. **DNA profiling**, also called genetic fingerprinting, compares DNA found at the scene of a crime with the DNA of a suspected perpetrator. If DNA from several people is found at the scene of a crime, it may be more difficult to narrow down the perpetrator, but if DNA is found and can be proved to match a perpetrator, a person whose DNA does not match that sample can be excluded as a suspect. Various laws require people who are convicted of certain types of crimes to provide law enforcement with a DNA sample. These samples are placed in a database and then can be matched to DNA found at the scene of a crime.

Along with providing proof for use by prosecutors regarding who has committed a crime, the use of DNA evidence has also exonerated many people who have been imprisoned as convicted criminals. The "Innocence Project," formed in 1992 by attorneys Barry Scheck and Peter Neufeld, has worked to exonerate many people who had been wrongly convicted of crimes. Inmates and other convicted persons contact the project, which then investigates issues relating to the inmates' claims of innocence. Other innocence projects have also been founded and have assisted people in their attempts to prove their innocence. These projects and other advocates have also encouraged changes within the system to decrease the number of people who are convicted wrongfully, such as improved preservation of evidence and recording of police interrogations so unconstitutional interrogations can be reviewed and suppressed by the court. Review of cases by the Supreme Court provides one more layer of review in the hopes that innocent people are not wrongfully convicted, and innocence project advocates help properly raise these issues before the courts.

Juvenile Offenders

The Supreme Court has had to deal with issues that are specific to juvenile offenders. Because the juvenile justice system was created with the idea in mind that juveniles are different from adult offenders in their ability to think, reason, and be rehabilitated, constitutional issues surrounding juvenile offenders are different from those same issues as they apply to adult offenders.

In re Gault[22] was the first and most important landmark case in terms of juvenile offenders and their rights under the Constitution.

---

22. 387 U.S. 1 (1967).

IN RE GAULT

FACTS: Ora Cook, a neighbor of 15-year-old Gerald Gault, accused Gault of making an obscene phone call to her. The local sheriff took Gault into custody without notifying his parents. Gault's mother eventually located him in the county's juvenile detention facility, but she was unable to take her son home with her. Gault had a preliminary hearing the next morning and he indicated that his friend had made the telephone call from Gault's house and that Gault had asked him to leave after he informed Gault that he had done so. Gault was released only after remaining in custody for several more days, and his family was notified by a letter of the next hearing date.

At the next hearing, Gault was found to be a delinquent and was ordered to be confined at the state industrial school until the age of 21, unless he would be discharged sooner by court order. Had Gault been convicted in adult court of the same crime, lewd phone calls, he would have received a maximum prison sentence of two months and a fine of $5.00 to $50.00. Gault never met his accuser and she did not attend his hearing.

Gault filed petitions under the habeas corpus act but eventually his case ended up in the Supreme Court, where he argued that the entire process violated his due process rights in various ways.

ISSUE: Did the process Gault was subjected to violate his due process rights under the Fourteenth Amendment?

HOLDING: Gault's Fourteenth Amendment rights were violated, including his right to an attorney, formal notification of the charges against him, the right not to incriminate himself, and his opportunity to confront his accusers.

RATIONALE: The opinion in this case was 7-1 for Gault. The sole dissenter argued that the purpose of juvenile court was to correct juveniles, not to punish them, so the safeguards applicable to adult cases should not apply to juvenile cases. The majority opinion indicated that providing juveniles with constitutional rights would not change the basic tenets of the juvenile justice system. Because a juvenile can be sent to a juvenile facility that functions similarly to a jail, with institutional hours and guards, his rights should be protected before he is sent there. This includes being given the same basic rights, set forth above, that adults are given.

Juveniles now have the following constitutional rights:

1. Written notice of charges
2. Right to confront and cross-examine witnesses
3. Right to an attorney
4. Right not to incriminate themselves
5. Right for charges to be proved beyond a reasonable doubt
6. Protection against double jeopardy

A juvenile does not have the right to receive a trial by jury, according to the Supreme Court's decision in **McKeiver v. Pennsylvania**.[23] The Court opined that the jury is not an essential system of "accurate fact finding" in our justice system. Further, juvenile cases are not considered to be either criminal or civil cases, so the jury trial provisions of the Constitution do not apply to them.

Some states, however, do permit juveniles to have their case tried by a jury if they request it, for limited types of cases.

Probable cause requirements in terms of searching a juvenile are the same as for adults, although some exceptions exist in a school setting, where "reasonable suspicion" is the standard, due to the school's quasi-parental status toward the minor. A juvenile does have the same **Miranda** rights as an adult. Juveniles do not have the right to request bail, although many juveniles are released to their parents pending further proceedings.

QUESTIONS TO CONSIDER

1. Watch a trial on a court television channel. Consider the opening statements of both parties. Based on those statements alone, if you were a juror, would you have an opinion one way or another as to whether the defendant is guilty or not guilty? As you consider the testimony that is presented, does your view change? Do the closing arguments change your mind in any way in terms of which side should prevail? Do you believe you could have followed the testimony presented in the case without first hearing the opening arguments?

2. Look at the innocence project website, http://www.innocenceproject .org. Review the facts of one of the cases discussed on the website. What constitutional rights were violated against the wrongly convicted person in that case?

3. Read **Hurtado v. California**, 110 U.S. 516 (1884), the case in which the Supreme Court determined that a right did not need to be incorporated to the states. Do you agree with the Court? Why or why not? Compare this case with one of the cases in which the Court did incorporate a right.

4. On the Internet, find all of the arguments you can from advocates of gun control and advocates of the right to bear arms. What statistics does each group cite that supports its argument? Which side do you believe has an argument that better comports with the language of the Second Amendment?

---

23. 403 U.S. 528 (1971).

KEY TERMS

allocatur
When the state supreme court agrees to hear and make a ruling on an appeal; it is the state equivalent of a petition for certiorari.

Articles of Confederation
Approved in 1781, they set forth the structure for the new government, allowing the states to retain some power while also delegating power to what has become the federal government, which in turn allowed the government to be centralized while maintaining the individual governments established in the colonies, which later became states.

beyond a reasonable doubt
The burden of proof in a criminal trial, based on the evidence presented at trial.

Bill of Rights
The first ten amendments to the Constitution, guaranteeing certain basic civil liberties.

common law
Law made by the court in an area where the legislature has not passed a law.

concurring opinion
Written opinion issued by a Supreme Court justice when a justice agrees on the result, but not the reasoning, of a Court ruling.

crime control model
This model is based on the concept that crime control is of the utmost importance and should be the focus of the Court in making decisions in cases in which criminal procedure is an issue; advocates of this model believe that accused must be guilty

and are concerned with moving cases efficiently and quickly through the criminal justice system, without being particularly concerned with procedure and process.

dissenting opinion
Written opinion of the Supreme Court justices who oppose a ruling.

due process
The Fourteenth Amendment principle that gives each individual the right to be treated fairly and have a say in the judicial process.

due process model
This model focuses on human rights and freedoms, and assumes that all individuals are innocent until proved guilty. Advocates of this model argue that the most important characteristic of our justice system is the right of all people to be free from governmental interference, and that this consideration should be the focus at all levels.

executive branch
Branch of government developed in Article II of the Constitution, referring to the office of the President.

Great Compromise
This agreement allowed both types of representation—based on population but also equal number of votes per state—with the House being selected based on population and the Senate based on equal representation, which also adopted a system based on shared power between legislative, executive, and judicial branches.

habeas corpus
Literally, "to have the body," this term refers to the wrongful imprisonment of an individual.

judicial branch
Branch of government established in Article III of the Constitution, responsible for legal actions, and specifically created the Supreme Court as the highest court in the United States.

legislative branch
Branch of government developed in Article I of the Constitution that is Congress, including the House of Representatives and the Senate.

majority opinion
The written decision of at least five of nine Supreme Court justices.

New Jersey Plan
Resolution proposed at the Constitutional Convention calling for a similar government structure to the Articles of Confederation, and supported by many of the smaller states.

petition for certiorari
This petition is filed when a defendant or the commonwealth/government loses their case and either party wishes to appeal the decision; it is a request for the court to agree to consider and make a ruling on the case.

plurality opinion
An opinion whereby the rationale clearly differs but the justice reaches the same result.

preponderance of the evidence
The burden of proof in a civil trial, based on the evidence presented at trial.

procedural law
Includes any legal rules that tell courts and attorneys how to proceed with a case, including the "rules of evidence."

statutory law
Refers to laws passed by legislature.

substantive law
Guarantees that citizens' liberty will be protected, according to the Fourteenth Amendment.

Virginia Resolution
Resolution proposed at the Constitutional Convention calling for a national government with a legislature, executive branch, and judicial branch.

KEY COURT CASES

Brown v. Board of Education of Topeka
Landmark case in which the Supreme Court ordered that public schools be desegregated, overturning the "separate but equal" laws.

Gideon v. Wainwright
A prime example of a case whereby the Supreme Court decided that its ruling should be retroactive, which granted defendants the right to assistance of counsels in certain cases.

Illinois v. Gates

In this case, the Supreme Court ruled that a police officer may consider the "totality of the circumstances" when determining whether or not the facts of the case support a search warrant.

In re Gault

First, landmark case involving juvenile offenders and their constitutional rights, guaranteeing right to written notice of charges, right to confront witnesses, right to counsel, right to not incriminate themselves, right for charges to be proved beyond a reasonable doubt, and protection against double jeopardy.

Marbury v. Madison

Case that established the Supreme Court's use of judicial power, establishing the concept of judicial review by the Supreme Court and clarifying the role of the three branches of government (the checks and balances system).

Miranda v. Arizona

Case that established the "Miranda rights," which guarantee certain rights and privileges upon arrest. (Right to remain silent, right to counsel, etc.)

Roe v. Wade

Landmark case in which the Supreme Court ruled that the constitutional right to privacy extends to a woman's ability to decide whether or not to have an abortion.

THE FOURTH AMENDMENT: THE BASICS OF SEARCH AND SEIZURE

LEARNING OBJECTIVES: Students will

1. Know what is protected by the Fourth Amendment
2. Know what a search is and when a search occurs
3. Know what administrative searches are and when they are permitted
4. Know when law enforcement agents can seize property and detain people

> The right of the people to be secure in their persons, houses, papers, and effects, against unreasonable searches and seizures, shall not be violated, and no Warrants shall issue, but upon probable cause, supported by Oath or affirmation, and particularly describing the place to be searched, and the persons or things to be seized.
>
> **—U.S. Constitution, Amendment IV**

The Fourth Amendment is only 54 words long. However, police officers use its provisions daily in performing their duties, and the concepts contained in the amendment are central to our criminal justice system. Because of the lack of clarity of the actual language of the amendment, the Supreme Court has struggled to interpret it. As Justice Felix Frankfurter opined in **Chapman v. United States,**[1] "[t]he course of true law pertaining to [this amendment] ... has not ... run smooth."

The Fourth Amendment applies only to criminal cases and has no application to civil law. Further, the Fourth Amendment applies only to government actors. A private party who conducts a search of another private party's personal property is not violating the Constitution. Remember, the purpose of the Constitution was to limit the acts of government and not the acts of private citizens. A private search can be unlawful and lead to trespass or other criminal charges but cannot be the subject of a constitutional violation.

---

1. 365 U.S. 10 (1961).

SUPREME COURT BUILDING IN WASHINGTON, D.C.

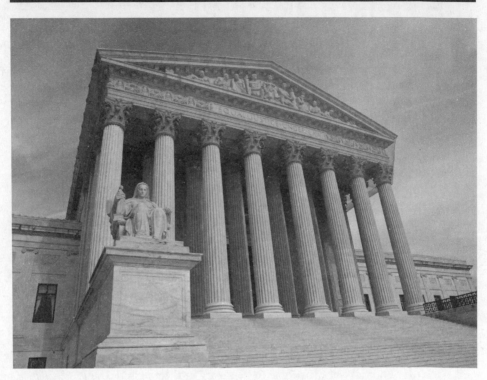

www.bigstock.com.

The amendment is divided into two clauses: the first portion of the amendment is the "reasonableness" clause and the second is the "warrant" clause. As with the wording of the Second Amendment, it is unclear which of the two clauses of the Fourth Amendment was meant to be controlling. If the warrant clause is controlling, then warrants should always be obtained before a search and seizure is conducted. If the "reasonableness" clause controls, then the primary issue in examining a search and seizure issue is reasonableness. The Supreme Court has decided many cases that speak to the reasonableness of searches and seizures and has also handed down many decisions that instruct police officers as to whether they need a warrant in particular cases. The amendment does state that if a warrant is issued, it must be issued upon "probable cause."

These two words have often been interpreted by the Supreme Court and lower courts. Another issue that arises in applying the Fourth Amendment to the actions of law enforcement is the term "secure" that is used in the first part of the amendment. The placement of the term at the beginning of the amendment suggests that the entire amendment was written in order to provide security. However, our security in our personal items and our homes must be balanced by the government's ability to investigate crime and prosecute criminals expediently and thoroughly. Thus, the Supreme Court has had to struggle with interpreting the Constitution in a way that permits this security but also furthers the safety of citizens and the ability of our justice system to prosecute people who break the law.

This chapter will cover the issues of what objects are covered by the Fourth Amendment, when a court will determine that a search or seizure has taken place, and when a search and seizure might be considered "unreasonable." Chapter 5 will explain the Supreme Court's definition of "probable cause" and discuss when law enforcement officials must acquire a warrant before effectuating a search, seizure, or arrest.

HISTORY OF THE AMENDMENT

As with the other amendments and concepts discussed so far, recognizing the culture that existed at the time the framers wrote the Constitution can assist us in determining why the framers wrote the specific parts of the Fourth Amendment. You will recall from Chapter 1 that the framers disliked England's system of **writs of assistance** and **general warrants**, documents the framers viewed as being overbearing and oppressive. Writs of assistance allowed local individuals to enter and search the homes of colonists, generally for no reason at all, to assist the British government in searching for smuggled goods. General warrants were used in a similar way, although the underlying purpose of the warrants involved law enforcement looking for books and papers that were being used to criticize the government. In executing either, the agents of the government were able to enter houses at will and were not particularly civil in their execution of the writs and warrants. A significant case in this area decided by the English government prior to the American Revolution was **Entick v. Carrington**.[2] John Entick was the editor of a newspaper that criticized the English government and was arrested on charges of libel. The government issued a warrant requesting the seizure of all of his books, letters, and papers. Entick sued the government, arguing that its agents had trespassed on his property when seizing those items. The English court agreed and further stated that the practice of general warrants was illegal. This encouraged the framers of the United States Constitution to specifically outlaw such warrants in the language of the Bill of Rights.

Even with this historical framework in mind, the Supreme Court has interpreted the Fourth Amendment as having other, broader goals as well. For example, the Supreme Court has determined that a primary and important focus of the framers in drafting the Fourth Amendment was to protect the sanctity of private property. Criticizing the writs of assistance, the Court stated that owning property was "[t]he great end for which men entered into society." **Boyd v. United States**.[3] Further, as will be discussed at length in this

---

2. 95 Eng. Rep. 807 (1765).
3. 116 U.S. 616 (1886).

chapter, one of the main concerns of the framers when drafting the Bill of Rights was to protect an individual's expectation of privacy in his property and belongings. The Supreme Court stated in **Boyd** that "a search and seizure [is] equivalent [to] a compulsory production of a man's private papers."

It is important to keep in mind that when drafting the Constitution, the framers were familiar with very few of the items that are often subject to search or seizure in today's society. Certainly, the framers were not concerned about whether the same standard that applied to general searches and seizures would apply to items found within a motor vehicle, computers, or cell phones, which are items that are routinely searched by police now. (The nuances of searches that involve these items will be discussed later in this chapter.) The Supreme Court has had to apply the Constitution to new technology as it has been developed.

THE PROTECTIONS AND PRINCIPLES OF THE FOURTH AMENDMENT

Reasonableness

The Fourth Amendment bars unreasonable searches and seizures. This means that if police conduct is not "unreasonable," it will not be barred by the Fourth Amendment. It is important to keep in mind the distinction between searches and seizures that fall within the scope of the Fourth Amendment but are permissible under the amendment and those that do not fall within the scope of the amendment at all. A search that does not fall within the scope of the Fourth Amendment has no limitations. A search that falls within the scope of the Fourth Amendment needs to be "reasonable."

Many decisions have been written discussing the meaning of the term "reasonable." In 1923, a court decided the case of **Sussex Land & Live Stock Co. v. Midwest Refining Co.,**[4] one of the first cases considered by a federal court that concerned environmental issues. Persons living downstream from oil drilling filed a lawsuit against the oil driller who was drilling upstream, arguing that the drillers were polluting the water. Although this was not necessarily a criminal case, the court's discussion of what was considered "reasonable" was relevant in future criminal cases. The court considered whether the oil company's use of the property deprived the adjoining owner of the "reasonable" use of his land, stating that "[w]hat is reasonable depends upon a variety of considerations and circumstances. It is an elastic term which is of uncertain value in a definition."

Courts have employed two different approaches to determine whether police action is reasonable. First, courts use a **bright-line** approach, where reasonableness is determined by a specific rule that applies to all cases. One bright-line approach to search and seizure is the rule that permits law

---

4. 294 F. 597 (8th Cir. 1923).

enforcement to open any containers they find in the passenger compartment of a car, as will be discussed in Chapter 4.

If no bright-line rule can be established, courts will employ a **case by case** approach, in which each time a search is conducted, the reasonableness of that search and seizure is completely dependent on the facts and circumstances of that case. For example, as you will learn, when a police officer sees a person acting suspiciously in a high crime area and he believes the person could be armed, he might be able to at least conduct a frisk of the person to make sure the person is not carrying weapons. The exact facts of each case, however, will dictate whether the frisk can occur and a court will explore those facts in detail in trying to determine whether the conduct of the police, given the facts, is reasonable. Courts can consider a person's demeanor, the area of a city in which the person was observed by law enforcement, and many other factors when ruling on the reasonableness of a frisk.

YOU BE THE JUDGE

An officer was patrolling in a high crime area at 11:00 P.M. when he noticed an older vehicle pulling out of the lot of a factory; many cars were leaving the lot because second shift workers were just finishing their shift for the day. The vehicle had a sticker on the back window that had on it the name of a local university. The officer looked at the individual driving the car and noticed that he was a male who was wearing a baseball hat and who appeared to be about 17 years old. The city has a curfew ordinance that requires all youths under the age of 18 to be at home by 10:00 P.M. The officer pulled over the car and requested that he be able to see the young man's identification. Upon requesting the identification, he realized that the man was a local college student and was actually 20 years old. However, the officer noticed a bag of marijuana sitting on the seat next to the man. The marijuana can be introduced in court only if the pullover was reasonable. Do you rule that the pullover was reasonable or not, based on these facts?

Persons, Houses, Papers, and Effects

The Fourth Amendment specifically protects "persons, houses, papers, and effects." We know that the drafters of the amendment were particularly interested in making sure that colonists were not the subject of warrantless searches while in their homes. The distinction between items that fall within the scope of the terms "persons, houses, papers, and effects" and anything that does not fall within the scope of these terms is very important. If an item is not considered a person, house, paper, or effect, that item is NOT protected by the Fourth Amendment. Thus, even an unreasonable search can take place in regard to that item. Further, no warrant would ever be necessary to conduct a search for that item. The search or seizure would never need to be supported by probable cause, or even a lesser standard such as reasonable suspicion. You will find that the majority of items are included in the scope of those terms. However, the Supreme Court has identified a few items that are deemed not to have been included in this list. Such items include those that are found in "open fields," a concept which is discussed at length below, as well as items that have been abandoned by its owners and other items that people do not, or should not, expect to be private.

Persons. The term "persons," as used in the Fourth Amendment, refers to anything that is connected to a person's body. This term can include items that are not seen by the public, such as items in a person's pocket or hidden within a person's body. This would also include a blood draw, as might be required in a case in which a person is charged with driving while intoxicated. Checking someone's pockets would also be considered a search of a "person." In early cases in which the Court defined the term "person," the Supreme Court determined that the Fourth Amendment only applied to searches and seizures of items that could be physically touched. However, this term was later expanded to include the search and seizure of oral communications, such as statements made by one person to another.

For example, in **Olmstead v. United States**,[5] the government wiretapped private conversations of individuals. In ruling that no search or seizure had taken place, the Court stated as follows: "The [Fourth] Amendment does not forbid what was done here. There was no searching. There was no seizure. The evidence was secured by the use of the sense of hearing only. There was no entry of the houses or offices of the defendants." The majority opinion of the Court reasoned that because the wires via which the phone conversations were transmitted were outside the defendant's house, they could not be considered to be protected anyway. The Court further considered the fact that Congress could extend the protection of the Fourth Amendment to telephone conversations by passing legislation accordingly. The Court stated that it would not prohibit such actions, since to do so would "[attribute] an enlarged and unusual meaning to the Fourth Amendment." Until the Supreme Court overturned its own decision in the **Olmstead** case in 1967 via the **United States v. Katz** case, discussed below, the Court considered the Fourth Amendment to be applicable only in cases in which an actual physical "penetration" of property occurred. Most of the early Supreme Court cases discussing this topic also focused on whether a person possessed a "property interest" in an item.

Judge Brandeis wrote a dissenting opinion in the **Olmstead** case, setting forth concepts that the Supreme Court focused on in later cases to expand the protection of the Fourth Amendment. Brandeis stated in his opinion that the framers drafted the Bill of Rights in a time when "force and violence" were being used by the government to obtain information from criminal defendants. The amendments were drafted, in part, to avoid such force and violence by the government. However, when the amendments were written and

---

5. 277 U.S. 438 (1928).

passed, force and violence were the only means available for the government to intimidate people and obtain information. According to Brandeis, granting the government the authority to utilize wiretapping techniques and obtain information from technology has merely provided the government with an alternative way to violate citizens' privacy rights, albeit perhaps in more subtle ways than force and violence. Brandeis likened a telephone conversation to a sealed letter sent through the mail, stating that we expect privacy in items we place in the mail and perhaps expect even more privacy in conversations we have on the telephone. Brandeis believed that the framers intended to protect Americans "in their beliefs, their thoughts, their emotions, and their sensations"; further, he stated that the most comprehensive right we have as citizens is the right to be left alone.

Finally, Brandeis used the **unclean hands** theory to argue that the evidence was gathered by the government in an unconstitutional manner. The unclean hands theory is a common law theory which states that a court should not allow a party to prevail in a case when he has "unclean hands." In other words, someone who contributed to his own problem should not be able to recover from someone else for the problem he helped to create. Brandeis stated that allowing the government to tap phone wires, which was illegal under the law of the state in which it occurred, should result in the government not being able to "avail itself of the fruits of these acts" as the government would be committing an illegal act. In one of Brandeis's famous quotes in the **Olmstead** case, he stated,

> [I]f the government becomes a lawbreaker, it breeds contempt for law; it invites every man to become a law unto himself; it invites anarchy. To declare that in the administration of the criminal law the end justifies the means—to declare that the government may commit crimes in order to secure the conviction of a private criminal—would bring terrible retribution. Against that pernicious doctrine this court should resolutely set its face.

Interestingly, a portion of Judge Brandeis's dissent was also quoted by Timothy McVeigh, who was brought to trial for his participation in bombing the Federal Building in Oklahoma City in 1995 that caused the deaths of numerous people. McVeigh remained silent during his trial but chose to speak at his sentencing, quoting Brandeis's statement that "our government is the potent, the omnipresent teacher. For good or ill, it teaches the whole people by its example." Brandeis's words demonstrate the serious nature of any intrusion on a person's right to privacy.

Houses.   The term "houses" implies a place that people live and has also been expanded to mean other dwelling places such as apartments and even recreational vehicles or other places in which a person might reside for some time. Courts will always consider the use to which a structure is being put when determining whether that structure falls within the term "house" for Fourth Amendment purposes. Courts have questioned, for example, whether a recreational vehicle is a "home" or not. The answer to this question is very fact specific and generally depends on the use to which the recreational vehicle is put. A recreational vehicle that is moveable and is being used to travel on a road is probably not going to be considered a home for purposes of the amendment and will most likely be subject to the relaxed search rules that are applicable to vehicles. However, a recreational vehicle in which someone is residing for three months and is hooked up to water and sewer will most likely be considered a house for purposes of the amendment.

Privacy rights have been extended to include a person's office in his workplace, depending on how private that area is. It can also include items such as file cabinets or lockers that are kept within a business and contain personal items. While a business may be considered by a court to be somewhat less protected than a home based on its accessibility to the public during business hours, a business is still protected from unreasonable searches and seizures when it is not open for business. Courts recognize the private nature of items and information maintained at the physical location for a business when the business is not open to the public. The concept of "open fields" and "curtilage" will be discussed below to help you understand privacy outside the walls of a home.

Papers. The next term, "papers," originally meant, literally, paper. When the Fourth Amendment was drafted, personal information was written on paper and thus, the framers wished to protect that type of information. However, many of us do not keep our personal information on "paper" documents anymore; a large amount of our personal information is now kept in electronic form on computers or even handheld personal data assistants or other electronic devices. Courts have recognized a privacy interest in all types of documents, whether "hard copy" or otherwise, that might contain personal information. The term "papers" can also include film and video.

Effects. The final term referenced in the Fourth Amendment is the word "effects," a term you probably don't use very often, if at all, in your daily speech. What did the framers mean by this word? The term basically means "personal property." Consider all of the things a person might not want a police officer to search but which might not be included in the list of "persons, houses, and papers." For example, what about your car? What about your book bag that you carry with you back and forth from class? Weapons, drugs, and other evidence of criminal activity are considered "effects." In fact, any item that the Supreme Court has not specifically excluded from the list of possible items a person could own is considered to be protected under the "effects" category.

PROCEDURE FOR OBTAINING A WARRANT

A law enforcement official who wishes to obtain a search or arrest warrant must do so by following local rules and procedures. The official must draft an **affidavit of probable cause**, which is a statement of all of the information that the official knows either from personal observation or from the investigation she has conducted in connection with a particular crime. In Chapter 5, you will learn about what types of information can be included in an affidavit. The official who signs and submits the affidavit must believe that the information contained therein is true or at least must have obtained the information from someone who she believes is a reliable source. The official who drafts and signs the application is called the **affiant**, because she is the person swearing that the information in the application is correct to the best of her knowledge or was received from a trustworthy source. The affidavit of probable cause is accompanied by a **warrant application**, which requests that a magistrate or other neutral official sign the warrant. The affiant will also provide the magistrate with a proposed warrant for the magistrate to sign. The magistrate can alter the proposed warrant as he sees fit, adding or deleting items to be searched for or dictating the hours during which the warrant can be **executed**. A search warrant is executed when the law enforcement official actually goes to the location set forth in the warrant and searches for the items listed in the warrant. An arrest warrant is executed when the suspect named therein is taken into custody.

The process to be followed once a warrant application is drafted varies by state and locality, but usually an affiant must have his supervisor review the application. Further, often a prosecutor, either the local district attorney or federal prosecuting attorney, reviews the application and approves it before it is submitted to the magistrate. Having both a supervisor and prosecutor review the application means that two more people who have generally not been involved in the investigation believe that the application establishes that probable cause exists. The application can be sent to the magistrate as a hard copy, by facsimile, or even by email. Local rules will dictate which magistrate the application should go to for consideration; usually each local magistrate has a specific geographical area over which he presides. Thus, if a crime takes place in that magistrate's geographical area, he will approve of the warrant, although the magistrate who presides over the jurisdiction where a crime is investigated also has jurisdiction to issue the warrant. A crime that takes place in multiple jurisdictions will usually be consolidated under one magistrate. If the magistrate denies the warrant application, the affidavit cannot be submitted again to that magistrate or to any other magistrate[6] unless the warrant application is revised and new information is added to it. The magistrate will usually provide a time limit for when the warrant must be executed. Often this time period is ten days but again, the time limit may vary based on local rules. If the time limit passes, the law enforcement authority must return to the magistrate who issued the warrant and provide good cause for why the warrant could not be issued within the applicable time period, requesting its renewal.

A sample probable cause affidavit, warrant application, and warrant signed by a magistrate are provided in Figures 2.1 and 2.2.

---

6. Occasionally it could be determined that a particular magistrate might have rejected a warrant application because she was biased and that another magistrate must review the warrant; in such a case it is possible that the warrant will not need to be revised. Further, sometimes two different magistrates might have the ability to grant the warrant, for example, if a criminal committed similar crimes in two different magistrates' jurisdictions. However, absent a conflict of interest, it is inappropriate to "forum shop" by filing a warrant application in front of one magistrate when another magistrate has already rejected the application.

FIGURE 2.1. SAMPLE PROBABLE CAUSE AFFIDAVIT

Commonwealth of Pennsylvania   **Warrant Control No. 5**
County of Wrightsville   **Inventory No.**
                                                    Date of Application: October 22, 2010

Name of Affiant: Detective Sergeant Jack Black,
                                Wrightsville Police Department (867-5309)

**Probable cause belief is based on the following facts
and circumstances:**

On October 15, 2010, a telephone call was received by the Wrightsville Police Department reporting that a robbery had occurred at the S&P Mini Mart, located at 210 West 4th Street. Patrol officers Jim Beam and Jack Daniels responded. Upon arriving at the Mini, the officers found that the clerk, Jimmy Jenson, had been shot in the chest and was on the floor behind the counter lying in a pool of blood. Emergency personnel told the officers that Jenson's pulse was very weak and that he was unconscious and unresponsive. They also told the officers that they observed a gunshot wound to the chest on the right side just below the victim's nipple. The Mini Mart was sealed off and Detectives Jack Black and Joe White responded. The victim was transported to the hospital where he was pronounced dead upon arrival. At the Mini Mart, detectives found several fingerprints in blood on the counter, a wallet, a broken gold tooth, and a spent shell casing from a 45 ACP caliber handgun. Hair was located in the victim's right hand indicating that a possible struggle with the offender had taken place. The cash register drawer was open and empty. The store manager stated that $250 was missing from the cash drawer, along with several cartons of Red Dog Cigarettes.

Detective Black looked through the wallet and found a photo ID bearing the name of Hammond Ranson. Detective White reviewed the surveillance video. The video showed a person wearing a blue bandana over his face and dark sunglasses. The person appeared to be a white male, and he had a tattoo of a dragon on the right side of his neck that appeared to be breathing fire. He had on a red tee shirt with "Jive Turkey" printed on it in white lettering, blue jeans with a ripped pocket, and a red and white baseball cap that had the words "Kool Kat" printed on it. The suspect could also be seen holding what appeared to be a silver semiautomatic handgun and pointing it at the clerk. The video showed that the clerk struggled with the suspect and the clerk was able to knock the suspect's hat off and grab a handful of hair, apparently also knocking out one of the suspect's teeth. The suspect then shot the clerk and took the money from the cash drawer and also took several cartons of cigarettes. He then picked up his hat and ran from the store.

After canvassing the neighborhood, detectives Black and White found two witnesses identified as Jack Jones and Jill Jones, who saw the suspect run from the store. They described the man they saw running from the store and the description matched the man in the video. They described him as a white male around 5'10'' tall weighing approximately 180 to 200 pounds with a blue bandana over his face and wearing dark sunglasses. They even described the dragon tattoo on his neck. They also told the detectives that the man got into a black Cadillac Escalade and sped off. They were able to get a partial license plate number. The plate number started with the letters DMM-5.

The fingerprints that were found at the scene of the crime were lifted and analyzed through NCIC and were matched to a Hammond Ranson, which was the same name on the ID found in the wallet at the crime scene. The detectives then ran a record check on Hammond Ranson and found that he has an arrest history of armed robberies dating back to 1990. They also found from the record that he is a white male weighing 190 pounds and has a tattoo of a dragon on his neck just like the suspect in the surveillance video from the store where the crime took place. Hammond also goes by the street name of "June bug." This fits the description of the suspect that was given by the witnesses who saw him leave the scene in a black Escalade. Further investigation found that Hammond's mother owns a 2009 black Cadillac Escalade with the license plate DMM-5211, which is a match with the partial plate given by the witnesses. It was also found that Hammond's last known address was 4410 West 22nd Street, Wrightsville, PA 15411. This is the same address where his mother resides.

An autopsy was performed by Dr. Frank N. Stein on the victim. Dr. Stein reported that the victim died of a single gunshot wound to the chest. He reported that he found the bullet lodged in the victim's chest. Following its removal from the body, the bullet was analyzed and it had come from a 45 ACP caliber handgun. That bullet matches the caliber of the spent shell casing found at the crime scene. No handgun was found at the scene of the crime.

This officer requests a search warrant for the residence and curtilage of Hammond Ranson for the items specified on the face of the search warrant. It is believed that these items, which have not been recovered, may be at this location. It is also believed that this search warrant is necessary at this stage of this investigation, and is necessary for the successful completion of this investigation. This affiant requests this search warrant to be granted.

Jack Black
_____
Detective Jack Black

Sworn to and subscribed
Before me this 22nd day
Of October, 2010

Anthony L. Hugar
_____
Issuing Authority

FIGURE 2.2. SAMPLE WARRANT APPLICATION

			APPLICATION FOR
COUNTY OF	**Commonwealth of Pennsylvania** } ss.		**SEARCH WARRANT**
WRIGHTSVILLE	**County of** _____ Wrightsville _____ }		AND AFFIDAVIT

			Warrant Control No.
Detective Jack Black,	Wrightsville Police Dept.,	867-5309	5
(Name of Affiant)	(Police Department or address of private affiant}	(Phone No.)	**Date of Application** 22 Oct 2010

being duly sworn (or affirmed) before me according to law, deposes and says that there is probable cause to believe that certain property is evidence of or the fruit of a crime or is contraband or is unlawfully possessed or is otherwise subject to seizure, and is located at particular premises or in the possession of particular person as described below.

Inventory No.

IDENTIFY ITEMS TO BE SEARCHED FOR AND SEIZED (be as specific as possible):

Clothing worn by the Suspect, a handgun, black Escalade, money and Red Dog cigarettes, items used in the commission of the crime and items taken in the crime.

On 10/15/2010 at the time of a robbery/homicide on Victim Jimmy Jenson, approx. 0530 hours, to include a red tee shirt with Jive Turkey printed on it, blue jeans with a ripped pocket and a red and white baseball cap that had the words Kool Kat printed on it, and other items, including a silver 45 caliber semiautomatic handgun, a 2009 black Cadillac Escalade, $250 in cash and 6 cartons of Red Dog Cigarettes, transfer evidence to include blood, hairs, fibers connected to the incident

SPECIFIC DESCRIPTION OF PREMISES AND/OR PERSONS TO BE SEARCHED (Street and No. Apt. No. Vehicle, Safe Deposit Box, etc.):

4410 West 22nd Street, a green and white two story residence, with two car attached garage, entrance is on the north side of the residence.

NAME OF OWNER, OCCUPANT OR POSSESSOR OF SAID PREMISES TO BE SEARCHED (If proper name is unknown, give alias and/or description):

Hammond Ranson, age 42 years, Mother's name is Jolleen Winters, and is the owner of residence to be searched.

VIOLATION OF (Describe conduct or specify statute):

DATE OF VIOLATION 15 OCTOBER, 2010

ROBBERY (3701), HOMICIDE (2501)

PROBABLE CAUSE BELIEF IS BASED ON THE FOLLOWING FACTS AND CIRCUMSTANCES (See special instructions below):

SEE ATTACHED PROBABLE CAUSE

ATTACH ADDITIONAL PAPER (S) COPIES IF NECESSARY [ ] CHECK HERE IF ADDITIONAL PAPER IS USED.

PLEASE READ AND FOLLOW THESE INSTRUCTIONS CAREFULLY

1. If information was obtained from another person, e.g., an informant, a private citizen, or a fellow law officer, state specifically what information was received and when such information was obtained. State also the factual basis for believing such other person is reliable.
2. If Surveillance was made, state what information was obtained by such surveillance, by whom it was obtained, and state date, time and place of such surveillance.
3. State other pertinent facts within personal knowledge of affiant.
4. If nighttime search is requested (i.e., 10 P.M. to 8 A.M.) state additional reasonable cause for seeking permission to search in nighttime.
5. State reasons for believing that the items are located at the premises and/or on the person stated above.
6. State reasons for believing that the items are subject to seizure.
7. State additional information considered pertinent to justify this application.

Detective Jack Black	Wrightsville PD, 127 Main St Wrightsville, PA 15411	225	D1
(Signature of Affiant)	Address of Affiant	Badge No.	District/Unit

Sworn to and subscribed before me on _22nd_ Day of _October_ 2010 Office 1926 West 20th Street
Address Wrightsville, PA 15411

Anthony L. Hugar _____ (SEAL) Mag. Dist. No. 05-2-09

Signature of Issuing Authority

After a search warrant is executed, the officer who executed the warrant must sign a form stating the date and time that the warrant was executed. The officer must also set forth an inventory of what was located and seized during the search. If no evidence of criminal activity was located, that must be noted on the inventory form. A copy of an inventory is attached to the warrant application (Figure 2.3).

TECHNOLOGY

An issue that has become an increasing concern of courts over approximately the last 20 years is that of technology. The framers of the Constitution did not have to consider whether cell phones, computers, and information stored and transmitted on the Internet constituted a person, house, paper, or effect. Yet courts were forced to consider the problems associated with telephone calls, even those made from a pay phone, in court cases beginning in the 1960s. Today's technology goes far beyond that of a telephone that plugs into a receptacle in the wall of a house or business or even a pay telephone in a public place. We walk around every day posting "tweets" and "status updates" that tell people where we are. Global positioning system (GPS) enhanced devices that we carry can allow others to find us at any time and to track our movements. Our movements can be tracked and our location is no longer completely private. If we send a text message to a friend, the police can recover those text messages later and use them against us. If we delete something from our computer, a forensic computer expert can retrieve those deleted items and they can be used against us in court. Law enforcement agents and investigators even create fake profiles, such as that of a 14-year-old girl, and pretend to be that person in order to identify people who are prone to prey on young girls for sexual reasons. All of these technological advances have caused courts to have to consider what is "reasonable" in terms of the search and seizure of digital documents and other pieces of information created by technology. Generally, these bits of information have been considered to be similar to a written diary entry, which are considered an "effect" for purposes of determining whether the Constitution protects the search and seizure of those items, but each technological advancement requires courts to analyze how far law enforcement can go in monitoring these devices. The Supreme Court has not yet decided a landmark case in this area, although lower courts have struggled with the issue. For example, some courts have determined that a person's cell phone can be searched at the time of his arrest, as it is possible that text messages could disappear from the phone over time. Further, courts generally agree that people do not expect privacy in their emails once the emails are delivered to a third party.

FIGURE 2.3. SAMPLE RECEIPT/INVENTORY

A COPY OF THIS FORM, WHEN COMPLETED, IS TO BE ATTACHED TO EACH OF THE SEARCH WARRANTS/AFFIDAVIT

COUNTY OF WRIGHTSVILLE	Commonwealth of Pennsylvania } ss County of ____Wrightsville____ }	DATE OF SEARCH 10/22/2010	INVENTORY CONTROL NO.

RECEIPT/INVENTORY

TIME OF SEARCH

OF SEIZED PROPERTY FROM   1800   A.M.   X P.M.

_____ Jolleen Winters _____   4410 West 22nd Street, Wrightsville, PA 15411

_____

(Name)   (Address)

The following property was taken/seized and a copy of this Receipt/Inventory with a copy of the Search Warrant and affidavit(s) was [X] personally served on the above named [] was left at (describe location at premises __Green and White_ two story house_____

_with attached garage_____ as required by the Pennsylvania Rules of Criminal Procedure 2008(a).

LINE	QUANITY	ITEM DESCRIPTION	MAKE, MODEL, SERIAL NO., COLOR, ETC.
1	1	Red & White Baseball Cap – Kool Cat - printed on it,	N.E Bedroom Closet
2	1	Red Tee Shirt – Jive Turkey – printed on it,	N. E. Bedroom Closet
3	1	Pair Blue Jeans – with left pocket ripped,	N. E. Bedroom Closet
4	1	Blue Bandana,	N. E. Bedroom Closet
5	1	Silver 45 caliber semiautomatic handgun and ammunition,	Garage
6	1	2009 Black Cadillac Escalade – License Plate # - DMM – 5211,	Garage
7	4	Cartons of Red Dog Cigarettes,	Basement
8			
9			
10			
11			
12			
13			
14			
15			

[] CHECK HERE IF LIST CONTINUED ON REVERSE SIDE

I/We __Detective/Jack Black_____ OF __Wrightsville Police Dept_____

do hereby state that this inventory is to the best of our/my knowledge and belief a true and correct listing of all items seized, and that I/we sign this Receipt/Inventory subject to the penalties and provisions of 18 pa. c.s. Sec.,4904(b) -----Unsworn Falsification to Authorities.

Detective/ Jack Black	Detective Jack Black	WPD	225
(Signature of Person issuing Receipt/Inventory)	(Printed Name of Person Issuing Receipt/Inventory	(Affiliation)	(Badge No. or Title)

SIGNATURE OF WITNESS TO VERIFY ACCURACY OF INVENTORY IN ABSENCE OF OWNER/OCCUPANT OF PREMISES. (Rule 2009(a))

Detective/Jim Beam	Detective Jim Beam	127 Main St Wrightsville PA 15411	WPD	192
(Signature of Witness)	(Print Name of Witness)	(Address of Witness)	(Affiliation of Witness)	(Badge No. or Title)

Detective Jack Black	Detective Jack Black	WPD	225
(Signature of Person Making Search)	(Printed Name of Person Making Search)	(Police Department/Unit/Affiliation)	(Badge No. or Title)

YOU BE THE JUDGE

An employee who was a teacher in a high school was viewing illegal child pornography on his work computer. Another teacher reported this activity and the school district's informational technology department was directed to make copies of the employee's hard drive and hand it over to the FBI. The employee was charged with violating child pornography laws but argued that the evidence should be suppressed. He stated that he had an expectation of privacy that evidence he viewed on his work computer was private and that his employer could not consent to having a third party view what was on his computer. Do you rule that the employee had an expectation of privacy in his work computer, as against the administrators of his school, or not?

RIGHT TO PRIVACY

The Supreme Court has often considered how far an individual's right to privacy extends. Remember, the framers of the Constitution desired that our lives be private from any overbearing tendencies of the government. Court decisions have also focused on other parts of our lives that do not involve the investigation of crime, such as the right to have an abortion or to use birth control. One of the first cases that involved the issue of a person's privacy was the case of **Griswold v. Connecticut**.[7] The **Griswold** case involved the protesting of a Connecticut law that prohibited Connecticut residents from using any form of contraceptives. Specifically, the law stated that the following items were prohibited: "any drug, medicinal article or instrument for the purpose of preventing conception." Estelle Griswold was the Executive Director of the Planned Parenthood League of Connecticut and had opened a birth control clinic along with Dr. C. Lee Buxton, who was a physician and professor at the Yale School of Medicine. The clinic was opened specifically to test the law and bring a lawsuit arguing against it if it was enforced; Griswold and Buxton knew that the law had been on the books since 1879 and was rarely enforced. Nonetheless, they also knew that the fact that such a law was still in existence and could be enforced arguably went against the foundations of this country. Indeed, Griswold and Buxton were arrested, tried, and found guilty; each received a $100.00 fine. They appealed, arguing that the law violated the right to privacy which is implied by the Constitution. The case made its way to the Supreme Court, which

---

7. 381 U.S. 479 (1965).

ruled that the law was unconstitutional, as it violated the "right to marital privacy." The Court acknowledged that the Constitution does not mention the word "privacy" but that the right nonetheless is found under the "penumbras" and "emanations" of other constitutional protections. Concurring opinions in the case stated that privacy is protected by the due process clause of the Fourteenth Amendment. Justice Stewart, in his dissent, called the statute "an uncommonly silly law" (but nonetheless argued that it was constitutional)! Interestingly, the Court applied its decision in the **Griswold** case only to people who were in marital relationships; a later case, **Eisenstadt v. Baird**[8] extended the right to use contraception to unmarried couples, under the premise that the equal protection clause of the Fourteenth Amendment was violated when unmarried couples did not receive the same protection as married couples. Two further cases struck down laws that prohibited certain forms of intimate sexual contact between persons of the same sex, again changing the culture of our society.[9] The Supreme Court indicated in these rulings that human sexual behavior, especially in the home, should be protected and not controlled, or privacy and liberty would be taken away.

The **Griswold** case, while based on a "silly law," was the predecessor to many other right-to-privacy cases decided by the Supreme Court, all of which had an extreme impact on the culture of our country. One of the most notable of these cases is **Roe v. Wade**,[10] the case in which the Supreme Court determined that a woman had the right to choose to have an abortion. The outcome of the **Roe v. Wade** case was primarily based on the theory that substantive due process requires that privacy rights be respected. Specifically, the substantive due process clause of the Fourteenth Amendment states that "no state shall make or enforce any law which shall abridge the privileges or immunities of citizens of the United States; nor shall any State deprive any person of life, liberty, or property, without due process of law . . . nor deny any person the equal protection of the laws." The **Roe v. Wade** case specifically struck down a Texas law that made aiding a woman in receiving an abortion a criminal act. The case was sweeping in its results, however, legalizing abortion for any woman up through the end of the first trimester, for various health reasons in the second trimester, and occasionally in the third trimester if the mother's health clearly warranted it. While the cases discussed previously are not criminal cases, the Supreme Court's verbiage in those cases set the stage for criminal cases that followed, as the issue of search and seizure is an issue of privacy.

---

8.   405 U.S. 438 (1972).
9.   **Lawrence v. Texas**, 539 U.S. 558 (2003); **Bowers v. Hardwick**, 478 U.S. 186 (1986).
10. 410 U.S. 113 (1973).

WHAT IS A SEARCH?

Searches Outside the United States

Constitutionally based search and seizure rules do not always apply to searches in foreign countries or at the United States border. Routine border searches may be conducted without probable cause and without a warrant, and no suspicion of wrongdoing is required. The right to cross the border into another country is not protected by the Constitution. Courts sometimes distinguish between routine and nonroutine searches. Routine searches are permitted for no reason at all. Nonroutine searches must be reasonable. Under this analysis, routine searches would include searches of luggage and other containers, while nonroutine searches would include more intrusive searches such as strip searches and body cavity searches. A search, or even a detention, of a person will be upheld at the border as long as it is considered "reasonable." Border searches and detentions have been upheld regardless of the reason provided, including random reasons, no reason at all, and even ethnic profiling.

UNITED STATES V. MONTOYA DE HERNANDEZ[11]

FACTS: Customs inspectors at the Los Angeles International Airport detained Elvira Montoya de Hernandez, who was entering the country from Bogata, Colombia, and was suspected of smuggling drugs. A customs inspector noticed as Montoya de Hernandez passed through customs that she had made eight recent trips to Miami and Los Angeles. She had $5,000 in cash and stated that she was going to drive around to various stores to purchase items to sell in her husband's store in Bogata. Bogata was known to the inspectors as being a source city for drugs. Montoya de Hernandez indicated that she did not have hotel reservations but planned to stay at a Holiday Inn. Her carry-on bag contained four changes of clothing but no shoes. Inspectors further noticed a bulge in her abdomen. She was suspected of being a "balloon swallower," where drugs are smuggled by being placed in balloons and swallowed. It is difficult for someone who has swallowed balloons to control her bowel movements. Inspectors detained Montoya de Hernandez. She refused to use the bathroom and she claimed to be pregnant. Inspectors found she was wearing two sets of elastic underpants with some paper towels lining the crotch area of her clothing. Montoya de Hernandez was detained for 16 hours, and a pregnancy test was administered and turned up negative. A physician then performed a rectal examination that eventually produced a balloon containing a foreign substance. While detained over the next three days, Montoya de Hernandez passed 88 balloons filled with cocaine. Montoya de Hernandez argued that the evidence should be suppressed because

---

11. 473 U.S. 531 (1985).

the custom officials did not have a clear indication that she was smuggling drugs at the time of her detention.

ISSUE: Did officials have enough suspicion to detain Montoya de Hernandez based on the evidence they possessed?

HOLDING: A border traveler can be detained if officials reasonably suspect that the person is smuggling contraband, and in this case, the facts support that suspicion.

RATIONALE: Searches at the border are different from domestic searches. "Routine searches of the persons and effects of entrants are not subject to any requirement of reasonable suspicion, probable cause, or warrant." While Montoya de Hernandez was entitled to be free from unreasonable searches and seizures, the government's interest in protecting the border weighed more heavily than Montoya de Hernandez's expectation of privacy. The Court stated that "particularized suspicion" was the standard to be used at the border, rather than "probable cause" or "reasonable suspicion," specifically stating that officials at the border must have a "particularized and objective basis for suspecting the particular person" of smuggling. Inspectors need more than an "inchoate and unparticularized suspicion or hunch," and in this case, they had it. A quick strip search of Montoya de Hernandez would not have been sufficient to determine whether smuggling was going on or not, so the longer detention was appropriate. The Court stated that while the long detention and subsequent actions at the hospital were uncomfortable for the defendant, the method she used to smuggle the drugs necessitated this longer detention. Two judges dissented in the case, arguing that the decision permits a situation akin to a "police state" in our country.[12]

Another type of permitted border stop involves "roving" border patrols, where patrols stop motorists who are driving within 30 to 50 miles from the border at night. The purpose of these patrols is to prevent illegal aliens from crossing the border. These patrols are legal as long as officials performing the stop have some suspicion that the person is in the country illegally. Officials must then develop probable cause through their encounter in order to legally search the person.

The Supreme Court has not yet decided a case regarding whether electronic devices such as laptops or flash drives that would hold electronic files can be searched at the border. Certainly an argument can be made that electronic devices hold some of our most personal and private information. So far, lower courts have generally permitted such searches, while individuals have argued that these items are protected by both the Fourth Amendment unreasonable search and seizure and the First Amendment freedom of

---

12. **United States v. Montoya De Hernandez**, 473 U.S. 531 (1985).

expression provisions. In **United States v. Arnold,**[13] the federal Court of Appeals for the Ninth Circuit held that government agents do not need reasonable suspicion before searching laptops or other digital devices at the border or at international airports. The court stated that the government's interest in preventing unwanted persons and effects to enter the United States was greater than a person's desire to conceal his electronic items, which the defendant in this case argued was expected to be as private to him as his home. The Supreme Court refused to hear the **Arnold** case, despite the defendant requesting that it review the lower court's decision. The federal government seems to agree with the Ninth Circuit. Department of Homeland Security policies allow federal agents to take a traveler's laptop computer or other electronic device to an offsite location for an unspecified period of time without any suspicion of wrongdoing. A bill was introduced in the Senate, called the Travelers' Privacy Protection Act, which would require reasonable suspicion to search electronic devices. The bill was introduced but never moved forward when a new session of Congress began. The Supreme Court has, however, recognized that unlike property searches of personal items, searches of a traveler's body can be highly intrusive and should be protected because of fundamental interests of privacy and dignity. The Court has ruled that a customs officer must have reasonable suspicion to believe that searching a person's body will reveal contraband, and an officer may even have to have further court approval in the form of a warrant for invasive searches.[14]

When the United States government collaborates with the police in another country to conduct a warrantless search on an individual's home in that country, the search cannot be contested under the protection of the Constitution. In **United States v. Verdugo-Urquidez,**[15] a Mexican citizen was arrested and brought to the United States under suspicion that he had been involved in the torture and murder of a United States Drug Enforcement Agency (DEA) agent. His trial took place in the United States. The DEA decided to search the defendant's house, which was in Mexico. The DEA secured permission from the Mexican government to search the house, and records regarding marijuana shipments were found in the home. The defendant objected to use of the documents at trial, arguing that they were obtained without a warrant. The Supreme Court ruled that "the people" who were intended to be protected by the Fourth Amendment were the people of the United States, and not people from foreign countries. Thus, the defendant's involuntary presence on American soil for purposes of a trial did not constitute sufficient contacts for him to receive the protections provided by the Constitution.

13. 523 F.3d 941 (9th Cir. 2008).
14. **United States v. Flores-Montano,** 541 U.S. 149 (2004).
15. 494 U.S. 259 (1990).

When Does a Search Occur?

Initially, when questions were first raised in front of the Supreme Court regarding the legality of searches, the Court focused on declaring certain types of places, such as houses or offices, to be private and thus protected from unreasonable searches. The Supreme Court later changed its focus to consider whether an individual had a particular expectation of privacy in a place, rather than stating that certain types of places should always receive protection.

This change was made in the 1967 Supreme Court case of **Katz v. United States**.[16] The **Katz** case involved an individual who was making illegal wagering bets in a public phone booth. Government agents, acting without a warrant, had attached a recording device to the outside of the phone booth based on a tip that Katz's bets were being placed from the booth. Katz's conversations were monitored and were used as evidence at trial.

In its decision, the Supreme Court abandoned both the idea of "trespass" that had been promulgated in the **Olmstead** case and the idea that a person must prove he had "property rights" in something in order to assert the possession of a Fourth Amendment right. Even though the Court found that the government agents had not "trespassed" into the phone booth, it ruled that the Fourth Amendment was still violated. In its decision, the Court stated that the Fourth Amendment protects "people, not places." The Court decided not to make a decision about whether phone booths are protected; instead, the important inquiry was whether the words of the person within the phone booth should be protected. The Court stated that it preferred to protect "people, not places" and considered whether the person within a phone booth expected that what he was saying would be private. The Court also considered whether a person "knowingly" exposed something to the public or "sought" to preserve that item as something private.

The Court's final determination in **Katz** was that indeed, the user of the phone booth, who shut the door of the booth in the attempt to make his conversation private, did expect privacy in the phone booth. Thus, government agents should have obtained a warrant before placing the listening device in the booth. The **expectation of privacy** terminology set forth in the Court's decision has been used over and over again by the Court in determining whether Fourth Amendment rights should be applicable to various items. In other words, having an expectation of privacy in something triggers the application of the Fourth Amendment, and the next question then becomes whether the search that uncovers the item or results in its seizure is reasonable or unreasonable.

Perhaps the most important portion of the **Katz** decision was not the majority opinion, but a two-prong test set forth in Justice Harlan's dissent, commonly referred to as the Katz test. This test is used by courts to determine

---

16. 389 U.S. 347 (1967).

when an "expectation of privacy" exists and thus implicates the Fourth Amendment.

The first prong of Justice Harlan's test is that a person must exhibit a subjective expectation of privacy in the item. Thus, a person must believe that the item is protected from searches and seizures. If others can see something I have or hear what I am doing, then that action is no longer protected. For example, if I place an item on a table in a restaurant as I enjoy my dinner, that item can be viewed by the public and I cannot claim that I expect that item is private. If I sit in the restaurant and talk loudly about the criminal behavior I am planning to engage in, my words are not protected, as they would also not be considered private. The first prong of the **Katz** test also initiates the following question: What if a person from another country in which no right of privacy exists in anything arrives in the United States believing that there are no rights to privacy in the United States? Because that person believes that government officials can come into his house at any time and search through his belongings, does that mean he has no expectation of privacy?

The second prong of Justice Harlan's **Katz** test is that the expectation of privacy in the item must be one that society is prepared to recognize as "reasonable." Even if I believe that my actions are free from anyone seeing them while I engage in strange actions in my transparent glass house in the middle of a city, I would not be able to argue that most of society would believe that my expectation to privacy was reasonable in that case. Thus, the second prong of the Katz test involves whether the majority of "reasonable" citizens would expect privacy in that particular item, place, or discussion. Keep in mind that if an expectation of privacy in an item does exist, the police may still be able to search wherever the item is, but they will have to do so "reasonably" under the standards set forth by the Fourth Amendment. In the alternative, if no expectation of privacy is found to exist, then no Fourth Amendment protection is in place, even if the item is searched for or seized "unreasonably."

"False Friends" and Electronic Transmission of Information

In a landmark Supreme Court case, Jimmy Hoffa, the famous organizer of the International Brotherhood of Teamsters Union, tried to argue that his expectation of privacy was violated when a person who Hoffa assumed was his friend and confidante turned out, instead, to be an informant for the government. This case preceded other landmark cases in which the Supreme Court had to clarify further what expectations of privacy we really have when voluntarily sharing information with other people.

Hoffa v. United States involved a criminal charge filed against Jimmy Hoffa after he was suspected of tampering with a jury. Hoffa was staying in a hotel room in Tennessee during the Test Fleet trial, when Hoffa was accused of violating the Taft-Hartley Act. Constant companions while Hoffa was in the hotel room were the president of the Teamsters Union in Nashville and a man named Edward Partin, a Teamsters Union member from Baton Rouge, Louisiana. Hoffa trusted Partin because he was a member of the union, but he was unaware that Partin had been involved in criminal activity and was working with officials to have his charges reduced if he could bring information to the officials regarding Hoffa's alleged tampering with the jury during the Test Fleet trial. Partin did provide the officials with information regarding conversations that Partin claimed he had with Hoffa relating to the Test Fleet trial. Partin's testimony helped result in a criminal conviction of Hoffa and three others for jury tampering.

Hoffa made numerous arguments to the Supreme Court, and one argument was based on the Fourth Amendment right to be free from illegal search and seizures and the claim that Hoffa expected privacy in his conversations with Partin. Hoffa's case and other cases involving undercover informants who are working for the government are referred to collectively as "false friends" cases. Hoffa's premise was that it is inappropriate and unconstitutional for a "false friend," who he trusted, but who is actually working for the government, to give information to the government. The Supreme Court disagreed with Hoffa's argument, stating that people have no right not to have information they give to others be transmitted to third parties. The dissenting judges agreed with Hoffa, partly because of their concern that in this particular case, the "false friend" might have been making up information in order to ensure that his charges would be lessened.

A second, similar case, **United States v. White**,[17] went even further in allowing "false friends" to transmit information to others. In the **White** case, White went to a "false friend" informant's house, and hiding in the closet at the informant's house was another person who was wearing a wire and transmitting everything that White said to agents who were sitting in a van outside the house. White argued that his rights were infringed upon even if Hoffa's were not, as Hoffa's conversations had not been recorded or transmitted immediately to others through a wire. The Supreme Court ruled against White, stating that no one has an expectation that something they say to someone else will not be transmitted further to others (with the exception of certain privileged communications, such as conversations with priests or attorneys). Further, the Court indicated that it actually prefers that another party hear the information being recorded, as it will then be impossible to argue that the "false friend" has fabricated the statements.

---

17. 401 U.S. 745 (1971).

YOU BE THE JUDGE

A defendant who was in jail awaiting trial received a visit from his mother. His mother had been his biggest advocate throughout the proceedings and was paying for his attorney. She consistently told anyone who asked that her son was innocent. She had visited him in jail many times and continued to put money in his prison account and support him financially and emotionally. One day, she visited him in jail and asked him about another crime that had taken place in the community. Her son told his mother that he had been involved in that crime, but told her not to tell anyone because that could surely be detrimental to his current case and to his ability to ever get out of jail. His mother, upon leaving the facility, went to the police and told them everything her son had told her. The defendant argues that his mother should not be considered merely a "false friend"—that he should have been able to trust his mother as he could a priest or his attorney. What do you decide? Could this possibly be an exception to the false friend rule? Why or why not?

NONSEARCHES

The first question that must be answered when any search and seizure issue is brought before the court is whether a search has actually taken place. The Constitution protects people from unreasonable searches, and if no search has occurred, there is no constitutional protection and no reason to determine the reasonableness of the police conduct. The Supreme Court has defined a few very clear instances in which no search has taken place. This includes open fields, items which have been abandoned, and items held out to the public. The Supreme Court has held that there is no expectation of privacy in these situations.

Open Fields

One major category declared by the Supreme Court to not be considered an "effect" and therefore not protected by the Fourth Amendment is the category of **open fields**. Many Supreme Court decisions involving open fields were decided in the 1980s when the "war on drugs" was rampant in the field of criminal justice. People were being arrested and charged with the manufacture of drugs when the marijuana they were growing in fields adjoining their homes was being seized by police. Police identified the marijuana by either trespassing onto the fields or by flying over the fields in a helicopter or small airplane and identifying the marijuana solely by observing the marijuana. Defendants, of course, argued that they had a right to privacy in the fields as the fields belonged to them and that a search warrant was required prior to any search of the fields.

The Supreme Court determined in a series of cases that no expectation of privacy existed in "open fields," as opposed to **curtilage**, which is the area connected closely to the home, where, according to the Court, the "intimate activities of life" take place. "Open fields," then, includes any area that is not considered curtilage. The very first case that separated open fields from Fourth Amendment protection was **Hester v. United States**,[18] wherein the Supreme Court stated that open fields are not a "person, house, paper, or effect." The Court's opinion was short and succinct, but the opinion substantially changed the practices of law enforcement. Hester was prosecuted for concealing "illegal spirits" based on "moonshine whiskey" that officers found in a broken jug near the house where he resided. The officers admitted they had no warrants to arrest Hester or search the home in which he lived, which belonged to his father. However, the officers apparently had received information that Hester was engaged in some illegal activity. They approached the house and they saw a man (later determined to have the name "Henderson") driving toward the house. The officers concealed themselves and watched Hester come out of the house and hand Henderson a quart bottle. The officers sounded an alarm; upon hearing it, Hester went to a car that was nearby, took a gallon jug from it, and ran with Henderson. The officers chased Hester and one officer fired a pistol at him. Hester dropped his jug, which broke. Approximately a quart of its contents (moonshine whiskey) remained inside. Henderson also threw away his bottle containing moonshine whiskey.

Hester argued that the officers were trespassing on his property. The officers argued that no seizure took place when the officers examined the contents of the abandoned jug. The Court agreed with the officers on this point and also stated that despite the fact that Hester and the abandoned jugs were on Hester's father's land, "the special protection accorded by the Fourth Amendment to the people in their 'persons, houses, papers and effects' is not extended to the open fields." The Supreme Court justices did not spend any time analyzing how far away from the house Hester had run before he dropped the bottle, nor did the Court engage in any discussion of a distinction between curtilage and open fields. The Court felt it was appropriate to say that because the jug was outside the home, officers could most certainly pick it up and view its contents. Years later, the Court further developed the **open fields** doctrine and specified what portions of a person's yard or field would be considered an open field for purposes of the Fourth Amendment.

A more recent case that began to clarify the distinction between open fields and curtilage was that of **Oliver v. United States**.[19] In the **Oliver** case, two Kentucky state police officers received a tip that defendant was growing marijuana on his property. Based solely on this tip, the officers drove on to

---

18. 265 U.S. 57 (1924).
19. 466 U.S. 170 (1984).

defendant's land, past his house, and up to a gate, which was marked with a "no trespassing" sign. The officers walked on a footpath around a gate and continued on Oliver's property for at least a mile from the house, where they spotted a large marijuana crop. The defendant was charged with drug offenses.

The defendant argued that he expected privacy in his marijuana crop because it was being grown where no one could view it from the road and because someone would have to trespass for "quite a ways" onto his property before finding the marijuana crops. The Supreme Court disagreed, stating that the only privacy a person could demand in activities outside his house were activities that took place in the area immediately surrounding his home. The Court indicated that the constitutional framers wished to protect homes, and not necessarily real property located away from homes. The Court stated that normally open fields are accessible or viewable by the public and that "no trespassing" signs normally are not particularly effective in deterring others from walking on posted land. Finally, the Court specifically stated that society would not recognize as reasonable the assertion that crops growing in a field away from a house should be protected by an expectation of privacy.

There is no clear set of factors defining what is considered part of an open field and what is considered curtilage. Each case will present its own circumstances. Open fields includes pastures, open water, woods, and large fields. In the situation of a house on a small lot with a small yard, it is fairly clear that all of the yard would be considered curtilage. Curtilage is the area surrounding a house which "harbors the intimate activities associated with the sanctity of a man's home and the privacies of life."[20] Outbuildings that are attached to, or close to, a house, such as garages, can be considered curtilage. However, sheds or other outbuildings can also be considered open fields, depending on their proximity to the house and other factors.

In the case of **United States v. Dunn,**[21] the Supreme Court identified four factors for lower courts to consider when determining whether an area constituted curtilage or open fields:

1. The proximity of the home to the area
2. Whether the area is included in an enclosure (i.e., fence) that also surrounds the home
3. The use to which the area is put
4. Whether steps have been taken by the landowner to protect the area from the public

When considering the factors of the area's use, the Court has stated that illegal uses are not apt to be protected, while legal uses are more apt to be protected. If you really ponder this, you will see that this factor always works

---

20. **United States v. Dunn**, 480 U.S. 294, 300 (1987).
21. **Id.**

against the criminal defendant and basically indicates that a person who engages in illegal activities has less of an expectation of privacy in their activities than someone who is engaging in legitimate activities!

As mentioned previously, many open fields cases were initiated when agents in aircraft flying over fields recognized, solely by sight, marijuana crops. The Supreme Court has ruled that government officials can generally fly over any area as long as they are within navigable airspace, even if they are purposefully flying over the area in the anticipation of discovering marijuana. The Supreme Court has determined that any viewing of illegal crops growing in a field is appropriate regardless of whether the owner took certain steps to attempt to conceal the contraband from others, as long as some portion of the contraband can be viewed from the air. One criminal defendant argued that because the police who identified his marijuana had been trained in recognizing marijuana plants from the air, that officer was using something other than his "natural knowledge" and the evidence should be suppressed. The Court disagreed, and in subsequent court cases, the Court even allowed government officials' use of high-power cameras to take pictures of the fields, opining that the use of any equipment that is available to the public is "fair game" and does not constitute a physical intrusion.[22]

Another case regarding aircraft and the open fields doctrine is **Florida v. Riley**.[23] The Court in that case approved the government's surveillance of a greenhouse in a residential backyard from a helicopter that hovered 400 feet above ground. Because the helicopter was within legal navigable airspace, and as any member of the public could have hovered at that level, the majority opinion of the Court stated that no violation of Riley's expectation of privacy had taken place. In a concurring opinion, Justice Sandra Day O'Connor reasoned that the reliance on the Federal Aviation Administration (FAA) rules regarding how low a helicopter is permitted to hover was not the proper analysis. O'Connor stated that if it is not common for a helicopter to hover that low over residential property, the person who owned the residence would have a reasonable expectation of privacy in the property. Thus, some state courts might follow O'Connor's philosophy and consider open fields cases based on the specific facts of each case, meaning that it will be difficult for law enforcement officials to predict whether their actions will be upheld by a court. According to the Supreme Court, however, if an airplane is chartered by law enforcement exclusively to fly over someone's property to look for contraband, the search is legal. Further, aircraft used for this purpose do not have to fly in space that is normally used by commercial aircraft as long as they are in airspace that is compliant with FAA rules.

A common question when considering the open fields doctrine is whether a police officer's actions are considered trespass, because in many of the open fields cases police are, in effect, illegally trespassing on a person's land when

---

22. **Dow Chemical Co. V. United States**, 476 U.S. 277 (1986).
23. 488 U.S. 445 (1989).

discovering the items that are found in the open fields. The Supreme Court has stated that the fact that an officer can look in open fields does not affect the consideration of whether a trespass action might be plausible. However, the Supreme Court's initial decisions regarding what constituted persons, houses, papers, and effects required the defendant to prove that the government agent had trespassed on a constitutionally protected area in order for a Fourth Amendment right to apply. This reasoning was also used in the **Olmstead** case, wherein the Court ruled that because the telephone wires through which the defendant's statements passed were not on the defendant's property, the Fourth Amendment would not apply. In fact, the main difference between the open fields doctrine and the plain view rule, which permits police officers to seize something that is clearly visible to them, is that the open fields doctrine does not require that the officer be legally at the location where the observation is made.

The Supreme Court further clarified the issue of curtilage in the context of dog sniffs in the case of **Florida v. Jardines**.[24]

FLORIDA V. JARDINES

FACTS: Police at the Miami-Dade Police Department received an unverified tip that marijuana was being grown in the home of Joelis Jardines. A month later, a surveillance team watched Jardines's home for 15 minutes and saw no vehicles in the driveway or activity around the home, and as the blinds were drawn, he could not see inside the house. He then approached the home with a drug-sniffing dog. The dog "hit" on an area near the house, spinning and sniffing and finally sitting down to indicate that he had located the source of the odor that he had hit on. Officers then obtained a police warrant based on the dog's indication that drugs were present. The search revealed marijuana plants, and Jardines was charged with trafficking cannabis.

Jardines filed a motion to suppress the evidence based on the fact that the search was unreasonable. He argued that the police did not have probable cause, based on the dog sniff, to obtain a warrant.

ISSUE: Whether unverified information and a dog sniff on the outside of a residence is considered a "search" and is thus unlawful if probable cause does not exist.

HOLDING: A dog sniff on the outside of a house is considered a "search" and probable cause must be present to conduct such a sniff.

RATIONALE: The Fourth Amendment guards against the government physically intruding upon a person, house, paper, or effect. The officers were gathering

---

24. 569 U.S. ___ (2013) (decided March 26, 2013).

information in an area belonging to Jardines and in the curtilage area of his house, which enjoys as much protection as the house itself. The Court specifically reasoned that "[a]t the [Fourth] Amendment's 'very core' stands 'the right of a man to retreat into his own home and there be free from unreasonable governmental intrusion.' . . . This right would be of little practical value if the State's agents could stand in a home's porch or side garden and trawl for evidence with impunity; the right to retreat would be significantly diminished if the police could enter a man's property to observe his repose from just outside the front window." The Court reasoned that although officers do not need to shield their eyes from what is happening outside a home, once the officer steps off a public thoroughfare and into the area surrounding the home, he has entered an area that is protected. The officers would have had a right to knock on the door of the home, but bringing a dog to sniff the area is a far more intrusive action. Generally, people can approach a house and knock on someone's door, waiting briefly to be let in, and then leaving if they are not invited in. (The Court suggested that this behavior is undertaken by Girl Scouts and trick-or-treaters, and that it is perfectly acceptable.) However, there is no assumed invitation to pause around the front of a home with a canine in the "hopes of discovering incriminating information."

Finally, remember that state courts can choose to give individuals more rights than the Supreme Court requires. For example, New York has decided that a landowner who posts a "no trespassing" sign has established enough of an expectation of privacy in his land that his property will no longer be considered "open fields." The Supreme Court's rulings do not permit a person to place their open fields back under constitutional protection by posting signs. Do you agree that the posting of no trespassing signs should automatically give protection from law enforcement's observation of growing crops?

Abandonment

Another Supreme Court has ruled that people have no expectation of privacy when an item has been "abandoned." An item has been abandoned, according to the Court, when its owner has relinquished it, with the intent (or, sometimes, apparent intent) to give up possession of that item forever. For example, if you leave class and leave your backpack behind, a janitor who is cleaning the classroom later that day might look in your backpack to determine who it belongs to. If the first thing the janitor pulls out of your backpack is a baggie of marijuana, he can report his finding to the campus police and you can be charged with a crime based on that evidence. You have been assumed to have "abandoned" your backpack, even if you accidentally forgot it and did not intend to leave it, and your marijuana, behind. The consideration is whether the item is abandoned or appears to be abandoned to others. Courts apply both an objective and subjective test to attempt to ascertain the intent of the owner. An item will rarely be considered abandoned if it is in the home of its owner but can definitely be abandoned elsewhere, even in someone else's private home. An issue that can arise in abandonment cases is whether the abandoned item actually belongs to the person being accused of possessing it. Most illegal items are not marked with the owner's name. Often other items found in a trash bag with contraband, such as bills or receipts with a person's name on them, can be circumstantial evidence that the contraband also belonged to that person. However, even a bag lying on the ground near a suspect could arguably have been left there by someone else. Police officers often have to testify about surrounding circumstances when trying to prove that an abandoned item belonged to a particular person.

While it might seem obvious that certain items have been abandoned, such as a bag left in a hotel room after the occupant has checked out of the hotel, the Supreme Court had to consider whether a person who placed a bag on the floor of a taxi cab while still riding in it had abandoned the property. The Court stated in 1960 that such action was not considered abandonment in the case of **Rios v. United States**.[25] The case arose from the following facts. In 1957, two Los Angeles police officers were dressed in plain clothes and riding in an unmarked car. They observed a taxi cab in a parking lot next to an apartment building in a neighborhood that had a reputation for narcotics activity. The officers watched Rios look up and down the street, walk across the parking lot, and get into the cab. The officers did not know who Rios was at that time and testified that they had never seen him before. The officers followed the taxi cab and when the cab stopped for a traffic light about two miles later, the officers approached the taxi on foot and stood on opposite sides of the cab. While there were several versions of the succession of events from that point on, it was established that one of the officers identified himself as a police officer, suddenly the cab door was opened, and Rios dropped a bag of narcotics on the floor of the vehicle (the officers indicated they immediately could tell that narcotics were in the bag) and attempted to flee from the cab, leaving the narcotics behind. One of the officers retrieved the bag while the other officer drew his revolver. There were some differences in testimony between the cab driver, Rios, and the police in terms of whether the officers touched Rios at all and whether Rios opened the door to the cab or one of the officers opened it. Because of this, the Supreme Court remanded the case to the trial court for the court to take more testimony from the parties involved regarding the sequence of events. The Court indicated that if the officers had, in effect, arrested Rios by either grabbing his arm or by standing by the doors of the taxi cab, they would have to prove that they had probable cause to arrest in order to seize the bag of narcotics, and they probably would not be able to do so. However, if the police approached the standing taxi for the purpose of routine interrogation and had no intent to detain Rios beyond what the court called the "momentary requirements of such a mission," then Rios would be considered to have voluntarily revealed the package of narcotics to the officers and the package would be considered to have been abandoned. As you can see,

---

25. 364 U.S. 253 (1960).

the issue of the legality of a search or seizure is often extremely fact specific and it is the trial court's duty to decide the facts of the case. The Supreme Court merely applies the law to facts but does not decide the facts; they must be developed thoroughly in the trial court record. The **Rios** case was also interesting in that the American Civil Liberties Union (ACLU) filed an amicus brief on behalf of the defendant, arguing that the search was illegal because there was no evidence that Rios was doing anything wrong; he just happened to be catching a cab in an area where there existed a large amount of narcotics crime. Organizations such as the ACLU and other interest groups often try to sway the Supreme Court to decide a case in a particular way.

The Supreme Court also considered the issue of abandonment in the landmark case of **California v. Greenwood**.[26]

CALIFORNIA V. GREENWOOD

FACTS: Officers had been informed that Greenwood was engaged in drug trafficking, and they set up surveillance of his home. They observed suspicious activity, including numerous persons making brief stops at the house late at night and early in the morning, and one of the vehicles then moved on to another residence, where the occupants were also suspected of drug trafficking. Based on his suspicions, one officer requested that the person who collected the garbage from Greenwood's home collect it separately, without collecting anyone else's garbage. The police would then take Greenwood's garbage and search it. Upon completing this search and seizure, the officers found evidence of narcotics trafficking in the garbage and included that evidence in an application to obtain a warrant to search Greenwood's home. That search revealed hashish and cocaine.

Greenwood was arrested and charged with felony narcotics violations but posted bond and was free awaiting trial. The police continued to receive reports of drug trafficking by Greenwood, so police again seized his garbage in the same manner as before and again found evidence of drug use. The officers then again searched Greenwood's home and found additional evidence of drug trafficking. Greenwood was arrested again and charged further. Federal courts that had examined this issue had been divided on whether or not the collection of garbage by police was a violation of search and seizure.

ISSUE: Is garbage considered "abandoned" and therefore subject to seizure by police?

HOLDING: Garbage, once it is placed at the curb for pickup by a trash service, is considered abandoned and its owner no longer has a privacy interest in it.

---

26. 486 U.S. 35 (1988).

RATIONALE: The Supreme Court stated that placing garbage at a curb is, in essence, abandoning the garbage to the garbage collector as well as to anyone else who might come along and take the garbage. This includes, in the Supreme Court's words, "animals, children, scavengers, snoops, and other members of the public." The Supreme Court stated that even if Greenwood actually believed that his trash would go nowhere except to the garbage collector and would end up in a garbage dump somewhere with other peoples' garbage, this expectation is not reasonable. Because the garbage was left in an area that the public had access to and the purpose of placing it there was to, in effect, have a third party (the garbage collector) take it away, there is no expectation of privacy in the garbage. Further, the police should not be required to "avert their eyes" from evidence of criminal activity that any member of the public could also have seen. The Court stated that it did not believe that society would accept as reasonable the claim that anyone would expect privacy in trash that was left for collection in an area accessible to the public.

The Supreme Court's decision in the **Greenwood** case was important to law enforcement agencies that had routinely used this method of investigation to obtain enough information to request and receive a search warrant when other information was not sufficient to obtain a warrant. The reasoning set forth in **Greenwood** has also been used to justify a law enforcement agency's taking and using against a defendant his DNA that has been left inadvertently on a discarded coffee cup, napkin, or other item. Additionally, this case leaves open the possibility that other individuals, such as newspaper reporters or just generally nosey individuals, can obtain their neighbors' garbage and look through it at their leisure.

YOU BE THE JUDGE

You are a police officer and you are patrolling on foot in a high crime area known for narcotics trafficking. You see two people exit a private residence and enter the parking lot of a YMCA, which also is known to be an area in which drugs are exchanged. One of the people is carrying a brown grocery bag, seemingly in a very careful manner. You do not know either of the people. You are in plain clothes. You approach the person and ask him to "come here a minute," and as you do so, the person throws the bag on the hood of his car and turns to face you. You ask him what the bag contains, and he does not answer. You grab the bag, open it, and find drug paraphernalia. You then search the person and arrest him, charging him with a drug crime.

Do you believe the court will uphold your actions if the defendant files a motion to suppress the evidence? What other facts might the court want to know before making its decision?

Items Held Out to the Public

A person cannot assert a right to privacy in items that are generally held out to the public. For example, a person's handwriting is not private, since people routinely submit signed documents to third parties, thereby exposing their handwriting. Bank records are not private, as federal laws require banks to submit information to the government if deposits of a certain amount are made by an individual. The Supreme Court also applied this analysis in the **United States v. Place** case, discussed later. The Court's permission of drug-sniffing dogs to sniff luggage was based partially on the fact that the contents of the luggage weren't being held out to the public but, apparently, that the odor of the luggage was.

Defendants began to argue that any time an officer used "extra effort" to reach a place, that place could no longer be considered "held out to the public." For example, in **California v. Ciraolo,**[27] an "open fields" search took place but involved police officers utilizing an airplane to help them see the defendant's property. Police had received an anonymous tip over the telephone that Ciraolo was growing marijuana in his backyard. The police went to Ciraolo's house to investigate, but they could not see the area in question from the ground owing to a 6-foot outer fence and 10-foot inner fence that were barring their entry. Thus, the officers rented a private plane and flew over Ciraolo's house at 1,000 feet above the ground, at an altitude that was permitted by law. From this altitude and view, the officers were able to see the marijuana; the officers had been specially trained in determining whether certain plants were in fact marijuana when viewed from the air. The officers saw marijuana plants that were approximately 8 feet to 10 feet tall and growing in a 15- by 25-foot plot of land in Ciraolo's yard. The officers took an aerial photograph with a standard 35-millimeter camera and used the photograph plus their interpretation of what they had seen to obtain a search warrant, and the officers then were able to enter onto Ciraolo's property; they seized 73 marijuana plants.

Ciraolo did not argue that the plants were not marijuana, but he did argue that the officers should not have been able to view the plants from above. Ciraolo argued that short of placing a covering over his yard in order to keep people from seeing his yard from airspace, he had done everything he possibly could to proclaim to the world that he wanted to keep his yard private. He further argued that covering his yard would not allow him to "enjoy" it, and thus he should not be required to do so in order to expect privacy. A California appeals court agreed with Ciraolo, stating that the existence of the fences demonstrated that the Ciraolo did expect privacy in his backyard and that because the police officers' action of flying over Ciraolo's yard was not routine and was made for the sole

---

27. 476 U.S. 27 (1986).

purpose of looking into Ciraolo's backyard, not for any particular law enforcement or public safety reason, the flyover constituted only a purposeful intrusion into the sanctity of the curtilage of Ciraolo's home. Thus, according to the appeals court, the police officers' behavior violated Ciraolo's expectation of privacy.

The case made its way to the Supreme Court, which disagreed with the court of appeals. The Supreme Court first stated that it was difficult to determine exactly whether Ciraolo really did expect privacy in his yard, as a person standing on the top of a tall truck or bus could have seen into his yard. The Court then moved on to analyze whether, even if Ciraolo's expectation of privacy was legitimate, under the Katz test, that expectation of privacy was reasonable. The Court determined that it was not, stating that police officers do not need to "shield their eyes" when passing by a house in an area where they are permitted to be, just because a person might want privacy in that area. Further, efforts a person has made to avoid view of his property from a certain viewpoint does not mean he should legitimately expect privacy when someone observes the area from another vantage point. Further, the Court stated, there is no concern about this particular decision resulting in a slippery slope of the Court permitting "advanced electronic devices" to infringe upon the right to privacy. An airplane and an officer's eyes, the Court opined, do not constitute an advanced electronic device. Even using some common device, such as binoculars, which might allow an officer to see the plants closer than with her naked eye, would not be considered too intrusive.

Bodily Fluids

Bodily fluids are a substance that officers can seize; a common bodily fluid to seize from an individual is blood from a person suspected of driving while intoxicated. The Court first considered this issue in 1957 in the case of **Breithaupt v. Abram**[28] where the Court permitted officers to draw the blood of a driver who had been in an accident and was suspected of alcohol use despite the driver's unconscious state. The landmark decision in this area in which the Supreme Court ruled on the ability of the police to draw blood from a conscious person was in **Schmerber v. California**.[29] Schmerber was involved in an automobile accident and was also arrested for driving under the influence of alcohol. The police read Schmerber his rights and Schmerber was transported to the hospital for treatment of his injuries. While he was there, an officer directed that a physician draw blood from him for purposes of chemical analysis. Schmerber objected and his attorney objected as well, but the blood was drawn anyway and analysis of the blood

---

28. 352 U.S. 432 (1957).
29. 384 U.S. 757 (1966).

sample demonstrated that Schmerber was in fact intoxicated. Schmerber, of course, objected to the evidence being presented at his trial, and the case reached the Supreme Court.

In a decision that has affected defendants up to the present day, the Court determined that drawing blood, even without the consent of a suspect, is constitutional as long as the blood draw is done by medical personnel using accepted medical standards. Schmerber argued that the police should at least have obtained a warrant prior to requesting the blood draw, but the Court determined that "exigent circumstances" (a concept discussed later in this book) permitted the blood draw without the necessity of first obtaining a warrant. Most driving while intoxicated (DWI) and driving under the influence (DUI) cases are prosecuted based on the results of a blood draw, which determines a person's blood alcohol level.

The Court later refined its longstanding determination that a blood draw constitutes "exigent circumstances."

MISSOURI V. MCNEELY[30]

FACTS: McNeely was pulled over for speeding and lane violations. The officer who effectuated the stop observed that McNeely's eyes were red, his speech was slurred, and his breath smelled like alcohol. Further, McNeely admitted that he had consumed alcohol earlier that evening. The officer conducted field sobriety tests on McNeely, who performed poorly. The officer then asked McNeely to take a preliminary breath test; McNeely refused, and the officer arrested him for drunk driving. The officer took McNeely to the hospital to have blood drawn; McNeely refused to consent and the officer directed the lab to draw blood anyway. McNeely's blood alcohol concentration was .154 percent, well above the legal limit. McNeely was charged with drunk driving and he moved to suppress the blood test results based on the warrantless blood draw. McNeely argued that every suspicion of drunk driving does not result in an exigent circumstance that permits a blood draw. The state argued that because alcohol dissipates in a person's body as time passes, an exigency always exists.

ISSUE: Does the suspicion of drunk driving always create an exigency exception permitting an unwarranted search?

HOLDING: Exigent circumstances do not always exist in a drunk driving investigation; the totality of the circumstances must be considered in each individual case.

---

30. 133 S. Ct. 832 (2013).

RATIONALE: Destruction of evidence of a person's blood alcohol content is different from the destruction of other types of evidence. A person has no control over how alcohol dissipates in her bloodstream over time. The alcohol dissipates in a predictable and gradual way. It takes time to transport someone to a hospital to conduct blood testing; during that time, it would be possible for an officer to obtain a warrant to test a person's blood alcohol level. In the **Schmerber** case, the Court originally determined that a blood alcohol draw was an exigent circumstance; the defendant had been in a car accident and much time had passed between the time of the accident and the time the defendant was transported to the hospital. McNeely's case involved a routine traffic stop with a suspicion of drunk driving and no circumstances delayed the transport of the defendant to the hospital. The Court pointed out that 47 years had passed since the **Schmerber** case was decided; officers can now obtain warrants much more quickly than in the past, due to the use of computers, fax machines, and other immediate transportation of information.

A related type of bodily intrusion was considered by the Court in **Winston v. Lee**.[31] In the **Winston** case, a shoot-out ensued during a robbery and a store owner was wounded in the legs; the robbery suspect was wounded in his left side. Officers located the suspect and questioned him; he indicated that he had been wounded when he was robbed. He was taken to the hospital, and the store owner happened to be there as well; the store owner identified the suspect as the man who had shot him. The state asked the court to order that the suspect undergo surgery to have the bullet removed; the bullet would be utilized as evidence to determine whether the suspect was indeed the robber. Consulting doctors stated at first that there was some danger related to the surgery but later stated that because the bullet was close to the skin surface, there was not much danger involved. However, while preparing the suspect for surgery, the doctors again stated that the bullet was deep into the skin and the surgery to remove it would thus require general anesthesia with some risk. The Supreme Court determined that the surgery was too intrusive to permit officers to order it and that it was "unreasonable" to require such a procedure. The Court determined that the community's interest in resolving crimes did not justify a surgical intrusion. Forcing the removal of the bullet through surgical means would violate the suspect's right to be secure in his person, as guaranteed by the Fourth Amendment, and the government had not established a compelling need to force the removal.

---

31. 470 U.S. 753 (1985).

YOU BE THE JUDGE

Since the **McNeely** case was decided, law enforcement officers will decide whether the case involves exigent circumstances which are sufficient to request that a hospital draw an individual's blood for purposes of testing alcohol levels. Assume the state you are in has a law which requires that blood be drawn from any driver of a vehicle who is involved in an accident when death or severe bodily injury occurs. A case comes in front of you involving a woman who was driving in the fog and ran into another woman who was walking on the fog line of the road. The woman driving stopped and rendered aid to the woman who was walking, and who eventually died as a result of her injuries. Upon arriving at the scene, the driver seemed coherent and no smell of alcohol emanated from her breath. She explained that she could not see the woman who was walking because of the heavy fog and that she had just come from a friend's house where they each had "one glass of wine with dinner." The woman was nonetheless taken to the hospital for a blood draw because of the state law set forth earlier. She was eventually charged with homicide by vehicle while under the influence of alcohol because the blood test demonstrated that her blood alcohol level was above the legal limit. Her attorney argues that the blood evidence should be suppressed because the state statute conflicts with the Court's decision in **McNeely** and that the totality of the circumstances of this case do not support the warrantless blood draw. The officers argue that not only does the state's statute provide an exigency, but that because they arrived at the scene and administered some emergency aid to the victim prior to the medics arriving, a longer amount of time had passed than would have in a routine traffic stop, and thus an exigency existed. How do you rule?

ADMINISTRATIVE SEARCHES

Sometimes, searches are carried out by government agents but are for civil, not criminal purposes. The Supreme Court has established a relaxed standard for government inspectors who search personal and business properties. Such "searches" are really government inspections, performed for purposes of protecting the public and regulating industries. Rather than requiring that probable cause be present, government agencies must merely demonstrate that a "general and neutral" enforcement plan is being implemented. Examples are health and safety inspections, airport inspections, and other inspections of highly regulated industries such as liquor stores, mines, and gun shops. The reasoning behind the exception carved out by the Supreme Court in this area is that there is an urgent public interest in regulating these industries, and that owners of businesses of this nature give "implied consent" that their business will be regulated when they enter into business in such an industry. Most of these industries involve some sort of danger to the safety and general welfare of either the public or of those persons who work in the industry.

Administrative Searches of Homes

Courts have repeatedly insisted that the warrantless search of homes is the "chief evil" that the Constitution was intended to prevent. Nonetheless when it comes to administrative searches of homes, some exceptions to this rule have been created by the Court. In **Frank v. Maryland**,[32] a governmental inspector received complaints that Frank, a Baltimore resident, had a large number of rats in this home, thereby causing a health hazard to others who lived near him and thus creating a public nuisance. The inspector went to Frank's home and requested admittance to check out the situation. Frank refused to allow the inspector admission to his house and was subsequently arrested for his refusal; the arrest was permitted by the Baltimore health code. The Court upheld the statute, citing a long history of warrantless housing inspections and ruling that because a complaint had been lodged, it was appropriate to require warrantless admission to Frank's private home. While this standard was later altered by the court, the **Frank** case set the stage for the relaxed requirements the Court has set for administrative searches.

Currently, the standard applied in administrative searches balances the rights of individuals in not being subjected to the inconvenience of a search with the interest in government in regulating certain industries, and a consideration of the benefit that regulation will bring to the public. The landmark case in which the Supreme Court considered administrative searches following the **Frank** case is **Camara v. Municipal Court**.[33] In **Camara**, a health inspector inspected an individual's home without a warrant in accordance with the provisions of the San Francisco health code. The Supreme Court first ruled that the Fourth Amendment applied to this situation and that the sanctity of the home was important. The Court wanted to prevent a person claiming official authority from entering a home for purposes of committing a criminal action within. The Court also agreed with the argument of the citizens that requiring a warrant would allow an inspector to provide written notification to the resident of the scope of the search and would give the homeowner proof that the inspector was authorized to enter the home.

However, despite acknowledging these concerns, the Court then indicated that upon weighing the interests of the government and the individual,

---

32. 359 U.S. 360 (1959).
33. 387 U.S. 523 (1967).

the usual warrant rules could be relaxed for administrative searches. The Court opined:

> [W]e think that a number of persuasive factors combine to support the reasonableness of area code-enforcement inspections. First, such programs have a long history of judicial and public acceptance. Second, the public interest demands that all dangerous conditions be prevented or abated, yet it is doubtful that any other canvassing technique would achieve acceptable results. Many such conditions—faulty wiring is an obvious example—are not observable from outside the building and indeed may not be apparent to the inexpert occupant himself. Finally, because the inspections are neither personal in nature nor aimed at the discovery of evidence of crime, they involve a relatively limited invasion of the urban citizen's privacy.

Some codes require that an **administrative warrant** be obtained, absent consent or an emergency, before an administrative search can take place. An administrative warrant is issued by a judge to an administrative agency. A requested administrative warrant will almost always be issued upon request as long as the requested inspection is considered routine. Administrative searches must be reasonable, but no individualized suspicion is necessary. For example, in a low-income housing unit funded by federal funding, health and safety checks can be performed as long as the inspections are routinely performed for all residents, and certain residents are not singled out.

Administrative Searches of Closely Regulated Industries

A business that is engaged in a type of business that is closely regulated by the government should expect that its operations will be closely regulated. For example, a trucking company that transports hazardous waste, a gas station that sells highly flammable and highly regulated fuels, and a store that sells alcoholic beverages are all subject to special regulation and strict governmental controls and should thus be subject to extra regulation. In **United States v. Biswell**,[34] the government undertook a warrantless inspection of a federally licensed firearm dealer. The government argued that the inspection would pose only a limited threat to the dealer's expectation of privacy. The Court agreed, stating that because the person had decided to engage in a business that was "pervasively regulated" and to apply for a federal license to sell firearms, the inspection was reasonable and complied with the Fourth Amendment. In prior cases, the Supreme Court had previously inferred that it agreed with this practice based on the fact that in England and its colonies, inspectors were permitted to enter "brewing houses" and inspect them without a warrant.

---

34. 406 U.S. 311, 316 (1972).

YOU BE THE JUDGE

A local housing unit is occupied by people who are considered to be "low-income" tenants whose rent is subsidized by the government each month. Some issues of drug dealing and violence have arisen in other low-income housing units throughout the city. As a result, the manager of the housing unit has decided to implement a rule that states that every resident of the unit is subject to random, unannounced searches where the management will enter the apartment units and search for drugs or guns, which are illegal to possess, according to the tenants' leases. The residents of the housing unit are bringing the issue to court for you to determine whether or not the management has a right to conduct this type of search. What do you decide and why? Whose interests will be balanced in this situation?

Administrative Searches of Ordinary Businesses

The search of "ordinary businesses," or those that are not closely regulated by the government, is not as easily done without a warrant as a closely regulated business. A plumbing business that was inspected by the government without a warrant was not considered a closely regulated business; in fact, even a type of business that would sometimes be considered to be closely regulated in one instance might not be in another. The Supreme Court has stated that the individual characteristics of each business should be considered.

Fire Inspection Searches

The Supreme Court has authorized post-fire inspections by authorities following a fire to determine the cause of the blaze (which often turns up evidence used against someone who is accused of starting the fire). In **Michigan v. Tyler,**[35] a fire began in a furniture store around midnight. Firefighters were finishing putting out the fire around 2 A.M. when fire inspectors entered the scene and seized two plastic containers of liquid. The fire inspector decided he was unable to continue his investigation because it was very dark, and he thus left the scene and then returned at 8:00 A.M. He continued his investigation, left again, and then returned with a police investigator, who had also previously entered the scene. Several more entries of the scene were made, all without consent or warrants, and many pieces of evidence were obtained during the searches.

---

35. 436 U.S. 499 (1978).

The Supreme Court considered the circumstances of the case and decided to rely on rules that had been established previously by state courts regarding the allowance of nonwarranted searches in cases of fire. The general rule was that a fire presents an exigency that justifies a warrantless entry by officials to fight the fire, and that officials can remain in the building for a "reasonable time" after initially entering it to investigate the cause of the blaze. However, further investigations made after the original entry should be made only with a warrant. Utilizing these rules, the Supreme Court decided that the first entry by the fire inspector and even his entry later in the morning after the smoke and darkness cleared were appropriate (that entry was considered an extension of the first entry) but any later entries should have been made only with a warrant.

In another case decided by the Supreme Court, the owner of a house that had burned hired a work crew to board up the house and pump water out of the basement following the fire and prior to the entry of the fire inspector.[36] The Court determined that the seizure of items following the boarding up and pumping out of the house was a violation of the Fourth Amendment, as the owner of the house clearly expected privacy in it when he hired someone to board it up. Any lapse of time between the time of a fire and the time an investigator enters the scene generally triggers a requirement to seek a warrant.

Searches of Public School Students

In general, no warrant is needed to search a school student or his possessions. Cases decided by the Supreme Court and lower courts generally state that students, who are normally minors, have a lesser expectation of privacy than adults. In order to perform a search, school administrators must possess reasonable suspicion that the search will turn up evidence that the student has violated or is violating the laws or rules of the school. Further, the search must not be excessively intrusive in light of the age and gender of the students and the nature of the infraction.[37] Most states permit schools to physically search or even perform a canine search on students' lockers as long as there is a reason to believe that students possess drugs or other illegal items.

Drug Testing

Drug testing of school students is also permitted if the school district demonstrates that it was experiencing significant drug usage by the students, all students (or athletes, if the test is only for athletes) are subject to the test, and appropriate procedures are followed. In fact, most employees and professional athletes can also be subjected to drug testing. We have all

---

36. **Michigan v. Clifford**, 464 U.S. 287 (1984).
37. **New Jersey v. T.L.O.**, 469 U.S. 325 (1985).

watched dramatic sports stories unfold in the news as athletes sometimes lose their titles, and even their livelihood, after testing positive for drugs. The Supreme Court has decided a series of cases that allow the testing of employees, athletes, and students to confirm that they have no illegal substances in their systems. Obviously, those being tested have argued that the testing is an intrusion on their privacy rights. The Supreme Court has consistently permitted drug testing of these classes of people.

The Supreme Court first permitted random drug testing of employees in its 1989 landmark decision **Skinner v. Railway Labor Executives Association**.[38] The employer was concerned that an employee who was under the influence of a controlled substance at his job and was driving a train could harm others. The attorney representing the employees in that case argued that random drug testing in the workplace violates employees' Fourth Amendment rights. The Supreme Court held that this type of testing was appropriate in employment that was "safety sensitive," because the government interest in testing, even without demonstrating any individualized suspicion of the employee being tested, was "compelling." The Court ruled that because employees under the influence of controlled substances or alcohol could harm others, the interest of the general public in not being harmed allowed this type of "search." A dissenting opinion agreed that illegal drugs harm society, but called the use of random drug tests in employment situations a "draconian" weapon against drug use. The dissenting justice expressed concern that the reason for allowing this type of testing was merely because of the outcry over the use of illegal drugs that was taking place in the United States at that time. The Court stated that "[h]istory teaches that grave threats to liberty often come in times of urgency, when constitutional rights seem too extravagant to endure," and cited the Court's decisions permitting relocation camps in World War II, which were later determined to involve the sacrifice of freedoms for a perceived exigency, and decisions that were "regretted" later.

The Supreme Court in that same year also specifically approved of a drug testing program for employees of the United States Customs Service, stating that those employees had a diminished expectation of privacy and should expect that a drug test could be given to them, as was decided in the case of **National Treasury Employees Union v. Von Raab**.[39] The United States Customs Service required that all of its prospective employees be drug tested not only because they might be impaired while on the job, but also because the government preferred that all of its customs officers, who were working in drug enforcement positions and carrying firearms, would lead totally drug-free lives. The Supreme Court had to consider whether it would allow that intrusive of a requirement by an employer. The government argued in support of mandatory drug testing of these employees not because they had had previous problems with employees using or being under the influence

---

38. 489 U.S. 602 (1989).
39. 489 U.S. 656 (1989).

of drugs while on the job, but because it believed that a custom agent who is drug addicted is a target for bribery and cannot carry out his job duties. The government also argued that a person who uses illegal drugs is not apt to enforce drug laws against people who are selling drugs; thus, those who use drugs should not be in that type of employment. The government claimed that all people who are employees of the United States government, including military and intelligence officers, in effect agree to a lowered expectation of privacy when applying to work for the government. The Supreme Court agreed with the government's position that drug testing involves limited intrusion and, if known to all candidates that apply for the job, does not in any way invade a candidate's expectation of privacy.

The Court's decision in the **Von Raab** case was also important in that the Court relaxed the requirement that an employer have particularized suspicion against a specific person in order to subject her to drug testing. The Court stated: "We have recognized before that requiring the Government to procure a warrant for every work-related intrusion would conflict with the common-sense realization that government officers could not function if every employment decision became a constitutional matter." Thus, the Court rejected the application of any probable cause or reasonable suspicion requirement in order to engage in drug testing. Testing of all candidates or even random testing of employees in the workplace has become commonplace.

However, the Supreme Court held that a South Carolina's hospital's testing of pregnant women for illegal substances was violative of the Fourth Amendment in the case of **Ferguson v. City of Charleston**.[40] The hospital was concerned about the prevalence of births of babies addicted to crack and the use of cocaine by women who used the services of the hospital. The hospital thus began collecting urine screens of women who used the hospital's obstetrics department and referred the women to drug and alcohol counseling if the urine test was positive for illegal substances. Shortly after this process began, the local police department began arresting pregnant women whose urine screens were positive and charging them with child abuse. A policy was developed to dictate how certain women would be targeted for the screening and how prosecutions would follow the testing results. Many of the women who had been prosecuted brought a lawsuit arguing that the policy violated their right not to be subject to unreasonable searches and seizures. The Supreme Court agreed, stating that a person who engages in testing in a hospital for medical purposes does not assume that the tests will be used to criminally prosecute her. The Court indicated that while in the **Skinner** case drug tests were being used to protect the public from drivers who were under the influence of illegal substances, the South Carolina hospital's purpose in obtaining the testing was not only to provide counseling for the mothers in the hopes of protecting the unborn children but also to obtain

---

40. 532 U.S. 67 (2001).

evidence to criminally prosecute the mothers. The Court stated that this search went further than other "special needs" searches permitted by the Court.

In 1995, the Supreme Court upheld the constitutionality of random drug testing of school students.[41] The case came before the Court when 10 percent of all athletes in the Vernonia, Oregon, local public schools were being randomly selected for drug testing. The Supreme Court held that the tests did constitute searches under the meaning of the Fourth Amendment but indicated they were reasonable because the schools had an interest in preventing teenage drug use. The Court discussed the fact that the testing was random, that urine was collected in a way that would preserve students' "modesty," and that, if a student tested positive, he was given the option of undergoing counseling or quitting the athletic team for the remainder of the season or the next season. The Court held that the Fourth Amendment does not require a showing of probable cause in all cases, and that because obtaining a warrant would be impractical in this type of case, and administrators needed to maintain order in the school, Vernonia's drug testing policy was constitutional. The Court also focused on the fact that the drug testing was being carried out against "children" who were "committed to the temporary custody of the State as schoolmaster." Further, because public schools can require that students undergo certain vaccinations and vision, hearing, and other screenings, public school students already have a lesser expectation of privacy than the general public. The Court concluded that athletes have even a lesser expectation of privacy than public school students, as they subject themselves to additional regulations and medical screenings in order to be able to participate in a sport. The Supreme Court did consider the intrusiveness of the testing (requiring a student to be monitored while urinating) but ruled that the school's interest in deterring drugs use was even more important. The Court reasoned that drug use by a student affects not only that student but all members of the school, including students who are trying to learn and faculty who are trying to educate them. Drugs used during athletic activities could ultimately cause harm to the athletes or other players, and athletes are considered role models for the other students.

The Vernonia case was later expanded in **Board of Education v. Earls,**[42] in 2002, when the Supreme Court authorized drug testing for all students who were involved in extracurricular activities. The Court referred to its reasoning in the **Vernonia** case, stating again that school students have a diminished expectation of privacy and that the school has a high interest in making sure that students were not abusing drugs. Thus, a student working on the yearbook or participating in marching band could also be drug tested.

---

41. **Vernonia School District 47J v. Acton**, 515 U.S. 646 (1995).
42. 536 U.S. 822 (2002).

YOU BE THE JUDGE

You are a judge and are asked to rule on a case that involves evidence obtained through a new scientific principle: that of "dog scent lineups." A dog scent lineup starts with a dog being introduced to a sample of evidence that has been obtained from a crime scene. Law enforcement agents then bring samples of clothing or other personal items from a suspect, along with other samples that do not belong to the suspect, and provide the samples to the dog to sniff. The dog then, theoretically, will pick out the scent from the second set of samples that matches the first sample. A dog handler watches this process then testifies in court as to whether the dog selected the sample that came from the suspect. The prosecution argues that this is a good way to identify a suspect. The defense argues that handlers can, even if only subconsciously, cause errors in this process by pulling the dogs away from certain samples or otherwise providing messages to the dogs through gestures or glances. Considering what you know about how the Supreme Court views the use of various technologies, how would you decide whether or not to allow the use of this sort of evidence in court?

OTHER SPECIAL SEARCHES

The Supreme Court has specifically considered two other types of special searches. For example, in **Griffin v. Wisconsin**,[43] the Supreme Court considered a case in which a probation officer searched the home of one of his probation clients without a warrant. Griffin had been convicted of a felony and was placed on probation; Wisconsin law provides that probationers are subject to conditions set by the court and rules and regulations established by the probation department. As many states provide, this permits probation officers to search the house of their probation clients without a warrant as long as a supervisor approves the search and "reasonable grounds" exist to believe that contraband will be found in the house. (Contraband can include items that are illegal to possess, such as drugs, but can also include items that probationers specifically are prohibited from possessing, such as alcohol or guns.) In the case of, for example, someone who is a registered sex offender, this could also include items such as any type of pornography or a computer that has access to the Internet. The law permits a probation officer to consider a number of factors to determine whether reasonable grounds are present to conduct the search, including information given by an informant and the officer's own experience with the probationer. The Wisconsin regulations made it a crime for the probationer to refuse to consent to a home search.

---

43. 479 U.S. 1053 (1987).

Griffin's apartment was searched in accordance with these regulations when his supervisor received information from a local police detective that Griffin might have guns in his apartment. The search revealed a handgun. Griffin was charged with possession of a firearm by a convicted felon. He argued that his apartment was protected by the Fourth Amendment and that thus a warrant was required. The Court disagreed, reasoning as follows:

> A warrant requirement would interfere to an appreciable degree with the probation system, setting up a magistrate, rather than the probation officer, as the judge of how close a supervision the probationer requires. Moreover, the delay inherent in obtaining a warrant would make it more difficult for probation officials to respond quickly to evidence of misconduct . . . and would reduce the deterrent effect that the possibility of expeditious searches would otherwise create. . . . By way of analogy, one might contemplate how parental custodial authority would be impaired by requiring judicial approval for search of a minor child's room. And on the other side of the equation—the effect of dispensing with a warrant upon the probationer: although a probation officer is not an impartial magistrate, neither is he the police officer who normally conducts searches against the ordinary citizen. He is an employee of the State Department of Health and Social Services who, while assuredly charged with protecting the public interest, is also supposed to have in mind the welfare of the probationer. . . . In such a setting, we think it reasonable to dispense with the warrant requirement.

The Court even went so far as to point out that the Wisconsin probation regulations refer to probationers as "clients," so the role of a probation officer is more "caring" than that of a police officer, thereby, in the Court's view, justifying this relaxed standard for searches. A dissenting opinion in the case stated that a warrant should be required, although probable cause should not be required.

Another area in which the Supreme Court has decided that "relaxed" rules exist is in the case of a search of a government employee's desk, file cabinet, and the like, at her workplace, especially when she is employed in the public sector. Generally, a worker in a public sector job (federal, state, or local government) has the right to due process at her place of employment. However, in **O'Connor v. Ortega**,[44] the Supreme Court determined that even in a public sector job, if reasonable suspicion exists to believe that an employee is engaging in work-related misconduct, a warrantless search might be appropriate. Dr. Ortega was fired from his public sector employment at a public hospital following an investigation by a hospital administrator into claims of stealing funds from residents and sexual harassment. Dr. Ortega was put on administrative leave and an investigation ensued which involved seizing some of Dr. Ortega's personal items from his office. Testimony indicated that the investigators had boxed up everything in Dr. Ortega's office and taken it from

---

44. 480 U.S. 709 (1987).

his office to sort through, rather than engaging in any focused search for items specifically related to the accusations.

The Court held that Ortega had a reasonable expectation of privacy in his office because it was occupied only by him and he had occupied it for over 17 years. The reduced expectation of privacy that public employees face, on the job, are only those that relate to the work the agency does. In other words, it should be expected that a coworker might need to obtain paperwork from another office if that paperwork relates to the job; however, being a public employee does not mean that a person should not expect that private items in their office are actually private. The Court determined that it was not reasonable to search through all of Dr. Ortega's private items in his office and that the search thus violated the Fourth Amendment. Later case law, however, established the rule that at-will or probationary employees are not subject to due process; only public service employees engaged in "permanent employment" will be given due process protection.

OTHER VIOLATION OF PRIVACY RIGHTS IN THE WORKPLACE

Every employee who uses the Internet or other electronic devices owned by her employer should realize that her employer has access to her accounts and information regarding her searches and emails. In the 2009-2010 Supreme Court term, the Court considered how far an employer can go in reviewing electronic files of employees and whether an employee's electronic data can be protected under the Fourth Amendment. The case involved the City of Ontario, California, which had acquired pagers for its police officers for purposes of permitting them to send and receive text messages. The service plan covering the equipment limited the number of messages that could be sent and charged the company when an employee went over the limit. The department was paying more than it had anticipated each month and investigated whether the employees were sending personal messages on the devices and, if so, should employees be charged when they sent personal messages. In attempting to ascertain how the devices were being used, the employer requested transcripts from the wireless company of certain employees' August and September 2002 text messages. They discovered that one employee, Quon, not only sent personal text messages but also sent sexually explicit messages via text. The matter was referred to the police department's internal affairs division and Quon was disciplined for violating workplace rules.

Quon and the individuals with whom he had exchanged text messages filed a lawsuit alleging that the city had violated their Fourth Amendment rights, along with a federal act called the Stored Communications Act. They argued that the wireless company that had handed over the text messages had violated the Fourth Amendment and had violated the individuals' privacy rights. The Supreme Court denied the plaintiffs' request, stating that the search of the text messages was reasonable. First, the Court indicated that the plaintiffs did not have a right to privacy in the messages as the government employer could conduct searches to retrieve work-related material or investigate violations of workplace conduct. Although the plaintiffs worked for a government agency, a private employer could have conducted the same type of search and thus the search was reasonable. The Court then indicated that even if the plaintiffs did have an expectation of privacy, the review of the transcript was reasonable and not beyond the scope of what it needed to be in order to determine whether the government was paying for excessive personal use of the devices. Everyone involved had a legitimate interest in making sure that the employees were not being forced to pay if they were not using the devices for personal reasons but also in making sure that the taxpayers were not paying for the officers to use the devices excessively for personal reasons. Reviewing the transcripts was an efficient way to determine what the devices were being used for and thus would be upheld by the Court. The Court stated that its decision was not to be interpreted as making a far-reaching decision that any employer's review of an employee's electronic transmissions is appropriate. Each case will be considered on its merits, with the Court considering whether the employer was justified in reviewing the transcripts of electronic transmissions in light of its end goal.

USE OF ENHANCEMENT DEVICES

Normally, officers are allowed to observe items with their natural senses, such as touch and sight. The use of further surveillance or equipment will generally trigger scrutiny as to whether the surveillance was too intrusive and thus violated a person's expectation of privacy. Dog sniffs in particular have been used frequently by law enforcement to determine whether narcotics are present when a search is being conducted. The use of a dog's sensory perceptions to smell drugs is considered an extension of an officer's sensory perception. The issue is whether a dog sniff is considered a "search," thus requiring probable cause, or whether a dog's sniffing is merely an extension of an officer's senses. In other words, if an officer can be in a public area (for example, outside someone's car or home), can a dog also be there?

In 1983, the Supreme Court for the first time considered the issue of dog sniffs for narcotics. In **United States v. Place**,[45] the Supreme Court reasoned that because a dog sniff is a very limited test, no warrant is required to conduct such a sniff. The case involved a man at an airport who refused to provide identification to officers when requested. After Place declined to allow the officers to search his luggage, the officers then took the man's bags and performed a dog sniff on them; the officers later obtained a search warrant to

---

45. 162 U.S. 696 (1983).

search the bags and found cocaine in the bags. The Supreme Court ruled that taking the man's bags and having the dog sniff them did not require opening the luggage or exposing anything to public view and that the sniff itself was very limited, as it only revealed the presence or absence of narcotic. Therefore, the dog sniff itself was not unreasonable or a search. The Court did find that in this particular case, taking the bags away from the man did constitute an unreasonable seizure. However, this case and others led the way for dog sniffs of cars, especially during a lawful traffic stop, and luggage in general, as long as those items were not physically moved in order to undertake the search. The Supreme Court further considered dog sniffs in a case that hinged on the definition of "curtilage," discussed in detail below.

YOU BE THE JUDGE

Police received a telephone call that a man was growing marijuana at his home, in his basement, using artificial heat lamps. Police drove by the man's home and, from the street, used a thermal imaging device to scan his home. The scan indicated an unexplained heat source in the basement that was not consistent with a furnace. The results of the scan were used to obtain a warrant to search the rest of the house. The defendant asks the court to suppress the evidence based on his argument that the heat scan was illegal, similar to a dog sniff. The prosecution argues that any citizen could purchase a heat scanning device and drive around gauging the heat emanating from houses, so this was not some sort of specialized search like the dog sniff, which requires dogs to be trained. Do you suppress the evidence? Why or why not?

The Supreme Court, however, has permitted a defendant to argue against a dog sniff if his argument is about the reliability of the dog itself. In **Florida v. Harris**,[46] the Court moved away from its prior implications that a dog's detection of drugs is always accurate. Data presented to the Court indicated that up to 80 percent of dog alerts are wrong. The officer testified that his dog, Aldo, had completed a 120-hour drug detection training class and that he was certified by an independent company that certifies K-9s. Aldo was trained for four hours a week and Aldo's success during training was "really good," according to his handler. Some interested groups argued to the Court that dog sniffs are so unreliable that they should not be used at all. Law enforcement agencies argued that having to prove a dog's credentials in any given case would be an undue burden on law enforcement. Officers argued that they

---

46. 133 S. Ct. 1050 (2013).

have great incentive in making sure that dogs are well trained, as further investigating an incorrect sniff wastes an officer's time and unnecessarily exposes officers to danger, as they would remain longer at a roadside stop.

The Florida trial court in the **Harris** case had developed a long list of requirements for an officer to prove in order to demonstrate a dog's reliability. The Supreme Court rejected that exhaustive list and ruled that a dog's satisfactory performance in a training or certification program could provide sufficient reason for an officer to trust the dog's alert. However, the Court stated that a defendant has the right to challenge the presumption that a trained dog is reliable and that a defendant can cross-examine an officer or introduce his own witnesses to testify as to why the dog's alert should not have been trusted. This includes contesting the adequacy of a certification or training program or examining the dog's history in the field of detection of narcotics or other substances.

The Supreme Court has considered other uses of technology by officers while investigating crime. In **Kyllo v. United States,**[47] the Court considered the use of thermal imaging devices by law enforcement to discover pockets of heat in a house that might signal that a person was growing marijuana plants. Based on a warrantless scan of defendant Kyllo's house, along with tips from informants and evidence of Kyllo's high utility bills, agents obtained a search warrant to search Kyllo's house. The government argued that because all the heat-sensing device would detect would be heat radiating from the outside of the house, there should be no expectation of privacy by the homeowner and that thus the warrantless scan could legally be used to develop probable cause. The homeowner argued that the scan constituted a "search" of his home under the language of the Fourth Amendment. The Supreme Court disagreed with the government's position, ruling that the use of the thermal imaging devices constituted a "search" and that probable cause and, other than in cases of emergency, a warrant must be obtained prior to performing the imaging scan.

The Court ruled that in accordance with the original meaning of the Fourth Amendment, to protect the sanctity of the person's home, a technological device could not be used to "explore" areas of the home that had not previously been discoverable without an actual physical intrusion into the house. The Court further indicated that such thermal imaging scans were not generally available to the public so there would be no expectation by the homeowner that such a device would generally be used to track the amount of heat emanating from his home. The Court indicated that a dog sniff of luggage, which was not considered a search but is arguably similar to a thermal imaging scan, searches only the air outside the luggage and not what was inside the luggage, unlike the thermal imaging scan which searches what is inside the home. In Chapter 6 of this book you will learn about some cases in which technology was used to track the location of specific items that had been

47. 533 U.S. 27 (2001).

purchased by suspected drug dealers and the Supreme Court's view of those devices.

WHAT IS A SEIZURE?

In the realm of criminal law, two things can be seized—property or people. The issue of when something has been seized has been a question that courts have had to grapple with. The issue of when a person is seized has also been the subject of many court cases and has many gray areas. The question of what constitutes a seizure is important in analyzing any search and seizure question because once an item is officially seized by police, the constitutional question of whether the seizure is reasonable must be answered. The Constitution prohibits unreasonable seizures, so no constitutional issues can be argued when nothing has been seized.

When Is Property Seized?

A piece of property is seized when "there is some meaningful interference with an individual's possessory interest in that property."[48] Two related concerns here are whether an officer's interference with property is "meaningful" and whether the individual from whom the item was seized actually has a "possessory interest" in his property. Further, property can be seized by officers in the presence of a person or outside his presence—does this distinction have any bearing on whether the person has a possessory interest or whether an officer's act of taking the property is meaningful?

For example, if a person is not currently in actual possession of his property, such as when he has checked his luggage through to his next destination in an airport, the airport police do not "seize" the luggage when they detain it for some time as long as they return it to its owner when the owner expects it to be returned. However, if the luggage is detained after the person expects to receive his property back, a seizure occurs. If an item is in a person's possession, any movement of the item, even if it constitutes only a temporary deprivation, is considered a seizure. Occasionally a government agent might be able to justify a temporary seizure of an item pending obtaining a search warrant. This is a commonly invoked practice when a container is found in a motor vehicle or in the mail and is suspicious. Officials can seize that item without opening it or looking inside it until they are able to obtain a search warrant based on probable cause if they believe that something illegal is in the container. Further rules regarding container and vehicle searches will be covered in Chapter 6.

---

48. **United States v. Jacobsen**, 466 U.S. 109 (1984). *See also* **Maryland v. Macon**, 472 U.S. 563 (1985).

Clearly, there is more of a chance that the Court will find inappropriate interference in an item if the police touch the items while the defendant is physically in possession of his items. In **Bond v. United States,**[49] Steven Bond was a passenger on a Greyhound bus traveling from California to Little Rock, Arkansas. The bus stopped at a required Border Patrol checkpoint in Texas. The agent checking citizenship status of the passengers had reached the back of the bus and had determined that no one on the bus was an illegal immigrant and was walking back toward the front of the bus, squeezing and manipulating soft-sided luggage found in overhead luggage compartments. The agent felt what he later described as a "brick-like" object in a green canvas bag that belonged to Bond, who acknowledged that the bag was his. The agent requested that he be permitted to open the bag, and Bond gave him permission to do so. The agent opened the bag and found that the "brick" he felt was actually methamphetamine.

Later, Bond argued to suppress the evidence and, while the lower courts denied the suppression stating that Bond had no expectation of privacy in his bag because other passengers could touch Bond's bag, Bond argued that other passengers would not be "manipulating" his bag to try to feel what was in it, especially to the level of manipulation that the agent engaged in. The Supreme Court reversed the lower courts, stating that Bond did expect privacy in the brick, as he had placed it in an opaque bag and placed it above him so he could keep track of where it was and who might have had access to it. Further, the Court found that Bond would not have expected that even if someone touched his bag that the person would spend time thoroughly manipulating the objects within it. Thus, the officer's behavior did constitute an illegal seizure.

Another landmark and interesting seizure case is **Arizona v. Hicks.**[50] In the **Hicks** case, the police were called to a downstairs apartment when a bullet came through the ceiling from the direction of the upstairs apartment. The police entered the upstairs apartment to investigate and saw, in plain view, an expensive piece of stereo equipment that seemed out of place considering the surrounding impoverished neighborhood. Remembering that the department had recently heard of thefts of stereo equipment in the area, the officer attempted to determine whether this stereo might be stolen. In order to make this determination, the officer picked up the stereo to obtain the serial number on the bottom of the unit. The Supreme Court, considering this movement of the stereo, ruled that the movement of the stereo was indeed a seizure and that probable cause to believe that the equipment was stolen was needed before any seizure.

---

49. 529 U.S. 334 (2000).
50. 480 U.S. 321 (1987).

Seizure of a Person

Seizure While in Motion. The issue of when a person is seized is a complicated issue and very fact specific. In the landmark case of **Terry v. Ohio**,[51]
"Whenever a police officer accosts an individual and restrains his freedom
to walk away, he has 'seized' that person." Being subjected to a frisk on
the street is considered a seizure. The issue of frisks under the **Terry** "stop
and frisk" doctrine and the issue of "investigatory detentions" will be covered
in Chapter 6. A related issue is the consideration of when a "stop" has taken
place. A police officer has the authority to ask someone questions in order to
conduct an investigation (sometimes referred to as a **mere encounter**). For
example, if a police officer is called to a house because someone reported
that a bullet came from a car window and landed on the porch of that
house, the officer can knock on the doors of neighbors and ask the neighbors
if they heard or saw anything strange around the time of the shooting. The
neighbors do not necessarily have to answer the officer's questions, but the
officer has a right to ask them and to stop anyone walking down the street to
see if they might know something. However, at some point a "discussion"
with an individual can turn into more than a "mere encounter" and into a
seizure; as each level escalates, different constitutional ramifications exist.
Thus, it is important to distinguish each of these types of police encounters.

When Does a Stop and Seizure Take Place? An important aspect in determining whether a seizure has taken place is whether a "reasonable person"
would feel free to leave. If not, the person has been seized. A court is not
concerned with whether or not an officer intended to seize a person, but
instead applies an objective standard that demonstrates what the person
being seized should reasonably have believed. Further, although some citizens
might feel as though they must comply with any requests of an officer, the
courts consider a "reasonable person" to be someone who knows that he can
choose not to comply with certain requests asked by an officer. One reason
that it is difficult to determine when an actual seizure takes place is that a
situation may escalate from a "mere encounter" to a seizure, if the officer
develops probable cause during her encounter with the person that leads
her to suspect that the person has committed a crime. Further, as is the
case with all searches and seizures, probable cause to seize must be developed
prior to the seizure and cannot be based on anything that happens following
the seizure, like the subsequent discovery of criminal evidence or contraband.

A seizure may take place in one of two ways—through physical force by
the officer or by an officer's show of authority. The question becomes when
the encounter with the officer is consensual and at what point the encounter is
based on the authority of the police to keep a person from going elsewhere. If
an officer asks someone to accompany him to the police station, even if that

---

51. 392 U.S. 1 (1968).

person submits willingly, the submission might be considered a seizure, since the person may feel as though he must comply with the officer's request.

Generally a seizure takes place while a person is in motion, either on foot or in a vehicle, but an officer can also seize a person when the person is sitting or standing still. Consider the following case.

FLORIDA V. BOSTICK[52]

FACTS: Officials boarded a bus that was en route from Miami to Atlanta and stopped in Fort Lauderdale. The officials, members of the Broward County Sheriff's Department, were engaged in a drug interdiction program and believed that drugs were being transported via bus. The officials asked the defendant if they could inspect his ticket and identification. The two items matched, but nonetheless, without any articulated suspicion, the officials asked if they could search the defendant's luggage. The court determined that the defendant was advised that he could refuse consent (although the defendant disputed this), and that the officers did not point their guns at the defendants or even draw them, although the guns were visible to the defendant. The defendant permitted the search but argued later that the police officers' conduct was in effect a seizure of his person.

ISSUE: Did the police engage in an "unreasonable" search and seizure by approaching defendant while he was on the bus and requesting to search his luggage?

HOLDING: No seizure had taken place merely by virtue of the fact that the individual was on a bus. The trial court should have analyzed all of the facts to determine whether, under the particular facts of the case, the individual felt as though he was unable to leave.

RATIONALE: The Supreme Court stated that it is not unreasonable for the police to approach a citizen and request that the citizen answer some questions; rather, there must be a show of physical force. In **Bostick**, the mere fact that the defendant was a passenger on a bus did not, in and of itself, make the encounter unreasonable. A seizure occurs only when a reasonable person does not feel free to leave. Bostick argued that he did not feel as though he could leave the bus because it was scheduled to depart soon. Bostick's movements were confined because he had taken the bus, and not because of any specific movements made by the police. The lower court should not have made a ruling that in every instance where a law enforcement official steps on a bus, a seizure takes place. The dissenting justices pointed out that had the defendant chosen to leave the bus, he would have been stuck in Fort Lauderdale rather than ending up at his desired ending point of Atlanta.

---

52. 501 U.S. 429.

However, in a 1983 case decided by the Supreme Court, an individual boarding an airplane was "seized" by officials asking for his identification.[53] In that case, the officials had focused on the defendant, Royer, because he fit a drug courier profile. The officers asked if Royer would speak with them, and he consented and produced his airline ticket and driver's license for the officials' inspection. The officials noted that the ticket and driver's license had different names on them, and they indicated to Royer that they suspected he was transporting narcotics. The officials failed to return Mr. Royer's ticket and license to him and they asked him to accompany them to a small room. Royer went with them, and without Royer's consent, the officials obtained his luggage and brought it to the room. They asked him to consent to a search of his luggage, and he produced a key, although he did not verbally agree to the search. The officers opened the suitcase and found marijuana.

The Supreme Court held that the officers did not have probable cause when they moved Mr. Royer to the small room in the airport; thus, even if Royer's handing the officials the key was considered consent to the search, that consent was obtained illegally. Because the officials still held Mr. Royer's ticket and license, he had no choice but to cooperate with the officials, because he could not go anywhere without those items.

The issue of whether a stop and seizure has occurred is very factually based and the Supreme Court has hesitated to give any exact time limit as to when an "encounter" by a law enforcement official might turn into a "stop." A case in which the Court considered this time limit is that of **United States v. Sharpe**.[54] In **Sharpe**, an agent of the Drug Enforcement Administration (DEA), Agent Cooke, was on patrol in an unmarked vehicle near a coastal town in North Carolina. Cooke noticed a blue pickup truck with an attached camper shell traveling on the highway, driven by Savage. The pickup truck was seemingly being driven in tandem with a blue Pontiac Bonneville, driven by Sharpe with a man named Davis riding along as a passenger. Agent Cooke observed that the pickup truck was riding low in the rear and that the camper did not sway or bounce when the truck drove over bumps or around curves; he thus concluded that the camper must be heavily loaded. The windows of the camper were covered by a quilted material, so it was impossible to see inside the camper. Based on suspicions that the camper might be transporting narcotics, Cooke followed the vehicles for approximately 20 miles, and he then made an "investigative stop," radioing for backup from the local state police barracks, which arrived shortly. The Pontiac and the pickup truck turned off the highway shortly after the state police officer, Thrasher, driving a marked police car, joined Cooke in following the two vehicles.

The police cars followed the two vehicles as they drove on a campground road at a speed that far exceeded the designated speed limit. The road eventually looped back to the highway, and the vehicles traveled back onto the

---

53. **Florida v. Royer**, 460 U.S. 491 (1983).
54. 470 U.S. 675 (1985).

three-lane highway and continued to drive south. Thrasher pulled alongside the Pontiac, which was currently in the lead of the two vehicles and traveling in the middle lane of the highway, and turned on his flashing light. As the Pontiac moved into the right lane, the pickup truck cut between the Pontiac and the patrol car, nearly hitting the patrol car, and then continued down the highway. Thrasher pursued the truck while Cooke pulled over the Pontiac. Cooke approached Sharpe in his Pontiac, who produced a driver's license bearing the name of Raymond J. Pavlovich. Cooke radioed for Thrasher, could not receive a response from him, then radioed for more backup; when it arrived, he drove down the road to try to find Thrasher and the pickup truck.

Cooke found Thrasher, who had stopped the pickup truck approximately ½ mile down the road; Thrasher had ordered Savage out of the vehicle and Savage had produced his driver's license and a bill of sale of the truck which bore the name of Pavlovich. Savage said the truck belonged to a friend and that he was taking it to have its shock absorbers repaired. Thrasher told Savage that he would be held until Cooke arrived; when Thrasher also informed Savage that Cooke was a DEA agent, Savage became nervous and asked for the return of his driver's license, stating that he wanted to leave. Thrasher told Savage that he was not free to leave at that time.

Cooke arrived at the scene approximately 15 minutes after the initial stop of the truck, and Cooke requested that Savage allow him to search the truck, stating that he believed that it was filled with marijuana. Savage refused to allow the truck to be searched, stating that he was not the owner. Cooke stepped on the rear of the truck, observed that it did not sink any lower when he did so, and confirmed his suspicion that it was overloaded. He also put his nose against the rear window and indicated that he could smell marijuana. Cooke, still acting without Savage's permission, removed the keys from the ignition, opened the rear of the camper, and observed a large number of burlap-wrapped bales that resembled bales of marijuana. (Cooke indicated that he had previously seen similarly wrapped bales that contained marijuana.) Cooke placed Savage under arrest, left him with Thrasher, and returned to the Pontiac and arrested Sharpe and Davis. The total amount of time elapsed between the time Cooke stopped the Pontiac and the time he returned to arrest Sharpe and Davis was approximately 30 to 40 minutes. After the parties were arrested and the vehicles were moved to the closest federal building, the vehicles and camper were searched without warrants; 43 bales of marijuana, weighing a total of 2,629 pounds, were found, and 8 randomly selected bales all tested positive for marijuana. Sharpe and Savage were charged with possession of a controlled substance with intent to distribute it, and they moved for the marijuana to be suppressed, arguing that the detention constituted a seizure without probable cause.

The Supreme Court indicated that it would not set forth a certain period of time for investigations, as the lower court had done in this case, having set a length of 20 minutes as the longest a person could be detained before it was considered an arrest, rather than merely an investigatory stop. The Court stated that its main concern was whether police had "diligently pursued a means of investigation that was likely to confirm or dispel their suspicions quickly, during which time it was necessary to detain the defendant . . . whether the police are acting in a swiftly developing situation, and in such cases the court should not indulge in unrealistic second-guessing." The Court determined that Cooke had indeed pursued his investigation in a diligent and reasonable manner. During most of Savage's detention, Cooke was attempting to contact Thrasher and obtaining the help and backup of the local police department who had to remain with Sharpe while Cooke went to find Thrasher and Savage. Once Cooke found Thrasher, he quickly requested information from Savage, requested permission to search the truck, stepped on the rear bumper of the truck and drew conclusions from the fact that it did not move, and detected the odor of marijuana. No delay existed other than the delay caused by Savage driving away rather than pulling over, and thus, the Court would not determine that the amount of time automatically placed the situation into an arrest situation instead of an investigatory stop. Thus, reasonable suspicion existed for the officers to begin questioning.

YOU BE THE JUDGE

Two officers are patrolling in the early evening and observe a man walking away from a bus terminal. He is accompanied by a white male who does not have any luggage with him. The officers assume that the man has just gotten off the bus and believes that drugs are being smuggled on that bus. The officers ask to speak to the man and explain to him that they are investigating the prevalence of drugs being smuggled on that bus. The officers ask the man if he is carrying any weapons, large amounts of cash, or illegal drugs. He states that he is not and the officers ask permission to search the bag he is carrying. He agrees. One officer searches the bag while the other continues questioning him. The officer finds a small box wrapped in Christmas paper with a tag that states "To Dee Dee From Kevin." The man states that the box contains "perfume or something." The officers ask him three times to consent to open the package and he refuses all three times. An officer then asks him if the officers can search his person, and he agrees. The officers find a pipe that is thought to be illegal drug paraphernalia. The man is arrested, the package is opened, and it is found to contain cocaine. The man later argues that the evidence should be suppressed because he stated three times that he did not wish for the package to be opened, and thus the fourth consent he gave was not voluntary but was coerced. The officers argue that obviously the man knew that he was able to deny consent and that the consent was therefore voluntary. What do you decide?

INVESTIGATORY STOPS

The **Royer** case, discussed above, is a good example of a case involving an investigative detention. The parallel notion of a "stop and frisk" will be discussed in Chapter 6. Other Supreme Court cases have focused on what constitutes sufficient reasonable suspicion for police to stop a person and begin to ask questions. The answers to those questions might, then, help the officers in developing probable cause. A person might match a profile, as discussed above, but many other circumstances will suffice. Law enforcement agents must use the totality of the circumstances test, developed for purposes of establishing probable cause and explained further in Chapter 6.

In **United States v. Cortez**,[55] the Supreme Court stated: "[T]he whole picture must be taken into account. Based upon that whole picture the detaining officers must have a particularized and objective basis for suspecting the person stopped of criminal activity." The **Cortez** Court set forth specific items that the police could use to develop reasonable suspicion. Note that all of these items are considered objective, not subjective; in other words, these are not things that an officer believes but tangible evidence that can be presented later in court if necessary. Police reports, consideration of the modes and patterns of operation of the person in comparison with the modes and patterns of operation that criminals normally use, and even "suspicious behavior" can support an investigatory stop. Following the use of these objective items, then, the officer can make deductions, which, as the Court stated, "might well elude an untrained person." The Court allowed this sort of interpretation by law enforcement officers as follows: "[l]ong before the law of probabilities was articulated as such, practical people formulated certain common-sense conclusions about human behavior; jurors as fact-finders are permitted to do the same—and so are law enforcement officers." A mere hunch, however, will not suffice, and law enforcement has been cautioned by the Supreme Court not to go on a "fishing expedition."[56]

An interesting and landmark case in the area of defining how officers can develop particularized suspicion in a case was set forth in **Illinois v. Wardlow**.[57] Officers noticed Wardlow standing on the sidewalk of an area of town where officers knew that heavy drug trafficking regularly took place. The officers were in a four-car caravan of marked police vehicles, and Wardlow fled when he saw police vehicles approaching. The officers assumed that when they drove into the area they would encounter a large number of people, including drug customers and individuals who were serving as lookouts for drug deals. Thus, when Wardlow began to run from the area, two officers decided to

---

55. 449 U.S. 411 (1981).
56. **United States v. Pavelski**, 789 F.2d 487 (7th Cir. 1986).
57. 528 U.S. 119 (2000).

investigate his presence in the area. The officers followed Wardlow in their police car and cornered him on a street. Upon stopping Wardlow, an officer immediately conducted a protective pat-down search for weapons; the officer later testified that he did this because it is very common for people in high drug trafficking areas to carry weapons. Wardlow was carrying a gun and the officer felt a heavy, hard object in the shape of a gun. The officer opened the bag and found a .38 caliber handgun containing five rounds of ammunition. Wardlow was arrested and filed a motion to suppress the evidence. The lower court (the Illinois Supreme Court) had ruled that the officer did not have reasonable suspicion to search Wardlow based solely on the fact that he was in a high crime area and ran when he noticed the police. However, the Supreme Court disagreed, acknowledging that "nervous, evasive behavior" is a pertinent factor in obtaining reasonable suspicion and justifying an investigative stop. In fact, the Court stated,

> Headlong flight—wherever it occurs—is the consummate act of evasion: it is not necessarily indicative of wrongdoing, but it is certainly suggestive of such. In reviewing the propriety of an officer's conduct, courts do not have available empirical studies dealing with inferences drawn from suspicious behavior, and we cannot reasonably demand scientific certainty from judges or law enforcement officers where none exists. Thus, the determination of reasonable suspicion must be based on commonsense judgments and inferences about human behavior.

Amicus briefs were filed by various interest groups on behalf of the defendant, focusing on the fact that innocent people sometimes flee from the police. While the Supreme Court accepted the fact that officers conducting an investigatory stop might end up stopping innocent people, the Court acknowledged that many people, especially some racial groups, are afraid of the police, and that unprovoked flight does not always imply criminal behavior but that it often does. The Court quoted surveys and studies that show that many African Americans consider police brutality a serious problem and that many African Americans are disproportionately stopped by police. In fact, a report issued by the Attorney General of Massachusetts stated that young men were forced in some investigatory stop situations to lower their pants or have their underwear searched in public forums.[58] The controversy over whether certain racial and socioeconomic groups are stopped more often than other groups by police remains a hot topic in the field of criminal justice.

---

58. **Illinois v. Wardlow,** *quoting* J. Shannon, Attorney General of Massachusetts, Report of the Attorney General's Civil Rights Division on Boston Police Department Practices 60-61 (Dec. 18, 1990).

YOU BE THE JUDGE

A person was traveling by bus from Ft. Lauderdale, Florida to Detroit, Michigan. The bus stopped in Tallahassee, Florida to refuel and be cleaned. All passengers were asked to get off the bus for a short time. When the passengers reboarded the bus, three members of the Tallahassee police department boarded the bus; the officers were in plain clothes, carried concealed weapons, and openly displayed their badges.

One officer knelt on the driver's seat to watch the occupants of the bus while the other two officers asked passengers in the bus about their travel plans. The first officer did not block the door, and the other officer did not block the aisle while asking questions. The officers testified that most people were willing to cooperate and answer questions, although on the day in question, they did not tell the passengers that the passengers could refuse to answer their questions. The officers indicated that some passengers got off the bus during the questioning and then returned.

The officer asked two men, Drayton and Brown, if he could check their bags, which were in the overhead compartment. The men said that would be fine. The officer then noticed that the men were dressed in heavy clothes considering the warm temperature outside and requested to search their person. Upon patting down the two men, the officer found drugs taped to their legs with duct tape.

The two men were charged with various drug crimes. They argue that they were seized when the officers came onto the bus and began to ask questions and that they did not feel as though they could leave, or that if they did leave, they would end up having to answer the officers' questions once they came back. The officers argued that people normally cooperate with their questions, that the two men cooperated fully, and that they did not seize the two men.

You are the judge trying to decide whether a seizure of the two men took place. What do you decide?

Another "seizure of the person" issue can arise when an individual is being chased by the police. A seizure generally does not occur until a person submits to police authority, as long as the officer has not laid hands on the person. In **California v. Hodari D.,**[59] a juvenile fled on foot as an unmarked police car approached him. An officer pursued him on foot, and while he was being pursued, he tossed something on the ground, which turned out to be narcotics. If Hodari had been seized (by the police officer's actions of

---

59. 499 U.S. 621 (1991).

running after him) at the time the narcotics were thrown, the Court would have had to consider whether the seizure itself was legal. Instead, the Court ruled that the defendant had not been seized, as the officer had not placed his hands on the defendant. The Court opined that, had the officer placed his hands on the defendant and the defendant broken away, the defendant would have been considered seized, but this was not the case, so no seizure had taken place.

SEARCH AND SEIZURE OF LITERARY ITEMS

Because literary items are subject to First Amendment protection, search and seizure rules vary when literary items are to be seized. A warrant is always required to seize these items.[60] Also, an affidavit requesting a magistrate to approve the seizure of materials based on their obscenity must be very specific. The officer must either show the materials to the magistrate, when possible, or specifically describe them in detail. Further, the items to be seized must be very specifically stated—it is not enough to state that all "obscene materials" are to be seized. If there are numerous copies of the items, such as in a store or other distribution center, only one or two copies shall be seized, and the other copies should remain in the store until a court has made a final decision on whether or not the items are obscene.[61]

CITIZEN'S ARREST

Many people are familiar with the concept of a "citizen's arrest." This doctrine exists in many countries, and occasionally a news story will inform the public of someone who has "heroically" made such an arrest. When no police officer is present but a common citizen sees someone committing a crime, it is possible, depending on the law of the particular state the person is in, to effectuate a citizen's arrest. This concept was permitted in medieval England when law enforcement was neither prevalent nor organized and the Crown relied upon the common citizens to assist in the enforcement of laws and identification of law breakers. In fact, in medieval England, a common citizen had the exact same right as a sheriff to arrest a fellow citizen and was sometimes even paid to do so. Although the term implies that the person making the arrest is a "citizen" of the country in which the arrest is taking place, this is generally not a requirement in states that have laws permitting citizen's arrests.

---

60. **Roaden v. Kentucky**, 413 U.S. 496 (1973).
61. **Heller v. New York**, 413 U.S. 483 (1973).

Some argue that the Ninth Amendment to the Constitution permits citizens' arrests as part of the individual's natural right to self-preservation and the defense of others. Another related amendment is the Second Amendment, as the possession of firearms allows a citizen to arrest another person with less concern of being harmed in the process. Every state except North Carolina allows citizen's arrests. Most state statutes allow a citizen's arrest when the arresting citizen has a "reasonable belief" that a felony has been committed. Occasionally a citizen's arrest can be made if a person commits a misdemeanor that disturbs the peace and the person has witnessed the crime taking place. Some states also permit a person to detain someone (as opposed to arresting them) if probable cause exists that the person has committed a felony, breach of peace, physical injury to another person, or theft or destruction of property. Although the line between detention and arrest in a citizen's arrest may seem blurred, the concept behind detention is that the person who is detained cannot be transported elsewhere, while a person who is arrested can be forcibly moved.

Some states go so far as to permit a person making a citizen's arrest to use lethal force against a fleeing felon, just as a law enforcement official can. Citizens can also come to the assistance of police officers if necessary. However, effectuating a citizen's arrest is not without risk. In some states, a person who effectuates such an arrest can be liable in a civil lawsuit for false arrest or false imprisonment if the person they arrest is not eventually convicted of a crime. Civil and criminal penalties, including the charge of false imprisonment, can also be lodged against the person making the arrest if the arrest is made maliciously or without a reasonable basis to believe that the person has actually committed a crime. A person making a citizen's arrest should be very cautious. First, he should be concerned about being harmed when making the arrest. Second, he should make sure not to use more force than is necessary in effectuating the arrest. Third, he should make sure to immediately turn the suspect over to the proper authorities and should never mete out his own punishment to the suspect. Considering all the specifics of when a citizen's arrest can and cannot be made, and considering the special rules surrounding this doctrine, do you believe individuals should be permitted to arrest their fellow citizens? You will study the doctrine of probable cause at length in your college courses and still you will need years of law enforcement experience before you are comfortable with making a split-second decision regarding whether probable cause exists. Do you believe a citizen can make such decisions appropriately and fairly?

VIGILANTE JUSTICE

If not highly regulated, the concept of citizen's arrest can be used as **vigilante justice**, which means that individual citizens take the law into their own hands, often resulting in extreme harm or even death to others, outside the bounds of the law. Vigilante justice has also been referred to as "frontier justice" and included lynching and gun fighting that was common when the western United States was settled. Vigilante justice is highly discouraged by the courts and legislature, but it is sometimes encouraged by the public and glamorized by the media. Vigilante justice is motivated by a person's dissatisfaction with the justice system. For example, a father whose daughter is killed by a drunk driver might feel that he should find the offender and take justice into his own hands, knowing that the prosecution of the man in the court system will be time consuming and frustrating and could even result in the man walking free based on what the public would call a "technicality."

One very famous case of vigilante justice was the subway shooting committed by a man named Bernard Goetz in the 1980s. Goetz shot, but did not kill, four men in the New York subway as a reaction to his belief that the men were about to rob him. The shootings took place in an era when New Yorkers were frustrated with the high amount of crime that existed, including crime on the subway system. He was then referred to as the "Subway Vigilante." Goetz fled after the shootings but surrendered to police later and was eventually tried in federal court for attempted murder, assault, reckless endangerment, and several firearms offenses. A jury found him not guilty on all charges except the firearms offense, because the gun he was carrying was not legally in his possession. Goetz served two thirds of a one year sentence. The case was controversial because the men had exchanged words with him but had not actually made a physical move to rob him, and since Goetz admitted that when he shot the men, he was trying to "get as many as he could." Goetz had many supporters including the "Guardian Angels," which was a group of mostly Hispanic and black teenagers who had taken it upon themselves to patrol the New York subway system; that group even raised money to benefit Goetz's defense.[62] Controversy still exists regarding whether the jury made the correct decision in the **Goetz** case.

QUESTIONS TO CONSIDER

1. Read the case of **United States v. Dunn**, 480 U.S. 294 (1987). How would you have decided the case if you were the Court? Can you think of any facts that, if changed slightly, might have made the Court rule for the defendant in that case?

2. Do you think, like the Court did in **Griffin v. Wisconsin**, that probation officers have the welfare of their clients in mind and that this justifies probation officers to be able to search a probationer's home without

---

62. For more information regarding this case, *see* Fletcher, George P. (1988). *A Crime of Self Defense: Bernhard Goetz and the Law on Trial*. Chicago, University of Chicago Press.

probable cause? Do you believe the framers intended this result when they drafted the Constitution?

3. Compare the facts of **Florida v. Royer** with those of **Florida v. Bostik**. The **Bostik** case was remanded to the trial court to determine more facts. In light of the **Royer** case, how do you think the lower court should have ruled on the case? Compare both cases with the facts of **United States v. Sharpe**. Do you believe the Supreme Court's determination in all three cases can be reconciled?

4. What do you think Judge Brandeis would say about the many forms of technology we now have and whether the government should be able to search this technology to obtain information that is used to prosecute people?

5. The Supreme Court has stated that abandoning an item takes it out of the protection of the Fourth Amendment. Have you abandoned your items if you leave them on a table in a public library while you go to a vending machine to purchase a bottle of water?

6. Review the **Florida v. Harris** case. How did research and various reports made by agencies in the United States and elsewhere influence the Court's decision? Locate and read one of the studies that are mentioned in the opinion and discuss how this study could support either a majority opinion, a dissenting opinion, or both.

7. Read the following cases: **United States v. Arnold**, 523 F.3d 941 (9th Cir. 2008), and **United States v. Ickes**, 393 F.3d 501 (4th Cir. 2005). Identify the arguments made by the government and the plaintiffs in each case. If the issue of the search of electronic items at the border comes before the Supreme Court, which side do you believe will prevail, and why?

KEY TERMS

affidavit of probable cause

This document is a statement of all the information that the officer knows either from personal observation or from the investigation she has conducted in connection with a particular crime.

curtilage

Refers to the area connected to a home where the intimate activities of life take place.

expectation of privacy

This ruling was the extension of the right to privacy in specific places, such as houses, and recognizes that individuals should have a reasonable sense of privacy in certain situations and locales.

general warrants

These documents allowed local law enforcement to enter and search the homes of colonists in order to look for books and papers that were being used to criticize the government.

investigatory stops

These are stops made when an officer suspects criminal behavior. The Court has ruled that the whole picture must be taken into account, and that based on that picture, the detaining officers must have a particularized and objective basis for suspecting the person stopped of criminal activity.

mere encounters

This is the process in which a police officer has the authority to ask someone questions in order to conduct an investigation.

open fields

Refers to anything beyond the area of a home where the intimate activities of life take place.

seizure

When a person or property is taken into custody. Two things may be seized: people and property. Property is seized when there is some meaningful interference with an individual's possessory interest in that property. A person is seized when a police officer accosts an individual and restrains his freedom to walk away.

stop and seizure

It is sometimes difficult to determine when a stop becomes a seizure, but the determining factor is whether a reasonable person would feel free to leave. Probable cause must exist to execute a seizure. A seizure may take place in one of two ways, through physical force by the officer, or by an officer's show of authority. Generally, a seizure takes place while a person is in motion, either on foot or in a vehicle, but an officer can also seize a person when the person is sitting or standing still.

writs of assistance

These documents allowed individuals to enter and search the homes of colonists, generally for no reason at all, to assist the British government in searching for smuggled goods.

KEY COURT CASES

Arizona v. Hicks

Landmark case involving seizure of property, where police officers entered an apartment to investigate a shooting and saw in plain view an expensive stereo, which they seized as possibly stolen. The Court ruled that the movement of the stereo was a seizure and that probable cause to believe that it was stolen was necessary before the seizure.

California v. Greenwood

This case regarding the definition of abandonment was important to law enforcement agencies who routinely used curbside trash to obtain enough information to request and receive search warrants for suspects when other information was not sufficient to obtain a warrant, and has further been used to justify law enforcement's taking and using against a defendant his DNA that has been left inadvertently on a discarded item.

California v. Hodari D.

In this case, a juvenile fled on foot as an unmarked police car approached him. As he was being chased on foot, he tossed a bag on the ground that turned out to contain narcotics. If Hodari had been seized by the police officer's actions of running after him, the seizure of the drugs would have been illegal. The court ruled that the defendant had not been seized, as the officer had not placed his hands on the defendant.

Camara v. Municipal Court

In this case regarding a health inspector's invasion of a home without a warrant, the Court established the standard for administrative searches that balances the rights of individuals in not being subjected to the inconvenience of a search with the interest of government in regulating certain industries, and a consideration of the benefit that regulation will bring to the public.

Florida v. Harris

In this case, the Court moved away from its prior implications that a dog's detection of drugs is always accurate, and stated that a defendant has the right to challenge the presumption that a trained dog is reliable, and that a defendant can cross-examine an officer or introduce his own witnesses to testify as to why the dog's alert should not have been trusted.

Griswold v. Connecticut

One of the first cases involving the issue of a person's privacy, this case involved the protesting of a state law that prohibited residents from using any form of contraception, specifically prohibiting "any drug, medicinal article, or instrument for the purpose of preventing conception," and the ruling stated that the law violated the right to marital privacy.

Oliver v. United States

This case began to clarify the distinction between open fields and curtilage, and the Court ruled that the only privacy a person could demand in activities outside his house were activities that took place in the area immediately surrounding his home, that normally open fields are accessible or viewable by the public, and that "no trespassing" signs normally are not particularly effective in deterring others from walking on posted land, and that society would not recognize as reasonable the assertion that crops growing in a field away from a house should be protected by an expectation of privacy.

Skinner v. Railway Labor Executives Association

This 1898 landmark case first permitted the random drug testing of employees, in a case in which the employer was concerned that an employee who was under the influence of a controlled substance at his job and was driving a train could harm others.

Terry v. Ohio

This landmark seizure case created the "stop and frisk" doctrine, otherwise known as a "Terry stop and frisk," and ruled that whenever a police officer accosts a person and restrains his ability to move away freely, that person has been seized.

United States v. Katz

This case involved an individual who was making illegal wagering bets using a public phone booth. Government agents, without a warrant, had attached listening devices to the outside of the booth. The Court ruled that the user of the phone booth who shut the door of the booth to make his conversation private did indeed have an expectation of privacy in that case, and that the surveillance was unlawful without a warrant. It also created a two-pronged test of expectation of privacy.

SEARCHES AND ARRESTS WITH A WARRANT AND PROBABLE CAUSE

3

LEARNING OBJECTIVES: Students will

1. Understand what constitutes probable cause
2. Know what constitutes a sufficient proper warrant
3. Understand how a search warrant can be challenged in court
4. Know how to execute a search warrant
5. Be familiar with the rules surrounding wiretap applications

The Fourth Amendment states that "no warrant shall issue, except with probable cause." Thus, the framers of the Constitution clearly believed in the use of warrants. However, the language of the amendment does not include any guidance as to whether warrants are always necessary preceding a search. The Supreme Court's original stance on the issue was that a warrant was always needed in order to perform a search, and thus, a warrantless search was presumed to be unreasonable. While the Court has made many exceptions to this general rule, it is always prudent for a law enforcement officer to obtain a warrant when practical. A warranted search results in less of a possibility that a defendant will be able to argue that a search was performed improperly. This chapter will explore how a warrant is obtained and how a warrant is executed by a law enforcement official.

THE WARRANT REQUIREMENT

Controversy exists over what the framers' intent was in even including the warrant language in the Fourth Amendment. Did they mean to force law enforcement officers to always have a warrant before searching someone or someplace or seizing someone? Or was the assumption that sometimes warrants would be needed and sometimes they would not be, and that the probable cause language in the Fourth Amendment would be important

A JUDGE'S GAVEL

www.bigstock.com.

only when a warrant was actually needed? The framers of the Constitution gave no guidance to this question, and thus courts have had to determine the answer to this question. Obtaining a warrant takes time, so forcing police officers to have a warrant for every search and seizure they perform would be time consuming and might result in valuable evidence being destroyed before a warrant could be obtained. However, the historical basis under which the framers were operating at the time they wrote the Constitution demonstrates that the framers were wary about the types of warrants that had been traditionally issued by the British government, including those referred to as general warrants, which are discussed in Chapter 2.

Recent Supreme Court decisions have eroded the Supreme Court's original presumption that a warrant must always precede a search, and many exceptions to the warrant requirement have been set forth by the Court. These exceptions will be further discussed in Chapter 6. Nonetheless, the best advice a rookie police officer can receive is to always obtain a warrant if possible. In most jurisdictions, after a police officer drafts an application for a warrant, the officer is required to have a district attorney review the warrant application before it is submitted to a magistrate for her review. Thus, by the time the officer would actually receive the signed warrant from the magistrate and execute it, at least two more people have reviewed the warrant and confirmed that in fact probable cause does exist to support its issuance. This process protects the officer from claims that probable cause was not developed prior to the issuance of the warrant, and a defendant will have a more difficult time requesting that the court suppress the evidence when the search was based on a valid warrant, especially because many state courts have also established a "good faith" exception to a facially valid warrant that turns out to actually be invalid.

The Constitution itself provides that when a warrant is issued, four requirements must be met:

1. The warrant must be based on probable cause.
2. The warrant must be supported by oath or affirmation.
3. The warrant must particularly describe what is to be searched and what items are to be seized.
4. The warrant must be issued by a neutral magistrate.

Each of these topics will be discussed further below. The question of when a warrant is necessary at all remains and will be discussed in Chapter 6. Warrants are necessary both for finding physical evidence and for arresting people who are suspected of committing crimes. The standards are the same for both search and arrest warrants. This chapter will focus primarily on search warrants, as they are more commonly the subject of court cases than are arrest warrants.

WHAT CONSTITUTES PROBABLE CAUSE?

When an officer requests that a search warrant be issued, he drafts an **affidavit of probable cause**, a document that sets forth all of the information the officer has gathered through his investigation that leads him to believe that it is necessary to search a particular place for certain items. An arrest warrant application would include any information that would support the belief that a particular person has committed a particular crime. Because no definition of probable cause is provided in the Constitution, the meaning of the phrase is completely based on judicial interpretation. The framers of the Constitution did not define the term, nor do any federal statutes. The Supreme Court, however, has been defining the term as far back as 1813, when it stated that probable cause "means less than evidence which would justify condemnation. It imparts a seizure made under circumstances which warrant suspicion."[1] Further, probable cause is less than what would be sufficient to prove guilt in a criminal trial. Probable cause should be determined according to "factual and practical considerations of everyday life on which reasonable and prudent men, not legal technicians, act."[2] In other words, probable cause should be based on common sense—given all the facts,

---

1. **Lock v. United States,** 11 U.S. (7 Cr.) 339 (1813).
2. **Brinegar v. United States,** 338 U.S. 160 (1949).

does it appear as though this person committed a crime or criminal evidence will be found in a certain place?

The official standard that has been used over and over by courts is whether "the facts and circumstances within their knowledge and of which they had reasonably trustworthy information were sufficient in themselves to warrant a man of reasonable caution in the belief" that a crime had been committed.[3] This definition applies to searches in that the officer must also believe that the item to be searched for will be found in the location where he is requesting to search. The definition applies to arrests also, and an officer must believe that the person he is requesting to arrest is the person who has committed the crime. Probable cause in practical terms can be described as more than 50 percent certainty that a person has committed a crime or that certain items will be found in a certain place. A "reasonable man," sometimes referred to as a "prudent man," is a phrase that is often used by courts in both the criminal and civil law. The concept of a "reasonable man" encompasses both men and women and generally refers to someone who has common sense and general beliefs that are similar to most people. Probable cause refers to what a common person on the street would believe, not necessarily what a law enforcement officer, judge, or someone else trained in the area of criminal justice would believe.

However, courts sometimes consider the specialized wisdom of a law enforcement officer when determining whether probable cause has been developed. In **United States v. Ortiz,**[4] the Supreme Court considered the search of a vehicle by United States border patrol agents. The officers found illegal aliens in the trunk of the car. The officers admitted that they had no particular reason for suspecting that the car harbored illegal aliens, but they advertised to traffic via a sign with flashing lights that all vehicles should stop ahead at the border, where a permanent border patrol building is erected. Officers testified in court that when the checkpoint is open, all northbound traffic is screened. If anything about a vehicle or its occupants lead an officer to believe that the vehicle might be carrying illegal aliens, he will stop the car and question the occupants about their citizenship. If the questioning does not allay the officer's suspicions, or if the occupants' responses to the questions actually add to the officer's suspicion, he will then inspect all portions of the vehicle where a person could be hiding. The Supreme Court first determined that probable cause or consent must have been present in order for a car to be searched. The Court then stated that officers may rely on their knowledge of and prior experience with aliens and smugglers in determining whether probable cause exists. This concept makes sense considering that law enforcement officers are familiar with common behaviors of certain types of criminals. A law enforcement officer might know that, for example, drug dealers often hide their illegal drugs in a prescription bottle, hoping that the illegal

---

3. **Carroll v. United States,** 267 U.S. 132 (1925); **Beck v. Ohio,** 379 U.S. 89 (1964).
4. 422 U.S. 891 (1975).

substance will resemble a legal substance, or that crack cocaine rocks are sometimes hidden in a cigarette package or even a baby's diaper! A person who is not involved in the criminal justice system might not know about these common ways of smuggling drugs, but this type of knowledge should none-theless be permitted to be used by law enforcement agents as part of their determination of whether probable cause is present.

The "affidavit of probable cause" sets forth, generally in paragraph and narrative form, all of the information the police officer possesses, within her personal knowledge or told to her by others, which lead him to the conclusion that a crime was committed, that a particular person was involved in that crime, or that evidence pertaining to the crime will be found in a particular place. A magistrate will read the affidavit of probable cause and determine whether the information provided therein establishes probable cause. The magistrate's decision must be based only on the information found within the affidavit, so it is very important that the officer include all of the evidence she has gathered. The magistrate cannot consider anything he already knows about the case through the media, and in fact, if the magistrate knows too much about the case, she may not be considered "neutral and detached," as discussed later in this chapter.

Any information appearing in the affidavit of probable cause must be a statement of fact, and the magistrate cannot consider anything that is a con-clusory statement. For example, if an officer states in his affidavit "Peter Benekos is a drug dealer," the magistrate cannot consider that statement in her decision to grant the warrant. Conclusory evidence has been referred to as being "bald and unilluminating." One of the Supreme Court's first discus-sions of this issue was in the case of **Nathanson v. United States,**[5] decided by the Supreme Court in 1933. The officer in that case stated as probable cause in his affidavit that he had

> . . . cause to suspect and does believe that certain merchandise, to wit: Certain liquors of foreign origin a more particular description of which cannot be given, upon which the duties have not been paid, or which has otherwise been brought into the United States contrary to law, and that said merchandise is now deposited and contained within the premises of J.J. Nathanson.

Consider all of the information in this paragraph. What information demonstrates to the magistrate that J.J. Nathanson was actually involved in a crime? Does the information contain anything other than conjecture on the part of the officer? If you were the magistrate, what other types of information would you want or need to know in order to decide whether or not to grant the warrant? All of the information given in this paragraph is conclusory; the officer is telling the magistrate what he thinks J.J. Nathanson did but is not providing any information to the magistrate to explain to the magistrate

---

5. 290 U.S. 41 (1933).

why he came to that conclusion! The Supreme Court determined that this paragraph included only "mere affirmance of suspicion or belief without disclosure of supporting facts or circumstances" and therefore did not establish probable cause.

Direct and Hearsay Information

A police officer or other investigator has access to two different kinds of information during her investigation of a case: **direct information** and **hearsay information**. Consider the following scenario:

> Officer Dunn is called to the First Financial Bank located at First and Plum Streets. The caller indicates that he is outside the bank and that a robbery is taking place. Officer Dunn drives to the bank as quickly as he can, and as he pulls into the parking lot, he sees a man running out of the bank carrying a brown paper bag. The man is dressed like Michael Jackson, complete with a sparkling glove and Michael Jackson Halloween mask. The man leaves in a small red "getaway car" that is waiting by the door. Another officer chases the man but loses sight of the car. The officer enters the bank and begins to talk to the tellers and various customers. They all describe the man that robbed the bank as wearing a Michael Jackson costume, but only a few saw him before he put his mask on. They describe the man as having a very unusual tattoo of a dragon across his face. Each of the witnesses states that the man they are describing held up the teller of the bank at gunpoint and that the teller gave him money, which he placed in a brown paper bag before running out of the bank. The teller describes the man's voice and indicates he had a very unusual accent. Based on all of this information, the officer is aware that the suspect must be Harold Harper, a local man who speaks with an unusual accent, has the tattoo described by the witnesses, and is known to be a Michael Jackson fan.

In this example, the officer would have good reason to believe that the suspect is Harold Harper, but must include in his affidavit of probable cause all of the information leading him to believe that, even the facts that he obtained by interviewing witnesses. If the officer was to submit the affidavit based solely on the information he knows for a fact, he would only be able to state that he saw a man who looked like Michael Jackson running out of the bank with a bag and that the man got into a red car and drove away.

Information that the officer indicates he knows from first-hand knowledge, like seeing the bank robber leaving the bank, can be assumed by the magistrate to be true. The magistrate can assume that a law enforcement official will not fabricate evidence. Any such falsity could lead to the officer being prosecuted or disciplined at his job. The officer attests that the information in the affidavit is true to the best of his knowledge, and the magistrate can take the officer at his word. In the Harold Harper case, the officer obtained more information from the witnesses in the bank. In many cases, the information provided by witnesses will be the only information an officer receives. Officer Dunn could have gone to the bank after the robber had already departed, and then the only information Dunn would have had is what he was told by the customers and tellers that were at the bank at the time of the robbery.

The officer should always include in his affidavit of probable cause information he has obtained from the witnesses if he believes the information is accurate. However, how does the officer know whether the information he obtained from witnesses is true? Perhaps a witness that told the officer about the tattoo and the strange accent is a person who holds a grudge against Harold, and he really didn't think the bank robber was Harold. Can a magistrate consider an affidavit based solely on information provided to an officer by witnesses? This question will be considered later when the concept of hearsay information is discussed.

Anything that adds to the law enforcement officer's suspicion that a crime has been committed and that can link a particular person to the crime can contribute to probable cause. These things include a person's prior record, any sort of suspicious conduct, unusual behavior, the time of day during which a behavior takes place (a woman standing on the street corner at night might be more likely to be engaged in prostitution than one who stands on a street corner during the day), the resemblance of a person to a suspect (i.e., a person running through a park near the location of a bank robbery is wearing the same clothing as the person who robbed the bank), evasive or suspicious answers to questions (a person says he is driving to a wedding but is not dressed appropriately), or the seeming attempt to hide something (an officer notices a passenger in a vehicle shoving something under the seat as the officer approaches the vehicle during a traffic stop).

A good example of facts that would establish probable cause is set forth in the case of **Henry v. United States**.[6] Whiskey being shipped interstate was stolen from a terminal in Chicago. Investigating officers saw a man named Pierotti walking out of a tavern and getting into an automobile; Pierotti's employer had given the officers information, in their words, "concerning the implication of the defendant Pierotti with interstate shipments." However, the employer did not tell the agents he actually suspected Pierotti of committing the thefts himself. Officers followed Pierotti's vehicle and saw it enter an alley and stop; Mr. Henry was also in the vehicle and got out of the car, went into a residence, and came out with some cartons. He placed the cartons in the vehicle and he and Pierotti drove off. The agents were not able to follow the vehicle but later found it parked near the tavern; the car took the exact same route to the same residence with the same occupants and again cartons were taken out of the house and placed in the car. The agents finally stopped the car, and as Henry got out of the car, the officers heard him say, "Hold it; it's the Gs" and then "Tell him you just picked me up." The officers searched the vehicle and took the cartons (which had the name "Admiral" on them and were addressed to an out-of-state company). The officers found, inside the cartons, stolen radios. They arrested the men.

6. 361 U.S. 98 (1959).

Henry argued that the officers did not have probable cause to search the vehicle. The officers argued that because they found contraband in the vehicle, probable cause was in effect established. The Supreme Court stated that good faith on the part of the arresting officers was not enough; instead, true probable cause must exist and must be strictly enforced by the courts. The Court's analysis of the officer's actions provides a good explanation of what the Court requires in terms of probable cause:

It is true that a federal crime had been committed at a terminal in the neighborhood, whiskey having been stolen from an interstate shipment. Petitioner's friend, Pierotti, had been suspected of some implication in some interstate shipments, as we have said. But, as this record stands, what those shipments were and the manner in which he was implicated remain unexplained and undefined. The rumor about him is therefore practically meaningless. On the record, there was far from enough evidence against him to justify a magistrate in issuing a warrant. So far as the record shows, petitioner had not even been suspected of criminal activity prior to this time. Riding in the car, stopping in an alley, picking up packages, and driving away—these were all acts that were outwardly innocent. Their movements in the car had no mark of fleeing men or men acting furtively. The case might be different if the packages had been taken from a terminal or from an interstate trucking platform. But they were not. As we have said, the alley where the packages were picked up was in a residential section.

The fact that packages have been stolen does not make every man who carried a package subject to arrest, nor the package subject to seizure. The police must have reasonable grounds to believe that the particular package carried by the citizen is contraband. Its shape and design might at times be adequate. The weight of it and the manner in which it is carried might at times be enough. But there was nothing to indicate that the cartons here in issue probably contained liquor. The fact that they contained other contraband appeared only some hours after the arrest. What transpired at or after the time the car was stopped by the officers is, as we have said, irrelevant to the narrow issue before us. To repeat, an arrest is not justified by what the subsequent search discloses. Under our system, suspicion is not enough for an officer to lay hands on a citizen. It is better, so the Fourth Amendment teaches, that the guilty sometimes go free than that citizens be subject to easy arrest.[7]

Does Probable Cause Exist Forever?

The probable cause that exists when a law enforcement officer applies for a warrant generally does not later cease to exist and thereby make an arrest or search warrant stale. In fact, arrest warrants are sometimes effectuated years after being issued. However, each state and the federal government establish

---

7. **Id.** at 103, 104.

ARREST OF A SUSPECT

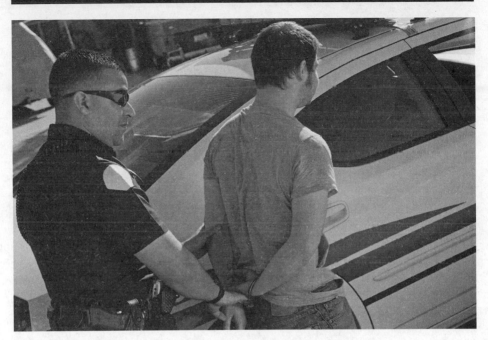

www.bigstock.com.

statutes of limitations for crimes which establish a limited time period during which a person can be charged with a crime. Once the statute of limitations has expired and a person can no longer be arrested, probable cause no longer exists, because probable cause must relate to a particular, defined crime. With the passage of time, police often obtain more information that supports a person's guilt. However, since probable cause is based on information that someone most likely, but not definitely, committed a crime, a subsequent investigation could produce evidence that shows that someone else committed the crime or that the original suspect did not. This type of information would cause probable cause, in effect, to become "stale." Thus, no officer should execute a warrant that is known not to be based on current probable cause. The case of **Arizona v. Evans**,[8] discussed elsewhere in this text, is an example of a case in which the Court decided that probable cause was not stale even though the computer system erroneously listed a prior warrant for a misdemeanor. The Court decided the case based on the officer's good faith in executing the warrant rather than based on the issue of staleness of probable cause. Had the Court considered the staleness of the probable cause, it might not have permitted the search.

---

8. 514 U.S. 1 (1995).

YOU BE THE JUDGE

You are a highway patrol officer sitting in your vehicle in the median strip on a major highway that runs between two large cities. Your job on this particular day is to identify those vehicles that are traveling at least ten miles over the posted speed limit, effectuate a stop of those vehicles, and issue speeding tickets.

Using your radar gun, you identify a vehicle that is traveling 85 miles per hour in a 65 mile per hour zone. You pull out onto the highway, follow the vehicle, and turn your lights on. After about one and one half minutes of following the vehicle with your lights on, the vehicle pulls over and comes to a complete stop on the berm of the highway. You notice that the driver leans over toward the passenger shortly after the vehicle comes to a complete stop.

When you arrive at the driver's window, the driver, a male who appears to be approximately 20 years old, presents to you his registration card and driver's license. You perform a computerized check of the driver to check for outstanding warrants or prior crimes but you find nothing. The driver is a resident of your state and lives in one of the main cities through which the highway runs. The passenger of the vehicle, also a male in his 20s, and the driver are both dressed in khaki pants and polo shirts. Both of the occupants of the car seem a bit nervous; the driver's hands are shaking and the passenger seems to be looking around nervously.

Based on the nervous appearance of the two men, you ask them to step out of the vehicle. You then separately ask them where they are going. One of the men states that the two men are friends and are going to a wedding in a city that is approximately one hour away. The other man says that the two men are going to the same city but states that they are going to visit relatives and that they are cousins. You have the suspicion that the two men might be taking drugs from one city to the other, because that particular highway is known for drug trafficking between those two cities, which happen to be the city the men state they are coming from and the city which they both state they are going to.

Do you have probable cause to search the car for evidence of drug trafficking? If not, what other information would you need to know or acquire before you would have probable cause?

Oral Affidavits of Probable Cause

As technology becomes more and more advanced, it is more likely that information on which probable cause is based will be more likely to be presented to magistrates in a form other than traditional paper. The Federal Rules of

Criminal Procedure permit officers to present oral sworn testimony to a magistrate in support of their affidavit request. Warrant applications can also be submitted by fax or electronically in some jurisdictions. This use of technology can speed up the amount of time it takes to get the warrant application to the judge. This might result in courts requiring a warrant where exigent circumstances might have previously supported a warrantless search. Thanks to new technology, a warrant application could have been in front of a magistrate in enough time to avoid destruction of evidence or a safety issue, two instances in which a warrant might not normally be required.

HEARSAY INFORMATION

Information provided by witnesses and not known first hand by the officer is referred to as hearsay information. Sometimes the only information known by law enforcement is hearsay information. For example, in many drug cases, the police use informants to obtain information. In a drug case, an informant could be someone who purchases drugs from a suspected dealer and then reports the sale to the police. Informants are often people who have previously been prosecuted or arrested by the police for criminal actions themselves and are now assisting the police in order to have the charges against them reduced or even dropped. Thus, some informants are inherently suspect, and an officer will have to indicate in his warrant application that the information was obtained from an informant. A better type of informant is one who is giving information to the police that might implicate him but he is not trying to get any favor back from the police.

So when an informant who might receive favor from the police provides information to the police with the possibility of potentially receiving special treatment for his own case, how can a magistrate determine whether or not the suspect is reliable? The Supreme Court has developed this issue and has modified the test used to determine whether probable cause exists when hearsay is present. The first major cases in which the Supreme Court decided this issue were the cases of **Aguilar v. Texas**[9] and **Spinelli v. United States**.[10] The **Aguilar** and **Spinelli** cases set forth a two part inquiry to be used to determine whether hearsay within a probable cause affidavit is reliable. Originally, the Supreme Court ruled that an applicant for a warrant would have to demonstrate to the magistrate that both prongs were met before the magistrate could find that probable cause was present. That requirement was later changed, as will be discussed next.

9. 378 U.S. 108 (1964).
10. 393 U.S. 410 (1969).

The Basis of Knowledge Prong

The first prong to determine whether hearsay information is reliable is the **basis of knowledge prong**. This prong considers how the individual who is providing the hearsay information obtained his information. Did the individual state that he saw the event take place or did he receive his information from someone else? The officer must know the initial source of the information. The officer can then ask this person further questions to attempt to verify whether the information is accurate (as set forth in the discussion below regarding the second prong of the test). Under the basis of knowledge prong of the test, the officer will also have to question the individual as to the underlying facts that support any conclusion that the individual might have. If an individual tells the officer "my neighbor is selling drugs," the officer must ask why the individual thinks that. If the individual cannot give the officer further conclusory information, the information cannot be included in the affidavit. The individual would have to provide specific details regarding heavy traffic at night, seeing others drive up to the house and obtain baggies while giving money in return, and other specific evidence of drug dealing.

The basis of knowledge prong can also be satisfied with "self-verifying" detail. The police might receive information from an anonymous source that can be verified. For example, in the case of **Draper v. United States**,[11] Hereford, an informant, gave the following facts to Marsh, a federal agent.

> On September 3, 1958, Hereford told Marsh that James Draper (petitioner) recently had taken up abode at a stated address in Denver and "was peddling narcotics to several addicts" in that city. Four days later, on September 7, Hereford told Marsh "that Draper had gone to Chicago the day before [September 6] by train [and] that he was going to bring back three ounces of heroin [and] that he would return to Denver either on the morning of the 8th of September or the morning of the 9th of September also by train." Hereford also gave Marsh a detailed physical description of draper and of the clothing he was wearing, and said that he would be carrying "a tan zipper bag," and he habitually "walked real fast." Hereford also told Marsh that Draper was a Negro of light brown complexion, 27 years of age, 5 feet 8 inches tall, weighed about 160 pounds, and that he was wearing a light colored raincoat, brown slacks, and black shoes.

The Supreme Court discussed these facts in the **Spinelli** case, indicating that the information given by the informant was of such sufficient detail that the magistrate reading the information in the warrant application should know that the informant was relying on information that was based on more than just a casual rumor. Even if Draper's general reputation was that of a drug dealer, the specific amount of drugs Draper would be carrying, his physical description, and details regarding the time and date of his arrival

---

11. 358 U.S. 307 (1959).

could assist the magistrate in determining that the information came from someone close to Draper who knew a lot about his future plans. An officer could verify these facts by observing Draper arriving at that time and engaging in activities consistent with drug dealing.

The Veracity Prong

The second prong of the two part test for hearsay is the **veracity prong**. The magistrate must determine why she should believe a person. In a case in which the person providing information to the police is an innocent bystander who happened to see a crime and is reporting what she knows, the information is probably truthful, as the person would seemingly have no reason to be lying. In a criminal case when the victim, offender, and witnesses all know each other, it is possible that some of the information obtained by an investigating officer might be biased. Thus, known relationships between the parties should be disclosed in the affidavit of probable cause. However, in the case of an informant who has been working with the police to give the police information regarding crimes, it is easy to be suspicious that the informant might fabricate information in order to continue to remain in the favor of the police. Informants often have a fairly lengthy criminal record and are not necessarily the type of person that is normally trusted.

Thus, the magistrate must attempt to determine how truthful the informant is. This is the **credibility of the informant** test. One way to prove truthfulness is to provide the magistrate with information regarding previous information that the informant has provided and whether that information was correct. Often police agencies use the same informants over and over to obtain information, and an informant who has provided good information before can be assumed to be providing good information now as well.

However, every informant has his first time giving information to the police and in such a case will have no track record to prove his veracity. Also, occasionally an informant will have provided bad information in the past to law enforcement, but later tries to provide law enforcement with further information. The best way to prove the veracity of the informant in a situation such as this is to demonstrate the information's reliability. Evidence is most often reliable if it could be used against the informant. If an informant is reporting to the police that he purchased drugs from someone, the information is more likely true. If a person did not commit a crime, he would most likely not tell a police officer that he did.

It is important to note that the informant's identity does not have to be revealed in the warrant application. It is sufficient to refer to the informant as a "confidential informant" and then indicate whether or not the informant has provided information in the past and, if so, whether that information was reliable. In **McCray v. Illinois**,[12] the Supreme Court ruled that as long as the

---

12. 386 U.S. 300 (1967).

law enforcement agency attempting to secure the warrant states in the affidavit of probable cause that the confidential informant has provided credible information on several previous occasions, the law enforcement agency need not provide further specific information about the informant.

In a small number of circumstances, a court will order that a confidential informant's identity be revealed. Defense attorneys can generally file a motion requesting that the confidential informant's identity be disclosed, so the informant can be called as a witness at trial and subjected to cross-examination by the defense. Of course, prosecutors and law enforcement agencies generally want to keep the confidential informant's identity secret so the confidential informant can be used again by police. Courts rarely rule that the confidential informant's identity should be disclosed since it is used solely for purposes of the law enforcement agency's application for a warrant. However, a defense attorney might win her motion to have the identity of the confidential informant disclosed if the informant was an eyewitness to the crime and if his testimony would be material to the court making a determination as to whether the defendant was actually guilty of the crime.[13]

DIRECT EVIDENCE OF PROBABLE CAUSE

A police officer can sometimes establish enough probable cause to obtain a warrant based only on direct evidence, which consists of his observation. Various types of direct evidence can be used, including a person's prior criminal record, an observation of furtive conduct, admissions made to a police officer, association with other known criminals, and of course, physical evidence. A magistrate will assume that direct evidence provided by a law enforcement official is true and correct. Various types of direct evidence will be discussed here.

Furtive Conduct

A person's mere behavior can establish probable cause; this type of evidence often forms the basis for at least reasonable suspicion and can lead to a pat down and, perhaps eventually, an arrest or search without a warrant. While the Supreme Court has not considered specifically which "furtive movements" are sufficient to establish reasonable suspicion or probable cause, state courts have ruled on this issue. There is no good test to be used to determine what constitutes a "furtive movement." Courts have stated that an innocent gesture (such as looking both ways before crossing the street) cannot be considered a furtive movement. Also, courts have recognized that people do in fact often feel nervous when police officers are present.

---

13. **Rovario v. United States**, 353 U.S. 53 (1957).

However, one court determined that "fidgeting" is considered furtive.[14] In a Massachusetts case, troopers pulled over an individual who did not stop immediately when the trooper signaled for him to do so. When the vehicle eventually did stop, the trooper approached the driver's side of the vehicle and noticed that four individuals were in the vehicle and that the defendant was "making movement side to side and slightly forward" and "fumbling with an object in his lap [and] manipulating that object between his legs." The officer ordered the occupants of the vehicle to put their hands on their heads; they did not comply until after the order had been given a second time. The officer frisked the defendant, found a cellular telephone, and then told a second officer who had arrived for backup purposes about the movements the defendant had made. The second officer, based on that information, decided to search the vehicle and found a gun near the driver's seat. The defendant argued that his motions were not "furtive" but, rather, constituted "fidgeting." The Massachusetts court indicated that furtive movements include any movements that seem to demonstrate the hiding of contraband or some movement that might hint to the threat of an officer's safety. The court indicated that the defendant's movements here indeed signaled to the police that some criminal activity might be afoot.

Two cases from Wisconsin contrast a series of furtive movements with a single furtive movement. In a 2007 case, a Wisconsin Court of Appeals found that a defendant's act of leaning over after being pulled over, during which his head and shoulders disappeared from the officers' view momentarily, was not considered "furtive." Police testified that they believed the defendant was reaching under the front seat, but the reviewing court determined that this one action was not enough to justify search of the vehicle.[15] However, in a subsequent case, the same Wisconsin court determined that an officer's view of a defendant making three to five distinct and repeated kicks of something, as if he was trying to kick something under the seat, was enough of a "furtive movement" to allow a search.[16] The court had previously decided that movements which appeared to be near the glove compartment were also sufficient to justify a search when the officer then noticed that items that normally would be in the glove compartment were lying elsewhere in the vehicle.

As you can see, the issue of what is considered "furtive" will vary greatly from state to state, court to court, and case to case. The best practice is for police to always document the number of movements they saw and the time period in which they witnessed those movements, along with their impression as to why those movements implied criminal activity. It is helpful if an officer has seen that same type of movement before in relation to a specific type of crime; for example, an attempt to shove items under a seat could be related to drug activity or hiding illegal weapons.

---

14. **Commonwealth v. Rivera,** 76 Mass. App. Ct. 394, 921 N.E.2d 1008 (2010).
15. **State v. Johnson,** 2007 WI 32.
16. **State v. Bailey,** 2008 AP003153.

Prior Criminal Record and Association with Other Known Criminals

The fact that a person has committed a crime in the past cannot be used as evidence to establish that a person has committed another crime. After all, it is possible for someone to commit only one crime in her life, learn from her mistake, and then move on. A person's prior crimes can be considered when a judge is sentencing her but cannot, in most circumstances, be presented at trial to attempt to prove guilt. However, the Supreme Court determined that it is appropriate for law enforcement agents to consider a person's criminal record and even present it as part of the evidence set forth in an affidavit of probable cause when a search warrant is being requested. The Supreme Court long ago ruled that a person who associates with other known criminals might be likely to be a criminal; however, more information would need to be gleaned in order to develop probable cause. A person who serves as a "lookout' can also be considered suspicious if it is clear his actions relate to someone who is engaged in crime.

Answers That Seem Illogical

A person might be engaged in illegal activity if the person's statements to police officers do not make sense. If, for example, a police officer makes a traffic stop, he generally will question the occupants in the car to determine whether he believes they are engaged in a legitimate or illegitimate activity. The police officers in a federal circuit court case had stopped a car on a road known to be used by drug traffickers. The defendants were driving in New York in a car owned by someone else, which is a tactic used by drug dealers in order to avoid forfeiture of the car if the drugs are found by the authorities. The officers searched the car and found a large amount of money in small denominations; the cash was wrapped with rubber bands in small bundles, and the bundles were placed in three separate bags. The occupants of the vehicle were questioned as to where the money came from and what it was to be used for, and they answered that they had won the money in Atlantic City; the police did not believe that the money would have been packaged the way it was if this was the case. Further, the individuals indicated that they were on their way to Chester, but the area in which they were stopped and the direction in which they were heading was not consistent with this story. Upon further investigation, a Chester police officer indicated that the individuals were "known drug pushers." The court determined that this information did give the police the ability to search the vehicle, as the story given by the defendants did not comport with the facts as they were unfolding.[17]

---

17. **United States v. Anderson**, 676 F. Supp. 604, 1987 U.S. Dist. LEXIS 8938 (1987).

Physical Evidence

The existence of a strong amount of physical evidence can support probable cause. In a Maine case, police were called to the scene of a burglary where an owner of a store found that his store had been broken into and some contents stolen. The officers found two sets of boot tracks leading through the snow to a lumberyard; it appeared that the person who had burglarized the store had left on foot and gone through the lumberyard, entered a parked vehicle, and driven away. Vehicle tracks remained in the snow and were smooth in the center with ridges on the sides of the tread mark. Another officer came upon a 1964 Chevrolet Corvair, which was stopped on the road; as the police approached, the car's lights came on and it started up. A check of the owner of the car via radio confirmed that the owner was not native to the area. The officers stopped the car and searched the passengers, finding tools consistent with burglary and two revolvers.

The defendants, of course, argued that the physical evidence alone did not establish probable cause. The court, however, upheld the search based only on the physical evidence, stating, in part,

> [T]racks in new snow furnish a prime example of trustworthy circumstantial evidence and one which with great frequency has been used by trial courts in explanatory instructions to juries. When, as in this case, there has been a recent fall of snow, the presence or absence of fallen or drifted snow in the tracks is revealing as to approximately when the tracks were made. Tracks often speak louder than words as to the direction taken by and the activities o those who made them. . . . By back-tracking from the store and observing the size and condition of the tracks it was possible for the investigating officers to determine that at some time in the evening two men had approached the Mountain store on foot by a circuitous route, crossing West Main Street at a point some distance from the store and proceeding along the bank of the Piscataquis River to a wooded area, . . . There was physical evidence that they forced the door and gained entrance, broke into the safe and removed virtually its entire contents as well as numerous other items on the premises.[18]

CORROBORATION OF EVIDENCE

Either the reliability or veracity prong of the test can also be satisfied by police corroboration of the information. In the **Draper** case, the police corroborated the information given them by the informant:

> On the morning of September 8, Marsh and a Denver police officer went to the Denver Union Station and kept watch over all incoming trains from Chicago, but they did not see anyone fitting the description that Hereford had given.

---

18. **State v. Heald**, 314 A.2d 820 (1973).

YOU BE THE JUDGE

A burglary alarm has just gone off in a local bank in a small town in Kansas; a neighbor of the bank indicates that he noticed one automobile on the street soon after the alarm began to sound, and that the automobile was heading toward Highway 160. The witness followed the automobile toward Highway 160 and witnessed the automobile driving east; the automobile was a "late model car, with a light-colored top, and the tail lights resembled those on a Thunderbird." A law enforcement officer from a neighboring town hears the dispatch and these details and sees two individuals driving East on Highway 160 in a Thunderbird. The officer stops the vehicle and the driver indicates he is going "down the road." When a second officer goes to the passenger's side of the car, he sees wrecking bars, hammers, some leather gloves, and a flashlight on the ground near the car. Do the officers have probable cause to search the occupants of the car and the car based on these facts alone?[19]

Repeating the process on the morning of September 9, they saw a person, having the exact physical attributes and wearing the precise clothing described by Hereford, alight from an incoming Chicago train and start walking "fast" toward the exit. He was carrying a tan zipper bag in his right hand and the left was thrust in his raincoat pocket. Marsh, accompanied by the police officer, overtook, stopped and arrested him. They then searched him and found the two "envelopes containing heroin" clutched in his left hand in his raincoat pocket, and found the syringe in the tan zipper bag.[20]

These facts substantially matched the facts given by Hereford and thus Hereford's information had been corroborated. In the **Draper** case, Hereford had previously given information to the police, but the corroboration by the police would have most likely been enough to establish probable cause even if Hereford had been a brand new informant. The federal agent in this case was wise to obtain as much information as possible to place in the warrant application by corroborating the facts.

It is important to note that all information used to establish probable cause must be present prior to the actual search taking place. This is obvious when an affidavit of probable cause is being prepared prior to a search or seizure, but when a search is done without a warrant under one of the numerous exceptions to the warrant requirement, a police officer must later be able to prove that she had probable cause at the time the search was conducted, and not based on information found during the search.

---

19. The facts of this case were derived from the case of **United States v. Troutman**, 438 F.2d 217 (1972).
20. **Id**. at 309–310.

THE TOTALITY OF THE CIRCUMSTANCES TEST

The Supreme Court initially required that both the basis of knowledge and veracity tests be satisfied in order for probable cause to be established. Eventually, however, the Supreme Court realized that there were times that both prongs would not be met when a warrant really should be issued. The Court thus changed the standard for probable cause to what is now known as the **totality of the circumstances** test. The facts that lead to this determination were from the landmark case of **Illinois v. Gates,**[21] which changed the way that probable cause was viewed by courts and law enforcement.

ILLINOIS V. GATES

FACTS: The Bloomingdale, Illinois police department received by mail an anonymous letter that stated as follows:

> This letter is to inform you that you have a couple in your town who strictly make their living on selling drugs. They are Sue and Lance Gates, who live on Greenway, off Bloomingdale Rd. in the condominiums. Most of their buys are done in Florida. Sue his wife drives their car to Florida, where she leaves it to be loaded up with drugs, then Lance flies down and drives it back. Sue flies back after she drops the car off in Florida. May 3 she is driving down there again and Lance will be flying down in a few days to drive it back. At the time Lance drives the car back he has the trunk loaded with over $100,000.00 in drugs. Presently they have over $100,000.00 worth of drugs in their basement.
>
> They brag about the fact they never have to work, and make their entire living on pushers.
>
> I guarantee if you watch them carefully you will make a big catch. They are friends with some big drug dealers, who visit their house often.

The police engaged in further investigation and found that Lance Gates had indeed made a reservation on a flight from Chicago to West Palm Beach, Florida. Federal agents in Florida watched Lance Gates while he was in Florida and many of the facts set forth in the letter were true. Based on all of the information obtained through the letter and the investigation, Gateses' home and car were searched and marijuana, weapons, and other contraband were discovered therein.

ISSUE: Did the evidence known to police constitute probable cause for purposes of conducting a search of the Gateses' home and car?

---

21. 462 U.S. 213 (1983).

HOLDING: The "totality of the circumstances" surrounding all of the evidence did constitute probable cause.

RATIONALE: The Supreme Court wrestled with the fact that despite all of the evidence in this case, both the reliability and veracity prongs of the probable cause test had not been met. The problem was that there was no indication given by that person as to who wrote the letter or what his basis of knowledge was. Further, there was no known prior information or statements against that person's own interest given. The facts that had been corroborated by the police's investigation were "innocent" facts—driving and flying from one place to another. The drugs in the basement and trunk were only discovered after the search had taken place.

However, the Supreme Court realized that with the facts police had possessed at the time of the search, a reasonable person would in fact believe that a crime had been committed and that evidence of the crime would be found in the Gateses' car and home. Thus, the test would from that point on be the "totality of the circumstances" test, considering all of the factors set forth by both of the prongs established in the Aguilar case. Satisfying one prong of the test is now enough if the evidence supporting that prong is of great weight. The strength of one prong can overcome a weakness in the other prong.

The Court emphasized that "probable cause" does not infer that the police should have the same amount of evidence that they would need to actually convict a person. Traditionally, as long as a magistrate had a "substantial basis" for determining that a search would uncover evidence of wrongdoing, the Fourth Amendment does not require a stricter standard. The Court felt that the "totality of the circumstances" standard more fully reflected this common law requirement. The Court praised the standard as being a common sense, flexible standard.

Remember that states can give their citizens more rights than the Supreme Court requires. Some states have rejected the "totality of the circumstances" requirement and have required that both prongs of the test be met before probable cause can be established. Those states have indicated that they prefer to have a strict and specific test, rather than a flexible "common sense" framework.

THE WARRANT

Arguing the Sufficiency of a Search Warrant

A defendant whose case is moving through the criminal system would not want to wait until he had been tried, found guilty, and sentenced before he could file an appeal and argue that a warrant was issued inappropriately. Many times criminal charges are dismissed based on the fact that all of the

YOU BE THE JUDGE

You are an agent of the division of Alcohol, Tobacco and Firearms. You have been given a case to investigate which alleges that an individual named Joe Cook is operating an illegal distillery in his house. You have been conducting surveillance on the house for many months and have personally observed the following during your surveillance:

1. On seven occasions, a car was driven to the rear of Cook's house, where no driveway existed.

2. On four of those occasions, the car carried loads of sugar in 60-pound bags; sugar can be used as part of the distilling process.

3. On two trips the car seemed to be laden with empty cans.

4. On one trip the car seemed to be laden with something heavy.

5. Cook, who generally drove the car, and another person, who was always a passenger in the car, were seen on several occasions loading the car at Cook's house and unloading the car at the passenger's house, including sometimes unloading full five-gallon cans.

6. On many occasions as you and other investigators walked in front of the house, you could smell fermenting mash.

7. On many occasions as you and other officers walked by the house, you could hear the sound of a motor pump and metallic noises from the direction of the house.

Do these facts establish probable cause for you to obtain a warrant to search Cook's house? If not, what else might a magistrate ask for? If so, why?

evidence a police department has against a defendant was obtained based on a faulty warrant. The court saves time and the defendant moves on with his life more quickly when the charges can be dismissed before a trial is even scheduled. Thus, in **Franks v. Delaware**[22] the Supreme Court ruled that defendants can challenge a search warrant in a pre-trial proceeding. The Court stated that a hearing should be held by the court (referred to as a **Franks hearing**) in which the affiant who requested the search warrant should state, under oath, the basis of the allegations made in his warrant. The defendant can cross-examine the affiant about these statements. This hearing must be held if the defendant makes a substantial preliminary showing that the affiant made a "false statement knowingly and intentionally, or with reckless disregard of the truth" in

---

22. 438 U.S. 154 (1978).

the affidavit accompanying the search warrant application. The court would not only have to find that false statements were made but also that the statements that were false actually constituted the probable cause that resulted in the issuance of the warrant.

Who May Issue a Warrant

According to the Constitution, a "neutral and detached" magistrate can issue a warrant. The Court has specifically ruled that a prosecutor or state attorney general cannot issue a warrant.[23] Because the entity issuing the warrant must review the entire warrant and be convinced that the facts as set forth establish probable cause, it would be a conflict for someone whose goal is to prosecute crime to issue the warrant. The Supreme Court has further ruled that the United States Attorney General cannot authorize domestic security surveillance without judicial approval.[24] The entity issuing the warrant must not be compensated based on how many warrants it issues. Some magistrates historically were paid based on work performed, not a salary, so they were only paid if they granted a warrant. This clearly gave the magistrate incentive to grant a warrant.

An interesting case regarding the "neutrality" of a magistrate was in **Lo-Ji Sales, Inc. v. New York**.[25] In **Lo-Ji**, the magistrate approved a warrant application for the search of an adult book store. After signing the warrant, the magistrate proceeded to accompany the officers on the search, inspect the materials in the store, assist the officers in determining which materials are obscene, and order that certain items be seized. The Court determined that the magistrate was not "neutral and detached" in that case. Besides the obvious concern that magistrates would grant warrants based on places they would like to "examine," another problem with this sort of behavior is that often materials found in one search are utilized as evidence that support a request to obtain another warrant either to search for different materials in that same location or to search a different location. The magistrate who issued the original order would be unable to perform a neutral role in determining whether enough probable cause existed within the four corners of the next affidavit of probable cause submitted in that case.

Specificity of the Warrant

When applying for a warrant, the officer requesting the warrant has the burden of preparing the warrant to be signed. The magistrate must review the warrant application but cannot ask further questions or add language to the application or to the actual warrants submitted to him. An important

---

23. **Coolidge v. New Hampshire**, 403 U.S. 443 (1971).
24. **United States v. United States District Court**, 407 U.S. 297 (1972).
25. 442 U.S. 319 (1979).

YOU BE THE JUDGE

A warrant is issued to take samples of the hair and blood of a man who is being charged with sexual assault. You are a magisterial judge and it is your job to determine whether the warrant should be issued. The warrant application states the following:

On 4-5-12 at approx. 22:30 hours while at 222 West Greenbelt Parkway, the subject Joseph Palmer did enter the victim's residence and threaten to kill her if she did not comply with his demands to perform oral sex on him. The victim attempted to fight the subject; however, he overpowered her by striking her in and about her face using a glass candle holder. The subject then penetrated the victim's vagina with his tongue and penis. The DNA samples of blood, head hair, and pubic hair will be retrieved from the subject by trained medical personnel in a medical facility. The collection of these samples will be conducted in a noninvasive manner.

Is the warrant specific enough? Why or why not? What other information could an officer have included?

component of the warrant application is that the warrant itself must, according to the Fifth Amendment, particularly describe the place to be searched, and the persons or things to be seized. This requirement, referred to by courts as the "particularity requirement," must be present in both search and arrest warrants. How specific must these descriptions be?

Place to Be Searched. The place to be searched must be specifically listed and identified. If an officer wants to search Donald Trump's residence, he must specify within the warrant application and on the warrant itself which residence to search among the several Trump owns. What about Trump's restaurants, casinos, and offices? What about a pool house or other structure on the grounds of his Florida estate? Even in the case of a person who only has one residence, specificity is necessary. Each specific place must be connected to the suspected crime by the information presented in the affidavit and warrant application and identified in the warrant itself. If a warrant permits the search of "521 State Street" and the residence is a two-story flat with two apartments, one on the upper level and one on the lower level, the warrant should specify which apartment to search. Civil lawsuits have been filed over police searching the wrong household, especially if they destroy physical items in conducting the search (such as a door in the case of a no-knock warrant or other items within the house while conducting the search).

If a search warrant is written in a general manner but the officer is able to determine from the description the appropriate place to search, the search warrant will be held to be valid. Where the warrant states the place to be searched but an officer searches another location, courts will consider the reasonableness of the officer's mistake. In **Maryland v. Garrison**,[26] Mr. Garrison was the victim of such a wrongful search. Baltimore police officers had obtained a warrant to search the person of Lawrence McWebb and his premises, identified in the warrant as "2036 Park Avenue, third floor apartment." The officers believed that there was only one apartment described that way, when in fact, the third floor of the premises was divided into two apartments, one occupied by McWebb and one occupied by defendant Garrison. The officers entered what they believed was the only apartment on that level and discovered contraband before they realized that they were not in the correct apartment. As soon as the officers realized they were in the incorrect apartment, they halted their search, but they still filed charges against Garrison because of the contraband that they found in his apartment when they believed they were in the appropriate apartment. The Supreme Court held that the since the officers did not know or have reason to know that there were two apartment units on the third floor of 1036 Park Avenue, they did not err in obtaining or executing the warrant. The officers' actions were appropriate and their conduct was "consistent with a reasonable effort to ascertain and identify the place intended to be searched within the meaning of the Fourth Amendment." Clerical typographical errors on a warrant will be considered similarly by the court, with an officer being held not liable for any error as long as he reasonably relied on the information within the warrant.

Items to Be Seized. Further, the "items to be seized" must be specifically specified in the warrant. Some generalities can be used, such as "evidence of drug possession," but generally the language of the warrant must be clear on what is being seized. If the crime involves drugs, officers should anticipate what items they believe might be discovered in the household, including packaging materials, lists of clients who had purchased the drugs, money, and other related items. All items that officers anticipated finding should be listed in the application and on the proposed warrant. The search must cease once all items listed on the warrant have been found, so listing all items is extremely important. Further, the information listed in the affidavit accompanying the request for the search warrant itself cannot be used to determine whether the description of the items listed in the search warrant are sufficient. The description of the items in the warrant itself must be sufficient on their own.

The Supreme Court has acknowledged that occasionally a case might be too complex for the information in the warrant to be very specific. In **Anderson v. Maryland**,[27] the defendant was suspected of having committed criminal fraud in various complex real estate transactions. The language in a search warrant that was applied for and approved, and issued by the magistrate, included a list of certain specific documents that could be searched for, but also included the following description of more items to be searched for and seized: "other fruits, instrumentalities and evidence of the crime at this

---

26. 480 U.S. 79 (1987).
27. 427 U.S. 463 (1976).

time unknown." The defendant argued that this description was too general, but the Supreme Court indicated that given the complex nature of the case and the fact that the evidence could take a variety of forms, the description was sufficient.

Following are some descriptions of items listed in search warrants that courts have found to be sufficient enough to be particular:

a. Gambling implements and devices used for the purpose of gaming and gambling.
b. All controlled substances and other matters of things pertaining to or relating to said possessions and sale of controlled substance in violation of the law. (The defense argued that certain types of controlled substances should be listed, but the court stated that many people who engage in the sale of one type of controlled substance also are in possession of other types of controlled substances.)
c. Any and all envelopes, letters, records, documents, correspondence, video-tapes, published materials, and other objects relating to contact with an unidentified woman in Texas who has two daughters 7 and 12 years of age and a son 10 years of age.
d. All business records of a particular business, when the case being investigated involves a pervasive scheme to defraud.

A list of descriptions of items included in search warrants which have been found to be insufficient include the following:

a. The seizure of clothing that the suspect was wearing the evening of the murder and the weapon used in the murder. (This does not state what the clothing looks like or what type of weapon was used and thus grants the officers too much discretion.)
b. In connection with the theft of building materials, the description of a "blue wheelbarrow" was insufficient, where the only item mentioned in the warrant was a blue wheelbarrow with no further description.
c. In a child pornography case, computer equipment, electronic digital storage media included but not limited to floppy diskettes, compact disc, hard drive whether mounted in a computer or otherwise, video or audiotapes, video surveillance systems, video and digital camera systems, printing devices, monitors, and firearms. This listing was not sufficient to cause the officers to conduct a tailored search of the electronic media to focus specifically on the crime.
d. Where a warrant permitted the search of computer files for names, telephone numbers, ledgers, receipts, addresses, and other documentary evidence pertaining to the sale and distribution of controlled substances, the description was not particular enough to permit the opening of jpg files where law enforcement's assumption was that those files would contain pornography.

Occasionally one portion of a search warrant is found to be lacking in sufficient particularity but that does not void the entire warrant. A warrant that includes a sufficient description of numerous items but contains an insufficient description of one item will only result in officers being able to look for the items that are named properly.

When an officer executes a warrant, he must only search for items that are listed in the warrant. Further, if an emergency search takes place with no warrant, officers still must be selective in which items they seize, depending on the scope of the crime being investigated. For example, in **Flippo v. West Virginia**,[28] police received a 911 call wherein the caller indicated that a man and his wife had been attacked in a cabin at a state park. The police went to the scene and found a dead woman. No man was present at the scene. In reviewing the crime scene, the police came across a briefcase; they opened it and found an envelope inside, which they also opened. Inside the envelope were photographs that implicated the woman's husband in her murder. The evidence was seized and was used against the defendant at his trial. The prosecutor argued that there should be a "crime scene" exception to the general rule of warrants, in that all investigations of crime scenes should permit the seizure of items found there. The Supreme Court rejected this argument, stating that while sometimes items can be taken from a scene and inventoried, they cannot be taken in a search when they are not apparently obvious as being related to the crime.

YOU BE THE JUDGE

You are a federal agent who is monitoring a chat room on the Internet to attempt to identify people who possess child pornography. You receive from a person in the chat room an email that contains a number of images depicting child pornography. You subpoena the records of the Internet service provider which demonstrate that the computer from which the images were sent was owned by Joseph Weber in Michigan. You apply for a warrant and conduct a search of Mr. Weber's home. The warrant states that you can search for the following: "Any and all computer software and hardware, computer disks, disk drives" and "Any and all visual depictions, in any format or media, of minors engaging in sexually explicit conduct." Using a computer utilities program and the "undelete" function, you recover from the hard drive of the computer and other disks 1,500 images of minors engaged in sexually explicit conduct, all of which had been deleted from the drives.

Was the language of the warrant sufficient to describe what you seized? What could have been a better description?

---

28. 528 U.S. 11 (1999).

Person to Be Arrested. In the case of an arrest warrant for a person, it is obviously very important that the person who is being arrested is specifically identified. Lawsuits have been filed against police officers who arrest the wrong individual, depriving him of his liberty. However, supplying a person's name is considered sufficient in terms of fulfilling the particularity requirement for a search warrant. A good rule of thumb, however, is to determine any distinguishing characteristics (tattoos, presence of facial hair, scars) and also include a person's approximate age. This can help avoid arresting John Brown Sr., who happens to live in the same house as his son, John Brown Jr.

Occasionally an arrest warrant can be issued without stating an individual's name. Sometimes the police know that a crime was committed and they do have a description of the perpetrator but do not know his name. In such a case, the courts will permit a "John Doe" warrant to be issued. The warrant should include a description or surveillance photograph of the suspect that is sufficient for officers to identify him should they encounter him. This permits an officer to arrest the person and also permits the filing of criminal charges in the matter, which might be necessary so that the statute of limitations for filing charges does not expire. A recent development in this area has been the utilization of unique DNA profiles, if DNA is found at the scene of the crime.

DNA is collected from people who are convicted of certain types of crimes and are catalogued. With the use of DNA, if a person is in custody for something else and his DNA is taken and analyzed, the person can be arrested under the DNA "John Doe" warrant and face charges under the "John Doe" criminal complaint that was filed. Some states may require that the DNA profile listed on the John Doe warrant also include as much information as possible regarding the person's age, height, weight, and race, evidence that can be obtained from the DNA. Once a suspect is identified, the warrant and criminal complaint can be amended to include the person's actual name. A California court permitted the match of DNA in a database with the DNA entered into the database under a John Doe warrant even when the evidence entered into the database was entered mistakenly. A sharply divided Supreme Court has permitted police to take DNA from anyone they arrest, similar to fingerprinting.

MARYLAND V. KING[29]

FACTS: King was arrested on first- and second-degree assault charges and was processed through a Maryland prison facility. Booking agents used a cheek swab to take a DNA sample from King in accordance with the requirements of the Maryland DNA Collection Act. The swab matched King to an unsolved 2003 rape and King

---

29. 569 U.S. ___ (decided June 3, 2013).

was charged with that crime. King moved to suppress the DNA evidence, arguing that Maryland's Act violated the Fourth Amendment. King was convicted of rape.

ISSUE: Does automatically taking a DNA sample from a person accused of a crime a legitimate police booking procedure that is reasonable under the Fourth Amendment?

HOLDING: If a person is arrested and the arrest is supported by probable cause, the taking of DNA is a legitimate police booking procedure.

RATIONALE: Obtaining a DNA sample is in fact a search, although it is a fairly small intrusion considering it involves only a scrape on the inner cheek with a swab. The Fourth Amendment does not constrain against all intrusions, only those that are not justified under the surrounding circumstances or made in an improper manner. The Fourth Amendment does not require any individualized suspicion. "When faced with special law enforcement needs, diminished expectations of privacy, minimal intrusions, or the like, the Court has found that certain general, or individual, circumstances may render a warrantless search reasonable." In this case, the individual is already in police custody based on the probable cause that the person has committed a crime. The DNA collection is not subject to the whims of a police officer but is routinely used on every individual who comes to the facility. The concerns of law enforcement in obtaining this type of information is balanced between privacy needs of individuals and the law enforcement concerns that prevail.

Anticipatory Search Warrants

While generally a search warrant must be based on probable cause that has already been established, the Court has carved out an exception that permits a person to obtain a search warrant when the establishment of probable cause is anticipated. Generally this type of warrant is issued in cases in which a law enforcement officer anticipates that such trafficking will take place in the future. **Anticipatory search warrants** were initially approved in the 1980s by state courts and permitted officers to obtain a search warrant and then execute it when a certain event occurred. For example, if a package came through the mail with an illegal drug substance oozing out of it and the package was being sent to a certain address, officers might be able to obtain an anticipatory search warrant that could be executed when officers actually observed the package being delivered to that residence. Courts permitted this type of warrant based on the fact that neither the federal nor state constitutions prohibit a search warrant that will be issued in the future. If the probable cause comes after the search warrant is issued but before it is executed, no constitutional language is violated. However, courts in various states and in the federal system differed on the legality of anticipatory search warrants, so finally in 2006 the Supreme Court considered their constitutionality.

In **United States v. Grubbs**,[30] the Supreme Court approved anticipatory search warrants, leaving it up to each state to decide whether they would permit the warrants. (Remember, states can choose to give individuals more rights than the Supreme Court requires and thus can prohibit such warrants.) Specifically, the Supreme Court defined anticipatory search warrants as being "a warrant based upon an affidavit showing probable cause that at some future time, but not presently, certain evidence of crime will be located at a specific place." The Supreme Court stated that anticipatory warrants are not different "in principle" from ordinary warrants; a magistrate issuing such a warrant still needs to determine that it is probable that contraband or other evidence of a crime will be on the premises described in the warrant when the search takes place. In fact, according to the court two "prerequisites" of probability must occur. First, the warrant application must demonstrate that if the triggering conditions occur, the contraband or evidence will most likely be found on the premises, but the application must also demonstrate that there is probable cause to believe that the triggering event will actually occur.

Challenging a Search Warrant

One method a defendant can use to request the Court exclude evidence is to argue that the warrant that constituted the basis of gathering that evidence was invalid. Assuming some technical error did not occur, the defendant's ability to make such an argument is based on demonstrating that some statement within the warrant application and accompanying affidavit was incorrect. A defendant would normally attempt to make such a showing by filing a suppression motion that would be decided by the court prior to trial. First, the defendant must make a substantial showing via a preponderance of the evidence that a false statement was included in the affidavit. The statements must involve "deliberate falsehood or reckless disregard for the truth." Police "negligence" or an innocent mistake made by an officer will not result in the warrant being set aside. Generally, a court will hold a hearing to establish whether an affiant actually made false statements in his warrant application. This can be done via testimony of the defendant but is best shown by bringing in other witnesses or documents that clearly prove the falsity of the information.

If the defendant can prove that the information stated within the affidavit was actually false, he must then demonstrate that had that information not been included in the affidavit, the warrant would not have been granted. In other words, the court must find that without that piece of information, the magistrate would not have found that probable cause existed on which to

---

30. 547 U.S. 90 (2006).

issue the warrant. Finally, the defendant must demonstrate that the information was included in the warrant by the affiant acting in a reckless manner or that the affiant knew that the information was false. This could be accomplished by demonstrating that the officer specifically lied in the affidavit in order to obtain the warrant or that the officer failed to be diligent in drafting the affidavit. For example, an officer might create the affidavit while thinking about another case she is investigating and accidentally place information about one case in the other affidavit. This would be accidental but would be reckless in that an officer should double-check all of the facts she is asserting in an affidavit to verify their truthfulness before submitting the affidavit to the court. As you can see, this type of argument is very factually based and thus will be determined by the courts on a case-by-case basis. An example of a suppression motion based on the falsity of information in the affidavit of probable cause is shown in Figure 3.1.

A case in which the Supreme Court reviewed a defendant's challenge to the issuance of a warrant was in **Franks v. Delaware**.[31] The facts of that case involved a man named Jerome Franks, who was arrested for a sexual assault on a 15-year-old girl named Brenda. Franks was on his way to a bail hearing when he stated "I thought you said Bailey. I don't know her." Ironically, a woman whose last name was Bailey had told the police earlier that day that she had been sexually assaulted by a man who had entered her home through a window and who wielded a knife. She had provided the police with a detailed description of the man's appearance, including a description of his clothing. Three days after the bail hearing, the officer who had accompanied Franks to the bail hearing happened to mention Franks's comment to the officer who was investigating Ms. Bailey's case. That officer sought a warrant to search Franks's apartment; his probable cause was based on the fact that Franks usually dressed similarly to the description of the clothing Ms. Bailey had stated her assailant was wearing. This evidence was given to the officer by youth officers in the facility in which Franks had been detained regarding his typical style of dress. However, the affidavit accompanying the warrant stated the wrong youth officer's name. The warrant was issued. (The magistrate would have no reason to know the wrong youth officer's name appeared in the warrant.)

The warrant was issued and officers conducted a search of Franks's home and seized a knife matching the description given by Ms. Bailey. The "characteristic clothing" was also located and seized. Both items were introduced as evidence against Franks at trial. The prosecution did not claim that the knife found in Franks's home was the exact knife used in the crime, but Ms. Bailey did testify that the knife used "looked like" that one. Franks's lawyer attempted to exclude the evidence of the knife in a pre-trial motion, based on the fact that the officers had misstated which youth officer they spoke to. In fact, Franks's lawyer specifically argued that the officers

---

31. 438 U.S. 154 (1978).

<hr>

FIGURE 3.1. SAMPLE SUPPRESSION MOTION BASED ON THE FALSITY OF INFORMATION IN THE AFFIDAVIT OF PROBABLE CAUSE

<hr>

IN THE COURT OF COMMON PLEAS OF COBAIN COUNTY, PENNSYLVANIA CRIMINAL DIVISION

COMMONWEALTH OF PENNSYLVANIA   :   No. 14737 OF 2008

          :

     v.   :

          :

JOSEPH LONG.   :

MOTION TO SUPPRESS EVIDENCE

AND NOW, comes the Defendant, JOSEPH LONG, through counsel, Mary Manchini, Esquire, and files this Motion to Suppress Evidence, and in support thereof states as follows:

FACTUAL BACKGROUND

1.   The defendant (hereinafter "Mr. Long") was charged with the following offense: Possession of Drugs with Intent to Distribute.

2.   The charges resulted from a search conducted by the police on January 20, 2012.

3.   Officer Rory Lillian (hereinafter "Officer Lillian") testified at a preliminary hearing held on June 27, 2012.

4.   Officer Lillian obtained a search warrant by submitting an affidavit that stated that he believed Mr. Long was engaged in drug trafficking because he "received information from a confidential informant stating that Mr. Long possessed drugs and was intending to sell them. The confidential informant had provided good information regarding drug sales in the area to the affiant in the past."

5.   Mr. Long later testified during a preliminary hearing that in fact he had not received his information from a confidential informant, that he was not sure who the confidential informant was, and that he had received his information from another police officer.

6.   Defendant moves to suppress all evidence against him because it was unlawfully obtained in violation of his rights under the Pennsylvania Constitution and the Fourth Amendment of the United States Constitution. Specifically, the information provided in the affidavit was false and thus no probable cause existed to issue the warrant.

WHEREFORE, Counsel for Defendant prays this Honorable Court enter the relief requested.

Respectfully submitted,

<hr>

Mary Manchini, Esq.

<hr>

deliberately misstated the content of the conversation that the officers had with the youth officers. The trial court refused to hold a hearing on whether or not the officers told the truth in the affidavit.

The Supreme Court reviewed the issue when the Delaware Supreme Court refused to overturn the lower court's failure to hold a hearing on the matter. The Supreme Court first determined that the introduction of the knife at trial was not harmless error; its introduction could have made a difference in the jury's mind in terms of whether Franks committed a crime, especially since Franks's testimony at the trial was that he did have intercourse with Ms. Bailey but that Ms. Bailey consented and he did not have a knife with him at the time. In light of the fact that the presence of a similar knife in Franks's apartment could sway the jury to discredit Franks's story, the Supreme Court determined that the knife was prejudicial to Franks's case. The Court then ruled that the Fourth Amendment permitted Franks to challenge the evidence in his case and that the lower court should have held a hearing to determine the accuracy of the information contained in the affidavit. Although probable cause can exist even when some facts in an affidavit of probable cause are inaccurate, officers must believe the evidence put before a magistrate is true in order for the warrant to be valid. This condition is especially true when an application for a warrant by law enforcement involves an **ex parte hearing**, which is one where only one side (law enforcement, in this case) is present. When such a hearing is held, the defendant has no opportunity to discredit the information contained in the affidavit; thus, the factual basis of the information contained in the warrant is very important.

The prosecution argued that officers would not be deterred by the exclusion of evidence in this manner; officers who deliberately lie on warrant applications will face prosecution for perjury, contempt proceedings, other administrative discipline, or a civil lawsuit. The prosecution also complained that holding hearings to determine the truthfulness of affidavits of probable cause undermine the authority of magistrates. However, the Supreme Court stated that allowing police perjury would undermine a magistrate's authority and could not be permitted.

Execution of a Warrant

A police officer must execute a warrant once it has been issued by a magistrate. A private citizen cannot execute a warrant, for obvious reasons. Further, when a police officer executes a warrant, the media or other third parties cannot accompany the officer. This rule was set forth by the Supreme Court in **Wilson v. Layne**,[32] when the Supreme Court considered whether a newspaper reporter and photographer should be permitted to accompany the police on the execution of an affidavit. After all, the public might be

---

32. 526 U.S. 603 (1999).

interested in seeing footage on the news or pictures in the newspaper of what the inside of a house looked like in the case of a murder or other serious crime. However, in keeping with the framers' interest in protecting the right to privacy in homes, the Supreme Court indicated that this practice was impermissible. The Court reasoned that police action pursuant to a warrant is reasonable only if the action is related solely to the objectives of the warrant. The purpose of executing a warrant is to find information that would assist in prosecuting the person, not to broadcast the condition of the house to others. The presence of any third parties that are not in attendance solely to assist in finding the items requested in the warrant would thus be unreasonable. This issue demonstrates how two amendments sometimes clash with each other. The First Amendment permits freedom of the press, but not when that freedom infringes upon a person's ability to be free from unreasonable searches and seizures, as assured by the Fourth Amendment.

The Supreme Court in **Illinois v. McArthur**[33] ruled that police could prohibit an individual's possessory interest in her own home while the police were waiting to obtain a warrant, if necessary in order to preserve evidence within the home. Tera McArthur requested that two police officers accompany her to her trailer home where she lived with her husband, Charles, so that she could retrieve her personal items from the home. Upon exiting the residence, following the retrieval of her items, Ms. McArthur informed the police that Charles had drugs inside. The police requested that Charles allow them to search but he refused; he then came out of the trailer. An officer then prevented Charles from going back into the trailer until another officer could obtain a warrant. Charles later argued that this action by the officer was unconstitutional. The Supreme Court upheld the search, indicating that in those circumstances, the police needed to prevent the scene from being contaminated and thus could prevent the owner from entering his own home. The Court stated that the action by the police was a "temporary seizure" that was supported by probable cause and was designed to prevent the loss of evidence while the police "diligently" obtained a warrant. The concurring opinion in the McArthur case also made it clear that the search was being upheld only because of the immediate danger of evidence being destroyed.

Timing and Manner of Execution. Most states and the federal government have created further rules that govern the execution of a search warrant, especially as it relates to the timing of the execution. Generally, search warrants should be executed as soon as possible after they are issued. Federal rules require that a warrant be executed within ten days of the date it is issued. Eventually the facts on which the warrant was based could change, and thus executing a warrant without delay results in less of a chance that evidence will be destroyed or disposed of. Searches should be carried out during daytime hours (federal rules define this as being between 6 A.M. and 10 P.M.), to protect

---

33. 531 U.S. 326 (2001).

the officer and reduce inconvenience to those whose premises are being searched. As a California court stated, "On the inside of the door is a lone woman with two daughters; she lives in an increasingly violent society and she must decide at 12:50 A.M. whether to throw her door open to a band of armed men who claim to be police but who are standing on her front porch in scruffy street clothes."[34] Some states require that a warrant be executed in the daytime unless there is some specific reason to execute it at night. Executing a warrant in the daytime is advantageous to both the convenience of the subject of the warrant and the safety of the officers. If the alleged criminal activity generally occurs at night, the court might issue a warrant that allows the warrant to be executed at night. This type of warrant would be permitted if, for example, drug activity that generally takes place at night would be the focus of the search. A "no-knock" warrant can also be requested if officers can demonstrate that knocking and announcing their presence would put them or others in danger. An officer need merely prove that he has reasonable suspicion that he should not knock in order to obtain such an order, according to the Supreme Court.[35] Arrest warrants are valid indefinitely; sometimes it is very difficult to find a person after an arrest warrant has been issued, and a fugitive from justice might be captured years after an arrest warrant is issued.

The Knock and Announce Rule. An old English case decided in 1603 holds as follows: "[B]efore the Sheriff break the party's house, he ought to signify the cause of his coming, and to make request to open doors."[36] The concept of **knock and announce** began at common law and then became a federal rule and was adopted by the Supreme Court in the case of **Wilson v. Arkansas**.[37] An officer is allowed to enter a house to execute a warrant without a homeowner's consent, but it is better if the officer obtains consent first. The **Wilson** case required that before an officer breaks down a door in order to serve an arrest warrant or execute a search warrant, he should indicate to the homeowner that he is there and request entry. The Supreme Court did acknowledge that sometimes it is not practical to request entry. If an officer knows that a suspect is armed and dangerous and lying in wait for the police, the officer probably should not knock and announce his presence for fear of being harmed.

How long must an officer wait after he knocks on a door to forcibly make an entrance? Courts have not set a bright-line rule stating how many seconds an officer must wait between the time he knocks and announces his presence and the time he enters. Rather, the amount of time he must wait is based on the individual circumstances the officer encounters. The safety of law enforcement officers is paramount in such cases and courts will make their

---

34. **People v. Gonzalez**, 211 Cal. App. 3d 1043, 1049 (1989).
35. **United States v. Ramirez**, 523 U.S. 65 (1998).
36. Semayne's Case, 77 Eng Rep 194 (1603).
37. 115 S. Ct. 1914 (1995).

rulings in accordance with this goal. In **United States v. Banks**,[38] the Supreme Court found that 15 to 20 seconds was a reasonable wait time, based on the specific circumstances of that case. In **Banks**, officers from the North Las Vegas Police Department and the FBI surrounded the apartment of Lashawn Banks, possessing a valid search warrant. They knocked on Banks's door and stated "Police—Search Warrant." They waited approximately 15 to 20 seconds without hearing anything inside and then forcibly entered the apartment, stating that they feared that Banks was destroying the drug evidence while they stood outside and waited. Banks was actually in his apartment and had just finished taking a shower—he was standing naked in the hallway outside his bathroom when the police entered the house. The police saw him and immediately forced him to the floor and handcuffed him. (They also provided him with a pair of underwear to put on and then began to question him.) The police searched the apartment and found crack cocaine and a firearm, for which charges were pressed.

Banks's defense attorney argued that the statements made by Banks to the officers should be suppressed because the officers failed to wait a "reasonable" period of time before entering Banks's apartment. Banks's lawyer also argued that Banks's Fifth Amendment rights were violated because he had not made a knowing and voluntary waiver of his rights before speaking and whether he had a right to the presence of an attorney. The Supreme Court focused on the Fourth Amendment knock and announce issue more than the Fifth Amendment issue. The Court stated that once an officer waits 15 to 20 seconds after knocking on a suspect's door, he can assume that the suspect has had had time to begin destroying or disposing of evidence and can thus enter the home through the use of force. The Court took a "totality of the circumstances" approach to the issue of whether the entry of the home was proper. The **Banks** decision was applauded by law enforcement for encouraging the safety of police officers as well as the preservation of evidence.

However, each knock and announce case must be considered based on its own facts and the totality of the circumstances, including the following factors:

1. The size, design, and layout of the premises
2. The nature of the offense, including the possibility of destroying evidence and the possibility that the suspect will be dangerous
3. The time of day that the search is being conducted

Courts have found time delays of less than 15 to 20 seconds to be sufficient. Sometimes grounds for failing to knock and announce take place after the officers arrive at the scene and thus a warrant requiring the knock and announce can suddenly change to a no-knock situation. Any exigency that occurs following the officer's arrival at the scene can change whether an

---

38. 540 U.S. 31 (2003).

officer is required to knock and announce his presence. The mere opening and subsequent slamming shut of a door upon a police officer's approach can be sufficient for an officer to justify a failure to follow knock and announce rules. Certainly this type of behavior in addition to any other sounds of a scuffle or "discussion" heard by officers that suggest a lack of cooperation on the part of the individuals in the house (or the possibility of destruction of evidence) will also support a failure of an officer to knock.

In the case of **Hudson v. Michigan**,[39] the Supreme Court further ruled in favor of law enforcement, changing citizens' right to privacy.

HUDSON V. MICHIGAN

FACTS: Booker Hudson was sitting on a chair in the living room of his house, with numerous other individuals, on the afternoon of August 27, 1998. Police obtained a warrant authorizing a search of Hudson's home for drugs and firearms, and several officers approached the house with the warrant and shouted "police, search warrant." One of the officers, Jamal Good, testified that his policy in drug cases was to only wait three to five seconds before entering a home when he was executing a warrant in a drug case. Thus, he entered the house almost immediately and officers found five rocks of crack cocaine inside Hudson's pants pocket, a plastic bag containing 23 individual bags of crack and a loaded revolver on the chair where Hudson was sitting, and a plastic bag containing 24 individual baggies of cocaine on the living room coffee table. Hudson argued that the entry by the police was premature and that the police thus violated the knock and announce rule, and that the evidence found in his home following the entry should be suppressed. Indeed, Good clearly did not wait long enough after knocking for Hudson to even come to the door and open it if he had wanted to.

ISSUE: Can the evidence be used against the defendant even when it was seized in violation of the "knock and announce" rule?

HOLDING: Evidence obtained in violation of the "knock and announce" rule can still be used against a defendant in court.

RATIONALE: The costs of excluding evidence that is obtained wrongfully in knock and announce violation cases outweigh the benefits of admitting the evidence. The Court stated that "suppression of all evidence . . . in many cases is a get-out-of-jail-free card." Further, suppression of evidence has been the Court's last, rather than first, impulse, as it generates substantial social costs in setting the guilty free and permitting dangerous people to remain at large. The Court reasoned that excluding the evidence would have little or no deterrent effect, since deterrents already exist. (A person whose house is entered too quickly can sue the

---

39. 547 U.S. 586 (2006).

police department civilly for any harm done, and police can be disciplined internally as well.) Police agencies have been increasingly professional in the last few years, so the concerns that originally brought about the knock and announce rule were most likely not concerns at this point. Further, in this case, the court opined that whether or not the misstep in the knock and announce procedure had occurred, "the police would have executed the warrant they had obtained, and would have discovered the gun and drugs inside the house." An unannounced entry might provoke violence by the person inside the house, and the knock and announce rule protects people from having their property destroyed by a police officer barging into their home without asking first. The knock and announce rule is not supposed to protect one's interest in preventing the government from seeing or taking criminal evidence that is described in a warrant.

Some legal scholars consider the **Hudson** decision to be one more step in the erosion of the exclusionary rule. The Court's decision suggested that perhaps remedial alternatives less costly than suppression can deter Fourth Amendment violations. This view could be related to other types of evidence to which the exclusionary rule has traditionally applied. The Court stated, "We cannot assume that exclusion in this context is necessary deterrence simply because we found that it was necessary deterrence in different contexts and long ago," thus suggesting the acceptance of a limitation on the use of the exclusionary rule.

The Supreme Court has consistently held that a failure to knock and announce in accordance with this rule might not render a search completely invalid. The Supreme Court stated in **Wilson v. Arkansas**[40] that whether an officer knocked and announced his presence is only one factor to be considered in the overall constitutionality of a search. Several states had attempted to specifically exclude certain types of searches (such as searches in all drug cases) from the knock and announce rule, and the Supreme Court considered whether such "blanket" rules should be permissible. The Court ruled against such rules in the case of **Richards v. Wisconsin**,[41] stating that courts must consider each scenario on a case-by-case basis to determine whether the knock and announce rule was required to be used in that particular case. The Court listed the following circumstances which might permit the avoidance of the rule:

1. Circumstances when a threat of physical violence is present
2. Circumstances when an officer has reason to believe that evidence would likely be destroyed if advance notice of entry by the officers was given
3. Circumstances when knocking and announcing would be dangerous or futile

---

40. 514 U.S. 927 (1995).
41. 520 U.S. 385 (1997).

YOU BE THE JUDGE

You are a police officer and have been investigating a drug trafficking case for several months. Part of your investigation involves an informant who has given your agency reliable information previously in drug-related cases and specifically during the investigation in this case. You have gathered enough information to obtain a search warrant to search the premises where you believe the drug transactions are taking place. You do not have enough evidence to prove to the magistrate issuing the warrant that you need a "no-knock" warrant. However, the reliable informant has told you that he believes that the suspect would definitely try to destroy evidence if he thought that officers were going to enter and search his house. The informant states that the suspect has stated that "no cops are going to get me in this—I'll get rid of all my goods before I'll go to jail for this."

You arrive at the suspect's house ready to knock and announce your presence. As you approach the house, you can see the suspect through the open bathroom window, and it appears as though he is cutting heroin there. Although it is difficult to see the suspect clearly, through the window you believe you see him glance out the window at you as you are walking up the sidewalk in your uniform toward the house. You then see the suspect run out of the bathroom.

Do you have the ability to enter the house by smashing down the door if it is locked, based on this information?

The Court also stated that a factor that was not to be used in determining whether officers must knock and announce was whether or not officers needed to destroy property in order to enter. The issue of an officer's safety or whether evidence would be destroyed was much more important than whether a suspect's door was knocked down in the course of executing a warrant.

Limitations on the Search of Persons Found on the Premises When a Search Warrant Is Executed.   Police officers cannot, by virtue of possessing a warrant to search a particular place, automatically search every person who is present when the warrant is executed. In **Ybarra v. Illinois,**[42] the police obtained a search warrant based on the statements of an informant that he had observed "tinfoil packets" on the person of a bartender and lying behind the bar in a certain tavern; the informant also stated that the bartender had informed him that he would have heroin for sale on a certain date. The search warrant permitted the search of the tavern and also the search of the bartender for evidence of possession of a controlled substance.

---

42. 44 U.S 85 (1979).

Officers entered the tavern to execute the warrant, announced their presence, indicated why they were there, and advised those present that they were going to conduct a search for weapons. The officers began searching customers who were present in the tavern and one felt a cigarette packet with "objects" in it in the pants pocket of one of the customers (Ybarra). The officer did not remove the pack from the customer's pocket but continued patting down other customers, then returned to Ybarra and removed the packet, finding six tinfoil packages of heroin in the cigarette package. Ybarra was charged with possession of an illegal substance, and he filed a pre-trial motion to suppress the evidence found in the tavern. Ybarra argued that no probable cause existed to search him. He had not made any gestures or movements to arouse suspicion and had not done or said anything suspicious to the officers upon their entrance into the tavern. Ybarra argued that his mere presence in a tavern where a search warrant was being executed due to concerns about illegal behavior of the owner did not permit officers to search him. The informant did not tell the police that customers were involved in the drug transactions.

The officers attempted to justify their actions based on an Illinois statute that authorizes police officers, when executing a search warrant, to detain and search any person found on the premises. The purpose of the statute was to protect officers from being attacked or to prevent the disposal or concealment of anything described in the warrant. Thus, the question before the Supreme Court was whether this type of statute permits officers to engage in actions that would otherwise be declared unconstitutional.

The Supreme Court ruled for Ybarra. The Court stated that a person's "mere propinquity" to others who might be suspected of criminal activity does not establish probable cause to search that person. Instead, some level of probable cause must exist to suspect that the person who happens to be on the premises is somehow involved in the illegal activity. The Supreme Court further stated that "[e]ach patron who walked into the Aurora Tap Tavern on March 1, 1976, was clothed with constitutional protection against an unreasonable search or an unreasonable seizure. That individualized protection was separate and distinct from the Fourth and Fourteenth Amendment protection possessed by the proprietor of the tavern." The officers had no reason to believe that Ybarra was carrying narcotics or a weapon, so they could not even frisk him for weapons or contraband. Note that if officers have a warrant to arrest a person, they can definitely search that person incident to the arrest, but they cannot search others who happen to be present without some other suspicion.

Further court cases have established that furtive hand movements and other "suspicious" behavior would be necessary for an officer to even have reasonable suspicion that would permit him to frisk a person for his own safety and the safety of others present. Cases have also established that even though officers cannot search every person who is present in a location where a search can take place, they can detain anyone who is on the premises while the search is being conducted. Failing to detain everyone who is on the premises when an officer enters an establishment and announces his intention to search could result in patrons leaving the establishment with evidence and result in general chaos and confusion, along with potential danger to the officers as a result of, for example, someone reentering the establishment with a weapon. You will learn in Chapter 6 that a defendant's act of running away from a police officer can lead the police officer to at least request information from the suspect and briefly stop him to ask questions. However, the Supreme Court on more than one occasion ruled that a person's refusal to identify himself when a police officer asks him for his name does not, without some more suspicious behavior being present, give the officer probable cause to arrest him.

Destruction of Property

When a police officer executes a warrant, items can be destroyed or damaged. An officer has no duty to try not to destroy or damage a house, vehicle, or their contents when executing a search warrant. In fact, the Supreme Court has stated that sometimes officers must damage property in order to properly execute a warrant.[43] Damage to these items can occur when an officer has to knock down a door to enter a house, but it can also happen when, for example, the officer has to pry open a locked container, take a car door apart to search for something hidden within the door panel, or remove a wall hanging to see if a secret compartment within the wall holds drugs or contraband. If physical damage to premises or objects is significant, the Fourteenth Amendment due process clause applies to the police conduct. If a police officer's conduct "shocks the conscience" of the court, compensation might be available for the victim of the search. "The general touchstone of reasonableness which governs Fourth Amendment analysis . . . governs the method of execution of [a search] warrant. Excessive or unnecessary destruction of property in the course of a search may violate the Fourth Amendment, even though the entry itself is lawful and the fruits of the search not subject to suppression."[44] A practical problem in filing a lawsuit against law enforcement officials who destroy property is that generally such lawsuits must be initiated in federal court, which is a long and often costly process. An inmate rarely has access to the resources necessary to file and successfully prosecute such a lawsuit. Thus, a defendant whose conviction was based on evidence obtained in the search will have to orchestrate filing a lawsuit from his prison cell. The Supreme Court has ruled that the extent of property damage has no bearing on whether the entry into the home was proper or not; that analysis is completely based on the knock and announce rules set forth above.

---

43. **Dalia v. United States**, 441 U.S. 238 (1979).
44. **United States v. Ramirez**, 523 U.S. 65, 71 (1998).

Return of Seized Items

What happens to items that have been seized, following trial or the dismissal of a case? Police must return the property to the defendant. However, a defendant generally must file a motion in court and obtain a court order requiring the police agency to turn over the property, subject to local rules of court. The government, however, may retain property that is illegal for a person to possess, such as illegal drugs or weapons. These items are either destroyed or, in some cases, sold with the proceeds being used to fund drug resistance programs or programs educating the public about the danger of illegal weapons. Items that can be seized under civil forfeiture laws are also obviously not returned to the defendant.

WIRETAP APPLICATIONS

One of the greatest expectations of privacy we rely on each and every day is the ability to speak on the telephone privately. Traditionally, **eavesdropping warrants**, which permitted law enforcement to tap phone lines, were issued without full probable cause when certain types of offenses were suspected. Intrusion into the person's private conversations continued under these warrants for a lengthy period.

In 1967, The Supreme Court struck down a New York law that permitted electronic eavesdropping, ruling that the law was "overly broad and unconstitutional."[45] The New York law permitted electronic eavesdropping by law enforcement even when law enforcement had no belief that any particular offense had been committed. The eavesdropping could take place for as long as two months, and the conversations of any and all persons coming into the device could be monitored and taped, regardless of whether there was a belief by law enforcement that the person was engaged in criminal activity. The Court stated that the statute was overly broad and unconstitutional, and the Court hinted that Congress should pass legislation that would provide guidelines for electronic eavesdropping.

Congress took the Supreme Court's suggestion and the expectation of privacy very seriously and passed the Federal Wiretapping Act in order to provide very specific guidelines as to when law enforcement could engage in wiretapping. The Federal Wiretapping Act is also known as Title III of the Omnibus Crime Control and Safe Streets Act, and is found at 18 U.S.C. §§2510-2520. The act was supplemented by the Electronic Communications Privacy Act of 1986, which focused on computer-generated forms of communication, such as email.

Title III only applies to wiretaps that take place without the agreement of a party. If one party to the conversation decides to wear a wire and transmit

---

45. **Berger v. New York**, 388 U.S. 41 (1967).

the information back to an agent, the other party to the conversation will have no expectation of privacy. However, when a phone line is tapped and neither party to the conversation is aware that his conversations are being monitored and recorded, the expectation of privacy of an innocent person is also being affected. Thus, Title III is very strict in its rules, especially when it affects a person who is not the subject of an investigation but happens to be conversing with someone who is. As you will see, the statute focuses on protecting the rights of those who are not the subject of the law enforcement effort. Title III applies to states that allow wiretapping under their own state codes. Title III does not apply to video surveillance. If a state chooses not to permit wiretapping, then Title III is irrelevant.

The general rules of wiretapping can be summarized as follows:

1. Anyone who is "aggrieved" by the wiretapping has standing to attempt to suppress the evidence in court.
2. Unauthorized interception of conversations is subject to criminal actions, a private lawsuit, and fines.
3. A prosecuting agency must authorize an application for a wiretap, and then a magistrate must approve the application.
4. The following information must be included in the wiretap application:
   a. Identity of the officer making the application
   b. Statement of the facts of the crime
   c. Description of the location where the communications will be intercepted
   d. Description of the type of interception and identity of persons to be intercepted
   e. Other investigative techniques that have been tried and failed
   f. The length of time for which the device will be placed, and any reason the wiretap should not be terminated automatically as soon as the desired information is gathered
   g. Information about whether prior eavesdropping has been attempted for this person, including any prior applications that were submitted to request authorization for wiretapping
5. Wiretapping must begin as soon as practical after the order granting it is issued, it can last no longer than 30 days once it has commenced (unless an application to extend the time is submitted and approved), and the 30-day period begins either the day the wiretap is placed or 10 days after the warrant is issued, whichever is first.
6. The probable cause requirement for the wiretapping warrant is as follows:
   a. An enumerated crime has been committed. In federal court, this is limited to felonies that are intrinsically serious or characteristic of organized crime. In state court, the list of crimes are limited to murder, kidnapping, gambling, robbery, bribery extortion, or dealing in narcotic drugs, marijuana or other dangerous drugs, or other crimes dangerous to life, limb, or property, and punishable by imprisonment for more than one year.

   b. Communications relating to that crime will be obtained by eavesdropping.
   c. Normal investigative procedures have failed and are unlikely to succeed.
   d. The place of the eavesdropping is being used in the commission of the
   crime.
7. The eavesdropping must be conducted so as to minimize the interception
   of communications that are not a focus of the investigation.
8. Within 90 days of the eavesdropping, all parties named in the order and
   anyone else whose conversations were intercepted must be informed by
   mail that an order was in place and that conversations were intercepted.
9. Disclosure of the contents of the eavesdropping is narrow, being limited to
   disclosure to other law enforcement agencies and disclosure for purposes of
   trial.

   The officers listening to the phone conversations are supposed to determine at the beginning of the conversation whether they believe the conversation could have any relevance to the information they are attempting to
gather. Consider the following example:

> Federal agents have wiretapped Tony Spano's private phone line in his house
> to attempt to intercept conversations that are relevant to a money-laundering
> operation in which Tony is involved. The phone rings, and the call is from
> Tony's 16-year-old daughter, Emily, asking Tony if she can stay after school to
> work on the school newspaper.

   The agents should immediately determine that the conversation will most
likely not be relevant to money laundering and should hang up. That being
said, the Supreme Court has been very lenient in allowing intercepted conversations to be recorded in almost every situation, because in the Court's
view it is very difficult for an agent to determine whether or not a conversation
will pertain to issues related to the criminal activity. Further, calls could
involve code words or other language that would not be immediately apparent
as relating to the criminal activity but which could pertain to it. Generally,
courts will defer to an agent's discretion in terms of whether or not to continue
to listen to the call.
   The Electronic Communications Privacy Act, which supplemented the
wiretap act, provides similar rules for the interception of electronic communications such as those from computers when they are being transferred. It
does not affect the seizure of electronic communications that have already
been sent and are being stored, for example, on the hard drive of a computer.
Those electronic documents would fall under other search and seizure guidelines. Another area of concern is that of cordless and cellular telephones. It is
possible that a radio receiver owned by a private individual, such as a scanner
or other cordless device, can pick up transmissions from wireless phones. The
Supreme Court has not yet considered the issue of whether law enforcement
officials can purposefully intercept such transmissions without a warrant or

probable cause. Many state and federal courts have considered this issue and have indicated that users of cordless or cellular telephones have no expectation of privacy in their conversations because it is possible for anyone to intercept the conversation. However, other courts have decided that the purposeful interception of such conversations by law enforcement is unconstitutional or that such behavior violates certain state laws that protect the privacy of communications. In 1986, Congress became involved, amending the Federal Wiretap Law to include wireless phones and cellular telephones in the definition, so that interception of those types of phones by law enforcement would also have to comply with the provisions of the wiretapping law. Federal law further permits an individual to record phone conversations with the consent of only one of the parties to the conversation, but 12 states go one step further, requiring that both parties agree. "Two party" states include California, Connecticut, Florida, Illinois, Maryland, Massachusetts, Michigan, Montana, Nevada, New Hampshire, Pennsylvania, and Washington. The federal law also requires that a person notify other parties to an interstate call before recording it.

NATIONAL SECURITY ELECTRONIC SURVEILLANCE

Electronic surveillance is often conducted in conjunction with national security guidelines, and originally Title III allowed electronic eavesdropping without a court order if it was being performed for purposes of national security and if it was authorized by the president. The constitutionality of using electronic eavesdropping for national security was successfully challenged in **United States v. United States District Court**[46] (often called the Keith case because Judge Damon Keith of the United States District Court for the Eastern District of Michigan had decided the case at the District Court level, ordering the government to disclose to the plaintiffs all of the conversations it had illegally intercepted). In the Keith case, the United States, using evidence obtained in a wiretap, charged three individuals with conspiracy to destroy government property; one of the defendants was also charged with bombing a CIA office. The United States Attorney General had authorized the wiretaps under the exception in Title III (the Omnibus Crime Control and Safe Streets Act of 1968) that permitted wiretaps without a warrant (1) to prevent the overthrow of the government and (2) when any clear and present danger to the structure of the government existed. The government alleged that the men charged were involved in a domestic organization that was attempting to subvert and destroy the government.

The Supreme Court ruled against the government, stating that even national security did not justify departure from the established Fourth

---

46. 407 U.S. 297 (1972).

Amendment requirement of judicial approval prior to electronic surveillance taking place. The Court stated, "The price of lawful public dissent must not be a dread of subjection to an unchecked surveillance power. Nor must the fear of unauthorized official eavesdropping deter vigorous citizen dissent and discussion of Government action in private conversation. For private dissent, no less than open public discourse, is essential to our free society." The Court further opined that this practice could pose "the frightening possibility that the conversations of untold thousands of citizens of this country are being monitored on secret devices which no judge has authorized and which may remain in operation for months and perhaps years at a time."

The Court's comments on this issue were strong. These comments are as applicable today with issues such as terrorism and the Patriot Act as they were in 1972 when this case was decided. Here are two more quotes from the Court (all authored by Justice Lewis Powell, writing the majority decision):

> History abundantly documents the tendency of Government—however benevolent and benign its motives—to view with suspicion those who most fervently dispute its policies. Fourth Amendment protections become the more necessary when the targets of official surveillance may be those suspected of unorthodoxy in their political beliefs. The danger to political dissent is acute where the Government attempt to act under so vague a concept as the power to protect "domestic security." Given the difficulty of defining the domestic security interest, the danger of abuse in acting to protect that interest becomes apparent.
>
> As I read it—and this is my fear—we are saying that the President, on his motion, could declare—name your favorite poison—draft dodgers, Black Muslims, the Ku Klux Klan, or civil rights activists to be a clear and present danger to the structure or existence of the Government.[47]

How do these concerns relate to current domestic security issues, considering our present concern over terrorist attacks and our strict monitoring of travelers who board planes and cross our borders? Has the Supreme Court, in deciding cases, and the legislature, in passing laws, stayed true to the concerns of the Court when it decided the Keith case?

Finally, consider the following quote, which comes from Justice William Douglas's concurring opinion in the Keith case. This quote includes statistics from the time in which the wiretapping took place:

> We are told that one national security wiretap lasted for 14 months and monitored over 900 conversations. Senator Edward Kennedy found recently

---

47. **Id**. at 313, 314.

that "warrantless devices accounted for an average of 78 to 209 days of listening per device, as compared with a 13-day per device average for those devices installed under court order." He concluded that the Government's revelations posed "the frightening possibility that the conversations of untold thousands of citizens of this country are being monitored on secret devices which no judge has authorized and which may remain in operation for months and perhaps years at a time." Even the most innocent and random caller who uses or telephones into a tapped line can become a flagged number in the Government's data bank.[48]

Considering our society's high reliance on technology and wireless devices such as cell phones and laptops, some of which include global positioning systems (GPS) that can track our every move, do you feel that we are even more of a flagged number in a data bank, either governmental or private? How do you believe the Supreme Court would rule on an issue today where a person's movements or conversations were being tracked? Is there an argument to be made that when we use cellular devices or devices with GPS tracking, we are giving up our right to any privacy and the government should be able to obtain that information because private companies can?

The Court's decision did not bind foreign intelligence operations, which are governed by the Foreign Intelligence Surveillance Act of 1978, more commonly known as FISA. That act allows the president to authorize the electronic surveillance of conversations between two foreign entities as long as the president obtains a certification of facts by the attorney general. Further, a special warrant procedure was created whereby a panel of seven federal district judges would convene to approve the surveillance. The purpose of the act is to allow the government to spy on foreign nationals on American soil without infringing upon the rights of American citizens. Similar attempts to combat terrorism caused the passage of the USA Patriot Act.

THE USA PATRIOT ACT

The **USA Patriot Act** was passed by Congress in 2001 in reaction to the events of September 11, 2001, when terrorists hijacked four U.S. airliners and flew the planes into the World Trade Center, the Pentagon, and a field in Pennsylvania. The name of the act is an acronym that stands for **Uniting and Strengthening America by Providing Appropriate Tools Required to Intercept and Obstruct Terrorism**. The act was signed into law by President George W. Bush. The act reduced restrictions that had been placed on the ability of law enforcement agencies to search telephone and email communications, along with medical, financial, and other records, and also eased prior restrictions on foreign intelligence gathering. The act also affected

---

48. **Id**. at 325, 326.

law enforcement's ability to detain immigrants and expanded the definition of terrorism to include domestic terrorism. The act caused quite a bit of controversy upon its passage, as it even allowed, for example, the government to find out what books a person had checked out from a public library.

Title II of the Patriot Act, titled "Enhanced Surveillance Procedures," is related to the issue of wiretapping and constitutional search and seizure provisions. This portion of the act also contains many of the most controversial provisions of the act due to the concern that law enforcement could use it to violate the rights of privacy for many. The act relaxed some portions of the wiretap act, such as the ability of the FBI to gain access to a person's stored voicemail through a search warrant rather than through more stringent wiretap laws. Further, the act provided that various private agencies could disclose electronic communications to law enforcement agencies. For example, law enforcement agencies could demand that cable companies disclose certain types of customer communications. Subpoenas could be issued to Internet service providers to obtain the user's name, address, local and long distance telephone billing records, telephone number or other subscriber number or identity, length of service of a subscriber, session times and durations, types of services used, communication device address information (Internet protocol [IP] addresses), payment methods, and bank account and credit card numbers. If communication providers believe that a "danger to life and limb" exists, they are required to disclose customer records or communications to law enforcement agencies.

More controversial provisions include the following. First, **roving wiretaps** are wiretap orders that do not specify all of the carriers and third parties that are involved in the order. The Department of Justice believed that many times terrorists circumvent wiretap orders by changing locations and communication devices. A warrant that does not specify exactly which device or location will be tapped can alleviate this problem. Some argue that this type of warrant violates the particularity clause of the Fourth Amendment. A second very controversial provision of the law allows the FBI to make an order requiring the production of any tangible things, such as books, records, and other documents, for any investigation that relates to international terrorism or other intelligence activities. One agency that opposes this law is the American Library Association, because libraries would be required to give up the records of its consumers. Many people are concerned about the act because so many people currently conduct so much private business on the computer and through various websites.

The Supreme Court had not considered a case directly relating to the constitutionality of the Patriot Act until 2010, when it agreed to hear the case of **Holder v. Humanitarian Law Project**.[49] In that case, the Supreme Court considered the constitutionality of the portion of the act that prohibits material support to groups designated as terrorists. "Support" was defined as

---

49. 561 U.S. ___ (2010).

follows: training, expert advice or assistance, service, and personnel. The Humanitarian Law Project sought to aid the Kurdistan Workers' Party in Turkey and the Liberation Tigers of Tamil Eelam to attempt to assist them in learning ways to peacefully resolve conflicts. The act was written in such a way that it would prohibit the Humanitarian Law Project. The Project filed suit, arguing that this portion of the Patriot Act was unconstitutional because it was vague and because it limited the organization's First Amendment right to freedom of speech. The Supreme Court disagreed, upholding the statute and permitting the prosecution of the Humanitarian Law Group, because its actors had provided service to these types of groups. The Court based its final decision on the fact that any support given to groups that support terrorism furthers those groups' terroristic activities, even if the intention of supporting the group is to educate them. Prohibiting this type of support serves the government's interest in preventing terrorism and thus is permitted. This decision has been widely criticized, with critics stating that the Humanitarian Law Project's goal was to assist the groups on pursuing nonviolence and that the Court's decision thwarts this goal. In September 2010, the Federal Bureau of Investigation conducted a raid on activists in Minneapolis and Chicago, seeking ties to foreign terrorist organizations. Many have argued that this raid would not have been undertaken had it not been for the Supreme Court's support of such raids in the **Holder** case.

OTHER CONSIDERATIONS REGARDING THE WAR ON TERRORISM

All persons employed by the government take an oath to defend the United States Constitution. These people include judges, prosecutors, presidential candidates and other elected officials, law enforcement officials, and military personnel. Even though the Bill of Rights guarantees rights for individuals and protection against overreaching by the government, in times of war these rights sometimes are set aside. For example, during World War II, United States citizens of Japanese ancestry were moved by the government to barbed-wire-enclosed camps, because of a fear that these citizens would act as spies, give information to their relatives in Japan, and endanger U.S. citizens. Interestingly, the Supreme Court upheld this type of imprisonment while seemingly attempting to uphold the principles of the Constitution in its decision.

In the case of **Korematsu v. United States**,[50] the Court first determined that any legal restriction that curtails the rights of a single racial group should be immediately considered suspect. Any such law must be subject to rigid scrutiny but public necessity might justify the existence of such restrictions. Korematsu, a person of Japanese ancestry, had remained in a military area when a rule prohibited all persons of Japanese ancestry from doing so.

---

50. 323 U.S. 214 (1944).

The Court concluded that the rule was necessary because a number of disloyal members of the "group" (those with Japanese ancestry) were present in the country. Approximately 5,000 American citizens of Japanese ancestry refused to swear unqualified allegiance toward the United States and renounce allegiance to the Japanese Emperor. The Court recognized that the rule would undoubtedly cause hardship to a group of Japanese-American citizens who were not dangerous to the United States, but indicated that in times of war such hardships will undoubtedly exist. The Court stated as follows in upholding the law:

> It is said that we are dealing here with the case of imprisonment of a citizen in a concentration camp solely because of his ancestry, without evidence or inquiry concerning his loyalty and good disposition toward the United States. Our task would be simple, our duty clear, were this a case involving the imprisonment of a loyal citizen in a concentration camp because of racial prejudice. Regardless of the true nature of the assembly and relocation centers—and we deem it unjustifiable to call them concentration camps with all the ugly connotations that term implies—we are dealing specifically with nothing but an exclusion order. To cast this case into outlines of racial prejudice, without reference to the real military dangers which were presented, merely confuses the issue. Korematsu was not excluded from the Military Area because of hostility to him or his race. He was excluded because we are at war with the Japanese Empire, because the properly constituted military authorities feared an invasion of our West Coast and felt constrained to take proper security measures, because they decided that the military urgency of the situation demanded that all citizens of Japanese ancestry be segregated from the West Coast temporarily, and finally, because Congress, reposing its confidence in this time of war in our military leaders-as inevitably it must-determined that they should have the power to do just this. There was evidence of disloyalty on the part of some, the military authorities considered that the need for action was great, and time was short. We cannot—by availing ourselves of the calm perspective of hindsight—now say that at that time these actions were unjustified.[51]

The suicidal attacks on the World Trade Center and Pentagon on September 11, 2001 created much controversy over the limits of the Constitution in protecting individuals, as set forth earlier in the discussion regarding the Patriot Act. United States citizens cried out for protection from terrorism but not all citizens wished to become inconvenienced or risk a reduction in their privacy to accomplish such a goal. How much can the government infringe upon our right to freely go where we want to go and do what we want to do when National Security is at issue? How much infringement can we tolerate? What other treaties and rules exist that might also restrict the rights of individuals? One group of treaties that relates to this issue are those passed under the **Geneva Convention**. These treaties speak to the conduct of

---

51. **Id**. at 223-224.

war that the United States and most other countries agree to obey. Following the September 11 attack, the United States captured fighters from the Taliban and Al Qaeda; if these people were considered prisoners of war, the rules of the Geneva Convention would apply. If they were, instead, considered criminals who had committed crimes in the United States, the Constitution would apply. To avoid having the Constitution apply to these individuals, the United States moved many prisoners to a United States Navy base that was not on United States soil, but instead was at Guantánamo Bay, Cuba. This base was in a territory controlled by the United States but was not technically in the United States, so the Constitution did not apply. The Geneva Convention treaties, the rules of the United Nations, and other international treaties were also not applicable in Cuba. The government was thus able to limitlessly detain and interrogate these persons, and much controversy ensued over the ethics of these detentions. The interrogation techniques that were employed at Guantánamo were especially criticized, as they included prolonged questioning and arguably torturous techniques including blindfolding, being tied up in painful positions, being deprived of sleep, and "waterboarding."

Further, President George W. Bush issued an order in November 2001 that permitted persons who were not United States citizens and were considered members of Al Qaeda or an individual who otherwise "threatened" the United States to be tried in military tribunals. The rules for these tribunals were developed solely by American military officials and no appellate process was included in the rules. (American soldiers tried in military courts do enjoy the right to appeal to American civilian courts.) These "specialized" courts can avoid the restrictions of the Constitution, and their continued use has caused much controversy.

On June 11, 2008, the Supreme Court issued a decision in the case of **Boumediene v. Bush**.[52] The Court affirmed in that decision that detainees in Guantánamo Bay could challenge their detention through habeas corpus proceedings. These proceedings would allow the detainees to submit petitions directly to federal judges in Washington to request that those judges determine whether the United States government possessed enough evidence to hold the detainees against their will. Guantánamo Bay is a United States Territory that the United States exercises jurisdiction and control over in accordance with a lease with Cuba that allows Cuba to retain sovereignty over the territory. Guantánamo Bay houses a United States Naval Station military base on which various military detainees have been held. Because Guantánamo Bay is not a state and detainees are not American citizens, much controversy exists over whether constitutional guarantees exist for the detainees. The Court stated that the guarantees of the Constitution should not be switched on or off at will by political branches.

---

52. 553 U.S. 723 (2008).

QUESTIONS TO CONSIDER

1. Read the case of **Adams v. Williams**, 407 U.S. 143 (1972). The court approved the stop of a motorist in this case but stated that the tip that allowed the stop might be insufficient under the **Aguilar** and **Spinelli** tests, before the **Gates** "totality of the circumstances" test was used. What prongs of the **Aguilar** and **Spinelli** tests would not have been satisfied, and what further information would have satisfied those prongs of the test?

2. Draft a search warrant application based on the following facts, making sure you provide the reviewing authority with plenty of information regarding why probable cause exists in this case.

    A 32-year-old law student, Martha Cross, was found dead in her apartment by her father. She had been dead for approximately two days when her body was found. The student had been sexually assaulted and was stabbed while lying on her bed; the stab wounds caused her death. Her neighbors state that they did not hear any evidence of a struggle or any noise coming from her apartment on the night that she purportedly was killed, January 21, 2013. Ms. Cross's purse and wallet are missing.

    Ms. Cross's apartment building has security cameras in the hallways, and the police were able to obtain surveillance tapes from the cameras for the time period during which the coroner stated Ms. Cross was most likely assaulted based on an autopsy he performed. The surveillance cameras show a man exiting the apartment during that time period. The man has tattoos on his face. A bag from a local convenience store, "Red's Concessions," was found in the bedroom, with a receipt in it that was dated the day of the murder. A prescription number on the receipt, when matched with the pharmacy's records, was for a woman named Jean McDonald. McDonald has a son named Robert McDonald, who has a teardrop tattoo on his cheek and a tattoo of a snake on his forehead. The police have interviewed Mr. McDonald's roommate, John Cummings, who states that Mr. McDonald recently stated that his tattoo teardrop "tells the world that he has killed someone" and that he is "keeping track of his victims in a journal." Finally, Mr. McDonald's cellular telephone records were obtained from his cell phone provider and they show that he had made a telephone call to Ms. Cross's phone on the day she was killed. The autopsy report found Mr. McDonald's DNA on a scarf that had been used to bind Ms. Cross's legs, although another man's semen was found on the bedding on which her body was found.

    The officers wish to search Mr. McDonald's apartment and car for the murder weapon, clothing he wore on the night of the murder, any journals he might have written, Ms. Cross's purse and its contents, and any other items related to the murder.

3. Since the detainees at Guantánamo Bay have obtained the right to file habeas corpus petitions, many have filed such petitions and been released

from custody. One such detainee was the subject of the Supreme Court case discussed above, Lakhdar Boumediene. Research Mr. Boumediene's claims on the Internet and determine whether you believe his detention was without merit. What other principles that you have studied so far in this course could apply to Mr. Boumediene's case and how would they apply?

4. Research Edward Snowden's revelations into actions taken by the U.S. government that he argued reflected badly on it. Do you agree with Snowden that these issues should be revealed to the American public? Why or why not?

KEY TERMS

affidavit of probable cause
This document is a statement of all the information that the officer knows either from personal observation or from the investigation she has conducted in connection with a particular crime that leads her to believe that it is necessary to search a particular place for certain items.

anticipatory search warrant
This is an exception that permits a person to obtain a search warrant when the establishment of probable cause is not actual, but anticipated.

basis of knowledge prong
This prong considers how the individual who is providing the hearsay information obtained his information. This prong can also be satisfied with the "self-verifying" detail.

direct information
This type of evidence includes a person's prior criminal record, an observation of furtive conduct, admissions made to a police officer, associations with other known criminals, and physical evidence.

Electronic Communications Act
This act supplemented the wiretap act, and provides similar rules for the interception of electronic communications such as those from computers when they are being transferred. It does not affect the seizure of electronic communications that have already been sent and are being stored, for example, on the hard drive of a computer.

hearsay information
This is information provided by witnesses and not known first hand by the officer in charge of a case.

roving wiretaps
These surveillance orders are orders that do not specify all of the carriers and third parties that are involved in the surveillance orders, but rather they are attached to the individual the law enforcement agency wishes to eavesdrop upon.

statute of limitations
This doctrine refers to the time limit period during which a person may be charged for a particular crime.

totality of the circumstances
This test for probable cause states that both the veracity and basis of knowledge prongs of the hearsay evidence test need not be satisfied to prove probable cause if the rest of the available evidence suggests that there is sufficient reason to suspect criminal activity.

USA Patriot Act
The Uniting and Strengthening America by Providing Appropriate Tools Required to Intercept and Obstruct Terrorism Act, passed in 2001, reduced restrictions placed on the ability of law enforcement agencies to search telephone and email communications and medical, financial, and other records, and eased prior restrictions on foreign intelligence gathering.

veracity prong
This prong means that the magistrate must determine why she should believe a person, based on the credibility of the witness and the information being provided.

KEY COURT CASES

Arizona v. Evans
This is an example of a case in which the Court decided that probable cause was not stale even though the computer system erroneously listed his prior warrant for a misdemeanor. The Court based its decision based on the officer's good faith in executing the warrant, rather than on the issue of staleness of probable cause.

Draper v. United States
An example of self-verifying detail, this case involved an informant giving facts to a federal agent.

Hudson v. Michigan
In this case, the Supreme Court held that evidence obtained in violation of the knock and announce rule can still be used against a defendant in court.

Illinois v. Gates
This case changed the way probable cause as viewed by courts and law enforcement, and established the "totality of the circumstances" test for establishing probable cause.

Lo-Ji Sales, Inc. v. New York
This case involved the neutrality of a magistrate. In this case, the magistrate approved a warrant application for the search of an adult book store. After signing the warrant, the magistrate accompanied the officers on the search, inspecting materials in the store, assisting to determine which materials were obscene, and ordering that certain items be seized. The court determined that the magistrate was not neutral and detached in this case.

United States v. Banks
In this case, the Supreme Court found that 15 to 20 seconds was a reasonable wait time before entering premises, according to knock and announce rules.

SEARCHES AND ARRESTS WITHOUT A WARRANT

4

LEARNING OBJECTIVES: Students will

1. Know when a search can be conducted without a warrant
2. Know when an arrest can be conducted without a warrant
3. Understand the doctrine of plain view
4. Understand the scope of a warrantless search
5. Understand the automobile exception to the warrant requirement

As established in the last chapter, the framers did not include language in the Constitution that required that law enforcement obtain a warrant for all searches and arrests. Because of this, the Supreme Court has felt comfortable in establishing exceptions to the rule that a warrant is necessary before a search can take place. Most of the exceptions are based on the concept of **exigent circumstances**. An exigent circumstance includes any situation that the court believes would give law enforcement a reason to conduct a search without a warrant. Most of the time, these situations arise when law enforcement has a reason to believe that evidence that is relevant to a case would be destroyed or otherwise disappear before they can obtain a warrant. Other exigent circumstances include times that an officer needs to search a person or an area in order to protect herself or the general public. As you learn about circumstances that the Supreme Court has declared to be exigent, consider the rationale the Court used for permitting the relaxation of the warrant requirement when that exigency exists.

SEARCH INCIDENT TO A LAWFUL ARREST

When a law enforcement officer is arresting a person, she can automatically search that person without having to obtain a warrant. First, an officer would want to make sure that a person she is arresting does not possess weapons that could be used against the officer. Second, an officer would not want to put a suspect in the back of a police vehicle en route to the police station and have the suspect abandon his drugs or other contraband somewhere in the back of the police car. Thus, conducting a search of the person also ensures the preservation of evidence. This doctrine was first established in the case of **United States v. Robinson**.[1] In **Robinson**, a District of Columbia police officer stopped a 1965 Cadillac based on information that the driver's operating license had been revoked. The occupants of the car exited the car and the officer arrested Robinson, who was the driver; Robinson was also searched, and the search yielded a crumpled cigarette packet. The officer opened the cigarette packet and found fourteen capsules of white powder that were later determined to contain heroin. The arrest itself was deemed by the Court to be valid, so the question was whether the officer's search of Robinson after arresting him was valid or whether, alternatively, the search violated the Fourth Amendment. The Supreme Court declared that in any case involving a lawful custodial arrest, a person can be searched. The Court stated that not only was its decision based on the fact that a search of a person is an exception to the warrant requirement of the Fourth Amendment, it would also be deemed to be reasonable, because it protects the police officer, and thus valid.

A search incident to an arrest is considered legal only if the arrest that preceded it was legal. Thus, the arrest must be made pursuant to a valid arrest warrant or made under exigent circumstances. However, if an arrest is made by an officer because he believes that a person has violated a statute and that statute is later declared to be unconstitutional, the arrest will still be lawful and the search thus will still be legal. In the case of **Michigan v. DiFillippo**,[2] Detroit police officers found a person in an alley with a woman at ten o'clock at night, and the woman was in the process of lowering her pants. The officers asked the person for identification, and he gave responses that were inconsistent and seemed evasive of the officers' questions. The person was arrested for violating a Detroit ordinance that provides that a police officer can stop and question an individual if he has reasonable cause to believe that the person's behavior warrants further investigation for criminal activity. The statute also provided for the arrest of a person if the person refuses to identify himself and produce proof of his identity. The officer searched the individual after he arrested him and found drugs. The defendant was charged with drug offenses but not with violation of the ordinance. The Court ruled that the statute was unconstitutional, and the defendant argued that thus the arrest was illegal and, most importantly, that the evidence seized in the ensuing search should be suppressed. The Supreme Court ruled that the arresting officer was not required to anticipate that the ordinance would be declared unconstitutional and that the officer thus did not lack probable cause to arrest and subsequently search the suspect. Thus, the search was valid. This case and others decided

---

1. 414 U.S. 218 (1973).
2. 443 U.S. 31 (1979).

later by the Court also stood for the proposition that a person's mere failure to give an officer identifying information does not in and of itself give rise to probable cause to arrest a person.

The Supreme Court has not gone so far as to determine that a search is "incident to an arrest" when a citation is being given to a person, for example, during a traffic stop. In **Knowles v. Iowa**,[3] an officer effectuated a traffic stop on a vehicle that was traveling 43 miles per hour in a 25 miles per hour zone. The officer issued the person a citation but also searched the car after he wrote the citation. The Supreme Court determined that there is less of a threat to an officer's safety when a citation is written than when an arrest is effectuated, so the officer does not have the ability to conduct a full search when he is merely writing a citation. (Also, when a citation is written, the officer generally lets the person go and is not transporting him back to the police station, so there is no issue concerning the disposal of evidence.) Further, when a citation is made, there is generally no physical evidence to seize in connection with the violation, so there is no need to further preserve evidence by searching the person.

Further, any search being made contemporaneous to an arrest must truly be made in the brief period that follows arrest. Two Supreme Court cases highlight this issue. First, the case of **Preston v. United States**[4] involved a Kentucky police department that received a telephone complaint at three o'clock one morning stating that three suspicious men were seated in a car in a business district and had been there since ten o'clock the prior evening. Four policemen went to the car and found Preston and two others. When asked why they were parked there, the men gave answers that were "unsatisfactory and evasive," according to the police. The men did indicate that they were all unemployed and indicated that between all of them they only had 25 cents. They all stated that they had purchased the car the day before but they could not produce the title. (It was true they had purchased the car the day before.) They indicated they were sitting in the car waiting for a particular truck driver to pass through, but they could not state the company the driver worked for, what his truck looked like, or when he was expected to arrive. The men were arrested on charges of vagrancy and taken to police headquarters. The car was driven by an officer to the police station and then towed to a garage. Two officers searched the car and found two loaded revolvers in the glove compartment. They were unable to open the trunk, so they returned to the station; they were then instructed to go back to the garage and figure out a way to get into the trunk. They eventually were able to access the trunk through the back seat of the car and they found caps, women's stockings complete with eye and mouth holes, rope, pillow slips, and an illegal "fake" license plate that would be snapped over another license plate, along with some other incriminating items.

Following the officers' search of the vehicle, one of the men confessed that he and two other people did intend to rob a bank in Berry, Kentucky.

---

3. 525 U.S. 113 (1998).
4. 376 U.S. 364 (1964).

The men were charged in federal court and the evidence found in the car was presented as evidence against them. The men argued that the evidence was seized illegally, particularly claiming that the search of the vehicle was not reasonable due to the fact that it was not performed contemporaneously to their arrest.

The Supreme Court stated the fact that the rule that allows contemporaneous searches to take place is justified because weapons need to be seized and the destruction of evidence needs to be avoided. However, according to the Court, "these justifications are absent where a search is remote in time or place from the arrest. Once an accused is under arrest and in custody, then a search made at another place, without a warrant, is simply not incident to the arrest." In other words, the search required a warrant, as there was no exigency to searching the car; the men were in custody and thus could not access the car to obtain weapons or destroy evidence, and the car was certainly not going to be moved anywhere by the men. Thus, declared the Supreme Court, the search was not reasonable.

The Supreme Court further considered the issue of exigent circumstances in the case of **United States v. Chadwick**.[5]

UNITED STATES V. CHADWICK

FACTS: Amtrak railroad officials in San Diego observed two people (Gregory Machado and Bridget Leary) loading a brown footlocker onto a train that was bound for Boston. The officials noted that the trunk seemed unusually heavy for its size and that it was leaking talcum powder. (The Supreme Court noted in its recitation of the facts that talcum powder is often used to mask the odor of hashish.) The railroad officials reported their suspicions to federal agents in San Diego who alerted their counterparts in Boston.

The train arrived in Boston two days later and federal narcotics agents were waiting with a drug-sniffing canine. Machado and Leary, who were unknowingly under surveillance, lifted the footlocker from the baggage cart, placed it on the floor of the train station, and sat on it. The agents released the dog near the footlocker, and the dog signaled the presence of a controlled substance. Immediately following this, Chadwick entered the scene, approaching Machado and Leary and assisting them in moving the footlocker to his vehicle. (They also enlisted the help of an employee of the train station.) The footlocker was placed in the trunk of Chadwick's car and the narcotics agent arrested all three individuals. The keys to the footlocker were taken from Machado and the three individuals were searched for weapons; none were found, but the three were nonetheless subsequently arrested.

Machado, Leary, and Chadwick were taken to a government building in Boston and the footlocker remained under the exclusive control of the law enforcement

---

5. 433 U.S. 1 (1977).

officers. The agents did not believe that the footlocker contained any sort of explosives or any other substance that would result in an exigency in opening it. The officials stored the footlocker in a secure place. Without securing a warrant and without obtaining the consent of the defendants, the officials opened the footlocker (along with the defendants' luggage, which they had also seized) and searched both. They found large amounts of marijuana in the footlocker. The search took place an hour and a half after the arrest itself. The defendants were charged with possession of marijuana with intent to distribute it and with conspiracy. They attempted to suppress the marijuana found in the footlocker, but the government argued that it was permitted to search the footlocker under the "automobile exception" to the Fourth Amendment. The evidence was suppressed by the lower court and the case made its way to the Supreme Court.

ISSUES: Whether luggage placed in the trunk of a car is subject to an exigency search under the automobile exception.

Whether search incident to an arrest is an exigency and thus justifies an automatic search.

HOLDING: The luggage does not fall under an exigency exception based solely on the fact that it was placed in an automobile. The luggage itself does not have a lesser expectation of privacy like an automobile. Search incident to a lawful arrest is considered an exigency and a search without a warrant is thus allowable.

RATIONALE: The Supreme Court discussed the historical basis of the Fourth Amendment, including the colonial writs of assistance and the government's contention that the framers of the Constitution meant primarily to protect the home from unlawful governmental intrusion. The Supreme Court concluded that the framers also meant to protect people from all "unreasonable government intrusions into their legitimate expectations of privacy." The Court reasoned that because the framers did not specifically distinguish between searches of the home and searches conducted in other places in the warrant clause, their intention was clearly to broadly protect all people in all situations. The Court also emphasized that warrants provide security; they are applied for and approved by a detached, neutral magistrate, and are thus effective against erroneous governmental intrusions. The Court stated that "[b]y placing personal effects inside a double-locked footlocker, respondents manifested an expectation that the contents would remain free from public examination. No less than one who locks the doors of his home against intruders, one who safeguards his personal possessions in this manner is due the protection of the Fourth Amendment Warrant Clause." Further, there was no concern after the luggage was seized that it would be moved or that the contents would be tampered with. The search could not possibly, according to the Supreme Court, be considered incident to an arrest, as the search was conducted more than an hour after the arrest took place. There was no reason for the agents not to obtain a warrant, and thus they should have done so.

The part of the **Chadwick** case regarding the search of containers in an automobile was later overturned by **California v. Acevedo,**[6] as will be discussed later in this chapter. However, the law regarding searches incident to a lawful arrest has not been overturned. Note, however, that if a valid reason for a delayed search can be given, the Court might uphold it. In **United States v. Edwards,**[7] Edwards was arrested and charged with attempting to break into the post office in Lebanon, Ohio. Edwards was placed in a cell at the local jail. Meanwhile, the investigation of the crime scene led the investigating officers to believe that the person who had broken into the post office would have paint chips on his clothing as a result of the paint chipping where the intruder had crawled through a window. Edwards had been wearing the same clothing at the time of his arrest that he still wore while in the jail cell hours later. The officers, now realizing that his clothing might contain evidence of the crime, gave Edwards some other clothes to wear and collected the clothing he had been wearing since the time of his arrest. Edwards objected at trial that neither the clothing nor the result of the examination on the clothing should be permissible at trial. The Supreme Court considered the issue and determined that an exception to requiring a search warrant was during a custodial arrest, including when a person arrives at the location where he will be detained. Clearly, clothing can be seized at the time a person is checked into custody and can be searched upon its delayed seizure, after the actual arrest has taken place.

In Edwards's case, however, the clothing was being taken much later than the initial arrest or checking into the jail. Curiously and somewhat in contrast to the Court's decision in the **Chadwick** case, the Court stated,

> [O]nce the defendant is lawfully arrested and is in custody, the effects in his possession at the place of detention that were subject to search at the time and place of his arrest may lawfully be searched and seized without a warrant even though a substantial period of time has elapsed between the arrest and subsequent administrative processing on the one hand and the taking of the property for use as evidence on the other. This is true where the clothing or effects are immediately seized upon arrival at the jail, held under the defendant's name in the "property room" of the jail and at a later time searched and taken for use at the subsequent criminal trial. The result is the same where the property is not physically taken from the defendant until sometime after his incarceration.[8]

As you can see, a fine line determines when a warrant is needed to conduct a search after an arrest. When in doubt, and when practical, securing a warrant constitutes the best practice.

---

6. 500 U.S. 565 (1982).
7. 415 U.S. 800 (1974).
8. **Id**. at 807.

HOT PURSUIT

Another emergency exception to the warrant requirement is that of "hot pursuit." Hot pursuit warrant exceptions, like other exceptions to the warrant requirement, involve emergency situations when procuring a warrant would take too much time and evidence could be destroyed or moved, or suspects might come up missing during the time it takes to obtain the warrant. Consider the facts set forth in the case of **Warden v. Hayden**.[9] Police suspected a certain person of being involved in an armed robbery and they thus went to his house minutes after the robbery, initially encountering the suspect's wife, who indicated that she had no objection to the officers searching the house. Certain officers found the suspect in an upstairs bedroom, and others simultaneously searched other parts of the house, looking either for the suspect or the stolen money. One officer found weapons in the flush tank of a toilet, and another found in the washing machine clothing that matched the description of the clothing the robber had been wearing at the time of the crime. The officers also found ammunition in the home, and all of the evidence they found was presented against the suspect in court.

The Supreme Court considered several issues in the case, but the first was whether the search itself was legal without a warrant. The Court found that indeed the search was constitutional, as the seizures of evidence took place as part of an effort to find a suspected felon, who was armed, and who, the officers believed, had run into the house just minutes before they entered the house. Certainly, waiting to obtain a warrant could have resulted in the suspect hiding evidence, destroying evidence, or escaping and never being located once the police returned with the warrant. The **Warden** case also stood for the premise that officers could legally, under the hot pursuit doctrine, follow a suspect from a public place (where a person has less of an expectation of privacy and can be arrested without a warrant) into the person's home if the person flees there from the public place. The caveat to this rule is that the offense must be major and not minor; a summary offense or some type of civil offense will not justify the ability of a police officer to enter someone's home without a warrant.

Two interesting cases decided by the Supreme Court involve emergencies that relate to the human body. A law enforcement official can obtain, in an emergency manner, a blood sample in order to analyze a person's blood alcohol level; waiting to obtain such a sample until a warrant was obtained would mean that the level of alcohol in the blood would dissipate. The Supreme Court made this ruling in the case of **Schmerber v. California**,[10] wherein the defendant was arrested at a hospital while receiving treatment for injuries he

---

9. 387 U.S. 294 (1967).
10. 384 U.S. 757 (1966).

DANGEROUS TRAFFIC STOP

www.bigstock.com.

suffered in an accident involving an automobile that he had been driving. A police officer requested that the hospital withdraw a blood sample to determine his blood alcohol level. The defendant had specifically refused to consent to the test, but the blood was taken by the hospital anyway upon the police officer's recommendation. The defendant argued that several provisions of the Constitution had been violated, including the due process clause, his privilege against self-incrimination, and his right to counsel, and he also argued that his search and seizure rights had been violated. The Supreme Court denied his claims. Regarding the search and seizure issue, the Court did recognize that the "overriding function of the Fourth Amendment is to protect personal privacy and dignity against unwarranted intrusion by the State." The Court stated that although an intrusion into the human body is grave, the officer was certainly confronted with an emergency, in which failing to immediately draw the blood and waiting to procure a warrant would surely result in the destruction of valuable evidence. Time had already passed in this case since the time of the accident, and thus, there was no time to seek out a magistrate and secure a warrant. The blood draw itself was performed in a reasonable manner by an authorized person and thus there was no violation of the defendant's rights.

A second, somewhat related and very interesting case is that of **Cupp v. Murphy**[11] which involved evidence found on a person's body.

CUPP V. MURPHY

FACTS: Daniel Murphy's wife died of strangulation in her home in Portland, Oregon. There were no signs of a break-in or robbery at the house. Murphy was not at that time residing with his wife, and he received word of the murder; he then voluntarily telephoned the Portland police and offered to come to their station for questioning. Murphy arrived at the station and met his attorney there. Shortly after his arrival, however, police noticed a "dark spot" on Murphy's finger. The officers suspected that the spot might be dried blood, which is often found underneath the fingernails of the perpetrator in strangulation cases. The officers thus requested that Murphy allow them to take samples of the substance from underneath his fingernails; he refused. Despite his refusal, and without a warrant, the officers took scrapings from his fingernails, which did have traces of skin and blood cells, plus fabric from the victim's nightgown. This evidence was admitted at trial, and Murphy argued that the evidence was obtained unlawfully due to the fact that he was not under arrest and no warrant had been obtained to obtain the evidence.

ISSUE: Did Murphy's actions and the circumstances of his case rise to the level of exigent circumstances?

HOLDING: Exigent circumstances did exist in this case and the search was legal.

RATIONALE: While the Supreme Court had previously stated that obtaining a voice exemplar or a handwriting exemplar were not emergency instances, as they would not tend to change over time, this case involved evidence that did not involve mere physical characteristics of the defendant but, rather, evidence that could be destroyed. Further, Murphy was certainly aware enough of the situation that was going on that he would have the motivation to destroy whatever evidence he believed might incriminate him in the crime. Officers had testified that after

---

11. 412 U.S. 291 (1973).

Murphy refused to consent to the taking of the fingernail samples, he engaged in the following behavior: (1) put his hands behind his back, rubbing them together (2) put his hands in his pockets, and a metallic sound, such as keys rattling, was heard. The officers then believed that Murphy was trying to dig out the substance or rub it off, and they knew they had to work quickly. The Supreme Court stated that scraping Murphy's fingernails was a very limited intrusion compared to the larger concern that Murphy was in the midst of destroying important evidence. The Court clarified that a full search of Murphy would not have been appropriate, but a limited search conducted to verify that certain evidence was not being destroyed was appropriate.

Evidence such as a suspect's blood alcohol level or other quick-to-be-destroyed evidence is sometimes referred to as **evanescent evidence**. Exigent circumstances have also been found in cases in which explosives are believed to be on a property, a fire is in progress, a person is believed to have been kidnapped and held against her will and is in danger of being harmed, or a child is believed to be in the process of being abused. Even though it is preferable for an officer to obtain a warrant in any case before conducting a search, there are many reasons for which a court will uphold a search without a warrant.

CONSENT SEARCHES

Individuals often voluntarily consent to be searched by law enforcement officials. In fact, "consent" is the most often utilized reason that police give for performing a search. If an individual consents to a search, then it does not matter whether a police officer had probable cause, reasonable suspicion, or any other reason to search the person. It is possible, nonetheless, for a person to also consent to a seizure, in which case the plain view rule does not even need to be invoked. However, most consent cases involve consensual searches and not consensual seizures. Any seizure that would take place generally follows from the consensual search and is generally justified by the plain view rule, which will be discussed later in this chapter. Two requirements exist for a consent search to be valid. First, consent must be given by someone who has control over the area that is being searched. Second, consent must be given "voluntarily and intelligently," meaning the individual should know what she is consenting to for the consent to be valid and should not be bullied or tricked into giving consent.

Consent must be given by a person who has dominion or control over the property or items to be searched. It is sometimes difficult for law enforcement agents to determine who actually has control over property and who thus has the authority to consent. The police are permitted to act on who they reasonably believe has proper authority to give consent. A Supreme Court case demonstrates the difficult decision police had to make in determining whether a person had the ability to consent to a search. In **Illinois v. Rodriguez**,[12] Rodriguez's former girlfriend permitted police to enter Rodriguez's apartment using a key she had retained when she had moved out following the parties' separation. The officers arrested Rodriguez and found drugs in plain view. Rodriguez argued that the drugs should be suppressed, as his ex-girlfriend had untruthfully informed the police that she lived in the apartment with Rodriguez and that she had clothes and furniture there. The officers believed her and thus believed that she possessed control over the apartment and had the authority to consent to the search. The Supreme Court ruled that the evidence should not be suppressed, indicating that as long as the officers had a good faith, reasonable belief that the person giving consent did have control and authority over the area, the search would be valid.

There are many limitations on who can consent to a search. For example, a young child cannot give consent to the police to search a home, as the child would not understand what she was consenting to. A police officer should not request to conduct a search if he arrives at a home and is greeted by a young child or someone who is mentally challenged or unable to understand the consequences of her actions or the gravity of permitting a search. Parents can consent to search of common areas of the home shared by all residents of the home, but special issues arise when a parent is asked to permit an officer to search a minor child's room. Often, the ability to consent depends on the age of the child and the amount of privacy that the child normally receives from the parents. If the room belongs to a person who is over the age of 18 or if the room is normally locked or "off limits" to the parents, the parents may not be able to consent to the search. Even if a parent can permit the search of a room, the parents might not be able to consent to the opening of containers by officers, especially those of an older child who is normally in exclusive possession of the item, such as a backpack that he normally carries to school or work with him. An officer should use discretion in determining whether valid consent can be obtained. Consent searches are valuable to the law enforcement community as a valid consent search cannot be challenged on Fourth Amendment grounds in Court and relieves the officer from having to take the time to obtain a warrant.

A defendant can also argue about whether a consent search was truly voluntary. The Supreme Court considered this issue in the case of **Schneckloth v. Bustamonte**,[13] when a defendant's vehicle was stopped by

---

12. 497 U.S. 177 (1990).
13. 412 U.S. 218 (1973).

officers for traffic violations. The car was pulled over because of a headlight and license plate light being burned out. Six people were in the car; some could produce identification and some could not. The officer asked if he could search the car, and the occupants agreed, even assisting him by opening the glove box and the trunk. The officer found three checks that had been stolen from a car wash, and charges were filed accordingly.

The defendant argued that consent was not voluntarily given, focusing especially on the fact that the officer did not specifically inform the defendants that they did not have to give consent for the officer to conduct a search. The Court stated that whether or not a person was informed that they did not have to give consent could be one of many factors for a court to consider, but was not always necessary in order for consent to be freely given. Further, the Court indicated that the prosecutor always has the burden of proving that consent was voluntary if a defendant makes an argument to the contrary.

In the case of **Bumper v. North Carolina**, the Supreme Court set forth further factors the Court could consider when determining whether consent is given voluntarily:

1. Did the police use a show of force, such as displaying weapons?
2. Did the police make persistent requests, or just one?
3. What were the ages, mental conditions, and intellectual capacities of the consenting parties?
4. Was consent granted only "after the official conducting the search has asserted that he possesses a warrant"?

The **Bumper** case also placed a limitation on the officer's actions in obtaining a consent search. The Supreme Court stated in **Bumper** that consent is not considered to be voluntarily given if the police officer lies in order to obtain that consent. In the **Bumper** case, law enforcement officers told the defendant's grandmother, with whom the defendant lived, that they had a warrant to search her house, and she allowed the search. The officers found a rifle that was then used against defendant in his murder trial. The officers admitted that they did not actually have a warrant and relied on the consent of the search to request that the evidence be admitted. The defendant's grandmother testified that she did not ask to see the search warrant but believed that the warrant existed, and the Court found that her consent was not given voluntarily. The officers lied about having a search warrant and the officers did not mention to the defendant's grandmother that her grandson was being accused of murder. Thus, according to the Court, the consent was only given because of the threat of the warrant and was not properly given under those circumstances.

YOU BE THE JUDGE

The district attorney in your jurisdiction receives information from a confidential informant that two men were boasting about having robbed a drug dealer and were looking for someone to purchase the stolen drugs. The informant indicates that the men were traveling in a silver Lincoln Continental and were staying in a local motel in room 222. The informant describes the appearance of one of the men and states that he believes the man is a fugitive because he always wears sunglasses, even at night. The district attorney relays this information to you. You have also received information from a separate source that a person had escaped from a local prison and was in the area with two other fugitives, and that the men were trying to sell drugs. You believe that the two stories are connected and involve the same people, and you also recall that a man you had arrested a couple of years ago wore dark glasses and had been sent to prison.

You find the men at the hotel room and search them; your search yields no weapons or drugs. You do find some keys to a vehicle in one of the men's pockets and you notice a Lincoln car parked outside. The men indicate that the Lincoln parked outside does not belong to any of them and that they have no objection to your seeing whether the keys fit the Lincoln. You unlock the Lincoln with the keys and find a large quantity of illegal drugs in the trunk. Your sole purpose of approaching and opening the car was to search it.

Is the search of the Lincoln legal as a consent search?

Scope of Consent

The scope of the search can be limited by the scope of the consent. A person who permits an officer to enter a person's home to search for a dead body is not also giving the officers consent to search for drugs or drug paraphernalia. If the officer, in looking for the dead body, looks in a shoebox, anything found in the shoebox will not be considered to be properly discovered. However, if the officer looks in a large refrigerator box for the body and finds a stash of illegal drugs in the box, those drugs will be able to be seized under the plain view rule. Once the body is found, the officers must not continue to conduct a search.

Consent can also be revoked after it has been given. Such a scenario occurred in the case of **Florida v. Jimeno**.[14] In **Jimeno**, Police officer Frank Trujillo overheard Jimeno arranging an apparent drug transaction over a public telephone. Trujillo followed Jimeno's car and observed him making a right turn at a red light without stopping. Trujillo effectuated a traffic stop and told Jimeno he had been stopped for committing a traffic infraction. He also told Jimeno that he had reason to believe that Jimeno was carrying narcotics in his car, and he asked permission to search Jimeno's car. The officer

---

14 500 U.S. 248 (1991).

informed Jimeno that he did not have to give the officer his consent to search the car, at which point Jimeno stated that he had nothing to hide and told Trujillo that he could proceed with the search. Jimeno's spouse was also in the car, and after she stepped out of the car, Trujillo went to the passenger side of the car, opened the door, and saw a folded, brown paper bag on the floorboard. He picked up the bag, opened it, and found cocaine inside.

The Jimenos were both charged with possession with intent to distribute cocaine, and they filed a motion to suppress the cocaine, arguing that Jimeno's consent to search the car did not extend to the contents of the paper bag since it had been closed. The Supreme Court considered that the cornerstone of the Fourth Amendment is reasonableness, and that the issue central to the Jimenos' case was whether the typical "reasonable person" would have understood their consent to search the car to include a search of the paper bag lying on the floor of the car. The Court determined that the search was reasonable because Jimeno did not expressly limit the scope of the search. Trujillo had told Jimeno that he would be searching for narcotics, and thus it would be logical that he would look in a container like the paper bag, because many people store narcotics in containers. The defendant argued that police officers should separately ask a person as he finds each container in the car whether he can open that container, but the Supreme Court found that this was unnecessary. The Court did state that the defendant could have told the officer only to search certain places or to look in certain containers and not others, but the person did not do that. The dissenting judges cited the **Chadwick** case in supporting their opinion that people enjoy a higher expectation of privacy in closed containers than in other items that are open to public view.

Third-Party Consent

Exactly what is one consenting to when he allows police officers to conduct a search? If you live with a roommate, can you allow the police to search her bedroom as well as your own? Generally, with the exception of minor children, as discussed previously, a consent by one person only allows the police to search that person's items plus any "common areas" of the house or apartment, such as the living room, kitchen, and bathroom. One person is not allowed to consent to the police's search of an area that belongs to, or is exclusively controlled by, someone else. Even in a shared bedroom, the police must ask the person giving consent to clearly inform the officer of where their personal items are kept, and the police should avoid searching any area in which the other, nonconsenting person maintains their items. Thus, an issue that sometimes arises when a police officer obtains consent from someone for search is whether that person is actually authorized to agree to the search.

Further, what if, for example, someone is at your house laying new flooring you just purchased and you are at work? How would a police officer know whether that person is a roommate, a friend, or you? What if the person laying the flooring thinks it would be fun to allow the police to come into your house and search? In such a case, the government agent has the burden of proving that he believed the person who gave him the authority to search actually had some authority over the area that he searched. Several cases of this type went before the Supreme Court, and the Court declared that each case with this type of issue will have to be considered on its facts and that law enforcement officials can rely on circumstantial evidence to justify a belief that the person in the home has the authority to give permission to search.

Consider the following scenario:

Joe James is a junior in college and lives in an apartment off campus with four other college students. Joe and his three roommates all take a class on Monday morning between eight o'clock and ten o'clock. Joe and his roommates leave their apartment together on a Monday morning, but purposefully leave the door unlocked because they know that their neighbor, Kyle King, enjoys watching television on their large flat screen television in their apartment.

After the roommates leave for class, Kyle does let himself into the apartment and closes the door behind him. He helps himself to some snacks from Joe's kitchen and he plops down on the couch, sprawled out and relaxing.

Local police have heard that Joe and his roommates are selling illegal substances from their apartment and decide to confront the students. The police officer has been told that Joe is a college student with short brown hair. Kyle, incidentally, also has short brown hair.

The police officer knocks on the door and Kyle answers the door. The officer asks his name and, as a joke, Kyle says, "My name is Joe James." The officer asks for permission to search the apartment, and Kyle tells the officer that he is welcome to search the apartment. The officer begins his search in the kitchen, where he finds a large bag of marijuana.

The police officer in that case would most likely be able to justify the search, since he believed Kyle was Joe and had authority over the property, under the **apparent authority** given to the police by Kyle.

Assume the same facts as the above scenario, but that all four roommates are present when the police officer comes to the door and knocks. Assuming that one of the roommates gives his permission to search the common areas of the apartment, the police can search, regardless even of whether another roommate is objecting to the search.

Even though the Supreme Court has allowed one resident of a dwelling to consent to a search in the absence of a co-occupant, consider a case in which two roommates are present during a search and one consents while the other declines to give consent. The roommate who declines consent is charged with a crime after the officer conducted a search based on his roommate's consent. Of course, the law enforcement officials argue that the consent of one person is enough, while the defendant argues that his lack of consent should override the consent of his roommate. In **Georgia v. Randolph**,[15] Scott Randolph and his wife, Janet Randolph had separated

---

15. 547 U.S. 103 (2006).

late in May 2001, and Mrs. Randolph left the marital residence in Georgia, taking her son and moving in with her parents in Canada; Mrs. Randolph then returned to the house in July 2001 with the child. On July 6, Mrs. Randolph called the police and indicated that she and her husband had been engaged in a domestic dispute and that he had taken the parties' son and left the residence. The police came to the Randolph house to investigate, and upon arrival, Mrs. Randolph told them that her husband was a cocaine user and that his drug use had caused the family financial troubles. She indicated that she and her son had been gone from the house and had recently returned to the house. While Mrs. Randolph was talking to the police, Mr. Randolph returned, and indicated that his wife used cocaine but that he did not. One of the officers asked Mr. Randolph if he would allow a search of the house; he refused, but the officer then asked Mrs. Randolph if she would give permission for the search, and she consented. Mrs. Randolph then led the police to an upstairs bedroom that she identified as Mr. Randolph's bedroom, and the officer noticed a section of a drinking straw in the room with visible powder residue that he suspected was cocaine. The officer went to his car to get an evidence bag, and he called the district attorney's office, who instructed him to stop the search and apply for a search warrant. The officer returned to the house, and Mrs. Randolph withdrew her consent to searching the house. The police took the drinking straw and the Randolphs to the police station, obtained a search warrant, and went back to the house and seized further evidence of drug use, charging Mr. Randolph with possession of cocaine.

YOU BE THE JUDGE

You are a police officer and have received a tip from a reliable informant that Mr. and Mrs. O'Dell of 345 Main Street sell drugs. You approach the O'Dells' home and knock on the door. Mrs. O'Dell answers the door and invites you inside the home. You explain to her that there have been reports of drug activity in the home and that you would like to take a look around the house. Mrs. O'Dell agrees, and as you begin to look from room to room, you see a door that is closed in the upstairs hallway. A sign on the door says "Pittsburgh Steelers Fans Only." Mrs. O'Dell states, "That is my husband's private room. I have never gone in that room and he rarely lets anyone in there. He has told me more than once that I should not go into that room." You ask Mrs. O'Dell if it is okay for you to go into the room and she says "It's fine with me, but I know he would never let me let you in there."

Do you have proper consent to search the room?

Mr. Randolph attempted to suppress the evidence of the straw because of his express indication to the police that they could not search the house. The Supreme Court had to determine whether Mrs. Randolph's consent took precedent over Mr. Randolph's failure to consent. In a 5–3 decision, the Court held that Mr. Randolph's specific refusal did prevail, and thus the evidence obtained in the search should be suppressed. The officers probably would have had enough probable cause to obtain a warrant based on their initial conversation with Mrs. Randolph where she provided them with specific information about her husband using drugs. The officers could have settled the domestic dispute and then applied for a warrant, coming back to the house later to execute it.

One type of person who might not have the authority to allow a search but who might feel as though he does is a landlord or proprietor of a hotel.

STONER V. CALIFORNIA[16]

FACTS: Police officers searched the hotel room of a man who was believed to have been involved in the robbery of the Budget Town Food Market. One of the suspected men was traced to the Mayfair Hotel in Pomona, and without a search or arrest warrant, police officers approached the desk and asked the desk clerk if the suspected man was staying at the hotel. The clerk confirmed that such a person was staying there and indicated that the man was not in his room at the time; hotel regulations required that a person place his room key in a box at the desk upon departing from the hotel, and the man's key was indeed in the box.

The police then asked if they could search the person's room, explaining that they were there to arrest the man, who they believed had been involved in a robbery, and that they were concerned that he had a weapon with him. The clerk then stated, "In this case, I will be more than happy to give you permission and I will take you directly to the room." The officers then left one detective in the lobby, while the other officers went to the room. The clerk accompanied the officers, unlocking the door and stating, "Be my guest" as the officers entered the room. The officers thoroughly searched the room and found clothing worn by the perpetrator during the robbery, along with a .45 caliber automatic pistol with a clip and several cartridges. The defendant argued that the officers did not have proper consent to search the room, and all parties agreed that the search was not incident to a lawful arrest.

ISSUE: Did a search following the hotel clerk's permission constitute an unreasonable search and seizure?

HOLDING: The search was not permissible when the hotel clerk gave permission.

---

16. 376 U.S. 483 (1964).

RATIONALE: The search was not reasonable because the focus is on the defendant's constitutional rights, not those of the clerk or hotel owner. The police had no basis to believe that the hotel clerk had the authority to allow the search of the room. "When a person engages a hotel room he undoubtedly gives 'implied or express permission' to 'such persons as maids, janitors or repairmen' to enter his room 'in the performance of their duties.'"[17] However, a person should not expect that the police would enter his room when the room is secure and he is paying for the room. Had a cleaning person entered the hotel room to clean in the normal course of business of the hotel and noticed a gun, ammunition, and clothing that matched the description of a suspect of a robbery that she had seen on the local television newscast, she perhaps could have reported the items to the police and her observations might provide probable cause for a warrant to be sought. However, the entrance of the room without a warrant violated the defendant's Fourth Amendment rights. A guest in a hotel room should be treated the same as a tenant of a house or the occupant of a room in a boarding house.

A dorm room on a university campus is similar to a hotel room for purposes of search and seizure. After all, the room belongs to the university and the students rent the room for a period of time. Sometimes students are subjected to a search merely because they reside on a college campus, and courts have permitted routine searches of dorm rooms or campus apartments for health and safety purposes. Do college students possess any expectation of privacy in their university-owned rooms? Students keep personal items in their dorm rooms and generally assume that campus personnel will not be looking through their personal items that are stored in their dorm rooms or apartments. Just as a hotel manager or clerk cannot allow a police officer to search the room of an individual who has paid a rental fee for the room, courts have restricted the ability of college officials to search a student's dorm room. Unless exigent circumstances exist that justify an emergency search based on safety purposes or the concern that items related to a criminal search are being destroyed, a search warrant is generally necessary for a search of a dorm room or other campus owned housing to take place. The same rule applies to a landlord or owner of apartment buildings. Even when a university has students sign paperwork that permits the university to check rooms for damage and the use of unauthorized appliances, the university can only enter the room without a warrant when exigent circumstances are present. However, if the university specifically has a policy that periodic inspections can take place for cleanliness by college officials, those inspections are not considered a law enforcement search. Any obvious illegal contraband items noticed during those inspections could then be turned over to law enforcement. Similarly, a landlord could place a provision in a lease that he can enter a tenant's apartment on a periodic basis to inspect for damages.

---

17. **Id**. at 489.

YOU BE THE JUDGE

A local university student has been charged with the possession of marijuana. The student lived in university owned housing and signed a contract which stated that "residence life staff members will enter student rooms to inspect for hazards to health or personal safety." A maintenance worker heard a cat meowing in a suite that contained four bedrooms. Having a cat in campus housing was a violation of the campus housing code, so a maintenance worker entered the student's bedroom without the student being present. While looking for the cat, the maintenance worker noticed a light in the closet and was concerned that it was a fire hazard. Upon opening the closet door, the worker found two large marijuana plants along with lights, fertilizer, and other items that would be used to harvest and use marijuana. The maintenance worker notified campus police who entered the room without a warrant, photographed the relevant evidence, and removed the evidence from the room. The student was charged criminally and is now filing a suppression motion, stating that the evidence was seized illegally, as there was no evidence that the cat was in the room and once the worker entered his room, he should have realized there was no cat there and left before he could notice the closet light. University officials claim the janitor had a right to look in the room merely because he heard a cat noise in one of the four bedrooms. What do you decide?

WARRANTLESS SEARCHES

Inventory Searches

While police are most often conducting a search for the purposes of finding evidence relating to a criminal case, police also sometimes perform searches as part of an administrative function. Two examples of this type of search are when police inventory the contents of a vehicle when they plan on storing it in the police impound lot, and when police inventory a defendant's personal items that he might have with him when he is arrested, if he is placed in a holding or prison cell. Obviously the reason for performing **inventory searches** is threefold: the police need to safeguard the defendant's items while the defendant is in prison, the police need to protect themselves against any claim that the defendant might make that the police have misplaced or stolen his property, and the police need to make sure there is nothing illegal or harmful in the defendant's vehicle while it sits in the police impound lot or another lot.

Because police inventory searches are performed routinely, as long as the same method of taking inventory is performed on each vehicle or person, there can be no argument that a "search" has taken place. Thus, any inventory obtained can be utilized in court against the defendant, regardless of whether or not it is related to the original crime the defendant has been charged with upon his admission to prison or the impounding of his car. The Supreme Court has determined that the concept of "probable cause" is irrelevant to inventory searches. The Supreme Court has placed some limitations on the use of inventory searches, stating that an inventory search cannot be used as a pretext for an investigation. Thus, the initial impoundment must be undertaken in the ordinary course of investigation and a reason to impound the car must be legitimately present.

If a person who has been charged with a crime is taken to prison, he is booked as a part of his formal entry into prison. At the time of booking, everything that he has with him is searched. This search includes a strip search and potentially a body cavity search. Even though the Supreme Court permits any type of search whenever someone is booked, no matter how intrusive, some states have restricted this action, requiring that reasonable suspicion exist that a person is concealing drugs, weapons, or some other evidence or contraband on his person. However, during the booking process, closed containers can be opened with no restrictions, because the container will be stored in the prison or jail until the person is released and must therefore be deemed safe.

Searches of Prisoners

When a person is incarcerated, she gives up many of her privacy rights. In addition to the inventory search that is permitted upon admission to prison, inmates may also be searched at any time while they are in prison. No particularized suspicion is necessary; there need be no reason to believe that the particular inmate is harboring an illegal object or substance. Any inmate can be searched any time for any reason or no reason at all. Random searches are used frequently in prisons and jails to keep order and maintain security. Many items that are considered contraband in prison are not illegal to possess in the outside world. Jewelry, money, certain types of photographs, and many other items are not permitted in prison. Conducting searches for these items may require, however, that inmates be given notice upon admission to prison that those items are contraband. Contraband enters prison through contact visits by family members, through mail if it is not properly scanned by prison officials, and even, unfortunately, through prison employees. An exception is those items that could have attorney-client privilege. Prison officials should not open or seize correspondence to or from the inmate's attorney. Diaries and journals that are personal to the inmate might also be protected from being seized.

Inmates possess some protection from strip and body cavity searches, but usually only a slight suspicion is necessary to justify these types of searches. The Supreme Court permitted strip searches of inmates to ensure that contraband was not being carried into prisons in the case of

Bell v. Wolfish.[18] The Court permitted these strip searches because of the concern of dangerous contraband being brought into prisons. However, the Court did place some limitations on these searches, stating that the need for the search should be balanced against the invasion of the inmate's personal rights. Thus, the searches must be carried out with as little intrusion as possible—for example, the search must take place in a private area out of the view of others. Further, the Supreme Court has permitted searches of visitors who will have face-to-face contact with an inmate. A pat-down search or a search using a metal detector or other nonintrusive device is appropriate, however, in order to strip search a visitor, a guard must have reasonable suspicion to believe that the visitor possesses contraband. A woman recently was found removing her husband from prison in a suitcase after the two had enjoyed a conjugal visit. In a state prison in northwest Pennsylvania, an inmate hid in a vat of food scraps that a local farmer was transporting out of the prison to feed to his pigs. Everything that travels in and out of the prison should be considered a potential contraband carrier.

Not all arrestees can automatically be strip searched. An inmate who is being placed in a holding cell for a certain period of time before charges are pressed or just to be kept under surveillance for a while (such as when the person is intoxicated) should not necessarily automatically be strip searched. Only if a police officer has probable cause to believe that an individual is truly hiding weapons or drugs in a body orifice can a strip search be effectuated. Strip searches can also expose agents to potential civil rights liability. In one instance, a woman was waiting for her probation officer in the waiting room of a probation department. Another probation officer had the authority to strip search her probation client and had been told that her client was waiting on the couch in the waiting area. That client had left the waiting area and was in another area of the building. The probation officer entered the waiting room, saw a woman sitting on the couch, assumed it was her client, and told the woman to go into the bathroom. The woman complied and was strip searched. The woman later filed a civil lawsuit against the governmental entity that was in charge of the probation department, based on the fact that having to undergo the strip search was emotionally damaging to her. Courts have considered strip searches that involve searches of body cavities an extreme violation of privacy and permissible only under extreme circumstances.

Stop and Frisk

One of the most commonly known exceptions to the warrant requirement is the "stop and frisk" exception, also known as the "Terry stop and frisk" exception, because it came from the case of **Terry v. Ohio.**[19]

---

18. 441 U.S. 520 (1979).
19. 392 U.S. 1 (1968).

TERRY V. OHIO

FACTS: Cleveland, Ohio, police detective Martin McFadden was patrolling a crime-ridden area at approximately 2:30 P.M. on October 31, 1963. He noticed two men, Richard Chilton and John W. Terry, standing on the corner of Huron Road and Euclid Avenue. The two men were not known to the officer and he had a difficult time stating why they drew his attention; however, he continued to watch them. He later testified in court that he had been a policeman for 39 years, a detective for 35 years, and had been patrolling that particular area for shoplifters and pickpockets for 30 years. He indicated that he had developed certain habits of observation throughout all of his years and would watch people at various intervals of the day; he stated that in this case, the individuals did not "look right" to him as he first observed them and he then watched them more closely.

McFadden moved to stand in the entrance of a store approximately 300 to 400 feet away from the two men. He noticed that one of the men walked southwest on Huron Road, past some stores, then paused for a moment, looked in a store window, then walked on for a short distance. He then turned around again, walked back toward the corner, paused once again to look into the same store window, then rejoined the other man and the two "conferred" with each other briefly. The second man did the same thing, looking in the same store window twice, then returning to confer with the other man. The two men repeated this behavior about five or six times each, for a total of about a dozen trips. Finally, a third man arrived, engaged the two in conversation, and then left the others and walked west on Euclid Avenue. The two original men, Chilton and Terry, resumed pacing and peering into the window, along with conferring with each other following their peering. This went on for about 10 to 12 minutes, according to McFadden, and then the two men walked off together in the same direction that the third man had gone.

Officer McFadden testified that by this point he had become very suspicious of the men and that he suspected they intended on robbing the store in which they had been peering. He also feared that the men might have a gun and felt that it was his duty as a police officer to investigate what they were doing. Consequently, he followed the two men and saw them stop in front of a store to talk to the third man who had conferred with them previously. McFadden definitely felt that he should confront the men at this point, so he approached them, identified himself as a police officer, and asked their names. McFadden admitted that he had never seen any of the three men before, knew nothing about them other than what he had observed that day, and had not received any information about them from any other source.

When Officer McFadden asked the men for their names, they "mumbled something"; at that point, Officer McFadden grabbed Terry, turned him around to face the other two, and patted down the outside of Terry's clothing. He could feel through Terry's clothing that he had a gun in his pocket, and thus he reached into the left breast pocket of Terry's overcoat to remove the gun, although he was unable to do so. He then ordered all three men to enter a nearby store, and as they went in, he removed Terry's overcoat completely, took out the .38-caliber revolver that had been in his coat pocket, and ordered all three men to face the wall with their hands raised. Officer McFadden then proceeded to pat down the outer clothing of the other men, discovering a revolver in the outer pocket of Chilton's overcoat and no weapons on the person of the third man. Chilton and Terry were arrested and charged with carrying concealed weapons.

Officer McFadden testified that his purpose of patting down the three men was to determine whether any of them was in possession of a weapon and that he did not place his hands beneath Chilton or Terry's outer clothing until he had determined that they each possessed a weapon. The defense filed a motion to suppress the evidence, while the prosecution took the stance that the evidence had been seized pursuant to a lawful arrest. The trial court rejected the prosecution's argument, stating that Officer McFadden did not have enough probable cause to arrest the individuals at the time the search took place. However, the trial court permitted the evidence to be used in court, stating that Officer McFadden "had reasonable cause to believe . . . that the defendants were conducting themselves suspiciously, and some interrogation should be made of their action." The court indicated that McFadden had the right to pat down the outer clothing of the men for his own protection, as he had reasonable cause to believe that they might be armed, based on their behavior. The case made its way up to the Supreme Court.

ISSUE: Can a law enforcement officer conduct a search of a person based on less than probable cause?

HOLDING: A law enforcement officer can conduct a limited "pat-down" search of a person if certain requirements are met and reasonable suspicion exists.

RATIONALE: The Supreme Court allowed Officer McFadden's actions in a landmark ruling that changed the way police officers could perform their jobs and potentially led to a larger number of arrests for individuals who carried illegal items while engaging in suspicious behavior. The Court distinguished the difference between "stops" and "arrests," and "frisks" and "seizures." The Court laid out the arguments for both sides of the issue as follows. Those supporting police activity such as Officer McFadden's will state that the idea of stopping someone and frisking them constitutes a minor inconvenience that can be imposed upon citizens in the interest of effective law enforcement, and based on an officer's suspicion regarding that person's activities. The other side of the argument, of course, is that the Fourth Amendment requires specific justification for any intrusion upon a person's personal security and should also require a system of judicial controls for agents who should closely follow the provisions of the Constitution. To permit this type of stop and frisk would constitute, as the Court summarized it, "an abdication of judicial control over, and indeed an encouragement of, substantial interference with liberty and personal security by police officers whose judgment is necessarily colored by their primary involvement in 'the often competitive enterprise of ferreting out crime.'" This, according to those arguing against stops and frisks would "exacerbate police-community tensions in the crowded centers of our Nation's cities."

The Supreme Court then discussed the fact that the major issue here is not the concern of the frisk itself but of the presentation in court of the evidence that is obtained during the search. The Court also acknowledged that a main reason to uphold the Fourth Amendment is to deter law enforcement misconduct. Further, "[a] ruling admitting evidence in a criminal trial . . . has the necessary effect of legitimizing the conduct which produced the evidence, while an application of the exclusionary rule withholds the constitutional imprimatur." The Supreme Court was aware that permitting stop and frisks would definitely result in this type of conduct by other officers at other times. The Court also indicated that it was aware of the problems that could ensue if officers are given too much latitude to stop random citizens on the street, which could lead to the harassment of certain individuals. However, the Court acknowledged that a police officer who wishes to harass those of a certain race or other group will most likely do so regardless of what legal action the Court allows or prohibits.

The Court then delved into deciding exactly what terminology to use for Officer McFadden's confrontation of the defendant. Whenever an officer restrains an individual's ability to walk away, he has "seized" that person. Officer McFadden had indeed seized Terry and his companions. Further, the Court noted, an "exploration" of the outer surfaces of a person's clothing is quite akin to a "search"; thus, said the Court, this type of activity by the police was not to be taken lightly. Despite this, the Court's next consideration was whether the search and seizure were unreasonable. As discussed previously in this book, when considering the reasonableness of any official action, the Court will balance the need to search against the degree of invasion the search and seizure entails. Further, would the facts available to the officer at the time his actions occurred "'warrant a man of reasonable caution in the belief' that the action taken was appropriate?"

Using this test, the Court first considered the nature and extent of the governmental interests. It found that a police officer may approach a person in an "appropriate manner" when "appropriate circumstances" permit. So was Officer McFadden's manner of approaching Terry and his friends appropriate according to this test? Officer McFadden was discharging a "legitimate investigative function." The men were pacing alternately along an identical route and staring into the window of one particular store a cumulative amount of 24 times, and the men were conferencing with a third man who walked away but was then joined by the original two men. Based on these facts, the Court concluded not only that the officer's behavior was appropriate but that indeed "[i]t would have been poor police work indeed for an officer of 30 years' experience in the detection of thievery from stores in this same neighborhood to have failed to investigate this behavior further." The Court then, however, stated that it needed to delve into the question of whether the behavior of the individuals, and the determination of the officer that he should investigate, justifies his taking steps to ensure that the individuals did not possess any weapons. The Court determined that this was, in fact, reasonable, especially due to the fact that many officers die each year or are wounded in the line of duty as a result of a suspect having in his possession a knife, gun, or other weapon.

The Court then considered the intrusion on individual rights that is set into place when the Court permits this type of search. The Court recognized that "[e]ven a limited search of the outer clothing for weapons constitutes a severe, though brief, intrusion upon cherished personal security, and it must surely be an annoying, frightening, and perhaps humiliating experience." The defendant's perspective of this issue is that an officer should not conduct a search for weapons until he has probable cause to make an arrest of a person, and that the right to conduct a search for weapons would only be appropriate in a search incident to an arrest.

Based on these two sides of the argument, the Court concluded that it must narrowly state a rule that would permit a reasonable search for weapons without probable cause, when the officer has "reason to believe that he is dealing with an armed and dangerous individual." If the officer, using a "reasonable person" standard, believes that his safety or the safety of others is in danger, he may conduct a limited search of the outer clothing of the suspect to search for weapons. Specifically, the Court stated that when reviewing whether an officer acted reasonably in such a situation, "due weight must be given, not to his inchoate and unparticularized suspicion or 'hunch', but to the specific reasonable inferences which he is entitled to draw from the facts in light of his experience." When an officer requests information from a suspicious person and the person does not provide information that would assure the officer that the person is not engaging in criminal behavior, the officer may then further question the person and may frisk him—if the frisk leads to the discovery of weapons (or other illegal evidence, found by the officer's "plain feel"), the individual may be arrested, as probable cause to do so would be present.

The Court's specific ruling was as follows:

> [W]here a police officer observes unusual conduct which leads him reasonably to conclude in light of his experience that criminal activity may be afoot and that the persons with whom he is dealing may be armed and presently dangerous, where in the course of investigating this behavior he identifies himself as a policeman and makes reasonable inquiries, and where nothing in the initial stages of the encounter serves to dispel his reasonable fear for his own or others' safety, he is entitled for the protection of himself and others in the area to conduct a carefully limited search of the outer clothing of such persons in an attempt to discover weapons which might be sued to assault him. Such a search is a reasonable search under the Fourth amendment, and any weapons seized may properly be introduced in evidence against the person from whom they were taken.

A concurring justice wrote in his opinion that any person, including a policeman, is at liberty to avoid a person he considers dangerous. Thus, there must be a reason to encounter the person rather than avoid him, which in this case was the strange and seemingly criminal-related behavior of the individuals. The concurring opinion also noted that the frisk must be limited and must be rapid and routine, and that the purpose is for the officer to obtain information while not receiving, as an answer, "a bullet."

Following the Court's decision in **Terry**, related issues came before the Court for further clarification. The case of **United States v. Cortez**[20] involved border patrol officers who noticed at various times a V-shaped shoeprint and other shoeprints along a path that led from the Mexican border to a nearby highway. The officers suspected that the person responsible for the shoeprint was guiding illegal aliens into the United States and that the person was most likely transporting the persons in a pickup truck, which could transport many aliens without arising suspicion. Based on their suspicion, the officers stopped a pickup truck and observed that a passenger in the truck was wearing shoes that had soles that matched the distinctive design. The Court determined that the "totality of the circumstances" in this case, with all facts taken together, provided enough reasonable suspicion for the officers to reasonably believe that the vehicle was being used in criminal activity.

In 1985, the Supreme Court decided the case of **United States v. Hensley**,[21] determining that a **Terry** stop can be made to investigate a crime that has already taken place. Officers often stop someone who is suspected of violating the conditions of his parole (such as violating a curfew) or someone who matches the description of a person who has just committed a robbery or other crime. The Court in **Hensley** found that reasonable suspicion to stop someone can be based on a "wanted" flyer or bulletin, especially when the flyer states that the person is most likely armed and dangerous, as long as that flyer or bulletin was issued based on probable cause.

Officers might become suspicious of a person because that person flees when they see an officer approaching, and they can use that suspicion as their basis to stop and conduct a **Terry** frisk of that person. In the case of **Illinois v. Wardlow**,[22] officers in Chicago were working in an area known for heavy narcotics trafficking. The officers were prepared to find a large crowd of people in the area, including lookouts and drug customers. En route to their destination, Officer Nolan, who was traveling in a marked police car, saw Wardlow standing next to a building holding an opaque bag; when Wardlow saw Nolan, he fled. He ran through an alley and was eventually cornered on a street by Nolan and another police officer. Nolan exited his car, stopped Wardlow, and immediately conducted a protective pat-down search for weapons; Nolan later testified that it is common for people engaging in narcotics transactions to have weapons. While frisking Wardlow, Officer Nolan felt the bag Wardlow was carrying and felt a heavy, hard object that was similar in shape to that of a gun. He opened the bag and discovered a .38-caliber handgun with five live rounds of ammunition. The officers arrested Wardlow, who filed a motion to suppress the evidence; the trial court rejected his motion and Wardlow was convicted of unlawful use of a weapon by a felon.

20. 449 U.S. 411 (1981).
21. 469 U.S. 221 (1985).
22. 528 U.S. 119 (2000).

The Supreme Court held that the stop, frisk, and subsequent arrest did not violate the Fourth Amendment. The Court repeated the meaning of the term "reasonable suspicion," as set forth in the **Terry** case, defining it as follows:

> reasonable suspicion is a less demanding standard than probable cause and requires a showing considerably less than preponderance of the evidence, the Fourth Amendment requires at least a minimal level of objective justification for making the stop.[23]

The Court opined that while Wardlow's mere presence in a high crime area was not enough to support reasonable suspicion, his presence plus his unprovoked flight, which constituted "nervous, evasive behavior," developed sufficient reasonable suspicion. The Court stated that no one has published a study on what constitutes "suspicious behavior," and there is no scientific certainty as to what could constitute it, so the "determination of reasonable suspicion must be based on commonsense judgments and inferences about human behavior." In this case, the Court agreed that Wardlow's behavior could support the common sense conclusion that Wardlow was engaged in

THE STOP AND FRISK PROGRAM OF THE NEW YORK CITY POLICE DEPARTMENT

The New York City Police Department began a controversial "stop-question-and-frisk" program as a way to cut down on crime in the city. Officers are authorized to stop pedestrians, question them, and frisk them for weapons and other contraband. However, the vast majority of persons stopped were African American or Latino, and the program and others like it have been criticized. Critics, and some courts, have averred that the stops are based more on race than on any reasonable suspicion of criminal activity. The New York Civil Liberties Union and other organizations have filed a federal class action and citizens have marched in protest of the program. A United States District Court ruled on August 12, 2013, that the stop and frisk practice was unconstitutional. The Court directed the New York City Police Department to adopt a written policy to clarify when such stops are authorized. Mayor Bloomberg is appealing the ruling. Other municipalities, such as the Fayetteville, North Carolina Council, have voted to stop their police departments from performing these types of frisks. Review a stop and frisk statute such as the New York City ordinance and consider whether it could be rewritten to avoid racial bias in its execution.

---

23. **Id.** at 123.

criminal behavior. Finally, the Court reasoned that indeed **Terry** stop and frisks have the potential of leading to the stopping and questioning of innocent people. The Court stated that the inconvenience to citizens is minimal when this might happen compared to the protection of the officer and other citizens that the doctrine provides.

Plain View

Many pieces of criminal evidence are seized by police under the **plain view** doctrine. The premise behind this doctrine is that anything that an officer sees that is within the officer's plain view can be seized regardless of whether an officer has probable cause or permission to search from the owner of the item. The plain view rule is often used by law enforcement to justify the seizure of items that "just happen" to be in the view of an officer who is otherwise performing his job duties. An officer can see something in plain view when he is conducting a search with or without a search warrant or even just investigating a case and talking to a witness to a crime. A plain view seizure could also take place when an officer is merely patrolling or otherwise interacting with the public. When an object is in the plain view of police, the Fourth Amendment does not apply; the Supreme Court reasoned that no one can expect privacy in items that have been left in plain view, especially if those items constitute contraband or otherwise demonstrate evidence of criminal activity. However, the Fourth Amendment is often relevant in cases involving plain view seizures since some other doctrine must be used by law enforcement before something can be seized if it is in an officer's plain view. The officer must be initially engaged in a proper search in order to be able to see something in plain view, as will be explained here.

An example of a plain view seizure is as follows:

> Officers are dispatched to an automobile accident just occurred at the corner of West 23rd Street and State Street. Upon arriving at the accident scene, they find the male driver of the vehicle unconscious and slumped over the steering wheel. While waiting for the ambulance to arrive, the officers open the back door of the car, which has tinted glass that is impossible to see through, to make sure there are no victims in the back seat. Upon opening the door, two large bags of cocaine fall out of the car and onto the ground. The cocaine was in plain view and the officers can seize it. Two requirements for a plain view seizure are as follows:
>
> 1. The officer must be at a lawful vantage point when noticing the item and have lawful access to the object. (In other words, the officer must be legitimately and lawfully on the premises, in accordance with the rules of the Fourth Amendment, and the item must be in plain view of the officer, without the officer having to move or open anything to see it.)
> 2. The item must be immediately apparent as contraband.

The first requirement is that an officer be legally in the location where the item is in plain view. Assume an officer is legally in a residence based on a search warrant obtained specifically for that location, but the officer is there to look for evidence of drug trafficking. If the officer opens up a closet door to look for drugs and an axe falls out of the closet (with human hair and part of a human scalp clinging to it), the officer can seize that item as it is apparent that it is most likely a murder weapon. The officer had every right to look in the closet for evidence pertaining to drug trafficking.

Further, an officer could be responding to an emergency or even just walking in an area where he is allowed to be when he notices something in plain view. Police are allowed to look around wherever they happen to be and evaluate whether what they are seeing is related to criminal activity. Vehicle stops often result in plain view seizures. As long as an officer has the legal right to pull over a vehicle, due to a traffic or other motor vehicle related violation, the officer can then seize anything that he sees in the vehicle that relates to a criminal violation. However, if the officer is merely walking through a parking lot and sees what appears to be illegal drug paraphernalia in a vehicle, he cannot seize that item as he has no access to it without breaking the car window or in some other way tampering with the vehicle. (Note that an officer might be able to obtain a search warrant to search the vehicle based on what he saw inside the vehicle and can then proceed to seize the item based on probable cause and a lawful search.) Anything an officer finds during a proper search will be considered to have been seized lawfully. As the Court stated in **Coolidge v. New Hampshire**,[24] "What the plain view cases have in common is that the police officer in each of them had a prior justification for an intrusion. . . The doctrine serves to supplement the prior justification— whether it be a warrant for another object, hot pursuit, search incident to lawful arrest, or some other legitimate reason for being present unconnected with a search directed against the accused—and permits the warrantless seizure."

In **Texas v. Brown**,[25] a police officer stopped a vehicle in a routine traffic stop. Upon looking into the vehicle with a flashlight (which the officer was permitted to do), the officer observed that one of the individuals in the vehicle was holding in his fingers an opaque, green party balloon that was knotted about one-half inch from the tip. The officer believed that this balloon could contain illegal drugs, since it is common practice for drug traffickers to transport drugs in balloons. The officer testified that the individual holding the balloon dropped it between two seats and that when he looked in the glove compartment, he observed several small plastic vials, some loose white powder, and an open bag of party balloons. Upon retrieving the balloon from between the seats, the officer noted that there seemed to be a powdery substance in it.

---

24. 403 U.S. 443 (1971).
25. 460 U.S. 730 (1983).

While it is possible the individuals could have a balloon in their vehicle because they had children who brought it in to the car or because they had been at a festival or a party, the Court permitted the officer leeway in making a decision about whether he believed the balloon was related to drug trafficking and permitted the seizure of the balloon under the plain view doctrine. The Court permitted the officer in the **Texas** case to make a decision about whether the item was **immediately apparent**, the second factor of the plain view doctrine. This doctrine requires that an officer immediately recognize that the item he is about to seize is in fact an item that is illegal to possess or that would be considered evidence of some type of criminal activity.

Finally, once an officer finds all of the items he is looking for in a case, he cannot continue his search for any other illegal items and then seize such items under the plain view rule. Once the officer finds all of the items listed in the warrant, he cannot continue his search. Also, an officer does not have to be certain that an item constitutes criminal evidence. Two common household items that are often found in the residences of people who engage in the sale of illegal substances are sandwich bags and scales. Certainly a person who is not engaging in criminal activity could also possess these items; many people purchase sandwich bags and use them to pack lunch items. A kitchen scale could be used to weigh drugs but are also often used by people to measure and weigh food. Another category of commonly possessed items that can be

YOU BE THE JUDGE

A warrant was issued to search a residence for certain items stolen from an auction. The warrant authorized the seizure of a set of antique ceramic bookends in the shape of horse heads, certain compact discs, and miscellaneous vases and glassware items that were missing from the auction. Sheriffs executed the warrant and knocked on the door of the house and were admitted. The occupants of the house turned over the book ends, discs, and vases and glassware. While the items were being retrieved, one of the sheriffs noticed a small television set that matched the description of a set that was reported stolen by a neighbor who lived two doors down from the house that was being searched. The television set specifically had a broken knob on it, and the neighbor had reported that his also had a broken knob. The neighbor had reported that he had placed a small sticker on the back of the television set with his name on it. The sheriff moved the television set and looked for the sticker on the back; he found it and seized the television set. The defendant now argues that the television set was not immediately apparent as contraband because the officer had to move it to look at the sticker on the back. He asks that the television set be suppressed. How do you rule?

related to crime are what many states' laws call "burglary tools." These tools include such items as screwdrivers and other tools that could be used to pry open a door or window. Although possessing these types of items is not illegal, if an officer sees such items lying in plain view in the apartment of a person who is being accused of burglary, the officer has the right to seize those items if he believes that they could be evidence of the crime. Each plain view case must be considered based on its unique facts.

The Inadvertency Controversy. An interesting issue related to the concept of plain view involves whether or not an officer can seize an item if he anticipates he might find it and hasn't "inadvertently" come across it. This controversy arose from language in the first case in which the Supreme Court acknowledged the plain view rule, **Coolidge v. New Hampshire**. The Court implied in this case that there was another factor to be considered when determining whether an item was properly seized as being in plain view and that was that the item was found "inadvertently." The **Coolidge** case involved the search of a motor vehicle when the police had suspected for quite some time that the vehicle would contain illegal items but failed to obtain a warrant and thus performed a warrantless search of the vehicle. Upon searching the vehicle, the officers found items they had anticipated they would find but which were not specifically listed in the warrant. However, the **Coolidge** case also dealt with the automobile exception, which tends to alter any analysis of search and seizure, as explained later in this chapter. In any event, the Court emphasized that the plain view doctrine assumes that officials are finding an item "inadvertently."

Later, in the case of **Horton v. California**, the Supreme Court specifically ruled that a plain view search did not need to be inadvertent. In that case, police officers were investigating a robbery case and requested a search warrant to look for certain items related to the robbery, but did not specifically request in the warrant application permission to seize the weapon that was used in the crime. The officers then searched the defendant's house using the warrant as their basis, and happened to see the weapon during the course of that search. The officer stated that he anticipated finding the weapon and assumed he would do so, but had not stated a request to seize it on the warrant. The Court found that it did not matter whether the officer had previously "thought about" the item or even anticipated finding it, as long as he found it before he found all of the other items that were described in the warrant. Requiring the inadvertency rule in plain view cases would force officers to testify about what they "thought about" as they investigated a case and prepared a warrant application. Some argue that this would encourage officers to lie so as not to have a search thrown out of court. An officer might honestly not even remember what he had thought about in a case, especially if he is being called to testify about that case long after the search took place. As the Supreme Court stated, the inadvertency requirement really serves no purpose in protecting officers and can frustrate legitimate searches, when an officer could find an illegal item but be prohibited from seizing it. The Court also reasoned that the rule serves no purpose in protecting an individual's right to privacy. The individual will still be subjected to having an officer in his home, searching through his items, even if the items are not seized.

However, some states provide defendants with more rights than the Supreme Court requires and still require that officers use the inadvertency doctrine when seizing an item under the plain view doctrine. States that require inadvertency agree with the dissent in **Horton**, in which the justices reasoned that if an officer fails to mention in an affidavit an item that he believes will be found but subsequently finds that item, his actions are "per se" unreasonable. As the Court stated, "To the individual whose possessory interest has been invaded, it matters not *why* the police officer decided to omit a particular item from his application from a search warrant . . . [s]upression of the evidence so seized will encourage officers to be more precise and complete in future warrant applications." Further, these Courts believe that eliminating the inadvertency requirement would lead to an increase in the number of **pretext searches** undertaken by police. As the dissenting judges in **Horton** stated:

> [T]here are a number of instances in which a law enforcement officer might deliberately choose to omit certain items from a warrant application even though he has probable cause to seize them, knows they are on the premises, and intends to seize them when they are discovered in plain view. For example, the warrant application process can often be time consuming, especially when the police attempt to seize a large number of items. An officer interested in conducting a search as soon as possible might decide to save time by listing only one or two hard-to-find items . . . confident that he will find in plain view all of the other evidence he is looking for before he discovers the listed items. . . . An officer might rationally find the risk of immediately discovering the items listed in the warrant—thereby forcing him to conclude the search immediately—outweighed by the time saved in the application process.

Plain Feel, Hear, and Smell. Officers can use senses other than their ability to see something in conjunction with the plain view rule. The Supreme Court developed a **plain feel rule**, which requires the same elements as the plain view rule but allows an officer to identify an object as being contraband based on simply "feeling" the item. This type of seizure often occurs when an officer is performing a warrantless search on an individual in accordance with a lawful stop and frisk. A stop and frisk, as discussed later in this chapter, allows an officer to frisk a person for weapons, to ensure the safety of the community. In a stop and frisk scenario, an officer would pat down a person's outer clothing. However, a frisk often leads to the officer's realization that although the person may not have weapons hidden in his clothing, he may have illegal substances hidden in his pocket. If the officer can testify that when patting down a suspect's outer clothing, he was able to "feel" a lump or container that he immediately suspected contained an illegal substance, he can justify seizing that substance. However, if the officer has to manipulate the object in any way and does not immediately know that the object is illegal to possess, he cannot seize the item under the plain feel rule. An officer's ability to smell something, such as the presence of marijuana outside a residence, could lead to his having probable cause to search the residence. Something an officer overhears, such as a conversation being held in a room nearby where he is searching, could allow him to use the contents of that conversation either as information on which to base a search warrant or as evidence which is presented against that person in Court.

The plain feel doctrine has its limitations as well. In **Minnesota v. Dickerson,**[26] an officer was investigating a suspicious, notorious "crack house" in Minneapolis. The officer observed Dickerson leaving the house and then turning and walking in the opposite direction when he saw the officer. The officer followed Dickerson and stopped to ask him some questions. The stop itself was in accordance with the rules set forth in the **Terry** case to conduct stops. The officer ordered Dickerson to submit to a pat-down search. The search did not reveal weapons, but the officer conducting the search did feel in the defendant's pocket a "small lump." The officer later testified that as he "examined" the lump with his fingers, it moved, and it felt like a lump of crack cocaine in cellophane. Based on what he had felt, the officer reached into Dickerson's pocket and retrieved a small plastic bag containing one fifth of one gram of crack cocaine. Dickerson moved to suppress the cocaine based on the fact that although the frisk may have been legal, the officer's seizure of the item was not based on the plain feel doctrine, because the officer testified that he had to manipulate the package in order to determine what it contained.

The Supreme Court stated that an officer who bases his seizure of an item on the plain touch doctrine must "[feel an object whose contour or mass makes its identity immediately apparent, [and must prove that] there has been no invasion of the suspect's privacy beyond that already authorized by the officer's search for weapons." In Dickerson's case, however, the officer only determined that the lump was crack cocaine after "squeezing, sliding and otherwise manipulating the contents of the defendant's pocket," which the officer had already determined had contained no weapon. The Supreme Court has broadened the plain view rule to include all senses that an officer possesses, including smell, such as when someone is driving while intoxicated, is pulled over, rolls down his window, and the smell of alcohol emanates from the car. Occasionally a driver opens the window of the car after being pulled over and a marijuana smell wafts out. These distinct smells would give an officer the ability to further conduct a search. The sound of a gun being shot would also be considered evidence that would permit an officer to move forward with an investigation. The officer's next step is only permitted,

---

26. 508 U.S. 366 (1993).

however, when the officer is legally allowed to be wherever he is; an officer cannot break into a house with no warrant or probable cause and then state that he happened to see something in plain view.

Scope of a Warrantless Search

A warrant provides an officer with specific instructions on where he can search. Courts have had to provide boundaries for **warrantless searches**. The scope of the search depends on the reason for the search and includes the goals of the safety of the officer and a concern over the potential destruction of evidence. If an officer is arresting a person at home, the person has the advantage of knowing where weapons that could be used against the officer might be hidden. Thus, the Supreme Court has ruled that police can search not only the individual's person when he is being arrested but can also search the person's "arm span" or "grabbing area." In **Chimel v. California**, the police arrived at Chimel's house with an arrest warrant, based on information they received that Chimel had burglarized a coin shop. The officers did not have a search warrant to search Chimel's house. Chimel's wife allowed the police to come in, and they waited about 10 to 15 minutes until Chimel arrived home, at which time they arrested him. The officers asked Chimel if they could "look around," but he denied their request; the officers searched the rest of the house anyway, justifying the search on the basis that their arrest of Chimel gave them the authority to search the entire house. While searching in the master bedroom and sewing room, the officers they asked Chimel's wife to open drawers and physically move the contents of those drawers so the officers could see whether any of the coins from the burglary were in the drawers. The officers seized coins along with several medals, tokens, and some other objects. The search took between 45 minutes and an hour.

Chimel was charged with burglary and the items that were taken from his house were used against him in court. Chimel argued that the items had been seized unconstitutionally. The Supreme Court considered the scope of a search incident to an arrest and found that the officers had gone too far in searching Chimel's entire house. The Court determined that a warrantless search incident to a lawful arrest permits officers to search the area that is in the possession or under the control of the person arrested. The Court pointed out that the framers of the Constitution desired that a person's house be a place of sanctity and thus highly protected. The Court specifically stated the following rule in support of this decision that the search of the entire house was unlawful:

> When an arrest is made, it is reasonable for the arresting officer to search the person arrested in order to remove any weapons that the latter might seek to use in order to resist arrest or effect his escape. Otherwise the officer's safety might well be endangered, and the arrest itself frustrated. In addition, it is entirely reasonable for the arresting officer to search for and seize any

evidence on the arrestee's person in order to prevent its concealment or destruction. And the area into which an arrested might reach in order to grab a weapon or evidentiary items must, of course, be governed by a like rule. A gun on a table or in a drawer in front of one who is arrested can be as dangerous to the arresting officer as one concealed in the clothing of the person arrested. There is ample justification, therefore, for a search of the arrestee's person and the area "within his immediate control"—construing that phrase to mean the area from within which he might gain possession of a weapon or destructible evidence. There is no comparable justification, however, for routinely searching any room other than that in which an arrest occurs—or, for that matter, for searching through all the desk drawers or other closed or concealed areas in that room itself. Such searches, in the absence of well recognized exceptions, may be made only under the authority of a search warrant.[27]

Dissenting justices stated that the majority opinion ignored the Fourth Amendment. The dissenting justices argued that a search ten hours after the arrest is not considered a search incident to an arrest. The police had ample time to seek a warrant, and no exigent circumstances permitted the failure to obtain a warrant. Thus, according to the dissenters, the officers, while not acting in bad faith, should nonetheless have procured a warrant.

Warrantless Cell Phone Searches

The Supreme Court has not yet ruled on the issue of how much privacy a cell phone user should expect in her cell phone, and state and federal court decisions are divided on this issue. Cell phones are becoming a depository of very personal information, including emails, text messages, phone numbers, photographs, and posts and messages from social networking sites. Some courts have justified the warrantless search of the contents of a cellular telephone under the "search incident to a lawful arrest" exception to the Fourth Amendment, ruling that any data in the phone can be seized and used against the individual as evidence in court. The information stored in the phone could potentially be destroyed, so the immediate search of the phone without a warrant is thus justified. Some courts justify a cell phone search on the basis that a cell phone is similar to a "container" that can be searched incident to a lawful arrest. Others reason that because a person's cell phone can be seized as part of an inventory search when a person is booked when being admitted to jail, the search of the phone upon arrest is appropriate. Still other courts, such as those in Ohio, have actually banned all warrantless cell phone searches. In many cases, if a cell phone is locked and a password is required to view its contents, a court order is required in order to compel a person to unlock it.

---

27. **Id.** at 762-763.

DETENTION OF OTHER PEOPLE DURING A LAWFUL SEARCH

When a lawful search is taking place, police may detain anyone who is present, either on the premises in the case of the search of a building or in an automobile in the case of an automobile search. This assures an officer's safety and also guarantees that no person leaves the scene with evidence that would be relevant to the case. Further, it is easier for an officer to conduct a search when people are not moving in and out of the area. However, an officer cannot pat down everyone who is present, only when she has a reasonable and articulable suspicion that criminal activity is taking place and that the people she is patting down may be armed.

YOU BE THE JUDGE

You are a state liquor control agent and you receive a call that a party where minors will consume alcohol will take place at a local fraternity house. The fraternity is selling tickets for the party, and you purchase two. When you and another agent arrive at the fraternity on the night of the party, you enter the home and make your way to the basement, where you observe a makeshift bar where people who appear to be students are gathered and are consuming alcoholic beverages. You feel as though some of the persons consuming alcohol are under the age of 21, the legal age to consume alcohol in your state.

The basement is becoming more and more crowded and you decide you should call in uniformed police officers. When the officers arrive, you stop the party and begin to card all of the individuals who are drinking. You find that some are under the age of 21, and you detain those people while letting others go. You then administer preliminary breath tests to the students and ask them if they have been drinking. You issue underage citations based on the students' appearance, the breath tests, and their admissions.

Did you have reasonable suspicion and the authority to suspect these students, question them, and administer the preliminary breath tests? What will the students' attorneys argue? What will the prosecuting attorney argue? Who will prevail?

Bringing a person to a police station for questioning poses a situation that can be especially volatile. Obviously, in many instances, people voluntarily come to the police station and answer questions. However, if a person is forced to come to the police station to be questioned, she can argue that her constitutional rights were violated unless probable cause is present. Even forcing a person to come to the police station for fingerprinting requires probable cause.[28] In **Dunaway v. New York,**[29] the owner of a pizza shop in Rochester, New York, was killed during a robbery. Police had received some information that a man named Dunaway was involved, but they did not have enough evidence to obtain a warrant. Nonetheless, the police took Dunaway into custody. He was not told he was under arrest, but the police indicated he would be restrained if he tried to leave. He was questioned in an interrogation room and made statements and drew sketches that incriminated him in the crime. He attempted to suppress the statements; the statements were not suppressed at the trial level, and Dunaway was convicted. The Supreme Court heard his case and held that his Fourth Amendment rights had been "compromised," stating that "common rumor or report, suspicion, or even 'strong reason to suspect' [is] not adequate to support a warrant for an arrest." The Court determined that taking Dunaway to the police station indeed constituted a seizure and that probable cause was required before such a seizure could take place. However, in **Davis v. Mississippi,**[30] police were permitted to require a person to go to the police station for investigatory purposes.

DAVIS V. MISSISSIPPI

FACTS: Officers were investigating a rape that had taken place in 1954; the victim indicated that the perpetrator was a "negro youth." The officers also found some fingerprints and palm prints on the windowsill through which the perpetrator had entered the house. The police, without warrants, took at least 24 black youths to the police station and questioned them about the crime, fingerprinted them, and then released them. They also interrogated 40 to 50 other black youths at police headquarters, a school, or on the street. Davis was a 14-year-old youth who had occasionally worked at the victim's house doing yard work, and he was questioned by the police several times in his home, in a car, and at headquarters. The questioning was related to the investigation of other suspects, but the officers also took Davis to the victim's hospital room, stating that it was for the purpose of "sharpening" the victim's description of the perpetrator by providing a gauge to go by in terms of the perpetrator's size and race. Finally, the police drove Davis to another city and confined him overnight in jail. No warrant had been obtained and the officers also admitted they had no probable cause for arrest. The next day, the officers had Davis take a polygraph test and sign a statement; he was then put in jail and was fingerprinted a second time. His fingerprints purportedly matched the fingerprints taken from the window. Davis was tried and was convicted. Davis argued that the police officers' action of taking him to a hotel room was an arrest

---

28. **Hayes v. Florida**, 470 U.S. 811 (1985).
29. 442 U.S. 200 (1979).
30. 394 U.S. 712 (1969).

without a warrant or probable cause and that the fingerprint evidence should be suppressed as a fruit of that illegal action.

ISSUE: Did the police's action of moving Davis to the hotel room constitute an arrest without a warrant?

HOLDING: The movement of Davis to the hotel room constituted an arrest without a warrant and thus the evidence was suppressed.

RATIONALE: The Court decided that because there was no probable cause to arrest Mr. Davis, the detention was illegal. There could never be an emergency situation in which fingerprints would have to be taken without the issuance of a warrant, since fingerprints cannot be destroyed or disposed of, barring someone's fingers being cut off! In this case, there was no attempt made to employ procedures that would comply with the requirements of the Fourth Amendment.

Any physical movement of a person once he has encountered a police officer can result in an illegal detention. Asking a person questions on the street can turn into an arrest requiring probable cause if the person is forcibly moved elsewhere by a police officer. An exception would be a situation where the location of a person and an officer could be dangerous. For example, a traffic stop initiated by a police officer which results in a person being removed from his vehicle could result in the officer and the individual standing near a very busy highway on a very icy night. This would clearly be dangerous, so the officer could move the person to his patrol car or perhaps to a rest area where the two can speak without concern of being harmed. Similarly, if an officer stops someone on the street to ask questions and the current weather conditions include hurricane-like winds and rain, an officer can legitimately request that the person move into a nearby building or other public place to continue the questioning. As long as the individual realizes or should realize that he is still free not to answer questions asked by the officers and that he can leave the situation if he so desires, he is not considered seized.

AUTOMOBILE SEARCHES

The Automobile Exception

An exception to the warrant requirement concerns the search of vehicles. The law as it relates to the search and seizure of automobiles is very different from general search and seizure laws. A number of cases have been decided by the Supreme Court in regard to when a vehicle can be searched. In order to properly analyze the Fourth Amendment implications of an automobile search, it is important to understand the reasoning that courts have used when determining that officers do not need to possess a search warrant in order to search a vehicle.

The main reason courts have set forth for not requiring that an officer obtain a search warrant to search a vehicle is that vehicles are movable and thus searching them constitutes an exigency. Imagine that you are a police officer and you pull over a vehicle that has just failed to stop at a stop sign. You approach the vehicle and as the driver rolls down the window to speak to you, a large cloud of marijuana smoke escapes from the window. You want to search the occupants of the vehicle to determine whether anyone has marijuana in her possession. Consider the difficulties that could arise if you had to obtain a warrant in order to search the car. You could leave the occupants in the vehicle while you drive to the nearest magistrate's officer to request the warrant. It is very doubtful that you would be able to locate the vehicle once you returned to the spot where you had effectuated your initial stop. Calling another officer to either process the warrant paperwork for you or sit at the scene and make sure the occupants of the car don't drive away would result in fewer officers being available for other duties. Even if you could sit in your car and apply for a warrant by phone or some other electronic means and not leave the scene, the process would be lengthy and would cause inconvenience to the occupants of the car. Further, especially at night, sitting by the roadside in a vehicle is dangerous, both in terms of the potential dangerous actions of the occupants of the car or in terms of the general danger of being on the side of a roadway for a period of time. The inherent mobility of automobiles permits officers to search the entire vehicle without having to secure a warrant.

The movable nature of vehicles has remained the primary reason for relaxing the warrant requirement in the case of a movable vehicle. Courts have also justified the automobile exception to the warrant requirement based on the argument that people inherently have a lesser expectation of privacy in their automobiles (and other motorized items such as planes, motor homes, airplanes, and boats) than in their houses. The landmark case in which the Supreme Court first considered this issue was **Carroll v. United States**,[31] decided in 1925. During the time of prohibition, officers noticed Carroll driving a vehicle with passenger Kiro between Detroit and Grand Rapids, which was a route used by bootleggers transporting illegally produced alcohol. The officers chased the vehicle and eventually pulled it over. They searched the car without a warrant and found illegal liquor behind the rear seat. The National Prohibition Act specifically authorized law enforcement to search vehicles, boats, and airplanes when there existed "reason to believe" that illegal liquor was being transported. Carroll appealed his case to the Supreme Court, arguing that the search was unconstitutional. The National Prohibition Act had permitted this type of search, but any

---

31. 267 U.S. 132 (1925).

statute can be declared unconstitutional by the Court. In upholding the act and the officers' actions based thereon, the Supreme Court noted that Congress has always recognized a difference between the search of a vehicle and the search of a home.

In one vehicle search, which was the focus of a Supreme Court case after the **Carroll** decision, officers found the defendant's car without him in it and, instead of procuring a warrant even though they could have, they chose to wait for the driver to come back to the car. When he did, the officers arrested him and then searched the car. The driver argued that the search was invalid because the officers could have obtained a warrant while they were waiting for him to return to the car. The Supreme Court rejected his argument and recognized "a necessary difference between a search of a store, dwelling house or other structure in respect of which a proper official warrant readily may be obtained, and a search of a ship, motor boat, wagon or automobile, for contraband goods, where it is not practicable to secure a warrant because the vehicle can be quickly moved out of the locality or jurisdiction in which the warrant must be sought." It did not matter to the Court that the defendant was not in the vehicle or that officers waited for him to come back instead of using that time to procure a search warrant.

It is always good practice to obtain a warrant if an argument can be made that a vehicle is not movable. Some types of vehicles that do not fall under the vehicle exception to the search warrant requirement are as follows:

1. A vehicle that has been in a major accident and has become inoperable. (This vehicle might, however, be towed, in which case it might be important to search it before it is moved if it will be impractical to search it after it is moved or if there is a concern that something explosive, flammable, or otherwise dangerous, is in the vehicle.)
2. A vehicle that is immobile because its engine has been removed or it is otherwise unable to be moved.

YOU BE THE JUDGE

You are a police officer and you receive a report from a reliable informant that two men are selling cocaine from their motor home. The motor home has been parked in a summer campground for approximately two months, having arrived around June 15. The campground usually begins to clear out around August 15 as people return to their permanent homes for the fall. When you arrive at the campground, you do not find anyone near the motor home. Looking through the window, you can see a few boxes sitting around as if someone was packing items, but it is difficult to tell for sure what the boxes contain. The motor home is hooked up to the sewer system and the natural gas resources at the campground. It would take someone approximately 30 minutes to disconnect the motor home from these services. The local magistrate's office is approximately 45 minutes away from the campground.

Can you search the camper without a warrant on the ground that the camper is a movable vehicle?

The doctrine set forth in **Carroll** was eventually expanded to permit the search of passengers in a vehicle as long as the vehicle had been lawfully stopped, even without probable cause to believe that the passenger was actually in possession of contraband or evidence. In **United States v. Di Re**,[32] federal investigators received information that a man named Buttitta would be selling illegal gasoline vouchers to another man named Reed (an informant) at a particular place, and at a particular time. Acting on this tip, the officers located the vehicle in which the men were to exchange the coupons and found Reed in the back seat, Buttitta in the driver's seat, and a third man in the front passenger seat. Reed held two counterfeit vouchers in his hand, and he stated that he had obtained them from Buttitta. All three men were taken into custody and police found vouchers on the person of the third man (Di Re), who was eventually convicted of illegally possessing the coupons. The Supreme Court allowed the suppression of the coupons, stating that it would not expand the **Carroll** doctrine to mean that any occupant of a car could be searched, even when no cause existed. Specifically, the Court stated:

> An inference of participation in conspiracy does not seem to be sustained by the facts peculiar to this case. The argument that one who "accompanies a criminal to a crime rendezvous" cannot be assumed to be a bystander, forceful enough in some circumstances, is farfetched when the meeting is not secretive or in a suspicious hide-out but in broad daylight, in plain sight of passersby, in a public street of a large city, and where the alleged substantive crime is one which does not necessarily involve any act visibly criminal. If Di Re had witnessed the passing of papers from hand to hand, it would not follow that he knew they were ration coupons, and if he saw that they were ration coupons, it would not follow that he would know them to be counterfeit. Indeed it appeared at the trial to require an expert to establish that fact. Presumptions of guilt are not lightly to be indulged from mere meetings. Moreover, whatever suspicion might result from Di Re's mere presence seems diminished, if not destroyed, when Reed, present as the informer, pointed out Buttitta, and Buttitta only, as a guilty party. No reason appears to doubt that Reed willingly would involve Di Re if the nature of the transaction permitted. Yet he did not incriminate Di Re. Any inference that everyone on the scene of a crime is a party to it must disappear if the Government informer singles out the guilty person.

---

32. 332 U.S. 581 (1948).

A question sometimes arises as to when a person is considered sufficiently connected to his vehicle to justify a vehicle search. In **Arizona v. Gant,**[33] Tucson, Arizona, police arrested Rodney Gant in his friend's yard after Gant had parked his vehicle and was walking away. The police had received an anonymous tip that drugs were being sold at a particular residence and they knocked on the front door of the house and asked to speak to the owner. The person who answered the door, Rodney Gant, indicated that the owners of the home were not present but would be later, and he produced his identification to the police. Upon checking Gant's identification, the police found that Gant had a suspended driver's license. When the officers returned to the home that evening to arrest the owners, Gant drove into the driveway. The officers recognized him and after he got out of his car, the officers walked toward Gant and met him about 10 to 12 feet away from his car. Gant was arrested and officers searched his car, finding a gun and a bag of cocaine in the pocket of a jacket on the backseat.

The Supreme Court's opinion in **Gant** revisited its ruling in the case of **New York v. Belton,**[34] which had been decided previously. The **Belton** case established the rule that once a police officer has made a lawful custodial arrest of an automobile's occupant, the officer can search the passenger compartment immediately as a search incident to a lawful arrest, which will be discussed later in this chapter. The **Belton** court believed that a bright-line rule would be helpful to law enforcement officers. The **Gant** court again considered whether the search of a passenger compartment in a car should be undertaken only when the passenger compartment is within the reaching distance of the suspect. The prosecution argued that it is appropriate for the court to rule that the passenger compartment of a car can be searched in any event, regardless of whether or not a person is present therein or it is otherwise within the person's grabbing area, because it is preferable for the Supreme Court to develop a bright-line rule that is easy for police officers to follow. The Supreme Court rejected this argument, stating that "[a] rule that gives police the power to conduct such a search whenever an individual is caught committing a traffic offense, when there is no basis for believing evidence of the offense might be found in the vehicle, creates a serious and recurring threat to the privacy of countless individuals. Indeed, the character of that threat implicates the central concern underlying the Fourth Amendment—the concern about giving police officers unbridled discretion to rummage at will among a person's private effects." The Court ruled that the search of a vehicle without a warrant may take place in three circumstances: (1) when an arrestee is within reaching distance of the vehicle or it is reasonable to believe the vehicle contains evidence of the offense of arrest, (2) when safety or evidentiary concerns demand, or (3) when there is probable cause to believe that a certain area of the vehicle might contain evidence of a

33. 556 U.S.332 (2009).
34. 453 U.S. 454 (1981).

crime. Gant was not within the grabbing area of his vehicle when he was searched. The Court stated that it believed that this decision was in line with the Court's intention when deciding the **Belton** case. The **Gant** decision demonstrated that the Court was no longer declaring "open season" on automobiles, as many argued the Court had done years before when it began to relax the general rule requiring warrants before searching a vehicle.

The Court's rulings in the **Gant** and **Belton** cases also resulted in an interesting decision from the Supreme Court in the 2010-2011 court term involving the issue of when a court case can reasonably be relied upon by law enforcement to justify their actions. In **Davis v. United States**,[35] police arrested Willie Davis for giving the police a false name during a routine vehicle stop. The police handcuffed Davis, secured the scene, and then proceeded to search Davis's vehicle, finding a revolver. Davis was a felon and was prohibited by law from possessing a firearm, and was thus indicted. Davis moved to suppress the firearm, acknowledging that the search of the vehicle complied with the Court's ruling in **Belton** but requested that the Supreme Court review and reverse this doctrine.

During that time, the **Gant** case was moving its way up through the system and while Davis's appeal was pending, the Supreme Court announced its new rule in **Gant** governing automobile searches. The **Gant** case changed the way the police should have acted toward Mr. Davis. However, the Supreme Court determined that the police should only be expected to behave in accordance with the current status of the law. Because the **Belton** case was binding precedent at the time the police searched the vehicle, there was no reason to apply the exclusionary rule. The Supreme Court ruled that the officers' actions were in good faith and the exclusionary rule should apply only when it can deter officers and when an officer was not acting in reasonable reliance on binding precedent.

Probable Cause to Search a Vehicle Must Be Present, Even Without a Warrant

The absence of a warrant does not render probable cause moot. The ability of an officer to search a vehicle without a warrant does not mean that he does not need probable cause to search it; it simply means that he does not have to present that probable cause to a magistrate and procure a warrant prior to the search. He may, however, have to set forth the facts that prove probable cause after the fact in court. Observations made by an officer after he stops a vehicle can develop probable cause. Probable cause can also be developed by observing the vehicle's movements, such as when someone is driving while intoxicated and weaving, driving particularly slowly, failing to stop when required or stopping for no reason, or other erratic driving behavior. Probable cause

---

35. 564 U.S. ___ (decided June 16, 2011).

can also be developed after a legal stop ensues. For example, if an officer pulls over a car for speeding and then sees a nervous driver, a gun lying on the seat, and evidence of drug paraphernalia in the vehicle, probable cause might be present and might justify a search. Under the exclusionary rule, however, the initial stop must be appropriate and legal in order for the ensuing search to be legal; if a court determines an initial stop is not in accordance with the law, the items found in the subsequent search will be thrown out.

Search of a Vehicle Without a Warrant Is as Broad as If a Warrant Had Been Obtained

In **United States v. Ross**,[36] the Supreme Court issued a decision with six judges in the majority and three judges dissenting. The ruling was important in terms of automobile searches, as the Court ruled that the search of a vehicle without a warrant is exactly the same in scope as the search of anything with a warrant. The Court also ruled that containers found in a vehicle can be opened and searched when a vehicle search is underway, if those containers might hold items related to the suspected crime. The Court explained that the efficiency of the search was important, rather than being concerned about the fact that more privacy might exist in a closed container. The court opined:

> When a legitimate search is under way, and when its purpose and its limits have been precisely defined, nice distinctions between closets, drawers, and containers, in the case of a home, or between glove compartments, upholstered seats, trunks, and wrapped packages, in the case of a vehicle, must give way to the interest in the prompt and efficient completion of the task at hand.[37]

The Court concluded that requiring an officer to obtain a warrant prior to opening a container found in a legitimate search would be unnecessarily time consuming for law enforcement officials; as summarized later by the Supreme Court in **New York v. Belton**, "the time and expense of the warrant process would be misdirected if the police could search every cubic inch of an automobile until they discovered a paper sack, at which point the Fourth Amendment required them to take the sack to a magistrate for permission to look inside."[38] Certainly if a police officer's encounter with an individual rises to the level of probable cause that the individual has committed a crime and the individual is then arrested, a search of the person and the entire vehicle will also be permitted under the search incident to a lawful arrest doctrine.[39]

---

36. 456 U.S. 798 (1982).
37. **Id**. at 821.
38. **California v. Acevedo**, 500 U.S. 565 (1991).
39. **Belton**, 453 U.S. 454 (1981).

The scope of the search of a vehicle was further explained by the Supreme Court in the case of **California v. Acevedo**.[40]

CALIFORNIA V. ACEVEDO

FACTS: Coleman, an agent of the Santa Ana, California, Police Department received a telephone call from a federal drug agent in Hawaii, who stated that he had seized a package containing marijuana that was being sent to the Federal Express office in Santa Ana and was addressed to an individual named J.R. Daza, whose address was 805 West Stevens Avenue, in Santa Ana. The agent sent the package to Coleman instead, who took the package to Federal Express with the intent of arresting whoever arrived at the Federal Express office to pick up the package. A man (Acevedo) did accept the package and drove to his apartment on West Stevens Avenue.

Officers kept an eye on the individual and they witnessed him leaving his apartment with the box and paper that had contained the marijuana and dropping it into a trash bin. Coleman then left to obtain a search warrant. While Coleman was gone, officers observed Acevedo leaving the apartment with a blue knapsack that appeared to be about half full and also appeared to be about the same size as one of the packages of marijuana that had been sent from Hawaii. Acevedo walked to a silver Honda vehicle in the parking lot, placed the bag in the trunk of the car, and began to drive away. The officers who had remained at the scene followed him in a marked car and pulled him over, fearing that the evidence would disappear if they waited for Coleman to come back with his search warrant. Following the stop, the officers opened Acevedo's trunk, pulled out the bag, and found marijuana inside it.

Acevedo moved to suppress the marijuana found in the car, and the case found its way to the Supreme Court. The lower courts argued as to whether, under the rules set forth in **Chadwick**, the officers would have to obtain a warrant to open the package, or if, under the Court's decision in **Ross**, the package in the trunk of the vehicle could be opened immediately.

ISSUE: Do officers need a warrant to search a closed container in a vehicle?

HOLDING: Officers can search a closed container in a vehicle without a warrant as long as probable cause exists to believe that the container holds contraband or evidence.

RATIONALE: The Supreme Court recognized the dichotomy of those two cases and thus heard the case in order to decide how the polarized decisions in the **Chadwick** and **Ross** cases could be rectified by law enforcement officials who were trying to follow the law. The Supreme Court began its analysis by discussing the **Carroll** case

---

40. 500 U.S. 565 (1991).

and the general warrant exception in cases of movable vehicles. The Court stated that the facts presented in the **Acevedo** case were more akin to the facts of the **Ross** case than the **Chadwick** in that officers had probable cause to believe that drugs were in the trunk of Acevedo's car. The question that the **Ross** decision had not answered was whether the police should have to obtain a warrant to open a container when they did not possess enough probable cause to search the entire car. The Court stated that questions regarding the warrant requirement previously had depended on a "curious line between the search of an automobile that coincidentally turns up a container and the search of a container that coincidentally turns up in an automobile."

The Court reasoned that to require an officer to have enough probable cause to search an entire car before she can begin to open containers would actually encourage officers to search a car more extensively when pulling it over so as to justify opening the container. The Court stated that it could not "see the benefit of a rule that requires law enforcement officers to conduct a more intrusive search in order to justify a less intrusive one." The Court further pointed out that in the **Carroll** case, which was the original case justifying the lack of a warrant in the case of an automobile, the Court also permitted the officers to rip the upholstery of the vehicle to determine whether any contraband was hidden inside the seats. If this behavior was appropriate, the Court stated, then opening containers should be appropriate too.

Thus, the Court's attempt to rectify the decisions in the **Chadwick** and **Ross** cases resulted in permitting police officers to search any areas in a vehicle where they believe criminal evidence could be. Once the officers search in that location, if they find a container that could hold the evidence, they are permitted to open the container without a warrant. The Court's final ruling was set forth as follows: "[t]he police may search an automobile and the containers within it where they have probable cause to believe contraband or evidence is contained." As with any search, then, officers can look in containers that are large enough to hold the items for which they are looking, but not in containers that are not. Drugs can be hidden in almost any container, but a fugitive from justice could be hiding in the trunk but not in a shoebox found in the trunk and thus the shoebox could only be opened under the drug search scenario.

Administrative Automobile Stops

In 1979, the Supreme Court was faced with the question of whether officers could stop vehicles for the mere purpose of checking to make sure the person driving it possessed a driver's license and that the vehicle's registration was current. In **Delaware v. Prouse**,[41] an officer had stopped an automobile solely in order to check the status of the vehicle's registration and the driver's license.

---

41. 440 U.S. 469 (1979).

He had not witnessed the vehicle violating any laws, and he was not engaged in any spot checks of other vehicles. Upon stopping the vehicle and approaching it, he noticed marijuana in plain view, and the driver of the car was consequently indicted for illegal possession of a controlled substance. The Supreme Court agreed with the trial court that stopping an automobile and detaining its occupants constitute a "seizure" within the meaning of the Fourth and Fourteenth Amendments, even when the purpose of the stop is limited to checking paperwork. The Court balanced the intrusion on the Fourth Amendment privacy interests of individuals driving cars against the promotion of governmental interests. The Court indicated that the state's interest in conducting discretionary, as opposed to routine, stops in this type of check does not outweigh the resulting intrusion on the privacy and security of the persons detained, however briefly. The Court stated that in fact, such a stop actually physically and psychologically intrudes upon the occupants of the vehicle. Those who travel in vehicles do not lose all of their rights of privacy just because they are in a vehicle, and thus this practice is not permitted and the seizure of the marijuana was illegal.

However, the Court did not preclude states from developing policies where routine checks would take place as part of departmental policy. As long as a routine method is developed and the sought-after evidence involves something that is unique or related to operating a motor vehicle, the Court will allow roadblocks and other checkpoints. Allowing random checks such as the one performed by the officer in the **Prouse** case could lead to discrimination and profiling, but allowing states to develop systems whereby officers periodically stop all drivers on a certain roadway or even every third driver on a roadway to check for current licenses, registration, and insurance is appropriate. The Court also approves of checkpoints where law enforcement searches for individuals who are driving under the influence of alcohol or controlled substances. Such checkpoints can also be utilized to check for illegal alien status.

Any time a provision of the state's motor vehicle code has been violated, officers can stop someone for that violation even if they are choosing to stop that vehicle with the suspicion that the person is really engaged in a different type of crime also, such as the possession of drugs. In **Whren v. United States**,[42] officers were patrolling a high drug area of Washington, D.C. They passed a dark Pathfinder truck with temporary license plates and "youthful occupants." They became suspicious when the truck remained stopped for an unusual amount of time (more than 20 seconds); when the police car made a U-turn to go back toward the truck, the truck made a quick turn to its right and, without signaling, sped off at an "unreasonable" speed. The police followed the Pathfinder and pulled up alongside it at a red traffic light. An officer exited his car and approached the driver's side of the Pathfinder, noticing two large bags of what appeared to be crack cocaine in one of the passenger's

---

42. 517 U.S. 806 (1996).

hands. The occupants of the vehicle were charged with violating various federal drug laws, but they argued that the officer had no reasonable suspicion to approach the vehicle. They argued that any police officer could find a violation of a traffic law in almost any vehicle that is observed for a substantial period of time, and that this police officer would not have stopped their vehicle unless he was suspicious that they were engaged in a drug transaction. The officer indicated that he was approaching the vehicle to tell the occupants that they had violated some traffic laws. The defendants argued that the court should decide whether the officer would in fact have approached their vehicle if they had not been in a high drug area and "looked suspicious" and, if not, the evidence seized should be excluded.

The Supreme Court decided that it would be very difficult to determine in individual cases whether an officer was pulling someone over as a pretext to some other hunch that he had as opposed to the actual traffic violation. In fact, basing a decision on such information might actually cause officers to lie in order to avoid having evidence thrown out of court. Another option is to try to use some sort of standard based on what most law enforcement officials would do in a certain case. Regarding this, the Court stated:

> Indeed, it seems to us somewhat easier to figure out the intent of an individual officer than to plumb the collective consciousness of law enforcement in order to determine whether a "reasonable officer" would have been moved to act upon the traffic violation. While police manuals and standard procedures may sometimes provide objective assistance, ordinarily one would be reduced to speculating about the hypothetical reaction of a hypothetical constable—an exercise that might be called virtual subjectivity.[43]

Since the officers in this case had reason to believe that the defendants violated traffic rules, they had enough probable cause to pull over the vehicle, regardless of whether they normally would have pulled over a vehicle for that particular traffic violation. The Court upheld police officer's discretion in determining what laws to enforce in a situation. One exception to this rule is that of boats; United States Customs agents are permitted to randomly stop sea vessels to examine their documentation, as it would be difficult to create a "checkpoint" system for boats.[44]

Law Enforcement Use of Vehicle Tracking Devices

Because the Supreme Court has decided that citizens have less of an expectation of privacy in their vehicles than in their residences, the Court has also permitted law enforcement to place "tracking devices" on a vehicle in the attempt to obtain information about the movements of the vehicle that

---

43. **Id.** at 815.
44. **United States v. Villamonte-Marquez**, 462 U.S. 579 (1983).

could assist the officers in developing probable cause of criminal activity. Two Supreme Court cases were based on law enforcement's use of tracking devices on items that were being placed in a vehicle.

In **United States v. Knotts**,[45] decided by the Supreme Court in 1983, law enforcement officials arranged with the seller of barrels of chloroform to place a "beeper" (a radio transmitting device) in one of the barrels and then sell it to an individual who they believed was purchasing the chloroform to be used in the manufacturing of illicit drugs. Officers followed the car in which the chloroform was placed, using visual surveillance and a monitor that received the beeper signals. They ultimately traced the chloroform to a cabin in a secluded location, which was owned by Knotts. They undertook surveillance on the cabin for three days and eventually secured a search warrant, found the chloroform container, and found a drug laboratory in the cabin. The defendant argued that the use of the tracking device was a violation of expectation of privacy in that items that he purchases in a store should not be traceable in that manner by law enforcement. The Supreme Court disagreed and permitted the monitoring, stating that no search or seizure existed under the meaning of the Fourth Amendment. Because law enforcement was following the vehicle on public thoroughfares, the defendant had no expectation of privacy in his movements. The use of the beeper to "supplement" the senses of the officers was merely an extension of the officers' act of following the vehicle in public. The beeper was not used to follow the movement of the chloroform container once it was no longer in public transit and had been placed in the cabin. Because the only tracking accomplished through the use of the beeper was when it was in the public thoroughfare and where tracking was also accomplished by the use of the visual surveillance of the officers, no Fourth Amendment violation took place. According to the Court,

> A person traveling in an automobile on public thoroughfares has no reasonable expectation of privacy in his movements from one place to another. When [the defendant] traveled over the public streets he voluntarily conveyed to anyone who wanted to look the fact that he was traveling over particular roads in a particular direction, the fact of whatever stops he made, and the fact of his final destination when he exited from public roads on to private property.[46]

In contrast, in the case of **United States v. Karo**,[47] the Court considered a similar factual scenario with only one difference and came to the opposite conclusion. In **Karo**, law enforcement officials learned from a government informant that three men had ordered 50 gallons of ether from him and that the ether was going to be used to extract cocaine from clothing that had been imported into the United States. The government then obtained a court order, which authorized the installation of a beeper in one of the cans

---

45. 460 U.S. 276.
46. **Id**. at 281-282.
47. 468 U.S. 705.

of ether. Drug Enforcement Agency (DEA) agents actually substituted their own can into the shipment of ether that the suspected individuals would purchase. Agents watched Karo pick up the ether from the informant and they subsequently followed Karo to his house and determined through the use of the beeper that the can of ether was in Karo's house. The ether was subsequently moved to two other houses and then into a locker in a commercial storage facility and then a locker in another storage facility. The ether was eventually moved again to another house. The agents, using the beeper monitor, determined that the beeper can was inside a particular house, and obtained a warrant to search the house based in part on this information.

The Supreme Court found that transferring the can of ether with the beeper in it to Karo did not violate the Fourth Amendment; as long as the informant agreed to have the can placed in the supply that he was transferring to Karo, the action was constitutional. Karo would have no expectation of privacy that his purchase of the can would be private, and the installation of the beeper did not interfere with Karo's possessory interest in a meaningful way. However, the action of monitoring the beeper did constitute a violation of Karo's Fourth Amendment rights. If a government agent had actually entered the house to determine whether ether was in the house, he would have violated Karo's Fourth Amendment rights. Thus, monitoring a beeper that is inside an individual's house would also be a violation, since the information could not have been obtained from outside the curtilage of the house. It appears as though the agents could have seized the ether and then proceeded to obtain a warrant to search the house based on the defendant's possession of the ether had they tracked the ether only to the driveway of his house, rather than waiting for it to be moved inside the home. This decision is supported by the Supreme Court's prior decisions upholding the sanctity of an individual's home.

The Court revisited this issue in **United States v. Jones**.[48]

UNITED STATES V. JONES

FACTS: The FBI and District of Columbia Metropolitan Police Department suspected Antoine Jones of trafficking in narcotics. Based on numerous pieces of information obtained in an ongoing investigation, the government applied for a warrant authorizing them to install a GPS tracking device. The warrant was issued but did not specify how long the agents could actually track the location of the vehicle. The tracking device was installed on Jones's vehicle while it was parked in a public parking lot. The device could establish the vehicle's location within 50 to 100 feet and the vehicle's movements were tracked within a four-week period. Jones was indicted and he moved to suppress the data that the government had

---

48. 565 U.S. ___ (decided January 23, 2012).

obtained from tracking his vehicle. The Court suppressed all data obtained while the vehicle was parked in Jones's garage adjacent to his home but allowed introduction of the remaining data. The prosecution argued that Jones had no reasonable expectation of privacy in the vehicle because the locations of the Jeep on public roads were visible to all.

ISSUE: Is installing a tracking device on a person's vehicle considered a search?

HOLDING: Yes. Installing a tracking device on a person's vehicle is considered a search.

RATIONALE: By installing and monitoring the tracking device, the officers did more than merely conduct a visual inspection of the defendant's vehicle. The officers, in effect, trespassed by attaching the device to the Jeep, encroaching on a protected area of the defendant's vehicle. The Court also suggested that long-term monitoring of a vehicle would require a warrant. The Court did not state whether installing tracking devices requires a warrant, only that installing a device is a search that may or may not require a warrant. The opinion served to freeze the ability of law enforcement to install these devices freely, but the details of when a warrant is necessary and under what circumstances the devices can be installed will be determined in future cases.

Belief That a Vehicle Is Contraband

If the police believe that a car itself is contraband, for example, if the police know that a vehicle has been stolen, then they can seize the vehicle from any public place without a warrant and can move it to a different location, where they can then search the car either with a warrant or without one under the inventory search rules. This scenario was considered by the Supreme Court in **Florida v. White,**[49] when a car was seized without a warrant because the officers felt the vehicle was subject to Florida forfeiture laws. The officers observed the defendant using his car to deliver cocaine, and he was arrested at his workplace two months later on unrelated charges. The officers seized his car because Florida forfeiture laws provided that if a vehicle was utilized in the commission of a drug-related crime, the vehicle itself could be forfeited. The police completed an inventory search and found cocaine in the car, so the defendant was charged with a state drug violation. The defendant moved to suppress the evidence discovered during the search, arguing that the cocaine was "fruit of the poisonous tree" because the car had been originally seized illegally, without probable cause. The Supreme Court ruled that the Fourth Amendment does not require the police to obtain a warrant prior to a seizure

---

49. 526 U.S. 559 (1999).

of an automobile from a public place, as long as the police have probable cause to believe that the automobile itself is forfeitable contraband. The Court agreed that the police lacked probable cause to believe that respondent's car contained contraband at the time they seized it, but they did have probable cause to believe that the car itself was contraband. The Court embraced the principles set forth in the **Carroll** case regarding the need to seize readily mobile contraband. The Court further pointed out that the vehicle had been seized from a public area, and that a person enjoys less of an expectation of privacy in an item that is left in a public area.

CONCERNS ABOUT DISCRIMINATION AND "PROFILING"

A controversial topic in the area of law enforcement that has been gaining media attention in the last two decades is the issue of **profiling**, or whether law enforcement is targeting people of a certain race or other group when conducting stops, searches, and arrests. Profiling has been defined as "any police-initiated action that relies on the race, ethnicity or national origin rather than the behavior of an individual or information that leads the police to a particular individual who has been identified as being, or having been, engaged in criminal activity."[50] Most concerns about profiling have focused on the issue of racial profiling, especially the profiling of African Americans (also sometimes referred to sarcastically as the crime of "DWB," or "Driving While Black").

One of the first cases of racial profiling widely publicized by the media was the case of Rodney King, an African-American citizen who was driving in Los Angeles in 1991 and whose blood alcohol level was later found to be just under the legal limit. Two Los Angeles police officers spotted King's car speeding and pursued him; a chase on the freeway ensued. King eventually exited the freeway and the chase continued through residential neighborhoods. Eventually, officers surrounded King's car and forced King and his passengers to exit the car and lie face down on the ground. The passengers did so and were taken into custody without incident. King, however, remained in the vehicle and exhibited strange behavior as he exited the car. At one point, he grabbed his buttocks, and one of the responding officers later testified that she believed King was reaching for a gun. The officer drew her weapon and ordered King to lie on the ground; he did so, and the officer approached him with her gun drawn. Four officers then attempted to handcuff King; King resisted, and tossed two officers off of his back; the officers testified later that they believed that King was under the influence of drugs. (King's toxicology results tested negative for the drug under which the officers believed King

---

50. Ramirez, Deborah; McDevitt, Jack; and Farrell, Amy. *A Resource Guide on Racial Profiling Date Collection systems: Promising Practices and Lessons Learned.* Washington, D.C.: National Institute of Justice, Nov. 2000 (NCJ 184768).

was under the influence.) King was standing up and was not complying with the officers' commands, so one of the officers tazed him twice. At some point officers began to strike King with batons, including on his head. Around this time, someone began to videotape the officers' actions, and that footage was repeatedly included in the vast amount of media coverage this case received. King was taken to the hospital and suffered a fractured facial bone, a broken right ankle, and other injuries. King filed a negligence claim with the City of Los Angeles, and the Los Angeles district attorney charged four of the officers with the use of excessive force. The jury acquitted three of the officers and was hung (unable to come to a unanimous conclusion) on the guilt of the fourth officer.

The news of the acquittals triggered many riots, in Los Angeles and in other cities as far east as Atlanta, Georgia, causing the United States Army, Marines, and National Guard to be called in to maintain order. The riots were based on the concern that King had been brutalized based on his race. The officers were tried again, this time in federal court on allegations of civil rights violations. The federal jury found two of the officers guilty and acquitted two of the officers; the officers who were found guilty were each sentenced to 30 months in prison. The entire saga brought to light the issue of whether racial profiling was indeed taking place in police departments and also brought to light the concern of police brutality in general and how it affects the public's trust in the police.

The Johnny Gammage case in Pittsburgh was another case that garnered much media attention and was widely publicized, in large part because Gammage was a cousin of Ray Seals, a member of the Pittsburgh Steeler's football team; in fact, the vehicle that Gammage was driving when he was pulled over by Pittsburgh police belonged to Seals. Gammage, an African American, was pulled over by an officer of the Brentwood police department on October 12, 1995, in a suburb of Pittsburgh that was "all white." Gammage was pulled over because he had put on his brakes when he passed Lieutenant Milton Mullholland's police car. (The road on which he was driving also had an incline, which some argued would cause a person to put on their brakes during normal driving.) Mullholland called for backup, specifically requesting Officer John Vojtas; other officers also arrived and soon various officers had surrounded Gammage's vehicle with their weapons drawn. When Gammage exited his car, an officer knocked his cell phone and date book out of his hand; Gammage, in turn, knocked one of the officer's flashlights out of his hand. The officers tackled him and wrestled him to the ground, and struck him with flashlights as he was handcuffed. One officer sat on Gammage's legs after he was handcuffed, while another officer sat on his upper body. Gammage died, and the coroner ruled that the cause of death was asphyxiation due to pressure applied to the chest and neck. Three officers were charged with involuntary manslaughter and the first trial ended in a mistrial; the second trial was also a mistrial, with the jury deadlocked 11-1 (the one vote to convict came from the only African-American juror). The prosecutor dropped the charges against the police after the second mistrial.

The family filed a civil rights lawsuit and obtained a 1.5 million dollar judgment, the majority of which was paid by the insurance company for three Pittsburgh municipalities. Because police officers have discretion to be able to choose whether to search or even arrest someone, concerns have been raised about how police are making those choices, especially when race is involved. Some argue that the current practices in airports in terms of scanning certain passengers and their luggage over concerns of terrorism involve racial profiling, especially against those travelers of Arabic descent.

Following the Rodney King and Johnny Gammage cases, along with other cases that involved questions of racial profiling, many police departments, including Pittsburgh, entered into **consent decrees**. Consent decrees are an agreement between an agency and the courts in which an agency agrees to abide by certain rules. Consent decrees require agencies to provide certain training for their police officers along with promises that the department would consider racial profiling issues in establishing policies. These decrees are entered into between the United States Department of Justice and local agencies. For example, the Pittsburgh Bureau of Police, following a class action brought against it by the American Civil Liberties Union and the National Association for the Advancement of Colored People, entered into a consent decree with the federal government in 1997. The consent decree outlined steps the bureau would take to improve its conduct, especially in the area of race relations. It was lifted from the Police Bureau in 2001 and from the Office of Municipal Investigation in 2002.

Despite all of the concern about racial profiling, however, profiles can be legitimately used by police agencies to train their officers regarding certain characteristics used to identify, for example, a terrorist, drug smuggler, or other specific type of criminal. Profiles can be used to assist a law enforcement agency in watching a certain type of person more closely, but reasonable suspicion or probable cause can be developed only if that person displays further suspicious behavior that is consistent with a particular type of crime. In the early 1970s, terrorism commonly took the form of persons hijacking planes by taking over the cockpit and flying the plane and its hostages to a different location than its original destination. Owing to the high rate of terrorism, the United States government developed a list of traits that hijackers usually exhibited. Similar lists were developed by law enforcement agencies throughout the United States to identify drug smugglers, especially in certain "source" cities such as Miami and New York City, cities through which drugs were often smuggled. An example of a list of such traits that might be used by airport police in Miami could be as follows:

1. The person travels to and from a particular source city (i.e., a city in South America to Miami, Florida).
2. The person utilizes a large amount of cash to purchase his ticket.
3. The person travels alone.
4. The person brings a large amount of luggage for a short stay in the source city.

5. The person travels for many hours on the airplane to remain in the source city for only a few hours before reboarding a plane and heading back.
6. The person makes a phone call immediately after de-boarding the plane.
7. The person sits in the front of the plane in order to de-board quickly upon landing.
8. The person "appears nervous."

Now, imagine that you are an airport police officer in Miami and you have been given this list of traits to look for. You find a person who appears to have those traits, and on further investigation, you find that the person is a business traveler who is working for a company that has offices both in South America and Miami and who is attending and speaking at a very large convention in Miami, then quickly returning home to speak in South America at another convention. The person has to bring many suitcases with him in order to bring handouts and pamphlets for the audience. The person flies often but has admitted in speeches that he has an extreme fear of flying due to the fact that his uncle was killed in a plane crash.

You most likely would not target this person. However, assume your focus is now on another person who fits most of the same traits. You obtain some background on this person and find that he is not employed, he dresses in very expensive clothes and uses very expensive luggage, he travels to Miami twice a month, and he always is picked up at the airport by the same person. You follow the vehicle to a very bad area of town that is known for having "crack houses." The individual stays at one known crack house for about an hour each time he comes to Miami, then he returns to the airport. The information and profile you have used, in addition to the information you have gleaned about the individual through further investigation, could either constitute reasonable suspicion or perhaps even probable cause to continue with the next step of either performing a frisk on the person or perhaps requesting a warrant for his arrest or for the search of his luggage. Facts or behavior that match a profile can provide part, but not all, of the facts necessary to establish reasonable suspicion or probable cause.

Two Supreme Court cases focused on the issue of the use of profiles to identify drug dealers. In **Reid v. Georgia,**[51] a federal narcotics agent at the Atlanta Airport noticed Reid occasionally looking backward at a second man. The men each had a shoulder bag but no other luggage. The men left the terminal together and the agent asked them for identification. The two men consented to a search of their shoulder bags and persons but then Reid attempted to run away from the agent, abandoning his bag as he ran. The agent searched the bag and found that it contained cocaine. Reid attempted to suppress the cocaine due to a lack of reasonable suspicion on the part of the agent. The Supreme Court agreed, stating that the agent could not have reasonably suspected drug activity on the part of the defendant based on his

---

51. 448 U.S. 438 (1980).

observations. The agent's main reason for his suspicion was that he believed that Reid and his friend were trying to conceal the fact they were traveling together. This, in the court's opinion, was not enough to develop suspicion, as innocent people traveling together could also walk separately.

A later case, **United States v. Sokolow**,[52] however, resulted in a different conclusion. In the **Sokolow** case, DEA agents stopped Sokolow at the Honolulu International Airport. The reason for stopping him include the following: (1) he paid $2,100.00 for two round trip tickets, and he used $20 bills to make the payment, (2) he traveled under a name that did not match the name under which his telephone number was listed, (3) he had flown in from Miami, which was a source city for illegal drugs, (4) a flight from Honolulu to Miami takes 20 hours and he stayed in Miami for only 48 hours, (5) he "appeared nervous" during his trip, and (6) he did not check any of his luggage. Sokolow's carry-on luggage was searched and contained 1,063 grams of cocaine. The Supreme Court stated that the facts known to the agents were sufficient to allow the agents to conduct the search. The Court determined that while each factor itself is not proof of illegal behavior, all of the facts taken together did in fact result in enough evidence to establish reasonable suspicion, so that further investigation could take place. This decision validated the use of profiles to assist agents in establishing reasonable suspicion.

SCOPE OF THE SEARCH

How far can an officer go in "patting down" a suspect? According to the **Terry** decision, the answer is that a limited pat down of the outer clothing is permitted. The Supreme Court considered this question in the case of **Adams v. Williams**,[53] in which the police had information regarding the defendant even before they encountered him. A police officer was patrolling in Bridgeport, Connecticut, at 2:15 A.M. when an individual who was known to him approached his car and told him that a person in a nearby vehicle was carrying narcotics and had a gun in the waistband of his pants.

The officer called for assistance and then approached the vehicle to investigate the informant's report. The officer found Robert Williams sitting in the car and approached him, requesting that Williams open the car door. Instead of opening the door, Williams instead rolled down the window and the officer immediately reached into the car and removed a fully loaded revolver from Williams's waistband. The gun was not visible to the officer but was located exactly where the informant had said it would be. The officer arrested Williams for unlawful possession of the gun and conducted a search incident to arrest of Williams and a search of the car, finding substantial quantities of

---

52. 490 U.S. 1 (1989).
53. 407 U.S. 143 (1972).

heroin in both places; the officer also found a machete and another weapon in the vehicle.

Williams argued that the initial seizure of his pistol, which then precipitated his arrest and the subsequent searches of his person and his car, was not justified by the informant's tip, and that the officer should have had a more reliable informant or corroboration of the tip before he could perform a frisk on Williams. The Supreme Court disagreed. The Court upheld the seizure because the informant was known to the police officer and had provided him with information in the past. Further, the informant could have been subject to criminal prosecution had he provided a false report and the informant provided enough information for a **Terry** type frisk, although most likely not enough information for probable cause to obtain a warrant. The Court stated that reasonable suspicion can be established based on information other than that obtained by an officer's personal observation. As with establishing probable cause, however, an officer must analyze the information he receives, determining whether the information he receives is likely to be reliable. The Court gave examples of information that would be considered reliable, such as when a victim of a street crime immediately gives a police officer a description of his assailant. Dissenting judges in the **Williams** case considered that it is legal for a person to carry a gun in the State of Connecticut and, thus, the information given to the officer might not have given rise to the establishment of reasonable suspicion. However, the majority opinion's decision opened the door to law enforcement to obtain information from others in order to justify a **Terry** stop and frisk.

THE ARREST

Arrest Without a Warrant

The rules regarding an arrest without a warrant are similar to those regarding a search without a warrant; some exigent circumstance must occur to justify the failure to obtain a warrant. An exigent circumstance always exists when a police officer sees a defendant actually commit a crime. This is sometimes referred to as committing a crime within "plain view" of an officer. Obviously it makes no sense for an officer to see a person committing a crime and say "Hold on—I will be back later with a warrant to arrest you." However, rules vary depending on whether an officer wants to arrest a person in a public place or in a private place. Arresting a person in a public place when that person is seen committing a crime is acceptable to the Supreme Court. In **United States v. Watson**,[54] an informant named Khoury told a postal inspector that Watson possessed a stolen credit card and had asked Khoury to utilize the

---

54. 423 U.S. 411 (1976).

card with him for illegal purposes. Khoury had previously given reliable information to the postal inspector. The inspector arranged for Khoury to meet with Watson to obtain the credit card, and a meeting eventually ensued at a local restaurant. Khoury was to signal the inspector when Watson indicated that he had more stolen credit cards; the signal was given and the officers arrested Watson. Watson was searched and no credit cards were found on him. The inspector asked if he could look inside Watson's car and Watson agreed, providing his keys to the inspector. The inspector found an envelope containing two stolen credit cards under the floor mat of the car. Watson attempted to suppress the cards prior to trial, arguing that no probable cause existed for his arrest. (Had the Court found this was the case, all evidence seized after his arrest could have been suppressed.) The Court found that the arrest was reasonable, based on the common law rule that a peace officer could arrest someone without a warrant if a misdemeanor is committed in his presence and for a felony even if it is not committed in his presence. This remains the rule today. Some states have provided an exception to this rule for domestic violence cases. In these states, if a domestic violence situation involves misdemeanor charges but the officer observes bruising or other immediate injuries on the victim and other clear signs of violence when he arrives at the scene, he can arrest the suspect immediately without a warrant.

However, can a police officer enter a person's home to arrest him without a warrant? The Supreme Court ruled on this issue in the case of **Payton v. New York**.[55] Payton was suspected of murdering the manager of a gas station six days before. Officers, without a warrant, went to Payton's apartment to arrest him. The officers believed that Payton was at home when they entered the residence. Lights were on in the apartment and music was playing inside, but no one responded when the officers knocked on the door. Thirty minutes later, the officers used a crowbar to pry open the door and enter the apartment. They did not find anyone in the apartment but they did find a .30 caliber shell casing that was seized and used as evidence against Payton.

Payton eventually surrendered to the police and was indicted for murder; he moved to suppress the evidence that had been seized from his apartment. The Supreme Court, in deciding the case, indicated that the police had not asserted that any exigent circumstance existed in terms of their entry into the house. The Court stated that searches and seizures inside a home without a warrant are "presumptively unreasonable." Further, the Court stated that "[t]he Fourth Amendment protects the individual's privacy in a variety of settings. In none is the zone of privacy more clearly defined than when bounded by the unambiguous physical dimensions of an individual's home—a zone that finds its roots in clear and specific constitutional terms: 'The right of the people to be secure in their . . . houses . . . shall not be violated.'" Thus, according to the Court, a man should be comfortable to retreat

---

55. 445 U.S. 573 (1980).

to his own home without being concerned about "unreasonable government intrusions." Had an arrest warrant been obtained, the implication would exist that officers could enter the dwelling to effectuate the arrest if there was a true belief that the suspect was inside the dwelling. This rule applies in exigent circumstances where there is reason to believe the suspect is armed and dangerous or that the suspect will escape or evidence will be destroyed if the suspect is not apprehended immediately. Further, the offense must be serious, generally a felony; an officer cannot break into a house to arrest a person who is suspected of a minor crime.

Protective Sweep

In addition to being able to conduct a search of a person's "arm span," the area under his control when he is being arrested, the police may also perform a **protective sweep** of the area surrounding the arrestee. This would go beyond the arm span of the person to other areas, such as a closet, if the police believe that other persons might be hiding there and might pose a threat to the police. The police do not want to be in the midst of arresting a suspect, especially a violent one, and have another dangerous individual who was in another area of the house unexpectedly appear. The police need to have some reason to believe that others are present before they can conduct such a sweep. This rule was established in the case of **Maryland v. Buie**, in which the Supreme Court clarified that a protective sweep must be limited to areas where people could be located and where officers have reason to believe someone might be hiding. Occasionally this type of protective sweep will result in an officer locating evidence that is in plain view, a concept discussed elsewhere in this chapter. Further, if a defendant is arrested outside his home, the police may only enter his home if doing so is appropriate. For example, if a person is arrested outside his house and is not wearing a shirt or shoes, he may want to enter his house to get dressed before being transported to the police station. Officers may allow him to do so but may enter the house with him to monitor his actions. Once officers enter an arrestee's home, the officers can search any area within the immediate control of the person and seize anything that is immediately apparent as contraband under the plain view doctrine.

Use of Force in Making Arrests

A topic universally discussed in police academies and in criminal justice ethics classes is the issue of a police officer's ability to use force to effectuate an arrest. The Supreme Court has considered this issue, and state courts and police departments have rules to guide officers regarding this issue. The most famous Supreme Court case in this area is that of **Tennessee v. Garner**.[56] Prior to this case, states had little guidance on when an officer who had probable

---

56. 471 U.S. 1 (1985).

cause to arrest a person could use lethal force to effectuate the arrest. Officers currently also have many nonlethal options that can assist in effectuating arrest, such as taser guns. While these types of weapons should be considered first, lethal force is a last offense that sometimes becomes necessary to use.

TENNESSEE V. GARNER

FACTS: The **Garner** case began when Memphis Police were dispatched to a burglary call. The neighbor who had made the call told the officers that someone was breaking into the house next door. Upon approaching the house, the officers noticed Garner running across the yard and stopping at a chain-link fence. The officer could see that Garner was unarmed, and he ordered Garner to halt. Garner proceeded to begin to climb the fence, and the officer believed that Garner would flee if he made it over the fence, so he shot Garner, striking him in the back of the head. Garner died shortly thereafter in an ambulance. Ten dollars was found on his person—he had taken the ten dollars from a purse in the house. The officer's actions were legal according to a Tennessee state statute and Memphis Police Department policy. A lawsuit was brought against the police department by Garner's family members.

ISSUE: When can a government agent use lethal force when chasing a suspect?

HOLDING: Lethal force can be used when a law enforcement officer possesses probable cause to believe that the suspect is armed and dangerous and that the suspect poses a significant threat of death or serious physical injury to the officer or to others.

RATIONALE: The Supreme Court determined as a threshold issue that apprehension through the use of deadly force constituted a seizure. The Court then weighed the nature of the intrusion of the person's Fourth Amendment rights against government interests that justify the intrusion. Obviously, the use of deadly force is the most intrusive possible type of seizure, but the officer's interest is his own survival. The Court determined that in the **Garner** case, the officer's interest did not overcome the intrusion of taking Garner's life. The Court noted that while at common law the use of deadly force in such a circumstance was permitted, originally at common law felonies were punishable by death. We no longer punish most felonies by death, and some states do not punish any felonies by death. The Court then established the rule that is used today: an officer can only use deadly force against a suspect if he possesses probable cause to believe that the suspect is armed and dangerous and that the suspect poses a significant threat of death or serious physical injury to the officer or to others. The dissenting opinion stated that officers, by using deadly force against a fleeing person they are arresting, are merely trying to make sure that the person, who is most likely a criminal, is not at large to engage in more criminal activities. Further, the dissent indicated that a suspect's interest in his own life does not extend to the right to flee from the scene of a crime. The Court noted that research has demonstrated that laws that permit police officers to use deadly force to apprehend unarmed, nonviolent fleeing felony suspects actually do not protect citizens or law enforcement officers, they do not deter crime or alleviate problems caused by crime, and they do not improve the crime-fighting ability of law enforcement agencies.

While the **Garner** decision assisted officers by providing a specific rule for deadly force and narrowed their discretion somewhat, officers still are faced with many very difficult decisions in this area. An officer must make a split-second decision when a criminal is fleeing in order to determine whether the suspect is in fact armed and dangerous. Unfortunately, sometimes the officer's initial impression of a situation is not accurate. An example of such a case is that of Amadou Diallo. In 1999, New York City police had been given information that a serial rapist was at large and that he was in a particular area of the Bronx. The officers involved indicated that they had noticed Diallo and believed he fit the description of the rapist. The officers ordered Diallo to put his hands in the air. Diallo turned around and reached into his pocket instead of putting his hands in the air; after the incident, many surmised that Diallo may not have understood what the officers were saying, as he did not clearly understand the English language, and that he may have been reaching into his pocket for his identification, since his wallet was later found in the pocket he was reaching into. The officers believed that Diallo was reaching into his pocket for a weapon and they shot and killed him, firing 41 bullets at him, 9 of which struck him. The officers were charged with second-degree murder and reckless endangerment. A jury acquitted the officers, but the case demonstrates the difficulties police officers have in performing their job duties. Had Diallo been reaching for a gun, officers could have been killed had they waited to see whether a gun was in his hand when he pulled it out of his pocket. It is easy to judge an officer once all of the information surrounding a lethal case is exposed following an investigation, but at the time a suspect is noncompliant with a police officer's commands, the officer must quickly decide whether or not to use his firearm. Officers go through extensive training to practice how to make the split-second decision of whether or not to use lethal force against a suspect.

Misdemeanor Arrests Without a Warrant

Supreme Court case law permits a police officer to arrest a person that she sees committing a misdemeanor in her presence. It would be a waste of police time and resources for an officer to have to return to the barracks, prepare an arrest warrant application, and deliver it to a magistrate whenever he sees a misdemeanor taking place. The chances of actually finding the person who committed the crime once the officer has a warrant in hand are slim. People would not wait at the spot where the crime was committed so the officer could return with a warrant. This would in turn waste time as officers attempt to find the person to arrest.

The general rule that permits officers to make such probable cause arrests is the case of **Atwater v. City of Lago Vista**.[57] Police officer Bart Turek observed the driver of a vehicle violating state law by failing to wear her seatbelt. The driver, Gail Atwater, was arrested, after being stopped, for the crime of not wearing a seatbelt and for the crime of not requiring her minor children to wear a seatbelt. Atwater ultimately pleaded guilty to a misdemeanor and paid a $50 fine, which was the minimum fine required under state law. Upon reviewing the case, the Supreme Court determined that the common law can and does permit restrictions on misdemeanor arrests. However, the Fourth Amendment does not prohibit warrantless arrests for misdemeanors when a police officer actually witnesses a crime. Thus, a state can choose to prohibit such arrests but they are not prohibited under the Fourth Amendment.

Right of an Arrestee to Appear Before a Magistrate

Any person who is arrested without a warrant, and especially one who is subject to a warrantless arrest, should be brought before a reviewing authority as soon as possible to ensure that his rights are not being violated. In the case of a warrantless arrest, a magistrate should consider whether probable cause existed to arrest the person. The Supreme Court decided in the case of **County of Riverside v. McLaughlin**[58] that an arrested person should be brought in front of a magistrate within 48 hours following his arrest. The County of Riverside, California, had required that a person be brought before a magistrate for a probable cause determination within 48 hours following arrest, but excepted weekends and holidays from the time computation. Thus, an individual arrested on Thursday sometimes ended up with a five-day delay before receiving a hearing; a person arrested over the Thanksgiving holiday could end up with a seven-day delay. A class action lawsuit was filed on behalf of defendants who stated this rule violated their Fourth Amendment rights to a prompt judicial determination. The Supreme Court had already decided that a "prompt" determination of probable cause is required;[59] the **County of Riverside** case permitted the Court to define exactly what the term "prompt" meant.

The Supreme Court ruled that a state has no legitimate interest in detaining an individual for extended periods of time before determining whether probable cause was present. The Court hesitated to compel states to follow a certain time limit, but it also acknowledged that the term "prompt" was vague. The Court acknowledged that sometimes delays have to occur, based on the inability to obtain paperwork and other systemic problems.

---

57. 532 U.S. 318 (2001).
58. 500 U.S. 44 (1991).
59. **Gerstein v. Pugh**, 420 U.S. 103 (1975).

Thus, the Court decided, if an individual does not receive a probable cause hearing within 48 hours, the state has the burden to explain why the hearing did not occur and must prove that a bona fide emergency or other extraordinary circumstance existed. Weekends are not considered an emergency or extraordinary circumstance.

As you can see, the question of whether a warrant is required in any case is very fact specific. The officer will be forced to justify his decision after the fact, so he should keep good notes on why he believed probable cause existed if he did not obtain a warrant. The law is constantly changing in this area, and officers should keep abreast of cases decided in his locality and in his state that relate to this issue.

QUESTIONS TO CONSIDER

1. Read the **Chadwick** and **Edwards** cases. Is there a way to reconcile the two decisions in the two cases, which seem to oppose each other?

2. Do you believe the inadvertency rule should be a requirement for plain view searches? Why or why not?

3. Read the decision of the Supreme Court in **United States v. Jones**. What do you think will happen in the future in GPS cases? If you were a police chief, how would you tell your officers to implement this ruling?

4. Consider the **Terry** stop and frisk guidelines. Do you think that a brand new police officer can make the same decisions as an older officer regarding whether to effectuate a **Terry** stop and frisk? Do you believe the courts should take into consideration how long an individual has been an officer when deciding whether reasonable suspicion existed?

5. Consider the facts of the **Sokolow** case. If any of the facts listed were removed, do you believe the agents would still have been justified in conducting the search?

KEY TERMS

consent decrees
Agreements between an agency and the courts in which an agency agrees to abide by certain rules; they require agencies to provide certain training for their police officers along with the promise that the department would consider racial profiling issues in establishing policies.

evanescent evidence
Evidence such as a suspect's blood alcohol level or other quick-to-be-destroyed evidence.

exigent circumstances
Circumstances under which law enforcement personnel may enter a building or other structure without a search warrant, acting on the basis that people are in imminent danger, evidence is about to be destroyed, or that a suspect is going to escape.

inventory searches
Searches that occur when the police examine the contents of a vehicle designated to be stored on the police impound lot or examine the personal items of a defendant upon arrest.

plain feel rule
This doctrine allows an officer to identify an object as being contraband based simply on touching the item, as in a pat-down search, without visual confirmation of the object.

plain view
This doctrine states that an officer may seize anything that is clearly in her field of vision, regardless of probable cause or permission to search by owner.

protective sweep
This refers to a search of the area of the person's arm span, the area under their control when they are being arrested, and the area surrounding the arrestee.

warrantless searches
The scope of a warrantless search allows the officers to search beyond the individual being taken into custody, and usually includes the person's arm span or grabbing area.

KEY COURT CASES

Arizona v. Gant
The **Gant** court considered whether the search of a passenger compartment in a car should be undertaken only when the passenger compartment is within the reaching distance of the suspect. The Court ruled that the search of a vehicle without a warrant may take place in three circumstances: (1) when an arrestee is within reaching distance of the vehicle or it is reasonable to believe the vehicle contains evidence of the office of arrest, (2) when safety or evidentiary concerns demand, and (3) when there is probable cause to believe that a certain area of the vehicle might contain evidence of a crime.

Arizona v. Hicks
This case involved a call to the police that a gunshot had come through the floor of a duplex, from the first story to the second story. The police responded and entered without a warrant, due to emergency circumstances. They spotted an expensive stereo that looked out of place, and an officer picked it up to

examine the serial number. He called it in, and learned that it was, indeed, stolen. The Supreme Court ruled that the plain view rule did not apply in this case, since the officer had to move the piece of equipment to see the serial number. However, the decision seemed to imply that if the officer had been able to view the serial number without moving the equipment, he may have been able to justify its seizure under the plain view doctrine.

California v. Acevedo

This case ruled that officers can search a closed container in a vehicle without a warrant as long as probable cause exists to believe that the container holds contraband or evidence.

Carroll v. United States

This is the landmark case dealing with searches of automobiles. In upholding the National Prohibition Act, the Supreme Court noted that Congress has always recognized a difference between the search of a vehicle and the search of a home, mainly because of the movable nature of a vehicle.

Chimel v. California

In this case, the Court ruled that the officers went too far in the search of Chimel's entire house, and that a warrantless search incident to a lawful arrest permits officers to search the area that is in the possession or under the control of the person arrested.

Minnesota v. Dickerson

In this plain feel case, the Court stated that an officer who bases his seizure of an item on the plain touch doctrine may "feel an object whose contour or mass makes its identity immediately apparent, [and must prove that] there has been no invasion of the suspect's privacy beyond that already authorized by the officer's search for weapons." The Court ruled that in the **Dickerson** case, the officer could not tell what the object was simply by feel.

Payton v. New York

This case dealt with the legality of a police officer entering a person's home to arrest him without a warrant. The Court ruled that searches and seizures inside a home without a warrant are "presumptive and unreasonable." Further, the Court stated that the "Fourth Amendment protects the individual's privacy in a variety of settings. . . . The right of the people to be secure in their . . . houses . . . shall not be violated."

Tennessee v. Garner

The most famous Supreme Court case dealing with the use of force in making arrests. The Court held that lethal force can be used when a law enforcement officer possesses probable cause to believe that the suspect is armed and dangerous and that the suspect poses a significant threat of death or serious physical injury to the officer or to others.

Terry v. Ohio

This is the case that established the "stop and frisk" exception, which says that an officer may conduct a limited pat-down search of a person if certain requirements are met and reasonable suspicion exists.

United States v. Chadwick

This case involved the search of luggage spotted on Amtrak and loaded into an automobile trunk, where the Court ruled that search incident to lawful arrest is considered an exigency and a search without warrant is thus allowable.

United States v. Watson

In this case, the Court found that the arrest without a warrant was reasonable, based on the common law rule that a peace officer could arrest someone without a warrant if a misdemeanor is committed in his presence or for a felony even if it is not committed in his presence.

Whren v. United States

In this case, the officers had reason to believe that the defendants violated traffic rules, so they had enough probable cause to pull over the vehicle, regardless of whether they normally would have pulled over a vehicle for that particular traffic violation. The Court upheld police officer's discretion in determining what laws to enforce in a situation.

THE EXCLUSIONARY RULE

5

LEARNING OBJECTIVES: Students will

1. Understand what the exclusionary rule is
2. Understand what the alternatives to the exclusionary rule are and why the exclusionary rule is utilized as opposed to those alternatives
3. Know the many exceptions to the exclusionary rule
4. Know other remedies for police misconduct in addition to the exclusionary rule

All of the provisions of the Constitution that provide individual rights are to some extent useless if there is no remedy that can be enforced when those provisions are not upheld by law enforcement entities. If a police officer breaks into a home for no reason or simply because he wishes to harass someone and he finds an illegal substance in that individual's home, it would be unfortunate if all the individual could do is say "You just violated the Bill of Rights! Where is your probable cause?" That person could still end up being convicted of a crime, being imprisoned, and having a criminal record. It remains a mystery as to why the framers of the Constitution would give citizens, specifically defendants, so many rights without also specifically providing a remedy to be implemented when those rights are violated. The **exclusionary rule** provides this remedy by permitting the exclusion of evidence at trial if it was obtained by law enforcement agencies in violation of the Fourth Amendment. However, before the exclusionary rule was adopted by the Supreme Court, no remedies existed for improper and unconstitutional police behavior. Illegally seized evidence could still be used in court against a defendant.

HISTORY AND DEVELOPMENT OF THE EXCLUSIONARY RULE

Historically, English courts excluded evidence in criminal cases that was obtained forcibly or illegally. (In civil cases, parties were forced to provide evidence pertaining to their case to the court even if it would be used against them, so the rule clearly only applied to criminal cases, as it does now in the United States.) However, in 1783 and thereafter, evidence obtained as a result of an involuntary confession was sometimes used in English court cases. Even when these courts chose to use the exclusionary rule, the ramifications were not as strong as the rule developed later by the Supreme Court of the United States when it interpreted the related provisions of the Constitution. The exclusionary rule, as it is used in the United States, is still viewed as a reaction by the framers to the unfair practices used by the English courts to prosecute individuals.

The exclusionary rule was first recognized in the United States in 1886 in the federal case of **Boyd v. United States.**[1] **Boyd** was actually a civil case which involved a person's property being taken by the government in forfeiture proceedings. **Forfeiture proceedings** involve the government's ability to take private property from an individual when the individual has utilized the property in committing a crime or has obtained the property as a result of the commission of a crime. The "forfeited" items you see "for sale" by the government, including houses and expensive vehicles, are items that have been taken from private individuals in civil forfeiture proceedings. Proceeds obtained by the government in reselling the items are generally utilized to fund programs that combat crime. In the **Boyd** case, Boyd argued that the forfeiture proceeding in effect resulted in criminal penalties. Further, he stated that the Constitution should protect him because the forfeiture proceeding involved the government subpoenaing invoices from him to obtain information that would support the request for forfeiture, forcing him to be a witness against himself, which would be a violation of the Constitution. The Supreme Court agreed with Boyd, stated that he was in fact being forced to testify against himself, and ruled that the evidence that was seized could not be used against Boyd in court.

The Supreme Court again relied on the exclusionary rule to exclude evidence that was seized in violation of the provisions of the Constitution in federal cases in the case of **Weeks v. United States.**[2] Weeks's house was entered by a federal marshal who had been working with a local police agency and investigating Weeks's participation in an illegal lottery. The marshal seized papers and refused to return them to Weeks, because the prosecutor intended to use them to prosecute Weeks. Weeks argued for the return of his papers and prevailed; the papers were returned to him and the prosecution was thus halted. However, the rationale utilized by the Supreme Court in permitting the return of the paperwork was the fact that the government was holding property that rightfully belonged to Weeks. The Court did not state as its rationale any indication that the exclusionary rule would exclude such evidence from court.

---

1. 116 U.S. 616 (1886).
2. 232 U.S. 383 (1914).

Despite the fact that the Bill of Rights was added to the Constitution for the purpose of protecting citizens from overreaching actions of the government, the Supreme Court did not mandate that states adhere to the exclusionary rule until the 1960s. Further, the exclusionary rule has been determined to be a rule that was created by the Supreme Court and not based on any specific language within the Constitution. When the Supreme Court began to consider the remedies for violations of the search and seizure provisions of the Constitution, numerous options were available. Consider the following remedies and the effect that the use of each would have on the various parts of the criminal justice system, including the victim, the defendant, the public, and, most importantly, the ability of law enforcement agencies to do their job.

Alternatives to the Exclusionary Rule

What other options did the Supreme Court have for enforcing the search and seizure provisions of the Fourth Amendment? The choices would depend on the Court's reasons for enforcing the provisions of the Bill of Rights: to punish the officer who did not follow the Constitution, or to aid the individual whose rights were violated. Some remedies that would punish the officer who violated an individual's rights would still leave the accused with a conviction based on the evidence acquired in violation of the Constitution. Some options are impractical based on their expense. Still others might leave a law enforcement officer hesitant to perform the duties of the job, especially if the law is not 100 percent clear. Consider the following options from the perspective of a police officer. How might each change your daily policing activities?

Option One: Punishing the Law Enforcement Officer. A police officer who obtained evidence in violation of the Constitution could be "punished" by the court or by her employer. However, punishing an officer in order to enforce the provisions of the Constitution would not come without a price. You will see as you continue your study of the Constitution and of Supreme Court cases that sometimes it is difficult for even the brightest of legal scholars to predict how the Court's decision in a particular case will apply to a future specific factual scenario. Thus, officers would be in constant fear of being fired from their jobs if the choices they made on how to apply the law were later found by the Court to be unconstitutional. Officers might then choose not to fulfill the required duties of their employment because of the fear that they might be fired or disciplined after making choices with which a Court did not later agree. Separating officers from employment due to constitutional violations might also result in police forces with few experienced officers, as a high rate of turnover would exist. Further, relieving officers of their duties does not help the person whose rights were violated. If a defendant finds himself in prison as the result of evidence obtained during an illegal search and seizure, the discipline of the officer will not affect his loss of freedom.

Option Two: Filing a Civil Lawsuit Against the Law Enforcement Officer or Law Enforcement Agency. Another option when a constitutional violation occurs is for the citizen whose rights have been violated to file a civil lawsuit against the officer and his police department. However, this would rarely be a practical option. First of all, the length of time it could take for a civil lawsuit to be completed would often be longer than the amount of time for which the aggrieved citizen is being incarcerated. Second, legal costs to file a civil lawsuit are high and therefore such an option is often impossible for an individual who is incarcerated and has no source of income. Third, the result of even the most successful lawsuit would be that the defendant would receive money from the officer. This, again, would not erase time spent in prison and the individual's criminal record that would be with him throughout his life. There is also little hope that the individual would receive a large award at the end of the lawsuit. Many legal analysts indicate that juries generally favor police officers in civil trials and are not apt to give large monetary awards to convicted criminals. Further, many officers would not be willing to risk their lives on a daily basis in their jobs if they knew that their personal assets could be taken away based on a decision that was later determined by a court to be unconstitutional. This would mean that few individuals would apply for policing jobs. Finally, many police agencies are immune from lawsuits by state law, barring individuals from being able to bring a lawsuit regardless of the validity of the underlying claim. Even if a defendant received a judgment for a $1 million against an officer as a result of his lawsuit, if the officer does not possess $1 million worth of assets, that judgment might never be collected. Even if this issue could be remedied by permitting the defendant to sue the police agency instead of or in addition to suing the police officer, money paid to the municipality by taxpayers would be used to satisfy that judgment, which would place a burden on society and leave less funding available to police agencies for protection of the public.

Option Three: Excluding the Evidence from Court. The third option available to a person whose constitutional rights have been violated is the option that the Supreme Court adopted. The exclusionary rule has been adopted by the Supreme Court and applies to both federal and state law enforcement agencies. This rule states that any evidence that is seized as the result of an unconstitutional search and seizure will be excluded from being introduced against the defendant in a criminal court of law. The exclusionary rule is more concerned with how evidence is acquired than whether evidence of criminal conduct exists that would prove that the defendant is guilty of a crime, and thus it has been the subject of much controversy by legal scholars.

An argument can be made that if the courts wish to deter law enforcement officers from violating the constitution, then the first two options discussed previously, and not the exclusionary rule, are the best options. Even the Supreme Court has agreed that the goal of any remedy is to deter police from violating the Constitution. Firing or disciplining the officer or filing a lawsuit against her certainly could deter a law enforcement officer from purposefully violating the Constitution if her intention was to purposefully violate someone's rights. However, this argument fails when it is acknowledged that most officers do not purposefully violate the Constitution. As discussed earlier, most officers do their jobs as best they can, but the ever changing status of the law sometimes prohibits officers from being able to follow the law no matter how hard they try. Although some may argue that having evidence thrown out of court in a criminal case does not directly affect a police officer who violates the Constitution, others argue that no officer wants to be the person who caused a criminal to walk free because his unconstitutional actions resulted in the exclusion of evidence at trial. Thus, it is assumed that the exclusionary rule does in fact deter law enforcement officers as well as protect the rights of citizens. It is impossible to measure how many citizens have been spared from unconstitutional police behavior because an officer was deterred due to the existence of the exclusionary rule.

The exclusionary rule has been determined by the Supreme Court to be the most effective way to remedy and attempt to prevent constitutional violations in the area of search and seizure, but its use has nevertheless been criticized. The use of the exclusionary rule costs society in that guilty people do go free. Some argue that the rule also causes disrespect toward the criminal justice system and law enforcement officials by the public. The public becomes very cynical when a person who is clearly guilty of a crime is able to avoid prosecution due to what many refer to as a "technicality." Some argue that the rule does not deter because some officers still might wish to hassle an individual even if they never obtain a criminal conviction against that person. The rule also does not necessarily result in remedying the inappropriate conduct that has been promulgated against the defendant, as the harassment that accompanies an improper search has already taken place. As you become familiar with the cases in this chapter of the text, consider the alternatives the Supreme Court could have used to remedy the issues brought before it and the effects that you believe the Supreme Court's use of one of the alternative remedies to the exclusionary rule would have had on each case.

History of the Rule in Federal Court

Despite cases that allowed a defendant to use the rule in the federal court system, the Supreme Court stubbornly refused to require that the state courts use the rule. In **Wolf v. Colorado**,[3] the defendant was convicted in state court for conspiracy to perform criminal abortions. Had he been tried in federal court, the evidence used to convict him would have been excluded from court under the Fourth Amendment search and seizure provisions. The question considered by the Supreme Court was whether the inadmissibility of

---

3. 338 U.S. 25 (1949).

YOU BE THE JUDGE

You are in charge of a police agency and one of your officers has violated an individual's constitutional rights due to his negligence. The officer had received information that a man who had escaped from prison was at a home at 324 East Wallace Street. The officer decided to drive to the house to see if he could capture the man. He did not write down the address, and while he was driving, he was distracted and ended up going to 342 East Wallace Street. He knocked on the door and heard some "shuffling noises" inside; this made him think that someone was trying to hide from him. He broke down the door of the house and found two people inside; neither person matched the description of the escaped convict. Nonetheless, the officer searched through all areas of the house, opening drawers, breaking items, and throwing things. He found a small amount of marijuana in a drawer in the kitchen, and the residents were later charged with possession of a small amount of marijuana. Assume that the court is going to exclude the evidence from court, but you are responsible for disciplining the officer. What actions could you take and what do you believe the result of those actions would be in terms of (1) deterring that officer from doing something like this again and (2) deterring other officers from committing this sort of act?

the evidence in federal court required that the evidence be inadmissible in state court as well. The case does not set forth exactly what evidence was seized or how it was seized, but the defendant argued that evidence that was used against him in court was seized in violation of the Constitution. He wished to invoke the use of the exclusionary rule to request that the evidence be banned from being presented in court. The Supreme Court ruled that the evidence could be used, stating that although the exclusionary rule provides one way to deter law enforcement officers from engaging in unreasonable searches and seizures, other remedies were available and thus could be used by the defendant. The Supreme Court determined that it did not want to incorporate the exclusionary rule to the states and that the Fourteenth Amendment does not require the states to exclude evidence that is illegally obtained due to the existence of other possible remedies.

The majority opinion in **Wolf** took the stance that most states and even some other countries had taken in terms of the exclusionary rule. The Court stated that "in fact most of the English-speaking world does not regard as vital to such protection the exclusion of evidence thus obtained" and that, thus, the Court "must hesitate to treat this remedy as an essential ingredient of the right." The Court also pointed out that as of the date of its decision in **Wolf**, 31 states had rejected the **Weeks** doctrine and 16 states were in agreement with it, and that of the 10 jurisdictions within the United Kingdom and the British Commonwealth of Nations that had considered the question of the exclusion of evidence obtained by illegal search and seizure, none had decided that such evidence should be inadmissible. The four dissenting judges in the **Wolf** case stated that the majority's decision really leaves defendants with no effective remedy for constitutional violations in state courts. The dissenting judges indicated that the alternatives to the exclusionary rule are "deceptive." In fact, they opined, the only true alternative to the exclusionary rule is the alternative of no sanction at all. The judges stated that rarely will prosecutors prosecute a police officer for "overzealously enforcing the law" and that damages obtained by a person in a civil action against the police would be minimal.

Application of the Rule to the States

Although states cannot take away a right that has been given by the Supreme Court, states can provide more rights than the Supreme Court mandates. Despite the Court's decision in the **Wolf** case, some states decided to adopt the exclusionary rule for defendants who were prosecuted in their states. However, they did so with qualifications, excluding certain types of cases. The Supreme Court finally incorporated the exclusionary rule to all state criminal cases in 1961 in **Mapp v. Ohio**.[4] The Supreme Court had first suggested, though not required, that the rule should be followed by states in language included in the case of **Elkins v. United States**.[5] In **Elkins**, the Court denounced what it referred to as the **silver platter doctrine**, referring to the fact that defendants in federal court had the benefit of the exclusionary rule but defendants in state courts do not. In other words, the Court felt that individuals who faced prosecution in federal court were being treated better than those in state court.

MAPP V. OHIO

FACTS: Three police officers in Cleveland, Ohio, arrived at Mapp's door, stating that they believed that a person who was wanted for questioning in connection with a recent bombing was hiding at her house and that there was a large amount of illegal "paraphernalia" being hidden in her home as well. Mapp telephoned her attorney and refused to admit the officers without a search warrant. The officers left Mapp's house but arrived again three hours later, with more officers in tow, forcibly opened her door, and waved a paper at her, claiming it was a warrant. Mapp grabbed the paper and placed it in her bosom; the paper was then taken away by a police officer while Mapp was handcuffed by the police. The officers then searched Mapp's house and located illegal "obscene materials." No search

---

4. 367 U.S. 643 (1961).
5. 364 U.S. 206 (1960).

warrant was ever produced. The materials were admitted into evidence against Mapp at trial and she was ultimately convicted of possession of obscene materials. Mapp appealed to the Supreme Court, arguing that the evidence that had been seized from her without a warrant was seized illegally and that it thus should not be presented as evidence against her in court.

ISSUE: Whether state trial courts must exclude evidence that is seized illegally.

HOLDING: State courts must exclude illegally seized evidence.

RATIONALE: The **Mapp** Court determined that the evidence of the obscene materials should be suppressed and that states should recognize the exclusionary rule. The Court stated that "[n]othing can destroy a government more quickly than its failure to observe its own laws, or worse, its disregard of the charter of its own existence." The Court reasoned that the integrity of the criminal justice system was more important than the concern of a guilty criminal defendant being set free. The Court further stated that "our holding that the exclusionary rule is an essential part of both the Fourth and Fourteenth Amendments is not only the logical dictate of prior cases, but it also makes very good sense. There is no war between the Constitution and common sense."

Keep in mind that ultimately, the exclusion of evidence does not always result in the dismissal of a case. Consider the following scenario:

> An officer enters and searches a person's house in violation of the Constitution. The officer finds a list of customers to which marijuana is being sold, along with money and a pager with customers' phone numbers. Simultaneously, another officer confronts the owner of the house on the sidewalk and has probable cause to legally conduct a search of the person. That search also results in the finding of marijuana on that person in the form of several baggies that each contain about one ounce of marijuana.

At the trial of the homeowner, evidence of the possession of the baggies of marijuana can be presented to the jury but, absent the argument of some exception to this rule applying in this case, the court will not allow the presentation of evidence that was found in the house. This could make a difference as to the number or types of charges that are filed, but in the long run charges can still be pressed. In any case, if enough legally obtained evidence is available, a person can be convicted of a crime even after all illegally obtained evidence has been excluded. The evidence located in the house would be helpful in prosecuting the defendant but a jury would probably also be able to find that the defendant possessed marijuana with the intent to deliver it based solely on the finding of the baggies on his person.

The exclusionary rule applies to evidence obtained illegally under the Fourth Amendment, but it also has been expanded to protect rights provided for in other amendments, including "involuntary" confessions, unfair iden-tification procedures, and other methods of obtaining evidence that might "shock the conscience" of the court; some cases that fall within this category will be discussed later.

REASONS FOR THE RULE

As stated earlier, the exclusionary rule is needed in order to deter police offi-cers from engaging in inappropriate, unconstitutional, and illegal conduct. As also discussed in this chapter, sometimes an officer's behavior might not be changed by the exclusionary rule, because a court could rule that an officer's actions are unconstitutional years after the action actually takes place due to the amount of time that generally lapses before a case travels all the way through the lower and higher courts. However, we can assume that an officer would not want the cases he investigated to be thrown out of court and a criminal set free because the officer failed to do his job in accordance with the provisions of the Constitution.

The Supreme Court had also rationalized that the purpose of the exclu-sionary rule is to maintain the integrity of the judiciary. Courts are charged with maintaining citizens' fundamental rights and enforcing the provisions of the Constitution and, specifically, the Bill of Rights. Thus, courts should actively pursue a system in which no unconstitutionally obtained evidence is presented by the prosecution. In setting forth this rationale, the Supreme Court has stated that judges who allow evidence that was obtained unconsti-tutionally to be used would be "accomplices in the . . . disobedience of a con-stitution they are sworn to uphold."[6] However, recent Court decisions have, in effect, abandoned this rule, stating that deterrence is the primary purpose of the rule.

THE EXCLUSIONARY RULE IN COURT

Standing to Assert the Rule

Certain issues that arise in the area of constitutional law are considered **threshold issues**. Threshold issues are those that must be considered by a court before entertaining any other issues in the case—in other words, if the threshold issue is decided in a certain way, the entire case could be thrown out regardless of the merits of the other underlying issues. An overriding issue in any defendant's criminal case is the question of whether that particular defendant can even argue an issue before the court. This question concerns

---

6. **Elkins** *supra*.

whether a person has **standing**. Assume that your sister is involved in a car accident, having been hit from behind by a driver who is texting while driving. Your sister most certainly has the right to bring a lawsuit against the evil texter, as she was harmed by the texter's actions. However, can you bring a lawsuit against him? Generally, you would have no reason to bring such a lawsuit, and would not have standing to do so. However, what if your sister was driving your car at the time? Or what if you had a physical disability and your sister was your caregiver, and following the accident she was no longer able to care for you? These circumstances might cause the court to rule that you do have standing to bring some sort of action against the texter, as you have been directly harmed by the texter's actions.

The same type of analysis exists in criminal cases. Who has the right to bring the issue of a constitutional violation to the attention of the court and ask for relief? Remember, in criminal court, the remedy is not one of money; rather, the person whose rights are violated receives the benefit of his evidence being thrown out of court. Thus, does any person against whom evidence is being used in court have the ability to have the court consider whether that evidence should be excluded from court? The issue of standing is also considered a **threshold issue**, like that of government action, which is discussed later in this chapter. Thus, the Court must consider standing before it even determines whether a search or seizure has occurred. If a court decides that a person does not have standing to bring an issue in front of the court, the court will not consider that issue, no matter how heinous or unconstitutional the behavior of the government in the situation is.

The courts have wrestled with this issue and have come up with some guidelines that may surprise you. To understand this concept, remember that the Court has decided that only someone who has a "legitimate expectation of privacy" in an item can assert constitutional protection over that item. The Court has taken a **case-by-case** approach to this issue, which means that in each particular case the court will determine the particular complainant's expectation of privacy in an item, based on all of the circumstances surrounding the situation.

The Supreme Court has held that if a person owns (or has the right to possess) a particular place, then that person has standing to argue against any search within that place. Further, if the person lives in a particular place, he or she will have standing to argue about any search of that place. In other words, if you own a house, you have standing to argue its search. Further, if you live in that house, either as a renter or as a person who is permitted to live there for free (by a family member or friend), you will also have standing to argue when that place is searched. Finally, if you are an overnight guest in a hotel room or in someone else's house, you may have standing to argue if that place is searched and your items are recovered.[7] The Court assumes that we expect

---

7. **Minnesota v. Olson**, 495 U.S. 91 (1990).

privacy in a hotel room or a friend's house that we are staying in just like we expect privacy in our own home.

The rule set by the Supreme Court that has had the biggest impact on individuals in terms of standing involves issues surrounding the search of automobiles. As you have learned, the Court has significantly relaxed rules regarding the search and seizure of vehicles, and standing is no exception. Passengers in automobiles who have no particular argument that they own the vehicle do not automatically have standing to argue against a search. Furthermore, mere ownership of a piece of property does not invoke standing rights. For example, if a defendant's illegally owned sawed-off shotgun is in someone else's vehicle and is seized by the police in an unconstitutional manner, that defendant does not have standing to argue the constitutionality of the seizure.

The Court has rejected developing an "automatic standing" rule. The argument for automatic standing is best described by example. In accordance with the previous rules, if I want to assert that I have standing to argue that an item was seized illegally based on the fact that the item was in my vehicle, I will have to admit that the vehicle is mine. Perhaps one of the arguments I will want to make at my trial is that I did not own the vehicle in which the seized contraband was found. In such a case, the Supreme Court originally stated that a person would have automatic standing to challenge the search; however, the Court later overturned that rule and stated instead that any statements made at a suppression hearing regarding the ownership of the contraband could not be utilized against the person in subsequent proceedings, such as at his trial. Thus, defendants are required to have a full suppression hearing, giving testimony as to why they had an interest in the item.

Further, some defendants who were charged as co-conspirators argued that if their co-conspirator had standing to argue against a search and seizure, they should automatically have standing as well. These defendants argued for an automatic rule allowing co-conspirator standing. The Supreme Court disagreed with this request in the case of **United States v. Padilla**.[8]

UNITED STATES V. PADILLA

FACTS: An officer in Arizona followed a Cadillac that had passed his patrol car, as he thought the driver of the Cadillac acted "suspiciously." He eventually stopped the car for driving too slowly and Luis Arciniega, the driver and sole occupant of the car, produced his license and an insurance card that showed that the Cadillac was owned by a man named Donald Simpson, who was a United States Customs agent. The officer and another officer who had been called to the stop believed that Arciniega matched the drug courier profile and they asked Arciniega if they

---

8. 508 U.S. 77 (1993).

could search the vehicle. Arciniega agreed and the officers found 560 pounds of cocaine in the trunk. They arrested Arciniega, and Arciniega agreed to work with the police to make a controlled sale of the cocaine.

Arciniega telephoned Jorge Padilla and Maria Padilla, who met him at a hotel and attempted to drive away in the Cadillac. They were arrested and agreed to cooperate with law enforcement, leading them to the house where Maria Padilla and her husband, Xavier Padilla, were staying. The officers determined that Donald Simpson and his wife, Maria Simpson, were all linked to Xavier Padilla; all three were arrested and charged with conspiracy to distribute and possess with intent to distribute cocaine. Xavier Padilla was also charged with engaging in a continuing criminal enterprise. The defendants moved to suppress all evidence discovered in the course of the investigation, arguing that the evidence was the fruit of the unlawful investigatory stop of Arciniega's vehicle.

The issue centered on who could argue about the evidence found in the vehicle, due to the fact that the vehicle was only occupied by one person, who was not charged with a crime, at the time it was searched. The people who were charged argued that because the evidence in the car belonged to them, they should be able to argue about the search in court. Further, the owner of the car was not in the car at the time of the stop, so can he argue that he has standing to contest the use of the evidence in court?

ISSUE: Does a person have standing to argue the constitutionality of the search of a vehicle merely because that person is being charged as a co-conspirator of someone who might have standing?

HOLDING: The Court held that merely being a co-conspirator in a case does not give rise to standing to argue that a search and seizure was inappropriate.

RATIONALE: The Court remanded the case to the trial court to determine whether each individual had either a property interest protected by the Fourth Amendment that was interfered with by the stop of Arciniega's automobile or a reasonable expectation of privacy that was invaded by the search thereof. The Court stated that "Expectations of privacy and property interests govern the analysis of Fourth Amendment search and seizure claims. Participants in a criminal conspiracy may have such expectations or interests, but the conspiracy itself neither adds to nor detracts from them. Neither the fact, for example, that Maria Simpson was the "communication link" between her husband and the others, nor the fact that Donald Simpson and Xavier Padilla were in charge of transportation for the conspirators, has any bearing on their respective Fourth Amendment rights."

Because of the Court's strict rules regarding standing, not every criminal defendant can request the application of the exclusionary rule merely because he feels that the evidence somehow affects his case. Remember, the rule is a remedy which can assist certain defendants by prohibiting evidence from being used against them, but the focus is on the use of that evidence in a specific case, not on the desire to punish the actions of a police officer who seizes evidence wrongfully. Thus, if a court decides that the evidence being used in a proceeding is being offered against a person whose rights were not violated by the law enforcement agency, the person will not have standing to complain about the action, which means the court will not even consider the merits of whether the evidence should be excluded.

As the Supreme Court stated in the case of **Rakas v. Illinois,**[9] "fourth amendment rights are personal rights that may not be asserted vicariously." Thus, only the person who a court has found was "aggrieved" by the action of a law enforcement agent can argue that a Fourth Amendment violation has taken place. A court will consider whether the person had a "possessory interest" in the items seized, as well as whether the person had a legitimate expectation of privacy in the place that was invaded. The phrase "expectation of privacy" will be discussed fully in Chapter 6, but it will be discussed here as it relates to the issue of standing to assert the exclusionary rule.

In the **Rakas** case, a police officer who was on patrol received a radio call that reported a robbery of a clothing store in Bourbonnais, Illinois, and described the vehicle in which the robbers had fled. The officer spotted an automobile that matched the description of the getaway car and he followed it for some time and then, obtaining backup from some other officers, stopped the vehicle. Four people were in the vehicle; the male defendants in the case and two female passengers. The occupants of the car were ordered to get out of the car, and the interior of the car was searched. The search resulted in the discovery of a sawed-off rifle under the front passenger seat, as well as a box of rifle shells in the locked glove box. The owner of the car was the driver of the car at the time the vehicle was stopped and was not charged with a crime. However, the defendants were arrested and were tried for armed robbery and the items were introduced against the defendants by the prosecution. Neither of the defendants owned the vehicle or the items that were seized.

At trial, the defendants objected against the introduction of the evidence on the ground that the search and seizure violated their Fourth and Fourteenth Amendment rights. Previously, in the case of **Jones v. United States,**[10] the Court had established that any person against whom a search was "directed" would have standing to contest the legality of that search and to object to the admission at trial of evidence obtained as a result of the search. The defendants in this case argued that because they were legitimately in the vehicle at the time of the search, as they were invited passengers, they should be able to argue about the evidence under the rule set forth in the **Jones** case. The Supreme Court ruled that the defendants could not argue any search and seizure issues because they did not have standing to do so, because the car and

---

9. 439 U.S. 128 (1978).
10. 362 U.S. 257 (1960).

the items did not belong to them. The Court reasoned that the defendants did not have any expectation of privacy in the vehicle because it did not belong to them and that they also failed to demonstrate that they had complete control over the vehicle because it was not titled in their names. Interestingly, the Court stated in support of its reasoning that "[e]ach time the exclusionary rule is applied it exacts a substantial social cost for the vindication of Fourth Amendment rights" due to the fact that people who have committed crimes do sometimes walk free.

The Court concurred that although no Fourth Amendment suppression allegations could be sustained by these defendants, they still possessed civil remedies available to them such as seeking to recover damages from the police or to seek redress under state law for invasion of privacy or trespass. However, as discussed in this chapter, those remedies are not as helpful to the defendants as the exclusion of the evidence would be.

The Court contrasted the facts of the **Rakas** case with those of the **Jones** case in order to explain when a person might have standing although not the owner of the area that is searched. The **Jones** case involved a defendant who had permission to use the apartment of a friend, and although he had no key to the apartment, he did keep some of his possessions in the apartment on a regular basis. He had, according to the Court, "complete dominion and control" over the apartment, other than the ability of his friend who owned the apartment to enter at will, and he also possessed the ability to keep other people from entering the apartment. Thus, the Court agreed that a person visiting someone else or residing with someone else would have standing to argue that law enforcement officials violated the Fourth Amendment and that evidence should be excluded, as, in the Court's opinion, those types of persons have an expectation of privacy in that place where the passenger of a car does or should not.

The Court's dissenting opinion stated that the majority opinion declares "open season" on automobiles in terms of searches. The dissent stated that a person who is legitimately present in a private place should be protected from reasonable governmental interference even if he does not own the premises, and that cars and houses should be the same in terms of that protection. The dissent suggested that at some point there might be too many people present in one place to argue that all have a legitimate expectation of privacy in the place, but that a car with four individuals in it should not be included in that group. (Assumedly a bus full of people or a houseful of people would fall within that category.) Finally, the dissent stated that the majority court's ruling really undercuts the force of the exclusionary rule in the area of "bad faith" actions by police. The dissent opined that the "decision invites police to engage in patently unreasonable searches every time an automobile contains more than one occupant. Should something be found, only the owner of the vehicle, or of the item, will have standing to seek suppression, and the evidence will presumably be usable against the other occupants. . . .After this decision, police will have little to lose by unreasonably searching vehicles occupied by more than one person."

In a later Supreme Court case, **Rawlings v. Kentucky**,[11] the Supreme Court further discussed the issue of a person's expectation of privacy as it relates to his standing to be able to argue for the suppression of evidence. In the **Rawlings** case, the police searched the purse of an individual and found criminal items belonging to the defendant in that purse. Both the individual who owned the purse and the defendant were present when the purse was searched. The defendant had known the friend for only a few days and had not previously had access to the purse. The circumstances of the transaction in general did not hint that the defendant took any special actions to maintain his privacy when placing the items in the purse. The Court determined that just because the defendant owned the items, he still did not have enough of an expectation of privacy to argue that he had any right to Fourth Amendment protection in the search of the purse. Thus, the Court indicated that he could not argue about the search, even if the search was a violation of the provisions of the Fourth Amendment.

More recently, defendants have tried to argue that they have standing on the theory of "co-conspirator" standing. In other words, if a person is being tried for conspiracy and his co-conspirator can argue about the seizure of certain evidence, if that evidence is being used against the defendant, the defendant would argue that he too should have automatic standing to try to have a court suppress the evidence. The Supreme Court has disagreed with this argument as well in the case of **United States v. Padilla**,[12] stating that it was at odds with their decision in the **Rakas** case and that the establishment of a legal co-conspirator situation would not establish an ability to argue standing.

Government Action

A second threshold issue that occasionally arises in questionable search and seizure cases is the issue of whether **government conduct** was present in the search. The Supreme Court has stated that government conduct must be present during a search and seizure in order for the constitutional provisions to apply to it.[13] Recall that the purpose of the amendments was primarily to limit the ability of the government to interfere in the lives of citizens, not to control the actions of citizens toward each other. As stated in **United State v. Jacobsen**,[14] the Fourth Amendment is "wholly inapplicable to a search or seizure, even an unreasonable one, effected by a private individual not acting as an agent of the Government or with the participation or knowledge of any government official."

---

11. 448 U.S. 98 (1970).
12. 508 U.S. 77 (1983).
13. **Burdeau v. McDowell**, 256 U.S. 465 (1921).
14. 466 U.S. 109 (1984).

A **government agent** for purposes of proving the existence of governmental conduct in a certain case means either an individual who works for the government *or* an individual who is working with the government and is executing a search and seizure at the direction of or in coordination with a government official. This includes, for example, informants who are working with the local police department and even private security. It does not include private citizens. Thus, if your roommate decides to snoop through your sock drawer and discovers a baggie of marijuana, then turns it over to your campus police department, you cannot argue that the evidence should be excluded from court based on the Fourth Amendment.

BURDEAU V. MCDOWELL

FACTS: Private detectives stole papers from McDowell's office and turned those papers over to a United States prosecutor. The actions of the private detectives were found by the Court to be "egregious." They drilled into McDowell's private safes, broke the locks on his desk and broke into his file cabinets. Burdeau argued that his Fourth Amendment rights had been violated by these actions.

ISSUE: Did the private detectives' actions violate Burdeau's constitutional rights?

HOLDING: Because the government did not know that private detectives had taken the papers unlawfully, Burdeau's constitutional rights were not violated.

RATIONALE: The Supreme Court stated that the origin and history of the Fourth Amendment clearly demonstrate that the amendment was created to place limits on governmental action only. The government did not know that any of these actions had taken place against Burdeau by the private party until several months after the property had been taken. The Court stated in its opinion that "[i]t is manifest that there was no invasion of the security afforded by the Fourth Amendment against unreasonable search and seizure, as whatever wrong was done was the act of individuals in taking the property of another. A portion of the property so taken and held was turned over to the prosecuting officers of the federal government. We assume that petitioner has an unquestionable right of redress against those who illegally and wrongfully took his private property under the circumstances herein disclosed, but with such remedies we are not now concerned."

However, the government cannot use a private entity to do its "dirty work" in the hopes that the Court's reasoning in **Burdeau** would allow its attempt to usurp the Constitution. A fact scenario in which the government had arranged in advance that the private detectives would go into Burdeau's office and obtain the paperwork for it would have allowed Burdeau to prove that government action had been present.

YOU BE THE JUDGE

You are the judge in a drug case that involves the accusation that a defendant had 200 marijuana plants in a growing room in the basement of his house. Police were approached by a man unknown to them who stated that he had information about a "friend's" marijuana operation. The man gave the police details about the friend's house, stating that he knew the following items were in the house: marijuana plants in a room in the corner of the basement, money in a box in a hall closet underneath a pile of blankets, 30 bags of packaged marijuana in a trunk in the basement, and baggies/scales/packaging equipment in a corner cupboard of the kitchen. When officers asked him how he knew all of this, he stated, "I was at his house recently and saw these things." He did not offer further specific information regarding why he was at the man's house and simply kept saying that he was the man's "friend." Based on this information, the police obtain a search warrant and search the house. The items are found in the places that the man stated. Later, the police learn that the man had broken into the defendant's house because he did not like him. He spent quite some time looking through every part of the house in order to find these items. The defendant argues that the police should have known that the man was not a "friend" of his and that a casual "friend" visiting his house would not have seen all of the items that this person saw. The defendant argues that the court should go beyond the rule set forth in the **Burdeau** case and consider the fact that the man broke into the defendant's house and that the officer should have known that an illegal act had been committed. As a judge, which side do you rule for? Why?

The Fourth Amendment also does not apply to private security such as store detectives or employees of private mail organizations such as the United Parcel Service. In **United States v. Moore**,[15] a federal district court considered whether a Federal Express postal service agent was considered a private party or an arm of the government. A manager for Federal Express in Minneapolis was informed that a microwave oven package appeared to be damaged, and following company policy, he opened the package to inspect for damage to the contents. While inspecting the package, the manager noticed that there was an off-white substance inside the box, and he suspected that the white powder was a controlled substance. In accordance with company policy, the manager relayed the package to corporate security officers in Memphis, Tennessee, and they transferred the package to Drug Enforcement Agency (DEA) agent Richard Ripley in Minnesota. Two days later, the manager noticed

---

15. 943 F.2d 884 (8th Cir. 1991).

that a vacuum cleaner box that was being shipped was loosely packaged, so he took it to the rewrap station. When the box was opened, the manager found approximately 20 rolls of currency inside. The manager contacted the DEA directly and resealed the package. The DEA agent reopened the package and found $30,020.00 in currency. Eventually the DEA agent was led to Moore, who was using the alias "Michael Anderson," which was the name on the vacuum cleaner box. The contents of the vacuum cleaner box were used against Moore in a trial for possession with intent to distribute cocaine.

Moore filed a suppression motion, arguing that the search of the vacuum cleaner box was private and that no constitutional protection applied to the search. Moore claimed that the manager's search was conducted with the "encouragement" of DEA agents, which then transformed the search into a government act. Moore argued that the employees at the Federal Express office engaged in a "group effort" to obtain information about certain persons who regularly shipped packages and that the manager opened the package as part of an investigation that was encouraged by the DEA. The court disagreed, as the DEA agent indicated that he never asked or encouraged the manager to search packages on behalf of the DEA. Further, and more importantly, the court also held that even if the manager had suspicions or curiosity about the package and deliberately opened it to see if there was contraband inside, the search would still have been considered private. Moore also argued that because the manager closed the package and caused the DEA agent to reopen it, the DEA agent had no valid reason to search the package. The court held that because the DEA's search did not exceed the scope of the antecedent private search, no error had occurred.

Any person who is acting on the government's behalf, however, such as an informant, is subject to Fourth Amendment rules; the government cannot hire your roommate to search through your drawers when the government itself cannot do so. Obviously, government agencies such as the Federal Bureau of Investigation (FBI), Secret Service, Internal Revenue Service (IRS), and the Bureau of Alcohol, Tobacco, and Firearms are regulated by the Fourth Amendment, as are local and state police agencies. The court considered this issue in **United States v. Feffer**.[16] The **Feffer** court set forth two considerations for a court that wishes to determine whether a private citizen has in fact acted as an agent of the government: (1) whether the government knew and acquiesced in the activity and (2) whether the citizen was motivated to do what he did on the basis of assisting the government. The **Feffer** case involved an employee who turned over to the IRS documents that belong to the company for whom the employee worked; the documents were used by the IRS to prosecute the owners for tax fraud. The employee had spoken to the IRS ahead of time about turning over the documents and then proceeded to locate the documents and turn them over; thus, the defendants argued that the action was not private but that the employee was, in effect, an

---

16. 831 F.2d 734 (7th Cir. 1987).

agent of the IRS when she turned over the documents. The court concluded that the employee's actions were voluntary and not the result of any coercion by or involvement of the IRS. The employee testified that she was scared of being implicated as part of the tax fraud so she decided to turn over the paperwork and contact the IRS. Thus, the court concluded, she would have continued her search for the documents even if the IRS had not been involved.

Presenting Exclusionary Rule Issues

When an attorney believes that evidence should be excluded from court due to the exclusionary rule, the attorney (or a defendant who is representing herself) can file a motion in court requesting that the court rule that the evidence is inadmissible. This type of hearing is often referred to as a **suppression hearing**. This process happens before trial, following the defendant's initial formal processing in the system and the defendant's preliminary hearing or grand jury indictment. The motion should recite the facts that support the request and any law that supports the exclusion of the evidence. The court may then hold a hearing on the issue, and at the hearing, individuals such as the defendant, police officers, and other witnesses may be called to testify as to the facts surrounding the search and seizure or arrest.

One problem regarding this type of hearing is that the defendant may find himself having to testify as to the situation, and in so doing, he may put himself at a disadvantage if the motion is not suppressed and he later has to testify on his own behalf in court. For example, the defendant might have to admit during a suppression hearing that he possessed cocaine, and then describe how the police obtained the cocaine from him. Courts have ruled that, as a general rule, information presented at a suppression hearing cannot later be used in a trial proceeding to attempt to gain the conviction of the defendant. However, the information might be used in court against the defendant if he decides to take the stand at trial and testifies to information that is directly in opposition to what he stated under oath at the suppression hearing. This is one of the many reasons that defendants sometimes invoke their "right to remain silent" and choose not to testify in their own behalf at trial.

Scope of the Exclusionary Rule

The exclusionary rule may extend further than to just an initial illegal search and seizure. Suppose a police officer is aware that a particular search and seizure will be deemed unconstitutional by a court. However, suppose that officer also realizes that by engaging in the search and seizure, he will find information that will lead him to discover further evidence. Can an officer conduct the search in the hopes that the evidence he finds will be admissible in court?

The **fruit of the poisonous tree** rule provides that evidence that is obtained as a result of evidence discovered in an initial illegal search will also be excluded from court. The first suggestion by the Supreme Court of the fruit of the poisonous tree rule is found in **Silverthorne Lumber Co. v. United States**.[17] The Silverthornes, husband and wife, were charged with tax evasion. Federal agents illegally seized tax books from the Silverthornes and copied those records. The federal government then requested that the Silverthornes produce the originals of the records, and the Silverthornes refused. The Court determined that the original documents had, indeed, been seized illegally. The evidence on which the request to produce the originals was based was obtained through the illegal seizure. The Court ruled that because the government would not have had the information to obtain the subpoena without the benefit of the original illegal seizure, the subpoena was invalid.

The fruit of the poisonous tree rule was further established by the Court in the cases of **Nardone v. United States**[18] and **Wong Sun v. United States**.[19] In the **Nardone** case, the government tapped Nardone's phone wires in violation of the Communications Act of 1934[20] and utilized the information it gained in order to prosecute him. The information it obtained was considered a "vital part" of the prosecution's case. The Supreme Court reversed Nardone's conviction on the grounds that the evidence was secured illegally. During Nardone's new trial, the trial judge refused to allow the accused to cross-examine the prosecution about the uses to which it had put the information. Nardone's concern was that the initial information illegally obtained through the telephone tap was then utilized to obtain other information that was used during the second trial. The Supreme Court stated that it must balance the enforcement of the criminal law against the privacy guaranteed to individuals through the Constitution. The Court ruled that indirect use of the evidence would be "inconsistent with ethical standards and destructive of personal liberty."

The **Wong Sun** case was decided years after the **Nardone** case and changed the way police conducted investigations.

WONG SUN V. UNITED STATES

FACTS: A man named Hom Way was arrested and a search revealed heroin in his possession. Way had never previously provided the police with information, but he told the agents that he had purchased the heroin from "Blackie Toy," who owned "Oye's Laundry." Toy opened his door to the agents but, upon discovering the men were agents, he slammed the door shut and ran. The agents broke open the door and arrested Toy in his bedroom. The officers found no evidence of drugs or even that Toy was "Blackie Toy." Toy told the agents that he did not sell drugs but he knew that an individual named "Johnny" did. He gave the agents fairly specific

---

17. 251 U.S. 385 (1920).
18. 308 U.S. 338 (1939).
19. 371 U.S. 471 (1963).
20. 47 U.S.C. §605.

information regarding where Johnny lived, the bedroom where Johnny kept his heroin, and information regarding the place where he had smoked some of the heroin the night before.

Based on the information given to them by Toy, the narcotics agents went to the home of Johnny Yee and found him in possession of an ounce of heroin. Yee told the police that he had purchased the heroin from Toy and an individual who was known as "Sea Dog"; Toy finally told the police that "Sea Dog" was really "Wong Sun." Toy took the agents to Wong Sun's residence where Wong Sun's wife admitted them into the home and where Wong Sun was arrested. The officers found no narcotics on Wong Sun's person; however, each of the individuals was arraigned and released on his own recognizance.

A few days later, Toy, Yee, and Wong Sun were again interrogated and the agents prepared written statements, which were basically confessions, based on the interrogations. Wong Sun admitted to the accuracy of his statements, but neither Toy nor Wong Sun signed their statements. At trial, the government introduced the statements made by Toy at the time he was arrested, the heroin taken from Yee, Toy's pre-trial statement, and Wong Sun's pre-trial statement. Wong Sun and Toy were both convicted of transportation and concealment of heroin.

ISSUE: Were the statements and drugs considered fruit of the poisonous tree because they were obtained from a warrantless search?

HOLDING: The drugs were a primary "fruit" from the illegal search, but the confession was removed from the illegal search and was therefore admissible.

RATIONALE: The Supreme Court ruled that the statements made by Toy were inadmissible because his arrest was unlawful. Further, the narcotics taken from Yee after his arrest were also inadmissible, as Yee's arrest was unlawful. Wong Sun argued that his confession should be excluded as "fruit of the poisonous tree" because the agents' initial entrance into his place of business was illegal. The Supreme Court disagreed, holding that Wong Sun's statement was admissible in Court because it was made following Wong Sun's voluntary trip to the police station. In so holding, the Court required that the evidence to be excluded under the exclusionary rule must directly follow the original illegally seized evidence. The Court stated that the fact that Wong Sun had been released on his own recognizance and that he returned voluntarily to the police station to make his statement made the connection between the arrest and the statement "so attenuated as to dissipate the taint." Thus, the court required that the evidence to be excluded must directly flow from the original illegally seized evidence.

If the fruit of the poisonous tree rule did not exist, police could conduct an illegal search in the hopes of obtaining information that would lead to further evidence that could be utilized in court. An example follows.

The police break into Joe Jackson's home without a warrant and with no probable cause. They find, on Joe's nightstand, a diary. Inside the diary, Joe has written "I killed my neighbor yesterday and buried her underneath the old mill on Cumberland Street." Based only on this evidence, the police go to the old mill and dig up Joe's neighbor's dead body. The body cannot be utilized in court, nor can any forensic evidence obtained from the body, such as Joe's hair fibers or Joe's skin underneath the fingernails of the victim. The police never would have looked at the mill for the neighbor's body had they not read Joe's diary.

It is helpful to think of this rule in terms of the trunk of a tree representing the primary evidence (the diary) while the branches of the tree represent the body and evidence obtained from the body. If any evidence can be seen as a "branch" of the tree coming exclusively from the trunk, the evidence must be excluded under the exclusionary rule. The fruit of the poisonous tree rule was diluted somewhat when the "attenuation" exception, discussed later, was developed by the Supreme Court.

EXCEPTIONS TO THE EXCLUSIONARY RULE

Although the exclusionary rule generally applies to all evidence obtained contrary to the Constitution, there are exceptions to the rule. Courts are concerned with the delicate balance between preserving the rights of each citizen and allowing the introduction of evidence that will result in presenting the truth in criminal proceedings. Thus, there are times when a court may determine that even though a person's rights might have been violated, it is still fair to present certain evidence against that person in court. You will see that each of these exceptions considers the fairness of the presentation of the evidence against the victim of the illegal search.

Inevitable Discovery Rule

The first exception to the exclusionary rule is the **inevitable discovery** rule. This rule states that if police were sure to have discovered the evidence in some other manner notwithstanding the illegal seizure, the evidence can be admitted. For example:

Christopher Cash kidnaps and murders a woman and buries her body under the statue of George Washington in the local park. Local police, acting only on a hunch, illegally break into Cash's house and find his diary. The entry for November 18 reads as follows: "Dear Diary: Today I murdered a woman and buried her under George Washington's statue." The police officers run to the local park and find the body by digging under the statue.

In the meantime, the Federal Bureau of Investigation is also investigating the case due to the fact that it also involves kidnapping, which constitutes a violation of federal law. The FBI is properly and legally conducting surveillance on Cash and he tells a wired, undercover informant that he has killed a person and buried her body underneath the local George Washington statue. The FBI arrives at the park as the local police agency is pulling the body out of the ground.

In this case, prosecutors will be able to present in court the evidence obtained by the local police department (the body) by showing that it was inevitable that the victim's body would have been discovered lawfully by the FBI. The government's burden is merely to prove by a preponderance of the evidence that the evidence would have been discovered lawfully. (As discussed previously in Chapter 1, criminal cases generally require that the government produce proof "beyond a reasonable doubt".) Preponderance of the evidence is a lower standard than beyond a reasonable doubt and thus requires less evidence. The inevitable discovery rule will allow the inclusion of evidence even if the defense can demonstrate that the police purposefully obtained the evidence through unlawful means and that it was the police's specific intent to do so.

In **Nix v. Williams**,[21] the defendant, Williams, was charged with the abduction and murder of a young girl in Des Moines, Iowa. The girl had disappeared from a YMCA building in Des Moines and Williams was seen leaving that building carrying a large bundle wrapped in a blanket. Williams had a 14-year-old boy assist him in carrying the blanket, and the boy stated that there were two legs in the blanket that were "skinny and white." Williams's vehicle was found a day later near Davenport, Iowa, 160 miles east of Des Moines, and items of clothing belonging to the child and a blanket like the one that the 14-year-old boy had described were found between Des Moines and the location of Williams's vehicle. Williams surrendered to police in Davenport and was transported back to Des Moines in a police car. The assumption of the police based on the evidence they had discovered thus far was that the girl's body would be found somewhere in between Des Moines and Davenport. En route, the police officer transporting Williams mentioned to Williams that it could snow in Des Moines and that snow could jeopardize the search for the girl's body, which had not been found. Williams then volunteered the location of the body and the search was canceled. A search was being conducted at that time and had neared the location of the body, but following Williams's disclosure of the location of the body, the body was located and the evidence found was used against Williams at trial.

Williams's attorney moved to suppress all evidence attained after his disclosure to the police, under the theory that the police violated Williams's right to counsel by asking him questions without his attorney present and because of the fact that Williams's **Miranda** rights had not been read to him. The Supreme Court ruled that Williams's statements were inadmissible but ruled that the body would have been found shortly even if Williams had not disclosed its location to the police, so the evidence stemming from the

---

21. 467 U.S. 431 (1984).

discovery of the body could be used against Williams at trial. The Court reasoned that there needs to be a balance between deterring unlawful police conduct and permitting juries to have all probative evidence of a crime. The Court further opined that balancing those two things should not put the police in a worse position than they would have been in if no police error or misconduct had occurred, which would have happened if the courts had allowed the evidence in this case to be excluded.

Independent Source Doctrine

The second exception to the exclusionary rule is the **independent source doctrine**. This doctrine applies when a prosecutor can prove to the court that the evidence challenged by the defendant was not obtained as a result of the initial illegal "poison." For example, in the diary example set forth earlier, if the officers had received information from a reliable informant during the course of their investigation that the body was buried under the statue of George Washington, then the police could prove that the diary did not assist them in finding the body and that the body was discovered solely based on the information given them by the informant. The inevitable discovery rule, discussed previously, is similar. Inevitable discovery cases involve situations such as when the police find something in a person's car before impounding it, but would have been able to lawfully impound the car and performed a routine inventory search anyway. The independent source doctrine involves police finding the same information from two different sources at similar times.

AN OFFICER QUESTIONS A MOTORIST

www.bigstock.com.

The Supreme Court engaged in a balancing test when determining the outcome of cases in which it had allowed the exclusionary rule to be disregarded due to other factors, such as the **Nix** case. The author of the **Nix** opinion, Chief Justice Burger, reasoned that "[t]he independent source doctrine teaches us that the interest of society in determining unlawful police conduct and the public interest in having juries receive all probative evidence of a crime are properly balanced by putting the police in the same, not a worse, position than they would have been in if no police error or misconduct had occurred." The Court reasoned that allowing these types of exceptions would not weaken the possibility of the exclusionary rule's deterrence of police officers.

However, Justice Stevens, in his concurring opinion, expressed concern that the independent source doctrine does present a risk that law enforcement might disregard the Constitution. The Court then reconsidered this doctrine in two cases subsequent to **Nix**. In **Segura v. United States**,[22] federal agents heard that the some individuals, Colon and Segura, were "probably" trafficking cocaine from their apartment. New York Drug Enforcement Task Force agents began surveillance on the defendants and saw a package being exchanged between Colon and an individual named Parra in a restaurant parking lot. Segura was inside the restaurant with an individual named Rivudalia-Vidal. The agents followed Parra and Rivudalia-Vidal to their apartment and stopped and searched them, arresting them when they found that both individuals possessed cocaine. The individuals indicated that they had purchased the cocaine from Segura. The agents arrested the men but were advised that a search warrant for the individuals' apartment probably would not be obtained until the following day. However, the agents were instructed to secure the apartment to prevent any entry or destruction of evidence.

The agents later arrested Segura in the lobby of the building, took him to the apartment and knocked on the door, which was opened by Colon. The agents entered the apartment without requesting or receiving permission from Colon or Segura, conducted what they referred to as a "limited" security check, and observed, in the process, drug paraphernalia. Colon was arrested, and both men were taken into custody, but two agents remained in the apartment waiting for a warrant. The issuance of the search warrant was delayed and it was finally issued 19 hours later. A search was conducted pursuant to the warrant and the agents discovered cocaine and records of narcotics transactions. The men argued that all of the evidence should be suppressed but the Supreme Court disagreed, basing its decision on the fact that no evidence that was found in the initial unwarranted search was set forth in the search warrant application. The warrant, then, was considered an "independent source," unconnected with the initial valid entry.

In the **Segura** case, however, the Supreme Court did not rule on whether the evidence that was seized without a warrant could be lawfully introduced in

---

22. 468 U.S. 796 (1984).

court. That issue was discussed in a similar case decided by the Supreme Court four years after **Segura**, the case of **Murray v. United States**,[23] which uses a slightly different doctrine than the inevitable discovery rule. In the **Murray** case, federal agents suspected that Murray and another individual were involved in illegal drug activities and, placing them under surveillance, observed Murray and others driving vehicles into and out of a warehouse; inside the warehouse, officers could see a tractor-trailer with a long, dark container in it. The vehicles being driven by Murray and the other suspected individuals were turned over to another driver, who was arrested, and the vehicles were lawfully seized. Officers found marijuana in the vehicles. Following receipt of this information, agents forced their way into the warehouse and observed numerous burlap-wrapped bales of a substance in plain view. The agents did not disturb the bales but obtained a warrant to search the warehouse. They did not mention the entry into the warehouse or the fact that they had seen the bales in their request for a search warrant, and the warrant was issued. The agents reentered the warehouse and seized 270 bales of marijuana and other criminal evidence, including a notebook that set forth the destinations of the bales. The Supreme Court indicated that because the second entry, with the warrant, did not result from the first illegal entry but was based on a warrant that was obtained using other, legally gathered information, the search would stand. Thus, the police officers' actions of illegally entering the location would not be considered, because the evidence was seized after the officers obtained a warrant that did not rely on the initially obtained, illegal information.

The independent source doctrine applies when evidence is discovered completely independent of any constitutional violation. According to the Court, the police should be placed in the same position they would have been in had the constitutional error not taken place, but not a worse position. Again, when we understand that the purpose of these exceptions is to deter police conduct and not to "reward" or "make whole" the person whose rights might have been violated, the Court's reasoning makes sense, although it may not make sense to the criminal defendant who is upset because his constitutional rights are being violated. In fact, the **Murray** Court believed that an officer who possessed sufficient probable cause to obtain a search warrant would be foolish to enter the premises without the warrant knowing that he would later have to prove that none of the items seized in the illegal entry were used to obtain the warrant. Further, the Court stated, the officer would have no reason to unlawfully enter the house, as anything that he finds before he obtains a warrant will be excluded from court anyway.

The three dissenting justices in that case, Justices Marshall, Stevens, and O'Connor, disagreed with the majority's reasoning. They stated that the incentives for illegal conduct still exist. According to the justices, "Obtaining a warrant is inconvenient and time consuming. Even when officers have

---

23. 487 U.S. 533 (1988).

probable cause to support a warrant application, therefore, they have an incentive first to determine whether it is worthwhile to obtain a warrant. Probable cause is much less than certainty, and many 'confirmatory' searches will result in the discovery that no evidence is present, thus saving the police the time and trouble of getting a warrant. If contraband is discovered, however, the officers may later seek a warrant to shield the evidence from the taint of the illegal search. The police thus know in advance that they have little to lose and much to gain by forgoing the bother of obtaining a warrant and undertaking an illegal search."

The Attenuation Doctrine

A further exception to the exclusionary rule is the attenuation doctrine. Under this doctrine, a piece of evidence that can be linked to a constitutional violation but only in a "casual" manner could be admissible if the causal link is so "attenuated," or disconnected, that the purpose of the exclusionary rule (deterrence) would not be served even if the evidence was suppressed. Consent searches often raise issues of attenuation. For example, an illegal traffic stop might be initiated by a police officer, but once the stop takes place, the person might consent to a search of his vehicle. Although the stop was illegal, the consent was given freely. Can the defendant then argue that his consent to search should be invalidated because the initial stop was incorrect? The courts generally balance several factors in order to determine how this scenario will play out, looking at such factors as whether **Miranda** warnings were given, the proximity in time between the stop and the consent, the presence of intervening circumstances, and the purpose of the illegal stop. In other words, was the initial stop made solely to harass the person or was it made because the officer was merely mistaken about whether there was probable cause to initiate the stop? The attenuation doctrine is a vague, fact-driven test, and thus it is difficult to predict how a court will decide specific attenuation questions.

Act of Free Will

An act of free will can break the chain of an illegal seizure of evidence and result in the item being admissible in court. As set forth in the **Wong Sun** case, if a person is illegally arrested and confesses at the police station but then leaves the police station and goes back and willingly confesses again, the second confession will be admissible. The Supreme Court has set forth various factors to be considered by a court in determining whether or not an act of free will, including the time lapse between the original taint and the finding of the secondary evidence, whether any other circumstances intervened between the original taint and secondary evidence, and whether any **bad faith** existed on the part of the officers. Bad faith involves an intent to mislead or intentional misconduct on the part of a police officer.

Circumstances That "Shock the Conscience"

The Supreme Court has also provided that some scenarios are so heinous that they "shock the conscience" of the court and thus any evidence obtained must be deemed inadmissible in court. Although this type of situation may be rare, the Supreme Court determined that the facts presented in **Rochin v. California**[24] rose to this level. In **Rochin**, authorities had "some information" that Rochin was selling narcotics. They entered Rochin's house through an open door and then forced open the door to Rochin's bedroom. Rochin was found sitting on the bed, and when the deputies noticed some capsules on the bedside table, Rochin grabbed the capsules and swallowed them. The deputies attempted to extract the capsules by "jumping" on Rochin. Unable to expel the capsules in this manner, the deputies then handcuffed Rochin and took him to the hospital. There, they requested that the doctor pump Rochin's stomach and force him to vomit the capsules. They were found to contain morphine.

Rochin requested that the Supreme Court exclude evidence of the morphine in Court, and the Court agreed. The Court stated that it had a responsibility to uphold due process and that due process requires that evidence be obtained in a manner that does not "shock the conscience" of the court. The Court indicated that verbal or physical evidence would be excluded if it was physically extracted from a person in such a brutal manner and that the evidence would be considered a "coerced confession" and would thus be excluded from court. The Court, in fact, stated that this particular "course of proceeding by agents of the government to obtain evidence is bound to offend even hardened sensibilities. They are methods too close to the rack and screw to permit of constitutional differentiation." However, the Court's decision was limited to the facts of the **Rochin** case and the Court thus did not set forth factors that could be followed by lower courts. Therefore, each lower court faced with the issue would have to decide on its own whether a particular action "shocked its conscience." The **Rochin** case, however, was quite significant in that it was decided prior to the Supreme Court's extension of the exclusionary rule to the states, so the evidence, rather than being excluded under the exclusionary rule, was excluded under the due process clause. Thus, if the Supreme Court decided at some point that the exclusionary rule is not the best approach to illegally seized evidence, the Court's ruling in the **Rochin** case would still apply to police conduct.

Since the **Rochin** decision, the Supreme Court has dealt with other circumstances in which evidence was being obtained from the bodies of suspects. The most prevalent type of case, of course, is that of obtaining the evidence of blood alcohol levels in persons suspected of driving while under the influence of drugs or alcohol. In 1957, the Court upheld a conviction for drunk driving that resulted from a police officer's taking blood from a suspect while the

---

24. 342 U.S. 165 (1952).

suspect was unconscious.[25] The Court stated that this procedure was not considered brutal or offensive. The Court reasoned that because "millions" of American citizens undergo blood tests for various medical reasons every year, such tests should be allowed in order to keep drunk drivers off the road. In that decision, the Supreme Court determined that this type of test did not violate the Fourth Amendment prohibition against unreasonable searches and seizures. The Supreme Court in a later decision ruled that drawing blood from an individual in a suspected drunk driving case did not violate a person's Fifth Amendment right to counsel or a person's right not to incriminate himself.

In **Schmerber v. California,**[26] Armando Schmerber was hospitalized following an automobile accident. Schmerber had been driving at the time of the accident. A police officer smelled liquor on Schmerber's breath, placed him under arrest, and basically gave him his **Miranda** rights. Schmerber, upon the advice of counsel, refused to consent to the taking of a blood sample, but the officer directed a physician to take such a sample and the physician did. The Court reasoned that taking blood from a person was a "minor intrusion" into the body under limited conditions. The Court did note that its decision should not be interpreted to permit "substantial" intrusions into the body.

Another type of case in which the Supreme Court had to determine whether certain procedures in the criminal justice system were appropriate was in determining when body cavity searches could be undertaken.

YOU BE THE JUDGE

You are a judge in a small community. The local police have become very aggressive in policing drunk drivers. One indication that someone is driving drunk is if he violates a traffic rule. Sixteen-year-old Richard Langley was a passenger on the back of a motorcycle driven by his friend, Ivan Simpson, who is 21 years old. Ivan ran through a red light on his motorcycle and failed to stop when the police began to follow him immediately after the violation took place. The police continued to pursue the motorcycle, for more than two minutes, and the pursuit ended when the motorcycle tipped over and the officer's patrol car, traveling at a speed of 45 miles per hour, ran over Langley, who had been ejected from the motorcycle. The case is now in front of you to decide if police pursuits of motor vehicles and motorcycles, "shock the conscience of the court" in accordance with the Supreme Court's reasoning in the Rochin case. What do you decide, and why? What rights and interests must you balance to make your decision?

---

25. **Breithaupt v. Abram**, 352 U.S. 432 (1957).
26. 384 U.S. 767 (1966).

In **Bell v. Wolfish**,[27] the Supreme Court ruled that individuals who were detained in prisons and awaiting trial could be subjected to routine body cavity searches. Because the purpose of the searches was to determine whether contraband was being smuggled in, and the existence of such contraband would be detrimental to prison security, the Court allowed such searches. Another line of cases are those that allow testing for illegal substances by employers and for athletes. The Court has also disallowed some testing involving intrusion into the body, including the testing of pregnant women to determine whether they were ingesting illegal substances.

THE EXCLUSIONARY RULE IN NONCRIMINAL PROCEEDINGS

The exclusionary rule only applies in criminal trial proceedings in which the evidence seized would be used to convict a person of a crime; it does not apply to civil or other noncriminal proceedings. For example, if a defendant is charged with a crime, evidence seized illegally can be utilized by a police officer who is testifying against the defendant in a preliminary court proceeding in which the goal is to prove a prima facie case against the defendant so the

THE SCALES OF JUSTICE

www.bigstock.com.

27. 441 U.S. 520 (1979).

defendant's case can move to a trial. Following is an example of how this could happen.

> John Doe is driving his car and is pulled over by a police officer when the officer decides that John "looks shady." The police officer orders John Doe to get out of the car and the officer then searches John Doe's car. He finds in the car a crack pipe, crack cocaine, a scale, and a bag of money. The officer charges John Doe with possession of crack cocaine with the intent to deliver, possession of instruments of a crime, and possession of drug paraphernalia, based only on the items found in John Doe's car after the stop.
>
> John Doe meets with an attorney who correctly determines that the officer had no probable cause to pull over John Doe's car. At the preliminary hearing, the officer can testify as to all of the items found in the car. However, if the officer also testifies at the preliminary hearing that he pulled over John Doe's car because the car "looked like the type a drug dealer might drive" and for no other reason, then the entire stop would be declared illegal. Notwithstanding the illegality of the stop, the case will be bound over to court for a trial, and John Doe's remedy is to have his attorney file a motion in court before the case goes to trial to suppress all of the items found in the car and have the judge order that those items cannot be introduced at trial based on the exclusionary rule. If the court so orders, then the prosecution will most likely withdraw the charges filed against the defendant, as there will be no evidence for the prosecution to present at trial.

Use of Unconstitutionally Obtained Evidence for Purposes of Impeachment

Other instances in which illegally seized evidence could be presented to the court include any other non-trial proceedings that take place before the actual adversary process of a trial begins, such as suppression hearings, grand jury trials, and bail hearings. Generally, evidence that is presented by a defendant at a suppression hearing can be used later to **impeach** his or her testimony in court, even if the evidence cannot be used as direct evidence to show that a person actually possessed that evidence. Impeaching a witness refers to the act of proving to the fact finder (judge or jury) that the witness is lying, most likely based on differences between a statement that the witness makes at trial and a statement the witness made previously.

However, some evidence that is suppressed via the exclusionary rule may be utilized by the prosecution to impeach a defendant in court later. For example, a voluntary confession might be used to impeach a defendant who later states the opposite of something he said during the confession on the stand. A defendant who confessed to having cocaine on his person cannot late take the stand and indicate that he has never had cocaine in his possession, even if the confession itself was thrown out due to the defendant's **Miranda** rights being violated at the time of the confession. This is why some criminal defendants choose not to take the stand during their trial. However, involuntary confessions (for example, one given by a defendant who is being tortured) are considered inherently unreliable, and their content cannot be utilized even to impeach the defendant if he takes the stand.[28] Further, the impeachment exception applies only to the defendant's own testimony, and cannot be extended to use illegally obtained evidence to impeach the testimony of other witnesses.[29]

Here is another example of when tainted evidence would be utilized to impeach a witness (most commonly the testimony of a defendant).

> The police illegally and for no reason at all break into Johnny Bravo's house just to see if they can find any evidence at all that Johnny might be committing a crime. Upon searching Johnny's house, the police find his stash of cocaine. They seize the cocaine and try him on charges of possession of cocaine with intent to deliver. Typically, the cocaine would be suppressed and could not be utilized in court to prove that Johnny possessed the cocaine. However, technically, under the impeachment doctrine, the prosecutor could ask Johnny if he had ever seen cocaine. If Johnny answered "no," the prosecutor could then say "Isn't it true that in fact you had 100 grams of cocaine in your hall closet on February 17?"

Even a voluntary confession that was obtained illegally could be introduced to impeach the defendant. (An involuntary confession cannot be used, as involuntary confessions are assumed to be inherently unreliable. If a prosecutor has offered immunity in exchange for a confession, that confession cannot be used either.) According to **Brown v. Illinois**,[30] a court should consider whether the defendant was informed of his constitutional rights and his right to remain silent, whether he had the benefit of the assistance of counsel, the time frame of the confession in relation to when the defendant was detained, the purpose of the government action in utilizing certain methods to obtain the confession, and the flagrancy of the official illegal behavior. In the **Brown** case, the police arrested Mr. Brown without probable cause, but he was given his **Miranda** rights twice by the police and confessed after each episode of his **Miranda** rights being given. The first confession was given approximately 90 minutes after his arrest and the second was given approximately seven hours later. The question before the Supreme Court was whether the officers' intervening reading of the **Miranda** rights broke the causal chain between the illegal arrest and the confession. The Court decided that the causal chain was not broken, because the first statement came less than two hours after the arrest, without anything of "significance" intervening. In fact, the Court determined that the arrest itself was calculated by the police specifically to cause surprise, fright and confusion. The bottom line is for the court to consider how much of a deterrence excluding the confession would provide, depending on why certain tactics were utilized to obtain the confession.

---

28. **Mincey v. Arizona**, 437 U.S. 385 (1978).
29. **James v. Illinois**, 493 U.S. 307 (1990).
30. 422 U.S. 590 (1975).

The caveat to this is that a court can always rule that the evidence is "too prejudicial" to be presented to the jury. Obviously in a case such as the drug case discussed previously, it would be fairly obvious that the jury would most likely convict the defendant based on the evidence of the cocaine being in his closet. Allowing that evidence to be introduced to impeach the defendant would be so prejudicial that the court would probably not allow its use even for purposes of impeachment. Further, most often, defendants do not take the stand in their own defense when they realize that evidence that could normally be suppressed can be introduced for purposes of impeachment.

When, as in the abovementioned situations, evidence can be excluded for certain purposes in court while being included for other purposes, the judge who presides over the case might give the jury members a jury instruction regarding how they can consider the evidence in the course of their deliberations. The jury instruction will explain to the jurors that they are not supposed to consider certain pieces of evidence as proof of whether or not the person, for example, actually had those pieces of evidence in their possession. Rather, the jury is told they should solely consider whether the evidence that was brought out in court and, presumably, demonstrated that the defendant was lying casts a shadow on the other evidence and testimony that the defendant might have presented during the remainder of the trial.

Other Impeachment Proceedings

There are also other situations in which suppressed evidence cannot be utilized to impeach a defendant. For example, if a prosecutor offers a defendant immunity for testimony he provides as a witness against another defendant, the testimony cannot be used in any other proceeding against the witness when he is a defendant in court, even for impeachment purposes. In **Calandra v. United States**,[31] a witness was called to testify before a **grand jury**, which is an investigative body that determines preliminarily whether a defendant should be charged with a crime, and issue an "indictment." Some of the questions the grand jury asked the witness involved evidence that was obtained in what had been established as being an unlawful search and seizure. The Supreme Court ruled against the witness, finding that the functioning of the grand jury was extremely important, and that because the unconstitutionally seized evidence was not going to be used at trial, there would be no further deterrent effect should it not be used during the grand jury proceedings. In addition to the holding in the case, the Court's language regarding the exclusionary rule gave insight into the Court's beliefs about the rule. In **Calandra**, the Court indicated that the primary reason for the exclusionary rule was to deter police from engaging in illegal searches. By stating this, the Court was acknowledging that in its opinion, the primary purpose of the rule was not to try to assist criminals in not having illegally obtained evidence used

---

31. 414 U.S. 338 (1974).

against them. This is why most of the exceptions to the exclusionary rule are crafted by the Supreme Court as a result of its belief that allowing evidence from certain otherwise illegal searches to be used against a defendant would not deter law enforcement officers.

The exclusionary rule does not apply to **habeas corpus** proceedings. Habeas corpus petitions, discussed previously, are not an appeal but can be filed by a state or federal prisoner who argues that he is wrongfully imprisoned as a result of his constitutional rights being violated. Because habeas corpus petitions are always filed following trial, the Supreme Court has ruled that defendants cannot raise issues regarding Fourth Amendment violations in them because they would have had an ability to raise such issues at the time of trial, and the only way the exclusionary rule can have a deterrent effect is if the evidence is presented at trial. The Supreme Court determined that it is flawed to believe that law enforcement personnel would fear that federal habeas corpus review would reveal flaws in a search or seizure that went undetected at trial and on appeal.[32] The Court determined that permitting a defendant to argue a claim that was already rejected by two different tiers of courts would cause a "disrespect for the law and administration of justice."[33] The Court supported this analysis by quoting Dallin H. Oaks, who stated that "[t]ruth and justice are ultimate values, so understood by our people, and the law and the legal profession will not be worthy of public respect and loyalty if we allow our attention to be diverted from these goals."[34]

Post-Conviction and Noncriminal Proceedings

Evidence that might otherwise be excluded in court can be presented to and considered by the court after a person has been convicted of an offense, such as for sentencing purposes and determining whether a person will receive parole. The evidence could also be utilized in a noncriminal proceeding, such as deportation hearings, civil hearings regarding the IRS or another administrative body, and child custody or divorce proceedings. If a civil lawsuit is brought by the victim of a crime against a defendant who has been convicted in criminal court, the illegally seized evidence may be presented against the defendant in those proceedings. The evidence cannot be used in "quasi-criminal" proceedings, such as proceedings in which the government intends to request that the defendant forfeit assets that were utilized during the course of committing a crime. In determining that illegally seized evidence can be used in proceedings that do not involve a trial, the Supreme Court reasoned that the deterrent effect to officers would not be changed by allowing the evidence to be used in these types of proceedings, as long as the officer was aware that the evidence would

---

32. **Stone v. Powell**, 428 U.S. 465, 493 (1976).
33. **Stone** at 491.
34. **Stone** at 491, n. 30, *quoting* Dallin H. Oaks, *Ethics, Morality and Professional Responsibility*, 1975 B.Y.U.L. Rev. 591, 596.

not be used at trial. Further, grand jury witnesses may not refuse to answer a question based on the fact that it relates to evidence that was suppressed in another case. Parolees also cannot ask that evidence be excluded based on its prior unconstitutionality.[35] Parole proceedings are traditionally more flexible than most other court proceedings in terms of evidentiary rules and procedures. The relationship between a parolee and a parole officer is different from the relationship between a police officer and an arrestee. The parole officer's role is to supervise the parolee, so the Court has determined that to assume the parole officer's role is hostile is inappropriate. The Court further stated that use of the exclusionary rule in parole hearings would hinder the function of state parole systems. Finally, some state courts have ruled that the exclusionary rule is not applicable to sentencing hearings. Thus, if evidence is excluded in terms of bringing a case to trial, charging the defendant, or inducing a person to plea, the evidence can nonetheless be brought up in court when a person is sentenced so the judge understands all of the evidence that was obtained against the person before handing down the sentence.

Identification and Witness Statement Exceptions

The police can seize a person improperly and use the seizure to assist in the identification of the defendant by a victim, and the evidence of the identification need not be suppressed. The information is not excluded because the victim will again identify the defendant at trial, and thus the identification will be confirmed again at that time.[36] When an illegal search assists law enforcement in locating a witness for a case, the witness's statements often will not be excluded from court, despite the fruit of the poisonous tree rule. A court that rules on the admissibility of evidence in such a case should consider whether allowing the witness to testify would have any effect in terms of deterring future police conduct.[37]

Good Faith Exception

Another exception to the exclusionary rule is the **good faith exception**. This exception was established by the Court in the landmark case of **United States v. Leon**.[38] In the **Leon** case, the police obtained a warrant that they believed was properly requested and issued. The police had established what they believed was probable cause based on information from a confidential informant regarding drug trafficking. A lot of very specific information was included in the warrant application. The officers used this information to develop an affidavit of probable cause; three deputy district attorneys reviewed the

---

35. **Pennsylvania v. Scott**, 524 U.S. 357 (1998).
36. **United States v. Crews**, 445 U.S. 463 (1980)
37. **United States v. Ceccolini**, 435 U.S. 268 (1978).
38. 468 U.S. 897 (1984).

warrant and a state court judge issued it. Because of the judge's signature, the officers logically believed that the warrant was good; acting on this belief, they executed the warrant and searched Leon's house.

In reality, the warrant had not been valid, as probable cause did not exist under the law for the magistrate to be able to grant the warrant. The lower court, upon reviewing the warrant, stated that the reliability and credibility of the informant had not been established, that the drug transaction that was referenced in the warrant was "stale," and that a lot of the information stated could constitute details of innocence as well as details of guilt. However, because the officers did not know this and, in fact, believed that the warrant was valid, the Supreme Court ruled that the officers were acting in good faith when executing the warrant and that the search would thus be upheld. The Court ruled that the officers should not be expected to question the magistrate's probable cause determination, and that a police officer's conduct would not be deterred by a rule that forced officers to second guess a judge's decision of probable cause. The Court expressed a "strong preference" for warrants and then reasoned that if officers are expected to obtain warrants because they include the "detached scrutiny of a neutral magistrate," rather than the "hurried judgment of a law enforcement officer engaged in the often competitive enterprise of ferreting out crime," officers should not be penalized for relying on warrants.[39] The Supreme Court, in the **Leon** case and the case of **Massachusetts v. Sheppard**,[40] discussed next, decided not to use the exclusionary rule to protect a defendant when police actions were appropriate and the authority issuing the warrant, such as a judge, provided the inappropriate actions.

In the case of **Massachusetts v. Sheppard**, a police officer drafted an affidavit of probable cause to support a search warrant and an arrest warrant in a homicide case. The officer had been unable to find a blank search warrant form and he used one that had been previously filled out for controlled substances, changing some of the information. He informed the judge who reviewed the warrant of the information that needed to be changed on the warrant itself. The judge indicated that he would make those changes before issuing the warrant. The changes did not get made, and some of the items requested in the warrant application did not appear in the list of items to be searched. Nonetheless, the officer conducted the search, finding several pieces of incriminating evidence, which were used at trial against Sheppard. The Court determined that, like the **Leon** case, the officer need not "second guess" the judge. The officer has a right to believe that the paper issued by the judge is accurate and reflects what the judge said it would contain.

Some argue that this rule is necessary for police officers to be able to properly do their job without constantly worrying about whether they are violating someone's rights. After all, an officer should have the right to assume

---

39. **Leon**, *quoting* **United States v. Chadwick**, 433 U.S. 1 (1977).
40. 468 U.S. 981 (1984).

that the warrant signed by a magistrate is valid and that the magistrate performed her duties properly in signing the warrant. If an officer had to second guess himself every time he executed a signed warrant, police work could, theoretically, come to a standstill. Officers would be wary about performing searches, even with a valid warrant, and could be in a position of second guessing the warrant process. Defendants suffer because of the **Leon** good faith rule, but the Courts have determined that the bad effects to the defendant are outweighed by the concern that officers must be free to do their jobs based on the information they have in their hands.

As you would imagine, the Supreme Court has subsequently developed many exceptions to the good faith rule set forth in the **Leon** case. A major exception occurs when an officer relies on a search warrant that is defective. A search warrant is defective if it is so lacking in facts and details that there is no way the officer should have believed it would support his application for a warrant; if the warrant is defective on its face, in that it does state specifically the place (or places) to be searched or the items to be searched for; if the officer signing the affidavit (known as the affiant) knowingly lied or fabricated the truth on the warrant application; or if the magistrate "rubberstamped" the warrant and failed to consider whether probable cause was present or not.

The **Leon** and **Sheppard** cases were decided by the United States Supreme Court on the same day but involved different factual situations. In **Leon**, the information included in the affidavit itself did not establish probable cause. In **Sheppard**, the affidavit established probable cause but the final warrant had a typographical error. The Court determined that both situations fell under the good faith exception. This rule protects officers and, theoretically, the integrity of the system, but does not protect the defendant from mistakes performed in the course of the magistrate and police officers' daily work.

The **Leon** case did provide four exceptions to the good faith rule:

1. If the magistrate was not "neutral and detached" in granting the warrant
2. If the officer was dishonest or reckless in preparing the affidavit
3. If the officer could not possibly have reasonably believed probable cause existed to obtain a warrant
4. If the warrant fails to contain, as required by the provisions of the Constitution, a particularized description of the place to be searched or the things to be seized

Remember, states can choose to give a defendant more rights than the Supreme Court requires, and this has been done in the area of the good faith rule. Some states have specifically decided not to adopt the good faith rule. One such state, Pennsylvania, reasoned that the Constitution of Pennsylvania did not intend that the sole purpose of its search and seizure statute would be to deter police conduct, as the Supreme Court ruled about the United States Constitution. When the exclusionary rule was adopted in Pennsylvania, the assumption was that it was a constitutionally mandated rule, not a court-created rule. Deterrence was not the primary reason for requiring the exclusionary rule; rather, the Pennsylvania courts (and other state courts that have rejected the good faith rule) interpreted their Constitution as safeguarding the privacy of individuals and ensuring, in accordance with the words of the Fourth Amendment, that warrants would be issued only upon probable cause, without exception.[41]

However, facts and circumstances of a particular case can make the good faith rule inapplicable. In **United States v. Leary,**[42] the Court was faced with an issue in which the warrant was so facially deficient that the Court determined that there was no way the officers should have executed the warrant. The warrant permitted government agents to search a business, and it listed every possible type of paper that could be found in a business, in violation of the specificity rules of the Fourth Amendment. The Court indicated that the officers should have known that this broad language would render the warrant unconstitutional.

Justices Brennan and Marshall, dissenting in the **Leon** case, stated that they had "witnessed the Court's gradual but determined strangulation" of the exclusionary rule and that they believed the Court's permission of the good faith rule was the final step in the Court's "gradual but determined strangulation of the rule." The dissenting opinion criticized the Court's weighing of costs and benefits and indicated that the majority was ignoring the fundamental importance of the Constitution and the concern of expediency over rights. The dissent also stated that the "judiciary is responsible, no less than the executive, for ensuring that constitutional rights are respected."

However, the Supreme Court diluted the exclusionary rule further when it determined that a clerical error by the court will also not result in suppression of the evidence. In **Arizona v. Evans,**[43] officers spotted Evans going the wrong way on a one-way street near the police station. Evans was stopped, and a check of the central data system revealed that an outstanding warrant was in place for Evans's arrest. Unfortunately, this information was erroneous, as the arrest warrant had been quashed 17 days prior to Evans's arrest and a clerk failed to enter that information into the database. Nonetheless, because the officers had no reason to believe the entry was not accurate, Evans was handcuffed and taken into custody, and while being handcuffed, a hand-rolled marijuana cigarette dropped from Evans's person. The officers then searched Evans's car and discovered more marijuana under the passenger seat.

At trial, Evans moved to have the evidence suppressed due to the fact that the information regarding the warrant was erroneous. Had the officers not been able to arrest Evans due to the discovery of the warrant on the centralized computer system, they would not have been able to search Evans. Evans argued that the good faith exception to the exclusionary rule was inapplicable in this case, but the Supreme Court disagreed and

---

41. **Commonwealth v. Edmunds,** 586 A.2d 807 (Pa. 1991).
42. 846 F.2d 592 (10th Cir. 1988).
43. 514 U.S. 1 (1995).

permitted the evidence to be used against Evans. The Court determined that because the exclusionary rule was created to deter officers from committing illegal or unconstitutional acts, the officers in this case would not have changed their behavior had the court excluded the evidence, as they would not normally assume that the information entered into a system by a clerk was incorrect. The exclusionary rule was created to deter police conduct, not the conduct of court employees. However, the opinion in the **Arizona** case indicated that it would be inappropriate for police officers to rely solely on a recordkeeping system that did not have a mechanism to ensure its accuracy. Police must work to ensure the records it relies on are accurate.

The Supreme Court applied the good faith exception as a bar to the exclusionary rule in a case involving police error regarding a warrant in **Herring v. United States**.[44]

HERRING V. UNITED STATES

FACTS: Herring was arrested outside an impound lot where he was retrieving an item from his truck. An officer recognized Herring and believed that Herring had an outstanding warrant for his arrest. He called the county clerk's office, who stated that there was no outstanding warrant in that county but who agreed to call surrounding counties to inquire as to whether any warrants existed. The clerk stated that there was an active arrest warrant in a nearby county; in fact, this information was false. Based, however, on the mistaken belief that such a warrant he existed, the officer arrested Herring and based solely on the information regarding the warrant, he performed a search incident to an arrest. The officer found methamphetamine in Herring's pocket and an illegal pistol in his vehicle. He was charged with possessing those items. All parties agreed that the evidence was seized in violation of the Fourth Amendment, but they did not agree on whether the exclusionary rule should apply to suppress the evidence obtained as a result of the violation.

ISSUE: Should a police officer's mistaken belief that a warrant is active for a person provide an exception to the exclusionary rule because the police conduct was not undertaken purposefully?

HOLDING: The exclusionary rule would not apply; the evidence could be admitted.

RATIONALE: The Supreme Court reasoned that the police conduct in that case was not "sufficiently deliberate" to justify the exclusion of the evidence, and that the justice system would "pay a price" if the evidence was excluded. The Court stated that the exclusionary rule is not an individual right and applies only when it results in appreciable deterrence to police officers' conduct. The Court stated

---

44. 555 U.S. 135 (2009).

that "[T]he rule's costly toll upon truth-seeking and law enforcement objectives presents a high obstacle for those urging [its] application." The Court announced a new test for exceptions to the exclusionary rule, stating that "To trigger the exclusionary rule, police conduct must be sufficiently deliberate that exclusion can meaningfully deter it, and sufficiently culpable that such deterrence is worth the price paid by the justice system. As laid out in our cases, the exclusionary rule serves to deter deliberate, reckless, or grossly negligent conduct, or in some circumstances recurring or systemic negligence. The error in this case does not rise to that level."

Thus, a high standard exists for a defendant to prove that the exclusionary rule should be used by the Court. The Court's rule places a burden on the defendant to prove more than just that the officer's conduct was wrong; the egregious nature of that conduct must also be proved.

The Supreme Court has established a similar exception when an officer relies, in good faith, on a procedural statute that later is determined to be unconstitutional. Although this rule protects officers who are doing their job the best they can, it is unfortunate for a defendant that an "innocent mistake" on the part of a police officer can result in a criminal conviction for him, despite our system's belief in the exclusionary rule. According to the Supreme Court, a defendant also has no right to argue the exclusionary rule in a parole revocation proceeding.[45] As discussed previously, however, states can give individuals more rights than the United States Supreme Constitution provides, as interpreted by the Supreme Court. Some states, including Pennsylvania and New Jersey, have precluded police from using the good faith exception to justify their actions.

The Supreme Court also upheld police officers' actions when the actions were based on good faith reliance on a statute. In **Illinois v. Krull**,[46] Chicago police officers searched cards and the records of an automobile wrecking yard without a search warrant, based on a statute that permitted such searches for "regulatory purposes." The statute was later declared unconstitutional, in violation of the Fourth Amendment. The Supreme Court ruled in a close (5–4) decision that the officers had a right to rely upon the statute. The dissent in the case stated that "[p]roviding legislatures a grace period during which the police may freely perform unreasonable searches in order to convict those who might otherwise escape provides a positive incentive to promulgate unconstitutional laws."

Michigan v. DeFilippo,[47] discussed previously, involved an arrest of a suspect made by the police in good faith reliance on an ordinance that was later declared to be invalid. Detroit police officers received a call to

---

45. **Pennsylvania v. Scott**, 524 U.S. 357 (1998).
46. 480 U.S. 340 (1987).
47. 443 U.S. 331 (1979).

investigate two persons who appeared to be intoxicated and were in an alley. Upon arriving in the alley, the officers found a man and a woman, and the woman was lowering her pants. The woman indicated that she was about to "relieve" herself. The officers then asked the man for identification; the man stated he was a police officer, stated his name, and stated his badge number. The officer indicated that he was unable to hear the badge number. The officer asked the man again for identification, and the man stated that he knew or worked with the officer whose name he had given before. Despite the information given in the initial telephone call, the man did not appear to the officer to be intoxicated.

The officer arrested the individual under a Detroit ordinance that provided that an officer can stop and question an individual if he believes the individual's behavior warrants further investigation for a criminal activity. Further, the individual must identify himself. Thus, the man was arrested for failing to identify himself. He was searched by an officer who found a package of marijuana in one shirt pocket and a tinfoil packet with other controlled substances in the other. He was charged with possession of the controlled substance. The individual moved to suppress the evidence obtained in the search. The ordinance permitting the police to force someone to identify himself had been found unconstitutional because it was vague. Further, the individual argued, if the Court found that the ordinance was unconstitutional, the arrest should be considered invalid and thus any evidence obtained following the arrest should also be excluded from court.

In considering whether the unconstitutionality of the ordinance would render the police officer's behavior invalid, the Court stated the following:

> Police are charged to enforce laws until and unless they are declared unconstitutional. The enactment of a law forecloses speculation by enforcement officers concerning its constitutionality—with the possible exception of a law so grossly and flagrantly unconstitutional that any person of reasonable prudence would be bound to see its flaws. Society would be ill-served if its police officers took it upon themselves to determine which laws are and which are not constitutionally entitled to enforcement.[48]

The Supreme Court did state that sometimes a statute or ordinance authorizes searches under circumstances that do not satisfy the traditional warrant and probable cause requirements of the Fourth Amendment, and then the exclusionary rule would apply. For example, a statute that does not require a warrant to comply with the portion of the Constitution that requires that warrants particularly describe the place to be searched and the items to be seized, evidence obtained under the auspices of that statute would be subject to the exclusionary rule.

---

48. **Michigan v. DeFillippo,** 443 U.S. 31 (1979).

Illegality in the Manner of Entering

Another exception to the exclusionary rule was created by the Supreme Court in **Hudson v. Michigan**.[49] Many consider the Court's decision in **Hudson** as imposing a severe limitation to the exclusionary rule. The crux of the decision is that the Court must always consider whether the potential deterrence of law enforcement resulting from the rule outweigh its substantial social costs. If not, the rule should not be applied. In the **Hudson** case, the police violated the knock and announce rule as it was currently being applied by the Michigan courts; the usual time to wait between knocking on the door and announcing their presence and forcibly entering a residence was between 20 and 30 seconds. Police had obtained a warrant authorizing the search of Hudson's home for drugs and firearms, but they waited only three to five seconds after knocking before entering the premises. Once inside, the police found large quantities of drugs and firearms in the house, which were used against Hudson in court.

The Supreme Court had previously held that the knock and announce rule was constitutionally required, but the Court never specifically stated what it felt was an appropriate time period to wait after knocking. However, the Court ultimately permitted this technically unlawful entry, stating that, had the police waited a few more seconds, they still would have executed the warrant and would have found the drugs and weapons anyway. Specifically, the Court ruled that a violation of the knock and announce rule does not invoke the exclusionary rule. The Court stated that "[s]uppression of evidence . . . has always been our last resort, not our first impulse" and further reasoned that the social costs of applying the exclusionary rule in this type of situation would far outweigh the deterrent value of applying the rule, and that police departments have become increasingly professional, so the concerns over aberrant police behavior which might have been considered by past decisions did not remain. The Court further opined that the knock and announce rule was really designed to protect officers, by shielding them from "surprised" residents yielding weapons, rather than being designed to protect suspected criminals. The Court even went so far as to say that those whose rights were violated due to a violation of the knock and announce rule did have other remedies, such as filing a civil lawsuit or seeking the discipline of police officers (interestingly, these are the options the Court chose not to require when selecting the exclusionary rule as the "best" remedy for aberrant police behavior). The majority opinion also stated that "suppression of all evidence amount[s] in many cases is a get-out-of-jail-free card." The Court also discussed the fact that it believed that the existence of the exclusionary rule caused law enforcement officers to commit perjury in order to avoid having cases thrown out of court due to the exclusion of evidence. (This concept will be discussed later in this chapter.)

---

49. 125 S. Ct. 2159 (2006).

The Court has acknowledged that the exclusionary rule is not a "personal constitutional right."[50] In other words, it was not created by the Supreme Court in order to redress the injury that a victim of an unlawful search and seizure suffers at the hands of the police. It does not repair the violation of privacy that the person had to endure. The Court has, on the other hand, also acknowledged that the exclusionary rule is flawed in that, while curing a law enforcement officer's mistake, it comes with social costs. If truth-seeking is the Court's goal, then the exclusionary rule is an obstacle.

The Harmless Error Rule

Remember that an appellate court's determination that a particular piece of evidence should have been excluded from trial does not necessarily result in the entire case being dismissed. First, it is possible that the prosecutor's office will retry the case without the evidence and hope that the remaining evidence will be substantial enough to again obtain a conviction. However, the appellate court might also decide that the introduction of the evidence was "harmless" and refuse to set aside the conviction. When issues are raised on appeal, the appellate court must determine whether harmless error existed by placing itself in the shoes of the jury members to determine whether it believes the jury would have made a different decision based on an exclusion of a particular piece of evidence. Finally, it is important to note that the **harmless error rule** does not apply when defects such as the right to counsel or denial of the right to a public trial are present in a case. In those cases, an automatic reversal of the case will take place.

The harmless error rule was discussed by the Supreme Court in the case of **Harrington v. California,**[51] in which the Supreme Court directed courts to consider the evidence as a whole and to consider the error harmless if enough overwhelming untainted evidence existed to support the conviction of the defendant or if the error involved an element of the crime that was otherwise well established. The **Harrington** case presented the Supreme Court with a white defendant and three black co-defendants who were tried for first-degree murder. Defendant made statements that placed him at the scene of the crime and also implicated the other three men in the murder. The other men made confessions which had various differing facts but one of which placed defendant inside the store with a gun at the time of the crime; this man testified at defendant's trial. The two other men did not testify at defendant's trial, but their confessions, which mentioned the defendant, stated that they did not see him with a gun. The state of the law was such that the admission of a confession of a co-defendant who did not take the stand and thus, could not be cross-examined, would violate the defendant's rights under the Sixth Amendment's provision that guarantees defendants the right to confront

---

50. **Stone v. Powell**, 428 U.S. 465, 486 (1976).
51. 395 U.S. 250 (1969).

witnesses whose testimony is used against him. The jury was given an instruction from the judge that the confessions of the men who were not in court should not be used against the defendant. The Supreme Court stated that regardless of the confessions of the two men, which did not even name the defendant by name, the rest of the evidence presented against the defendant was so overwhelming that the violation of the cross-examination rule was harmless. The Court stated that it would not adopt the rule that any departure from constitutional procedures should result in an automatic reversal.

The Court further considered the issue of harmless error in the case of **Arizona v. Fulminante**.[52] Fulminante was suspected of having murdered his stepdaughter, and after statements he made to the police regarding her disappearance were inconsistent, he fled from Arizona to New Jersey; no charges had been filed against him. Fulminante was jailed in New Jersey on an unrelated federal charge, and his cellmate, Sarivola, was actually a paid informant for the FBI. Fulminante admitted to the informant that he had killed his daughter by shooting her twice in the head.

Fulminante was released from prison but confessed to the informant's wife about the same crime. Fulminante was charged with first-degree murder in Arizona, and he attempted to have the evidence of his confession excluded, alleging that it was coerced and thus barred by the Fifth and Fourteenth Amendments. He indicated that his confession to the informant's wife should be considered fruit of the poisonous tree and also excluded. The trial court admitted both confessions and Fulminante was not only convicted, but was sentenced to death. He appealed and argued that the harmless error doctrine should not be applied to involuntary confessions.

The Supreme Court first determined that the harmless error doctrine should be applicable in cases of involuntary confessions. Thus, if a trial judge admits an involuntary confession when it should have been excluded, the defendant's conviction will not be automatically reversed. Instead, the court must determine whether the inclusion of the tainted confession was really harmless or not before determining whether the defendant's conviction can be reversed. The Supreme Court decided that Fulminante's confession was coerced, because Sarivola had indicated that he would "protect" Fulminante in prison if Fulminante told him the truth about his stepdaughter. Thus, Fulminante was afraid of physical violence to his person by other inmates if he did not cooperate with Sarivola's request. In Fulminante's case, not enough other evidence existed to convince the Supreme Court that the introduction of the two confessions was merely "harmless error." However, Fulminante's case still set the stage for courts to determine that certain confessions that were obtained in violation of the Constitution and were wrongly introduced as evidence against a defendant constituted nothing but harmless error.

---

52. 499 U.S. 279 (1991).

YOU BE THE JUDGE

Donald Davis is convicted in a jury trial of possession of cocaine with intent to distribute it. The evidence presented to the jury was as follows. Donald's house was searched by the local police and ten bags of cocaine were found in his house. Officers also found a list of names, some of whom admitted to purchasing cocaine from Donald, and packaging materials, such as baggies and labels. The officers also searched Donald's car while it was parked at a friend's house and found another handgun. The police had a valid search warrant to search the house but did not have a warrant or probable cause to search the car and thus the search of the car was unconstitutional; however, the trial court errs and permits all of the evidence to be submitted to the jury. The jury finds the defendant guilty of possession of cocaine with the intent to deliver it. You are a judge in the appellate court. You find that the search of the vehicle was illegal and should have been excluded from trial due to the invalid search. Do you decide that presenting evidence of the gun was "harmless"? Why or why not?

CURRENT STATUS OF THE EXCLUSIONARY RULE

Following the **Mapp** case, a political backlash against the exclusionary rule ensued. In fact, President Nixon sought to appoint justices to the Supreme Court who would advocate against the rule. The **United States v. Calandra**[53] case, decided in 1974, suggested the Court's concern over applying the exclusionary rule. The Court reasoned that the exclusionary rule would not actually redress any injury to the victim of the search; the illegal search could not be "undone." The purpose was to deter future unlawful police conduct, by "removing the incentive to disregard it." The opinion then states that "the rule is a judicially created remedy designed to safeguard Fourth Amendment rights generally through its deterrent effect, rather than a personal constitutional right of the party aggrieved." The implication of this statement is that because the rule is judicially created and does not "spring from" the Constitution, the rule can be changed by the judiciary at any time and thus a defendant's right to have the exclusionary rule applied can be taken away. The **Calandra** decision suggests that the Court should balance the right of the defendant to be free from searches and seizures with the harm that is done by permitting evidence in a particular case to be excluded. This language was a precursor to many of the exceptions set forth previously and could most likely allow a further erosion of the exclusionary rule in the future.

---

53. 414 U.S. 338 (1974).

Another case, **Bivens v. Six Unknown Agents**,[54] contained a blistering dissent that attacked the exclusionary rule. Chief Justice Burger argued that the exclusionary rule works against the nature of the American adversarial trial system and argued that the rule does not deter police behavior and focused on the social cost of the rule because it allows criminal defendants to go free. Burger opined that a better remedy than the exclusionary rule would be for Congress to establish a court system in which police officers who violated the rights of defendant would be tried. Although the Supreme Court has not yet overturned the exclusionary rule, many of the exceptions set forth previously were created following, and perhaps as a result of, Burger's dissent in **Bivens**. The Supreme Court has also acknowledged that studies that have been conducted regarding the deterrent effect of the exclusionary rule have not conclusively provided any evidence that the exclusionary rule does, in fact, deter police officers from engaging in unconstitutional conduct.[55]

OTHER REMEDIES AGAINST VIOLATION OF DEFENDANTS' RIGHTS

Despite the Supreme Court's concern that remedies other than the exclusionary rule are often fruitless for those whose rights have been violated, there are some statutes that assist those whose rights are violated. Certainly a defendant can always file a civil lawsuit in state court under tort law. In addition to the exclusionary rule, some other remedies do exist for individuals whose rights have been violated by the police. These include federal statutes and state common law remedies, and although no remedy is perfect in every case, successful lawsuits have been brought under many theories.

Section 1983 of the Federal Code—Civil Rights Act

As discussed previously, when a person's constitutional rights are violated, one remedy is that the evidence that is seized as a result of that violation will be suppressed. However, in particularly egregious cases, an individual whose rights are violated might wish to sue the police officer in civil court. Generally, the individual will be seeking money from the officer or his department, and the individual could also seek injunctive relief, when he requests that the official and his department stop a certain behavior. These types of suits can be brought even in instances in which the exclusionary rule does not apply. Most suits of this nature are brought in federal court under 42 U.S.C. Section 1983, a portion of the United States Code. This section of the code provides as follows:

---

54. 403 U.S. 388 (1971).
55. **United States v. Janis**, 428 U.S. 433 (1976).

Any person who, under color of any statute, ordinance, regulation, custom, or usage, of any State of Territory, subjects, or causes to be subjected, any citizen of the United States or other persons within the jurisdiction thereof to the deprivation of any rights, privileges, or immunities secured by the Constitution and laws, shall be liable to the party injured in an action at law, suit in equity, or other proper proceeding for redress.[56]

This code section was enacted in 1871 as part of the Civil Rights Act of 1871. However, it was rarely used until 1961 when the Supreme Court considered the case of **Monroe v. Pape**.[57] In that case, 13 members of the Chicago, Illinois, police department broke into the residence of the Monroes. There were two adults and six children in the house. The officers did not have a search warrant or an arrest warrant. The officers woke everyone up and made the parents stand naked in the living room while the officers basically ransacked every room in the house. Mr. Monroe was taken to the local police station and questioned regarding a two-day-old murder case. He was never charged, but he was not allowed to contact an attorney during the interrogation and he was not allowed to make any other phone calls. The plaintiffs sued the police officers and the City of Chicago for violating Section 1983 of the Civil Rights Act. The city argued that it could not be held responsible for violating someone's civil rights and asked that the complaint be thrown out.

The case made its way up to the Supreme Court. The Court threw out the case against the city, deciding that because the word "person" was in Section 1983, the statute did not apply to municipalities. This concept was later changed when the Court found that it was possible for a municipal entity to be liable if the entity had a policy that was discriminatory under the act.[58] For example, if a police department had a policy that included profiling black citizens while they are driving or walking, the entity itself could be liable under Section 1983. The Supreme Court did hold in the **Monroe** case that the individual officers were liable for damages. In 1971, the Supreme Court considered whether Section 1983 applied to federal officials. The Court decided that it can apply to federal law enforcement officers, but other federal officials have absolute immunity, which means they cannot be sued in their official capacity.

Any officials who do not have absolute immunity, however, have **qualified immunity**. Qualified immunity is a defense that can be used by officials to become immune from being sued. The idea behind this is that government officials should feel comfortable doing their job and should not have to be concerned about whether decisions they make on a day-to-day basis are going to lead to lawsuits. Qualified immunity applies whenever an official acts with a mistaken belief, as long as that belief is reasonable.

---

56. 42 U.S.C. S 1983.
57. 365 U.S. 167 (1961).
58. **Monell v. Dept. of Social Servs. of the City of New York**, 436 U.S. 658 (1978).

THE TRACY THURMAN STORY

Tracy Thurman was a Connecticut woman who sued the police department of the City of Torrington, Connecticut, claiming the members of that department violated her civil rights by failing to provide her equal protection under the law against her husband, Charles "Buck" Thurman, Sr. Thurman's case also brought to light issues regarding domestic violence and sweeping change in the way courts handled domestic violence cases. Thurman had been assaulted and threatened by her husband numerous times, but the local police had generally ignored her calls and requests for help, considering the case "just another domestic violence" case. Finally, Thurman was assaulted by her husband and he stabbed her 13 times after she had called the police. Once the police did arrive, Thurman was kicked in the head by her assailant in the presence of officers. Thurman's husband even approached her as she was lying on the stretcher being taken to an ambulance.

Thurman argued that her constitutional rights had been violated in that she did not receive equal protection of the law, as the police treated her differently because she was married to her assailant. Had she been attacked by a random person, Thurman argued, the police would have certainly treated her case differently. Thurman was originally awarded $2.3 million in damages, although the amount was reduced to $1.9 million after the City of Torrington appealed the case.

Injunctions

The above-referenced types of lawsuits under Section 1983 involve a plaintiff seeking monetary damages from the police. Section 1983 also provides for injunctive relief under Section 1983. An **injunction** is an order issued by a court that either commands a person or entity to do something or orders a person or entity to stop doing something or avoid doing something, if they have not yet started it but have voiced the intent to do it. An injunction will be issued only if the defendant can show a clear and deliberate pattern of violations. Even when lower courts have issued injunctions, the Supreme Court has often overturned injunctions entered against local police departments, such as one entered against the Los Angeles police department.[59] The facts that were the subject of the case occurred in 1976 when an individual was stopped by City of Los Angeles police officers for a traffic violation. The individual stated that he did not resist the officers, yet the officers seized him and placed him in a chokehold, resulting in the individual becoming

---

59. **Los Angeles v. Lyons**, 461 U.S. 95 (1983).

unconscious and suffering damage to his larynx. The individual sued the officers and sought damages from them but also requested that the court enter an injunction ordering that the police department be banned from using chokeholds in all situations unless the proposed victim reasonably appeared to be threatening the immediate use of deadly force against the officers. The federal district court entered the requested injunction, prohibiting the police to use chokeholds unless the proposed victim threatened the officers with death or serious bodily injury. The court of appeals affirmed the injunction and the case moved up to the Supreme Court for review.

The Supreme Court overturned the lower courts' rulings, stating that the defendant did not demonstrate that he personally was in danger of being injured because of the police department's current procedure. The defendant argued that he was afraid of encountering the police again and being subjected to the same chokehold, but the Court stated that this concern was not "real or immediate." The Court stated that the emotional consequences of the police officers' prior action on the individual did not justify his concern that this type of event would happen again.

A similar ruling was handed down in the case of **Ashcroft v. Mattis**.[60] That case was initiated by a parent in Missouri whose 18-year-old child had been shot and killed by police when the child was attempting to escape from an arrest. The parents asked the court for damages, which were denied, but also requested that the lower court enter an order stating that the Missouri statutes that authorized police to use deadly force in apprehending a person who had committed a felony were unconstitutional. The federal appeals court determined that such relief was available and the case was appealed to the Supreme Court by the United States Attorney General.

The parents' reasoning in requesting the prohibition of the use of deadly force was that the parent had another son and he was worried that if that son was ever arrested, he might flee or give the appearance of fleeing, and would therefore also be in danger of being killed by the defendants or by other police officers. The Supreme Court ruled that this type of speculation was not enough to warrant the relief requested. The parents in this case also indicated that they would "feel better emotionally" if the Court ruled in their favor, as they would feel as though the Court was agreeing that their son was taken wrongfully. The Court also rejected this as a potential reason to rule in the parents' favor.

Other Possible Lawsuits

People whose rights are violated by the police can also choose to file a complaint against an individual officer in state court. State laws generally allow people to bring lawsuits for intentional torts, including trespass, assault, battery, false imprisonment, intentional infliction of emotional distress, breaking and entering, and false arrest. However, civil lawsuits cost money that a

---

60. 431 U.S. 171 (1977).

defendant, especially one who is imprisoned, probably does not possess. Even finding an attorney who will correspond with an inmate to assist with a civil suit might be difficult. Further, the civil court process takes a very long time even when positive results for the plaintiff are obtained in the end. Civil lawsuits take many forms and encompass many scenarios. For example, if a police officer puts someone's life in danger, that person can recover even if she was never actually in police custody. An individual might bring a claim against the police if her right to bodily privacy is violated by an officer conducting a strip search without cause or forcing her to sit in a public place unclothed while he conducts a search. An officer might also be subjected to criminal prosecution for violating a person's rights, and the jurisdiction in which these claims would be brought depends on whether the law violated was a federal or state law. The following federal statutes specifically provide that an officer's actions when he acts in his official capacity are criminal:

18 U.S.C. §2235—maliciously and without probable cause securing a search warrant

18 U.S.C. §2234—exceeding authority granted in a search warrant

18 U.S.C. §2236—conducting a warrantless search not incident to arrest or consent

18 U.S.C. §241—conspiracy to violate constitutional rights

18 U.S.C. §242—state officer who, under color of state law, deprive a person of constitutional rights.

Police have also been sued for reckless or careless driving when they have put the lives of others at risk, even when engaged in routine police behavior. In **Pletan v. Gaines**,[61] parents filed a wrongful death action on behalf of their deceased child against a police officer when a criminal suspect in a motor vehicle killed their child while being pursued by an officer in a high-speed chase. The child was walking home from school and the officer was chasing the suspect who was accused of shoplifting at a clothing store. The officer testified that the driver was traveling at a speed of approximately 60 miles per hour when the officer began to follow him. (The driver claimed he was traveling at about 30 miles per hour.) It was agreed, however, that the two cars sped down city streets, ultimately reaching speeds of more than 75 miles per hour in a 45 mile per hour zone. Gaines, the fleeing suspect, drove through three red lights and rammed two cars in his flight. The vehicles came to an intersection where a truck was stopped in the left turn lane for a red light; the officer noticed a pair of legs under the stopped truck running across the highway in a crosswalk. The officer applied his brakes and slowed, but Gaines proceeded through the red light, striking and killing minor Shawn Pletan as he emerged from behind the stopped truck. Shawn Pletan normally rode the bus home but, sadly, had decided to walk home that day. Gaines admitted that he was a heavy drug user and had used both heroin and cocaine within 24

---

61. 494 N.W.2d 38 (Minn. 1992).

hours before the car chase. The Minnesota Supreme Court ruled that generally an officer would have immunity from tort liability when exercising his duties but also stated that although it would not fashion a "bright-line" exception to such immunity, certain types of chases might be exempt from the immunity. For example, the court stated, a reckless "Dirty Harry" style car chase or a high-speed chase in congested traffic that hoped to catch only someone guilty of a minor property crime might not be exempt. In the alternative, pursuit of an armed and dangerous suspect who has committed a felony type of crime would warrant such a pursuit. The existence of immunity of this type of crime helps officers to perform their duties without constantly worrying about lawsuits, but also places individuals who are harmed without much of a remedy. The court decided that the officer was indeed entitled to immunity in this case.

Administrative Sanctions

Another possible sanction against an officer who violates a citizen's rights in his professional capacity is bringing sanctions against the officer administratively within the police department. Police agencies have written disciplinary codes and usually have either an internal review board or possibly a review board that includes citizens that will consider the officer's actions and impose a sanction. Some argue that having an internal body make decisions regarding the officer's discipline will result mostly in decisions in which the officer is not disciplined due to the fact that it is difficult for officers to discipline one of their own. Others advocate that the best person to decide whether an officer's duties have been met is another officer. Citizen review boards are used in some jurisdictions, but it might be difficult to determine how the citizens who sit on those boards are selected and whether they are qualified to judge the actions of officers.

EFFECTS OF THE EXCLUSIONARY RULE

Does the Exclusionary Rule Deter Officers?

Social science researchers have considered the question of whether the exclusionary rule actually deters officers from engaging in unconstitutional searches and seizures. The difficulty in measuring whether this actually happens comes from the obvious fact that it is virtually impossible to measure what conduct police officers might engage in if the exclusionary rule did not exist. We could survey officers and ask them how many times the exclusionary rule actually deterred them from inappropriate or illegal police conduct, but it is difficult to imagine that officers would actually answer this query truthfully or even really know themselves whether their behavior had been deterred. There is also the issue of whether the rule causes **specific deterrence** or **general**

deterrence. Specific deterrence would be the deterrence of one particular officer; in other words, if a particular officer violates the Constitution and the evidence obtained by him is excluded from court, that particular officer might choose not to violate the law in the future. General deterrence exists if evidence is excluded in a case and all officers become concerned enough to change their actions so the same thing does not happen in any of their cases. Generally, the purpose of the exclusionary rule is to have a general deterrent effect, not just a deterrent effect on a few specific officers.

Nonetheless, studies have been done and articles have been written analyzing the effect of the exclusionary rule on officers' conduct. One of the first and most comprehensive studies was done in 1970 by Dallin Oaks in his article entitled *Studying the Exclusionary Rule in Search and Seizure*.[62] Oaks's study has been cited numerous times by the Supreme Court and remains one of the premiere studies in this area. Oaks examined court records in several court jurisdictions and attempted to determine how the exclusionary rule was being implemented and whether the application of the rule to the states had changed the way police behaved. Oaks also considered the benefits of the rule and the costs of the rule and discussed alternatives to the rule.

Oaks stated that there was no evidence that would support whether or not the rule actually did deter police behavior. Oaks admitted that because it was impossible to actually measure the amount of police conduct that was inappropriate before **Mapp**, because such conduct was not "punished" in any way, it was further impossible to make any comparisons as to the frequency of such conduct following the **Mapp** case. Oaks determined that the best possibility of obtaining information that could provide any answer to this question was to consider laws that prohibited gambling and the sale and possession of weapons and narcotics, as the enforcement of those laws is highly dependent on searches and seizures. Thus, Oaks considered whether the total number of arrests and convictions for these crimes had declined following the passage of the rule; if the exclusionary rule in fact deterred officers, a decline should be seen. Oaks considered this question based on information gathered from Cincinnati, Ohio, and stated that there was a consistent annual reduction in the number of raids that resulted in gambling convictions in the years following **Mapp**, but that in the areas of narcotics and weapons offenses there was not a drop in convictions. However, Oaks also admitted that the decline in raids involving gambling offenses began in 1959, two years before the **Mapp** case was decided.

Another study was completed three years after Oaks's study and concluded that the **Mapp** case did seem to have an impact on crime in some cities, such as Baltimore, but not in other cities in which the same issue was studied.[63] For example, this study pointed out that the decreases in arrests other

---

62. 37 U. Chi. L. Rev. 665 (1970).

63. Bradley C. Canon, *Is the Exclusionary Rule in Failing Health? Some New Data and a Plea Against Precipitous Conclusion*, 62 Ky. L J 681 (1973).

than gambling cases after **Mapp** was decided "were both dramatically sudden and truly spectacular; one would be hard pressed to attribute them in large measure to anything but the imposition of the exclusionary rule."[64] Fourteen cities were studied, however, and Canon's conclusion was that a consideration of the data from all cities would not lead to the conclusion that the **Mapp** case had an effect overall on the number of arrest in crimes that involved search and seizure. Even the Supreme Court has stated that it does not believe that it will ever be possible to assemble conclusive data in this area.[65]

The Supreme Court often reviews social science and other research and considers it in making its decisions, often even citing the research in its opinions. The studies conducted by Oaks and others were cited in a footnote in the case of **United States v. Janis**.[66] The facts of the **Janis** case are as follows.

> On December 3, 1968, Leonard Weissman, a Los Angeles Police Department officer, informed Morris Nimovitz, a revenue officer of the Internal Revenue Service, that the plaintiff herein had been arrested for alleged bookmaking activities. Officer Weissman was the same person who had prepared the affidavit in support of the search warrant which had been quashed by Judge Lang on the basis of an insufficient affidavit in support thereof. Mr. Nimovitz proceeded to the Los Angeles Police Department and with the help of Officer Weissman, analyzed certain betting markers and information which had been seized pursuant to the aforementioned search warrant. On the basis of their analysis, the gross volume of bookmaking activities alleged to have been conducted by the plaintiff herein and Morris Aaron Levine was determined for the five days immediately preceding the arrest of the plaintiff herein and Morris Aaron Levine. Officer Weissman further informed Mr. Nimovitz that he had commenced his investigation of the plaintiff herein on September 14, 1968, which continued on an intermittent basis through November 30, 1968, the date of the arrest. On the basis of the information given by Officer Weissman to Mr. Nimovitz, the civil tax assessment was made by taking five days of activities as determined from the items seized pursuant to the aforementioned search warrant and multiplying the daily gross volume times 77 days, to wit, the period of Officer Weissman's intermittent surveillance (September 14, 1968 through November 30, 1968).[67]

In rendering its decision, the Supreme Court discussed the history of the exclusionary rule and the studies that had been done on its effects on law enforcement agents. The Court stated that each empirical study that had been conducted seemed to be flawed, not due to any fault of the researches, but because of the fact that there are so many variable factors to be considered. Recordkeeping by police agencies before the **Mapp** case was "spotty,"

---

64. **Id**, at 704.
65. E.g., **Elkins v. United States**, 364 U.S. 206, 218 (1960).
66. 428 U.S. 433 (1976).
67. **Id**. at 462.

according to the Court. Studies that rely on the responses of citizens might be hampered by the personal interests of the citizens that respond to survey questions. Extrapolation studies, which rely on historical information to predict future trends, can be influenced by many outside variables; in the case of the exclusionary rule, this includes better police/citizen relationships over time and constantly changing legal doctrines that affect court decisions and police behavior. The Court determined that all of the studies that had been done had one thing in common—they all demonstrated that it is nearly impossible to really make a determination as to whether the exclusionary rule has had an effect on police behavior. Some studies even attempted to demonstrate the difference between police behavior in the United States versus police behavior in other countries that do not have the exclusionary rule as a part of their legal system; however, this too is very difficult to study due to the numerous immeasurable variables that would have to be taken into consideration.

In the **Janis** case, because the Court was specifically faced with the issue of whether the exclusionary rule should apply in civil cases, and because the Court was utilizing as its underlying reasoning the consideration of whether the rule actually deters law enforcement officers from violating citizens' rights, the Court considered whether the rule would actually deter officers if evidence was excluded in civil court. After all, a police officer has something at stake when a person is prosecuted in criminal court; the officer's illegal search can result in a guilty person walking free and potentially committing more crimes in the community. In a civil case, a private individual sues another individual, so a police officer may have less at stake (other than, perhaps, her reputation). The **Janis** Court decided that the rule did not apply in civil cases, especially those which involved an officer from one jurisdiction providing illegally obtained evidence to another tribunal (for example, a state police officer providing evidence to a federal court). The Court opined that "the additional marginal deterrence provided by forbidding a different sovereign from using the evidence in a civil proceeding surely does not outweigh the cost to society of extending the rule to that situation. If, on the other hand, the exclusionary rule does not result in appreciable deterrence, then, clearly, its use in [a civil case] is unwarranted. Under either assumption, therefore, the extension of the rule is unjustified."[68] Although the person against whom the evidence is being used finds it very important that his rights not be violated and that the evidence against him be excluded, the Court determined that if police officers would not be "doubly deterred" if evidence is excluded in both criminal and civil procedures, there is no need to exclude the evidence in the civil court proceeding. The Court specifically stated that "exclusion from federal civil proceedings of evidence unlawfully seized by a state criminal enforcement officer has not been shown to have a sufficient likelihood of deterring the conduct of the state police so that it outweighs

---

68. **Id.** at 453, 454.

the societal costs imposed by the exclusion."[69] The dissenting opinion by Justice Stewart in the case pointed out that allowing illegally obtained evidence in a civil federal case just because it was seized by state officers, in effect, violates the silver platter doctrine that the Court has previously rejected, due to the fact that defendants would have more rights in one court system than the other. The dissent also stated that federal officials who are responsible for the enforcement of various civil provisions work closely with state officials and often call on them to conduct searches and seizures. Thus, the majority decision results in permitting officers in one jurisdiction to assist those in another jurisdiction by intentionally violating the Constitution.

The exclusionary rule can also cost society in that citizens will lose confidence in the police and the justice system. The public loses trust in the criminal justice system and becomes cynical when a person who is obviously guilty is not prosecuted because of what the public might refer to as a "technicality." Innocent people have nothing to gain from the exclusionary rule, as it will never be applied to them, but guilty people have everything to gain.

Another interesting aspect of the **Janis** case was the Court's discussion of prior Supreme Court decisions that relied not only on the issue of police deterrence but also on the concept of "judicial integrity" to support the exclusionary rule. These cases had stated that courts must not commit or encourage violations of the Constitution, and permitting evidence that was seized illegally by police encourages such violations. The Court's rejection of this doctrine in the **Janis** case was based on the fact that the violation is already complete by the time the case reaches the Court. Thus, the Court is in no way "encouraging" the violation, regardless of its decision regarding the exclusion of the evidence. The Court stated that judicial integrity does not mean that courts should never admit evidence obtained in violation of the Fourth Amendment.

The Costs of the Exclusionary Rule

In 1983, the Court tried an alternative approach to analyzing the exclusionary rule. In the case of **Illinois v. Gates**,[70] the Court considered the costs of the exclusionary rule. Obviously, the primary cost to society is that a criminal defendant would go free rather than being tried and incarcerated, and that the defendant might then commit more crimes, as he would not be incapacitated through incarceration, all because of a police officer's "technical" error. That case was a landmark case and the main issue was the standard to be used to determine whether sufficient probable cause was set forth in a search warrant application. However, in its decision, the Supreme Court justices

---

69. **Id**. at 454n.
70. 462 U.S. 213 (1983).

discussed and emphasized the importance of considering the "costs" of the exclusionary rule when deciding whether it applies to a factual scenario. The Court stated:

> The trend and direction of our exclusionary rule decisions indicate not a lesser concern with safeguarding the Fourth Amendment but a fuller appreciation of the high costs incurred when probative, reliable evidence is barred because of investigative error. The primary cost, of course, is that the exclusionary rule interferes with the truth-seeking function of a criminal trial by barring relevant and trustworthy evidence. We will never know how many guilty defendants go free as a result of the rule's operation.[71]

The Supreme Court again cited social science research in its opinion; a recent National Institute of Justice report had determined that approximately 30 percent of felony drug arrests were rejected by prosecutors because the cases involved search and seizure issues.[72] This statistic was cited in footnote 13 of the **Illinois v. Gates** case. However, further research demonstrates that the actual number of cases that were dismissed after arrest because of search and seizure issues, which can be definitively measured, was actually much lower than the NIJ report stated, as the NIJ study contained flawed interpretations of certain numbers. Although some will argue that even one lost arrest is a huge cost to society, this is controversial and subject to personal opinion. Remember, the opposing side of the issue is whether we as citizens want to be the subject of illegal searches and seizures. The exclusionary rule costs us as a society in that criminals may be free instead of incarcerated, but if there were no remedy for violations of the Constitution, police officers could trample on our rights if they desired with no concern of repercussions.

The counterargument to Justice White's argument, however, is that the exclusionary rule would never be an issue if officers did not violate the amendments. In other words, if the rules were upheld and there was no way to search someone's house constitutionally, the end result is that even if that person is guilty of a crime, they will go free. However, the opposing argument is that police should utilize their intelligence and skills and patiently investigate a crime until they have probable cause and then conduct their search in accordance with the Constitution.

Some argue that the exclusionary rule really does not change our lives much at all. If officers search against the exclusionary rule and find contraband, the contraband will be thrown out and the guilty party will be set free. However, if officers do not conduct the search because of their fear of the ramifications of the exclusionary rule, the guilty party will still go free. Further, officers may prefer to harass the suspect, confiscate contraband (the guilty party will not receive his cocaine back from the police, even if it was

---

71. **Illinois v. Gates** at 257.
72. National Institute of Justice, *The Effects of the Exclusionary Rule: A Study in California* (Washington, D.C.: U.S. Dept. of Justice, 1982).

seized illegally), and maybe even encourage the guilty party to become a police informant. The only time the exclusionary rule will really make a difference is when officers fail to obtain a warrant and could have. Officers who are cognizant of the exclusionary rule are more likely to obtain a warrant when they know they have probable cause to do so; entering the house with a warrant will yield evidence that can be presented in court, although evidence obtained when no warrant was obtained first and should have been will be excluded from court. Some scholars assert that the number of search warrants obtained in criminal cases rose following the **Mapp** decision.[73] Finally, when law enforcement personnel in California were surveyed, 60 percent reported that they did consider the threat of the exclusion of evidence to be an "important consideration" when they conducted searches and seizures.[74] In fact, 21 out of 22 police officers also reported when surveyed that they would be afraid to conduct searches they would be called upon to perform if civil lawsuits were the remedy used for unconstitutional searches and seizures rather than the exclusionary rule.[75] Thus, the exclusionary rule seems to allow officers to do their job without being completely stymied by possible repercussions.

One other issue that arises regarding the exclusionary rule is whether officers are more likely to lie about how evidence was obtained due to the exclusionary rule. Many times, officers claim that a defendant "drops" his drugs while running or that drugs are in "plain view" when the officer pulls someone over for a traffic violation. Some argue that this is really an officer making claims that are untrue in order to not have evidence thrown out under the exclusionary rule. Even the officer's argument as to why he effectuated a traffic stop could be untruthful; the officer might say a driver failed to stop at a stop sign when, in fact, the person stopped. Barring the use of dashboard-mounted cameras (which have been used successfully to prove that some traffic stops were inappropriate and in some situations proving that the officer's version of the facts were true), it can be very difficult to prove what actually happened prior to, or even during, a traffic stop. This argument, however, assumes that the majority of police officers are untruthful and will do anything they can to hassle citizens; commit inappropriate profiling based on race, age, or some other category; and generally assume that all citizens are engaging in criminal behavior. High-ranking police officers have actually admitted that they sometimes skew the facts of a case to prevent the suppression of evidence.[76] Although this topic can be debated fully in a criminal justice ethics course, we hope that most police officers are not unethical

---

73. Wayne R. LaFave, 1 *Search and Seizure: A Treatise on the Fourth Amendment*, §1.2(b) at 33 (West 4th ed. 2004).

74. Timothy Perrin, et al, *If It's Broken, Fix It: Moving Beyond the Exclusionary Rule*, 83 Iowa L. Rev. 669, 696 (1998).

75. Albert W. Alschuler, *Fourth Amendment Remedies: The Current Understanding*, in Eugene W. Hickok, Jr., ed., *The Bill of Rights: Original Meaning and Current Understanding* 197, 205 (Virginia 1991).

76. **Oaks** *supra* at 739.

YOU BE THE JUDGE

Consider the following scenario. What would you decide if you were the judge in this case?

Bobbie Barron was the bookkeeper at a used car dealership, Lonnie's Lemons. Ira Schwartz, an employee of the Attorney General's Office of the State of Connecticut, began investigating Lonnie's Lemons for suspected odometer tampering. Schwartz traced certain vehicles that were sold by Lonnie's and found that their odometers had higher readings when they were sold to Lonnie's by various other dealerships and owners than they did when Lonnie's sold them through a local automobile auction. There was also evidence that Lonnie's had been manufacturing false registrations for the vehicles.

Schwartz, along with two state law enforcement officials, executed a state search warrant at Barron's residence. The search warrant was determined later to be invalid. Upon executing the warrant, the officials seized 12 to 14 boxes of documents, along with a ledger book and some stamps that could have been used to forge registrations. The materials obtained in Barron's residence were taken back to Schwartz's office and reviewed over the course of four months. Schwartz then engaged in further interviews with various car dealers who had the cars previous to Lonnie's. Schwartz admits that he based his questioning of the dealers in part on the documents in the files he had illegally obtained.

The documents were eventually returned to Barron, who was convicted on state charges, and Barron voluntarily turned over the evidence to federal law enforcement officials.

The defense attorney is asking you to suppress all of the interviews based on the fruit of the poisonous tree doctrine. The prosecutor argues that the inevitable discovery rule applies here, because the evidence was eventually voluntarily turned over by Schwartz.

What do you decide and why?

and are doing their jobs in the hopes of properly fighting crime while protecting citizens' rights and following the rules.

Further, and perhaps contrary to the belief of the general public, few cases are actually resolved in the defendant's favor owing to the use of the exclusionary rule. Although members of the public might be horrified to see in their local newspaper that a case in which evidence was found that clearly implicates the defendant is being thrown out of court due to the use of the exclusionary rule, a 1983 study found that federal courts excluded unlawfully seized evidence in only 1.3 percent of all criminal cases.[77]

---

77. Thomas Y. Davies, *A Hard Look at What We Know (and Still Need to Learn) About the "Costs" of the Exclusionary Rule: An Empirical Assessment*, 8 Am. Bar Found. Res. J. 585, 596 (1983).

QUESTIONS TO CONSIDER

1. In the case of **People v. Defore**, 242 N.Y. 13, 150 N.E. 585 (1926), Justice Cardozo stated, "The criminal is to go free because the constable has blundered." Do you believe this is the case today, because of the exclusionary rule? If so, can you justify the use of the exclusionary rule? Consider the costs to society and the criminal justice system of enforcing the rule versus the costs if the rule was not in place.

2. Further, in the **Hudson v. Michigan** case discussed in this chapter, the Court refused to allow the use of the exclusionary rule when a knock and announce violation takes place. Some have suggested that this decision paved the way for further court decisions that might erode the use of the exclusionary rule. Do you believe the Supreme Court's reasoning in this case will open the door for an eventual elimination of the exclusionary rule?

3. Consider the facts from the **Rochin v. California** case. What other scenarios can you think of that would also shock the conscience of the court and lead the court to exclude the evidence on the basis of how it was gathered?

4. It appears as though the Supreme Court's primary concern when establishing the exclusionary rule is the deterrence of police officers. However, many of the cases the Court decided which excepts evidence from the exclusionary rule involves a violation of a defendant's constitutional rights. Do you believe the Court should focus so much on deterring inappropriate police conduct, or more on the fact that a defendant's rights are being violated?

5. Consider the facts of the **Mapp** case. Now that the **Herring** case has been decided by the Supreme Court, how do you think the **Mapp** case would be decided if it came in front of the Court again? What other facts would you need to know about the **Mapp** case to make this determination?

6. Assume that you are a juror in a criminal case and that the defendant is on trial for possession of illegal substances. Assume further that the illegal substances were found on the defendant but were suppressed. The substances are then brought in as evidence to demonstrate only that the defendant is lying on the stand. Do you believe that, as a juror, you could consider that evidence only in determining whether the defendant is telling the truth or not? Should the judge exclude the evidence entirely as too prejudicial for the jury to hear at all?

7. Go to the website www.parc.info/consent_decrees.chtml. Select one police department that has been the subject of a consent decree or other federal monitoring and read the articles and other information listed on the website regarding that department. Then find other resources on the

Internet that discuss the issues surrounding that monitoring. Do you believe the agreement entered into by that organization was appropriate considering the problems it was facing?

KEY TERMS

exclusionary rule
This provides for the exclusion of evidence that was obtained by law enforcement agencies in violation of the Fourth Amendment, and was adopted by the Supreme Court for federal cases in 1886 and later extended to the state level with the **Mapp v. Ohio** case in 1961. It protects against the use of illegally seized evidence in trial, protecting Fourth Amendment rights of those who are charged with crimes.

fruit of the poisonous tree doctrine
This doctrine provides that evidence that is obtained as a result of evidence discovered in an illegal initial search will also be excluded from court.

general deterrence
If evidence is excluded in a case and all officers become concerned enough to change their actions so that the same thing does not happen in any of their cases, this process would be considered general deterrence.

harmless error rule
The ruling that the introduction of inadmissible evidence into a trial did not have an adverse effect on the outcome of the trial.

independent source doctrine
An exception to the exclusionary rule, this doctrine applies when a prosecutor can prove to the court that the evidence challenged by the defendant was not obtained as a result of the initial illegal search.

inevitable discovery
This rule states that if police were sure to have discovered the evidence in some other manner notwithstanding the illegal seizure, the evidence can be admitted.

qualified immunity
This is a defense that can be used by officials to protect them from being sued, and applies whenever an official acts with a mistaken belief, as long as that belief is reasonable.

silver platter doctrine
This doctrine refers to the fact that defendants in federal court had the benefit of exclusionary rule although those in state courts did not.

specific deterrence
If a particular officer violates the Constitution and the evidence obtained by him is excluded, and he decides not to violate the law in the future, this process would be considered specific deterrence.

standing
The issue of whether a particular person has the right to bring an issue before a court.

KEY COURT CASES

Arizona v. Evans

In this case, the Court diluted the exclusionary rule still further when it determined that a clerical error by the court will also not help the defendant in requesting that evidence be suppressed. The Court ruled that because the exclusionary rule was created to deter officers from committing illegal or unconstitutional acts, the officers in this case would not have changed their behavior had the court excluded the evidence, as they would not normally assume that the information entered into a system by a clerk was incorrect. The exclusionary rule was created to deter police conduct, not the conduct of court employees.

Hudson v. Michigan

This case imposed a severe limitation to the exclusionary rule regarding the illegality in the manner of entering. The crux of the decision is that the Court must always consider whether the potential deterrence of law enforcement resulting from the rule outweigh its substantial social costs. If not, the rule should not be applied. Specifically, the Court ruled that a violation of the knock and announce rule does not invoke the exclusionary rule.

Illinois v. Gates

This case considered the costs of the exclusionary rule. This case was a landmark case, and the main issue was the standard to be used to determine whether sufficient probable cause was set forth in a search warrant application. However, in its decision, the Court discussed and emphasized the importance of considering the costs of the exclusionary rule when deciding whether it applies to a factual scenario.

Mapp v. Ohio

This case incorporated the exclusionary rule to all state criminal cases in 1961.

Massachusetts v. Sheppard

This case involved an officer using a previously used search warrant form, merely changing some of the information, leading to an incorrect application being filed and approved. The Court determined that, like the **Leon** case, the officer need not second guess the judge.

Monroe v. Pape

One of the first real tests of Section 1983 of the Federal Code—Civil Rights Act—this case addressed the violation of civil rights by the city of Chicago and police officers. The Court threw out the case against the city, but did hold the individual officers liable for damages.

Silverthorne Lumber Co. v. United States

This case was the first suggestion by the Supreme Court of the fruit of the poisonous tree rule. The Court ruled that the original documents had been seized illegally, and the evidence on which the request to produce the originals was based was obtained only through the illegal seizure. The Court ruled that because the government would not have had the information to obtain the subpoena without the benefit of the original illegal seizure, the subpoena was invalid.

United States v. Leon

This case established the good faith exception. The Court ruled that the officers should not be expected to question the magistrate's probable cause determination, and that a police officer's conduct would not be deterred by a rule that forced officers to second guess a judge's decision of probable cause.

United States v. Padilla

This case stated that merely being a co-conspirator in a case does not give rise to standing to argue that a search and seizure was inappropriate, and the Court remanded the case to the trial court to determine whether each individual had either a property interest protected by the Fourth Amendment that was interfered with by the stop of the automobile, or a reasonable expectation of privacy that was invaded by the search thereof.

Weeks v. United States

In this case, the Court ruled that papers seized and held by the government must be returned to their owner.

THE FIFTH AMENDMENT

6

LEARNING OBJECTIVES: Students will

1. Understand what due process is
2. Know the law surrounding police interrogations
3. Know when a defendant has a right to remain silent and how that right is preserved
4. Understand the **Miranda** rules and the exceptions thereto
5. Know when double jeopardy applies to a case

No person shall be held to answer for a capital, or otherwise infamous crime, unless on a presentment or indictment of a Grand Jury, except in cases arising in the land or naval forces, or in the Militia, when in actual service in time of War or public danger; nor shall any person be subject for the same offense to be twice put in jeopardy of life or limb; nor shall be compelled in any criminal case to be a witness against himself, nor be deprived of life, liberty, or property, without due process of law; nor shall private property be taken for public use, without just compensation.

—U.S. Constitution, Amendment V

The Fifth Amendment frequently comes up in media discussions or representations of crime and criminal justice. This makes sense, as it has implications in the contexts of the arrest, interrogation, and trial, all under the guiding principle of due process. Everyone is aware that officers read criminal suspects their "Miranda rights," but few are aware of the exact instances or circumstances in which these rights must be read. The final disposition of a criminal case can depend greatly on whether or not a person confessed to a crime following an interrogation by law enforcement. A defendant can always choose to remain silent outside court and in court, and other witnesses can be protected from having to testify if that testimony could incriminate them in other matters.

DUE PROCESS

The concept of **due process** is a cornerstone of the criminal court system in the United States. The assurance that each criminal defendant will receive due process as her case proceeds through the court system comes both from the language of the Constitution and from the way our criminal justice system has evolved over time. Due process involves the balancing of personal rights with the right of the government to control citizens through the use of laws and procedures. Simply, the concept of due process can be defined as being the concept of fairness. Due process involves rules and procedures and the defendant's right to be informed as to what those rules and procedures are. It protects the accused against random government actions and arbitrariness within the law. It also requires a balancing of rules with the rights of the individual.

The term "due process" appears in both the Fifth and Fourteenth Amendments. In the Fifth Amendment, the concept of due process means that before a court can take away someone's rights, or impose penalties upon that person, certain procedures must be followed. These procedures, as discussed in the prior chapters of this book, especially as they relate to the topic of search and seizure, are designed to protect individuals from oppressive government conduct and from the risk that unreliable evidence would be used to convict a person of a crime, perhaps one that the person did not actually commit. The concept of due process in the Fourteenth Amendment relates to incorporation and the requirement that the states follow certain provisions of the Constitution, as discussed previously in this book. As with other regulations and rights, due process can be broken down into the areas of substantive due process and procedural due process. Although substantive due process relates only to criminal law, procedural due process applies to both criminal and civil court proceedings. Due process also prohibits laws that are vague.

Although our concept of due process evolved from rights given to English subjects, the concept has evolved in our country in a way it has not evolved in England. However, the concept is found in clause 39 of the Magna Carta, which states that "No free man shall be seized or imprisoned, or stripped of his rights or possessions, or outlawed or exiled, or deprived of his standing in any other way, nor will we proceed with force against him, or send others to do so, except by the lawful judgment of his equals or by the law of the land." The Magna Carta provided for a panel of 25 barons to decide what redress should take place if a king "offended" a man. This could be interpreted as similar to our appeals court, in which a panel of judges determines if another judge (who is an arm of the government, like a king) decided a person's case appropriately.

The actual phrase "due process of law" first appeared in the Magna Carta in 1354 and stated as follows: "No man of what state or condition he be, shall be put out of his lands or tenements nor taken, nor disinherited, nor put to death, without he be brought to answer by due process of law." The case of

Regina v. Paty,[1] was decided in 1704 and provided an interpretation of the due process clause of the Magna Carta. The House of Commons had deprived John Paty and other English citizens the right to vote in an election. Further, the House of Commons had imprisoned the individuals because they pursued a legal action in the courts in the attempt to declare that the government's act of preventing them from voting was wrong. The Queen's Bench (the deciding court for Paty's case), stated in its decision, which was not in favor of Paty, that due process provides that "all commitments must be by a legal authority."[2] A dissenting judge argued that the House of Commons had legislated unilaterally without approval of the House of Lords, and that the House of Commons had thus overstepped its bounds, thereby violating due process. Interestingly, however, Queen Anne nonetheless freed Paty by exercising her right to discontinue the current session of parliament. Despite the mention of due process in England's important charter, the United States Supreme Court itself stated that due process in England was not "essential to the idea of due process of law in the prosecution and punishment of crimes, but was only mentioned as an example and illustration of due process of law as it actually existed in cases in which it was customarily used."[3] Frankly, the English courts were not given any means to declare that laws or statutes created by the government were invalid, so a law or statute that violated due process was not apt to be stricken.

The Government's Obligation to Provide the Defendant with Notice of Charges

A person who is charged with a crime can only defend himself against that crime if he knows specifically what he is being charged with. The Sixth Amendment provides that in criminal prosecutions, "the accused shall . . . be informed of the nature and cause of the accusation." Thus, a criminal defendant has the right to know the charges being lodged against him, so he can properly raise a defense. This part of the Sixth Amendment is applied to the states through the due process clause of the Fourteenth Amendment and also ensures that a defendant receives due process. This right is assured through the filing of an indictment or information that alleges all of the elements of the crime that has been committed. The main case in this area is **United States v. Carll,**[4] in which the Supreme Court stated that an indictment filed against a defendant is not sufficient if it sets forth the "offense in the words of the statute, unless those words of themselves fully, directly, and expressly, without any uncertainty or ambiguity, set forth all the elements necessary to constitute the offense intended to be punished." In **Carll,** an

---

1. 92 Eng. Rep. 232 (1704).
2. **Id.** at 234.
3. **Hurtado v. California**, 110 U.S. 516 (1884).
4. 105 U.S. 611 (1881).

individual was charged under the statute that prohibits passing counterfeit money. However, the language used in the charges lodged against the defendant stated merely that the defendant had violated a federal statute, and then went on to repeat the statute itself word for word. The indictment gave information regarding the times and places of the crime but did not give any evidence or specific allegation that the defendant knew the bills were counterfeit, which was a requirement under the statute. The question was whether this recitation of the facts, which left out that main issue, was sufficient to inform the defendant of the nature of the charges against him. The Supreme Court ruled that it did not. Thus, a successful police officer and prosecutor will ensure that all facts that demonstrate that a particular aspect of a statute has been violated are included specifically in the language of the indictment.

In **United States v. Cruikshank**,[5] the Supreme Court considered a racially charged case decided after the Civil War, using the Sixth Amendment arraignment/indictment clause to justify its decision. In the South, most of the former slaves became Republicans, as that had been President Lincoln's political party. The Democratic party was controlled by racist whites, and in an election, the Republicans had won seats in some political offices. The Democrats had threatened violence if the Republicans actually moved to take over those offices after they had won them in the election. In the town of Colfax, Louisiana, local Republicans had gathered around the court-house to protect it from being taken over by racist Democrats. A battle ensued, and several hundred African Americans were killed. Charges were filed against some of the Democrats for charges of conspiracy; the Democrats were alleged to have conspired to hinder the Republicans from exercising their constitutional rights to assemble, to bear arms, and to exercise free speech. The Supreme Court threw out the Democrats' convictions, stating among other things, that the indictment did not give specific enough details about how the Democrats had taken away the African Americans' rights. Although some other portions of the court's decision have been overturned, the issue of the specificity of the indictment remains good law today.

The Government's Obligation to Disclose Information to the Defendant

The justice system in the United States is predicated upon the premises that (1) we desire, in the long run, to know the truth and to convict only those persons who actually commit a crime, and (2) the defendant has the right to be assumed innocent until proven guilty. Thus, the defense generally has no obligation to disclose to the prosecution any tests or expert reports that it has obtained, and generally will not do so if those reports or tests are adverse

---

5. 92 U.S. 542 (1875).

YOU BE THE JUDGE

A defendant has been charged with distributing a paper through the United States mail that was "obscene, lewd, and lascivious," in violation of a statute that prohibits such mail. Ignoring any First Amendment freedom of speech issues that might be present regarding the statute itself, is this description of the defendant's crime sufficient to inform the defendant of the nature of the charges against him to the point at which he can properly prepare a defense? Assume that the specific indictment states as follows:

> . . . unlawfully, willfully, and knowingly deposit and cause to be deposited in the post office of the City of New York, for mailing and delivery by the post office establishment of the United States, a certain obscene, lewd, and lascivious paper, which said paper then and there, on the first page thereof, was entitled "Tenderloin Number, Broadway," and on the same page were printed the words and figures following, that is to say: "Volume II, number 27; trademark, 1892; by Lew Rosen; New York, Saturday, April 15, 1893; ten cents a copy, $4.00 a year in advance," and thereupon, on the same page, is the picture of a cab, horse, driver, and the figure of a female, together (underneath the said picture) with the word "Tenderloineuse," and the said paper consists of twelve pages, minute description of which, with the pictures therein and thereon would be offensive to the court and improper to spread upon the records of the court because of their obscene, lewd, and indecent matters, and the said paper, on the said twenty-fourth day of April, in the year one thousand eight hundred and ninety-three, was enclosed in a wrapper, and addressed as follows, that is to say: "Mr. Geo. Edwards, P.O. Box 510, Summit, N.J."—against the peace of the United States and their dignity, and contrary to the statute of the United States in such case made and provided.

The government argued that the indictment does not specifically describe the actual contents of the paper, except what appears previously, because "decent people" should not discuss such subjects. The indictment itself uses less offensive language than what the actual paper included. The defendant argues that the indictment should state the specific words used in the allegedly offensive documents. You are the judge—do you find that the indictment is specific enough or not?

to the defendant. However, the prosecution does have an obligation to turn over any evidence it obtains, whether detrimental to its case or not. The case that established this rule is **Brady v. Maryland,**[6] and many convictions have been overturned as a result of what the courts now refer to as a "Brady violation." The **Brady** decision stated that **exculpatory evidence,** or evidence that

---

6. 373 U.S. 83 (1963).

would assist the defense, cannot be withheld from the defense by the prosecution. Although other cases, which are discussed later, followed and clarified the **Brady** decision, courts, prosecutors, and defense attorneys continue to refer to issues regarding a prosecutor's failure to turn over evidence as **Brady** issues. The facts and an explanation of the Court's holding in the **Brady** case follow, along with a discussion of later cases that clarified the holding in **Brady**.

BRADY V. MARYLAND

FACTS: The State of Maryland prosecuted Brady and another person, Boblit, on charges of murder. Brady confessed to being involved in the murder but stated that Boblit had actually committed the murder. Boblit had written a statement that admitted that he had killed the victim by himself, without involvement from Brady. Brady appealed his conviction to the Maryland Court of Appeals, which affirmed his conviction and remanded the case to the trial court for the question of punishment only. The case was eventually appealed to the Supreme Court of the United States.

ISSUE: Whether the prosecutor's act of withholding exculpatory evidence violated the due process clause of the Fourteenth Amendment.

HOLDING: The prosecutor must disclose to the defense all exculpatory evidence it obtains.

RATIONALE: When the prosecutor receives evidence that could assist the defendant in defending the charges that have been lodged against him, the prosecutor must disclose that evidence to the defense. This is true when the evidence is either material to the guilt of the defendant or the potential punishment of the defendant. In Brady's case, the evidence, if disclosed, could have affected the level of punishment that Brady would have received.

Following the **Brady** decision, states and the federal government considered its ramifications and have considered when evidence is considered reasonable. Evidence is considered exculpatory if it is probable that a defendant's conviction or sentence would have been different if the materials had been disclosed to the defense prior to trial or sentencing. Consider all of the exculpatory types of evidence that, if offered to a jury or a judge as evidence in a trial, could have changed the outcome of the trial or the defendant's sentence. Certainly, any statements made by witnesses or co-defendants are important. Physical evidence can also be very important. Consider how important DNA testing, ballistics testing, or blood or other evidence of bodily fluids can be in a case. Now consider how unfair it would be to a defendant if the police had DNA from the scene of a crime tested, determined that it did not belong to the defendant, and failed to disclose that testing to the defendant. A defendant may not have enough funding to have his own tests run, or he might not even know that physical evidence was taken from the scene of the crime. Although finding DNA that belongs to an individual other than the defendant at the scene of the crime does not always demonstrate sufficiently that a defendant was not at the scene, it can be used by the defendant to at least make the argument that someone else must have been present. Any physical evidence that is found at the scene of the crime can be crucial to a defense. According to **Giglio v. United States**,[7] any deals that are made between the prosecution and a witness, for example, reducing charges against one person in return for him testifying against another, must be disclosed to the defense so that the deal can be disclosed to the fact finder (in most cases, the jury). The fact finder can then consider the deal when gauging whether the witness has reason to be untruthful.

Further evidence that must be disclosed under the **Brady** decision is that which would allow the defense to impeach the credibility of one of the prosecution's witnesses. An example of this type of failure to disclose was found by the Supreme Court in the case of **Banks v. Dretke**.[8] In that case, the defendant was convicted of capital murder and received a death sentence. The prosecution had indicated to the defense, prior to trial, that it would provide any information the defense needed in terms of discovery. However, the states instead held back two crucial pieces of information: (1) evidence that one of the prosecution's witnesses was a paid police informant and (2) a pre-trial transcript held by the prosecution that revealed that the witness had been coached by prosecutors and law enforcement officers. The Supreme Court determined that the information surrounding both of these witnesses were very important for the defense to have, especially because during the trial in the case, the prosecution allowed the police informant to testify that he had never given the police any statement and had not talked to any police officer about the case until a few days before the trial, when the pre-trial transcript showed otherwise. The Supreme Court stated that this was clearly a violation of **Brady** and that the concern was not only whether the defendant would have received a different verdict had the evidence in question been disclosed to him, but whether in the absence of receiving that information, the defendant actually received a fair trial, with a verdict that was "worthy of confidence."

In 1976, in **United States v. Agurs**,[9] the Supreme Court set forth tests that should be used to determine whether exculpatory evidence will be material, as follows. If the prosecutor relies on testimony that he knows is false or if he fails to disclose information to the defense that the defense requests, a reviewing court must consider whether any reasonable likelihood exists that the false

---

7. 405 U.S. 159 (1972).
8. 540 U.S. 668 (2004).
9. 427 U.S. 97 (1976).

testimony or the information that was not disclosed would have affected the judgment of the jury. If the prosecutor fails to disclose unrequested information (for example, if the defense asks for "all information" or "all information discoverable under **Brady**"), the conviction can be overturned if it creates reasonable doubt in the mind of the court as to whether or not the defendant is guilty. Both tests are similar, in considering reasonableness, but the first asks for a prediction of the possibility of a change in the jury's decision. However, failure merely to turn over evidence that was not even specifically requested by the defense is considered less of a concern and must be demonstrated to change the court's mind about the guilt of the defendant. The **Agurs** test was revisited in **United States v. Bagley**,[10] in which the court eliminated the different tests for withholding different types of evidence. The Court stated that the test from that point on would be that ANY evidence withheld by the prosecution would result in a conviction being overturned if there was a reasonable probability that, had the evidence been disclosed to the defense, the proceeding would have resulted in a different verdict.

In the case of **Stickler v. Greene**,[11] the Supreme Court established a three-part test to be used by reviewing courts in cases in which a **Brady** violation had taken place by the prosecution. The three components are as follows: (1) whether the evidence at issue is favorable to the accused because it is either exculpatory or it impeaches the testimony or a witness, (2) whether the state (prosecution) kept the evidence from the defense either willfully or inadvertently, and (3) whether the defendant's case was prejudiced as a result of not receiving the evidence. However, the concepts found in **Brady** were further clarified in **Kyles v. Whitley**.[12] The Supreme Court discussed the **Bagley** materiality test as follows. First, the Court said that the question should not be whether the defendant would more likely than not have received a different verdict (similar to the preponderance of the evidence test that is used in civil court). Rather, the question should be whether the defendant received a fair trial when he did not receive the evidence. The Court further opined that the test should not be a sufficiency of the evidence test; in other words, the question is not whether, without the exculpatory evidence, enough evidence was presented to convict the defendant. Further, the Court stated that a reviewing court should not use the **harmless error** test, which is used so often in cases involving prosecutorial misconduct. The harmless error test mandates that even if the prosecutor makes a statement that is inappropriate or unethical, or if, for example, a trial court makes an erroneous ruling in terms of whether some evidence should be permitted to be entered into trial (such as hearsay evidence), the case will only be reversed if the court finds that the evidence truly caused "harm," or changed the outcome of the trial. In other words, the court is allowed to second guess, for example,

---

10. 473 U.S. 667 (1985).
11. 527 U.S. 263 (1999).
12. 514 U.S. 419 (1995).

what the jury determined, based on the other evidence it received, and determine whether it feels that the jury's decision would have changed based on the erroneous evidence being entered. Finally, the **Kyles** court placed a burden on the prosecution to find out all evidence that various prosecutorial agencies had received. Thus, the police, for example, should hand over all of the evidence it obtained to the prosecutor so the prosecutor can consider whether it should be disclosed in accordance with **Brady**. In fact, prosecutors may have a duty to notify the defense if a law enforcement official who is involved in the investigation of the defendant's case has a significant history of knowingly failing to tell the truth. The duty to turn over the evidence is absolute, and not one of "good faith." Any mistakes made by the prosecution will be held to a strict standard, regardless of whether the prosecutor "meant" to withhold the evidence or not.

The case of **Gardner v. Florida**[13] mandates that a defendant who is being sentenced to death must have the opportunity to deny or explain the information that is presented against him in the penalty phase of his case. In the **Gardner** case, evidence presented against the defendant in the penalty phase of his death penalty case included evidence in a pre-sentence investigation report that was prepared by the state parole commission. The report contained a confidential portion that was not disclosed to the defense. Of course, the trial court considered the information in the confidential portion of the report when considering whether the defendant would receive the death penalty. Because the defendant had no ability to see the portion of the report, rebut it, or cross-examine the persons who prepared the report, the reviewing court found that the use of the report violated the defendant's rights. However, in other cases when information is presented at a penalty hearing and might be a surprise to the defendant but he is able to cross-examine the witnesses who are stating the evidence, courts have decided that no violation of the defendant's rights occurred.[14]

The **Brady** case and the string of cases interpreting and expanding upon it does not give the defense any obligation to disclose information to the prosecution. Disclosure rules vary by state, and federal rules also mandate certain disclosures. Some states do provide that the prosecution can be entitled to obtain information from the defense prior to trial, in certain situations. Under the federal rules, if a defendant asks for certain information, it must provide the same type of information to the prosecutor if it holds such information, unless the information involves the defendant's prior record or statements of the defendant that are not already in the files of the prosecutor. It is difficult to imagine a situation in which the defense has information regarding the defendant's criminal record that the prosecution does not have; however, it could be possible that a defendant would have a copy of a statement that had been made to someone other than a law enforcement agent that the defense could keep to

---

13. 430 U.S. 349 (1977).
14. *See* **Gray v. Netherland**, 518 U.S. 152 (1996).

itself. Some states also require that a defendant give notice to the prosecution within a certain amount of time before trial of any alibi defenses that the defendant is going to present, including the names of alibi witnesses. In some states, if the defendant is going to use an insanity defense at trial, he will have to disclose that to the prosecutor so that the prosecution can consider any evidence it might need to present that would counter the argument that the defendant was mentally ill at the time of the offense and thus unable to control his actions or understand the law; names of any expert witness that the defendant intends to call to discuss his mental capacity must also be disclosed to the prosecution.

Informants

A particularly interesting area of disclosure law is in the area of informants. Every defendant, for legitimate trial-related reasons and for other reasons, would like the government to disclose the names of informants that it has used to obtain information. Often, the information provided by the informant is the basis for probable cause to obtain warrants for arrest or to search the defendant's house, car, or other property. Thus, it would be helpful for the defense to be able to cross-examine the informant regarding the information she gave the police, in order to determine whether enough information was really disclosed to establish probable cause. Further, the defendant would always like to know which of his "friends" or acquaintances turned on him and gave the police information about his criminal activities. The prosecution, of course, does not want to give away the names of its informants, in order to protect the informants and in order to be able to use the informants again in the future. Once everyone knows that a particular person has given the police information, no one will involve that person in any illegal transactions or activities, and this would eliminate most of a police agency's sources for obtaining information about crimes. Further, the "business" of being an informant would be very dangerous if the informant's identity was freely disclosed to defendants against whom the informant is turning over information. As the California Court of Appeals stated, "It does not take a lively imagination to realize that disclosure of an informant's identity might constitute a death warrant for the informer."[15] In fact, the common law policy not to disclose the identity of informants has been codified in the Federal Rules of Evidence. Rule 1041(a)(2) states that "[d]isclosure of the identity of the informer is against the public interest."[16]

There are a few occasions in which a court might require the prosecutor to disclose the name of an informant. In **Rovario v. United States**,[17] the Supreme Court considered a case in which the defendant was charged with narcotics

---

15. **People v. Pacheco**, 27 Cal. App. 3d 70, 80 (1972).
16. Fed. R. Evid. 1041(a)(2).
17. 353 U.S. 53 (1957).

transactions and the only person who was present during the transactions was the undercover government informant. Because the informant was the only person who could testify in opposition to what government officials were testifying to in terms of the drug transaction, the prosecution was required to turn over the name of the informant. The **Rovario** court stated that a court considering whether the identity of an informant should be divulged should weigh "the public interest in protecting the flow of information against the individual's right to prepare his defense."[18] In a case in which the informant merely gives the government information that allows the government to then have enough probable cause to do a search and the search actually leads to a finding of drugs or other paraphernalia in the defendant's possession, the prosecution will not need to have the informant testify or to divulge the informant's name so that the defense can call him to testify. As long as the informant was not an actual participant in the charged offense, or a direct witness to it, his or her identity most likely will not be disclosed. The Court in **Rovario** even went so far as to state that information which would lead to the identity of the informant is also considered privileged. In other words, the defense does not have a right to know about any information that could reveal the identity of the informant, even if that information will be used against the defendant in court or was used to obtain a warrant.

SELF-INCRIMINATION

The Fifth Amendment states that "no person shall be compelled in any criminal case to be a witness against himself." This right has been used by many defendants to avoid testifying in criminal court proceeding and is often referred to as "pleading the Fifth." The rule against self-incrimination, at common law, applied only to actual trial procedures and not to pre-trial procedures. The rule that prohibited forced self-incrimination in the investigation stage emerged in the late eighteenth century in England with an exclusionary rule being created to ban the introduction of such evidence from trial. The premise of both rules was to avoid false confessions and heavy-handedness by the government. The public is often shocked by the fact that defendants can avoid having to say anything during a trial. This right was incorporated to the states in the case of **Malloy v. Hogan,**[19] decided in 1963. It is assumed that if someone is coerced to testify, they might not tell the truth. If forced to give an answer to a question that is incriminating, many will lie. Thus, if the ultimate goal of our justice system is to find the truth, compelling defendants to testify will not lead to this end. Further, our justice system is an accusatorial system, not an inquisitorial system. This means that

---

18. Id. at 62.
19. 378 U.S. 1 (1964).

a defendant is considered innocent until proven guilty, and an accused person has no duty to prove that he is innocent. Instead, the state must prove that the defendant is guilty. Thus, the defendant need not explain his side of the story; the state must present a strong enough case to demonstrate to a fact finder that the defendant in fact committed a crime.

The privilege against self-incrimination can only be asserted by people. It cannot be asserted by any other entity, such as a business or corporation. Further, a person cannot "plead the Fifth" on behalf of someone else or to protect someone else's interests. Only if the information the person will testify to could incriminate her personally can she avoid being forced to testify. Further, the person can assert the privilege only if the testimony she is trying to avoid giving could be used against her later in a criminal prosecution. If the information could merely be used against her in a civil proceeding or if a criminal prosecution has already taken place, the assertion cannot be made.

Courts have had to consider whether the privilege against self-incrimination applies to more than testimony. Court proceedings include both testimonial and real evidence. **Testimonial evidence** is any evidence that is set forth verbally by a person in court. Occasionally testimonial evidence includes a transcript of testimony taken from someone outside a trial if the person will not be available at trial. This evidence is clearly related to self-incrimination. However, another very important type of evidence, especially in today's society when crime scene investigation is the basis of many popular television shows, is real evidence. **Real evidence** includes any evidence that is not testimonial, such as physical evidence. Although testimonial evidence is questionable because anyone is capable of lying, real evidence can be quite damaging to a defendant or to the prosecution. Many people have been exonerated after the fact based on, for example, DNA evidence that was tested after the person's original trial. Others have been convicted based on photographs or other pieces of real evidence that link the person to the crime. The Supreme Court faced this question early on, in 1910. In **Holt v. United States**,[20] the Supreme Court considered a case in which a defendant was indicted and convicted of murder on a military base, having been accused of beating another man with an iron bar. Holt made some arguments regarding incriminating statements he argued he was forced to make to authorities. Holt also developed an argument that the Court called an "extravagant extension of the Fifth Amendment." A witness testified that Holt had put on a shirt that was purported to have been used in the murder and that it fit him. Holt objected that he did this under duress, under the same circumstances that made his testimony forced. The Court disagreed, stating as follows:

> But the prohibition of compelling a man in a criminal court to be witness against himself is a prohibition of the use of physical or moral compulsion to extort communications from him, not an exclusion of his body as evidence

---

20. 218 U.S. 245 (1910).

when it may be material. The objection in principle would forbid a jury to look at a prisoner and compare his features with a photograph in proof. Moreover, we need not consider how far a court would go in compelling a man to exhibit himself. For when he is exhibited, whether voluntarily or by order, and even if the order goes too far, the evidence, if material, is competent.[21]

Anything that is physically apparent in a person is considered real evidence. Photographs of a defendant's body, including tattoos and scars, are considered real evidence and are not subject to the rule against self-incrimination. Requiring a suspect to participate in a lineup, as discussed in Chapter 7, can be required, including forcing him to speak, as the tone of his voice and his physical characteristics are not considered testimonial evidence. Samples of blood or other bodily fluids, including a person's hair or DNA, are not considered testimonial. Another issue involves whether requiring a defendant to respond to a subpoena that requests documents is considered testimonial. The Supreme Court has not created a bright-line rule for such circumstances, determining instead that the circumstance of each case should be considered. The argument against ruling that this type of information is testimonial is based on the fact that the person does not need to restate, explain, or even affirm the truth of the documents that he is handing over. It merely confirms that the person believes that the papers being handed over are those being requested in the subpoena. Alternately, an argument can be made that by producing the paperwork, a person is communicating to someone else the contents of the papers. Certainly such a production entails the individual conceding that those papers exist.

An interesting case in which the Court was required to apply this rule was that of **Baltimore Department of Social Services v. Bouknight**.[22] The case involved a woman, Jacqueline Bouknight, who was suspected of child abuse when her son was three months old. Her son was removed from her car by the Baltimore Department of Social Services but was later returned to Bouknight, although she was required to fulfill certain requirements. Several months later, a court order was sought and received by Social Services to once again remove the child from Bouknight's home based on a concern that the child was in danger. Bouknight refused to turn over the child in accordance with the court order. Bouknight argued that turning over the child would, in essence, be incriminating herself. The Supreme Court disagreed, stating that "a person may not claim the [Fifth] Amendment's protections based upon the incrimination that may result from the contents or nature of the thing demanded." The Court tempered its decision by stating that in this case, Bouknight's production of her son was part of a "noncriminal regulatory scheme" and could thus be required regardless of whether producing her son was considered testimonial or not. Bouknight was jailed for contempt

21. **Id.** at 252.
22. 493 U.S. 549 (1990).

THE WHITEWATER SCANDAL

In the early 1990s a scandal referred to as "Whitewater" involved President Bill Clinton and his wife Hillary. The issue involved the Clintons' investment and loss of money in the Whitewater development project, a failed business venture in which the Clintons had engaged with Jim and Susan McDougal, their business partners. Criminal allegations were lodged against Bill Clinton by a man named David Hale, who claimed that Clinton, while governor of Arkansas, pressured him into providing an illegal loan to Susan McDougal. The Clintons were never prosecuted, but Susan McDougal refused to answer any questions about the Whitewater project and ended up serving 18 months in prison for contempt of court for her failure to speak. McDougal could be put in prison based on her failure to speak, as the charges were being lodged against Clinton, not the McDougals. Thus, the privilege against self-incrimination applies only to those being forced to testify against themselves, and not against others. Interestingly, McDougal was later pardoned by Bill Clinton before he left the office of president.

of court and remained in prison for seven and a half years, at which point she was released by a judge who stated that because she had not yet produced the boy within seven years, clearly the imprisonment would not result in her production of the child. Sadly, some assume that the child was dead, as he was never produced.

The privilege against self-incrimination can be asserted at any stage of the court proceedings, including pre-trial, grand jury investigations, and even custodial interrogations (consider this when you are reading the section later regarding **Miranda** rights). The privilege can be claimed by a person who is claiming to be innocent. The Supreme Court made that decision in the case of **Ohio v. Reiner**[23] after the prosecution argued that if a person were claiming to be innocent, they could not argue that anything that they would say could harm them. The Supreme Court disagreed, stating that the government could actually receive incriminating evidence from an "innocent witness" who speaks the truth.

Another issue related to self-incrimination is whether a defendant is required to answer questions that a police officer poses to him. Besides the issue of the right to remain silent, included in the warnings required by the **Miranda** case, this question comes up in the case of a **Terry** stop and

---

23. 121 S. Ct. 1252 (2001).

frisk. The purpose of asking a person questions in a **Terry** encounter is to determine whether to continue with a frisk. The Supreme Court ruled in the case of **Hiibel v. Nevada**[24] that a person does not have the right to refuse to provide identification to the police if requested in the case of a traffic stop. The defendant argued that this was a violation of his right not to incriminate himself, but the Supreme Court disagreed, permitting states to pass statutes that make the failure to show identification a crime, as long as the statute also provided the necessity for the officer to possess a specific level of reasonable and articulable suspicion of criminal involvement. The Court did keep open the idea that if the suspect could prove that giving his name would incriminate him, it is possible he could argue in his specific case that his right not to incriminate himself had been violated. The Court found that the officer's request for the defendant's identity in the case of a traffic stop was related to the purpose, rationale, and practical demands of the stop. The Court balanced the intrusion into the individual's privacy against the extent to which the stop-and-identify law promoted legitimate government interests and concluded that the law was valid.

INTERROGATIONS AND CONFESSIONS

Confessions

Any law enforcement official or prosecutor will admit that confessions make a case much easier to prosecute and are a huge factor in obtaining guilty pleas and convictions in the criminal justice system. Once a jury hears evidence that a defendant has confessed to a crime, it is difficult to prove to the jury that the defendant did not commit the crime. However, any confession must be made voluntarily to comply with the due process clauses of the Fifth and Fourteenth Amendments. It is important that people are confessing to crimes because they actually committed the crime and not because they are fearful of the police and what will happen to them if they do not confess. It is also important that police do not deceive a person to the point that the person believes that he has no choice but to confess. If a person is untruthfully told that evidence exists that proves that he committed a crime, he will often feel that he has no alternative but to confess.

The issue of voluntariness can be considered by a judge to determine whether a jury can even hear evidence of the confession. Alternatively, if the court determines that a jury can indeed hear evidence of the confession, the defense attorney could still argue that the jury should not rely on the confession, as it is unreliable. Obviously, a defense attorney's goal, however, would be to avoid having the confession come into the trial as evidence at all.

---

24. 542 U.S. 177 (2004).

Most jurors will assume that if a person confessed to a crime, he most likely committed the crime. Thus, the validity of a confession is very important to both the defense and the prosecution. Most cases that involve a confession result in the defendant entering a plea rather than taking the case to trial. This is favorable for the district attorney's office, saving time and ensuring a criminal record for the defendant. The defendant, on the other hand, will have a very difficult time in most cases proving that he confessed to a crime but that he did not actually commit it. It is also very difficult to prove what was said by an investigating officer during an interrogation or prior to one, especially if no videotape of the interrogation is present. The existence of a confession in a criminal matter is very important.

Coerced Confessions Are Not Admissible in Court.   One of the earliest and most famous coerced confession cases is **Brown v. Mississippi**.[25] The case, decided by the United States Supreme Court in 1936, involved racial tensions and corrupt authorities. The defendants, all described within the court case as "ignorant negroes" were charged with killing a white man. A deputy sheriff arrived at the home of one of the defendants and requested that he accompany him to the residence of the deceased, where an angry mob of white men was waiting. The defendant denied being guilty of the murder, and upon his denial, the men seized him, and, with the deputy participating, hung him by a rope to the limb of a tree, hoisting him up and down and requesting a confession each time they let him down. Each time the defendant refused to confess, the men hoisted him up onto the tree again and whipped him. Finally, he confessed and was then released. A second defendant was subjected to the same treatment and two others were made to strip and were laid over chairs, with their backs cut to pieces by a leather strap with buckles on it. All of the men eventually confessed to the crime and to any details that the authorities demanded of them. They were warned that if they changed their story, they would again receive the torturous treatment. As the Supreme Court stated, "Further details of the brutal treatment to which these helpless prisoners were subjected need not be pursued. It is sufficient to say that in pertinent respects the transcript reads more like pages torn from some medieval account, than a record made within the confines of a modern civilization which aspires to an enlightened constitutional government."

Once the defendants had been placed in prison, the basis for which was their confessions, the sheriff arrived with other officials. Despite the fact that the defendants recounted their terrifying experiences and some could not even sit down because of the whippings, the sheriff indicated that he had "heard of" the whippings but didn't know anything personally about them, and stated that he and the other men had come to formally take the men's confessions. Two sheriffs and one other person who was present were used by the prosecution in court to relate the men's confessions. The defendants

---

25. 297 U.S. 278 (1936).

objected and told the court their side of the story, but the court nonetheless determined that the confessions could be entered in court. The men then attempted to plead guilty but the court told them they could not and appointed counsel for them, setting the trial for the following morning. The defendants were tried and received death sentences, with the evidence utilized by the prosecution being the men's jailhouse confessions. Had the confessions not been utilized, the Supreme Court opined, the men could not have been found guilty. The men testified as to the reason they had confessed and maintained their innocence; the sheriff was placed on the stand and admitted the whippings. Sadly, the sheriff's response to the court's inquiry as to how severely he had whipped one of the defendants was "Not too much for a negro; not as much as I would have done if it were left to me." Two other men who had participated in the whippings were also put on the stand and admitted the acts.

Upon appeal, the state relied upon a decision the Supreme Court had made previously in **Twining v. New Jersey**,[26] in which the Court stated that the federal Constitution does not guarantee that a person participating in a state action would be exempt from compulsory self-incrimination. However, the Supreme Court ruled that the use of torture to extract a confession is different from self-incrimination. The Supreme Court, in **Brown**, then stated as follows:

> Nor may a State, through the action of its officers, contrive a conviction through the pretense of a trial which in truth is "but used as a means of depriving a defendant of liberty through a deliberate deception of court and jury by the presentation of testimony known to be perjured." **Mooney v. Holohan**, 294 U.S. 103, 112. And the trial equally is a mere pretense where the state authorities have contrived a conviction resting solely upon confessions obtained by violence. The due process clause requires "that state action, whether through one agency or another, shall be consistent with the fundamental principles of liberty and justice which lie at the base of all our civil and political institutions." **Hebert v. Louisiana**, 272 U.S. 312, 316. It would be difficult to conceive of methods more revolting to the sense of justice than those taken to procure the confessions of these petitioners, and the use of the confessions thus obtained as the basis for conviction and sentence was a clear denial of due process.[27]

The Court also quoted the case of **Fisher v. State**,[28] in which the Court stated that

> [c]oercing the supposed state's criminals into confessions and using such confessions so coerced from them against them in trials has been the curse of all

---

26. 211 U.S. 78 (1908).
27. **Brown** at 286.
28. 145 Miss. 116, 110 So. 361 (1926).

countries. It was the chief inequity, the crowning infamy of the Star Chamber, and the Inquisition, and other similar institutions. The constitution recognized the evils that lay behind these practices and prohibited them in this country . . . The duty of maintaining constitutional rights of a person on trial for his life rises above mere rules of procedure and wherever the court is clearly satisfied that such violations exist, it will refuse to sanction such violations and will apply the corrective.

The Supreme Court explained further their reasoning for refusing to allow coerced confessions to be a part of the American criminal justice system:

The abhorrence of society to the use of involuntary confessions does not turn alone on their inherent untrustworthiness. It also turns on the deep-rooted feeling that the police must obey the law while enforcing the law; that in the end life and liberty can be as much endangered from illegal methods used to convict those thought to be criminals as from the actual criminals themselves. Accordingly, the actions of police in obtaining confessions have come under scrutiny in a long series of cases. Those cases suggest that in recent years law enforcement officials have been increasingly aware of the burden which they share, along with our courts, in protecting fundamental rights of our citizenry, including that portion of our citizenry suspected of crime.[29]

Most police departments now videotape confessions and some states have even made this practice mandatory.

Voluntariness of a Confession. The issue of whether or not a confession was actually voluntary, however, can be complicated given less clear facts than those in the **Brown** case. Each case is dependent on its facts and circumstances. "The limits in any case depend upon a weighting of the circumstances of pressure against the power of resistance of the person confession. What would be overpowering to the weak of will or mind might be utterly ineffective against an experienced criminal."[30] The ability to coerce a confession from a defendant who has involvement in the criminal justice system cannot be compared to a defendant who is mentally ill or mentally challenged in some other way and has never had any participation in the system. The Supreme Court in **Lego v. Twomey**[31] considered the issue of voluntariness.

LEGO V. TWOMEY

FACTS: Lego was charged with armed robbery. Lego had made a confession to police that he committed the crime, but he argued that his confession was

---

29. **Spano v. New York**, 360 U.S. 315 (1959).
30. **Stein v. New York**, 346 U.S. 156 (1953).
31. 404 U.S. 477 (1972).

coerced. He testified in a hearing that the police had hit him around his head and neck with the butt of a gun, prompting his confession. The police chief had been a former neighbor and classmate of the victim of the crime, and Lego argued that the chief thus was attempting to "exact revenge" upon Lego. Lego produced, at the hearing, photographs of himself taken a few days after the confession was made, in which his face was swollen and had blood on it. The police chief and four officers also testified at the hearing and indicated that no physical abuse had taken place. Lego admitted that his face was scratched by the victim at the time of the robbery but argued that the photographs demonstrated more damage than that scuffle would have produced. The judge decided in favor of the officers, believing their testimony more than Lego's, and Lego went to trial. At trial, Lego testified on his own behalf, explaining his version of the events that took place in the police station at the time of his confession. Lego was convicted and appealed, finally filing a writ of habeas corpus in federal court,[32] maintaining that the jury should have been asked to consider whether Lego's confession was indeed voluntary.

ISSUE: Does a criminal defendant have a due process right to have a jury determine whether his confession was voluntary?

HOLDING: A defendant is entitled to a reliable determination that a confession was voluntarily, proven at least by a preponderance of the evidence.

RATIONALE: Coerced confessions offend constitutional principles. Juries can disregard confessions that they find are not sufficiently corroborated or are otherwise unbelievable. However, a preponderance of the evidence standard is appropriate (although each state can decide to impose a higher standard if desired).

A judge who is considering whether a confession was given voluntarily must consider evidence under the "preponderance of the evidence" standard, a lower standard than "beyond a reasonable doubt." The court should consider a multitude of factors and subjectively determine whether the confession was reliable, based on the "totality of the circumstances," in other words, all relevant factors. The facts and circumstances of each case should be considered by the judge after testimony is given by the officers and by the defendant regarding the situation surrounding the confession. The court will often have to consider which side is telling the truth and which side is not, as often the accounts given by both sides will differ, sometimes drastically. In essence, the Court must consider both the conduct of the police officer and the characteristics of the accused. In the **Brown** case the facts were admitted to by both sides and were fairly clear in terms of the possibility that the confessions were

---

32. Federal courts must consider questions of the voluntariness of confessions in an independent review when a habeas corpus motion is filed. **Miller v. Fenton**, 474 U.S. 104 (1986).

coerced and, thus, potentially unreliable. It is easy to imagine how a person might admit to a crime that he did not commit when subjected to physical torture. However, the use of physical torture is not as prevalent today and law enforcement officials are much more likely to use more subtle techniques, including psychological torture. This type of factual scenario is more difficult for a court to sort through.

Interrogations

Threats and Promises. Threats of physical violence, of the withdrawal of something the defendant needs to survive (such as food or medicine), or even of harm to a person's children or spouse are almost always considered inappropriate. Further, threats to prosecute family members or to give a person a harsher sentence or charge can be considered a predicate to an involuntary confession. One woman was told that her failure to cooperate could lead to the loss of her welfare benefits and her losing custody of her children. The Supreme Court found that this type of badgering on behalf of the officials was considered coercion.[33] Some states, however, permit a promise of leniency as long as the promise of leniency does not specifically relate to the issue of the actual charges that will be lodged against a person or to a specific sentence. For example, in many states it is perfectly acceptable for an officer to state that he will inform the district attorney that the defendant is being cooperative or if he states that he will "try" to go easy on the defendant if the defendant cooperates.

In the case of **Beecher v. Alabama**,[34] the Court considered the following interrogation of a suspect accused of murdering a woman.

> The un-contradicted facts of record are these. Tennessee police officers saw the petitioner as he fled into an open field and fired a bullet into his right leg. He fell, and the local Chief of Police pressed a loaded gun to his face while another officer pointed a rifle against the side of his head. The Police Chief asked him whether he had raped and killed a white woman. When he said that he had not, the Chief called him a liar and said, "If you don't tell the truth I am going to kill you." The other officer then fired his rifle next to the petitioner's ear, and the petitioner immediately confessed. Later the same day he received an injection to ease the pain in his leg. He signed something the Chief of Police described as "extradition papers" after the officers told him that "it would be best to sign the papers before the gang of people came there and killed" him. He was then taken by ambulance from Tennessee to Kilby Prison in Montgomery, Alabama. By June 22, the petitioner's right leg, which was later amputated, had become so swollen and his wound so painful that he required an injection of morphine every four hours. Less than an hour after one of these injections, two Alabama investigators visited him in the prison hospital. The medical assistant in charge

---

33. **Lynumn v. Illinois**, 372 U.S. 528 (1963).
34. 408 U.S. 234 (1972).

told the petitioner to "cooperate" and, in the petitioner's presence, he asked the investigators to inform him if the petitioner did not "tell them what they wanted to know." The medical assistant then left the petitioner alone with the State's investigators. In the course of a 90-minute "conversation," the investigators prepared two detailed statements similar to the confession the petitioner had given five days earlier at gunpoint in Tennessee. Still in a "kind of slumber" from his last morphine injection, feverish, and in intense pain, the petitioner signed the written confessions thus prepared for him.[35]

The Court found that the defendant's confession was the result of "gross coercion" and that the confession was obtained against his constitutional rights. Similar cases in which confessions were found to be unconstitutional involved the interrogation of a suspect who was in intensive care in the hospital and a case in which manipulative questions were given by a state-employed psychiatrist.[36]

Length of Interrogation, Trickery, and Deception. Another factor that a court could consider in analyzing the validity of a confession is how long the interrogation lasted. The case of **Spano v. New York**,[37] quoted earlier, involved a 25-year-old defendant, Vincent Joseph Spano, who had been born in Italy but was in the United States on January 22, 1957, following a fatal shooting in a bar. Spano called a friend of his, Gaspar Bruno, on February 3, 1957; Bruno was currently in the police academy training to be an officer. Spano told Bruno about what had happened and stated that he was about to turn himself in.

Spano did, in fact, turn himself in to authorities at 7:10 P.M. on February 4, 1957. Police began to question him but Spano, following his attorney's instructions, refused to respond, instead looking up at the ceiling and stating that he refused to answer questions. At 11:00 P.M., Spano was given two sandwiches, coffee, and some cake. At 12:15 A.M. on February 5, 1957, Spano was moved to another police station and three local assistant district attorneys came to the police station to participate in the ongoing interrogation. Questioning began again at 12:40 A.M. Spano again refused to answer and this time requested to see his attorney. That request was denied. The investigators then decided to use Spano's close friend, Bruno, who was an investigator. Bruno was directed to tell Spano that his telephone call had caused problems for Bruno and that he should consider Bruno's pregnant wife and consider confessing. Bruno did so three times to no avail. However, finally, on Bruno's fourth attempt to convince Spano to talk, Spano did so, confessing to the crime. His confession was finally memorialized by a stenographer at 4:05 A.M. Officers then drove Spano to the area where he stated he had thrown the murder weapon, and during that trip, Spano made more statements relating

---

35. **Id.** at 235.
36. **Leyra v. Denno**, 347 U.S. 556 (1954).
37. 360 U.S. 315 (1959).

to the crime; the drive lasted until about 6:00 A.M. Spano was arraigned at 10:15 A.M., after court opened at 10:00 A.M.

In addition to the concern of the Supreme Court about the fact that Bruno, Spano's good friend, was used to coerce his confession, the Court focused on the length of time that it took to obtain Spano's confession. "Petitioner was questioned for virtually eight straight hours before he confessed, with his only respite being a transfer to an arena presumably considered more appropriate by the police for the task at hand. Nor was the questioning conducted during normal business hours, but began in early evening, continued into the night, and did not bear fruition until the not-too-early morning. The drama was not played out, with the final admissions obtained, until almost sunrise. In such circumstances slowly mounting fatigue does, and is calculated to, play its part."[38] The Court also considered the totality of all of the circumstances of the case, including Spano's young age and lack of formal education, along with his history of emotional instability. The Court also considered the fact that the statement that Spano did make included mostly responding to leading questions asked by the investigators, rather than a statement created by him. However, the issue of fatigue due to the length of time of questioning and the fact that the questioning primarily took place during the early morning hours were a key factor in the Court's decision.

Other cases considered by the Supreme Court resulted in the Court throwing out confessions that were obtained when a person was confined in a small place; when a person was isolated from his family, friends, and lawyer; and when his basic needs of food, drink, and sleep were taken from him. In another case, **Greenwald v. Wisconsin**,[39] the defendant was taken into the police station around 2:00 A.M. The only "bed" in the room was a plank fastened to his wall. At 6:00 A.M. he was moved to another room and at 8:30 he participated in a lineup. At 8:45 the police began interrogating him and at 11:00 he began a series of confessions; his full confession was given at 11:30 and at 1:00 his written statement was taken. He was given no food or medication during his entire confinement and he indicated that he knew he would not be given any, or be allowed to sleep, until he confessed.

Police Deception. A controversial and very subjective factor for a court to consider in a coerced confession case is that of police deception. The mere usage of undercover police officers, used especially frequently in narcotics and prostitution cases, demonstrates that our society accepts the idea of police officers deceiving the general public. However, if the premise of our justice system is to determine the truth and place only guilty people in jail, it is unacceptable for an officer to convince someone to confess based on information that is absolutely untrustworthy. Often an officer will tell a suspect that the suspect's friend has already "told them everything" about what the

---

38. **Id**. at 322.
39. 390 U.S. 519 (1968).

suspect did. This causes the suspect, even if he did nothing, to figure that he had better confess or he will look uncooperative and, based on his friend's supposed testimony, will be convicted of the crime anyway. Other potential lies that officers could tell are as follows:

1. An officer might tell the defendant that there are witnesses to the crime, when in fact there are none.
2. An officer might tell the defendant that forensic evidence was located at the scene of the crime, when in fact it was not.
3. An officer could misrepresent her identity to the defendant, stating that she is a social worker or some other "non-police" related individual.

So how can a court deal with this type of deception? Certainly the psychology of obtaining a confession includes at least "stretching the truth" in order to convince the suspect that he should confess. One issue becomes whether the "truth stretching" in effect nullifies the warnings that the suspect has received in accordance with his **Miranda** rights, discussed later. However, otherwise, most types of police deception have been accepted by courts as part of routine police interrogation. In the case of **Frazier v. Cupp,**[40] for example, police suggested to Frazier, suspected of a murder, that his cousin, Jerry Lee Rawls, who was seen at a bar with him on the night in question, had already confessed and had implicated Frazier in the murder. Rawls, in fact, had not confessed. Frazier at first refused to confess but after much questioning a confession was in fact elicited and was used against Frazier at his trial. The Supreme Court upheld the conviction stating that although the "misrepresentation" of statements by Rawls was "relevant" to its review, it was "insufficient" to make the confession inadmissible. The Court did not spend much time discussing exactly what type of deception might not be acceptable, but the ruling was relied on by police to use deceptive techniques in gaining confessions. Note also that many police deception cases, including Frazier's, also involve issues regarding a suspect's right to have an attorney present during a police interview. Although few incidents of police deception have gone too far in the Supreme Court's eyes to negate a confession, occasionally the line is drawn. The **Spano** case is an example of this, in which the court frowned upon using the defendant's friend, Bruno, and encouraging him to lie and state that Spano's phone call harmed his career prospects when in fact it did not.

The Supreme Court has not ruled on whether fabricated documents are used inappropriately when presented to suspects in order to obtain a confession. However, some lower courts have disapproved of this technique due to the fact that fabricating documents, especially official ones, can be a crime under a state's penal code. In other words, a good rule of thumb is that if a police technique actually violates a law, it might be inappropriate to use to

---

40. 394 U.S. 731 (1969).

YOU BE THE JUDGE

You are a judge considering the following case. A five-year-old girl was murdered and sexually assaulted. Police focused on the victim's uncle, Joseph Doe. They interviewed him several times but could not obtain enough information to move forward with any charges against him. They then created two false documents fabricated by the police with the local prosecutor's consent: one is a letter that appears to be from a state agency and the other is a laboratory report that appears to be from a state agency, both of which report that semen stains found in the victim's underwear match Doe. When police present these false documents to Doe, Doe confesses to the crime. You are reviewing the case to determine whether the confession should be used in court. Do you find that it was in fact coerced?

coerce a suspect's confession. One concern of state courts that have considered this issue is that the documents, once placed in a suspect's file, could become evidence against the suspect if someone unwittingly includes it in a packet of information that is forwarded to the prosecutor. At some point, the fabricated document could show up in court as evidence against the defendant, or at least be used by a defense attorney to convince his client to enter a plea to the crime.

However, some state courts have accepted even fabricated documents. In **Sheriff v. Bessey**,[41] a sexual assault case, Bessey denied that he had engaged in sexual contact with the 14-year-old victim. Police then showed him a fabricated crime lab report that showed that his semen had been recovered from a sofa in his apartment where the sexual contact had allegedly occurred. The police had actually analyzed some evidence taken from that couch and the actual analysis was negative. Bessey confessed after being presented with this evidence. The Nevada Supreme Court stated that, considering the "totality of the circumstances" in the case, the falsehood would only have caused the suspect to consider his innocence or guilt, but he would not have necessarily confessed based on the fabrication. The Nevada Court and others since have opined that subterfuge and lies are part of the "bag of tricks" used by police officers to attempt to obtain confessions. A Maryland court even went so far as to say that because fabricated documents can be "seemingly official" to "amateurish," no hard and fast rule regarding the documents could be created; rather, each particular document should be scrutinized by the court in its "totality of the circumstances" query. Courts often echo what many lay citizens say about confessions: no one would confess to a crime he did not

---

41. 914 P.2d 618 (Nev. 1996).

commit, regardless of how or when a question is asked or what bogus, fabricated evidence is presented to him.

Other Factors Relating to Voluntariness

What other scenarios can you think of in which you believe a person might have confessed to a crime, but not voluntarily? The age, mental capacity, and current mental state of a person have also been considered by courts as part of the "totality of the circumstances" analysis. Minors can be questioned, although some states extend them further protection than adults, including their ability to confer with their parents before any interrogation. A person's mental capacity, including his or her intelligence quotient or general mental health can also be considered. A person who is known by police officers to be intoxicated or under the influence of a mind-altering substance might not be able to give a reliable confession. A person's mere use of drugs in general is not enough to prove that she was under the influence at the time of an interrogation, but evidence that a person is currently intoxicated or even going through withdrawal can be considered.

The landmark case that considered a confession by a mentally ill person was that of **Colorado v. Connelly.**[42]

COLORADO V. CONNELLY

FACTS: On August 18, 1983, Francis Connelly approached Officer Patrick Anderson of the Denver Police Department, who was in uniform but was off duty. Anderson said nothing to Connelly, and Connelly immediately told Anderson that he had murdered someone and wanted to discuss it with the officer. Anderson immediately informed Connelly of his **Miranda** rights and Connelly stated that he was aware of these rights but that he wanted to talk anyway. Anderson asked Connelly if he had been drinking or taking drugs, or if he had ever received mental health treatment. Connelly denied taking drugs or drinking alcohol but admitted that he had been a patient in several mental hospitals. Anderson informed Connelly again that he did not need to say anything, but Connelly indicated it was "all right" for him to talk and that he was talking to Anderson because his conscience had been bothering him lately. Anderson later testified that Connelly seemed to be in charge of his facilities and was able to understand fully the nature of his act of confessing to the officer.

A homicide detective arrived and again informed Connelly of his rights. Connelly again confessed to a murder that he had committed in Boston years before. Connelly then took the officers to the scene of the crime. The homicide detective stated that he did not perceive during his interaction with Connelly that Connelly was suffering from any sort of mental disability. Connelly was held by the police

---

42. 479 U.S. 157 (1986).

overnight and in the morning he met with an official from the local public defender's office. At that point, he was visibly disoriented and offered rather unusual answers to questions being asked of him. He then stated that the voices had told him to come to Denver and confess. He was sent to a state hospital, where initially doctors determined that he was unfit mentally to stand trial. He later did stand trial and he moved to suppress all of his statements at the time of his preliminary hearing. A psychiatrist testified that Connelly suffered from chronic schizophrenia and was in a psychotic state the day before his confession. He believed that Connelly was delusional at the time of his confession and was following delusional voices that he believed represented God telling him to confess. The trial court suppressed his confession, finding that the police had done nothing wrong but that nonetheless Connelly's confession was not a result of his rational intellect and free will. The Colorado trial court's ruling was appealed and eventually made its way to the Supreme Court of the United States.

ISSUE: Was Connelly's confession free and voluntary and thus admissible in court, if it was based on delusional voices, when the police did nothing to coerce the confession from him and, in fact, warned him against speaking?

HOLDING: The Supreme Court held that no violation of due process took place and that the confession was voluntary.

RATIONALE: The Court stated that if a private party acts "outrageously" in trying to convince a person to confess to a crime, the confession is legal. Only police behavior is important in terms of coercion. (In this case, arguably, God is the private person who was acting "outrageously.") The Court determined that Connelly's perception that God was speaking to him was not related to the Constitution. The Court reasoned that ruling for the defendant in this case would not result in any police deterrence. The Court stated that "[o]nly if we were to establish a brand new constitutional right—the right of a criminal defendant to confess to his crime only when totally rational and properly motivated—could [Connelly's] present claim be sustained." Coercive police activity must exist in order for a court to determine that a confession is not voluntary.

Interestingly, the dissenting opinion in **Connelly**, authored by Justice Brennan, expressed concern that the confession was the only evidence present in the case to convict Connelly. No physical evidence linked Connelly to the crime and in fact the body of the victim was never identified. Further, the dissent argued that the government has a very heavy burden to prove voluntariness and Connelly's incompetence, as verified by a physician, provided "overwhelming evidence" that Connelly's statement was unreliable.

Before the Court decided **Connelly**, courts were supposed to consider whether a confession was voluntary considering the totality of the circumstances, and generally this included whether the confession was made out of free will rather than due to police coercion. In other words, courts were supposed to consider police action in making a determination, along with other factors. Following the **Connelly** decision, the totality of the circumstances test is not applied until the defendant can show that coercive police action exists. A defendant must show that coercive police conduct existed and that the conduct caused the confession, and only then will the court consider the issues of free will and rational decision making on the part of that individual.

Massiah v. United States[43]

The **Massiah** case is another landmark case that focuses on a person's right to be free from governmental interrogation. Once the Sixth Amendment right to counsel attaches (a concept that will be discussed in Chapter 7), the government is no longer able to elicit statements from the defendant about themselves. Massiah was indicted on federal narcotics charges, retained a lawyer, pleaded not guilty, and was released on bail. A co-defendant, cooperating with the government, invited Massiah to sit in his car and discuss this crime. The co-defendant wore a wire and a government agent listened to the conversation via a radio transmitter. The defendant made statements that were later used against him in trial; he moved to suppress the statements, arguing that they were the result of unfair governmental conduct and his Sixth Amendment right to counsel. Because he was not told that he was going to be, in effect, interrogated by a government agent in the car, he was unable to have his attorney present.

The Supreme Court agreed and ruled that once (1) adversarial criminal proceedings have been commenced and (2) a government agent (which includes informants working for the government) deliberately attempts to elicit information from a person, Sixth Amendment safeguards apply. As will be discussed later, the right to counsel applies to all "critical" stages of a prosecution and investigation, including "any stage of the prosecution, formal or informal, in court or out, where counsel's absence might derogate from the accused's right to a fair trial."[44] If the **Massiah** rules were not in place, the government would be able to collude with inmates to ask their fellow inmates questions about their cases and turn that information over to the authorities.

Massiah protects individuals from law enforcement deliberately creating an atmosphere that might be likely to illicit an incriminating response. **Miranda** protects an individual from a law enforcement officer engaging in an action that is likely to induce an incriminating response from the individual, even if the officer did not intend to induce an incriminating response. In either case, the statements can be suppressed but can be used to impeach a defendant's testimony. **Miranda** is not offense specific, and once a person exercises his right to be silent under **Miranda**, the police must stop

---

43. 377 U.S. 201 (1964).
44. **United States v. Wade,** 388 U.S. 218, 226 (1967).

questioning him about any offenses, charged or uncharged. **Massiah** is more specific to particular charges. Once an individual exercises his right not to answer questions according to **Massiah**, law enforcement (or its agents) must stop questioning the individual about whatever offense or offenses he has been charged with. The individual could still be questioned about other acts. Without the **Massiah** ruling, the government could use inmates against one another, compelling or enticing them to act in its stead and gather information about their fellow inmates. It is important to note, however, that if an inmate volunteers information about his case to, for instance, a person with whom he's sharing a cell, the cell mate can, in turn, volunteer any information which he has learned to law enforcement, assuming law enforcement did not request that he do so.

A 2013 case decided by the United States Supreme Court clarified that an individual's choice to remain silent could be used against him in a trial.[45] The defendant had not been placed in custody and had not received **Miranda** warnings and he voluntarily answered some of a police officer's questions about a murder that was under investigation. However, the defendant did not answer questions posed to him regarding ballistics testing of his shotgun. At trial, the prosecutor brought up this silence as evidence of his guilt. The Court opined that the right to remain silent must be specifically invoked and that the defendant did not do so in this case. The Court stated that this ensures that the government is put on notice when a witness intends to rely on the privilege; the government can then either argue that the testimony is not incriminating or offer the individual immunity for giving up the information.

DIFFERENCES BETWEEN THE SAFEGUARDS PROVIDED UNDER **MIRANDA** AND **MASSIAH**

Miranda	Massiah
Interrogation + Custody	Deliberate Elicitation + Formally Charged
Charging Status Irrelevant	Custodial Status Irrelevant
Sixth Amendment right to counsel and Fifth Amendment right to remain silent	Sixth Amendment right to counsel

---

45. **Salinas v. Texas**, 133 S. Ct. 2174 (June 17, 2013).

POLICE PROCEDURES AND THE FIFTH AMENDMENT

When little forensic evidence exists, and when a victim is available to identify a perpetrator of a crime, lineups or photographic "showups" can be used to provide the police with a suspect.

The technique of asking eyewitnesses of a crime to identify the assailant has been used since the inception of the criminal justice system in the United States. These identification procedures include both in-person lineups, in which suspects line up next to each other and move together or each say a certain phrase out loud, and photographic "showups," in which photographs of one or more people are shown to the victim for identification.

During an in-person lineup, the victim or witness to the crime sits behind a two-way mirror, observes and listens to each person in the lineup, and tries to identify the perpetrator based on his voice, if he spoke during the crime, and his appearance and distinctive mannerisms. Another type of eyewitness identification is for the victim or witness to look at an array of photographs that have been prepared; the victim or witness will then declare whether any of the people in the pictures were the assailant. Occasionally, a witness is shown a photograph of just one person or the person is brought to the victim or witness in person to be identified. This process is difficult to justify, due to its suggestiveness, as will be discussed later, but sometimes is necessary due to time limitations in setting up a lineup or photographic array involving other individuals.

The topic of eyewitness identification heavily employs the field of psychology. There are many arguments to be made regarding whether a victim or witness of a crime can remember enough details about her assailant to truly know whether a particular person has committed a crime. One issue includes the problem of cross-racial identifications. Sometimes victims cannot correctly distinguish specific identifying features of people who are of a different race than themselves. Psychologists also question whether a person can actually focus on specific characteristics of a suspect when he is being victimized and often is in fear of his life. Because of these and other concerns, eyewitness identification is one of the least reliable types of evidence used in court. However, juries may consider an eyewitness's observations to be very important, and thus experts can be hired by both the prosecution and defense to explain to the jury their view of the reliability of eyewitness identification. However, sometimes a person will describe her assailant to a police sketch artist who will draw a picture as described to him and the picture will be shockingly similar to the actual assailant. Constitutional issues in this area include the right to counsel when a person is a subject in an identification procedure and the issue of whether such procedures are suggestive in nature, thereby violating a person's Fifth Amendment due process rights and his right to be free from self-incrimination. The Supreme Court has decided more cases regarding the right to counsel as it relates to lineups than it has the due process issues related thereto. Eyewitness identification procedures have been upheld in court and a defendant who refuses to participate in such a procedure can be held in contempt of court and sentenced to imprisonment by a judge.

Police Actions and Suspects' Rights

The Supreme Court had previously considered what types of requests from police to a suspect would lead to a violation of the privilege against self-incrimination. In **Schmerber v. California**,[46] the Supreme Court approved of requiring a suspect to submit to giving a blood sample to be analyzed for alcohol content; the defendant had argued that having to give blood was a violation of his privilege against self-incrimination. The Supreme Court again considered this issue in the factually unique case of **Holt v. United States**.[47] Holt was being prosecuted for murder and a relevant question to the proceedings was whether a particular shirt belonged to him. A witness testified at trial that Holt had put the shirt on and it had fit him. The defendant argued that he had been compelled by law enforcement to put the shirt on and that any testimony regarding the same was a violation of his privilege against self-incrimination. The Supreme Court disagreed, ruling that his claim represented "an extravagant extension of the Fifth Amendment." Specifically, the Court stated that "[T]he prohibition of compelling a man in a criminal court to be witness against himself is a prohibition of the use of physical or moral compulsion to extort communications from him, not an exclusion of his body as evidence when it may be material."[48] Interestingly, this type of evidence was seen in the infamous case of **The State of California v. O.J. Simpson**, in which Simpson was requested by the prosecution to put on a glove that had been found at the scene of the murder. When Simpson attempted to put the glove on, it seemed to be too small for his hand. This incident was used in the closing statement of one of Simpson's attorneys, Johnny Cochran, who stated, regarding the glove, "[I]f it doesn't fit, you must acquit."

UNITED STATES V. WADE

FACTS: A bank in Eustace, Texas, was robbed on September 21, 1964. A man who had a small strip of tape on each side of his face entered the bank, pointed a pistol at the female cashier and the vice president, who happened to be the only people in the bank at that time. He forced them to fill a pillowcase with money and he then drove away with an accomplice who had been waiting for him outside the bank. The defendant, Wade, was arrested on April 2 and counsel was appointed to represent him. Without notice to his lawyer, FBI officials arranged to have the two bank employees identify their assailant in a lineup that consisted of Wade and five or six other prisoners. Each person in the lineup wore strips of tape and stated "put the money in the bag," which were the words allegedly uttered by the robber. Both bank employees identified Wade as the perpetrator of the robbery. Both officials further identified Wade at trial as their assailant and he was convicted. The

---

46. 384 U.S. 757 (1966).
47. 218 U.S. 245 (1910).
48. **Id**. at 252.

defense argued that the lineup constituted a violation of Wade's Fifth Amendment privilege against self-incrimination and his Sixth Amendment right to the assistance of counsel. The case made its way to the Supreme Court following the trial court's rejection of Wade's claims and his subsequent appeals.

ISSUE: Did the lineup violate Wade's right against self-incrimination? (Another issue the court considered was whether the lineup violated Wade's right to counsel—the court determined that it did, although questions remained regarding the attorney's role at the lineup. The right to counsel will be discussed in Chapter 7.)

HOLDING: Lineups do not violate a person's right against self-incrimination.

RATIONALE: The right not to incriminate one's self is applicable only to a person actually testifying against himself or providing the state with evidence that is testimonial or communicative in nature.

The Supreme Court summarized all three cases as follows:

> We have no doubt that compelling the accused merely to exhibit his person for observation by a prosecution witness prior to trial involves no compulsion of the accused to give evidence having testimonial significance. It is compulsion of the accused to exhibit his physical characteristics, not compulsion to disclose any knowledge he might have. It is no different from compelling Schmerber to provide a blood sample or Holt to wear the blouse, and, as in those instances, is not within the cover of the privilege. Similarly, compelling Wade to speak within hearing distance of the witnesses, even to utter words purportedly uttered by the robber, was not compulsion to utter statements of a "testimonial" nature; he was required to use his voice as an identifying physical characteristic, not to speak his guilt. We held in **Schmerber** . . . that the distinction to be drawn under the Fifth Amendment privilege against self-incrimination is one between an accused's "communications," in whatever form, vocal or physical, and "compulsion" which makes a suspect or accused the source of **real or physical evidence**. We recognized that "both federal and state courts have usually held that . . . [the privilege] offers no protection against compulsion to submit to fingerprinting, photography, or measurements, to write or speak for identification, to appear in court, to stand, to assume a stance, to walk, or to make a particular gesture . . ." None of these activities becomes testimonial within the scope of the privilege because required of the accused in a pretrial lineup.[49]

---

49. **Id.** at 223.

In **Salinas v. Texas**,[50] the Supreme Court upheld a case in which a defendant's silence was used against him. Salinas was not in custody nor was he read his rights, but he voluntarily answered some questions that an officer asked him about a murder. When the officer asked him a question about whether ballistics testing would demonstrate that his weapon matched that used in the crime, Salinas fell silent and did not answer. His silence was brought up at his murder trial. He argued that the use of his silence was a violation of his Fifth Amendment rights, and that he was being compelled to be a witness against himself. The Court disagreed, stating that because Salinas did not specifically state that he was attempting to invoke his right to remain silent, his silence fell outside the Fifth Amendment. The Court stated that a witness does not invoke the privilege to remain silent by standing mute and that a person should put the government on notice when he intends to rely on the privilege so that the government could either provide immunity for the person's testimony or argue that the testimony is not incriminating. Thus, although courts have to inform jurors that they cannot use a defendant's choice to remain silent in court against them, their silence during interrogation can be considered detrimental.

YOU BE THE JUDGE

You are a judge considering the case of a bank robbery. The robber handed the teller a note and a gray plastic bag, which the teller filled with money and handed back to the robber. The note remained with the teller, and it stated: "Put all your money (from **both draws** $500.00, $100.00, $50.00, $20.00 Etc.) in the bag." Investigators arrested the suspected robber and requested that he provide a handwriting sample to the FBI. He was given documents to copy for some of the handwriting samples, and for others, he was directed to write phrases that were told to him orally by the investigators. He was not instructed as to how to spell the word "drawers," and he spelled it "draws" instead. This evidence was introduced at trial. The defendant argues that the request to have him write the samples violated his privilege against self-incrimination and that his spelling abilities represent his thought processes, which have communicative qualities. The prosecution argues that the nature of the defendant's spelling abilities lacks communicative intent. Who do you rule for, and why?

---

50. ___ U.S. ___ (June 17, 2013).

Effect of Violating a Suspect's Right Against Self-Incrimination

When a defendant is placed in an unconstitutionally suggestive lineup situation or a suggestive photographic array results in a victim selecting the defendant as the perpetrator of the crime, a few protections will apply. First, obviously, the result of the lineup will not be admissible in court. The victim cannot come into court and state he chose the defendant out of a lineup. Further, no law enforcement officials or other investigators can discuss the results of the lineup. However, it is also important for a victim to identify his perpetrator at trial, thereby demonstrating to the jury or to the judge that he is sure that the accused is, in fact, the perpetrator. If a lineup or photographic showup was unconstitutional, that means the victim may have chosen the defendant at that stage based, for example, on a suggestive statement by officers. The victim has now been convinced by outside sources that the person he identified is indeed the perpetrator. Thus, another result of the inappropriate lineup may be that the victim is prohibited from identifying the defendant in court. This is the case, however, only if the witness testifies that the only reason he can identify the defendant in court is based on his belief that the suggestive out-of-court identification was correct. If the court finds that the witness can identify the perpetrator in the courtroom setting without having to rely on the earlier erroneous identification, the court will probably allow the identification. This doctrine is related to the "independent source" doctrine discussed previously in Chapter 6 and developed by the United States Supreme Court in the **Wong Sun v. United States** case. In order to determine whether a tainted lineup or showup affected the victim's ability to identify the defendant later, the court will consider all relevant factors, including factors such as whether the defendant actually saw the perpetrator committing the act, if there were any failures to identify the defendant on a prior occasion, and whether the victim described the defendant prior to the lineup situation and, if so, whether that description varied from the defendant's actual appearance. Finally, of course, the fruit of the poisonous tree doctrine will apply, and if law enforcement performed a search or seizure based solely on the victim's identification of the defendant, the evidence obtained from the search will most likely also be excluded from court. The final factor that courts consider regarding the reliability of an identification procedure is that of suggestiveness in the identification procedure itself.

Suggestiveness in Identification Procedures

One of the most commonly known problems in identification procedures is that of suggestiveness during either a lineup proceeding or a showup. An investigator who suggests to a witness that number three might be the best pick or a lineup that includes four black men and a white man when the suspect is white might be causing an unreliable result. Interestingly, suggestiveness in and of itself will not disqualify an identification and often ends up becoming an issue for the jury during a trial rather than the type of evidence that would cause a judge to throw all evidence of the result of a lineup out of court.

The Supreme Court's stance on photographic identification procedures and lineups was explained succinctly in the case of **Simmons v. United States**.[51]

> It must be recognized that improper employment of photographs by police may sometimes cause witnesses to err in identifying criminals. A witness may have obtained only a brief glimpse of a criminal, or may have seen him under poor conditions. Even if the police subsequently follow the most correct photographic identification procedures and show him the pictures of a number of individuals without indicating whom they suspect, there is some danger that the witness may make an incorrect identification. This danger will be increased if the police display to the witness only the picture of a single individual who generally resembles the person he saw, or if they show him the pictures of several persons among which the photograph of a single such individual recurs or is in some way emphasized. The chance of misidentification is also heightened if the police indicate to the witness that they have other evidence that one of the persons pictured committed the crime. Regardless of how the initial misidentification comes about, the witness thereafter is apt to retain in his memory the image of the photograph, rather than of the person actually seen, reducing the trustworthiness of subsequent lineup or courtroom identification.
>
> Despite the hazards of initial identification by photograph, this procedure has been used widely and effectively in criminal law enforcement, from the standpoint both of apprehending offenders and of sparing innocent suspects the ignominy of arrest by allowing eyewitnesses to exonerate them through scrutiny of photographs. The danger that use of the technique may result in convictions based on misidentification may be substantially lessened by a course of cross-examination at trial which exposes to the jury the method's potential for error. We are unwilling to prohibit its employment, either in the exercise of our supervisory power or, still less, as a matter of constitutional requirement. Instead, we hold that each case must be considered on its own facts, and that convictions based on eyewitness identification at trial following a pretrial identification by photograph will be set aside on that ground only if the photographic identification procedure was so impermissibly suggestive as to give rise to a very substantial likelihood of irreparable misidentification.

The Supreme Court considered what constitutes suggestiveness in the case of **Foster v. California**.[52] Foster was charged with robbery and the facts are as follows:

> Except for the robbers themselves, the only witness to the crime was Joseph David, the late-night manager of the Western Union office. After Foster had

---

51. 390 U.S. 377 (1968).
52. 394 U.S. 440 (1969).

YOU BE THE JUDGE

You are a judge and are considering whether the results of a lineup should be brought into court. A manager of a gas station was robbed and fatally shot. His assistant, Wilson, was the only eyewitness to the shooting. He stated that he watched three men enter the gas station into the well-lighted office where he was working. The men inquired as to how much Wilson would charge to fix a flat tire and then demanded money, pointing a pistol at the manager. Wilson escaped by running through a side door and then ran back to the station, where one robber remained, being held at gunpoint by the manager who had not yet died. The police showed Wilson a photographic spread of only two photographs, both of whom were suspected of participating in the robbery. Wilson stated that he recognized both men. The defendants argue that the photographic display was impermissibly suggestive, due to the fact that only two photographs were presented to Wilson and that both photographs were of men who were ultimately tried in the case. Considering the totality of the circumstances, what circumstances should be considered here? Is there any other information you would want to know before making your decision? Was the lineup fair?

been arrested, David was called to the police station to view a lineup. There were three men in the lineup. One was petitioner. He is a tall man—close to six feet in height. The other two men were short—five feet, five or six inches. Petitioner wore a leather jacket which David said was similar to the one he had seen underneath the coveralls worn by the robber. After seeing this lineup, David could not positively identify petitioner as the robber. He "thought" he was the man, but he was not sure. David then asked to speak to petitioner, and petitioner was brought into an office and sat across from David at a table. Except for prosecuting officials there was no one else in the room. Even after this one-to-one confrontation, David still was uncertain whether petitioner was one of the robbers: "truthfully—I was not sure," he testified at trial. A week or 10 days later, the police arranged for David to view a second lineup. There were five men in that lineup. Petitioner was the only person in the second lineup who had appeared in the first lineup. This time David was "convinced" petitioner was the man. At trial, David testified to his identification of petitioner in the lineups, as summarized above. He also repeated his identification of petitioner in the courtroom. The only other evidence against petitioner which concerned the particular robbery with which he was charged was the testimony of the alleged accomplice Clay.[53]

---

53. **Id**. at 441.

The Supreme Court stated that this scenario presented a "compelling example" of unfair lineup procedures. The height of Foster as compared to the other men, plus the fact that he was wearing a leather jacket, as was the robber, was unduly suggestive. The one-on-one confrontation between the plaintiff and the witness added to the unfair nature of the procedure. In previous cases, the Court had frowned upon the use of in-person confrontations in general due to their suggestive nature. The Court also criticized the fact that Foster was the only person who had participated in both of the lineups. All of these facts would presumably make Foster more likely to have been chosen as the robber. The Court stated that "the pretrial confrontations clearly were so arranged as to make the resulting identifications virtually inevitable."

MIRANDA RIGHTS

The case of **Miranda v. Arizona** is one of the most famous Supreme Court cases. Anyone who has watched a television show or movie involving police work can most likely recite at least the beginning portion of the **Miranda** warnings, "You have the right to remain silent . . . anything you say can and will be used against you in a court of law." In fact, most people have heard that line repeated so many times that it almost seems meaningless. Why do police recite these rights? Do suspects really remain silent because they are being read? What consequence does a law enforcement officer's failure to make this statement have? In some ways, because **Miranda** rights have become so familiar to us, we fail to think about what a landmark decision this case really was. The **Miranda** case was really a demonstration of the Supreme Court's concern about police tactics in the area of interrogation of suspects. It is important to understand the history of interrogation law in order to understand the climate in which the **Miranda** case was decided by the Court. Be aware that the issue of interrogation also involves an individual's right not to incriminate himself and his potential right to have an attorney present when he is being interrogated. Both of these issues are dealt with in the statement that police read to suspects in compliance with the Court's decision in **Miranda**. Although many people believe that **Miranda** rights should be read any time that a person comes into contact with police, this is not the case. As will be discussed later, the only time a member of law enforcement must recite the **Miranda** rights to a person is when that person is being custodially interrogated. This concept will be further explained later, but routine traffic stops and general questions directed to a person by a police officer do not merit reading **Miranda** rights.

Police departments have come a long way in the last several decades, and it is no secret that in the early part of the twentieth century, police departments were corrupt and their treatment of suspects could be less than appropriate. The Wickersham Commission report, the result of a federal study in 1931, was entitled "Report on Lawlessness in Law Enforcement." The United States Attorney General, George Wickersham, had headed up the study, which was the first glance most of the public had at the brutal techniques used by officers in interrogating suspects. The report resulted in the public's insistence that police brutality be stopped. Besides lowering the public's confidence in the police, brutal tactics used in interrogation could lead to a suspect confessing to a crime that he did not commit. Departments began to hire more professional officers and change their tactics to avoid physical brutality. The current practice of videotaping most interrogations also assumedly keeps law enforcement from using violence to extract confessions.

The most famous case of police brutality is that of **Brown v. Mississippi**, discussed previously, wherein the Supreme Court ruled that confessions obtained by physical coercion violated the due process clause of the Fifth Amendment, which states that "[n]o person shall . . . be deprived of life, liberty, or property, without due process of law" and the similar provision of the Fourteenth Amendment.

However, by the 1960s, the brutal physical force of the past had been replaced by psychological tactics that could also lead to the end result of a person confessing to a crime because of too much pressure, rather than because he actually committed the crime. There are many examples of people who confessed to very serious crimes as a result of police pressure, including Michael Crowe, a juvenile who was accused of murdering his sister in 1988 and who confessed after being separated from his parents, hours of interrogation by police, and after saying many times during his confession statements such as "I'm only saying this because this is what you want to hear." These confessions often come as a result of police tactics that, although not necessarily unconstitutional, might be unethical in nature and surely can be considered to be unfair. Although it is difficult to understand why a person would confess to a crime she did not commit, it is possible to wear someone down to the point that she will confess. Promises of leniency or a false statement that someone else has implicated the suspect in a crime can often cause a person to break down and confess. A person who is mentally ill or otherwise incapable of logically processing events, or someone who is ill or tired, is especially prone to falsely confessing. In fact, police manuals and training sessions continue to provide officers with instruction on how to extract a confession from an unwilling suspect through psychological means.

Basis of the Miranda Rights

If a statement is used against a person in court and that statement has been extracted from the person involuntarily, the person is denied due process as it is set forth in the Fifth and Fourteenth Amendments. Further, a person has the right to be free from self-incrimination. The Fifth provides that "[n]o person . . . shall be compelled in any criminal case to be a witness against himself." The provision was added to the Constitution by its framers because common law in England permitted the courts to force a person to testify

THE MIRANDA RIGHTS

The typical statement made by a law enforcement officer to inform an individual of his **Miranda** rights is as follows:

> You have the right to remain silent. Anything you say can and will be used against you in a court of law. You have the right to an attorney. If you cannot afford an attorney, one will be provided for you. Do you understand the rights I have just read to you? With these rights in mind, do you wish to speak to me?

Some police departments add the following sentence:

> We have no way of giving you a lawyer, but one will be appointed for you, if you wish, if and when you go to court.

against himself, even if the way to get him to so testify was via torture. These tactics were also used against the Puritans by forcing them to take an oath in which they swore to God that they would tell the truth; only after they took the oath were they told that they were being accused of a crime. Puritans believed that God would punish them if they broke an oath to tell the truth, so they then were forced to give up information regarding their friends and other information desired by the Crown. Because the Puritans were instrumental in settling this country, they were influential in having this clause placed in the Constitution. Thus, the idea of physical torture preceded adding this clause to the Constitution, but the issue of psychological coercion existed as well. The concern now, of course, is more often that of the use of a false confession to convict someone; the courts do require that people take an oath, sometimes still adding the concept of answering to God, before providing testimony in court. The right not to incriminate one's self was incorporated to the states through the Fourteenth Amendment in 1964. Although most people probably think of this right in terms of a person testifying in an actual courtroom setting, the right also applies at any other proceeding in which incriminating testimony might be elicited from a person that could be used later in a criminal prosecution. Thus, in a civil case, the right could apply at all pre-trial discovery proceedings. In a criminal case, the right applies during interrogation and pre-trial proceedings, such as suppression hearings or preliminary hearings or even grand jury investigations. The privilege can only be asserted, however, if the witness is denying criminal behavior. If the witness is admitting to criminal behavior, for example, by entering a guilty plea to a crime, he will not be able to argue that he cannot testify regarding the criminal act if he is asked to do so in another court. Only a natural person can assert the privilege against self-incrimination. Corporations, associations, and partnerships cannot assert the privilege, and thus when such entities are sued they must testify in court and answer all questions, even if the answers might incriminate the officers or members of the entity.

With the exception of a criminal trial, as discussed later, the person claiming the privilege must claim it at the time he is being asked a question and must do so verbally by stating that he is claiming the privilege; he may not just remain silent without invoking the privilege, or he might be held in contempt of court. Only in a criminal setting can a person avoid actually taking the stand at all and stating that she is invoking the privilege. Assumedly, it could be prejudicial for a defendant to actually sit on the stand in front of a jury and have to state to the jury that he is invoking his Fifth Amendment right not to incriminate himself. Apparently having a defendant not take the stand at all sits better with the jury. If a person invokes the privilege and chooses not to take the stand at his trial, he cannot be penalized for invoking the privilege. Thus, the district attorney cannot comment on the defendant's silence to the jury. In fact, the judge must give the jury an instruction that tells the members that they cannot consider the fact that the defendant failed to testify. One defendant argued, however, that he did not want that instruction. He felt that the judge's act of commenting on the fact that he failed to testify would merely bring it further to the jury's attention. However, the Supreme Court did not agree to this and stated that the instruction could be given over the defendant's objection to it.[54] It is appropriate, however, for the prosecutor to comment on the defendant's failure to testify if the defense attorney argues to the jury that the defendant was not permitted to tell his side of the story.[55] A defendant who does choose to take the stand and tell his side of the story cannot, once he is finished with his direct examination and is being cross-examined by the opposing side, argue that he should not have to answer questions on cross-examination due to the privilege not to incriminate himself. By testifying, he has waived his ability to argue that he cannot answer questions on cross-examination owing to a concern that he would incriminate himself.

If a person is being criminally interrogated by police officers before criminal charges have been filed, or by being asked to take a polygraph test, the individual's **Miranda** rights could apply, and in such a case, the person does not have to verbally state his desire not to speak. "Incriminating evidence," as interpreted by the courts, is broadly construed to include anything that could possibly assist the prosecutor in obtaining some information that will assist him in prosecuting a case or in gathering further information that will be used to prosecute the case. Finally, a person cannot assert the right against self-incrimination as provided by the United States Constitution if he is concerned that he is going to be prosecuted in a foreign

---

54. **Lakeside v. Oregon**, 435 U.S. 333 (1978).
55. **United States v. Robinson**, 485 U.S. 25 (1988).

country. Additionally, occasionally a court grants an individual immunity from prosecution if the person testifies. An offer of immunity will prevent a person from being able to invoke the privilege. The privilege only applies to verbal testimony. If an issue regarding real evidence arises, search and seizure law would provide any relief a person might have. Further, the privilege does not cover verbal statements a defendant does NOT make, such as the refusal of a person who is suspected for driving under the influence of alcohol to have blood drawn. Fingerprints, voice samples, handwriting samples, and photographs taken of a suspect also are not considered verbal testimony for purposes of the privilege. If a person claims that testimony was obtained from him via the government compelling that testimony and violating the person's invoked privilege not to testify against himself, the evidence could still be used against the person to demonstrate that the person is lying in another court hearing if he says something that conflicts with the testimony that he had desired to exclude. This rule is not applicable, however, if the person has received immunity for his testimony. It is also not applicable if the **statute of limitations** has run on a person's case. The statute of limitations provides a time period during which the government must bring a case against a person. If it is too late to bring charges against a person because the statute of limitations has expired, a person cannot assert that he has a legitimate reason not to testify.

MALLOY V. HOGAN

FACTS: Malloy was arrested during a gambling raid in Hartford, Connecticut. He plead guilty to pool selling, a misdemeanor and was sentenced to one year in jail and subjected to a $500.00 fine. His sentence was suspended after 90 days and he was let out of prison and placed on two years of probation. Approximately 16 months after his plea, a referee appointed by the Superior Court of the State of Connecticut ordered Malloy to testify about gambling and other criminal activities that were taking place in Hartford. Malloy refused, stating that testifying might incriminate him. The state argued that the privilege against self-incrimination should not be incorporated to the states but should only apply to federal proceedings. Malloy was then imprisoned for contempt and held until he was willing to answer questions. Malloy filed a habeas corpus petition and his case went to the Supreme Court for consideration.

ISSUE: Whether the prohibition against self-incrimination is a fundamental right that should be incorporated to state court proceedings.

HOLDING: The privilege against self-incrimination is a fundamental right that should be incorporated to the states. (The decision was a close 5-4 decision, with 5 voting for the incorporation of the right and 4 voting against it.)

RATIONALE: The American judicial system is accusatorial, not inquisitorial. The Fourteenth Amendment does secure defendants against self-incrimination, thereby compelling state and federal officials to establish the guilt of an accused beyond a reasonable doubt independent of a suspect's own statement. Questions that would tend to directly incriminate a person and questions that could provide a causal link for government officials to further charge a person with a crime fall within the self-incrimination clause.

Miranda v. Arizona

Although most members of the public are familiar with the statement that is read to suspects in accordance with the Court's decision in **Miranda**, most are not familiar with the facts of the case or the basis of the Supreme Court's reasoning. Although states can develop their own **Miranda** statements, and an example of an extra sentence that is tacked onto the reading of the **Miranda** rights is set forth earlier, all states use the traditional language set forth previously.

The **Miranda** case was decided in an era when the Court was particularly interested in making sure that due process was upheld. Just two years before the Supreme Court decided **Miranda**, it had considered a similar issue in the case of **Escobedo v. Illinois**[56] and it was familiar with the problems that a person could have if an attorney was not present while someone was being interrogated. In the **Escobedo** case, the Court considered whether a suspect who is in police custody is entitled to assistance of counsel under the Sixth Amendment. The Court determined that a suspect can receive counsel if the suspect is in police custody, is interrogated after an investigation has focused on him, and if he requests but is denied the opportunity to consult with his lawyer and the police have failed to inform him of his Fifth Amendment right not to incriminate himself. Escobedo was in police headquarters along with a man who later became his co-defendant, also charged with the crime. Escobedo testified that he was told that he could "not walk out the door." He had retained a lawyer and the lawyer testified that he was unable to see Escobedo despite going to the police station to attempt to do so. Ironically, the attorney could at one point see Escobedo in a room and could wave to him, but was unable to enter the room.

The interesting part of the **Escobedo** case was its reasoning, which was also used in the **Miranda** case. The **Escobedo** court in effect overruled prior court decisions that held that a person has a right to counsel only after that person is formally charged. The **Escobedo** court reasoned that when a person is in police custody, suspected, and being questioned, he would need the "guiding hand of counsel." The Court stated: "We have learned the lesson

---

56. 378 U.S. 478 (1964).

of history, ancient and modern, that a system of criminal law enforcement which comes to depend on the 'confession' will, in the long run, be less reliable and more subject to abuses than a system which depends on extrinsic evidence independently secured through skillful investigation."[57] Further, the Court included in its decision a quote from **Ex parte Sullivan**.[58] If the Court did not permit counsel prior to a person being charged, "One can imagine a cynical prosecutor saying: 'Let them have the most illustrious counsel, now. They can't escape the noose. There is nothing that counsel can do for them at the trial.'"[59] Interestingly, the government argued that police would not obtain any confessions if counsel were available, as counsel would certainly tell their clients not to answer any questions. The Court concurred, but it also stated that clearly an attorney is needed at this stage, because obtaining a confession is one of the most important stages in police work.

The **Miranda** court, then, considered the Court's reasoning in **Escobedo** and expanded on it, stating that the real purpose of the Court in **Escobedo** dealt not as much with the right to an attorney but with the Fifth Amendment privilege against compulsory self-incrimination. The Court's decision in **Miranda**, however, can be used in cases with facts similar to **Escobedo** as well as many other scenarios. The **Miranda** Court's ruling was that a statement obtained by a suspect as the result of "custodial investigation" is not admissible in court if the statement is being used against the person, unless the government can prove that its agents (police or other governmental investigatory agents) have provided the person with procedural safeguards that are sufficient to ensure that the person's Fifth Amendment privilege against compulsory self-incrimination have not been violated. "[W]ithout proper safeguards the process of in-custody interrogation of person suspected or accused of crime contains inherently compelling pressures which work to undermine the individual's will to resist and to compel him to speak where he would not otherwise do so freely. In order to combat these pressures and to permit a full opportunity to exercise the privilege against self-incrimination, the accused must be adequately and effectively apprised of his rights and the exercise of those rights must be fully honored."[60]

The Court stated that it would not consider whether in some cases the facts could show that a person is already aware of his rights. The Court stated that the defendant's age, education, intelligence, or prior contact with authorities in the criminal justice system would not always provide a good basis to determine whether the defendant is aware of his rights. Further, the defendant could be nervous or confused because of the pressure of the

---

57. **Id**. at 488.
58. 107 F. Supp. 514 (1964).
59. **Id**. at 517-518.
60. **Id**. at 467.

interrogation, and thus even if a person was aware of the warnings that the **Miranda** court required, the person could forget or be confused about those rights once an interrogation began. Further, the Court stated that the current trend of interrogation environments

> is created for no purpose other than to subjugate the individual to the will of his examiner. This atmosphere carries its own badge of intimidation. To be sure, this is not physical intimidation, but it is equally destructive of human dignity. The current practice of incommunicado interrogation is at odds with one of our Nation's most cherished principles—that the individual may not be compelled to incriminate himself. Unless adequate protective devices are employed to dispel the compulsion inherent in custodial surroundings, no statements obtained from the defendant can truly be the product of his free choice.[61]

The **Miranda** case actually involved four separate cases that all made their way to the Supreme Court during the same time period. In all four cases, law enforcement agents took the defendant into custody to a police station. Each of the suspects were interrogated in the hopes that a confession would be obtained. The police did not tell the suspects that they could have an attorney present or that they did not have to answer the questions posed to them. The suspects were interrogated for hours and after finally confessing their confessions were presented at trial. As the Supreme Court put it, "In all the cases, the questioning elicited oral admissions, and in three of them signed statements as well which were admitted at their trials. They all thus share salient features—incommunicado interrogation of individuals in a police-dominated atmosphere, resulting in self-incriminating statements without full warnings of constitutional rights." Further, "In each of the cases, the defendant was thrust into an unfamiliar atmosphere and run through menacing police interrogation procedures." However, the Court acknowledged that "the records do not evince overt physical coercion or patent psychological ploys. The fact remains that in none of these cases did the officers undertake to afford appropriate safeguards at the outset of the interrogation to insure that the statements were truly the product of free choice."

The Privileges

Unbeknownst to many people, the Supreme Court in **Miranda** did not write the standard Miranda warning that police officers recite to suspects. Rather, the Court provided a list of rights that have been incorporated into the statement that we now know as the **Miranda** rights. The Court stated that the following rights must be discussed with defendants.

---

61. **Id.** at 457.

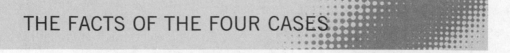

THE FACTS OF THE FOUR CASES

Miranda v. Arizona
The defendant was arrested and taken into a "special interrogation room" where his confession was extracted. The defendant was an indigent Mexican and was a "seriously disturbed individual with pronounced sexual fantasies."

Vignera v. New York
The defendant was interrogated and made oral statements in the afternoon; he was later interrogated by a district attorney that evening and signed a statement that evening.

Westover v. United States
Local police detained and interrogated the defendant for a lengthy period, both at night and the following morning. They then turned him over to the FBI, who questioned him for two hours and then received signed statements.

California v. Stewart
Local police held the defendant in the police station for five days and interrogated him nine different times. He confessed. Stewart was an indigent "Los Angeles Negro" who had dropped out of school in sixth grade.

a. **The privilege against self-incrimination.** This is the portion of the rights that tells suspects that they "have the right to remain silent." This comes from the Fifth Amendment clause that states that a person shall not "be compelled in any criminal case to be a witness against himself." No person ever has to give an interview to the police. (They cannot be compelled to testify in criminal court either.)

b. **The consequence of giving up the right.** This is the portion of the rights that states that "anything you say can and will be used against you in a court of law."

c. **The right to counsel.** This is the portion of the rights that states, "You have the right to an attorney. If you cannot afford one, one will be appointed for you." The right to counsel comes from the Sixth Amendment and permits a person to consult with an attorney, to have the attorney present at any questioning he participates in, and to have a free attorney appointed to represent him if he is unable to afford an attorney (and falls within the income and asset guidelines so that he is eligible for a public defender). Note that a person does not have the right to have an attorney present during tests such as a polygraph test or a voice stress analysis test, due to the need to uphold the integrity of the testing and have as few people as possible in the room during the testing process.

Note that these rights need not be recited in this exact order or with the exact language set forth by the Court. As long as the general rights are incorporated into a statement given orally to the defendant, the intention of the Court will be fulfilled.[62] Many jurisdictions choose to have a defendant sign a statement acknowledging that these rights were read to him; if he refuses to sign, the officer notes that on the form. In the case of an interrogation in a police station, the reading of the rights will often be videotaped, or at least the defendant will acknowledge on the videotape that the rights were read to him. In **Duckworth v. Eagan**,[63] the Supreme Court determined that the primary issue is whether the general words used by the police officer, in light of the defendant's age, intelligence, and demeanor, convey an understanding of the rights to that defendant. In 2004, the Court again considered the necessary format of **Miranda** warnings and determined an even looser standard for relaying the rights to a suspect. In **United States v. Patane**,[64] the Supreme Court considered a case in which a person interrupted a police officer when the officer was part of the way through giving the warnings required under **Miranda**. The Court stated that the warnings were sufficient even though the officer never finished them. The Court stated that the entire purpose of the **Miranda** warnings is to prevent violations of the Constitution and that because the suspect's testimony following the **Miranda** warnings was not used at his trial, the Constitution had not been violated. The physical evidence obtained following, and as a result of, the statements would be admissible because the statements had not been forced by the police.

When Can the Miranda Rights Be Invoked?

The **Miranda** rights can be invoked at any time, even if they have already been waived. The right to silence can be invoked any time either by the individual stating that he does not wish to answer any questions or by the individual simply failing to answer questions and remaining silent. At the point which an individual states that she does not wish to answer further questions, the interrogation must stop. The right to assistance of counsel must be stated in a clear manner. The individual must state directly that she does not wish to answer any more questions until her counsel is present, or that she does not wish to answer any more questions because she does not have counsel. A statement such as, "Wow, I wish my attorney could be here" might not be sufficient for a court to state that a person's rights have been violated if questioning continues. In fact, the Supreme Court consistently ruled that any language

---

62. California v. Prysock, 453 U.S. 355 (1981).
63. 492 U.S. 195 (1989).
64. 542 U.S. 630 (2004).

other than a specific statement that the person does not wish to answer any more questions is not sufficient to cause an officer to stop asking questions. Such language includes statements such as, "I don't think I should say anything" and "I don't have anything to say."

If a person does choose to speak to investigators, the burden is on the government to prove that the person knowingly, intelligently, and voluntarily gave up those rights. A waiver of these rights can only take place after the person has been read her **Miranda** rights, and a person could change her mind and unequivocally state that she now does wish to answer questions or proceed without an attorney. No coercion on the part of the government to continue can exist, however. Once a person decides to remain silent, his wishes must be respected. Only if a person then, on his own and with no prompting from police, decides to speak, is he truly giving up his right to remain silent.

Miranda applies only to testimonial evidence. The rule does not apply to evidence that is obtained by requiring a suspect to produce a handwriting sample, fingerprints, or DNA or hair samples. Physical or real evidence is not considered testimonial. Nonverbal conduct, however, can be considered testimonial; nodding or shaking one's head can be an answer to a question the same as a verbal "yes" or "no."

It is important to note that the warnings required by the **Miranda** decision do not have to be recited word for word. Although most law enforcement agencies do subscribe to the exact wording that is repeated on television shows and movies, the case itself did not require those exact words. The case required only that the general ideas set forth in the **Miranda** case be relayed to a suspect who is in custodial interrogation. In fact, the Supreme Court decided this in the case of **California v. Prysock**.[65] In that case, the suspect, a minor, was given warnings while his parents were present. However, instead of the usual "you have a right to remain silent" verbiage, the officers stated that the minor had the right to talk to a lawyer before he was questioned, and to have him present while he was being questioned. He was also told that he had the right to have a lawyer appointed to represent him at no cost. The defendant actually argued that the warnings given to him were inadequate because the minor was not explicitly informed of his right to have an attorney appointed before further questioning, and that thus his statements should be suppressed in accordance with **Miranda**. The Supreme Court disagreed, stating that rights given to suspects need not be a "virtual incantation" of the exact language set forth in the **Miranda** opinion and that the police had fully conveyed the defendant's rights to him and had not set any inappropriate limitations on them. According to the Court:

> [n]othing in the warnings given respondent suggested any limitation on the right to the presence of appointed counsel different from the clearly conveyed rights to a lawyer in general, including the right "to a lawyer before you are questioned, . . . while you are being questioned, and all during the questioning."[66]

---

65. 453 U.S. 355 (1981).
66. **Id**. at 359.

In both **Prysock** and a similar case, **Duckworth v. Eagan**,[67] dissenting justices were concerned that a failure to read the standard **Miranda** warnings could confuse defendants and that specific language should be required. In the **Duckworth** case, the Defendant, Eagan, was told:

> You have a right to talk to a lawyer for advice before we ask you any questions, and to have him with you during questioning. You have this right to the advice and presence of a lawyer even if you cannot afford to hire one. We have no way of giving you a lawyer, but one will be appointed for you, if you wish, if and when you go to court. If you wish to answer questions now without a lawyer present, you have the right to stop answering questions at any time. You also have the right to stop answering at any time until you've talked to a lawyer.[68]

Although the majority of the Court felt that these warnings were appropriate and "touched all of the required bases," dissenting justices were concerned that the warnings read in this manner would mislead the average suspect into believing that he could not immediately have a lawyer unless he could afford one.

The Supreme Court has more recently considered the question of whether, in fairness, officers should give a suspect more information than necessary if the officer believes that might affect the suspect's desire to offer information. In **Colorado v. Spring**,[69] a suspect was interrogated by officers in two different municipalities, approximately two months apart. He was given **Miranda** warnings in each case, separately. The first case involved firearms violations, but the officers questioning him on that case knew that he was suspected of a murder also and would be interrogated later by other authorities regarding those charges. The suspect argued that the officers should have told him that they knew about the murder charge so that he would be aware of it during his questioning regarding the firearms. The Supreme Court disagreed, stating that a criminal suspect does not need to be informed of every single possible consequence of his waiving his right to remain silent. The dissenting justices were concerned that the police officers, by not giving the suspect the extra information, voided the voluntary, knowing, and intelligent nature of the waiver of his rights.

Custodial Interrogation

Custody. The first term, then, that would need to be clarified from the Court's ruling is that of "custodial interrogation." When is a person in custodial interrogation so that he must be informed of his rights? Any time a person is deprived of his freedom of action in any significant way, he is

---

67. 492 U.S. 195 (1989).
68. **Id**. at 198.
69. 479 U.S. 564 (1987).

considered to be in custody. The test to determine whether someone is in custody is objective, not subjective. If a reasonable person in the same situation as the defendant would have believed, based on an officer's words or actions, that he is not free to leave, he will be considered to be in custody. The question concerns whether the general atmosphere created by the police would be coercive. The actual location of the interrogation is not dispositive of the level of coercion. A prison cell, the police station, or a person's house have all been found by courts to sometimes be custodial and sometimes not. If an officer specifically conveys to a suspect that he is free to leave, then it is likely the situation will not be found to be custodial. However, a suspect is not expected to read an investigating officer's mind and thus could consider a situation to be custodial even when the officer does not. Courts have to consider all circumstances surrounding police questioning to decide in each case whether a custodial situation existed.

As these scenarios can demonstrate, it is very difficult to determine exactly when a person might or might not objectively feel as though they can leave an officer's presence. Each case is very fact specific. Any formal arrest or restraint of movement that would be associated with an arrest is considered custodial. However, two Supreme Court cases focused on the issue of whether an officer's act of pointing a gun toward a suspect automatically resulted in the assumption that the person was in custody. In one case, the Court found that the officer's action did lead to the conclusion that the person was in custody, but in the other case, when the officer also had a gun, the court found that custody was not assumed.

The Court also determined that the mere act of handcuffing a person does not result in the person being in custody. In **Muehler v. Mena**,[70] the police were executing a warrant to search Mena's house for deadly weapons and evidence of gang membership. Mena was sleeping when the officers arrived and they immediately placed her in handcuffs at gunpoint. Mena was then detained in her garage for two to three hours in handcuffs under the guard of two officers. The Court stated that because officers can detain people who are in a particular place in order to search the place, they can also use reasonable force to effectuate the detention. The Court weighed the interest of the government in handcuffing the person with the intrusion against the person who was being handcuffed. Some legal scholars criticized the Court's decision, concerned that this case would begin to erode the law as it relates to personal intrusion. These scholars point out that Mena was 5 foot 2 inches tall and there were 18 officers on the scene. Police officers, however, called this case a victory in terms of their protection when executing a warrant. The case's discussion of what constitutes a person being in custody can arguably be extended to the issue of custodial interrogation. Other Supreme Court cases have determined that when a person is in a stop–and–frisk situation or being detained briefly at a crime scene for questioning, no **Miranda**

---

70. 544 U.S. 93 (2005).

YOU BE THE JUDGE

Consider the following scenarios and determine whether or not you believe the defendant in each case is in custody. What facts, if changed, would change your answer?

A. An individual voluntarily walks into the police station and states to the officer at the front desk that he wishes to confess to a murder. The officer at the front desk calls another officer, who then takes the individual into a conference room and tells the individual that he is free to leave whenever he wishes.

B. An individual is placed in a police car after having an accident and driving under the influence. The individual is not handcuffed, and he voluntarily gets into the back of the police car.

C. At 2:00 in the morning, an officer arrives at Joseph Smith's home to question him regarding a robbery that took place at the convenience store at the end of his street the previous night. Smith's ten-year-old daughter lets the officer into the house and tells him that her father is sleeping in his bedroom, which is at the end of the hall. The officer stands in the doorway of Smith's bedroom and asks him questions about his whereabouts the night of the robbery.

D. An officer is working undercover and is sitting in a neighborhood bar next to a known drug dealer. The officer asks the person if he has anything he can sell to the officer.

warnings are necessary. Police officers are permitted to ask suspicious persons their names and information such as where they are going to or coming from without informing them of their rights.[71]

Many people believe that any time an officer questions a person, the person's **Miranda** rights must first be given. This is untrue. For example, if an officer is going to drive a person suspected of driving under the influence to the hospital for blood tests to be performed, if the officer does not ask the person any questions during the drive, there is no reason to deliver **Miranda** rights to the person. If the individual begins to talk to the officer and tell him about what he was doing that night, the officer would be wise to interrupt and read the person his **Miranda** rights in case he responds to one of the person's statements with a question which might be related to the crime. There is no harm in reading the **Miranda** rights when they are not required, but there certainly is harm in failing to read those rights when they are required. The **Miranda** case was also determined to be retroactive, so even defendants

---

71. **Utsler v. South Dakota,** ___ (1969).

whose cases had been decided before the **Miranda** case was handed down could request that their cases be reviewed and statements be excluded from court based on the policies set forth in **Miranda**.

Interrogation. What exactly is "interrogation"? Any words or actions that would normally tend to elicit a response from the suspect which could be incriminating is considered an interrogation. This concept is very fact oriented. Further, the issue is not whether an officer meant to elicit an incriminating response from a defendant but, rather, whether the suspect believes that the officer's words were meant to elicit a certain type of response. This means an officer in effect has to know a lot of about the suspect's mental health status and, perhaps, experience with the criminal justice system in order to be able to predict exactly when he is required to read a suspect his **Miranda** rights. An interesting case in this area is that of **Brewer v. Williams**.[72]

BREWER V. WILLIAMS

FACTS: On December 24, 1968, a ten-year-old girl named Pamela Powers was at the YMCA in Des Moines, watching her brother's wrestling match. When she failed to return from a trip to the restroom, her parents became concerned and a search began. Shortly after her disappearance, a man named Robert Williams, who was a resident of the YMCA and had escaped from a mental hospital, was seen carrying a large bundle wrapped in a blanket. A boy helped Williams open the door and saw him put the bundle in his car, and he noticed that there were "skinny, white" legs poking out of the blanket. Williams drove away and his car was found, abandoned, the next day, in Davenport, Iowa. Williams surrendered to police and was given his **Miranda** warnings. Williams had an attorney who told Williams not to answer any questions posed by police officers, as officers from Des Moines would be picking him up and transporting him to Des Moines from Davenport. Williams had also retained an attorney in Des Moines, and both attorneys and Williams consistently reiterated to the police that Williams would not be answering any questions while in the police car.

One of the officers initiated a rather long conversation during which the officer became acutely aware of some of Williams's interests, likes, and dislikes. Specifically, the officer learned that Williams was deeply religious. At some point in the journey, the officer delivered what was referred to in court documents as the "Christian burial speech." The officer addressed Williams as "Reverend" and stated as follows:

> I want to give you something to think about while we're traveling down the road . . . Number one, I want you to observe the weather conditions, it's raining, it's sleeting, it's freezing, driving is very treacherous, visibility is

---

72. 430 U.S. 387.

poor, it's going to be dark early this evening. They are predicting several inches of snow for tonight, and I feel that you yourself are the only person that knows where this little girl's body is, that you yourself have only been there once, and if you get a snow on top of it you yourself may be unable to find it. And, since we will be going right past the area on the way into Des Moines, I feel that we could stop and locate the body, that the parents of this little girl should be entitled to a Christian burial for the little girl who was snatched away from them on Christmas Eve and murdered. And I feel we should stop and locate it on the way in rather than waiting until morning and trying to come back out after a snow storm and possibly not being able to find it at all.

The detective then, after a few questions from Williams, said "I do not want you to answer me. I don't want to discuss it any further. Just think about it as we're riding down the road." Williams then directed the officers to the area where he had left the girl's shoes and another area where her blanket was, and then offered to take the officers to the body. He did direct the police to the body and was indicted for first-degree murder. His attorney attempted to have all evidence suppressed that was related to or stemmed from his discussion with the police officers in the vehicle. The trial court ruled that Williams had waived his right to have an attorney present in the vehicle and, thus, the evidence was introduced at trial. Williams was found guilty of murder and the case made its way up to the Supreme Court.

ISSUE: Whether the "Christian Burial Speech" as recited by the police officer was equivalent to "interrogation" for purposes of **Miranda**.

HOLDING: The speech was equivalent to interrogation and the evidence should have been suppressed.

RATIONALE: The Supreme Court determined that the speech was indeed an interrogation. The Court stated that "waiver [of one's right to an attorney or not to incriminate one's self] requires not merely comprehension but relinquishment, and Williams' consistent reliance upon the advice of counsel in dealing with the authorities refutes any suggestion that he waived that right." Further, "disinterested zeal for the public good does not assure either wisdom or right in the methods it pursues . . . so clear a violation of the Sixth and fourteenth Amendments as here occurred cannot be condoned. The pressures on state executive and judicial officers charged with the administration of the criminal law are great, especially when the crime is murder and the victim a small child. But it is precisely the predictability of those pressures that makes imperative a resolute loyalty to the guarantees that the Constitution extends to us all."[73]

73. **Id**. at 306.

A similar case but with a different conclusion is that of **Rhode Island v. Innis**.[74] Innis was in the back of a police cruiser, having been taken into custody as a murder suspect. Two officers in the cruiser were talking and one remarked to the other that the gun used for the crime was missing and that there was a school for children with special needs in the area. The officer remarked that it would be a "shame" if one of the children found the gun and harmed himself. Innis, upon hearing these remarks, suddenly agreed to show the officers where the gun was. The Supreme Court ruled that the officer's remarks did not constitute interrogation. Rather, the Court said, the term "interrogation" "refers not only to express questioning, but also to any words or actions on the part of the police (other than those normally attendant to arrest and custody) that the police should know are reasonably likely to elicit an incriminating response from the suspect."[75] Further, the Court stated that "since the police surely cannot be held accountable for the unforeseeable results of their words or actions, the definition of interrogation can extend only to words or actions on the part of police officers that they *should have known* were reasonably likely to elicit an incriminating response." However, because there were no facts developed in the court's record to suggest that the police knew that Innis had any particular interest in the welfare of children, they could not have known that their conversation might lead him to interrogate himself. The conversation was limited to a few "offhand remarks," and "subtle compulsion" is not the same as interrogation.

Traffic Stops

The Supreme Court has considered several cases involving whether a traffic stop is considered custodial interrogation and thus subject to the rules of **Miranda**. From an officer's perspective, a traffic stop can be dangerous and it is important to immediately obtain information from the driver of a vehicle. Further, the average traffic stop lasts long enough for an officer to check a driver's record and background even before issuing a ticket. It seems wasteful and potentially dangerous to compel officers to read **Miranda** rights to the drivers of cars before obtaining the person's driver's license and registration card or before asking the driver where he is going. Although police officers prefer the warnings not be required at traffic stops, it is also the case that many times a routine traffic stop will result in a defendant's arrest on other, much larger charges. Thus, a defendant will try to have the evidence of anything he says suppressed. However, a traffic violation is a summary offense and thus it could be argued that **Miranda** warnings are not necessary.

The Supreme Court first dealt with this issue directly in **Berkemer v. McCarty**.[76]

---

74. 446 U.S. 291 (1980).
75. **Id**. at 301.
76. 468 U.S. 420 (1984).

BERKEMER V. MCCARTY

FACTS: Trooper Williams, an Ohio State Patrol officer, observed the defendant's vehicle weaving in and out of a lane on an interstate. Williams followed the vehicle for two miles and then effectuated a stop. Williams asked the defendant to exit the vehicle and the defendant did, but Williams noted that the defendant seemed to have difficulty standing. Williams concluded, at that point, that the defendant would in fact be cited for a traffic offense. At that point, Williams was not going to permit the defendant to leave the scene, but the defendant was not told at that point that he was going to be taken into custody. Williams then requested that the defendant perform a field sobriety test, requesting that the defendant balance on one leg. The defendant was unable to do so and Williams then asked the defendant if he had been using intoxicating substances. The defendant admitted that he had consumed two beers and had smoked several joints of marijuana a "short time" before the stop. Williams had difficulty understanding what the defendant was saying, as his speech was slurred. Williams then placed the defendant under arrest and transported him via his patrol car to the local jail. There, the defendant was given a test to determine how much alcohol was in his system, but no evidence of any alcohol was found. Williams then asked the defendant more questions, and the defendant admitted he was "barely" under the influence of alcohol. The defendant also wrote on a form he had been given that there was no angel dust or PCP in the marijuana that he had smoked. The defendant was never given any notice that he had the right to remain silent, have an attorney present if he wished, or have an attorney appointed for him. The defendant was charged with the first-degree misdemeanor of operating a motor vehicle while under the influence of alcohol and/or drugs. That charge carries a mandatory three days of incarceration. Defendant moved to exclude the various incriminating statements that he had made to the officer, and when the court denied the motion, the defendant pleaded "no contest" to the charge and was sentenced and fined. Defendant appealed and his case made its way to the Supreme Court of the United States.

ISSUE: Was the defendant entitled to receive **Miranda** warnings in the case of a traffic stop that resulted in being charged with a misdemeanor offense?

HOLDING: A defendant is entitled to receive **Miranda** warnings prior to an interrogation regardless of the nature or severity of the offense. Thus, the questions asked to the defendant at the police station should have been suppressed. However, the roadside questioning of a motorist detained pursuant to a routine traffic stop does not constitute "custodial interrogation."

RATIONALE: Any person who is subjected to custodial interrogation is entitled to receive the benefits of the procedural safeguards that were enumerated in **Miranda**. As soon as the defendant was formally arrested and instructed to get into the police car, he was in custody. Although the prosecution argued that an exception to the

Miranda warnings should exist when a person is arrested for committing a misdemeanor traffic offense, the Supreme Court stated that such an interpretation would substantially undermine the simplicity and clarity of the **Miranda** rule. In fact, often a police officer would not be sure whether a person has committed a felony or a misdemeanor at the time of the stop. The purpose of **Miranda** warnings is to ensure that an individual is not pressured to confess, and this is important whether a person is being charged with a misdemeanor or a felony.

Regarding the issue of traffic stops specifically, while the Court acknowledged that a traffic stop always curtails a person's freedom while she is being detained by the side of the road, the pressures of being stopped and being asked to answer questions do not impair the person's ability to exercise his privilege against self-incrimination. A traffic stop is brief and most motorists who are pulled over assume that they will receive a citation and will be able to continue on their way. Further, the typical traffic stop is conducted on a public roadway and the atmosphere is less dominated by police than a custodial situation in which a person is taken to a police station or questioned in the home with the presence of more than one officer. The Court acknowledged that a traffic stop could rise to the level of custody if a person is subjected to restraints comparable to those associated with an arrest. The Court took into consideration the fact that the officer did not tell the defendant that he planned on taking him into custody and charging him with a traffic offense when he made that determination, and his plan that was unarticulated to the defendant was thus not relevant to the analysis as to whether the situation involved custody. The question is how a "reasonable man" in the same position as the defendant would have understood the situation.

The Supreme Court created an interesting dichotomy between various portions of the field sobriety test given to people who are suspected of driving under the influence of drugs or alcohol. In **Pennsylvania v. Muniz,**[77] a defendant challenged the information obtained in a **field sobriety test** because he was pulled over and given the test without being first given his **Miranda** warnings. A field sobriety test is a way for police officers to establish probable cause to take a person into custody from a vehicle stop for purposes of doing further testing or charging the person with driving under the influence. The test involves requesting that a person answer certain questions and undergo some physical challenges as well. Questions include specific things that will test a person's ability to remember such things as their birth date and name, as well as mental exercises that will test a person's current ability to process information, such as requesting that the person recite the alphabet backward or do simple math in his head. The physical challenges include such things as walking in a straight line and standing still with one leg raised, as well as following the officer's finger with the person's eyes. The way a person handles

---

77. 496 U.S. 582 (1990).

taking the test itself (do they take it seriously and realize the gravity of the situation), along with their ability to actually carry out the tasks, will result in the officer determining what step to take next. Field sobriety tests often result in the defendant being subjected to a blood test, which will confirm the person's blood alcohol content. However, if a person refuses to permit the blood to be drawn and there is no requirement to take the blood for medical reasons, the results of the initial observations by the officer that permitted the traffic stop to begin with, along with his observations during the field sobriety tests, could be presented in court as evidence that the person was intoxicated while driving.

In Muniz's case, the Supreme Court concluded that some of the information the officers obtained was considered testimonial and thus should be excluded, while other information was merely real evidence that did not involve the defendant incriminating himself. First, the Court stated that the defendant's slurred speech was real evidence, not testimonial evidence. An officer does not need to immediately read a person his **Miranda** rights upon stopping the vehicle and can use slurred speech as evidence. Actual questions posed to the defendant, such as "What was the date of your sixth birthday?" and questioning him as to his name, address, birth date, eye color, and other specific information was considered to be an interrogation and thus should have been asked only after **Miranda** warnings were given. (The dissent disagreed that the question about the date of the defendant's sixth birthday should not be suppressed, stating that this was still some sort of physical act, not an actual answer that could incriminate the defendant by giving out information related to his case.) However, the standard physical portions of the sobriety test, the Court ruled, are not considered testimonial evidence. An officer does ask a suspect questions prior to administering the physical portion of the field sobriety test, but those questions are focused on whether the suspect understands how the test will be administered and are thus not considered interrogation. Unfortunately for Muniz, rather than merely responding to the officer's questions about whether he understood how to take the physical portion of the test, he gave the officer incriminating information that the officer did not ask for. However, the Court stated that those statements were made voluntarily and not as a response to the officer's questions, so they were admissible.

Waiver of Rights

The **Miranda** Court stated that if interrogation proceeds after proper warnings are given to a suspect, the government has a heavy burden to prove that a suspect actually waived his rights and spoke on his own accord. The government, in fact, must prove that the waiver was "voluntary, knowing, and intelligent." What does this entail? Does a person need to sign a statement in which he acknowledges that he knew what his rights were and decided not to invoke them? Is an officer's statement that he read the rights to the defendant enough? This scenario happens very often—police officers receive confessions in vast numbers despite people being read their rights—what is sufficient in the eyes of the Court?

The first case in which the Court considered this issue is **North Carolina v. Butler**.[78] Butler was in custody and being interrogated without counsel after he was arrested by officials in New York on the basis of a fugitive warrant for his arrest in North Carolina. Butler was advised of his rights in accordance with **Miranda**. In fact, the defendant was given an "Advice of Rights" form that explained his rights, and he told the agents that he had an eleventh grade education and was literate. Butler read the form, stated that he understood his rights, refused to sign the waiver at the bottom of the form, stating "I will talk to you but I am not signing any form" and then made inculpatory statements. Butler had never requested an attorney and he further never made an attempt to terminate the interrogation. The Court ruled that Butler's waiver was valid. "An express written or oral statement or waiver of the right to remain silent or of the right to counsel is usually strong proof of the validity of that waiver, but is not inevitably either necessary or sufficient to establish waiver. The question is not one of form, but rather whether the defendant in fact knowingly and voluntarily waived the rights delineated in the **Miranda** case."[79] The North Carolina court had attempted to create a rule, considered "inflexible" by the Supreme Court, that a defendant can waive his rights only by making an explicit statement to that regard. The Supreme Court stated that this rule "has gone beyond the requirements of federal organic law. It follows that its judgment cannot stand, since a state court can neither add to nor subtract from the mandates of the United States Constitution."[80]

The Supreme Court further considered this question in **Berghuis v. Thompkins**.[81] This case was decided following the terrorist attacks on the United States on September 11, 2001 and thus has been viewed with skepticism by some critics. As you read through the summary, consider whether you believe the case was decided purely on the grounds of the issue of **Miranda** or whether you believe the Court was also reacting to the attacks.

BERGHUIS V. THOMPKINS

FACTS: Van Chester Thompkins was suspected of fatally shooting someone on January 10, 2000, in Michigan. Officers interrogated him, following advising him of his **Miranda** rights in a routine manner. Thompkins did not state that he wanted to remain silent, that he did not wish to answer the questions posed by police, or that he wanted to have an attorney present at any time during the interrogation. In fact, Thompkins spoke very little throughout the interrogation (which

---

78. 441 U.S. 369 (1979).
79. **Id.** at 373.
80. **Id.** at 376.
81. 560 U.S. ___.

lasted three hours), and the few random comments he made had very little to do with the investigation. Toward the end of the investigation, the officers decided to change their tactic in terms of the investigation and began to discuss with Thompkins spiritual issues. They attempted to appeal to his conscience and his spiritual beliefs by asking him about whether he believed in God, whether he prayed to God, and whether he had asked God to forgive him for shooting the victim. Thompkins answered "yes" to each of these statements, and his answer was used against him. He moved to suppress those statements, arguing that he had invoked his right to remain silent, that he had not waived that right, and that his statements were involuntary.

ISSUE: Whether Thompkins had in fact waived his right to remain silent when he did not specifically state that he was doing so.

HOLDING: Thompkins's silence during the majority of the interview did not invoke his right to remain silent and he waived his right to remain silent when he knowingly and voluntarily made a statement to the police.

RATIONALE: A person can only invoke his right to remain silent specifically by an unambiguous act, which will result in certainty for all parties, including the accused, the police, and the courts. Invocation of the right need not be implied by the behavior and ambiguous acts of the accused. In this case, Thompkins had been read the warnings out loud, he expressed an understanding of the rights, he had not indicated that he did not understand them, and he was given time to invoke his rights. The Court stated that police are not required to renew the **Miranda** warnings throughout an interrogation; reading them once is sufficient. The defendant argued that linking answers to questions to religious beliefs made his answers involuntary, but the Court disagreed.

A dissenting opinion written by Justice Sonia Sotomayor argued that the Court's decision resulted in suspects having to "unambiguously invoke their right to remain silent—which, counterintuitively, requires them to speak. At the same time, suspects will be legally presumed to have waived their rights even if they have given no clear expression of their intent to do so." The dissent stated that Thompkins's act of remaining silent for nearly 2 hours and 45 minutes should have been understood by the officers as an invocation of the right to remain silent.

Exceptions to Miranda

Booking Questions. Routine booking questions, which request a person's address and other information, have also been excepted from the **Miranda** rights. However, an interesting issue often comes into play with questions asked during the booking process concerning whether they can be used against a person in court. For example, generally in order for a person to be charged with possession of drugs with intent to deliver them, the prosecutor will have to prove that a person did not intend to use the drugs themselves, but, rather, intended to sell them to someone else. A common booking question is "Are you currently under the influence of drugs or alcohol?" The intent of the question is to determine whether someone will be in danger because of detoxing while they are locked up. Many suspects will respond by saying, "I do not drink" or "I do not use drugs." This type of statement is then used against the suspects in court to attempt to demonstrate that any illegal substances they possessed were intended to be sold, not used by them. Courts thus must make special rulings that these types of answers to booking questions cannot be used against someone at their trial. The fact that **Miranda** rights are not read is one of the reasons that courts find it unfair to present these answers for use against a person at his trial.

Public Safety Exception. Another exception to the **Miranda** rule is the **public safety exception**. This exception is very significant because of the analysis the Supreme Court used in creating the exception. If an officer does not have time to read a suspect his **Miranda** rights owing to an emergency taking place, the rights will not be required. For example, consider a situation in which an officer arrives at the scene of a crime and a crowd has gathered, and the officer is aware that a gun was used to commit the crime. The suspect does not have the gun on his person when he is arrested, and thus the loaded gun must be somewhere in the crowd. It would most likely be appropriate for the officer to ask, "Where is the gun?" to the suspect in the hopes that he will tell the officer and avoid the potential issue of the gun being discharged. Further, it does not matter whether an officer really intends to obtain information from a suspect along with protecting the public, as long as there is some emergency to objectively justify the interrogation. In terms of public safety, courts can use a balancing test to consider whether the **Miranda** warnings are important enough to defer the safety of the public.

The case in which the Supreme Court considered the public safety rule was **New York v. Quarles**.[82] A woman reported to two police officers that she had just been raped and that her assailant had just entered a nearby supermarket and was carrying a gun. The officer stopped the man and found him wearing an empty shoulder holster. One of the officers asked him where the gun was; he nodded in the direction of some empty cartons and responded "the gun is over there." One of the officers retrieved a loaded .38-caliber revolver from the cartons and the man was arrested. After his **Miranda** rights were read, he answered questions regarding whether the gun was his and where he had purchased it. The New York trial court found that the man was in custody when the officers first asked him about the whereabouts of the gun and that thus his answer (and the subsequent answers which could be argued to be fruit of the

---

82. 467 U.S. 649 (1984).

poisonous tree) should be suppressed. The Supreme Court disagreed. They reasoned that the defendant's statements were not actually compelled by police conduct that overcame his will to resist; the question was merely whether the warnings should have been given in that case. The Court stated that

> [i]n a kaleidoscopic situation such as the one confronting these officers, where spontaneity rather than adherence to a police manual is necessarily the order of the day, the application of the exception which we recognize today should not be made to depend on . . . the subjective motivation of the arresting officer. Undoubtedly, most police officers, if placed in officer Kraft's position, would act out of a host of different, instinctive, and largely unverifiable motives—their own safety, the safety of others, and perhaps as well the desire to obtain incriminating evidence from the suspect . . . We do not believe that the doctrinal underpinnings of **Miranda** require that it be applied in all its rigor to a situation in which police officers ask questions reasonably prompted by a concern for the public safety. The **Miranda** decision was based in large part on this Court's view that the warnings which it required police to give to suspects in custody would reduce the likelihood that the suspects would fall victim to constitutionally impermissible practices of police interrogation.[83]

Concern arose that the Court's decision left open the possibility of the Court declaring that the rights guaranteed to suspects through the **Miranda** case were not constitutionally based. Although it is unlikely that the **Miranda** rights as they relate to interrogation at a station house would be taken away by the Court, the dissent in the **Quarles** case did voice this concern. "The majority's error stems from a serious misunderstanding of **Miranda v. Arizona** and of the Fifth Amendment upon which that decision was based. The majority implies that **Miranda** consisted of no more than a judicial balancing act in which the benefits of 'enlarged protection for the Fifth Amendment privilege' were weighed against 'the cost to society in terms of fewer convictions of guilty suspects' . . . Supposedly because the scales tipped in favor of the privilege against self-incrimination, the **Miranda** Court erected a prophylactic barrier around statements made during custodial interrogations. The majority now proposes to return to the scales of social utility to calculate whether **Miranda**'s prophylactic rule remains cost-effective when threats to public safety are added to the balance." The dissent pointed out that the defendant was approached by four armed officers and handcuffed before the public safety question was asked. The dissent found that the questions posed by the officer were answered "on instinct" by the suspect and thus could be considered coerced.

Undercover Interrogation. The third exception to **Miranda** is that of undercover interrogation. This exception is very logical. An undercover officer might "ask questions" of a person while attempting to fight crime. For

---

83. **Id.** at 655.

example, an officer might ask a person if he has anything to sell to the officer, meaning, of course, illegal drugs. Undercover investigations would be fruitless if, before engaging in any conversation with the person selling drugs, the officer had to read the person his **Miranda** rights! Even a situation in which an undercover officer is being placed into a jail cell with a defendant, posing as a fellow inmate, will not require the reading of **Miranda** rights. This situation was the case in **Illinois v. Perkins**,[84] a case in which the Supreme Court stated:

> [T]he danger of coercion results from the interaction of custody and official interrogation. We reject the argument that **Miranda** warnings are required whenever a suspect is in custody in a technical sense and converses with someone who happens to be a government agent. Questioning by captors, who appear to control the suspect's fate, may create mutually reinforcing pressures that the Court has assumed will weaken the suspect's will, but where a suspect does not know that he is conversing with a government agent, these pressures do not exist. The state court here mistakenly assumed that because the suspect was in custody, no undercover questioning could take place. When the suspect has no reason to think that the listeners have official power over him it should not be assumed that this words are motivated by the reaction he expects from his listeners.[85]

Thus, if a suspect is speaking to a government agent but does not know that the person is a government agent, he cannot then claim that he was under pressure to answer questions. His lack of knowledge that the person is a government agent negates any argument that he was being placed in a coercive environment. The **Perkins** case involved a defendant who was detained in jail on an aggravated battery charge but was also suspected of having committed a murder. Police arranged for an undercover agent posing as an escaped convict to be placed in the jail. The undercover officer discussed with Perkins the possibility of the two escaping together, in order to win Perkins's trust. Perkins did trust him and when the undercover agent asked Perkins whether he had ever "done someone," Perkins then recounted the details of the murder to the agent, as he had indeed committed the murder. The Supreme Court not only decided that Perkins was not in custody for purposes of the interrogation itself, but opined that it is perfectly acceptable and fair for police officers to "mislead a suspect or lull him into a false sense of security," and that this sort of behavior does not relate to **Miranda** issues.

The Current State of Miranda Rights

When the **Miranda** case was originally decided, it was interpreted as standing mainly for the proposition that any confessions or statements obtained without **Miranda** warnings were inherently coercive. The **Miranda** case

---

84. 496 U.S. 292 (1990).
85. **Id**. at 297.

included a strong dissenting opinion and a few years later, in 1971, the Supreme Court, on which numerous justices had been replaced, began to chip away at the rights provided in **Miranda**. In **Harris v. New York**,[86] the Court ruled that a confession obtained without complete **Miranda** warnings being given to the suspect could be introduced into evidence for the limited purpose of impeaching a defendant's credibility. Thus, if a defendant's testimony on the stand contradicted the content of his confession, even if it was obtained illegally, the content of the confession could be disclosed to a jury. This seems counterintuitive to the purpose of the **Miranda** rights. If a purpose of reading a suspect his rights is to avoid confessions that are not reliable, it seems inappropriate to let that unreliable confession be used to counteract the information a defendant sets forth while on the witness stand, under oath.

In **Michigan v. Tucker**,[87] decided in 1974, the Supreme Court to some extent lessened the impact of **Miranda**. The **Tucker** case maintained that statements obtained without **Miranda** rules being read should not be used in court, but not because they are a violation of the Fifth Amendment right to remain silent. Rather, the concern was merely that procedural safeguards that had been set up by the court system to protect clients had been violated. The end result, of course, is the same under **Tucker** in that a defendant's statement made without the **Miranda** rights being read would be inadmissible in court. However, the Court stated that the **Miranda** rule could be invoked even without a constitutional violation. The **Tucker** case involved a defendant who was not given his rights prior to interrogation (the **Miranda** case retroactively applied). However, the police then used the defendant's statement to obtain other information (in violation of the fruit of the poisonous tree rule). The Court did indicate that the fruit of the poisonous tree rule applied, but threw out the evidence based not on the fact that the defendant's Fifth Amendment right to remain silent was violated, but because the procedural rules that were supposed to be followed by the police were violated.

This reasoning was used further in the case of **Oregon v. Elstad**.[88] Decided in 1985, the case also dealt with the concern of further taints that result from law enforcements' failure to administer **Miranda** warnings.

OREGON V. ELSTAD

FACTS: "In December, 1981, the home of Mr. and Mrs. Gilbert Gross, in the town of Salem, Polk, County, Ore., was burglarized. Missing were art objects and furnishings valued at $150,000. A witness to the burglary contacted the Polk County Sheriff's office, implicating respondent Michael Elstad, an 18-year-old neighbor and friend of the Grosses' teenage son. Thereupon, Officers Burke and McAllister

---

86. 401 U.S. 222 (1971).
87. 417 U.S. 433 (1974).
88. 470 U.S. 298 (1985).

went to the home of respondent Elstad, with a warrant for his arrest. Elstad's mother answered the door. She led the officers to her son's room where he lay on his bed, clad in shorts and listening to his stereo. The officers asked him to get dressed and to accompany them into the living room. Officer McAllister asked respondent's mother to step into the kitchen, where he explained that they had a warrant for her son's arrest for the burglary of a neighbor's residence. Officer Burke remained with Elstad in the living room. He later testified:

> I sat down with Mr. Elstad and I asked him if he was aware of why Detective McAllister and myself were there to talk with him. He stated no, he had no idea why we were there. I then asked him if he knew a person by the name of Gross, and he said yes, he did, and also added that he heard that there was a robbery at the Gross house. And at that point I told Mr. Elstad that I felt he was involved in that, and he looked at me and stated, 'Yes, I was there.'

"The officers then escorted Elstad to the back of the patrol car. As they were about to leave for the Polk County Sheriff's office, Elstad's father arrived home and came to the rear of the patrol car. The officers advised him that his son was a suspect in the burglary. Officer Burke testified that Mr. Elstad became quite agitated, opened the rear door of the car, and admonished his son: 'I told you that you were going to get into trouble. You wouldn't listen to me. You never learn.'

"Elstad was transported to the sheriff's headquarters and approximately one hour later, officers Burke and McAllister joined him in McAllister's office. McAllister then advised respondent for the first time of his **Miranda** rights, reading from a standard card. Respondent indicated he understood his rights, and, having these rights in mind, wished to speak with the officers. Elstad gave a full statement, explaining that he had known that the Gross family was out of town and had been paid to lead several acquaintances to the Gross residence and show them how to gain entry through a defective sliding glass door. The statement was typed, reviewed by respondent, read back to him for correction, initialed and signed by Elstad and both officers. As an afterthought, Elstad added and initialed the sentence, 'After leaving the house Robby & I went back to [the] van & Robby handed me a small bag of grass.' Respondent concedes that the officers made no threats or promises either at his residence or at the sheriff's office."[89]

Elstad was charged with first-degree burglary and his attorney moved to suppress his oral statement and signed confession. He argued that the initial statement he made tainted the subsequent confession.

ISSUE: Must a subsequent confession, before which **Miranda** warnings were given, but following a statement that was improperly taken without first giving necessary **Miranda** rights, be suppressed?

HOLDING: No.

---

89. **Id**. at 300–302.

RATIONALE: The Court stated:

> There is a vast difference between the direct consequences flowing from coercion of a confession by physical violence or other deliberate means calculated to break the suspect's will and the uncertain consequences of disclosure of a "guilty secret" freely given in response to an unwarned but non-coercive question, as in this case . . . Certainly, in respondent's case, the causal connection between any psychological disadvantage created by his admission and his ultimate decision to cooperate is speculative and attenuated at best. . . . We must conclude that, absent deliberately coercive or improper tactics in obtaining the initial statement, the mere fact that a suspect has made an unwarned admission does not warrant a presumption of compulsion. A subsequent administration of **Miranda** warnings to a suspect who has given a voluntary but unwarned statement ordinarily should suffice to remove the conditions that precluded admission of the earlier statement. In such circumstances, the finder of fact may reasonably conclude that the suspect made a rational and intelligent choice whether to waive or invoke his rights.[90]
>
> We find that the dictates of **Miranda** and the goals of the Fifth Amendment proscription against use of compelled testimony are fully satisfied in the circumstances of this case by barring use of the unwarned statement in the case in chief. No further purpose is served by imputing "taint" to subsequent statements obtained pursuant to a voluntary and knowing waiver. We hold today that a suspect who has once responded to unwarned yet uncoercive questioning is not thereby disabled from waiving his rights and confessing after he has been given the requisite **Miranda** warnings.[91]

Thus, courts need not consider whether a statement that is tainted by a failure to inform a suspect of his **Miranda** rights in any way influenced his giving of a further statement following **Miranda** rights being given. The Supreme Court apparently believes that the fruit of the poisonous tree rule is important when the original evidence is obtained unconstitutionally, but as it no longer views the **Miranda** rules as being based in the Constitution, but rather being based on prophylactic rules, the fruit of the poisonous tree rule does not apply. Because the Court determined that the rule is not constitutionally based, the Court could at some point decide that the rule is no longer required.

In 1968, Congress attempted to overrule the **Miranda** decision through legislation, just two years after **Miranda** had been decided. In 18 U.S.C. §3501, Congress required that federal judges admit statements made by criminal defendants if the court determines that the statement was made

---

90. **Id**. at 312.
91. **Id**. at 318.

voluntarily, regardless of whether **Miranda** rights had been read to the suspect. The statute further defined how voluntariness would be decided, including some factors that were related to the **Miranda** warnings, such as whether the person had been informed that he did not have to talk to the police. However, the statute only stated that these factors should be considered, not that the absence of any particular factor would result in the statement being suppressed. The statute was an act of Congress and thus applied only to federal criminal proceedings, along with criminal cases being processed in the District of Columbia. Because the majority of criminal cases are litigated in state courts, Congress's statute did not significantly change the way the vast majority of law enforcement agencies proceeded with interrogations.

The case of **Dickerson v. United States**[92] seems to be the Supreme Court's reaction to Congress's attempt to change by legislation what the Supreme Court had decided. In **Dickerson**, the defendant was prosecuted in federal court and tried to suppress statements he had made to the FBI without first being read his **Miranda** rights. The trial level court suppressed the statements, and of course, the government appealed, arguing that Congress's statute had rendered the reading of **Miranda** rights unnecessary. The federal court of appeals for the Fourth Circuit reversed the district court's decision, agreeing with the government. The Supreme Court granted certiorari. The Court recognized that it had previously stated that the **Miranda** rules were prophylactic; however, the Court in **Dickerson** stated that perhaps the **Miranda** rule actually was constitutional. The Court stated that it would rule only on decisions that had any relevance to the Constitution if the underpinnings of those decisions had eroded over time, citing the concept of **stare decisis** to justify its failure to overrule **Miranda**. In this case, concerns still existed regarding police interrogation techniques and, as the Court stated, "subsequent cases have reduced the impact of the **Miranda** rule on legitimate law enforcement while reaffirming the decision's core ruling that unwarned statements may not be used as evidence in the prosecution's case in chief."[93] The Court also stated that "Miranda has become embedded in routine police practice to the point where the warnings have become part of our national culture."[94]

The dissenting opinion, written by Justice Scalia, disputed the notion that **Miranda** was a constitutional requirement, pointing out that even the majority opinion stated only that the concept is "constitutionally based." The dissenting opinion stated: "Since there is in fact no other principle that can reconcile today's judgment with the post-*Miranda* cases that the court refuses to abandon, what today's decision will stand for, whether the justices can bring themselves to say it or not, is the power of the Supreme Court to write a prophylactic, extra-constitutional Constitution, binding on Congress

---

92. 530 U.S. 428 (2000).
93. **Id**. at 443.
94. **Id**.

and the states."[95] Nonetheless, the **Dickerson** majority decision stated that **Miranda** could not be overruled by an act of Congress or ignored by the states. What does this decision mean for **Miranda**? The Court, having in effect changed its mind to imply that perhaps **Miranda** is constitutionally based, might not be able to justify decisions such as the determination that there is no fruit of the poisonous tree doctrine relating to cases in which **Miranda** warnings are the issue. The Supreme Court continues to consider cases related to the **Miranda** rule. In 2003, in another victory for law enforcement, the Supreme Court determined that violating **Miranda** does not subject police officers to civil liability as long as the statements obtained as a result of the **Miranda** violation are not used against the defendant (the plaintiff in the civil case) in Court.[96] The issue of **Miranda** rights is obviously an area in which the Supreme Court's future rulings will be closely scrutinized.

GRAND JURY INDICTMENT

An **indictment** is very important in the criminal law process. In the federal system, the indictment is the actual piece of paper that a prosecutor gives to the grand jury that charges a person with a crime. Grand juries were used in Great Britain to serve as a buffer between the king (and his prosecutors) and the citizens. Some argue that now grand juries merely serve as rubber stamps for the prosecutors, approving of the charges in most cases. Nonetheless, grand juries are used in the federal criminal justice system and in approximately one-half of the states, with some requiring their use and some permitting it. The right to be indicted by a grand jury is a right that has not been incorporated to the states.

After a grand jury hears evidence presented against the defendant, it returns the indictment paperwork with the words "A True Bill" if the members of the jury believe that the prosecutor has presented enough evidence to establish probable cause that the person did, in fact, commit a crime. Alternatively, if the grand jury decides that not enough evidence was presented to find that probable cause exists that the defendant committed the crime, the paper will be returned to the prosecutor with the words "No True Bill." However, do not try to apply the rules of double jeopardy to the indictment system. Because the double jeopardy clause only clicks in once a trial jury (not a grand jury) is sworn, or in a bench trial, once the first witness is sworn, double jeopardy does not apply in the case of a grand jury considering an indictment. Thus, if the prosecutor is not happy with the results of the grand jury's decision, and especially if the prosecutor obtains new evidence against the defendant at a later time, it is possible that the prosecutor can bring

---

95. **Id.** at 445.
96. **Chavez v. Martinez**, 538 U.S. 760 (2003).

an indictment proceeding again and have another grand jury consider the evidence. A grand jury generally has 16 to 23 jurors, and a grand jury needs 12 votes to indict. A grand jury can actually conduct an investigation, rather than just considering the information that comes before it, like a trial jury. A grand jury's procedures are secret in nature and even the accused does not know that a grand jury proceeding has taken place. The government must prove its case to a grand jury and if no case is proved and no bill is returned, the case will not proceed any further and the person accused of the crime will never know he was the subject of the grand jury's investigation. Although many state that the grand jury provides a layer of protection against governmental oppression, others complain about its one-sidedness in favor of the prosecution. The system goes against the rest of the procedures in the criminal justice system, in which transparency is necessary and important.

State courts can either use the indictment system or another system, such as the preliminary hearing system in which a single person, most often a district magistrate, decides whether probable cause exists, to move the case forward to trial. In these courts, a piece of paper called an "information" is filed, and that will form the basis of the charges against the defendant. The grand jury indictment provision of the United States Constitution is one of the few provisions which has not been incorporated to the states. In deciding that the provision of grand jury indictment is not fundamental to the United States justice system, the Supreme Court decided that the injustices that were to be avoided by the use of the grand jury system no longer exist.[97] Specifically, the court stated that

> as these broad and general maxims of liberty and justice held in our system a different place and performed a different function from their position and office in English constitutional history and law, they would receive and justify a corresponding and more comprehensive interpretation. Applied in England only as guards against executive usurpation and tyranny, here they have become bulwarks also against arbitrary legislation; but, in that application, as it would be incongruous to measure and restrict them by the ancient customary English law, they must be held to guarantee no particular forms of procedure, but the very substance of individual rights to life, liberty, and property.[98]

The Court also encouraged the law's changing with the times. It quoted a prior court decision,[99] stating that:

> A person has no property, no vested interest, in any rule of the common law. That is only one of the forms of municipal law, and is no more sacred than any other. Rights of property which have been created by the common law cannot be taken away without due process; but the law itself, as a rule of conduct, may

---

97. **Hurtado v. California**, 110 U.S. 516 (1884).
98. **Id**. at 532, *quoting* **Munn v. Illinois**, 94 U.S. 113-134 (1877).
99. **Munn v. Illinois**, 94 U.S. 113 (1877).

be changed at the will or even at the whim of the legislature, unless prevented by constitutional limitations. Indeed, the great office of statutes is to remedy defects in the common law as they are developed, and to adapt it to the changes of time and circumstances.

Any defendant in the federal criminal system has the right to be indicted by a grand jury when being prosecuted for a felony. However, a person being prosecuted for a misdemeanor in federal court is not entitled to have a grand jury hear his case; an information can be filed in those cases instead. A defendant has the right to waive a grand jury indictment in federal court unless his case is a capital case. Some states that use a grand jury system permit a defendant to waive grand jury indictment, but some do not. If a defendant waives a grand jury indictment, the government will file a document called an **information** to set forth the charges against the defendant. When a defendant does have the right to a grand jury indictment, he nevertheless does not have the right to hear the evidence that is put forth against him. Thus, witnesses are protected from a defendant knowing the contents of their testimony or the fact that they testified against the defendant. The defendant also does not have a right to appear in front of the grand jury or to present testimony or witnesses on his own behalf. The inquiry concerns merely whether enough probable cause exists to move the case along, based on what the prosecutor's witnesses testify to. The grand jury never decides whether the witnesses are telling the truth, just whether, if they are telling the truth, enough evidence has been presented to sustain the charges. Grand jury proceedings can be very long and involve large amounts of documents and evidence. Further, grand jury proceedings can, and very often do, rely on evidence that would most likely be excluded from trial as being obtained illegally (in opposition to a person's Fourth Amendment search and seizure rights). A grand jury can also consider **hearsay evidence**. Hearsay evidence is any statement that is being made in court and asserted to be true when the statement was previously made out of court by another person. Hearsay evidence is excluded from trial proceedings unless one of many exceptions is present. A prosecutor at a grand jury proceeding does not need to present to the jury any evidence that would show that the defendant did not commit the crime; this type of evidence is otherwise known as exculpatory evidence. Generally, the defendant does not even have the right to see the transcripts or evidence that was presented against him at the grand jury proceedings. There is an exception to this rule only if (1) the First Amendment provides otherwise or (2) the court specifically releases the information to the defendant.

DOUBLE JEOPARDY

The Fifth Amendment to the United States Constitution states: "[N]or shall any person be subject for the same offence to be twice put in jeopardy of life or limb . . ." The common law rule of double jeopardy in the United States prior to the Constitution being written included the concept that a prior conviction or acquittal could be presented in a case to avoid a second prosecution and the concept that a defendant couldn't be tried a second time even if his first trial had ended in a hung jury. The original guarantee as introduced by James Madison in the House of Representatives read, "No person shall be subject, except in cases of impeachment, to more than one punishment or trial for the same offense." Because this version of the amendment could imply that a defendant could not ask on appeal to receive a retrial, the language was changed to the language that ultimately ended up in the Constitution.

Many people are confused by the issue of double jeopardy and how the constitutional provisions regarding it are interpreted. The amendment itself simply says that no person shall be "subject, for the same offense, to be twice put in jeopardy of life or limb." One case in which this issue was noticed by the general public was in the O.J. Simpson murder case. In that case, O.J. Simpson was acquitted in criminal court of the charges of murder regarding his former spouse, Nicole Simpson, and her friend, Ronald Goldman. Following the verdict of not guilty in state criminal court, the family members of the deceased and Brown's estate brought a lawsuit against O.J. Simpson in civil court for the wrongful killings of their loved ones. Simpson was subpoenaed and forced to testify in this civil trial, when he could not be forced to do so in the criminal trial because of his constitutional right not to be forced to incriminate himself. The civil trial resulted in Brown and Simpson's children being awarded $12.5 million from their father, as beneficiaries of money paid into their deceased mother's estate. The victims' families were also awarded $33.5 million in compensatory and punitive damages. Some members of the general public may have been confused. How could O.J. be tried again after being acquitted? Isn't that considered double jeopardy? This chapter will explain when double jeopardy applies and why it did not apply in the O.J. Simpson case.

The basic provision of the double jeopardy rule is that a person who has committed a criminal offense can be prosecuted and punished only once for the act. However, despite how simple that statement sounds, a lot of situations can arise where the rule is not easily interpreted. The Supreme Court has considered what the clause "double jeopardy" means numerous times. For example, when is a case considered "prosecuted," and what if the person has committed multiple offenses? What if a person is found guilty of a crime but acquitted of others? What happens if a person appeals his case because he believes the court erred during his trial?

The concept of double jeopardy applies to criminal trials in countries other than the United States, where a defendant, at common law, can enter a plea of "autrefois acquit" or "autrefois convict," meaning that she has been previously acquitted or previously convicted of the same offense. In Mexico and the United States, the right not to be tried twice for the same offense is provided for in the Constitution. Other countries provide the right by statute. Even the European Convention on Human Rights, which has been signed by all members of the Council of Europe (including most European countries) protects individuals against double jeopardy. The double jeopardy clause, although referencing that no one should be put in jeopardy "of life or limb," has been interpreted to extend to much more than capital punishment (or crimes involving corporal punishment, although our statutes do not provide for corporal punishment for criminal behavior other than the death penalty). The concept extends basically to all nonsummary crimes, including felonies and misdemeanors, against both adults and juveniles.

Consider the effects of trying a person more than once for the same crime, when the first time the person is tried, he is determined not to be guilty. First, any person who is accused of a crime most likely suffers some, if not a great amount of, stress when awaiting trial. Even if the result of a trial is not in favor of the defendant, at least when the trial is over, some finality exists. If the government could continuously appeal the case, even if the defendant is found not guilty of all charges, the defendant would be constantly concerned that his case was not over. Second, the government could use each trial as a "practice run" in terms of trying to convict the defendant. Theoretically, each time a government agency tries a case, it will become more familiar with the case, more familiar with the defense that will be set forth by the defendant, more able to discover the weaknesses in its own case, and thus more able to prevail in the case.

The main, and probably most easily understood, example of a double jeopardy issue is that which the court discussed first in **Palko v. Connecticut**[100] and then again in **Baltimore v. Maryland**. To demonstrate the Court's original reasoning for determining that double jeopardy was *not* a fundamental right that had to be followed by the state, and then to demonstrate the Court's change in its determination, both cases will be excerpted below.

PALKO V. CONNECTICUT

In **Palko v. Connecticut**, the Supreme Court considered whether a person who had been acquitted of a first-degree murder charge could be tried again for first-degree murder.

FACTS: Palko was indicted for first-degree murder, and a jury found him guilty of the lesser charge of second-degree murder. Palko was sentenced to life in prison. The State of Connecticut appealed the case, arguing that (1) certain testimony regarding a confession made by Palko should have been excluded from trial, (2) certain evidence should have been entered into court in order to prove to the jury that Palko was not credible, and (3) the judge erred in the instructions he gave to the jury wherein he set forth the difference between

---

100. 302 U.S. 319 (1937).

first- and second-degree murder. The appeals court agreed with the state and reversed Palko's case for a new trial. Palko was tried again for first-degree murder and was this time found guilty of first-degree murder in his second jury trial. Palko was sentenced to death. He appealed, arguing that he could not be tried for first-degree murder when he had already specifically been acquitted of first-degree murder via the jury. The court admitted that to try Palko again for first-degree murder was considered double jeopardy, but the state argued that the Constitution's double jeopardy clause should not be applicable to states.

ISSUE: Whether the double jeopardy clause is so fundamental a right that it should be incorporated to the states.

HOLDING: The double jeopardy clause is not so fundamental that it must be followed by the states.

RATIONALE: The United States Supreme Court stated that although the concept of double jeopardy is well established in federal court, it did not feel that the right was so important that states should have to follow it. The Court stated:

> Is that kind of double jeopardy to which the statute has subjected him a hardship so acute and shocking that our polity will not endure it? Does it violate those fundamental principles of liberty and justice which lie at the base of all our civil and political institutions? The answer surely must be "no." What the answer would have to be if the state were permitted after a trial free from error to try the accused over again or to bring another case against him, we have no occasion to consider. We deal with the statute before us and no other. The state is not attempting to wear the accused out by a multitude of cases with accumulated trials. It asks no more than this, that the case against him shall go on until there shall be a trial free from the corrosion of substantial legal error. This is not cruelty at all, nor even vexation in any immoderate degree. If the trial had been infected with error adverse to the accused, there might have been review at his instance, and as often as necessary to purge the vicious taint. A reciprocal privilege, subject at all times to the discretion of the presiding judge, has now been granted to the states. There is here no seismic innovation. The edifice of justice stands, its symmetry, to many, greater than before.[101]

Later, in the case of **Baltimore v. Maryland**, the Supreme Court reversed its decision regarding whether double jeopardy is a fundamental right that

---

101. **Id**. at 328.

should be followed by the states. In so doing, the Court stated that it had recently been considering in its decisions specific guarantees provided by the Bill of Rights and how those rights related to a defendant's ability to obtain a trial in state court that was conducted with due process of law. The Court stated that in a number of cases, it had rejected the notion that only a "watered-down, subjective version" of the Bill of Rights applied to the states. The Court then stated that the double jeopardy prohibition of the Fifth Amendment represented a fundamental ideal in the constitutional heritage of the United States and that it should apply to the states through the Fourteenth Amendment due process clause. Specifically, the Court stated:

> The fundamental nature of the guarantee against double jeopardy can hardly be doubted. Its origins can be traced to Greek and Roman times, and it became established in the common law of England long before this Nation's independence . . . . As with many other elements of the common law, it was carried into the jurisprudence of this Country through the medium of Blackstone, who codified the doctrine in his Commentaries. "[T]he plea of *autrefois acquit*, or a former acquittal," he wrote, "is grounded on this universal maxim of the common law of England that no man is to be brought into jeopardy of his life more than once for the same offence."

Today, every State incorporates some form of the prohibition in its constitution or common law. As the Supreme Court stated in **Green v. United States**,[102] "[t]he underlying idea, one that is deeply ingrained in at least the Anglo-American system of jurisprudence, is that the State, with all its resources and power, should not be allowed to make repeated attempts to convict an individual for an alleged offense, thereby subjecting him to embarrassment, expense and ordeal and compelling him to live in a continuing state of anxiety and insecurity, as well as enhancing the possibility that, even though innocent he may be found guilty." This underlying notion has, from the very beginning, been part of our constitutional tradition. Like the right to trial by jury, the issue of double jeopardy is clearly "fundamental to the American scheme of justice."

Double jeopardy attaches as soon as a jury is empanelled, if the defendant is to have a trial by jury, or when the first witness is sworn, if a judge is to be the fact finder in the trial. If no trial takes place, double jeopardy applies when a plea is accepted by the court. An exception always exists, however, if the defendant decides to appeal the case himself. The Supreme Court has been very clear about the fact that a defendant cannot argue that he desires a new trial because he believes that something went wrong during the trial, and then when he receives a new trial, argue that his double jeopardy rights are being violated.

---

102. 355 U.S. 184-188 (1957).

A double jeopardy exception also exists when a military court is involved. If a person has been previously acquitted by a civilian court, he can be retried in a military court if he is a member of the military. Juvenile proceedings can also raise the issue of double jeopardy. As more and more state statutes permit juveniles to be tried as adults for committing a serious crime, it is important to remember that double jeopardy precludes the state from prosecuting an individual in both adult and juvenile courts, because both proceedings would be tried under the criminal code.

The Blockburger Rule

The concept that a person cannot be convicted of charges that include the same elements as another charge is referred to as the **Blockburger rule**. The Blockburger rule stands for the proposition that a defendant can be tried for two charges that seem similar, as long as each charge has one element that the other does not.

In **Blockburger v. United States**,[103] the Supreme Court made precedential law as is explained by the following case brief. However, note that the phrase "double jeopardy" and the Fifth Amendment were never actually included in the Court's opinion—the Court was in essence deciding on a double jeopardy–related issue without actually using that terminology.

BLOCKBURGER V. UNITED STATES

FACTS: The defendant was charged with selling morphine to one person, but he was charged with five different counts, in violation of the Harrison Narcotics Act. The jury found that the defendant was guilty of the second, third, and fifth counts. The second count charged that the defendant sold ten grains of morphine that was not in or from the original stamped package; the third count charged that the defendant made a sale on the following day of eight grains of the drug, not from the original stamped package; and the fifth count charged that the sale referred to in count three was made not in pursuance of a written order of the person who purchased it, which was required by the statute. The defendant argued that the two sales charged in the second and third counts were made to the same person and thus constituted a single transaction (thus double jeopardy prohibited the defendant from being tried on both counts). The defendant also argued that the sale charged in the third count and the fifth count constituted one offense, so only one single penalty could be imposed.

ISSUE: Whether two sales of narcotics to one person by one defendant constituted two separate crimes, and whether the sale of the drug and the failure of the

---

103. 284 U.S. 299 (1932).

defendant to have a written order for the sale were two separate offenses for purposes of double jeopardy.

HOLDING: Double jeopardy was not violated in this case; the defendant could be charged with and convicted of all offenses.

RATIONALE: The statute provided that it is illegal to sell drugs not in pursuance of a written order of the person to whom the drug was sold, but also provided in a different section that it is illegal to sell the drugs that are not in the original stamped package. As Justice Sutherland wrote:

> Each of the offenses created required proof of a different element. The applicable rule is that, where the same act or transaction constitutes a violation of two distinct statutory provisions, the test to be applied to determine whether there are two offenses or only one is whether each provision requires proof of an additional fact which the other does not.

The case of **Brown v. Ohio**[104] involved a defendant who was being charged with automobile theft and also with joyriding. The Court found that the defendant's conviction of joyriding would bar a later prosecution for auto theft, because auto theft involves taking the car of another person without the owner's permission, with the intent to steal it. Joyriding involves merely taking the car of another person; there is no requirement that the intention upon taking the car is to steal it. Thus, because the crime of theft includes all of the elements that the crime of joyriding already had in it, the defendant cannot be charged again with essentially the same elements. Thus, a wise prosecutor will prosecute someone for the higher offense, not the lesser one.

Acquittal

The concept of double jeopardy clearly applies when a defendant is acquitted of a crime. When a jury finds that a defendant is not guilty of a crime, the defendant has been cleared of the crime and under no circumstances can the defendant be brought to trial again for those charges. An acquittal might also take place if the court enters a **directed verdict**. A judge can enter a directed verdict if a jury is deadlocked or if the judge does not feel that, after all of the evidence of at least one party has been entered, enough evidence was presented to fulfill the elements of a crime. Thus, a directed verdict is not based on whether a party is telling the truth, but rather whether either the state or the defendant offered evidence of a particular crime. A directed verdict is occasionally entered, for example, if a witness says something completely different from what the prosecution believed the

---

104. 432 U.S. 161 (1977).

witness would say, or if a witness fails to show up at trial or cannot be found to testify. Occasionally, a court might direct a verdict if a jury is deadlocked. Further, if a jury is deadlocked on certain charges but makes a decision in the defendant's favor on any count, finding him not guilty, double jeopardy would attach to the crime for which the defendant was acquitted. A new trial would be held only for the remaining counts.

Even if an acquittal itself is later determined to be erroneous, the defendant cannot be tried again. In **Green v. United States**,[105] the Court was faced with an error by the court which worked to the defendant's advantage. The defendant was tried in federal court on charges of first-degree murder. The judge instructed the jury that it could find the defendant guilty of first-degree murder or the lesser offense of second-degree murder. The jury found him guilty of second-degree murder but did not render a specific verdict on the charge of first-degree murder. The trial judge dismissed the jury, when he should have requested that the jury render a decision on the first-degree murder charge, even though the jury's finding regarding second-degree murder implied that the jury had found the defendant not guilty of first-degree murder. The case was appealed by the government and the appeals court granted a new trial in which the defendant was again tried for first-degree murder, was found guilty, and was sentenced to death. The Supreme Court found that even though the judge had erred, once the jury was discharged, the case was final and could not be appealed by the government to the defendant's disadvantage. In rendering its decision, the Supreme Court stated that

> The constitutional prohibition against "double jeopardy" was designed to protect an individual from being subjected to the hazards of trial and possible conviction more than once for an alleged offense. . . . The underlying idea, one that is deeply ingrained in at least the Anglo-American system of jurisprudence, is that the State, with all its resources and power, should not be allowed to make repeated attempts to convict an individual for an alleged offense, thereby subjecting him to embarrassment, expense and ordeal and compelling him to live in a continuing state of anxiety and insecurity.[106]

> Moreover, it is not even essential that a verdict of guilt or innocence be returned for a defendant to have once been placed in jeopardy so as to bar a second trial on the same charge. This Court, as well as most others, has taken the position that a defendant is placed in jeopardy once he is put to trial before a jury, so that, if the jury is discharged without his consent, he cannot be tried again. . . . This prevents a prosecutor or judge from subjecting a defendant to a second prosecution by discontinuing the trial when it appears that the jury might not convict. At the same time, jeopardy is not regarded as having come to an end so as to bar a second trial in those cases where "unforeseeable

---

105. 355 U.S. 184 (1957).
106. 355 U.S. at 188.

circumstances . . . arise during [the first] trial making its completion impossible, such as the failure of a jury to agree on a verdict."[107]

Further, the Court stated, "Green was in direct peril of being convicted and punished for first-degree murder at his first trial. He was forced to run the gauntlet once on that charge, and the jury refused to convict him. When given the choice between finding him guilty of either first- or second-degree murder, it chose the latter. In this situation, the great majority of cases in this country have regarded the jury's verdict as an implicit acquittal on the charge of first-degree murder."[108] Thus, the verdict convicting Green of second-degree murder implied that the jury was acquitting Green on the first-degree murder charge, which would prevent him from being retried on that charge. Besides setting forth the concept of an **implied acquittal**, which bans a second trial on the higher level charges, the **Green** case stood further for the concept that even if court error results in a favorable, yet erroneous, verdict for the defendant, the defendant cannot be tried again for the higher charges that include the elements that are set forth in the lower charges for which he was found guilty.

Double jeopardy does not prevent the government from appealing certain issues that could cause the defendant to be retried. If the defense files a motion to dismiss the case and the motion is granted, the state can appeal and if it prevails upon appeal, the defendant can be tried. This is not, however, really a retrial, though, because the motion to dismiss would most likely have been filed prior to a jury being impaneled, toward the beginning of the case. There is also an exception if the defendant bribes the judge, who enters a directed verdict or an acquittal, and the bribery is later discovered. Oddly, however, if the defendant bribes the jury and the jury finds him not guilty, double jeopardy does attach and the defendant still cannot be tried again. (Note that in such a situation, however, the defendant can be charged with bribing a jury!) Finally, a defendant can in essence end up with two trials if his first trial results in a **mistrial**. A mistrial can be declared when anything improper is entered as evidence in a trial. A mistrial can result from a witness discussing a defendant's past crimes, if the applicable evidentiary rules of court would dictate that the defendant's criminal record should not be discussed at trial. A prosecutor's inflammatory statement made to the jury could also cause the judge to declare a mistrial. Really, anything that is brought up in trial that the judge feels is too prejudicial for the jury to hear and still make a neutral decision can result in a mistrial. A hung jury also falls within the scope of a mistrial. The idea behind a mistrial is that whatever caused the trial to stop was something that would have harmed the defendant anyway or was something unavoidable like a hung jury. Generally, if discriminatory

---

107. Page 355 U.S. 188, *citing* **Wade v. Hunter,** 336 U.S. 684, 336 U.S. 688-689.
108. **Green v. United States,** 355 U.S. 184 (1957).

information comes into the trial but the defendant argues that he would like the trial to continue anyway, the judge cannot on his own end the trial.

The only way a mistrial would involve double jeopardy is if the defendant argues against the judge declaring a mistrial and the court does not determine that the mistrial was one of "manifest necessity." This would be the case only if the court determined that public justice would not be served by a continuation of the trial. Most such cases involve a hung jury or remarks by the defendant or the defendant's attorney that were the cause of the mistrial. Another possibility would be if the court learned after empaneling the jury that one of the members of the jury had served on the grand jury that issued the indictment of the defendant. In such a case, that juror would have heard evidence that might not be admissible at trial and could have obviously formed an opinion about the case prior to trial.

Civil Cases

The type of court in which a case takes place also determines whether double jeopardy applies. The O.J. Simpson case, discussed earlier, involves a case that was tried in both criminal and civil courts. This dual attempt to penalize a person for his actions is not a violation of double jeopardy. When a case has been tried in criminal court, as long as a civil statute exists which also makes a person liable for his actions, the civil statute can be used to bring a suit in civil court. Most commonly, the civil lawsuit does not proceed very far until the criminal case has been finalized. This is because the **burden of proof**, or how much proof a jury needs in order to find a person liable, is different for criminal and civil cases. In a criminal case, the burden of proof is **beyond a**

YOU BE THE JUDGE

You are a judge in a trial involving writing checks with insufficient funds. The case is called for trial and a jury is selected and sworn in the morning, then informed that they can take a lunch break and should return at 2:00, at which time the trial will begin. When the jury returns, the prosecution immediately makes a motion requesting that the jury be discharged because its key witness for counts six and seven of the charges was not present. The prosecutor indicates that he was aware that the witness had not yet been found when the jury was selected. The defendant argues that those counts be thrown out, while the trial continues on the other counts. The judge nonetheless discharges the jury and orders that the trial be reconvened in two days with another jury. The defendant argues that double jeopardy applies. The prosecutor argues that stopping the trial was manifestly necessary. What do you think?

reasonable doubt, which means that the jury must have no doubt that the person being charged with the crime is actually the person who committed it. In a civil case, the burden of proof is merely a **preponderance of the evidence,** which means that the jury must merely find that it is more likely than not that the person engaged in a particular act. Thus, normally an attorney considering filing a civil suit on behalf of a client will wait until the criminal court's decision has been rendered. If the individual is convicted in criminal court under the beyond a reasonable doubt standard, the judgment rendered will assume that the preponderance of the evidence standard would also have been met. Thus, a civil court judgment can easily be entered.

Occasionally, it is difficult to determine whether a particular type of proceeding is civil or criminal in nature. Most often, the legislature determines, when writing a statute that prohibits someone's actions, whether the particular conduct is civil or criminal. However, sometimes penalties that appear to be civil in nature seem to penalize a person as if they were criminal in nature. In **Hudson v. United States,**[109] the Supreme Court discussed how courts should determine whether a particular type of penalty is civil or criminal. Even if a law clearly states that its penalties were intended by the legislature to be civil, a lower court must still make a determination as to whether the statute was intended to be punitive either in its "purpose or effect," thereby "transform[ing]" what was clearly intended as a civil remedy into something criminal. The Court then listed several factors that had previously been established as being relevant to this type of consideration:

(1) [w]hether the sanction involves an affirmative disability or restraint;
(2) whether it has historically been regarded as a punishment;
(3) whether it comes into play only on a finding of *scienter*;
(4) whether its operation will promote the traditional aims of punishment-retribution and deterrence;
(5) whether the behavior to which it applies is already a crime;
(6) whether an alternative purpose to which it may rationally be connected is assignable for it; and
(7) whether it appears excessive in relation to the alternative purpose assigned.

The Court further stated that all of the factors must be considered in relation to the clear meaning of the statute on its face; only clear proof will catapult a civil remedy into being considered a criminal remedy for purposes of the double jeopardy statute.

Often the issue of whether a penalty is civil or criminal relates to cases involving civil forfeiture or the payment of money in the form of civil fines. In these cases, courts should consider whether the amount of the fine or penalty seems to relate in some way directly to the amount by which a person's

---

109. 522 U.S. 93 (1998).

crime actually deprived someone else. A civil forfeiture or civil fine may be considered punitive when the value of the property seized or the fine is disproportionate to the loss that society experienced. If it appears as though the goal of the fine is really to punish, a court might determine that double jeopardy attaches. A civil action in which a defendant's professional license or driving privileges are taken may or may not be considered criminal for purposes of double jeopardy. Further, the revocation of a defendant's probation or parole has been treated differently for double jeopardy purposes in different states.

One line of court cases in essence permits large civil awards without bringing double jeopardy into play. Because the Bill of Rights only protects individuals against government action, an individual lawsuit filed by a plaintiff against a defendant would not subject the defendant to a double jeopardy claim, no matter how high the damages that are awarded are. Occasionally a court will grant punitive damages to a plaintiff in a civil matter; in other words, those damages are intended to punish the defendant for his actions. As long as the plaintiff in such a lawsuit is not a government entity, the defendant may not argue a double jeopardy issue. However, a penalty to be paid to the government might invoke the issue of double jeopardy. For example, a person who defrauds the welfare system and is forced to pay back the amount she obtained illegally will probably be considered a civil issue. The individual could be prosecuted based on the alleged criminal act of fraud in addition to the penalties already imposed in civil court. However, an

YOU BE THE JUDGE

The state in which you are a judge has passed an act to deal with sexually violent predators. The act states that anyone who the court determines is likely to engage in predatory acts of sexual violence based on his mental abnormality or personality disorder will be evaluated and placed in a facility for individuals with mental health disorders. This is not a prison, but it is a secure facility and a person would be unable to leave the facility voluntarily. Only if, in the future, a doctor determined that the individual is no longer a threat can the individual be released. You know that very often when a person is admitted to a mental health facility, they end up being detained there forever, as it seems to be a fairly heavy burden to prove that the person is well enough to be released once they have been committed. Is the use of the act to place a person in confinement a violation of the person's double jeopardy rights if the person has already been tried in criminal court, given a sentence of imprisonment in a correctional facility, served the sentence that he was given, and released from prison and the court system?

extremely large penalty that is far more than what the person received as an overpayment of benefits might be considered a criminal type of penalty for double jeopardy purposes since a governmental entity is involved.

Appeal by Defendant

If the defendant appeals his case, generally he cannot claim double jeopardy if he is then retried. In fact, most of the time when a defendant appeals his case, he is specifically requesting a new trial, free of error. Thus, the trial would be held again, but this time without the evidence or statements that were erroneous in the first trial. The prosecution rarely appeals a case, as an appeal after acquittal or conviction can be a violation of double jeopardy. If the prosecution desires to set aside a not guilty verdict, double jeopardy will apply. The government cannot retry the defendant for any counts on which the defendant was acquitted, and the government further cannot prosecute the defendant for a higher offense or other offenses than the crime for which the defendant was originally tried. The prosecution can appeal rulings made by the judge, for example, on evidentiary issues, if the rulings were made during the trial and before conviction and benefitted the defendant. The prosecution can never appeal a not guilty verdict by a jury; the prosecution can appeal a ruling by the court that follows a guilty verdict, however. Thus, if a defendant is found guilty by a jury and the judge sets aside that verdict, generally the prosecution can appeal the judge's decision. The prosecution can appeal a defendant's sentence without any double jeopardy issues coming into play.

If a defendant appeals his sentence, he is basically requesting that the reviewing court vacate his sentence and then resentence him properly. Thus, the new sentencing proceeding cannot be argued against on the basis of double jeopardy. In fact, the defendant could actually be sentenced more harshly when he is sentenced the second time. Although rare, if the sentencing judge states sufficient reasons for the new sentence on the record, demonstrates that something took place following the original sentence that justifies the new, harsher sentence, and does not seem to be sentencing the defendant more harshly due to vindictiveness, the new, harsher sentence can stand. This rule does not apply if a jury is making a decision regarding a defendant's sentence; a jury making the decision the second time can make any sentencing decision it desires, even if it is harsher than the original sentence.

The exception to this is when a jury decides whether a defendant receives a death sentence. Death penalty cases present an interesting double jeopardy question, because death penalty cases are tried in two phases. First, a jury decides whether the defendant is actually guilty of a crime for which the death penalty can be imposed. Once the jury decides on the defendant's guilt, the second stage is to sentence the defendant. If the defendant was convicted of a death penalty eligible crime, the jury can then make a determination as to whether or not the defendant should receive the death penalty. Double jeopardy applies to both portions of the trial. Regarding the first phase, if the defendant is found not guilty of first-degree murder but guilty of second-degree murder, he cannot be retried for first-degree murder under the implied acquittal rule. Regarding the penalty phase, if the jury has determined that the defendant should not receive the death penalty, the defendant cannot, upon an appeal and retrial, receive the death penalty.

However, there is one instance in which a defendant could receive the right to argue double jeopardy if he is retried, after his own appeal. That is in the case in which the evidence presented by the prosecutor is determined by the appeals court not to be sufficient to convict the defendant. A claim of **insufficient evidence** is a fairly common argument for a defendant to make on appeal. His argument is that the evidence that was presented by the prosecution was not sufficient to substantiate the elements of the crimes for which he was being prosecuted. The issue of sufficiency is different than the issue of **weight of the evidence**, an argument in which the defendant argues that the jury could not have believed the evidence that was set forth against him and thus that the jury's verdict was shocking and should be overturned. If a defendant prevails on a weight of the evidence claim, the case can be retried, because the reversal would be based on the fact that a greater amount of credible evidence supports one side of an issue rather than another. Because insufficiency implies that the prosecutor did not present enough evidence to sustain the conviction (for example, if no evidence was presented to substantiate a certain required element of the crime), then the prosecutor does not get another "bite at the apple" to try to present enough evidence. A reviewing court's determination that the evidence was insufficient implies that no fact finder could possibly have found the defendant guilty beyond a reasonable doubt, based on the evidence presented. If a defendant appeals his sentence, he can be resentenced. If a defendant, however, has entered a guilty plea in any case, he waives his right to argue that his double jeopardy rights have been violated. Thus, even if he was tried previously for the same crime, if he is charged again and enters a guilty plea, he cannot later argue that double jeopardy applies to his case.

Dual Sovereignty

An individual can be charged (and convicted) in two different states or in the federal and state court systems without an issue of double jeopardy arising. Consider the following example. A man kidnaps a woman, puts her in the trunk of his car, and drives from Pennsylvania to Ohio and then into Indiana. He assaults her when placing her in the car, stops in Ohio and rapes her, and then kills her in Indiana. The man could face a multitude of charges. First, he has committed the federal act of kidnapping by taking the woman against her will and taking her across state lines. He has also committed the act of assault in Pennsylvania, the act of rape in Ohio, and the act of murder in Indiana.

Even though all of the acts took place from a course of events, he can be charged and tried for all of those crimes. Even when one single act violates two statutes, a federal and a state crime, a person can be charged with both. For example, many drug cases violate both state and federal statutes. The possession and sale of cocaine violates every state criminal code. If the amount of cocaine sold reaches a certain level, it also violates federal law. Thus, a person who sells a large amount of cocaine could be charged with the sale of cocaine (and other attendant crimes) in federal court and can also be tried with the same charge in state court. Practically, often the state prosecutor's office will decide not to pursue the criminal charges if the federal government has decided to prosecute the individual, but both jurisdictions could prosecute. If both jurisdictions do prosecute the defendant and obtain convictions, the defendant will serve his time in either the state or federal prison until he has either maxed out or been paroled, and he will then report to the other institution to finish out his time. Note that municipalities are considered part of the state they are in, so a person who is tried in a municipality cannot later be tried in state court for acts constituting the same offense. American Indian tribal courts are considered to be sovereign, like states, so a person could be tried in this type of court and in federal court as well.

THE BELTWAY SNIPER ATTACKS

An example of a crime that was far-reaching in terms of being committed in more than one state was the Beltway sniper attacks, which took place in October 2002 in Washington, D.C., Maryland, and Virginia. John Allen Muhammad, an adult, and Lee Boyd Malvo, a minor, were driving around in a blue Chevrolet Caprice, and were randomly shooting victims. The shootings were perpetrated against people at shopping centers and gas stations, or people just walking on sidewalks. These criminals had previously committed murders and a robbery in Louisiana and Alabama. They were found sleeping in their car at a rest stop off of Interstate 70 in Maryland. They were arrested initially on federal weapons charges. They were eventually criminally prosecuted in Virginia, and Muhammad was sentenced to death, while Malvo was given life in prison without parole. Malvo was then sentenced to six consecutive life terms in Maryland without the possibility of parole, and Muhammad was also found guilty of six counts of murder in Maryland and was sentenced to six consecutive life terms without possibility of parole. Muhammad was eventually executed on November 10, 2009. Trials in three other states were pending at the time of his death. Muhammad could have been tried in every state in which he had committed a crime, plus in federal court for weapons violations, and no double jeopardy principles would have applied.

QUESTIONS TO CONSIDER

1. Do you agree with the different decisions made by the Court in the **Rhode Island v. Innis** case and the **Brewer v. Williams** case? Do you believe the two cases should have had two different outcomes? Why or why not? Do you believe that Williams's mental illness played a part in the Court's decision? Should it have?

2. Do you agree that the concept of double jeopardy is fundamental to our system of ordered justice? Do you agree that how a defendant's life could be affected if the state could always appeal an acquittal trumps the desire of the state to have a trial free from error in a criminal case?

3. Read the case of **Gray v. Netherland**, 518 U.S. 152 (1996), and the cases cited therein. Do you agree that when a defendant is "blindsided" at the time of the penalty phase with information was not previously disclosed to him, the ability to cross-examine a witness at the time of the hearing is enough to protect his constitutional rights?

4. Read the two Supreme Court cases that deal with a police officer holding a gun on a suspect and the subsequent determination as to whether that action makes the situation "custodial." The cases are **People v. Shivers** and **Yates v. United States**. Do you agree with the way the Court differentiated these factual scenarios?

5. Because the Supreme Court did not provide any exact wording to be used by police officers when informing suspects of their **Miranda** rights, can you think of any way to change the standard **Miranda** clause to make the rights more clear to suspects?

6. Do you believe that reading suspects their **Miranda** rights counteracts the interrogation techniques that are discussed in the **Miranda** case? Why or why not? Do you believe that any of the interrogation techniques discussed in **Miranda** are likely to result in a false confession?

KEY TERMS

beyond a reasonable doubt
The burden of proof needed to convince a jury of a guilty verdict in a criminal trial; it is a stronger requirement than is needed in civil cases.

Blockburger rule
This is the concept that a person cannot be convicted of charges that include the same elements as another charge; however, a defendant can be tried for two charges that seem similar as long as each charge has one element that the other does not.

burden of proof
This term refers to how much evidence a jury needs in order to find a person liable, and is different in criminal and civil cases.

due process
This practice assures that certain procedures are followed before a court can take away someone's right or impose penalties upon that person, and consists of substantive and procedural due process.

exculpatory evidence
Any evidence held by the prosecution that might be helpful to the defense; the prosecution has an obligation to turn over such evidence to the defense.

harmless error
This doctrine mandates that even if the prosecutor makes a statement that is inappropriate or unethical, or if there is an erroneous ruling regarding evidence entered into trial, the case will be reversed only if the court finds that the evidence actually changed the outcome of the trial.

implied acquittal
Under this doctrine, a conviction of one charge constitutes an implied acquittal of all other charges based upon the same facts of the verdict, thus preventing the defendant from being retried on the other charges.

indictment
This is the actual piece of paper that a prosecutor gives to the grand jury that charges a person with a crime.

Miranda rights
These rights include the right to remain silent, the consequences of giving up that right, and the right to counsel.

Miranda warnings
Also known as **Miranda** rights, this statement must be issued by officers to suspects when they are placed under arrest, to inform them of their Fifth Amendment rights not to incriminate themselves. ("You have the right to remain silent. . . .")

preponderance of the evidence
This burden of proof needed to convince a jury of a guilty verdict in a civil case, in which the jury must be convinced that the accused did in fact perpetrate the actions attributed to him.

KEY COURT CASES

Baltimore v. Maryland

Case in which the Supreme Court reversed its earlier decision and said that the double jeopardy clause must be applied to states as well.

Blockburger v. United States

In this case, the Supreme Court made precedential law by establishing the Blockburger rule, which states that a defendant can be tried for two charges that seem similar, as long as each charge has one element that the other does not.

Brady v. Maryland

The **Brady** decision stated that exculpatory evidence, or evidence that would assist the defense, cannot be withheld from the defense by the prosecution.

Brown v. Mississippi

This was one of the earliest and most famous coerced confession cases heard by the Supreme Court. The Court held that the confessions were coerced and not freely given, and thus were a violation of constitutional rights and not admissible in court. Using such confessions as the basis for conviction and sentence was a clear denial of due process.

Colorado v. Connelly

This landmark case considered a confession by a mentally ill person. Before the **Connelly** case, courts were supposed to consider whether a confession was voluntary considering the totality of the circumstances, and generally this included whether the confession was made out of free will rather than due to police coercion. Following the **Connelly** decision, however, the totality of the circumstances test is not applied until the defendant can show that coercive police action exists.

Hudson v. United States

In this case, the Court discussed how courts should determine whether a particular type of penalty is civil or criminal. Even if a law clearly states that its penalties were intended by the legislature to be civil, the Supreme Court stated that a lower court must still make a determination as to whether the statute was intended to be punitive either in its "purpose or effect," thereby "transforming" what was clearly intended as a civil remedy into something criminal. Only clear proof will catapult a civil remedy into being considered a criminal remedy for purposes of the double jeopardy statute.

Massiah v. United States

Another landmark case, the **Massiah** case focuses on a person's right to be free from governmental interrogation. Once the Sixth Amendment right to counsel attaches, the government is no longer able to elicit statements from the defendant about themselves. **Massiah** protects individuals from law enforcement deliberately creating an atmosphere that might be likely to elicit an incriminating response. **Massiah** is more specific to particular charges than **Miranda**. Once an individual has exercised his right not to answer questions according to **Massiah**, law enforcement must stop questioning the individual about whatever offense(s) he has been charged with.

Miranda v. Arizona

The **Miranda** Court's ruling was that statements obtained by a suspect as the result of custodial investigation is not admissible in court if the statement is being used against the person, unless the government can prove that its agents have provided the person with procedural safeguards that are sufficient to ensure that the person's Fifth Amendment privilege against compulsory self-incrimination have not been violated.

Salinas v. Texas

In this case, the Supreme Court upheld a case in which a defendant's silence was used against him. The Court stated that a witness does not invoke the privilege to remain silent by standing mute and that a person should put the government on notice when he intends to rely on the privilege so that the government could either provide immunity for the person's testimony or argue that the testimony is not incriminating.

United States v. Cruikshank

In this case, the Supreme Court considered a racially charged case decided after the Civil War, using the Sixth Amendment arraignment/indictment clause to justify its decision. The Supreme Court threw out the indictment, saying among other things that it was not specific enough about how the Democrats had taken away the African Americans' rights. Even though some other portions of the Court's decision have been overturned, the issue of the specificity of the indictment remains good law.

THE SIXTH AND EIGHTH AMENDMENTS

7

LEARNING OBJECTIVES: Students will

1. Understand when a defendant has a right to an attorney
2. Know what effective assistance of counsel is
3. Understand the right to a speedy trial, jury trial, and impartial judge and jury
4. Understand how a defendant can confront witnesses
5. Understand the bail process

> In all criminal prosecutions, the accused shall enjoy the right to a speedy and public trial, by an impartial jury of the State and district wherein the crime shall have been committed, which district shall have been previously ascertained by law, and to be informed of the nature and cause of the accusation; to be confronted with the witnesses against him; to have compulsory process for obtaining witnesses in his favor, and to have the Assistance of Counsel for his defence.
>
> **—U.S. Constitution, Amendment VI**

The Sixth Amendment provides those accused of crimes of the most basic and fundamental rights in criminal justice: the right to a speedy, public trial; the right to an impartial jury; the right to be fully informed of the charges and witnesses against them; and the right to call witnesses and have counsel to assist in their defense.

RIGHT TO COUNSEL

The Sixth Amendment provides that "in all criminal prosecutions, the accused shall enjoy the right . . . to have the assistance of counsel for his defense." English common law did not provide an absolute right to counsel until 1836, when Parliament passed a law that permitted those accused of felonies the right to have counsel represent them in criminal proceedings. In 1903, through the Poor Prisoner's Defense Act, Parliament granted a right to appointed counsel, although the courts had some discretion as to when to provide counsel. The United States Constitution was drafted prior to England's granting of the right to counsel, so it was clearly an issue that the constitutional framers cared about and specifically wanted to grant to United States citizens. Many states also initially included the right in their own constitutions. However, the right was initially interpreted more as the right to obtain counsel at one's own expense, and no system was present to appoint counsel for those who could not afford counsel. The law has evolved to the point that a defendant has a right to have an attorney present, and in some cases a free attorney appointed by the court, in any critical stage of a criminal justice proceeding; the determination of what is a critical stage is defined by the courts. The Court has acknowledged that representing oneself in a criminal proceeding can lead to a result that does not comport with the freedoms that have been guaranteed by the Constitution.

The words "assistance of counsel" have resulted in an entire system of government funded attorneys who represent indigent defendants who are accused of crimes. In any trial situation in which a constitutional right to an attorney was present and an attorney was not provided, the conviction will automatically be reversed.[1] The defendant need not show that the lack of counsel affected him. Thus, it is very important to provide an attorney when one is required. In any non-trial proceeding, failure to provide an attorney will only result in a reversal of the court's decision if the defendant can show that actual error occurred that would require a reversal. If the errors that occurred during those proceedings were harmless, the proceedings will not be reversed.[2] Note that there is no right to have an attorney for civil matters; courts have had to determine whether cases that are quasi-criminal in nature, such as the violation of a civil court order which results in a criminal charge, require the right to an attorney.

The first case in which the Supreme Court considered this provision of the Sixth Amendment was in **Powell v. Alabama**,[3] decided in 1932, when our criminal justice system reflected the poor race relations of that time. The "Scottsboro boys," the defendants in that case, were African-American men who had been accused of raping two young white women on a train. Some white boys had jumped off the train and told sheriff's deputies that black men on the train had committed the rape. One woman later retracted her claim, but nonetheless all of the men except one (who was 12 years old, the youngest of all of the boys) were convicted and sentenced to death after each received a one day long trial. The defendants received an attorney immediately prior to their trial but obviously did not have time to strategize with their lawyers regarding the trial. The defendants appealed their

---

1. **Gideon v. Wainwright**, 372 U.S. 335 (1963).
2. **United States v. Wade**, 388 U.S. 218 (1967).
3. 287 U.S. 45 (1932).

convictions based on the argument that they did not have time to plan their defense with their attorneys. The Alabama Supreme Court ruled that the trial was fair but the case was appealed to the United States Supreme Court, which reversed and remanded the decision of the Alabama Supreme Court, holding that due process was violated and that the defendants were not given proper counsel or a fair trial. (The case also involved the concern that the defendants were tried before juries on which members of their own race, although qualified to be jurors, were systematically excluded from serving.) Although the Supreme Court's decision was extremely important to the Scottsboro boys, controversy continued to ensue between courts as to whether the right to counsel prior to trial applied to non–death penalty cases.

The next case in which the Supreme Court considered this issue was **Betts v. Brady**.[4] The **Betts** court stated that whether or not a lawyer is required for a criminal case depends on the circumstances of each case but that generally states do not need to follow this portion of the Bill of Rights. In other words, the right was not important enough to be incorporated to the states. In ruling that state courts need not incorporate the right to counsel, the Supreme Court stated that "[t]he Fourteenth Amendment prohibits the conviction and incarceration of one whose trial is offensive to the common and fundamental ideas of fairness and right, and while want of counsel in a particular case may result in a conviction lacking in such fundamental fairness, we cannot say that the amendment embodies an inexorable command that no trial for any offense, or in any court, can be fairly conducted and justice accorded a defendant who is not represented by counsel."[5]

The Court did indicate that state courts should consider in each criminal case whether a failure to grant counsel would result in a violation of due process and thus result in an unfair trial. Following this decision, the Court heard many more cases, most of which involved the death penalty, and in most of which a lawyer was required. However, it was difficult for defendants who did not face the death penalty to be able to prove that due process had not been provided, as the standard for doing so was high. Thus, many defendants facing criminal charges still did not have the right to have an attorney appointed for their case.

The case that broke through the barrier set by the **Betts** court in the area of the right to counsel was that of **Gideon v. Wainwright**,[6] decided by the Supreme Court in 1963. Clarence Gideon was a man who was accused of breaking into a pool room in Florida and vandalizing some equipment and stealing money from a cash register. A witness indicated that he had seen Gideon leaving the pool room around 5:30 that morning with a bottle of alcohol and with money in his pockets. The police arrested Gideon and charged him with breaking and entering with the intent to commit petty larceny. Gideon requested that he be

---

4. 316 U.S. 455 (1942).
5. **Id.** at 473.
6. 372 U.S. 335 (1963).

appointed counsel to assist him with his case. The court denied his request, as the Florida courts at that point had determined that only defendants who were faced with capital punishment had the right to an attorney. Gideon appealed the case himself, using the law library in the prison and writing to the courts on prison stationary. His case reached the Supreme Court, which granted *certiorari* and appointed Gideon an attorney to assist him with his appeal. The State of Florida argued that an attorney should be appointed only if the defendant was proved to be incompetent, or unable to read and write, or had some other issue that would merit him having counsel such as a trial involving an extremely complicated issue. Gideon's attorney argued that any lay person cannot represent themselves as well as an attorney who has been schooled in the law. The Supreme Court ruled in favor of Gideon with all judges ruling for Gideon and with no dissenting opinion. The Court ruled that the right to assistance of counsel was indeed a fundamental right and that the failure to provide counsel would result in an unfair trial void of due process of law. Gideon's case was remanded back to the Florida courts for further action, and Gideon was appointed counsel to represent him in his subsequent trial. Gideon prevailed, receiving a not guilty verdict at his trial. Following the Supreme Court's decision in the **Gideon** case, approximately 2,000 inmates were freed from imprisonment because the decision was applied retroactively to some Florida cases.

Following the **Gideon** case, the public defender system became much larger in state systems and continued to be an important part of the federal court system as well. Public defenders represent a large portion of the criminal defendants who are charged with crimes. The public defender system is funded by taxpayer dollars and thus most offices run on a shoestring budget with attorneys having a fairly high caseload. Income guidelines exist for defendants to be eligible for a public defender and a defendant's assets are also taken into account. A few defender offices also receive private funds from donations. Some states also employ a panel of private attorneys who are compensated by the state to represent indigent clients on a case-by-case basis, working as independent contractors rather than as direct employees of the state or municipality in which they work. Private contract attorneys are also used if the local public defender's office has a conflict in representing a defendant, such as if it represents that person's co-defendant. The first public defender's office in the United States was initiated in California in 1914.

There are concerns that because of the high caseload and fairly low pay received by public defenders in state court systems, some public defender offices employ inexperienced attorneys who are unable to provide proper representation. Thus, some states have required that public defenders have certain qualifications or training before being hired. Many states also require that attorneys who represent defendants who are charged with capital crimes and could receive the death penalty have certain extra training or qualifications. Another concern regarding the public defender system is that the resources provided to most public defender offices are subpar to those provided to the offices of the prosecutor for the state. Investigators, support staff, and even the number of full-time attorneys are often lower than those provided to prosecutor's offices in the same jurisdiction. In contrast, federal public defenders are given salaries to match federal prosecuting attorneys. The federal public defender system is authorized by the Criminal Justice Act of 1964.[7] Federal public defenders also usually have a substantially lower caseload than those in the state system, although often federal cases are more complex.

In 1962, prior to the **Gideon** decision, the Supreme Court of Ohio considered a case in which a person argued for his release from prison based on his right to counsel.[8] The defendant, Doughty, pleaded guilty and was sentenced without the assistance of an attorney. He had never at any point requested an attorney. After his sentence, he filed a habeas corpus proceeding, requesting release from prison based on the fact that he did not have an attorney throughout his proceedings. The Ohio Supreme Court indicated that by entering a guilty plea, the defendant had waived his right to counsel, "unless there are circumstances which rebut and nullify such presumption." The Court indicated that the waiver could be express or implied. In other words, by merely attending the proceedings without an attorney, a defendant is in effect waiving his right to counsel. The Ohio Supreme Court was required to reconsider the case after the **Gideon** decision was handed down,[9] but refused to change its ruling. The court noted that the facts of the **Gideon** case were different from the facts for **Doughty**. Doughty did not specifically ask that counsel be appointed and he testified that he had discussed with his wife the possibility of retaining counsel but he had never made any request to the court that counsel actually be appointed.

Right to an Attorney at Trial

Gideon had the right to an attorney at his trial, and all defendants charged with felonies have that right. However, further Supreme Court cases considered whether all defendants, even those charged with fairly low level crimes, had the right to have an attorney appointed to represent them at trial. In **Scott v. Illinois**,[10] the defendant was convicted of shoplifting and received a $50 fine as his punishment. The maximum possible penalty he could have received was a $500 fine and/or a maximum of one year imprisonment. Scott appealed, arguing that he should have received counsel. The Supreme Court held that because Scott had not been sentenced to imprisonment, he had no right to have an attorney represent him. The Court's decision followed the Court's previous ruling in **Argersinger v. Hamlin**,[11] in which a man who was

---

7. 18 U.S.C. §3006A.
8. **Doughty v. Sacks**, 183 N.E.2d 368 (1962).
9. 191 N.E.2d 727 (1963).
10. 440 U.S. 367 (1979).
11. 407 U.S. 25 (1972).

sentenced to 90 days in jail in Florida for carrying a concealed weapon argued he should have received an attorney to represent him. The Florida courts held that because jury trials were not required for crimes in which the maximum possible sentence was six months, counsel was not required in such cases either. The United States Supreme Court reversed the case, ruling that Hamlin should have had counsel because he faced the possibility of a jail sentence. The Court reasoned that misdemeanor charges involve the same types of intricacies of the law as do felonies and that unrepresented clients might fall victim to "assembly line justice." Thus, the Court reasoned, no matter how small the charge seems, any misdemeanor in which a defendant could receive jail time should involve the right to counsel. However, the **Scott** court interpreted the **Argersinger** decision to mean that the state is not obligated to provide counsel to a defendant who does not receive a term of imprisonment. Interestingly, the dissenting judge in the **Scott** case, Justice Brennan, stated that the **Argersinger** case was intended to provide counsel for anyone who could receive a jail sentence, due to the social stigma attached to crimes in which a jail sentence was possible. Further, Justice Brennan stated that the majority in the **Scott** case was basing its decision to not provide counsel to every defendant when incarceration is a possibility due only to budgetary reasons (requiring counsel in ultimately fewer cases), which he felt was inappropriate when constitutional guarantees were at stake.

Practically, courts could still provide counsel for any defendant charged with a misdemeanor who could receive a sentence of imprisonment. To attempt to determine in every case whether a defendant will or will not receive imprisonment before he has entered a plea or received a trial and is sentenced is impossible. Certainly this means that public defenders are representing people who do not receive sentences of imprisonment and thus were not required to have representation. However, any incorrect predictions that a defendant would not receive incarceration would deny a defendant his constitutional right to counsel if he was, in fact, incarcerated for the crime. This rationale, combined with the fact that some states actually constitutionally or statutorily provide the right to counsel for all defendants who are charged with misdemeanors or felonies, has led to most states providing counsel for all misdemeanors, especially those that might result in incarceration.

However, a concern arose over the fact that a person could receive a misdemeanor conviction without the assistance of an attorney and the misdemeanor could impact a potential sentence he might receive if later convicted of another crime. Following the **Argersinger** and **Scott** decisions, the Supreme Court considered the consequences of misdemeanors which a person had been convicted of or pleaded to without an attorney. In **Baldasar v. Illinois**,[12] a defendant was convicted of misdemeanor theft and had not been assisted by counsel. He received probation and a fine, so he did not legally

---

12. 446 U.S. 222 (1980).

have the right to have counsel. However, later that same year, he was charged for a subsequent theft. The new theft was charged as a felony owing to his prior record. He argued that the prior misdemeanor should not be used to enhance his sentence, as he had not had the benefit of counsel for that crime. The Supreme Court agreed, but oddly did not write its own majority opinion. It merely overturned the lower court's ruling. Some concurring opinions were issued, with one dissenting opinion being issued. The case left open the question of whether a person could receive a period of imprisonment if the sentence of imprisonment was given based on a person's prior misdemeanor for which he did not have counsel. Interestingly, the Federal Sentencing Guidelines were amended in 1990 to permit the use of uncounseled misdemeanors to enhance a federal sentence, in direct conflict with the Supreme Court's decision in **Baldasar**. State courts also began to rule against the Court's opinion and permitted the use of uncounseled misdemeanors to enhance sentences. Thus, the Supreme Court needed to review this issue again to provide guidance and clarity to both the states and the federal government.

The **Baldasar** case was overruled by the Supreme Court in the following case. This case also may have begun to erode the right to counsel, and some legal scholars are concerned about the impact of this case on the rights of defendants.

NICHOLS V. UNITED STATES[13]

FACTS: Nichols was convicted in state court in 1983 of the crime of driving under the influence, a misdemeanor. He did not have the assistance of counsel at that hearing. He was fined $250. In 1990, Nichols pleaded guilty in federal court to possessing cocaine with intent to distribute. The federal sentencing guidelines are very specific and defendants receive "points" for prior crimes which often increase their sentence. Nichols was assessed one point for his prior uncounseled misdemeanor. The point increased his possible range of imprisonment from 168-210 months to 188-235 months. He challenged the inclusion of this conviction, arguing that using it violated his Sixth Amendment right to counsel and contradicted the rule set forth by the Supreme Court in the **Baldasar** case. Because the **Baldasar** case decided only the specific issue of a prior uncounseled misdemeanor as it relates to how a subsequent crime is charged, the federal trial court and federal appeals court did not agree with Nichols's arguments.

ISSUE: Whether a prior uncounseled misdemeanor can be used to enhance a later sentence.

---

13. 114 S. Ct. 1921 (1994).

HOLDING: The use of a prior uncounseled misdemeanor to enhance a person's sentence does not violate the Sixth Amendment to the Constitution and thus is permissible.

RATIONALE: The Supreme Court overruled its own decision in **Baldasar** and admitted that it had caused many questions and uncertainties. Enhancement statutes do not change the actual penalty that someone receives based on a prior conviction, and all courts generally accept the idea of enhancing an individual's sentence based on the individual's prior record. The dissenting justices argued that no defendant should be deprived of liberty without the representation of counsel and that uncounseled convictions are inherently unreliable.

In the federal court system, the United States Code guarantees that the right to an attorney also includes the right to obtain other services that are necessary to defend a case. This would include investigators, expert witnesses (such as those who can testify as to the defendant's psychiatric state or as to forensic evidence), and any other services that might be necessary for a proper defense. Many states also offer these services, but often a judge has to approve expenditures, and budgetary constraints might be an issue. Any such services that are provided will have to be paid for by public funds if the defendant is eligible for an appointed attorney.

Right to an Attorney Before and After Trial

Although the trial itself is extremely important and determines the initial outcome of the case, certainly all of the proceedings prior to the trial and following the trial are also important. If a defendant is unable to represent himself at the time of trial, he would also assumedly be unfamiliar with rules and procedures to be considered before trial, after trial or after a plea during a sentencing proceeding, or during appellate proceedings. The Supreme Court held in the case of **Gilbert v. California**[14] that counsel is important in any stage of a criminal proceeding in which the absence of counsel "might derogate from [the defendant's] right to a fair trial."

GILBERT V. CALIFORNIA

FACTS: Gilbert was convicted of armed robbery of a bank and of murdering a police officer during the commission of that robbery. Following his conviction, the defendant received a second proceeding for the jury to determine whether he should receive the death penalty. He did receive the death penalty and appealed his case. One of his arguments was that a lineup was held 16 days

---

14. 388 U.S. 263 (1967).

after his indictment and following an attorney being appointed to represent him; his attorney was not notified of the lineup proceeding and was not present. Some of the witnesses at Gilbert's trial testified specifically at trial that they had recognized him at the lineup. (Gilbert made other constitutional arguments as well that were not related to his right to counsel.)

ISSUE: Was Gilbert's Sixth Amendment right to counsel violated when the witnesses that were present at the lineup in which Gilbert's counsel was not present testified in court?

HOLDING: Yes.

RATIONALE: In **United States v. Wade**[15] the Supreme Court held that a post-indictment pre-trial lineup is a critical stage of a criminal prosecution. The testimony given by some of the witnesses at trial was directly related to the lineup itself. (Some witnesses' testimony was not and thus was permissible under the "independent source doctrine" exception to the exclusionary rule.) The Court stated that a hard and fast rule must be created that the use of such testimony will be absolutely excluded from trial. To decide otherwise would not encourage police to inform attorneys of an impending lineup. The Court indicated that lineups can be unreliable because there are not enough rules to control what happens at a lineup. The Court reasoned:

> In the absence of legislative regulations adequate to avoid the hazards to a fair trial which inhere in lineups as presently conducted, the desirability of deterring the constitutionally objectionable practice must prevail over the undesirability of excluding relevant evidence. That conclusion is buttressed by the consideration that the witness' testimony of his lineup identification will enhance the impact of his in-court identification on the jury and seriously aggravate whatever derogation exists of the accused's right to a fair trial.[16]

Right to an Attorney in Pre-Trial and Post-Trial Proceedings at the Trial Court Level

Often, the outcome of pre-trial proceedings are even more important than the trial itself. A motion to suppress evidence presented at pre-trial stage, if granted, can result in the entire case being dismissed without the necessity of the trial. Other motions can affect which witnesses are permitted to testify

---

15. 388 U.S. 218 (1967).
16. **Id**. at 273–274.

at trial and what evidence can ultimately be presented to the jury, either by the prosecution or the defense. Because of the importance of this stage of the proceedings, the Supreme Court has ruled in several cases that an attorney must be present at various pre-trial proceedings.

Criminal charges are often initiated after an individual is identified by a victim or a witness to the crime. There are three possibilities for this type of identification. First, a suspect might participate in a **lineup** in which the individual and others are placed in a line, literally, and the victim or witness identifies the person as the perpetrator of the crime. The other individuals should have a similar appearance to the suspect. Sometimes the individuals in the lineup are asked to turn sideways or say something, depending on the angle at which the victim or witness viewed the individual or what the victim or witness heard the individual say at the time of the crime. Lineups generally take place in a police station and the victim or witnesses stand behind a one-way mirror so that the individuals in the lineup cannot see them. A concern with a lineup situation is that the investigators who are behind the glass with the victim or witnesses might make a comment, intentionally or not, that would suggest who the suspect is. Further, victims and witnesses should not be pressured to pick someone out of the lineup if they do not believe that anyone looks familiar or if they are truly unsure as to whether a certain person is the suspect. A person may be pressured to pick a person from the lineup merely because the police have "gone to the trouble" of setting up the lineup, or they may feel that the suspect must definitely be in the lineup. The presence of an attorney at the lineup will ensure that the defendant's rights are protected in terms of the police making any suggestions as to the identity of the person who is suspected of the crime. Suggestiveness in a lineup situation can be argued to the court prior to a trial or can be argued during trial to a jury or the judge as fact finder. Lineups cannot be reproduced exactly but could be videotaped so that any suggestive comments, or the lack thereof, can be proved by either the prosecution or defense if the need arises. In terms of being forced to be in a lineup, if a person is already in custody, she can be forced to participate in a lineup. If a person is not already in custody, police must have reasonable suspicion, not probable cause, to believe that the person has committed the crime in order to force her to participate in a lineup. If a victim or witness identifies the person in the lineup, this finding, along with other information, might result in officials having probable cause to arrest the person.

A **showup** is similar to a lineup but with only one person, the suspect, being presented to the witness or victim. This is not a preferred way to handle a case because of the inherent suggestiveness that exists. A victim or witness will often assume that the person she is seeing must be the perpetrator of the crime. However, sometimes it is necessary to present the suspect to a person in a showup; for example, if a person is in need of medical attention and seriously injured due to the crime, it does not pay to wait for an identification to take place in a lineup. In the case of a seriously injured victim or witness, time may be of the essence. A showup would be difficult to recreate exactly and most likely would not be subjected to videotaping, although it could be.

A **photographic array** is similar to a lineup situation except that photographs of various people are shown to the victim or witness. Although a lineup situation is preferable due to the investigator's ability to ask the persons in the lineup to move around or make certain statements, a photographic lineup does provide a victim or witness with several people to choose from. Photographs from the records from the Department of Corrections or even from sources such as a high school yearbook can be used to find photographs similar to that of the suspect. A photographic array does not involve the suspect; in fact, the suspect rarely knows that a photographic array is being undertaken. It is not difficult to show a jury the exact photographs that were given to a victim or witness to view, but again, any statements made by investigators that are suggestive would only be able to be proved if the process of showing the photographs to the victim or witnesses was videotaped. Occasionally a single photograph, of just the suspect, can be shown to a victim or witness. This approach also should be saved for emergency situations, and the **Manson** case, discussed later, demonstrates the Supreme Court's inherent suspicion of this type of procedure.

Lineups, showups, and photographic arrays are all **out-of-court identifications**. Results can be introduced in court by a police officer or by the victim or witness reiterating his choice. However, the ultimate result of a lineup, showup, or photographic array would be that the victim or witness would make an **in-court identification** of the accused. A dramatic moment in a criminal trial can be when a victim or witness points at the defendant in court and identifies him as the perpetrator of a crime. Thus, both the actual identification process and the fact that a victim or witness will generally use their belief that they properly identified the accused at the lineup to identify the accused in court trigger a defendant's constitutional rights.

Due Process Issues at Pre-Trial Identification Procedures

The Fourteenth Amendment's due process provisions apply to the constitutionality of identification procedures. One of the main issues relating to due process is whether the identification procedure is truly suggestive. The issue, as with many issues in criminal justice, is really whether the process resulted in a reliable identification. It is easy to imagine what a very suggestive lineup would look like. A defendant who is short and Hispanic should not be placed in a lineup with several tall black or white suspects. The Supreme Court provided some guidance as to what types of circumstances would be suggestive in a 1977 case in which it, in effect, eroded some of the Court's prior decisions that considered eyewitness identification procedures. The Court had developed a fairly strong rule that suggestive eyewitness procedures should be considered unreasonable and that evidence obtained from such procedures should be automatically excluded from court. However, the 1977 case changed that rule.

MANSON V. BRATHWAITE[17]

FACTS: In 1970, Jimmy Glover, an undercover narcotics officer in the Connecticut state police, went to an apartment building with an informant, Henry Alton Brown. The two were going to purchase narcotics from "Dickie Boy" Cicero, a known narcotics dealer. Glover appeared at Cicero's apartment and knocked on the door. The area was illuminated by natural light from a window in the third floor hallway. A man opened the door approximately 12 to 18 inches in response to Glover's knock and Glover observed a man standing at the door and a woman behind him. Brown identified himself and asked for "two things" of narcotics. The man at the door held out his hand, and Glover gave him two $10 bills. The door closed, then the man returned and gave Glover two glassine bags. Glover testified that when the door was open, he stood within two feet of the person from whom he made the purchase and observed his face.

Glover and Brown left the building. Glover drove to police headquarters and described the seller of the drugs to two other officers. He described the seller as being "a colored man, approximately five feet eleven inches tall, dark complexion, black hair, short Afro style, and having high cheekbones, and of heavy build. He was wearing at the time blue pants and a plaid shirt." One of the officers believed from that description that the defendant, Brathwaite, might be the seller and he left a photograph of him at Glover's office. Glover viewed the photograph for the first time upon his return to police headquarters on May 7. He identified the person in the photograph as being the person from whom he had purchased the narcotics.

The defendant was charged with possession and sale of heroin. He was tried in January 1971 and the photograph was introduced into evidence at his trial. Glover testified that he had not seen the defendant for eight months (since the time of the sale) but that there was no doubt whatsoever in his mind that the person shown in the photograph was the respondent. Glover also made a positive in-court identification of the defendant. The prosecution did not explain why they did not use a photographic showup or an in-person lineup for the identification of the suspect. The defendant testified at trial that he was ill and at another apartment for the entire day of the drug transaction.

The defendant was convicted and appealed his case, eventually appealing it to the Supreme Court.

ISSUE: Does the due process clause of the Fourteenth Amendment require that pre-trial identification evidence obtained by a suggestive, unnecessary police procedure, be excluded from court?

HOLDING: Pre-trial identification obtained by a suggestive and unnecessary police identification procedure can be admissible at trial if, under the totality of the circumstances, the identification is proven to be reliable.

---

17. 432 U.S. 98 (1977).

RATIONALE: The Court reviewed prior cases that had generally condemned the practice of showing just one photograph to a victim or witness for purposes of identification. However, prior cases had permitted the court to determine whether a due process violation took place in a photographic situation based on the "totality of the circumstances." Even if an identification process is suggestive and unnecessary, as long as the identification possesses sufficient aspects of reliability, it could pass the due process test. A procedure will be unnecessary if there is no exigent, or emergency, situation, like a dying victim or witness who will be unable to identify the suspect if a proper procedure is performed in the future. The Court had previously set forth a two-part test for cases such as this: (1) Did the police actually use an impermissibly suggestive procedure in obtaining an out-of-court identification? (2) If so, under all the circumstances, did the suggestive procedure give rise to a substantial likelihood of irreparable misidentification?

The Supreme Court took the stance that the most important consideration of courts in these circumstances should be that of reliability. The factors to be considered, as set forth previously by the Court in **Neil v. Biggers**,[18] included the following: "the opportunity of the witness to view the criminal at the time of the crime, the witness' degree of attention, the accuracy of his prior description of the criminal, the level of certainty demonstrated at the confrontation, and the time between the crime and the confrontation. Against these factors is to be weight the corrupting effect of the suggestive identification itself."

Considering these factors, the Court determined that in this case there was no substantial likelihood of irreparable misidentification. The officer saw the defendant's face for some period of time, in proper light, and was not in any way pressured to make an identification of the defendant. He merely saw the photograph sitting on his desk and made the identification, with no one else even present at the time. He viewed the photograph two days after the event. The Court acknowledged that it would have been preferable for the officer to have been given an entire photographic showup, complete with other photographs, but that in this case, no due process error existed.

The United States Supreme Court's ruling regarding suggestive eyewitness identification procedures has not been revisited since its ruling in **Manson v. Brathwaite**. Since that time, numerous theories have been set forth arguing that eyewitness identification procedures do not produce reliable results. DNA tests have exonerated many individuals who were imprisoned based solely on faulty eyewitness identifications. Even at the time the case was decided, the dissenting justices were concerned about the precedent this would set. One dissenting justice stated: "the witness' degree of certainty in making the identification—is worthless as an indicator that he is correct.

---

18. 409 U.S. 188 (1972).

Even if Glover had been unsure initially about his identification of respondent's picture, by the time he was called at trial to present a key piece of evidence for the State that paid his salary, it is impossible to imagine his responding negatively to such questions as "is there any doubt in your mind whatsoever" that the identification was correct."[19]

Right to an Attorney at Pre-Trial Identification Procedures

Another question involving pre-trial identification procedures is whether a person has a right to have an attorney present at the procedure itself. This, of course, implies the investigator's duty to tell the suspect, in the case of a photographic procedure, that a procedure is even taking place. An important case in the area of identification procedures is that of **Kirby v. Illinois,**[20] in which the Supreme Court decided that the right to an attorney arises when an adversary criminal prosecution is initiated. The **Kirby** case denied the defendant the right to an attorney for a showup (identification by the victim of the suspect) that took place before criminal charges were brought. Willie Shard, the victim, had reported to police in Chicago that his wallet was stolen and that it contained his Social Security card and traveler's checks. The next day, police stopped Thomas Kirby and asked him for identification; he produced a Social Security card bearing the name "Willie Shard"; police also noticed traveler's checks in his wallet. Kirby and his companion, Ralph Bean, were arrested and taken to the police station. Shard was also brought to the police station and when he saw Kirby and Bean, he identified them as the people who had robbed him. Kirby and Bean received appointed counsel upon being indicted for robbery six weeks later, and both were convicted at trial, in which Shard's identification of them at the police station was permitted to be introduced. Kirby appealed, and the case made its way to the Supreme Court. The Court held that Kirby did not have a right to counsel at the showup because it occurred before the beginning of the criminal prosecution. Thus, a person must be charged with a crime before they have a right to counsel. An identification, either in person or through photographs, can be excluded on a constitutional basis for being overly suggestive or because of some other flaw, but the lack of counsel for the defendant at that stage is not considered unconstitutional. An in-person lineup that is held following the initiation of adversary proceedings, however, can require counsel.

The Supreme Court considers photographic showups to be different from in-person lineups. The Court explained its reasoning in a 1973 decision.

---

19. 432 U.S. at 128.
20. 406 U.S. 682 (1972).

UNITED STATES V. ASH[21]

FACTS: A man wearing a stocking mask entered a bank in Washington, D.C., in August 1965 and began waving a pistol. He ordered an employee to hang up a telephone and ordered that no one else move. Seconds later, a second man who was also wearing a stocking mask entered the bank, took money from the tellers' drawers, and left. Both men left and escaped through an alley. The entire robbery lasted three or four minutes. A government informer told authorities that he had discussed the robbery with Charles Ash, the defendant. Based on that information, an FBI agent showed five black and white mug shots of males of the same race, age, height, and weight to four witnesses. Ash's picture was in the group. All four made "uncertain" identifications of Ash as one of the bank robbers. Ash was not in custody and had not yet been charged with any crimes at the time of the identifications. The trial took place almost three years after the crime and the prosecutor showed five color photographs, including Ash's, to the four witnesses shortly before the trial. Three of the witnesses identified Ash but one was unable to make any selection. Pictures of Ash's co-defendant, John Bailey, appeared in the group of pictures but no witness selected him. At trial, three of the witnesses identified Ash as the gunman, and a fourth made an in-court identification of Ash and Bailey. Ash was convicted on all counts. Ash argued that he was denied the right to counsel at a critical stage of the prosecution, because of the post-indictment identification procedure. The case made its way to the Supreme Court.

ISSUE: Whether Ash had a right to counsel being present during the photographic showup in which his picture appeared.

HOLDING: No right to counsel exists for a photographic showup.

RATIONALE: The Court considered the history and purpose of the Sixth Amendment right to counsel. The provision was meant to assure that the "guiding hand of counsel" is present for those in need of it. Specifically, a criminal defendant may be unskilled and unable to represent himself properly in the system. The rule was also created to minimize the imbalance in the adversary system when prosecutors were funded; the state had the assistance of counsel but the opposing party, the defendant, did not. Further, the Court considered the fact that when the Bill of Rights was created, there were no highly organized police forces. Most evidence was presented and marshaled at the trial rather than beforehand.

Now, many important pieces of evidence are established at pre-trial proceedings and thus an attorney's presence may be important at those proceedings. A lineup situation itself might present a possibility for authorities to take advantage of the accused. However, a photographic showup is different from a

---

21. 413 U.S. 300 (1973).

lineup and is not considered a "critical" stage of the proceedings. A photographic showup, unlike a lineup, can be "re-created" before a court or a jury if a defendant wishes to assert that the photographs were unduly suggestive or otherwise likely to result in an unfair proceeding. Further, because the defendant is not present at the time of the showup, "no possibility arises that the accused might be misled by his lack of familiarity with the law or overpowered by his professional adversary. Similarly, the counsel guarantee would not be used to produce equality in a trial-like adversary confrontation." Finally, the Court stated, "[w]e are not persuaded that the risks inherent in the use of photographic displays are so pernicious that an extraordinary system of safeguards is required."

In-Court Identifications

Not all cases that are tried have involved an out-of-court identification procedure. It is always advisable from a prosecutor's standpoint to have witnesses and victims identify the offender in court. Thus, many times the first identification that takes place is during the trial itself. This is referred to as an **in-court showup**. Arguably, a victim or witness will almost always identify the defendant when asked in court to identify the assailant of a crime. The mere fact that the defendant is in court, accused of a crime, usually leads victims and witnesses to believe that the person did in fact commit the crime. In **Moore v. Illinois**,[22] the Supreme Court considered the problem with the suggestiveness of such in-court identifications.

MOORE V. ILLINOIS

FACTS: The victim was sexually assaulted and saw her assailant's face for 10 to 15 seconds during the attack. She told the police that she thought that the man who assaulted her had been the same man who had made offensive remarks to her in a neighborhood bar the night before. The police showed the victim two groups of photographs of men during the next week. She picked about 30 men from the first group of 200 that resembled her assailant and picked from the second group of 10 men about 2 or 3, including that of the defendant. This, plus other evidence in a notebook that the victim found in her bedroom that could be linked to the defendant, caused police to arrest the defendant. At a pre-trial hearing, the victim was asked whether she saw her assailant in the courtroom and she pointed at the defendant after the court announced that the defendant was being charged with rape and deviate sexual behavior. The defendant did not have an attorney present at that hearing. Once counsel was appointed for him for his trial and further proceedings, he requested that the victim's in-court identification of him be

---

22. 434 U.S. 220 (1977).

suppressed. The Court denied the motion. The victim testified at a jury trial that she had previously identified petitioner as her assailant. The defendant was found guilty on all counts. The defendant appealed, and the case made its way to the Supreme Court of the United States.

ISSUE: Did the admission of the identification testimony at trial violate the defendant's Sixth and Fourteenth Amendment rights?

HOLDING: The identification testimony should not have been allowed at trial because the defendant did not have an attorney present and the defendant was presented to the victim in a suggestive manner.

RATIONALE: The identification procedure at issue in this case was in fact a critical point in the criminal process. "It is difficult to imagine a more suggestive manner in which to present a suspect to a witness for their critical first confrontation than was employed in this case. The victim, who had seen her assailant for only 10 to 15 seconds, was asked to make her identification after she was told that she was going to view a suspect, after she was told his name and heard it called as he was led before the bench, and after she heard the prosecutor recite the evidence believed to implicate petitioner. Had petitioner been represented by counsel, some or all of this suggestiveness could have been avoided."

The **Moore** Court was also required to consider whether the identification could have been based on observations of the suspect other than the lineup identification. These factors included the following:

1. Any prior opportunities of the victim to observe the alleged criminal act
2. The existence of any discrepancy between any pre-lineup description and the defendant's actual description
3. Any identification prior to lineup of another person
4. The identification by picture of the defendant prior to the lineup
5. Failure to identify the defendant on a prior occasion
6. The lapse of time between the alleged act and the lineup identification

Right to an Attorney at Other Pre-Trial Procedures

Following its decision in **Kirby**, the Supreme Court considered many other pre-trial situations and whether counsel should be present for them. The Court agreed that counsel should be present at psychiatric examinations where the defendant's competency, potential future level of dangerousness, or amenability to rehabilitation is at issue.[23] Another very important step in

---

23. **Estelle v. Smith**, 451 U.S. 454 (1981).

YOU BE THE JUDGE

John Octavian is accosted on a highway by an individual who is armed with a small revolver and demands money from John. The robbery takes place at approximately 9:20 at night in February. A brief altercation ensues between the two men and Octavian attempts to flee: the assailant shoots Octavian in the leg. Octavian later indicates that although it was dark, the lights from the men's automobiles plus the street lights on the side of the highway gave him a good look at the man. He indicates he saw his assailant for a minute or so while the demand of money took place and he also was able to get a good look at the assailant's profile while the altercation between the two men took place. Around this time, a police officer on patrol hears gunfire and drives his vehicle in the direction of the sound. He and his partner drive their vehicle in the direction of the sound where they observe the assailant and two other men attempting to flee. They apprehend the man and find a pistol with one spent cartridge and one live cartridge. They arrest the assailant for violating the Uniform Firearms Act.

Meanwhile, Octavian gave the police a description of the man who had shot him in the leg. The police officer notices the assailant in custody and realizes that he matches the description given by Octavian. Octavian identifies the man in custody as his assailant approximately 19 hours after the initial confrontation, after being taken to the cell where the man is being held and being asked "is that the man who did this to you?" This identification is later thrown out of court because the man in custody was not given the opportunity to have his lawyer present during the identification process. However, at trial, Octavian again identifies the man as his assailant, pointing at him in court and saying "That is him."

Considering the factors set forth previously, do you believe that the facts of this case lead to the conclusion that the victim identified the suspect based on sufficient factors other than the suggestive identification of the suspect?

the evolution of a criminal case is that of the preliminary hearing, where the court listens to the evidence the prosecution has to determine whether enough evidence exists to charge the defendant with particular crimes and move the case toward trial. The Supreme Court ruled that a defendant has the right to an attorney at his preliminary hearing.[24]

However, the Court has ruled that the right to counsel does not exist for grand jury indictments, which are used by some states but are in some respect the federal equivalent to a state preliminary hearing. Grand juries, however,

---

24. **Coleman v. Alabama**, 399 U.S. 1 (1970).

are considered to be investigative in nature, so the Court has ruled that counsel is not necessary at that stage.[25] Further, the Supreme Court has limited any requirement of counsel at scientific procedures. This includes investigators obtaining handwriting samples, fingerprints, and blood samples. The Court's reasoning regarding this issue was set forth in **Gilbert v. California**. Regarding the issue of handwriting samples taken from the defendant by investigators without his attorney being present, the Supreme Court stated that the Fifth Amendment privilege against self-incrimination "reaches only compulsion of 'an accused's communications, whatever form they might take, and the compulsion of responses which are also communications, for example, compliance with a subpoena to produce one's papers,' and not 'compulsion' which makes a suspect or accused the source of 'real or physical evidence.' . . . One's voice and handwriting are, of course, means of communication. It by no means follows, however, that every compulsion of an accused to use his voice or write compels a communication within the cover of the privilege. A mere handwriting exemplar, in contract to the content of what is written, like the voice or body itself, is an identifying physical characteristic outside its protection."[26] Further, the Court reasoned that generally an exemplar taken with an attorney present would be very similar to one taken without an attorney present. If any issues regarding the handwriting exemplar did arise later, those issues could be addressed through cross-examination at a court proceeding.

Right to an Attorney at Sentencing

Although pre-trial procedures can certainly yield damaging evidence that can make or break a prosecutor's case, procedures following the trial are also important to a defendant. Following a defendant's guilty verdict at trial or guilty plea, the next step will be sentencing. Obviously a sentence is very important to a defendant, as that is where a defendant learns whether he will be incarcerated or not and how long he will be under the control of the court if he receives a probationary sentence. The Supreme Court has ruled that a defendant has the right to have an attorney present at any sentencing proceeding, including procedures in which a defendant's initial sentence is being revoked.

MEMPA V. RHAY[27]

FACTS: This case was brought to the Supreme Court based on more than one case that had been brought to the Court. One case involved a defendant who entered a

---

25. **United States v. Mandujano**, 425 U.S. 564 (1976).
26. 388 U.S. 263, 266 (1967).
27. 389 U.S. 128 (1967).

guilty plea to the crime of "joyriding" with the advice of court-appointed counsel in the State of Washington. He was placed on probation for two years, but his final sentence was deferred. Later, the court revoked his probation and he was sentenced to the maximum sentence of ten years with a recommendation to the parole board that he be required to serve only a year. However, he was not represented by counsel at that hearing and he thus appealed his sentence.

A second case involved a defendant who pleaded guilty to the crime of burglary (second degree) upon the advice of an attorney in the State of Washington. He was placed on probation for three years and his sentence was also deferred. When he was sentenced without his attorney being present, his probation was revoked and he received the maximum sentence of 15 years.

Both defendants argued that their right to counsel had been violated.

ISSUE: Were the defendants' right to counsel violated when they had counsel for their plea but not for their final sentencing?

HOLDING: A lawyer must be provided to defendants regardless of whether the proceeding they are going to is considered a revocation, a sentencing, or a deferred sentencing.

RATIONALE: The defendants' failure to have an attorney at the final sentencing stage of their proceedings in both cases could result in important rights being lost, including the right to appeal the sentence. A lawyer could also be of "substantial assistance" to a defendant in determining, between his initially being placed on probation and his final sentencing, as to whether he might like to withdraw his plea. A lawyer could make a defendant aware of this fact when otherwise he might not have been. The court also stated that an attorney who was appointed for purposes of a trial or guilty plea would not be "unduly burdened" by being requested to follow through at the deferred sentencing stage.

When a defendant has been sentenced and placed on probation or parole, he may be brought in front of the court for a revocation hearing if he violates a condition of his probation or parole, including committing a new offense. The Supreme Court has stated that a defendant has a right to two hearings when he might be revoked from parole. One is a hearing that is held initially to make sure that the defendant should be incarcerated at all due to these charges (referred to as a "Gagnon 1" hearing), then a more thorough hearing will be held to verify the finality of the revocation (referred to as a "Gagnon 2" hearing). The Supreme Court has determined that there is no need to have counsel present at either hearing. The first hearing takes place so rapidly after the defendant is detained that it would be impossible to have counsel present. The second hearing is scheduled, but the purpose of the hearing, according to the Supreme Court, is partially rehabilitative in nature. The presiding officer at the hearing is supposed to consider the rehabilitative needs of the defendant, and according to the Court, to add the presence of an adversary attorney into the hearing would change the tenor of the hearing. Thus, the Court ruled, unlike its determination in the **Gideon** case, revocation hearings should involve a case-by-case determination of whether an attorney should be present for that case. If the defendant requests an attorney and none is provided, good cause should be given for the failure to provide counsel. As the Court stated:

> Presumptively, it may be said that counsel should be provided in cases where, after being informed of his right to request counsel, the probationer or parolee makes such a request, based on a timely and colorable claim (i) that he has not committed the alleged violation of the conditions upon which he is at liberty; or (ii) that, even if the violation is a matter of public record or is uncontested, there are substantial reasons which justified or mitigated the violation and make revocation inappropriate, and that the reasons are complex or otherwise difficult to develop or present. In passing on a request for the appointment of counsel, the responsible agency also should consider, [411 U.S. 778, 791] especially in doubtful cases, whether the probationer appears to be capable of speaking effectively for himself. In every case in which a request for counsel at a preliminary or final hearing is refused, the grounds for refusal should be stated succinctly in the record.[28]

Because an attorney is not required for a revocation hearing, the Court also does not provide counsel for any appeal from that hearing. However, if a state court decides to provide counsel for a parole revocation, it will also provide counsel for the first appeal.

Right to an Attorney on Appeal

Although sometimes a sentence is the final step in a criminal case, it is common for defendants to appeal their case. An appeal can focus on the actual sentence the defendant received. Many defendants argue that a judge abused his discretion in fashioning a sentence or went outside the state's sentencing guidelines, if any exist, in handing down a sentence. Defendants also argue about the evidence that was introduced during a court proceeding (using the exclusionary rule and the constitutional premises that we have discussed so far in this book), that certain rules of evidence were broken (for example, that hearsay was let in as evidence), and that the jury made a decision that could not possibly be supported by the evidence. Criminal defendants would desire the assistance of counsel to deal with the appellate process. Each appellate court has its own specific rules regarding what paperwork should be filed, the timing for filing the paperwork, and the appropriate arguments that can be made in court.

If a defendant is entitled to have the assistance of an attorney for his appeal, for how many appeals does he receive this assistance? A case could go through two state court appeals and an appeal to the Supreme Court of the

---

28. **Gideon** at 777-778.

United States. If the theory of permitting counsel to defendants in criminal trials is because the defendant does not have the legal training, nor always the literacy, to represent himself, then shouldn't the same theory be advanced on appeal? The Supreme Court has extended the right to counsel to the first automatic appeal as of right. In a state court, most often the first appeal that the defendant has a right to make is to the intermediate appellate court of that state. Once the appellate court has made a decision, it is up to a particular state to determine whether a defendant has the right to an attorney if he decides to appeal his case to a higher court, such as the state supreme court. This makes sense considering that in an appeal, no further evidence is submitted to the court. The record that is created at the trial court level is the only evidence that appellate courts will consider, and any subsequent appeal beyond the first one will involve the same issues as the appeal for which the defendant had counsel. The following case will explain the Supreme Court's reasoning in determining this rule. However, be aware that, because a state can give an individual more rights than the Constitution requires, many states have mandated that an attorney represent an individual through that state's supreme court process if the individual desires to take his case that far. Even if a state does not require that a defendant be represented if he desires to take his case to the Supreme Court of the United States, often attorneys might offer their services for a defendant to assist him with that process because the possibility of arguing a case in front of the Supreme Court is an exciting and potentially career-changing event.

DOUGLAS V. CALIFORNIA[29]

FACTS: Two defendants, who were indigent, were tried and convicted in California for 13 felony charges, including robbery, assault with a deadly weapon, and assault with the intent to commit murder. The defendants received appointed counsel, but only one attorney was appointed to represent both of them. The attorney had filed a motion prior to trial to continue the trial to another date, stating that he was not as thoroughly prepared to represent them as he would have liked to be and that he believed the two men should each have a different attorney, as it was a conflict of interest for him to represent both of them. The defendants then dismissed the attorney and filed motions for separate counsel and for the case to be continued. The trial court denied those motions. The defendants were tried and were convicted; they were sentenced to terms of imprisonment. They appealed to the California state intermediate court and requested that an attorney be appointed to represent them. The court reviewed the record of the case and decided that appointed counsel would not be "of advantage to the defendant or helpful to the appellate court" and denied the appointment. The court was able to do this based on a California rule of criminal procedure that permitted state

---

29. 372 U.S. 353.

appellate courts to make an independent investigation of the record in any case to determine whether or not it would be helpful to have counsel appointed. The convictions were affirmed. The case made its way to the Supreme Court of the United States.

ISSUE: Whether a court can deny counsel for an appeal taken by an indigent defendant.

HOLDING: A court must provide counsel for indigent defendants who wish to appeal their cases.

RATIONALE: The Court referred to prior cases in which it had decided that poor defendants could not be treated differently on appeal than defendants who had means. Under the present practice, the appellate court is basically prejudging the case to determine whether the merits of the case justify counsel. A court should not be able to consider the merits of the case without first receiving briefs from both sides, rather than just the record. Any "hidden merit" that might exist in the case may never come out if a defendant is unable to have counsel assist with his case. The Court did clarify that its concern was solely with the first appeal of right, not necessarily with subsequent appeals. The Court explained the dichotomy between indigent and nonindigent defendants as follows:

> In California, however, once the court has "gone through" the record and denied counsel, the indigent has no recourse but to prosecute his appeal on his own, as best he can, no matter how meritorious his case may turn out to be. The present case, where counsel was denied petitioners on appeal, shows that the discrimination is not between "possibly good and obviously bad cases," but between cases where the rich man can require the court to listen to argument of counsel before deciding on the merits, but a poor man cannot. There is lacking that equality demanded by the Fourteenth Amendment where the rich man, who appeals as of right, enjoy the benefit of counsel's examination into the record, research of the law, and marshaling of arguments on his behalf, while the indigent, already burdened by a preliminary determination that his case is without merit, is forced to shift for himself. The indigent, where the record is unclear or the errors are hidden, has only the right to a meaningless ritual, while the rich man has a meaningful appeal.

The dissent argued that the majority opinion's "fetish for indigency" was placing an "intolerable burden" on the judicial system. One of the dissenting opinions stated that requiring everyone who appeals to obtain their own counsel does not discriminate between the rich and the poor, and the fact that California was giving some indigents an attorney after a preliminary review of the merits of the case complied with the spirit and intent of the Court's decision in **Gideon**.

The Supreme Court has also recognized that once an attorney has begun to represent a defendant in a criminal proceeding, the attorney may have an ethical duty to continue to represent that defendant if he desires to appeal the case further. Thus, in order to assist public defenders who are already over-burdened with cases from having to continue with frivolous appeals, the Supreme Court decided in the case of **Anders v. California**[30] that appointed counsel can relay to the court that she believes that a case lacks meritorious issues for appeal and can request to withdraw. Appointed counsel still needs to file a brief on behalf of the defendant, arguing the issues that the defendant wishes for her to raise. In some states, the attorney must also provide the court with her rationale as to why those issues are meritless.[31] The reviewing court must then review the record and determine whether merit exists for the claim; if not, appointed counsel's request to withdraw will be granted and the defendant will have to pursue further appeals on his own. Some states do not allow counsel to withdraw, however, giving the defendant the right to have counsel represent him throughout all of the proceedings.

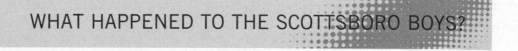

WHAT HAPPENED TO THE SCOTTSBORO BOYS?

After the Scottsboro boys' case (**Powell v. Alabama**) was reversed by the Supreme Court, the case was returned to the Alabama trial court in Paint Rock, where the train on which the boys were riding had been stopped and where the initial charges had been filed. The trial court permitted a change of venue for the case to be moved to Decatur, Alabama.

During the new trial, one of the victims admitted that she and the other woman had fabricated the rape story. The jury found the defendants guilty and the trial court set aside the verdict, granting a new trial; that trial also resulted in a guilty verdict. A new jury, which now included one African-American member, again returned a guilty verdict.

Charges were dropped by the prosecutor for four of the nine defendants but the others received sentences from 75 years to death. All but two of the men ultimately served prison sentences; one of the men was actually shot to death by a prison guard, and two escaped, then were charged with crimes and sent back to prison. The defendant who was sentenced to death escaped while on parole and went into hiding in 1946; he was later pardoned by George Wallace in 1976 after being found. He went on to write a book about his experiences.

---

30. 386 U.S. 738 (1867).
31. **McCoy v. Court of Appeals**, 486 U.S. 429 (1988).

Defendant's Waiver of Right to Counsel

A defendant can choose not to have counsel represent him at any point in his proceedings; however, judges prefer that defendants be represented, and a defendant will have to prove that he is knowingly and intelligently waiving his right to counsel. Defendants often waive their right to have an attorney present when police are questioning them, such as during interrogation at the police station. However, it is assumed that defendants will want counsel present at the time of trial, although some decide they would prefer to represent themselves.

A defendant who wishes to represent himself must show that he is knowingly and voluntarily abandoning his right to have an attorney represent him. The court must hold a colloquy with the defendant and place on the record a long discussion in which the judge confirms that the defendant knows that he has the right to have an attorney appointed and the right to have representation. In the case of **Von Moltke v. Gillies**,[32] a defendant who was not a citizen of the United States answered questions posed to her by the FBI and entered a guilty plea. As noted by the Supreme Court, the entire plea proceeding took about five minutes. Later, Von Moltke argued that she did not understand that she was waiving her right to counsel and in fact did not waive her right to counsel. The Supreme Court stated that a judge's quick discussion with a defendant about whether she wants to waive counsel is not sufficient. The judge must hold a colloquy to ensure that the defendant truly desires to waive counsel. The Court stated:

> The constitutional right of an accused to be represented by counsel invokes, of itself, the protection of a trial court, in which the accused—whose life or liberty is at stake—is without counsel. This protecting duty imposes the serious and weighty responsibility upon the trial judge of determining whether there is an intelligent and competent waiver by the accused. To discharge this duty properly in light of the strong presumption against waiver of the constitutional right to counsel, a judge must investigate as long and as thoroughly as the circumstances of the case before him demand. The fact that an accused may tell him that he is informed of his right to counsel and desires to waive this right does not automatically end the judge's responsibility. To be valid such waiver must be made with an apprehension of the nature of the charges, the statutory offenses included within them, the range of allowable punishments thereunder, possible defenses to the charges and circumstances in mitigation thereof, and all other facts essential to a broad understanding of the whole matter. A judge can make certain that an accused's professed waiver of counsel is understandingly and wisely made only from a penetrating and comprehensive examination of all the circumstances under which such a plea is tendered. This case graphically illustrates that a mere routine inquiry the asking of several standard questions followed by the signing of a standard written waiver of counsel—may leave a judge entirely unaware of the facts

---

32. 332 U.S. 708 (1948).

essential to an informed decision that an accused has executed a valid waiver of his right to counsel. And this case shows that such routine inquiries may be inadequate although the Constitution does not require that under all circumstances counsel be forced upon a defendant.[33]

Sometimes, a defendant wants to represent himself but the court is not convinced that he can do so effectively. In such cases, the court will appoint what is referred to as **standby counsel**. An attorney will be appointed to sit with the defendant and assist him in deciding what objections to make, how to examine and cross-examine witnesses, and how to enter evidence into the court record. If at any point in time the defendant no longer wishes to represent himself, standby counsel can step in and continue with the trial and will be aware of what had transpired in the trial thus far. The use of standby counsel is often distracting to jurors. Certainly jurors wonder why the defendant does not just allow his attorney to represent him, and the whispering back and forth of the two can also be very distracting and delay the process.

EFFECTIVE ASSISTANCE OF COUNSEL

When a defendant is appointed counsel by the court, or if a criminal defendant hires private counsel to represent him, when is that attorney considered to be ineffective to the point that the court will overturn the proceedings that took place in the case? In **Strickland v. Washington**,[34] the Supreme Court considered that issue. Strickland had committed three groups of crimes during a ten-day period in 1976, including three murders committed by stabbing, torture, kidnapping, several assaults, attempted murders, attempted extortion, and theft. The defendant was arrested after surrendering to the police and he voluntarily gave a confession. Strickland was appointed what was described by the Court as an "experienced criminal lawyer." That lawyer pursued any pre-trial motions and discovery he felt was necessary; however, he learned that his client, against his advice, had confessed to two more murders. His client further waived his right to a jury trial, once again acting against his attorney's wishes, and pleaded guilty to all charges, the most serious of which were capital murder charges for which the defendant could receive the death penalty. The defendant's attorney advised him to request a jury to determine whether or not he would receive the death penalty rather than permitting the judge to make the decision. The defendant again, against counsel's recommendation, made the decision not to utilize a jury, and to allow the trial judge to determine his sentence. In preparation for the sentencing hearing, counsel did not attempt to seek out character witnesses to speak on behalf of the

---

33. **Id**. at 723.
34. 466 U.S. 668 (1984).

defendant or request a psychiatric evaluation be done. (Counsel stated that he did not believe that any psychological issues were present.) Counsel stated that the plea colloquy in this case gave enough background about the defendant and that due to defendant's confessions to the gruesome crimes, he did not believe that further information would be helpful in the sentencing process. Counsel did make arguments on the defendant's behalf at the sentencing. After listening to the defendant's evidence and the evidence presented by the state, the Court determined that the defendant should be sentenced to death on each of the three counts of murder.

The defendant argued that his attorney was ineffective for failing to do the following: (1) request a continuance of the sentencing to allow more time to prepare for it; (2) request a psychiatric report; (3) investigate and present character evidence on behalf of the defendant; (4) present meaningful arguments to the sentencing judge; (5) investigate the medical examiners' reports; and (6) cross-examine the medical experts that the state called at the sentencing proceeding. In rendering its decision as to whether the defendant's counsel was effective or not, the Court cited the Sixth Amendment's provisions for a right to counsel, which protects a person's right to a fair trial. The Court stated that the right to counsel implies that counsel is effective and stated that its key concern would be "whether counsel's conduct so undermined the proper functioning of the adversarial process that the trial cannot be relied on as having produced a just result."[35]

The Strickland Test

The Court then set forth a two-part test, known now as the **Strickland test**, which should be used to determine whether counsel's actions were effective. First, the Court must determine whether counsel's actions were actually deficient. "This requires showing that counsel made errors so serious that counsel was not functioning as the 'counsel' guaranteed the defendant by the Sixth Amendment."[36] If a defendant can show that this attorney's performance fell below the standards required, he must then show that but for counsel's failure to properly represent him, the result of his case would have been different. In other words, Strickland would have had to demonstrate that his attorney failed to do things that other attorneys in his position would have done, but also that his attorney's failure to do those things were the reason he was sentenced to death and that he would not have been sentenced to death had it not been for his attorney's errors. In Strickland's case, the Court found that Strickland's attorney's actions were reasonable and that even if his attorney had taken a different course of action, Strickland still would have received a death sentence. His attorney demonstrated that he had been the subject of a

---

35. **Strickland** at 686.
36. **Id**. at 687.

mental health evaluation early in the case and that it showed no problems, that he had attempted to contact Strickland's family members to no avail, and that the seriousness of the crimes to which Strickland had pleaded were certainly sufficient to support the judge's sentencing decision.

The **Strickland** Court also instructed lower courts to give great deference to an attorney's actions, in the hopes that attorneys would not be so distracted by attempting to take every action possible that they would fail to vigorously advocate for their client's cause. The Court also stated that the purpose of the Sixth Amendment was not written in order to enhance the performance of attorneys, but just to ensure that defendants receive a fair trial.

The Court's decision relied heavily on standards set forth by the American Bar Association (ABA). The ABA's Standards of Criminal Justice provides that defendants should have the final say as to whether they should enter a plea, waive a jury trial, and testify on their own behalf. However, the decision of what witnesses to call, what trial motions should be made, and any other decisions that are strategic or tactical should be made by the attorney after she consults with her client. Some have criticized the Court's approach to attorney ineffectiveness claims, and many states have thus passed their own regulations requiring attorneys to obtain certain certifications before representing specific types of clients, such as those charged with the death penalty. In some states, attorneys fresh out of law school would be assigned death penalty cases and would not represent clients to the same standard as a seasoned attorney.

Attorney Conflict of Interest

When providing competent representation to a client, attorneys who represent criminal clients must also be sure they do not have a conflict of interest in providing that representation. This issue often arises when an attorney is representing two individuals who are charged as co-defendants. An attorney can provide effective counsel to co-defendants. However, sometimes an attorney must avoid representing co-defendants or risk being considered ineffective and potentially unethical in her representation. Sometimes co-defendants have the same defense. Perhaps they argue that they were not at the scene of the crime or they did not do what they were charged with. Perhaps they both agree that they were someplace else, but with each other, on the night in question, and they can vouch for each other's whereabouts. However, sometimes co-defendants point the finger at each other. One might claim that the other person masterminded the crime and that he just happened to be with the person when the crime took place but did not know that the crime would happen. In that case, representing both of the defendants would be problematic, for obvious reasons. When an attorney or a public defender's office is appointed to represent co-defendants, any claim that the representation is a conflict of interest must be heard by a judge. The judge will hold a hearing in which the attorney has to explain the conflict before a trial can be held. In a small town where a local public defender's office has only a few attorneys, it could be very difficult to find someone outside that office who is willing to represent indigent clients.

YOU BE THE JUDGE

Consider the following case, and state whether or not you believe the defendant meets the standards of the two-part **Strickland** test.

Jesus Romero has been convicted by a jury of the crime of capital murder of fifteen year old Olga Perales during an aggravated sexual assault. The facts presented at trial showed that Romero and two others were at a party with Perales and had been drinking beer and smoking marijuana. As Perales was leaving the party, Romero pushed her into the car, and he and the two others drove her to a lake. Romero held Perales' head down throughout the car ride, telling her to be quiet. She kept asking him to take her home. One of the men put a knife to Perales' neck and demanded that she perform oral sex on him; he then started having sex with her. The men then asked Perales if she was going to tell anyone what had happened; she assured them she would not, but one of the men nonetheless hit her on the forehead with a pipe. Perales fell to the ground, and then Romero grabbed the pipe and hit her at the most five times, giggling while he did so. He and another of the men dragged her into the bushes and Romero then asked one of the other men to stab the girl. Romero confessed to being present at the crime, but not to actually being the person who hit or stabbed the victim. A search of Romero's residence turned up underwear that had blood on both sides of it; he and the victim both had type A blood and the blood found was type A.

After Romero was convicted, the jury had to decide whether Romero should be sentenced to death. The evidence presented at that segment of the hearing included testimony that Romero had assaulted and kidnapped other women, and that his family was very violent. Romero did not testify on his own behalf at trial or at the sentencing phase. Romero's lawyer argued extensively during the guilt phase of the trial, but at the sentencing phase, his entire argument was as follows:

"Ladies and Gentlemen, I appreciate the time you took deliberating and the thought you put into this. I'm going to be extremely brief. I have a reputation for not being brief." He then told his client to stand up. After his client stood up, counsel stated: "You are an extremely intelligent jury. You've got that man's life in your hands. You can take it or not. That's all I have to say." Counsel did not argue to the jury that they could avoid giving Romero the death penalty by considering the fact that Romero was intoxicated at the time of the event, that his violent history at home which was partially caused by his father could have formed a basis for his actions, or that he was young, all common arguments generally made by attorneys in death penalty cases.

Do you believe that the Romero's attorney's representation met the provisions of **Strickland**?

THE RIGHTS OF THE ACCUSED AT TRIAL

Right to a Speedy Trial

The Sixth Amendment to the Constitution provides that "[i]n all criminal prosecutions, the accused shall enjoy the right to a speedy . . . trial." Although our idea about what is "speedy" may be different from that of the justice system, and the wheels of justice may seem to turn slowly, the authors of the Constitution wanted to prevent the government from delaying the process. This right protects the defendant from an inordinate amount of time passing before he receives a final verdict in his case. A defendant who is in jail awaiting trial will be deprived significantly of his liberty the longer he remains in jail, even if the ultimate verdict is that he is not guilty. This approach also assists both the prosecution and the defense in that witnesses are more likely to be available and to remember details of the incident the sooner the trial takes place after the incident. This provision of the Sixth Amendment was made applicable to the states through the Fourteenth Amendment due process clause in the case of **Klopfer v. North Carolina**.[37] The concept of providing swift justice dates back to the reign of Henry II in England and was also included in the Magna Carta and in many of the charters of the American colonies and the constitutions of the original 13 states in the United States.

Because the Constitution does not specifically set forth any specific time periods, states can legislate specific time periods as long as the Supreme Court finds that those time periods are "speedy" within the meaning of the Constitution. If the prosecution violates the speedy trial rule and does not bring a person to trial within the appropriate time period, the case can be dismissed without an opportunity for the prosecution to bring the case again. However, some of these statutes leave room for a court to determine whether the spirit of speedy trial rules has been broken rather than establishing very specific time periods. Although some states do not consider why time periods were violated, others require the defense to show that the failure to fall within the time period does not fall within any exception. Further, the rule only becomes relevant once someone is actually charged with a crime. No Sixth Amendment duty exists on the part of the police to investigate a crime more rapidly or to arrest a person at any point in time (although generally a statute of limitations will provide a nonconstitutional, but statutory, time period for bringing charges against a person once law enforcement is aware of a crime). Further, the Sixth Amendment does not apply to post-trial hearings, such as probation or parole revocation hearings, or even sentencings. An argument could be made that the due process clause applies to these types of proceedings, with each statute considering the time periods differently.

Although a defendant has a right not to have the prosecution delay his trial, he can delay his own trial. He does not have the right to ask that his trial

---

37. 386 U.S. 213 (1967).

be delayed so that he can have further time to prepare for it and then argue that he was not tried in a speedy manner. Any continuances that the defendant or his counsel requests will not be included in calculating the time period for trial. In other words, if the defendant asks for an extra three months in order to prepare for his trial, and his case is supposed to be brought to trial within six months, the case will now be considered "speedy" if it is tried within nine months. Occasionally when the defendant's request is based on a failure to receive information from the prosecutor that he needs in order to prepare for his defense, the time will be charged toward the prosecution rather than being attributed to the defense. Although speedy trial questions are rarely an issue, occasionally a trial court needs to consider the specific circumstances that delayed a case and consider whether to attribute the delay to the prosecution or the defense.

The Supreme Court considered factors that related to the speedy trial clause in 1972 in the case of **Barker v. Wingo.**[38] The Court developed a four-part test to determine whether a case should be dismissed for lack of prosecution in the appropriate time period. The four considerations are as follows:

1. The actual length of the delay. A shorter delay will be less suspect than a lengthy delay.
2. The reason for the delay. Was it incompetence on the prosecutor's part, or an attempt to accommodate the schedule of an expert witness or some other legitimate reason related to the prosecution of the case?
3. The severity of prejudice or whether actual prejudice is suffered by the defendant due to the delay in prosecution.
4. The stage during the criminal proceedings at which the defendant asserted the right to a speedy trial.

Many states provide time periods that require a case be prosecuted within a year after charges are brought, with the time period being six months if the defendant is incarcerated while awaiting trial. There is generally a presumption that if more than a year passes from the time the charges are brought until the time the trial takes place, the Sixth Amendment has been violated. However, as discussed earlier, depending on the circumstances, a court might find that the delay took place for a reason. It is generally the burden of the defendant, however, to argue that the time period has been violated. If a defendant goes to trial over a year after charges have been brought but does not object to being tried at that time, he most likely forever waives his ability to argue that his Sixth Amendment rights were violated. If he raises the issue for the first time on appeal, the court might dismiss his appeal without considering the merits merely because the issue was not raised previously. This permits the trial court to consider the factors set forth above when the issue is first raised. Occasionally a court will find that a time period of

---

38. 407 U.S. 514 (1972).

THE USA PATRIOT ACT

Some would argue that the Patriot Act was a knee-jerk reaction against the terrorist hijackings and attacks on the United States on September 11, 2001. The full name of the **USA Patriot Act** was an acronym for Uniting and Strengthening America by Providing Appropriate Tools Required to Intercept and Obstruct Terrorism Act. The act was signed into law on October 26, 2001, shortly after the attacks. At the time it was passed, Congress determined that the act would expire at the end of 2005, when it would be reevaluated. The law relates to many of the topics in this book and broadly permits the FBI and the Justice Department to monitor suspected terrorists. The law specifically permits law enforcement to use surveillance against terrorism-related crimes. Law enforcement is permitted to use "roving wiretaps" that apply to a specific suspect rather than to a particular phone or other communications device. Law enforcement can also obtain search warrants with a delayed time table in terms of informing others of the fact that the warrants were obtained. The government can also obtain foreign intelligence surveillance by requesting the information from the Foreign Intelligence Surveillance Court even if the information is not concerning a United States citizen. Further, the act assists police officers, the FBI, federal prosecutors and intelligence officials in sharing information, including evidence obtained through grand juries. The act also changed and tightened border security in the United States.

Regarding warrants, the act allows a more streamlined process to obtain warrants. Previously, if a person was suspected of engaging in activities in various jurisdictions, the government would have to obtain warrants in all of the municipalities where the warrants would be executed. The Patriot Act permits the government to obtain one warrant, regardless of where the warrant will be executed. The act also creates new crimes, including the prohibition of knowingly harboring someone who has committed or is about to commit a terrorist offense. Additionally, terrorist acts on mass transit systems and bioterrorists are addressed. The penalties for various crimes that are likely to be committed by terrorists have also been raised. These crimes include arson, destruction of energy facilities, providing material support to terrorists and terrorist organizations, and destruction of national defense materials.

One of the many arguments against the act was the fact that it would permit the government to "peek" into many of our daily activities, allegedly violating our right to privacy. The use of National Security Letters permits the government to obtain certain records without a warrant (and thus, presumably, without probable cause). These materials include records from libraries and book stores. Although the recipient of a National Security Letter is not supposed to discuss the fact that it received such a letter, many librarians verified in surveys that they had received numerous requests under the act. The act became particularly controversial when citizens learned that the government was monitoring the phone conversations of many citizens ("ordinary Americans").

As stated, the act was passed with the assumption that it would be reviewed, because the act was passed so quickly with little time to move it through the legislative system. Portions of the act were extended in 2006 by President Bush. The extension did not significantly change the portions of the law reacting to terrorism, although it did add sections that gave the government new tools to combat the production and distribution of methamphetamine. In 2011, President Obama signed a four-year extension of the provisions of the act that relate to roving wiretaps, searches of business records (i.e., libraries and book stores) and conducting surveillance of individuals who are suspected of terrorist activities but are not linked to terrorist groups.

less than a year is inappropriate as well, such as when the case is not brought to trial in a timely manner because the prosecution misplaces the defendant's case file or purposely delays the trial because of some bias against the defendant.

Despite the speedy trial clause in the Sixth Amendment, courts do become backlogged and prosecutors might have difficulty in prosecuting a case in time. To solve this problem in the federal court system, Congress passed the Speedy Trial Act, which applies to citizens of the United States but also applies to anyone who is being tried in the federal court system. It establishes time limits for all aspects of a case, prompting prosecutors to move various stages of the case along in a fairly rapid manner. The USA Patriot Act, which permits the government to detain noncitizens and certify them as terrorists if certain conditions exist, also permits the government to detain suspected terrorists for a significant amount of time without bringing charges against them.

THE RIGHT TO A PUBLIC TRIAL

The Sixth Amendment provides that all accused persons "shall enjoy the right to a . . . public trial." Although many attempt not to make their private lives public in today's society, the amendment was written to avoid trials in which the defendant is tried in secret, without any checks or balances as to whether the defendant is receiving the due process guaranteed by the Constitution. The Supreme Court considered this right in a 1984 case. In **Press-Enterprise Co. v. Superior Court,**[39] the Supreme Court considered whether the rule that the accused should be given a public trial should benefit individuals only or society in general. The Court determined public trials are also valuable in that they provide the public the opportunity to be able to view trials; all are interested in the issue of fairness. Thus, a defendant is unable to argue that the public nature of his trial is a right that is to benefit only him and that he can waive that right. Trials must be public even if a defendant

---

39. 464 U.S. 501 (1984).

indicates that he does not wish for it to be public. Further, the concept of "trial" includes other procedures such as preliminary hearings, jury selection, sentencings, and suppression hearings. The **Press-Enterprise** Court reasoned that the public's right to have trial proceedings be public is guaranteed under the First Amendment.

The Supreme Court further considered the history of England's open trials. Trials in both England and the early colonies of the United States were held in a "town meeting" format. Occasionally this gathering of interested citizens led to lynch mobs and, according to the Court, not necessarily "calm, reasoned decision making based on evidence." According to the Court, "openness in criminal trials, including the selection of jurors, 'enhances both the basic fairness of the criminal trial and the appearance of fairness so essential to public confidence in the system.'"[40]

The media is especially welcome at a trial, because the First Amendment guarantees freedom of the press. A judge can order that a trial be closed to the media only in very narrowly limited circumstances, and the closure itself will be limited as well. In **Globe Newspaper v. Superior Court**,[41] a Massachusetts statute provided for the general public and the press to be excluded from a courtroom during a criminal trial of a defendant charged with raping three teenaged girls. The statute was passed to protect the minor victim and excluded others from the trial during the minor's testimony. It was also hoped that by excluding the public and the media from this portion of the trial, other young girls who had been victimized would be more apt to bring their claims to the authorities. The Supreme Court determined that in order to comply with the First Amendment's provisions permitting the press access to governmental proceedings, the statute could not be upheld. The government could petition the court on a case-by-case basis to permit the exclusion of the press or the public from a certain aspect of a court proceeding, but a blanket statute providing for such exclusion on a regular basis could not be upheld. The Court stated that

> the right of access to criminal trials plays a particularly significant role in the functioning of the judicial process and the government as a whole. Public scrutiny of a criminal trial enhances the quality and safeguards the integrity of the fact-finding process, with benefits to both the defendant and to society as a whole. Moreover, public access to the criminal trial fosters an appearance of fairness, thereby heightening public respect for the judicial process. And, in the broadest terms, public access to criminal trials permits the public to participate in and serve as a check upon the judicial process—an essential component in our structure of self-government. In sum, the institutional value of the open criminal trial is recognized in both logic and experience.[42]

---

40. **Id**. at 501.
41. 457 U.S. 596 (1982).
42. **Id**. at 606.

The presumption of an open trial can be overcome if closure is essential to preserve some higher value. The **Globe** Court stated the following as possible reasons to close a trial, provable on a case-by-case basis: the minor victim's age, her psychological maturity and understanding, the nature of the crime, the victim's preference in having the trial open or closed, and the interests of the victim's parents and relatives.

One area in which a "higher value" has been proved on more than an individual case-by-case basis is in juvenile court proceedings. When a juvenile is being accused of a crime, his proceedings may be closed and sealed so as to attempt to shield him from being labeled a delinquent by society and being treated unfairly. The idea behind the juvenile court system is that juveniles have a good chance of being rehabilitated, so to label them as being deviant would be unfair and unproductive. Other types of court proceedings that are closed to the public include adoption hearings and other hearings involving minors who are being removed from their parents by the court. The privacy of the children is of the utmost concern in these cases and children are protected from their private, potentially embarrassing life becoming public.

> [T]he presumption may be overcome only by an overriding interest based on findings that closure is essential to preserve higher values, and is narrowly tailored to serve that interest. The interest is to be articulated along with findings specific enough that a reviewing court can determine whether the closure order was properly entered.[43]

Following is an example of a case in which the Court decided it was important not to force a witness to testify in front of everyone. Although not a Supreme Court case, the case provides a good example of the analysis a court goes through in order to make a determination as to the necessity of "clearing the courtroom" for certain delicate testimony.

ORLANDO V. FAY[44]

FACTS: Orlando was tried in federal court for charges of robbery (first degree), grand larceny (first degree) and assault (second degree). On the first full day of his trial, Orlando interrupted an identification of him by the victim, yelling, "You never saw me before," "You liar," and "This man is not supposed to say that. . . ." The court admonished him. The next day, the court learned that one prosecution witness had been threatened by two members of the electrical union to which Orlando belonged that he would lose his job if he testified against Orlando. Another prosecution witness had been subject to a similar threat. The judge admonished everyone without the jury being present, stating that this sort of

---

43. 464 U.S. at 510.
44. 350 F.2d 967 (1965).

behavior was unacceptable, and indicating that if any spectators to the trial were using the information they gained at the trial to make such threats, they should stop. That day, Orlando again would not keep quiet and a spectator (Orlando's mother) stood up and also spoke out of turn. The judge cleared the courtroom and continued the trial without spectators, except for the press and attorneys. Orlando continued to speak out of turn at the trial, was convicted, and appealed.

ISSUE: Did the court violate the defendant's right to a public trial by clearing the courtroom?

HOLDING: The court did not violate the defendant's right to a public trial, and the facts of the case support the judge's decision.

RATIONALE: The court determined that the trial judge had "good reason to believe that many persons in the courtroom were acting so as to interfere with the orderly conduct of the trial." A trial judge can exercise his power to exclude people who would disrupt the trial proceedings and the jury's ability to consider the charges. The court stated that the trial judge always has the power to keep order in the courtroom. The court pointed out that case law permits a judge to clear the courtroom to (1) prevent offensive evidence from being exhibited to the public, (2) to prevent unnecessary pressures or embarrassment to a witness or victim (such as the rape of a young child), and (3) to prevent young people from having to attend a trial of "scandalous nature." The court also pointed out that the purpose of the public being able to attend trials was so that proceedings were not secret; the fact that the judge permitted the entry of the press and the bar would certainly take away any concern of "secrecy."

Right to a Jury Trial

The right of a person to have a jury hear his or her case is a foundation of the American legal system. A jury consists of members of the community who are called to hear the case. Article II, Section 2 of the Constitution states that "the trial of all crimes, except in cases of impeachment, shall be by jury." The Sixth Amendment also states that "In all criminal prosecutions, the accused shall enjoy the right to . . . trial, by an impartial jury . . . ." Note that both of these clauses speak specifically to criminal cases, not civil cases, and the right to have a case heard by a jury is not guaranteed in a civil case. (In many states, a plaintiff can request a jury trial upon filing a civil complaint, but failure to make this request upon filing will often result in a waiver of that right forever.) A defendant has the right have his case decided by a jury if a penalty of incarceration of more than six months is a possibility. In deciding this time period, the Supreme Court reasoned as follows in denying those who were facing less than six months in prison a trial by jury: "Where the accused cannot possibly face more than six months' imprisonment, we have held that these disadvantages, onerous though they may be, may be outweighed by the benefits that result from speedy and inexpensive nonjury adjudications. We cannot, however, conclude that these administrative conveniences, in light of the practices that now exist in every one of the 50 States, as well as in the federal courts, can similarly justify denying an accused the important right to trial by jury where the possible penalty exceeds six months' imprisonment."[45] The Court acknowledged that the convenience of the system would give way to the rights of the individual, realizing that to someone who is faced with imprisonment, even a period of time of less than six months would not seem "petty." However, the rule was valuable to further judicial economy.

A juvenile does not have the right to a trial by jury. In **McKeiver v. Pennsylvania**,[46] the Supreme Court was faced with this issue and in making its decision discussed the roots of the juvenile justice system and how the system would change if jury trials were a part of the system. The Court stated that a juvenile defendant's interest in justice is protected by allowing accused individuals to have the public view their proceedings. (A juvenile can object to the public being a part of his proceedings but could also allow the public to be present.) Juveniles have the due process right to counsel, written notice, confrontation, and cross-examination, as well as the privilege against self-incrimination and the right to be found guilty only by the standard of proof beyond a reasonable doubt. However, according to the Supreme Court, the purpose of separating the juvenile and adult court system is to ensure that a judge who hears a juvenile case is familiar with the complex issues surrounding childhood and adolescence. A juvenile court proceeding is unique and a finding of delinquency is different and, according to the Court, "less onerous" than a finding of guilt in adult court. Because a jury trial would require "substantial alteration" of the normal juvenile process, the Court found that it was not appropriate in juvenile proceedings. The Court reasoned that a juvenile proceeding is not necessarily considered a "criminal prosecution" within the meaning of the Sixth Amendment. The juvenile system was developed as a protective, informal, and intimate proceeding, and to impose a jury trial on the system would not remedy any potential defects of the system. (A task force was appointed to look at the weaknesses of the juvenile system, and in the Court's opinion, adding the right to trial by jury would not cure any issues that the task force had found to be problematic within the system. In fact, the task force warned against any abolishment of the juvenile court and any attempt to combine juvenile and adult courts.) Some states, however, do extend the right to a jury trial to juveniles, with Kansas being the first state to add the right to the Constitution. The issue of what is considered a jury of a juvenile's "peers" is an interesting one.

45. **Baldwin v. New York**, 399 U.S. 66 (1970).
46. 403 U.S. 528 (1971).

Although the defendants in the **McKeiver** case argued that the jury system provides protection against corrupt judges, the Court indicated that the juvenile justice system was working well with no need to change the outcome of juvenile cases. Because the courts and legislatures had previously carved the juvenile justice system out of the adult system to make it unique, there would be no gain to be made in making the two systems so similar once again by providing jury trials to juveniles. Further, the delay, stress, formality, and adversarial nature of the adult system would be interspersed into the juvenile system if a trial by jury were permitted. The Supreme Court did suggest that a court may wish to use an "advisory jury" in juvenile cases, and this practice could be accepted.

Criminal Versus Civil Matters

Occasionally a matter that is technically civil in nature can result in criminal sanctions, and thus the issue can arise as to whether a particular matter is considered criminal for purposes of this rule. The Supreme Court determined that the right to a trial by jury in criminal cases is a fundamental right for defendants, and thus that portion of the Sixth Amendment is applicable to the states through the Fourteenth Amendment due process clause. In making this determination, the Supreme Court noted in the landmark case of **Duncan v. Louisiana**[47] that jury trials had been held in England since the time of the Magna Carta. The original states and any that entered the union since had included this right in their constitutions. The Court further stated:

> The guarantees of jury trial in the Federal and State Constitutions reflect a profound judgment about the way in which law should be enforced and justice administered. A right to jury trial is granted to criminal defendants in order to prevent oppression by the Government. Those who wrote our constitutions knew from history and experience that it was necessary to protect against unfounded criminal charges brought to eliminate enemies and against judges too responsive to the voice of higher authority. The framers of the constitutions strove to create an independent judiciary but insisted upon further protection against arbitrary action. Providing an accused with the right to be tried by a jury of his peers gave him an inestimable safeguard against the corrupt or overzealous prosecutor and against the compliant, biased, or eccentric judge. If the defendant referred the common-sense judgment of a jury to the more tutored but perhaps less sympathetic reaction of the single judge, he was to have it. Beyond this, the jury trial provisions in the Federal and State Constitutions reflect a fundamental decision about the exercise of official power—a reluctance to entrust plenary powers over the life and liberty of the citizen to one judge or to a group of judges.[48]

---

47. 391 U.S. 145 (1968).
48. **Id** at 154.

In addition to limiting overbearing police agencies and corrupt judges and prosecutors, involving citizens in the criminal justice process can result in the public being more aware of the limitations and advantages of our criminal justice system. This type of knowledge is important in a democratic society. A defendant may also feel as though he received a "fair shake" in his criminal proceedings if a jury of, theoretically, people like him, decided on his case rather than a judge.

The right to a jury trial is limited even within the realm of criminal cases. The expense and trouble of empaneling a jury for any criminal case would be problematic. Thus, the right has been limited to more serious cases. Any time a person can receive more than six months imprisonment as a result of being found guilty of an offense, that person has the right to a trial by jury. Six months of imprisonment is considered "serious" according to courts. Courts can, however, consider a sentence of less than six months to be a serious sentence as well. Consider the following case.

BLANTON V. CITY OF NORTH LAS VEGAS[49]

FACTS: Blanton was pulled over in Nevada and charged with the crime of driving under the influence of alcohol (DUI). At that time in Nevada, a first-time offender could face up to six months of incarceration or 48 hours of community service. (Interestingly, the community service had to be performed while the offender was wearing clothing that identified him as a DUI offender.) The offender was also required to (1) pay a fine of up to $1,000.00, (2) attend an alcohol abuse education course, and (3) lose his driver's license for 90 days. Blanton and another offender (with the same situation) asked for a jury trial for his case. The municipal court denied both requests and the cases were appealed. Interestingly, the appeals court denied Blanton's request while granting the other defendant's similar request. Both cases were appealed to the Nevada Supreme Court.

ISSUE: Whether there is a right to jury trial for persons charged with DUI in Nevada when the penalties include up to six months in jail and other additional penalties.

HOLDING: There is no right to a jury trial in this situation.

RATIONALE: The defendants argued that the legislature intended that "petty crimes" not be included in the list of crimes for which a jury trial was required. They argued that DUI was not "petty" considering the rather stiff penalties that would be received. In other words, the defendants argued that courts should consider the total penalties that a person would be subjected to, rather than solely considering whether the possible sentence is more than six months of imprisonment.

---

49. 489 U.S. 538 (1989).

The Court disagreed, although it stated that a court certainly should consider the length of the prison term as well as the seriousness of other punishment. However, it pointed out that the Court had previously determined that three years of probation was not considered serious enough to warrant a jury trial and that a person's loss of liberty will generally be seen as more severe than other nonincarcerative penalties. The Court stated that "a defendant is entitled to a jury trial . . . only if he can demonstrate that any additional statutory penalties, viewed in conjunction with the maximum authorized period of incarceration, are so severe that they clearly reflect a legislative determination that the offense in question is a 'serious' one." The Court stated that in this case, the license suspension might often run at the same time that the person is incarcerated and unable to use his license to drive anyway. Regarding the community service hours, "[e]ven assuming the outfit is the source of some embarrassment during the 48-hour period, such a penalty will be less embarrassing and less onerous than six months in jail." The $1000 fine was less than the statutorily set maximum level of $5,000.00 for petty offenses. Thus, according to the court, the penalties attached to a DUI charge in Nevada are indeed "petty." The Court further cautioned that it did not desire that judges spend their time inquiring into whether particular penalties are petty. "Doubts must be resolved, not subjectively by recourse of the judge to his own sympathy and emotions, but by objective standards such as may be observed in the laws and practices of the community taken as a gauge of its social and ethical judgments." The Court also pointed out that the defendants had requested that the Court consider whether other states had termed DUI as a "serious," rather than "petty" offense. The Court informed the defendants that this inquiry did not matter; other states could define driving under the influence as not being petty although the State of Nevada could most certainly determine that it was a petty crime.

As mentioned previously, in some instances, a proceeding is referred to as being "civil" when in fact criminal penalties might result. Although generally the issue in a right to trial by jury question is whether a person *could* receive more than six months' imprisonment, in the case of criminal contempt of court, the issue, as with the issue of the right to an attorney, becomes whether the defendant actually receives a term of more than six months in prison. In a case of criminal contempt (examples include contempt of court orders and acting out in court), a judge has a broad range of discretion in terms of how to sentence a person. Thus, only if the ultimate sentence is imprisonment for more than six months will a person have had a right to a jury trial. (For this reason, most judges will sentence those who are guilty of minor criminal contempt charges to a term of six months or less if imprisonment is to be imposed.) In terms of fines, a "serious" crime will lead to a right to jury trial. The Supreme Court has found that a criminal contempt fine of $52 million was serious enough to warrant a jury trial, but most fine amounts are less obviously serious and will be considered by courts on a case-by-case basis.

Right to an Impartial Judge and Jury

The Sixth Amendment also requires that a defendant receive a fair and impartial trial. This includes a trial in front of a judge or a jury, and different issues exist depending on the forum. The right is related to the concept of due process and thus has been incorporated to the states through the Fourteenth Amendment. As with many of the topics in this book, the issue of whether a judge or jury is impartial is a factually based inquiry. Interestingly, a judge whose bias is questioned is often required to make the determination as to whether she is biased or not. In most cases, judges will state that they are not biased. A judge will have the ultimate say also as to whether a jury member is biased, generally upon prompting by the prosecutor or defense attorney during the jury selection, or **voir dire** process.

Regarding the issue of a biased judge, a defendant must demonstrate that the judge has either a personal bias against the defendant or the particular case, or that the judge has a financial interest in the case. An example of a personal financial interest would be a judge who takes money from some entity in the court system, either defendants themselves or otherwise, depending on the decision he makes. In one case, a municipal judge was found to be biased when he was also the mayor of the municipality and roughly one-half of the funding that came into the municipality was from fines that were issued from the municipal judge. A judge can recuse herself if she realizes upon being assigned a case that she has some personal or financial bias, or either party can request that the judge recuse herself, both in civil and criminal cases.

In terms of jury trials, the voir dire process is designed to eliminate unfair jury members. However, other issues besides the actual composition of the jury can cause a biased situation in front of a jury. In **Estelle v. Williams**,[50] a defendant was forced to be tried in prison clothing. The Supreme Court decided that this could bias the jury and was thus unconstitutional, as the jury would immediately think of the defendant as already being a prisoner, and thus guilty, as soon as they saw him. The Court stated that although jurors should be able to look past a defendant's attire, it was far too risky to assume they could, and when a defendant puts in a request not to have to wear prison attire, that request should be granted. The Supreme Court has also considered how the media affects jurors' perceptions of trials. Generally, jurors are instructed not to read the newspaper or watch the news on television when they are hearing a case. If the case is expected to receive a large amount of media attention, the jurors might be sequestered in a hotel where they do not have access to television news or the radio. However, with smart phones, tablets, and other handheld devices giving people so much access to the Internet, it is becoming more and more difficult to completely sequester

---

50. 425 U.S. 501 (1976).

SCANDAL IN LUZERNE COUNTY, PENNSYLVANIA

In Luzerne County, Pennsylvania, an inordinate number of juveniles were being placed in county-funded juvenile facilities. In early 2007, several youths had sent requests to the Philadelphia-based Juvenile Law Center complaining about their sentences and lack of representation at their juvenile court hearings. An investigation revealed that several hundred juvenile defendants had been tried in Luzerne County without receiving proper attorney representation.

In 2009, charges were filed in federal court against two Luzerne County judges who were alleged to be corrupt as a result of receiving kickbacks from the detention facilities for each juvenile they sentenced to that facility. This "kids for cash" scheme also demonstrated that juveniles were being sentenced to lockup even when their probation officers did not recommend anything more than probation. Two judges were charged, as was a co-owner of the two juvenile detention facilities, the prominent real estate developer who built the facilities, and the former Deputy Director of Forensic Services for the Luzerne Juvenile Probation Office. All were convicted. Further, a class action lawsuit was filed by the Philadelphia Juvenile Law Center on behalf of the juveniles who were adjudicated delinquent by one of the judges despite not being represented by counsel or advised of their rights.

These circumstances caused the State of Pennsylvania to thoroughly investigate how the juvenile system worked, and recommendations to guarantee juveniles rights in the system were proposed by the commission.

witnesses and keep them from discovering information from the media. Sequestering juries is rare and expensive.

A very important case in the issue of the composition of a jury was decided by the Supreme Court in 1986.

BATSON V. KENTUCKY[51]

FACTS: Batson was an African-American man convicted of the crimes of burglary and receiving stolen goods; the jury that convicted him consisted entirely of white jurors. Batson appealed his case, arguing that the jury selection was flawed. Each side has the ability to strike a certain number of jurors, some **for cause** (a good reason exists) and then others **peremptorily** (without giving a reason). The prosecutor struck, peremptorily, all of the potential black jurors (a total of four) when he struck six total jurors. The defense counsel argued that the prosecutor's removal of

---

51. 476 U.S. 79 (1986).

the black jurors violated Batson's right to have his case heard by a jury that is drawn from a cross section of the community, arguing also a violation of his rights to equal protection of the law under the Fourteenth Amendment. The trial court refused his request and a jury convicted him. Batson appealed his case and it was eventually considered by the Supreme Court.

ISSUE: Were Batson's Sixth Amendment rights to an impartial jury and a jury composed of persons representing a fair cross section of the community violated by the prosecutor's striking of all African-American jurists?

HOLDING: Batson's rights were violated. The prosecutor's act of purposefully striking African Americans violated Batson's constitutional rights.

RATIONALE: Prior case law stated that the petitioner in a case such as this had to prove that the jurors were systematically stricken in other cases throughout the jurisdiction in which the case took place. The **Batson** court lowered this standard, stating that the defendant could make a case for purposeful racial discrimination by showing that discrimination took place only in his case. The Court's rule was as follows:

> The defendant first must show that he is a member of a cognizable racial group, and that the prosecutor has exercised peremptory challenges to remove from the venire (the pool of jurors available to hear the case) members of the defendant's race. The defendant may also rely on the fact that peremptory challenges constitute a jury selection practice that permits those to discriminate who are of a mind to discriminate. Finally, the defendant must show that such facts and any other relevant circumstances raise an inference that the prosecutor used peremptory challenges to exclude the veniremen from the petit jury on account of their race. Once the defendant makes a prima facie showing, the burden shifts to the State to come forward with a neutral explanation for challenging black jurors.

> The Court's decision was not retroactive, so anyone who had previously been tried and convicted could not have their case overturned on the basis of this new rule, even if they could prove that jurors of their race were systematically excluded in their case.

Although a person does not have a right to have his case heard by a jury that is composed of his own race, the systematic exclusion of persons of his own race is not constitutional. The **Batson** case has been extended to the issue of sex-based peremptory challenges. However, a case requesting that the same rule be extended to jurors' sexual orientation was not successful in federal court.[52]

---

52. **U.S. v. Blaylock**, 20 F.3d 1458 (1994).

Pre-trial publicity can sometimes prevent prospective jurors from being unbiased. However, if a juror has been exposed to pre-trial publicity in a case, he can still serve as a juror as long as he assures the court that he can still consider the facts of the case and set aside everything he has already heard about the case. In one case, however, a jury was not unbiased when some members had seen an interview that included the defendant's confession. In **Rideau v. Louisiana**,[53] the Supreme Court assumed that it would be very difficult for jury members to set aside their knowledge that the defendant had confessed.

YOU BE THE JUDGE

You are a Supreme Court justice and are reviewing a case involving the question of whether a jury was impartial. You know that juries are often considered not to be biased if the members of the jury state that they can set aside any biases they might have as a result of something they have heard prior to trial and consider the case solely on the facts that are being presented to them during the trial. Owing to a large amount of pre-trial publicity in the case, the jury was being sequestered. One of the courtroom staff was speaking to one juror in the presence of two other jurors and stated: "Oh, that wicked fellow, he is guilty." He then stated to another juror, "If there is anything wrong [in finding him guilty], the Supreme Court will correct it." The jurors stated that this did not affect their decision to find the defendant guilty of the crime. Do you believe the jurors could make a fair and impartial decision in this case?

Another issue regarding jurors is whether they are obtained from a cross section of the community. A defendant can argue that his rights were violated if a certain group of persons is systematically excluded from the jury, either in the initial selection of the pool of potential jurors or during the actual jury selection process. The defendant does not need to be a member of the class of jurors that were excused. So if the defendant can prove that women were excluded from the jury, he can argue that his constitutional rights were violated even when he is a man. A defendant needs to show that a group was significantly underrepresented in either the large jury pool or the smaller group of jurors who were ultimately selected. It is easier to prove this in the initial selection of jurors. If the community is made up of one half blacks

---

53. 373 U.S. 723 (1963).

and one half Hispanics and the initial jury pool comprises almost entirely all Hispanic people, an argument can be made that the pool does not fairly represent the community. However, a defendant has a more difficult time arguing after the voir dire process that a group was systematically excluded. If the prosecution can explain why it struck certain members of the jury for a reason that is not biased and does not relate to the suspected characteristic, the selection of the jurists will most likely be accepted as not being biased. A defendant does not have the right to ultimately have certain types, races, or classes of people on his jury.

Jury Nullification

Jurors do not have to justify or explain an acquittal. However, sometimes it is surmised, or jurors even admit, that their decision was based not on the law but on what they believe the law should be. If a jury acquits a person that the jurors believe is guilty, the jury may be engaging in **jury nullification**. For example, a juror might be selected to hear a case in which a person is being charged with the possession of marijuana. The defendant might argue that he possessed marijuana only for medical reasons, in that he has a terminal illness and smoking marijuana helps him with his pain. Although the law of the state in which the person is being prosecuted might state that there is no exception for marijuana used medically, perhaps the jurors all feel that there should be such an exception in the law. Despite the defendant's confession that he did in fact possess the marijuana, and despite the fact that his actions were guilty according to the law, the jurors might decide to render a verdict of not guilty to make a statement against the current status of the law. Thus, the jurors are, in effect, indicating opposition to the status of the law. An acquittal based on the defendant's or victim's race or some other factor could also be considered an act of jury nullification. Jurors cannot be punished for the verdict that they render, and the double jeopardy clause of the Fifth Amendment prohibits a subsequent trial even if the jurors admit that they attempted to nullify the law.

Judges do not tell jurors they have the right to nullify a law and often jurors don't even know that terminology exists to support what they are doing when they nullify the law. The Supreme Court has considered this issue in a few cases, some from the 1800s. In fact, some of the first instances of jury nullification occurred in the pre–Civil War era when Northern juries would refuse to convict those who violated the Fugitive Slave Act, wherein it was illegal to help a fugitive escape from jail. In the 1920s prohibition era, juries nullified alcohol control laws. During the Vietnam war era, juries nullified the law by failing to convict those who had avoided the draft. In the case of Jack Kevorkian, who was tried for assisting terminally ill people in committing suicide, Kevorkian's lawyer stated that he would urge the jury to nullify the law and permit assisted suicide.

Questions regarding nullification include whether a judge should or can inform jury members that they can nullify the law and whether attorneys can actually urge that the jury do so. In **Sparf v. United States**,[54] the Supreme Court held that a trial judge does not have to inform the jury that it can nullify the law. Prior law had provided to the contrary. Currently, jury nullification is not a power that the jurors are told about, although there are interest groups that try to encourage it. Some advocates of the process have been banned from handing out literature regarding nullification to potential jurors who are entering the courthouse.

Right to Confront Witnesses

The Sixth Amendment provides: "In all criminal prosecutions, the accused shall enjoy the right . . . to be confronted with the witnesses against him." This right involves more than appears at first reading. It gives the defendant the ability to be present at his trial, to be present when a witness against him testifies, and to ask that witness questions. These rights in turn assure truthfulness within the process. A witness who is faced with the defendant in person and who knows he will be cross-examined by the defendant (most often via his attorney) is less likely to be dishonest with his answers. Further, the defendant can then testify himself, or present witnesses who will testify, regarding the information the witness has provided. Finally, the rule requires that the witness testify in open court, not secretly, and thus the jury or other fact finder is given an opportunity to consider the witness's demeanor when testifying, as well as her demeanor when being asked questions on cross-examination. A witness who is unable to answer questions directly or clearly, or one who does not make proper eye contact when answering questions, may be considered unreliable by the fact finder.

The Supreme Court found this right to be fundamental in the 1965 case of **Pointer v. Texas**.[55] The Court spoke at length about the fact that open trials had been common early in the history of using trials to finalize criminal proceedings. The Court stated that trials that were open to the public had therapeutic value to the community in permitting the community to know fully what went on during the trial process. If citizens can observe the trial process, they would be more likely to accept and support the process. Thus, the right was incorporated to the states as well as applying to federal trials.

A defendant can, however, waive his ability to be present at the time of the trial by either choosing to waive his presence or by engaging in behavior that would cause a waiver. If an accused fails to show up for his trial, he simply forfeits his right to be there. The trial will proceed without him. Although his attorney, if he has retained one or if one has been appointed for him by the court, can cross-examine prosecution witnesses, call witnesses to testify on behalf of the defendant, make objections to evidence, and present opening and

54. 156 U.S. 51 (1895).
55. 380 U.S. 400 (1965).

closing arguments, the defendant's failure to show up for the proceeding will certainly have an effect on the fact finder's perception of him.

It is possible that a defendant might act out in court to the point that his presence in the courtroom is too disruptive for the proceedings to continue. Judges are cautious and prefer not to resort to removing the defendant from the courtroom but will do so if necessary to continue with the trial. However, inappropriate conduct in the courtroom that disrupts the proceedings can result in the defendant's removal from the courtroom with the trial continuing in her absence. An example of this follows.

ILLINOIS V. ALLEN[56]

FACTS: The defendant, Allen, was on trial for the robbery of $200 which he allegedly took at gunpoint from a bartender. Allen had refused court-appointed counsel and he indicated to the trial court several times that he wished to conduct his own defense. The judge told him that Allen could represent himself, but that the court would have a court-appointed attorney sit in and "protect the record" for the defendant. The trial began with jury selection and Allen began to question jurors at great length. The judge requested that Allen keep his questions to a minimum and Allen began to argue with the judge "in a most abusive and disrespectful manner." The judge finally asked appointed counsel to conduct the examination of the jurors. Allen continued to talk, stating that he did not want the appointed attorney to act as his lawyer. He also said to the judge, "When I go out for lunchtime, you're going to be a corpse here." He proceeded to take the file that his appointed attorney had and ripped it up, throwing it on the floor. The trial judge told Allen that he would remove him from the courtroom if he had one more outbreak, but Allen continued to talk back to the judge. He stated: "There's not going to be no trial, either. I'm going to sit here and you're going to talk and you can bring your shackles out and straight jacket and put them on me and tape my mouth, but it will do no good because there's not going to be no trial." The judge ordered the trial to proceed without the petitioner being there, and the petitioner was removed from the courtroom. The jury was selected and everyone took a lunch break.

The defendant appeared before the judge after the lunch recess and complained about the fairness of the trial, indicating that he wanted to be present for the rest of it. The judge told him he could be in the courtroom if he behaved himself and did not interfere with the presentation of the case. The jury was brought into the room and the defendant again began to be belligerent, stating that he was going to start talking and that he would "keep talking all through the trial." The judge then removed him from the courtroom again. Allen remained out of the courtroom during the presentation of the state's case in chief except when

---

56. 397 U.S. 337 (1970).

he was brought in several times so the witnesses could identify him. At one point, Allen again became vile and abusive with his language.

Following the presentation of the prosecution's case, the judge again told Allen that he could be present in court for the presentation of his case in chief if he could behave himself. Allen said he would do so and was present during the remainder of his trial, with his appointed attorney presenting the case.

Allen was convicted and appealed his case, arguing that he had a right under the Sixth Amendment to be present at all times during his trial, regardless of his conduct.

ISSUE: Does a defendant have an absolute right under the Sixth Amendment to be present during his trial, even if his behavior is inappropriate?

HOLDING: A defendant can be prohibited from attending his own court proceedings if other attempts to gain control over the courtroom have failed.

RATIONALE: The Supreme Court stated that there are three constitutionally permissible ways for a trial judge to handle an "obstreperous" defendant. The court can (1) bind and gag the defendant, (2) hold the defendant in contempt of court, or (3) remove the defendant from the courtroom. The Court acknowledged that binding and gagging the defendant would serve the purpose of having him present but should be used only as a last resort, as the jury might be swayed by seeing the defendant in that position. Further, the Court admitted that binding and gagging the defendant would be "an affront to the very dignity and decorum of judicial proceedings that the judge is seeking to uphold." Finally, the defendant would be unable to communicate with his counsel while he was bound and gagged. The Court indicated that this may still be the "fairest and most reasonable way to handle a defendant" who is uncontrollable in the courtroom.

As another possibility, the contempt procedure does permit the defendant to be present in court and would result in some punishment for the defendant. However, a defendant might wish for contempt so he could be imprisoned on the contempt charge for a while, during which time important witnesses for his case might disappear and the possibility of prosecuting the defendant might dwindle.

The trial court's decision to remove the defendant in this case was not unconstitutional. According to the Court:

Allen's behavior was clearly of such an extreme and aggravated nature as to justify either his removal from the courtroom or his total physical restraint. Prior to his removal, he was repeatedly warned by the trial judge that he would be removed from the courtroom if he persisted in his unruly conduct, and, as Judge Hastings observed in his dissenting opinion, the record demonstrates that Allen would not have been at all dissuaded by the trial judge's use of his criminal contempt powers. Allen was constantly informed that he could return to the trial when he would agree to conduct himself in an orderly manner. Under these circumstances, we hold that Allen lost his right guaranteed by the Sixth and Fourteenth Amendments to be present throughout his trial.[57]

The Court further stated that the courts cannot be treated disrespectfully and that permitting criminal defendants to act as Allen had would "degrade our country and our judicial system." Court proceedings "must not be infected with the sort of scurrilous, abusive language and conduct paraded before the Illinois trial judge in this case." The Supreme Court stated that the lower court could have done something other than removing the defendant, but that removing the defendant was appropriate under the circumstances and was one viable option.

Compulsory Process for Obtaining Witnesses

Compulsory Process. Many people who are called as a witness to testify at a trial would prefer not to be involved in the proceedings. Some are called to testify against a friend or family member. Others were perhaps the victim of a crime but would prefer not to have to sit on a witness stand and testify in front of strangers as to what happened to them, while facing their accuser. The Sixth Amendment permits the accused in any criminal trial to obtain witnesses in his favor via compulsory process. The prosecutor is given the right to subpoena witnesses, including the victim, and any person can be held in contempt of court and even jailed if he refuses to attend court proceedings. The defendant has this right also, established by the Supreme Court in the case of **Washington v. Texas**.[58] A Texas law had blocked defendants from being able to require witnesses to attend court and testify on their behalf. Prosecutors had prevented Washington from requiring that a co-defendant testify on his behalf. He was convicted of first-degree murder and sentenced to 50 years in prison, despite the fact that at his trial he blamed his accomplice, Charles Fuller. A Texas law, however, stated that co-defendants were not permitted to testify on behalf of each other in court. However, the state could call co-defendants to testify against each other. The Supreme Court issued a unanimous opinion, stating that the Sixth Amendment compulsory process clause was relevant to the case. A defendant must be able to present a defense and his own version of the facts in a criminal trial. Although some states had a common law prohibition against co-defendants testifying on each other's behalf, the federal court had determined that it did not wish to follow this rule since 1918. Many states had legislated exceptions to the rule. The Court pointed out that when testifying for the prosecution, a co-defendant would have many reasons to lie, although his testimony might actually be

---

57. **Id**. at 346.
58. 388 U.S. 14 (1967).

more truthful if he were testifying for his co-defendant. The Court also stated that the dichotomy of permitting the prosecution to call a co-defendant while not permitting a defendant to do the same had no logic or good reasoning that would convince the court that it was necessary. A defendant has the right to enter any evidence (subject to state and local evidentiary rules) that is relevant to his case and that assists him in presenting a defense to his case. An example of the Supreme Court's desire to permit defendants to offer any type of evidence available appears next.

ROCK V. ARKANSAS[59]

FACTS: Vickie Rock was charged with the death of her husband, Frank. In the midst of an abusive relationship, Frank prohibited her from eating a piece of pizza and would not let her leave the parties' trailer to get any food. Police were called and when they arrived at the trailer, they found Frank on the floor with a bullet wound in his chest. Vickie pleaded to the officers to help Frank and told them that Frank had choked her and threw her against the wall, then hit her and she shot him. However, she did not remember many specific details of the shooting and thus her attorney suggested that she submit to hypnosis in order to refresh her memory. She was hypnotized twice and she did not relate any new information during the hypnosis sessions but following the hypnosis she remembered certain details of the shooting that she had not previously remembered. The prosecutor filed a motion requesting that any testimony resulting from the hypnosis session be precluded from court. The trial judge granted the motion. The case made its way to the Supreme Court. The Supreme Court was faced with a history of states which allowed hypnotic testimony and others which did not, and thus considered that approach it preferred.

ISSUE: Whether testimony based purely on information obtained by hypnosis should be permitted to be used in a court hearing.

HOLDING: The Supreme Court determined that such testimony was admissible in court.

RATIONALE: The Court considered the defendant's argument that she has a constitutional right to testify in her own defense. Permitting a defendant to testify advances the ability of jurors to detect guilt and also advances the protection of innocence of a defendant. The right to testify is part of due process but is also found in the compulsory process clause, which permits a defendant to call witnesses on his own behalf. A defendant can also present his defense in his own words and must be able to present himself as a witness.

Certainly the concern with testimony that has been hypnotically induced is that it is not reliable. The Court, however, found that creating a rule that

---

59. 549 U.S. 877.

specifically inhibits hypnotically induced testimony is arbitrary and can result in an exclusion of material portions of the defendant's testimony. The Court noted that although the use of hypnosis is controversial, it has been recognized as a valid therapeutic technique since 1958. States can place restrictions on hypnotic testimony in terms of educating a jury to the risks of hypnosis and providing cautionary instructions regarding the jury's consideration of the testimony. Further, a defendant can be cross-examined regarding his testimony. The hypnotic sessions can be required to be videotaped to determine whether leading questions were asked of the subject. As long as the courts place appropriate restrictions on the use of hypnotically induced testimony and thus control for the reliability of the testimony, the use of the testimony is appropriate and cannot be completely denied by the court.

In the **Rock** case, one of Ms. Rock's comments after hypnosis led the defense to hire an expert who testified that the gun that Ms. Rock used was defective and could actually fire when hit or dropped, without the trigger being pulled. The Court pointed out that Ms. Rock's information, given after the hypnosis, was very important to the case and to her being able to properly enter her defense.

Disclosure by the Prosecution of Its Witnesses. A defendant has the right to know prior to the trial who will be testifying against him on behalf of the prosecution. Further, the defendant has the right to actually see the person testify so that he can decide how to best cross-examine the person and so that the identity of the person is not hidden. Occasionally the court will allow a person to use a pseudonym in court so as not to be harassed or embarrassed. This is very rare, however, and generally a defendant is entitled to know who is testifying against him in trial. When a person gives information to a police officer, however, as an informant and that information is brought out during a preliminary hearing in order to indict a defendant and move his case forward to the trial court level, most often the court will not require that the person's identity be disclosed. However, when the issue is a trial in which a jury or judicial fact finder must determine who is lying and who is telling the truth, it is very important that each victim and witness be identified. Although a prosecutor can file a motion with the court to request that victims' names be kept confidential, rarely do courts grant such motions. The names would also need to be redacted from any documents that were filed in court if the motion to keep them confidential was granted.

Direct Confrontation of a Witness. Occasionally a court will deny a defendant the right to have a face-to-face encounter with a witness for the prosecution. In **Maryland v. Craig,**[60] the Supreme Court considered the extent of the Sixth Amendment's confrontation clause. The case involved a child

---

60. 497 U.S. 836 (1990).

JERRY SANDUSKY TRIAL

In 2012, the Penn State University football program was shaken when allegations arose that one of the program's coaches, Jerry Sandusky, was guilty of numerous counts of sexual abuse of children. The Pennsylvania State Attorney General's office began to prepare the various victims for trial and informed them that they would have to testify in person against Sandusky at his trial. They would thus have to publically state their names for the court record and they would thus need to be prepared for the media to reveal their names.

The accusers had been shielded from their names being set forth since the time the charges were filed; one whose name was released by someone close to him ended up being bullied and left the school he was in and moved from his home. Originally, the judge in the case required that all victims' names be kept confidential to avoid media harassment and harassment by others. The one victim whose name was released indicated that his family's phones rang constantly, people knocked at the door of their home during all hours of the night, and someone broke into their car to leave a business card on the front seat.

However, the victims were revealed during the court hearing. A prosecutor in the case argued that it would be possible to give enough details in court about the victims and their allegations of abuse that Sandusky could still defend against the accusations, without the public being made aware of the victims' exact identities. However, the court did not allow this in this case. Arguments were made that once certain details were disclosed regarding the victims' lives, many community members would be able to figure out who those victims were anyway.

who was the victim of sexual abuse. The Court had previously decided the case of **Coy v. Iowa**,[61] in which a court was asked by the prosecution to permit hiding a child witness/victim behind a screen while testifying in court. Lighting would be arranged so that the defendant was able to dimly see the witness but the witness would not be able to see the defendant at all. Arguably, this would minimize the child's nervousness, anxiety, and distress by having to face her accuser in person in court. The Court ruled that this was not appropriate, stating that "face-to-face presence may, unfortunately, upset the truthful rape victim or abused child; but by the same token it may confound and undo the false accuser or reveal the child coached by a malevolent adult."[62] An Iowa statute had supported the use of a screen or closed circuit television in this type of case.

---

61. 487 U.S. 1012 (1988).
62. **Id.** at 1019.

However, when the Court considered the **Maryland** case in 1990, the facts of the case and the presence of a Maryland statute that would support the defendant's request resulted in a different decision.

MARYLAND V. CRAIG

FACTS: Craig was tried in a Maryland court, responding to charges of the sexual abuse of a six-year-old child. Maryland had passed a statute that permitted a judge to receive the testimony of an alleged child abuse victim via one-way closed-circuit television so the testimony would be live but the victim would not see the defendant. The statute required that the trial court determine that the child victim's testimony would result in the victim suffering serious emotional distress such that she would not even be able to communicate effectively if she were forced to face the defendant in person in court. The prosecutor and defense counsel would be in the room with the child, examining and cross-examining the child, but the jury, judge, and defendant would remain in the courtroom and view the testimony through the television. The defendant, Craig, objected to this type of testimony, arguing that his right to confrontation would be violated. An expert witness was called in by the prosecution, testifying that the victim in this case, as well as other children alleged to have been abused by Craig, would suffer serious emotional distress if they were required to testify in the presence of the defendant and that they then might be unable to testify at all. For example, one child stated that if she were forced to testify in front of Craig, she would "probably stop talking and she would withdraw and curl up." Craig argued that the use of the procedure would take away his right to observe, cross-examine, and have the jury view the true demeanor of the witness. The trial court found that the children were competent to testify in court but that the testimony of each of the children in the actual courtroom would cause each emotional distress to the point that they each would not be able to communicate effectively. Craig was convicted on all counts following a jury trial, and the case made its way to the Supreme Court, which agreed to hear the case.

ISSUE: Whether the use of the closed-circuit television is violative of the defendant's Sixth Amendment right to confrontation, and what steps must be taken before a court can determine that a closed-circuit television can be used.

HOLDING: The Court determined that the trial court can permit closed-circuit testimony but that a trial court must always first begin with the child testifying in the defendant's presence and then determine that the testimony is causing the child severe emotional distress before resorting to the use of a closed-circuit television.

RATIONALE: The Court ruled that the confrontation clause "prefers" that testimony always be given face to face. However, that face-to-face confrontation can be limited based on important interests. The Court stated that in **Coy v. Iowa**, it had left open the question as to whether any exceptions exist to the general nature of the confrontation clause, which allows defendants to meet face to face with everyone who would testify against a defendant at trial. The Iowa statute presumed that trauma would take place when children were forced to testify against an accused abuser at trial and did not leave open the ability of the trial court to determine in each separate case whether or not that particular child victim would be traumatized if required to face the defendant in person. There was no finding by the trial court in the **Coy** case that those particular witnesses would be traumatized.

The Court noted that the very essence of the word "confrontation" means a clashing of two people. While in the **Coy** case the Court had discussed the lengthy historical background of permitting confrontation, the Court in **Maryland** stated that the theory behind giving this confrontation right to defendants was to avoid the use of general affidavits that were being brought into court as evidence against a defendant without the affiant appearing in court to be cross-examined. The Court now stated that a victim who appears by closed-circuit television is still giving a statement under oath, submits to cross-examination (which the court stated, quoting a prior case, was "the greatest legal engaging ever invented for the discovery of truth"), and permits the jury to view the victim's demeanor. The Court acknowledged that it is more difficult to tell a lie about a person when the other person is physically present. Although the right to confrontation in person was found to be very important, the Court stated that it was not at the core of the confrontation clause. As long as Maryland's statute retained all of the important aspects of the confrontation clause, including cross-examination and an ability of the judge, jury, and defendant to view the victim/witness while testifying, the core requirements of the confrontation clause would be met. Maryland's system remained reliable, and the trial court would need to decide in each case whether the witness would be unable to testify if forced to sit with the defendant in person. The Court stated that the protection of minor victims of sex crimes from further embarrassment and trauma was a compelling interest that would be furthered by this ruling.

Following the Court's decision, most states have passed laws permitting child victims to testify via closed-circuit television. A debate has ensued regarding whether elderly or disabled persons should have this sort of protection as well. Certainly elderly victims and disabled victims could not only suffer emotionally when having to testify in court, which could be detrimental to their health, but it might also be difficult for them to even physically get to the courthouse to testify. The **Maryland** case may open the door for more special classes of people to be able to testify in this nontraditional way.

Right to Cross-Examine Witnesses. A defendant has a right to cross-examine witnesses who are called by the prosecution. However, a defendant does not have the right to ask witnesses any question; limitations exist. Generally, the questioning needs to be related to either (1) something the witness testified to on direct examination or (2) questions that would permit the fact finder to draw conclusions as to whether the witness' testimony is reliable. For example, if a witness had charges dropped in exchange for the testimony he offers against the defendant, that information would be important in terms of the jury deciding whether the witness would have a reason to lie. A defendant also has the right to call any of his own witnesses on cross-examination if that witness ultimately testifies against him. Occasionally a witness might be unavailable at trial but if the defendant has had the ability to cross-examine the witness at a prior proceeding, the witness's testimony might be able to come into court through an exception.

RIGHT TO BAIL

Basis and History of the Right to Bail

The ability of a defendant to be released from custody on bail is very common. However, the system has evolved greatly over the years. The origins of bail are rooted in Anglo-Saxon history. Originally, Anglo-Saxon law required that persons who were accused of a crime pay "bohr" to the victim's family; the money would be returned to the accused if he was found not guilty of the crime. Bail was later used as a way to lessen the harshness of the inefficient criminal system in which a person could languish in jail for years before being brought to trial. Besides being fairer to a person who might be found innocent, bail also helped law enforcement authorities; many times the "jail" was in the sheriff's private home. The bail system slowly evolved to include standards by which bail would be set, the purpose of which was to prevent flight by the accused.

Bail is the device used by courts to allow persons charged with a crime to be released by posting financial security or agreeing to certain terms of release. The most common type of bail is one when a person is required to post a certain amount of money before being released from court. This can range anywhere from 10 percent to 100 percent of the amount set. If the defendant does not appear at subsequent court proceedings, he will forfeit any bail he has posted and will also be required to pay the remaining amount of bail (if, for example, only 10 percent was posted). Some offenders work through a **bail bondsman**, who will loan the defendant the money and assure the payment of the full amount if necessary but takes an interest in the defendant's house or other property as collateral so that if the defendant does not appear for hearings, the bondsman can foreclose on or take the defendant's property.

The right to bail is generally thought of as a right that a criminal defendant has while waiting for a trial, but a defendant also has a right to have bail set when he is waiting for an appeal to be decided. The right to bail is set forth in the Eighth Amendment, which states that "excessive bail shall not be required." However, a close reading of this verbiage brings up the following question: Does a criminal defendant have a right at all to have bail set? Certainly if it is set, it cannot be excessive, but there is no right set forth in the Constitution that permits every defendant to have bail set. Because of the absence of this right in the Constitution, Congress, state legislatures, and federal courts have required bail in particular cases. Laws have also been passed to limit the ability of certain persons to obtain bail.

The Supreme Court has never made a specific decision as to whether the bail clause of the Eighth Amendment is a right that should be incorporated to the states. Most state constitutions, however, incorporate the right into their own constitutions, and the Supreme Court has not specifically ruled that the prohibition of excessive bail is not a fundamental element of our justice system. The Judiciary Act of 1789[63] has required that bail be set for noncapital offenders, as do the Federal Rules of Criminal Procedure. The Federal Bail Reform Act, originally enacted in 1966 and substantially revised in 1984, provides defendants with the right to bail.

Bail is widely used in justice systems throughout the world. England's system is similar to the bail system of the United States, and the same primary factors are used in both countries to determine whether bail should be granted. The British legal system also had a great influence on criminal law in Canada; thus, the roots of bail in Canada originated in England. Canada's bail system focuses on preventive detention for purposes of public safety, but recent court decisions have leaned toward protecting the rights of the defendant, and not denying bail for reasons that were merely convenient for the court, but only if such a denial is absolutely necessary for purposes of public safety.

Some countries, such as New Zealand, have no formal bail statutes, and any bail provisions in existence come from common law. New Zealand courts generally follow Canadian court rulings in their determination of bail factors. South Africa, in the post-apartheid era, has made great strides in the area of bail. That country's 1993 Constitution gives detainees the right to be released "with or without bail," depending on the circumstances. The legislature of that country has been given the power to regulate bail, and future standards will most likely be developed.

Standards for Setting Bail

When setting and granting bail, a court must balance the state's interest in both protecting society and prosecuting crimes with the presumption of innocence of the accused. Bail allows defendants an opportunity to prepare a defense to criminal charges and prevents punishment prior to a person's conviction. The right to bail is available at several different points in the criminal process, including prior to trial, prior to sentencing, and upon appeal. A Supreme Court justice can allow release on bail when a person has appealed a state court criminal proceeding to the Supreme Court, subject to that state's bail requirements. In such cases, bail is generally granted

---

63. 1 Stat. 73.

unless the appeal is frivolous or taken to delay proceedings. All judicial officers, including appellate and trial court judges, possess the right to grant bail. Magistrates also have the authority to grant bail when conducting preliminary hearings.

The Bail Reform Act of 1984, 18 U.S.C.S. §3144, was enacted following concerns of the criminal justice system in the 1970s and 1980s that society was being harmed when dangerous criminals were released on bail. That act recognizes that there are some persons who should not be released on bail in order to protect society. However, the act also recognizes that setting only monetary bail orders may be a violation of a person's constitutional rights, in accordance with the excessive bail provision of the Eighth Amendment. The act presumes that defendants should be released on personal recognizance, unless it can be determined that such a release would not ensure either the return of the person for court proceedings or the safety of the community. Release on personal recognizance provides that rather than posting monetary collateral, a person can be released from custody after signing a release form agreeing that he or she will attend all required proceedings. Factors that a judicial officer or magistrate must consider in order to determine whether to release a person on his or her own recognizance include information regarding the person's past and present employment, family ties and relationships, past and present residence, reputation, character, mental condition, criminal record, previous appearances in court, current charge, the existence of others who would support the character of that person, and other relevant factors. A defendant who is released from prison on bail must also comply with other provisions similar to those of a person who is on probation or parole, including a curfew, staying away from a victim, and other provisions.

The Supreme Court has stated that requiring excessive amounts or conditions of bail may violate due process The 1984 Federal Bail Reform Act provides that bail cannot be set at an amount so high that it, in effect, results in the pre-trial detention of a person. In other words, if a judge decides that the community will not be harmed by the release of a defendant, he must set bail at an amount that is only high enough to further the interest of the protection of the community, but not so high as to prohibit that person from being able to obtain release.

The Bail Reform Act eliminates any assumption that all defendants are entitled to bail, by eliminating the right to bail for persons charged with particular serious felonies. Section 3142(f) of the Bail Reform Act provides that if a defendant is charged with certain felonies or was involved in a crime of violence, a crime for which the maximum sentence is life imprisonment or death, or certain drug offenses, that person will not receive bail as long as the government can demonstrate that no release conditions would safeguard the community. Additionally, Section 3142(e) disallows bail if the judicial officer making the decision to grant or deny bail has probable cause to believe that the accused possessed a firearm during the commission of the felony. The Bail Reform Act assumes that no bail amount would safeguard the community for such felons. Additionally, the judicial officer determining whether to grant

YOU BE THE JUDGE

You are a Supreme Court justice and the following case comes before you. A new law in the State of Louisiana requires that a defendant who is accused of a sex offense and who is released from prison on bail pending his trial is prohibited from the "unlawful use or access of social media." This has been interpreted by Louisiana state courts to mean that the defendant cannot visit or use major social media websites such as Facebook, MySpace, and Google+. The American Civil Liberties Union (ACLU) argues that this rule also blocks these persons' access to other outlets, such as current event sites, job databases, and websites that allow anyone to leave comments or posts. Further, if a person is required to use the Internet for his job, and especially if he is required to use social websites or if he has his own business in which he advertises on social websites, he will be unable to engage in his trade or business. The law defines "social networking website" as any website that "allows users to create web pages or profiles about themselves that are available to the general public or to any other users or offers a mechanism for communication among users, such as a forum, chat room, electronic mail, or instant messaging." The ACLU argues that the law is vague and basically prohibits people from being let out on bail or remaining on bail due to its restrictive nature. The government argues that sex offenders often use social networking sites to find new victims, and that if the courts are going to risk letting sex offenders out on bail, these provisions must be in place.

What do you decide regarding the law? Assume Louisiana's Constitution provides that a defendant has the right to have bail set.

bail should consider the specifics of the crime allegedly committed, the weight of evidence existing against the person, the person's character, whether the person was already involved in the court system for another offense, and the potential of danger to any person in the community, including witnesses to the case, if the person is released from custody on bail.

A person's right to receive bail, and what conditions can be imposed upon such decisions, continues to be a controversial point of law. Since the passage of the 1984 Act, courts have considered whether provisions of the Bail Reform Act are unconstitutional, especially whether certain conditions under which a person will not receive bail are considered punitive in nature, go against the presumption of innocence implied in the Constitution, or violate equal protection.

Setting bail has several purposes. First, it permits defendants to be out of custody while awaiting trial, which furthers the presumption of innocence. A person who is accused of a crime and later convicted is at a severe disadvantage if he was incarcerated while waiting six months or more for trial, especially if he has had to give up his job and his ability to pay his bills while incarcerated. Further, incarceration is an extreme limitation on one's liberty, and society frowns upon taking that liberty away when a person is wrongly accused of committing a crime. Second, there is always a concern that prisons are overcrowded and that society is paying, through tax dollars, for people to sit in prison while waiting for court proceedings. Requiring bail if a person is going to be released while waiting for trial ensures that the person will show up for future hearings, as the bail amount is forfeited if the person fails to show up for court proceedings. Third, permitting a person to be released from incarceration permits the person to be active in preparing his defense to criminal charges.

Despite all of these various reasons to set bail, the Supreme Court decided long ago that the main purpose of setting bail is to ensure the defendant's appearance in court. In **Stack v. Boyle**,[64] the Supreme Court stated that the court must consider, in setting an amount of bail, factors that are relevant to assuring the presence of the defendant in court. If a court usually sets a particular amount of bail in particular types of cases, it must justify setting a higher amount in a similar case. The use of bail schedules which set an amount of bail at a particular rate for particular crimes are often used, but the Supreme Court prefers that a bail amount be determined on a case-by-case basis.

Why were the framers of the Constitution so concerned about the amount of bail that was set for a defendant? A similar provision existed in the English Bill of Rights and some of the framers were concerned that Congress could inflict unusual and severe punishments if such punishments were not specifically prohibited in the Constitution. Even if Congress did not want to admit to certain punishments such as the infliction of physical pain or tortures, it might resort to a civil type of punishment such as the infliction of a high amount of bail.

Courts have been permitted to deny bail to defendants completely in certain types of cases, without any consideration of the individual circumstances of those cases. In **capital cases**, when defendants are being charged with a crime in which the death penalty could be imposed, no bail is set. Obviously the concern is that a defendant's potential loss of life if he does attend trial proceedings would be worth the risk of fleeing if he is let out of prison. Secondarily, there is a concern that the person, if having a propensity to murder others, could commit another murder if released on bail. Bail for sex offenders has also been a concern, as sex offenders can be repeat offenders.

In **Murphy v. Hunt**,[65] the Supreme Court considered this politically charged question. Groups such as the ACLU argued against the rule but other victims' rights groups supported it. Hunt had been charged with first-degree sexual offenses in Nebraska. Hunt applied for pre-trial bail

---

64. 342 U.S. 1 (1951).
65. 455 U.S. 478 (1982).

YOU BE THE JUDGE

You are a judge who is required to set bail for a defendant. You can release him on his own recognizance or set a certain amount of bail for him to post. Following are the facts of his case:

1. The defendant is 40 years old and is being charged with possession of crack cocaine with the intent to deliver.

2. The defendant lives in Anytown, Pennsylvania, and has lived there all of his life.

3. The defendant has six minor children whom he supports by working at a local factory. He does not know where the children's mother is. The oldest child is 17 years old and helps him take care of the younger children. He claims that he has very little money left at the end of the month, after he pays for food and housing for his children.

4. The defendant was previously charged with possession of a small amount of marijuana previously and he pleaded to a misdemeanor and was sentenced to a period of probation of six months. He completed his probation successfully.

5. The defendant was previously charged with possession of crack cocaine and heroin. The police searched the defendant in a bar after they state that they saw him throw drugs to the ground when they entered the bar. That case was never prosecuted due to the fact that the evidence was suppressed because the police did not have probable cause to search the defendant, as determined by the court because the officers saw the defendant move his hand but they did not actually see drugs in his hand at the time, just on the floor afterward, so they could not prove that he threw the drugs.

6. The defendant showed up for all of his previous court proceedings.

7. The defendant states that he is not guilty. The police indicate that an undercover officer purchased crack cocaine from the defendant. The defendant then permitted the police to search his vehicle.

8. The defendant stated to the police that he has family members in San Antonio, Texas.

What factors do you consider in determining whether to set bail for the defendant and how much to require? How does each factor support your decision?

twice. He was denied because a provision of the Nebraska Constitution prohibited courts from granting bail in cases of first-degree sexual offenses when proof of the defendant's crime was evident or the presumption of his guilt was great (a determination to be made by the trial court). Specifically, the provision stipulated that all individuals could receive bail except for those charged with treason, sexual offenses involving penetration by force or against the will of the victim, and murder, when the proof is evident or the presumption of guilt is great. Pending his trial, Hunt filed a motion arguing that the failure to grant him bail violated his federal constitutional rights to be free from excessive bail and cruel and unusual punishment, to due process and equal protection of the laws, and to the effective assistance of counsel under the Sixth, Eighth, and Fourteenth Amendments. Hunt was convicted and appealed his case, with the case eventually reaching the Supreme Court. The Supreme Court dodged the issue of whether bail could be generally denied for first-degree sex offenders, stating that the issue of bail for Hunt was moot because by the time the case reached the Supreme Court, he was in prison as part of his sentence for his conviction.

QUESTIONS TO CONSIDER

1. Read the case of **Smith v. Phillips**, 455 U.S. 209 (1982). Do you believe the prospective juror in that case could have been biased? What would you have argued if you were the defense to argue that the juror was biased? Do you agree with the Court's decision?

2. Consider a recent high publicity criminal case that was covered heavily by the media. Was the fact finder in that case a jury or a judge? How do you believe the result could have been different if the case had been handled by a jury instead of a judge or a judge instead of a jury? Which of the two fact finders do you believe is more likely to reach the "correct" decision in the case? Why?

3. Research the topic of hypnosis. What types of limitations do you believe a judge should put on hypnotically recalled testimony? What arguments do attorneys have to argue that hypnotically recalled testimony should or should not be let into court? What types of instructions are jurors given regarding hypnotically induced testimony? What types of instructions should they be given?

4. Are you willing to give up your right to check books out of the library or use your phone in order to fight terrorism? Do you believe the Patriot Act was an unnecessary, knee-jerk reaction to the terrorist attacks of September 11, 2001, or a necessary way to combat terrorism?

5. Read the case of **J.E.B. v. Alabama ex rel. T.B.**, 511 U.S. 127 (1994), in which the Supreme Court decided that jurors of a particular sex cannot be

excluded from the jury. Then read the case of **United States v. Blaylock**, 20 F.3d 1458 (1994). Based on the Court's reasoning in **J.E.B.**, what do you believe the Court's ruling would be if the **Blaylock** case were heard by the Supreme Court? Why?

6. The facts of the lineup in the **Gilbert** case are set forth in the following.[66] What problems do you believe were inherent in the lineup? What procedural safeguards do you believe could be placed on the use of lineups that would result in a court being satisfied that a defendant's attorney did not need to be present at that lineup?

The lineup occurred on March 26, 1964, after Gilbert had been indicted and had obtained counsel. It was held in an auditorium used for that purpose by the Los Angeles police. Some 10 to 13 prisoners were placed on a lighted stage. The witnesses were assembled in a darkened portion of the room, facing the stage and separated from it by a screen. They could see the prisoners but could not be seen by them. State and federal officers were also present and one of them acted as "moderator" of the proceedings.

Each man in the lineup was identified by number, but not by name. Each man was required to step forward into a marked circle, to turn, presenting both profiles as well as a face and back view, to walk, to put on or take off certain articles of clothing. When a man's number was called and he was directed to step into the circle, he was asked certain questions: where he was picked up, whether he owned a car, whether, when arrested, he was armed, where he lived. Each man was also asked to repeat certain phrases, both in a loud and in a soft voice, phrases that witnesses to the crimes had heard the robbers use: "Freeze, this is a stickup; this is a holdup; empty your cash drawer; this is a heist; don't anybody move."

Either while the men were on the stage, or after they were taken from it, it is not clear which, the assembled witnesses were asked if there were any men who they would like to see again, and told that if they had doubts, now was the time to resolve them. Several gave the numbers of men they wanted to see, including Gilbert's. While the other prisoners were no longer present, Gilbert and two or three others were again put through a similar procedure. Some of the witnesses asked that a particular prisoner say a particular phrase, or walk a particular way. After the lineup, the witnesses talked to each other; it is not clear that they did so during the lineup. They did, however, in each other's presence, call out the numbers of men they could identify.

---

66. The facts of the lineup were set forth by the federal district court which decided the case at the lower court level and were repeated verbatim in a footnote in the Supreme Court's decision. **Gilbert v. United States**, 366 F.2d 923, 925 (1966).

KEY TERMS

bail
This device is used by courts to allow persons charged with a crime to be released by posting financial security or agreeing to certain terms of release.

jury nullification
This process means that the jury can actually choose, through their actions, to nullify a law that they believe to be unfair, when they acquit a defendant whom they believe to be guilty of breaking that law.

lineup
This process of identification uses a group of possible suspects, often similar in physical characteristics to the described perpetrator, presented side by side for the witness or victim to identify.

photographic array
This process of identification uses a series of photographs that are shown to a victim or witness for the purpose of identifying the perpetrator of a criminal act.

showup
This process is similar to a lineup, but with only one person, the suspect, being presented to the victim or witness for identification.

standby counsel
When a defendant wants to represent himself, but the court is not convinced that he can do so effectively, the Court may appoint a standby counsel, who is an attorney who sits with the defendant in court and aids in the raising of objections and questioning of witnesses, if necessary.

Strickland test
This is a two-part test set forth by the Court to determine the effectiveness of counsel. First, the Court must determine whether the counsel's actions were actually deficient. If so, then the defendant must show that it was the counsel's deficient actions that altered the outcome of the trial in a negative manner.

waiver of right to counsel
A defendant has the right to choose not to have counsel represent him at any point of the proceedings; however, judges prefer that defendants be represented by counsel, and a defendant will have to prove that he is knowingly and intelligently waiving his right to counsel

KEY COURT CASES

Batson v. Kentucky
Batson was an African-American male, convicted by an all-white jury. The Supreme Court ruled that Batson's rights were violated and that the prosecutor's act of purposefully striking African Americans from the jury violated Batson's constitutional rights.

Betts v. Brady

The **Betts** court stated that whether or not a lawyer is required in a criminal trial depends on the circumstances of each case but that generally states do not need to follow this portion of the Bill of Rights. In other words, the right was not important enough to be incorporated to the states. This decision was later overturned by **Gideon v. Wainwright**.

Estelle v. Williams

In this case, a defendant was tried in prison clothing. The Court decided that this could bias the jury and was thus unconstitutional, as the jury would immediately think of the defendant as already being a prisoner, and thus guilty, as soon as they saw him.

Gideon v. Wainwright

Case in which the Supreme Court ruled that the right to assistance of counsel was a fundamental right and that the failure to provide counsel would result in an unfair trial void of due process.

Nichols v. United States

In this case, the Court held that the use of a prior uncounseled misdemeanor to enhance a person's sentence does not violate the Sixth Amendment to the Constitution and thus is permissible.

Powell v. Alabama

This case involved the "Scottsboro boys," African-American men who were accused of raping two white women on a train, and dealt with the right to counsel prior to trial, arguing that denial of counsel prior to trial was a clear violation of due process.

Stack v. Boyle

In this case, the Court ruled that the court must consider, in setting an amount of bail, factors that are relevant to assuring the presence of the defendant in court. If a court usually sets a particular amount of bail in particular cases, it must justify setting a higher amount in similar cases. The Court prefers that bail be set on a case-by-case basis.

Strickland v. Washington

This case considered the effectiveness of counsel. The Court stated that the right to counsel implies that counsel is effective and stated that its key concern was whether the counsel's conduct so undermined the proper functioning of the adversarial process that the trial cannot be assumed to have produced a valid result. The Court set forth a two-part test, the **Strickland** test, for assessing the effectiveness of counsel.

PRE-TRIAL, TRIAL, AND POST-TRIAL PROCEDURES AND PROCESS

8

LEARNING OBJECTIVES: Students will

1. Understand how a case is investigated and moves toward trial
2. Understand the trial process
3. Know what the Eighth Amendment cruel and unusual punishment clause prohibits
4. Be aware of how capital punishment cases are handled in the court system

REPORT AND INVESTIGATION OF A CRIME

A criminal case begins with a police agency learning of the possibility of a crime. (See Figure 8.1 for an overview of the movement of a case through the criminal justice system.) This knowledge usually comes from a person telephoning a 911 emergency system or the police department directly in order to report a crime. Occasionally a police officer might be on a routine patrol or on his way to a call when he directly observes a crime taking place. Sometimes, crimes are reported by people who are mandated by law to report crimes that have been brought to their attention, such as schoolteachers or counselors. These individuals are referred to as **mandated reporters**. Regardless of how a report comes to a police agency, the police are the first contact in terms of a suspected crime. A report of a crime does not always mean that a crime has actually taken place. It is the responsibility of the police to try to determine whether or not a crime has actually been committed. It is possible that an initial investigation might result in the finding that no crime occurred and charges will never be filed. However, assuming that does not happen, the case will proceed with a police investigation.

Police have many ways to investigate cases, including technology and observation and, often most importantly, by gathering information from witnesses and potentially the suspect himself. Knocking on doors and asking questions does not generally lend itself to any constitutional issues. Police can ask any person any question at any time and as long as the person is willing

FIGURE 8.1. MOVEMENT OF A CASE THROUGH THE CRIMINAL JUSTICE SYSTEM, PART 1

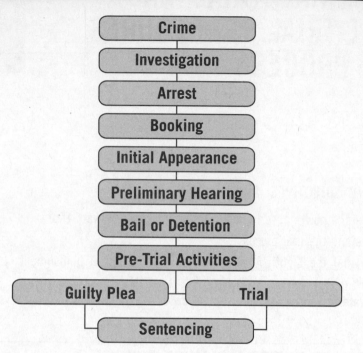

to answer the questions, the information can be used toward obtaining an arrest warrant or a search warrant, if those types of documents become necessary to continue an observation. Sometimes no warrants are issued until the time that police officials decide to charge an individual with a crime. Other times, an investigation can take months and sometimes years before any determination is made as to how to proceed or who to charge. Sometimes police will be sure that a crime has actually been committed but they have no evidence as to who committed the crime. Some crimes have gone unsolved for years with no hopes of ever determining who committed the crime.

Occasionally, a victim decides that she does not wish to cooperate with the police in terms of their investigation of the crime and that she does not wish for the police to further investigate. This sometimes happens in domestic violence cases in which the defendant has an emotional tie to the victim. Sometimes also the crime will be reported to the police by a neighbor or other observer and the victim never wanted the crime to be reported to the police. Cases have been thrown out completely even after charges were filed because the victim of the crime refuses to show up at hearings or refuses to testify against the defendant. Sometimes a victim will report a crime but then when the police ask for more details, he refuses to give them and the police can no longer move on with their investigation.

However, a police agency can continue with an investigation and can file charges and prosecute a case even when the victim does not wish for the police to do so. This is because a crime is considered to be an act against the entire community, not just one person. Theoretically, all persons in a community are victimized when a crime takes place, as the order of society is being disrupted. A police organization might have enough evidence to move forward without the victim's testimony, but sometimes agencies do not wish to do so and wish to honor the victim's desire instead. Many cases in which victims do not wish to go forward are domestic violence cases, although some shootings and other acts of street violence might also involve victims who do not wish to pursue charges. Police agencies have gone to hospitals when called to investigate situations of shooting victims and found victims who are unwilling to discuss how the shooting took place. In domestic violence cases, some police agencies have developed systems in which they work with local hospitals to make sure that pictures of the victims' injuries are either photographed or videotaped to use in a trial later. A victim (or witness to a crime) can be subpoenaed and forced to come to court and testify and can be held in contempt of court if she does not show up, up to the point of being imprisoned. In fact, an agency or attorney can request that a court imprison a witness prior to trial if there is a concern that the witness will not show up for court and will thus jeopardize either the prosecution or defense's case. However, many agencies do not wish to force a victim or witness who does not wish to testify to take the stand, due to the fact that the individual might not testify truthfully if she is being forced to do so.

Occasionally a case will not be pursued by the police, regardless of how much information they have about the crime, if the **statute of limitations** for prosecuting that crime has passed. A statute of limitations limits the amount of time a prosecuting agency has to prosecute a crime. These limitations are generally set by statute, although some common law doctrines can also set such limitations. The time limitations usually begin on the day that a victim realizes that a crime has been committed. A person who did not know that someone else took money from his bank account until two months after the money was actually taken will most likely have a certain number of years from the date that he learns of the theft for charges to be filed. Some crimes have no statute of limitations, the most common of these being murder. Sometimes a person will realize that a crime has been committed against him after remembering something from many years ago that he claims he had previously forgotten. This is referred to as **repressed memory syndrome**. Many experts disagree as to whether these repressed memories are legitimate. Certainly sometimes something can be so traumatic that the human brain will attempt to push that memory aside as a coping mechanism. Naysayers argue that these cases stem from overzealous therapists and police officers planting ideas in a person's mind and convincing him that a crime took place when in fact it did not. In any event, if these types of repressed memories are accepted by police, the police will file charges and often will not have a statute of limitations problem. A jury will then make the final determination as to whether the memories indeed reflect something that actually happened. In a case based on repressed memories, a psychologist will testify; often the defense will hire an expert to testify that repressed memory syndrome is false, while the prosecution will hire another expert who supports the idea of repressed memories.

Why have legislatures and the courts developed statutes of limitation? The longer time passes from the time a crime is committed, the more likely it is that witnesses to the crime and other evidence will disappear. Agencies that might once have had financial, medical, or other records related to the crime could have disposed of them as a routine part of their business practices. Further, the witnesses who do testify might not remember all of the details of what they knew. This makes it less likely that all relevant evidence will be presented and thus the proceedings might not be reliable. Further, it is better that people do not need to worry about something that happened years ago being brought up against them years later. Civil law has its own statutes of limitations that apply to actions such as medical malpractice lawsuits, contract issues, and the right to recoup money from someone who has wronged another. Sometimes time limits are suspended. If a defendant absconds during the trial, or if the defendant requests that a trial be postponed, the statute of limitations is tolled during that time period.

ARREST AND SEARCH WARRANTS

Assuming that enough information is obtained to identify the person responsible for a crime, the police can then file formal charges and obtain an arrest warrant from a magisterial justice or might be able to arrest a person without an arrest warrant. In many jurisdictions, felony arrests do not require an arrest warrant, and in most jurisdictions, if a person commits a misdemeanor in front of a police officer, no warrant is necessary. An arrest warrant must be based on probable cause, just like a search warrant. An arrest warrant will remain in effect until the person is actually arrested, no matter how long that might be. Some arrest warrants have been pending for years, while the subject of the arrest warrant has moved to another country and hidden from authorities. Often, a search warrant and an arrest warrant will be requested together. A search warrant could be issued to allow officers to search a particular location for a particular person for whom the police have an arrest warrant. An arrest warrant is considered to be **outstanding** if it has not yet been executed. All states have many pending outstanding warrants, and some prohibit a person from obtaining or renewing a driver's license or passport if a person is the subject of an outstanding warrant. Generally, when a person is pulled over for a traffic violation, officers check to see whether any warrants exist for that person. If so, the person can be arrested and his car searched incident to arrest.

Another type of warrant that can be issued is a **bench warrant**. If a defendant does not show up for a hearing, the court will hold that person in contempt of court and will issue a warrant for that person's arrest. If the person also happened to be out of prison on bail, failing to show up for a hearing will also cause that person to forfeit the bail he has posted. If a person has a bench warrant against him and he is pulled over by police, he will be arrested and a hearing will be held to determine whether the defendant will be imprisoned or whether a new bail amount will be set for the defendant. A person who has a bench warrant issued against him will be assumed to be a flight risk. Occasionally, however, a person can prove that he was unaware of a prior court hearing or had another legitimate reason for failing to show up for court proceedings.

PRE-TRIAL PROCEDURES

Decision to Charge

The prosecutor has absolute discretion in deciding whether or not to charge a person with a crime. Even a victim does not have the right to insist that a prosecutor file charges. Courts can review the decision not to prosecute, however, and certainly there are ethical issues that may arise if a prosecutor decides not to prosecute a case based on a relationship with the defendant or undue influence. Some jurisdictions in the United States require court approval of a prosecutor's decision not to bring charges. These jurisdictions may require the prosecutor to justify, in writing, his decision not to bring charges. The Supreme Court, however, does not favor this sort of system, stating that courts are not necessarily able to review the many reasons the prosecutor would choose not to prosecute a case, as discussed in **Wayte v. United States.**[1] These reasons include the strength of the case, the ability to deter criminals from committing crimes, and the general goals of the prosecutor's office. As long as the prosecutor can justify his reason for failing to prosecute the case, even if the reason is solely a backlog of cases in the prosecutor's office, the Court should uphold the prosecutor's decision.

Additionally, a prosecutor can be incorrect in deciding to prosecute a case. A prosecutor could decide to bring charges based on discriminatory reasons, like race, social class, or prior encounters with a person. A defendant who is prosecuted for discriminatory reasons will have a constitutional claim under the equal protection clause of the Fourteenth Amendment. Consider the following Supreme Court case in which the prosecutor was accused of pressing criminal charges against the defendant for the wrong reasons.

---

1. 470 U.S. 598 (1985).

OYLER V. BOLES[2]

FACTS: A West Virginia statute provided that a defendant would receive mandatory life imprisonment upon his third conviction of a crime that was punishable by confinement in a penitentiary. The prosecutor was required to file an information document requesting the sentence immediately upon the defendant's conviction and before the court-imposed sentence. Defendants in a particular case argued that the prosecutor was requesting the sentences only for a minority of those who would technically be eligible for them, in violation of the due process and equal protection clauses of the Constitution.

ISSUE: Whether due process requires advance notice that the trial of an offense could result in a sentence of mandatory life imprisonment.

HOLDING: Due process does not require advance notice of the potential result of a conviction, only that the defendant is able to defend against it.

RATIONALE: The failure of the prosecution to proceed similarly against other defendants who could have also been prosecuted under the rule because of either selectivity in the enforcement of the rule or the prosecutor's failure to become aware of other defendants' history does not violate equal protection or due process. The Court stated that "[t]he conscious exercise of some selectivity in enforcement is not in itself a federal constitutional violation. Even though the statistics in this case might imply a policy of selective enforcement, it was not stated that the selection was deliberately based upon an unjustifiable standard such as race, religion, or other arbitrary classification."

A prosecutor should not, however, attempt to punish a defendant for exercising his constitutional rights. In the case of **Blackledge v. Perry**,[3] the defendant was convicted of assault with a deadly weapon, charged by the prosecutor as a misdemeanor. The crime could have been charged as a felony, and after the defendant appealed the lower court's decision and prevailed, the prosecutor recharged the defendant with the crime (which it could legally do) but this time charged the defendant with the same offense graded as a felony. The Supreme Court determined that this was not appropriate. Although double jeopardy issues came into play, another issue was the fact that the prosecutor was clearly being vindictive, unless he could explain his decision in some other way. Had the prosecutor suggested during the pre-trial phase that he could have charged the defendant with more severe charges but chose not to due to the defendant's cooperativeness, it is possible the prosecutor could justify the change in charges. Of course, a prosecutor's charging decision can

---

2. 368 U.S. 448 (1968).
3. **Blackledge v. Perry**, 417 U.S. 21 (1974).

always result in his being subject to investigation for ethical violations or other violations related to his ability to practice law in a certain jurisdiction.

Initial Appearance

Following a person's arrest, it is important to some jurisdictions that the person have some contact with a magistrate or someone who can decide whether she should be incarcerated to ensure an appearance in future court proceedings and to protect public safety. Within a short period of time, such as 24 or 48 hours, a person must be seen by a magistrate in her first contact with the system, which is often called a **preliminary arraignment**, **initial appearance**, or **presentment**. The person will be notified as to why she is being detained, and may be given information regarding her right to counsel.

Every jurisdiction is required to hold a **probable cause hearing**. Jurisdictions that have an initial appearance will most likely have the probable cause hearing at the same time. In **Gerstein v. Pugh**,[4] the Supreme Court determined that a probable cause hearing must be held either before arrest or promptly after, if the arrest was made without a warrant and thus no probable cause was reviewed. The Supreme Court's reasoning for requiring this hearing was that "[T]he consequences of prolonged detention may be more serious than the interference occasioned by arrest. Pre-trial confinement may imperil the suspect's job, interrupt his source of income, and impair his family's relationship."[5] The Court went on to state that confirmation of probable cause by a neutral, detached judge helps to provide the defendant with essential Fourth Amendment protections. However, the Supreme Court refused to require that the hearing be adversarial in nature, and an arrest with a warrant need not be followed by a probable cause hearing. The Court did require that any such hearing must be held "promptly," and although the Court did not state exactly what it meant by prompt, in a later decision it offered that a hearing that takes place within 48 hours of arrest would be prompt enough.[6] That being said, courts have also permitted delays when the defendant needs to be transported or when an arresting officer is busy handling other cases.

Pre-Trial Release

Following a person's arrest, a magistrate will consider whether a person should be placed in jail to await further court proceedings or whether the person can be let back into the community with the promise that he will return for any necessary proceedings. This process is especially important if a person has been searched without a warrant or arrested without a warrant. The

---

4. 420 U.S. 103 (1975).
5. **Id.** at 114.
6. **Riverside County v. McLaughlin**, 500 U.S. 44 (1991).

Eighth Amendment states that "[e]xcessive bail shall not be required." The amendment does not state that any person has the right to be let out on bail, but apparently if a person is to be let out on bail, it should not be set excessively. In capital cases, bail is generally not ever offered and because the excessive bail provision of the Constitution has not been incorporated to the states, it is possible that a state could argue that excessive bail is appropriate. Sometimes a hearing is held to determine what amount of bail should be set; this hearing can be held along with a person's initial appearance or probable cause hearing. **Preventive detention** statutes authorize the denial of bail for persons who are charged with certain types of offenses. The District of Columbia was the first jurisdiction to pass such a law in 1970, although it limited the automatic denial of bail to certain persons for only the first 60 days from the date of their arrest. The **Federal Bail Reform Act of 1984** provided that in the federal system, judges could revoke pre-trial release for firearms possession, failure to comply with curfew, and failure to comply with other conditions. Further, any person who might be at risk of fleeing or posing a danger to any person in the community could be held for ten days, and the act also provides for indefinite detention of certain persons, following a hearing. A person can request at any time during the pendency of his court proceedings that the bail in his case be lowered. Sometimes a person is in prison for two different charges. If he posts bail for one of the cases he might still remain in jail and the time spent will be credited toward the case for which he has not yet posted bail.

A person can be granted a type of bail commonly referred to as **release on recognizance** (referred to also as ROR bond), in which the defendant agrees to attend any subsequent required court proceedings. Otherwise, bail involves a defendant posting a certain amount of money with the court and agreeing that if he does not show up for any required subsequent hearing, he will forfeit that money. A person is sometimes required to post only a certain percentage of the money set as his bail amount, such as 10 percent, but would owe the court any remaining amount if he did not show up for further proceedings. Bail is supposed to be set for the purpose of ensuring that the defendant shows up for trial and other proceedings, but also is currently used for other purposes.

The process of allowing bail assists the defendant in that he can continue to work and be with his family while charges are pending; thus, if he ends up being found not guilty or the charges are otherwise withdrawn by the prosecution, he has not lost his job or valuable time with his family. Even if a person is found guilty, he has had time with his family to prepare for court and has been able to earn money to pay toward an attorney to assist him with his trial. However, when the system of bail was originally developed, a major purpose was not to show compassion to a defendant but, rather, to alleviate the crowded conditions of prisons. If every person who was waiting for a court hearing was committed to a facility, we would have to greatly increase the size of our prisons and local jails. Judges who make decisions regarding the amount of bail to set for defendants are cognizant of how much room exists in local jail facilities when making their decisions.

Pre-Trial Incarceration

If a person is being incarcerated, he will go through necessary processing, such as the **booking** process and fingerprinting. Booking involves gathering information about a person, such as his birth date, address, and other necessary information, to properly admit them to the prison. A concern sometimes is that asking these types of questions can sometimes lead a person to give up information that could be detrimental to their criminal case. For example, the booking process often includes questions as to whether a person has any drug addictions or other medical needs. A person might answer that they do not use illegal substances, and then if they are tried for possessing drugs, the prosecuting agency might use that answer to try to prove that they must have been trafficking drugs because they had drugs on their person during a police search. Many courts have specifically ruled that booking questions cannot be used by the prosecution in this manner, as it is important to obtain all necessary information from a suspect before admitting him into prison. Further, as discussed previously, the courts have determined that routine booking questions do not require any **Miranda** warnings, as they do not necessarily relate to the defendant's criminal case. Booking can now include gathering DNA evidence in addition to photographs and fingerprints.

Preliminary Hearing

Following the initial hearing, a defendant will wait for his **preliminary hearing** to take place. This is an important stage in the proceedings, as it can encourage a defendant to plea; it is also at this stage that, for the first time, charges against the person can be dropped altogether. Preliminary hearings closely resemble adversary proceedings, with witnesses being offered and cross-examination usually being available, although the Supreme Court has ruled that there is no constitutional right to cross-examine at the preliminary hearing stage.[7] A preliminary hearing is not required by the Constitution; the Supreme Court determined this in 1913 in the case of **Len Woon v. Oregon!**[8] The Court reasoned that if a grand jury indictment is not necessary in state courts, a preliminary hearing was also not required. The Court further cemented this position in the later case of **Gerstein v. Pugh**.[9] Specifically, the Court stated that "[c]riminal justice is already overburdened by the volume of cases and the complexities of our system. The processing of misdemeanors, in particular, and the early stages of prosecution generally, are marked by delays that can seriously affect the quality of justice. A constitutional doctrine requiring adversary hearings for all persons detained pending trial could exacerbate the problem of pre-trial delay." A defendant does have a right to counsel at a preliminary hearing. The

---

7. **Goldsby v. United States**, 160 U.S. 70 (1895)
8. 229 U.S. 586 (1913).
9. 420 U.S. 103 (1975).

rules of evidence are relaxed during a preliminary hearing—hearsay and other evidence that might not be permitted to be introduced in a criminal trial can usually be introduced in a preliminary hearing.

In federal court and some state courts, a preliminary hearing is replaced by or followed by a grand jury hearing, in accordance with the Fifth Amendment of the Constitution. A preliminary hearing ensures that charging and holding a person is appropriate. The outcome of a preliminary hearing is determined solely by a magisterial judge and not by a group of the defendant's peers like a grand jury proceeding. Interestingly, a defendant has the right to have counsel present during a preliminary hearing but not during a grand jury proceeding; in fact, a person may never know that a grand jury is even considering her case. Each state has its own rules of evidence and process to be followed during a preliminary hearing. However, the goal of a preliminary hearing (as well as a grand jury hearing) is to determine whether enough evidence exists to continue the case through the court system. The prosecution has the burden of providing that enough evidence exists, assuming that its witnesses are telling the truth, to charge the defendant with a particular crime. If a witness fails to show up for a hearing or testify as predicted, it is possible that enough information will not be presented to even sustain the charges that had been selected to lodge against the accused. The magistrate presiding over a preliminary hearing will not decide whether a witness is telling the truth or not—that is a function for the jury or judge at the time of a trial. The assumption must be that the prosecution's witnesses are telling the truth. It is also possible that the case could be thrown out if it was not actually committed in that court's jurisdiction. The preliminary hearing stage is also a time for the defense attorney to determine the strength of the case by listening to what the witnesses have to say. Further, the testimony of a witness who testifies differently at trial than at the preliminary hearing can be impeached at the time of trial. Although preliminary hearings are not always transcribed, in major cases a defense attorney will request a transcription for purposes of potential impeachment of the witness later, at trial.

If a person is charged with lower misdemeanors or summary offenses, the charges may be handled completely at a preliminary hearing, with the magistrate being permitted to find the person guilty or accept a guilty plea and sentence the person. Generally, the sentence would be probation, although the magistrate might be able, in some states, to sentence the person to a short period of incarceration.

Formal Arraignment

Following the preliminary hearing, a **formal arraignment** will take place. This is a formality that takes place in order to formally notify the defendant of the charges against her. The formal arraignment date also starts certain time periods, such as the number of days a person has to file pre-trial motions. A defendant can enter a formal plea at the time of the arraignment, or following the arraignment. Although a plea deal can be discussed and agreed to at the preliminary hearing, in felony and higher misdemeanor cases, the plea can be entered only after that time. A person who does not specifically plead guilty will be considered to automatically be entering a plea of not guilty. Further, accompanying the formal arraignment is the filing of a document that sets forth the charges that remain following the preliminary hearing and the legal and factual basis for that hearing, referred to as the **information**. The information sets forth the statutes under which and specific crimes for which the defendant is being charged, along with a short narrative of the probable cause the law enforcement agency possesses.

Discovery

Following the formal arraignment, each side can obtain information from the other regarding the specific evidence that each side holds, as well the identities of any witnesses who will be used by either party. Unlike what is often presented in television and movies, there are no surprise witnesses or surprise pieces of evidence presented in the middle or the end of a trial that cause a completely different result than expected. The majority of **discovery** goes from the prosecution to the defense. Any evidence that is material to the prosecutor's case must be disclosed to the defense. **Materiality** is, generally, any information that could influence the outcome of the case. Generally, this includes the following items, although rules of evidence in this regard can vary by state:

1. Any written statements or transcripts of oral statements made by the defendant that are in the prosecutor's possession
2. The defendant's criminal record
3. Documents, photographs, other tangible items, reports of physician and mental evaluations of the defendant, and other forms of real evidence that are material to the prosecutor's case against the defendant

Notes regarding trial strategy and other notes recorded by an attorney, including information disclosed to him by his client, are referred to as the attorney's **work product**, and these notes need not be disclosed to the opposing side. Work product can also include drafts of motions and other pleadings that are never actually filed with the court. Items that do not constitute a work product are generally exchanged between sides soon after the defendant is formally arraigned. However, occasionally, the information will be supplemented if new evidence or new witnesses are found during the course of the pre-trial proceedings.

As mentioned, the prosecution does not have as much of a right to receive information from the defendant as the defendant does the prosecution. The defense does not have to provide the prosecution with any incriminating information. For example, if the defendant volunteers to have a private polygraph examiner give him a polygraph test and he fails, the results of the test need not be disclosed to the prosecution. Further, any mental examinations or statements written by the defendant that have not been disclosed to the prosecution need not be disclosed. The only categories of information that must be disclosed to the prosecutor are those regarding defenses that the defendant might use at trial. The prosecution has a right to prepare for trial knowing that the defendant will make certain arguments regarding his culpability. The defendant must also provide to the prosecution a list of witnesses that he intends to use at trial. This allows the prosecution to investigate the witnesses' backgrounds and determine whether each witness has bias or has a propensity to be dishonest. The defense also is required to provide information regarding any pieces of real evidence that it plans on presenting during the trial. All of the information that is presented by one side to the other does not have to be used in court simply because it is disclosed. However, a failure to disclose the evidence will prohibit that party's ability to present the information in court.

In **Williams v. Florida**,[10] the Supreme Court determined that states can have a rule that requires the defense notify the prosecution by a certain time if the defendant plans on asserting an alibi defense at trial. Further, it is appropriate for the prosecution to also receive names of the witnesses who will testify to support the alibi. The defendant in the **Williams** case argued that providing this information to the defense was really a type of self-incrimination. The Court disagreed, stating that because the prosecution presents its case first, the defendant in **Williams** was really asking to be able to wait until the prosecution had set forth its entire case to announce his defense. The Court stated that arguing this is similar to arguing that the defendant would have a right to hear the jury's verdict on the prosecution's case before deciding whether to take the stand on his own behalf, which obviously he cannot do.

The other types of defenses that a defendant must make the prosecution aware of include the insanity defense and any argument involving self-defense. The prosecutor would present her case in a different manner if she is aware that one of these defenses will be used. Insanity defenses generally rely greatly upon expert testimony, and although the defense might have a psychiatrist examine the defendant and attest to his mental state, the prosecution might want to obtain the defendant's prior medical records or mental health records to refute the defendant's proposition of insanity. Further, the defense must provide the prosecution with a list of the witnesses that it intends to present at trial. Everyone who appears on the list is not required to testify, but a person whose name does not appear on the list cannot testify. The district attorney needs to be able to check the backgrounds of the various witnesses on the list in order to determine how to best cross-examine the witnesses or impeach their testimony upon cross-examining them. Reciprocally, the prosecution must provide the defense with its list of potential witnesses who might testify in rebuttal to the defendant's presentation of an alibi or self-defense argument. However, the prosecution needs only to supply

---

10. 399 U.S. 78 (1970).

information to the defense that is material to the preparation of the defendant's case. In **United States v. Armstrong,**[11] the Supreme Court considered a case in which a defendant charged with drug crimes argued that he and his co-defendants were singled out for prosecution based on their race. The defendants argued that paperwork within the federal prosecutor's possession that would verify the government's strategy for the prosecution of drug crimes would support the defendants' argument. The Supreme Court stated that a defendant may only obtain information that would be considered a "shield" to his case, rather than that which would be classified as a "sword." A "shield" would be any information or evidence that could be used to refute the state's case, whereas a "sword" is anything that would challenge prosecutorial conduct. Courts are concerned that providing the defense with too much of the prosecution's information could afford the defendant an unreasonable advantage at trial and would subject the prosecution's witnesses to bribery, threats, and intimidation. As discussed previously, the prosecution must provide all information that is considered exculpatory.

The one "surprise" that the prosecution might receive at the time of trial is whether or not the defendant is going to testify. The defendant does not have to tell the prosecutor at any point whether or not he will testify at trial. He can decide whether to do so after the prosecutor has presented its case.[12] Even a state statute that requires that the defendant testify immediately following the prosecutor's case was declared unconstitutional by the Supreme Court. This would result in a violation of the defendant's Fifth Amendment privilege against self-incrimination. It also results in the defense attorney's inability to decide how to best present its case, as it is possible that the defense will flow more smoothly if other defense witnesses testify prior to the defendant's testimony. The Supreme Court stated that "[t]he decision as to whether the defendant in a criminal case shall take the stand is . . . often of utmost importance, and counsel must, in many cases, meticulously balance the advantages and disadvantages of the prisoner's becoming a witness in his own behalf. Why, then, should a court insist that the accused testify before any other evidence is introduced in his behalf, or be completely foreclosed from testifying thereafter?"[13]

Although it may seem as though the prosecution is at a disadvantage because the defense does not have to disclose everything to the prosecution, keep in mind that the prosecution has the burden of proof of demonstrating that the defendant actually committed a crime. However, the Supreme Court has gone a step further in making the prosecution responsible for focusing on finding the truth, requiring that the prosecution disclose to the defendant any information it would have that could help in exculpating the defendant. Thus, any DNA or other forensic tests that

---

11. 517 U.S. 456 (1996).
12. **Brooks v. Tennessee,** 406 U.S. 605 (1972).
13. **United States v. Shipp,** 359 F.2d 185, 190-191 (1966).

do not support the defendant's guilt, or other information given to the prosecution by witnesses that make it appear as though perhaps the defendant is not guilty, must be disclosed to the defendant. However, these requirements generally only apply if the defendant is headed to trial, as set forth by the Supreme Court in **United States v. Ruiz**.[14]

UNITED STATES V. RUIZ

FACTS: Immigration agents found 30 kilograms of marijuana in Angela Ruiz's luggage. Federal prosecutors offered Ruiz a plea bargain that would be contingent on her waiving indictment, trial, and an appeal, and the prosecution promised to recommend a reduced sentence for Ruiz. The prosecutor's offer also required that Ruiz would waive the right to receive any information from the prosecutor's office as it would relate to informants or other witnesses against her, and she would also waive the right to receive any impeachment-related information or any information that would support any affirmative defenses she might have if she decided to take the case to trial. Ruiz rejected the waivers and the prosecutors withdrew their offer. Ruiz was eventually indicted for unlawful drug possession, and she then entered a guilty plea. Ruiz requested at her sentencing that the judge grant her the lenient sentence that the prosecutor would have requested had she taken the plea. The court denied it, and she appealed. The court of appeals ruled that the Constitution prohibits defendants from being asked to waive their right to certain impeachment information. The case was appealed to the Supreme Court.

ISSUE: Do the Fifth and Sixth Amendments require federal prosecutors to disclose impeachment information to a defendant relating to informants or other witnesses prior to entering into a plea agreement?

HOLDING: The Constitution does not require that the prosecution disclose material impeachment evidence to a defendant who enters a plea to a crime.

RATIONALE: Requiring the prosecution to disclose such evidence would force the government to spend substantial time engaging in trial preparation without actually going to trial. A defendant who enters a guilty plea can do so knowingly and voluntarily without having all information from the prosecution. Specifically, the Court opined that the purpose of providing exculpatory information to the defense is to make sure that a fair trial ensues. Evidence of impeachment will not always be evidence that would be material. When entering a guilty plea, a defendant risks not having all of the information the prosecution has.

---

14. 536 U.S. 622 (2002).

Pre-Trial Motions

Assuming that at least some charges remain following the preliminary hearing, the case will be scheduled for trial. In the meantime, the defendant and his attorney, as well as the prosecutor, will all begin to prepare for trial. **Pre-trial motions** can be filed at any time in order to have evidence or certain statements excluded from trial or to request that the court rule that certain statements can be included. A **motion in limine** is a written request, submitted to a judge, to request that statements or evidence either be excluded or included. Although it is possible to make a motion just prior to trial or during the trial to exclude evidence, obviously it is detrimental to the trial process to have attorneys, even at sidebar and away from the ears of the jury, requesting that the judge make determinations as to the evidence that will be permitted in trial. Members of the jury will most definitely become irritated with waiting for the attorneys and judge to finish their discussion, and they will also most likely be suspicious about what evidence is being withheld from them. Further, even bringing up certain types of evidence in front of a jury could cause a mistrial, if a cautionary instruction to the jurors to request that they "forget" that they heard the information would not be sufficient. Motions can be filed to exclude evidence that was seized unlawfully and unconstitutionally. Motions can also be made to exclude certain types of evidence, such as the criminal background of defendants in accordance with state law or the testimony of certain witnesses or certain pieces of evidence that might be too prejudicial to the defendant. Hearsay evidence that is anticipated to be presented by one side or the other can be requested to be stricken through a motion in limine. See Figure 8.2 for a sample motion in limine.

A motion in limine can also be used to request that a judge allow evidence to be included at trial. An example of this type of motion would be a request to the court that a person's criminal record, which might otherwise be admissible, be declared inadmissible because of the prejudice that it would cause if the jury were aware of it. A motion in limine can also be used to request that certain evidence, such as testimony regarding prior bad acts or the defendant's reputation, be permitted to be included in the trial. Requesting this motion prior to trial results in the trial running much more smoothly than if the court had to stop the proceedings in order to discuss the admissibility of the motion. This is especially true because such discussions generally take place at **sidebar,** which means that the attorneys involved in the case stand in front of the judge and speak quietly, so the jury will not be able to hear what they are talking about. The discussion at sidebar will still be recorded by the court reporter and thus it will be available for appellate purposes. If a longer conversation will be taking place, the judge and the attorneys might step into the judge's office or the judge will clear the courtroom of the jurors while the discussion takes place.

FIGURE 8.2. SAMPLE MOTION IN LIMINE TO SUPPRESS HEARSAY EVIDENCE

IN THE COURT OF COMMON PLEAS OF HOBBIT COUNTY, PENNSYLVANIA CRIMINAL DIVISION

COMMONWEALTH OF PENNSYLVANIA   :   No. 3970 OF 2012

vs.   :

LESTER LOBOS   :

MOTION IN LIMINE

AND NOW, comes the Defendant by and through his attorney, Jonathan Johansen, and files the following Motion in Limine and in support thereof states as follows:

1.   Lester Lobos is charged with possession of crack cocaine.

2.   Lobos was charged after law enforcement entered a west side tavern after a confidential informant alleged that drug dealing was taking place inside the bar.

3.   Specifically, Officer Smith's incident data sheet reports, "[A] confidential informant was inside the bar and did give information related to several persons who were in immediate possession/control of controlled substances. Officers were directed to locations and persons inside the bar as they were familiar with certain persons."

4.   Although Lobos has maintained his innocence, he was willing to enter a plea to paraphernalia to resolve the case so that his license would not be suspended further. Unfortunately, the offer was rejected by the prosecution.

5.   Accordingly, Lobos's case is scheduled for trial on November 21, 2013 and this motion is filed in anticipation of the trial.

MOTION TO EXCLUDE HEARSAY TESTIMONY OF THE CONFIDENTIAL INFORMANT

6.   The Confrontation Clause bars testimonial out-of-court statements unless the witness is unavailable and the defendant had prior opportunity to cross-examine the witness, regardless of whether such statements are deemed reliable by court.

7.   As stated above, Officer Smith's incident data sheet reports, "[A] confidential informant was inside the bar and did give information related to several persons who were in immediate possession/control of controlled substances. Officers were directed to locations and persons inside the bar as they were familiar with certain persons."

8. The defense is unable to interview and otherwise investigate as to the informant's motive for stating that he/she may or may not have observed Lobos with a controlled substance.

9. It is suggested that if the prosecution needs to explain why the bar was raided, it can elicit testimony that a confidential informant observed and reported illegal activity. However, without producing the informant, it should not be permitted to state that the informant told them that Defendant Lester Lobos was in possession of a controlled substance.

WHEREFORE, Defendant prays that this Court grant his request to exclude all hearsay testimony pertaining to Lobos as such testimony violates the Confrontation Clause.

Respectfully submitted,

_____

Jonathan Johansen, Esq.

Apprising the Opposing Side of Potential Defenses

Defense counsel is required to apprise the prosecution as to whether certain types of defenses will be used at trial. Some defenses require the prosecution to prepare for trial in a specific manner which is different from how he would prepare if that defense were not used. These defenses include alibi defenses and insanity defenses. Each defense requires the use of certain types of witnesses for the defense and for the prosecution as well. An **alibi defense** is used if the defendant is alleging that he was not at the scene of the crime at the time it was committed and that someone else can testify as to his whereabouts. The prosecutor needs to know who the defendant's alibi witnesses are in order to properly prepare to refute what they are saying. An **insanity defense** differs depending on state law, but generally a defendant is claiming that he was legally insane to the point of not being able to form intent to commit a crime or understand that his actions were a violation of the law. An insanity defense generally requires the defendant to produce a mental health expert who can testify as to his general mental state. The prosecutor would obviously prosecute the case differently if he has to refute the defendant's sanity rather than refuting whether or not the defendant actually committed the crime.

ENTERING A GUILTY PLEA

Although television shows and movies generally show a criminal case being resolved through the trial process, in reality the majority of cases are resolved otherwise, through either a **plea bargain** or the defendant's entry of a **guilty plea** to all charges. These methods of resolving a case save the court system, and thus, taxpayers, a huge amount of money and permit all criminal cases to move through the court system more quickly.

A defendant might choose to plead guilty to all or some of the crimes for which he is charged. A defendant could plead guilty to some crimes and proceed to trial on others, or negotiate the entry of a plea to some crimes while having other charges dropped by the state. (See the discussion on plea bargaining later.) The Supreme Court decided very early on that a guilty plea must be "knowing, voluntary, and intelligent."[15] The prosecution has the burden of proving that these three elements were present in the plea process. A defendant must admit that he committed the offense in order to plead guilty. He cannot just state that he is entering a guilty plea because he believes the state has enough evidence to convict him; he must actually admit that he committed the acts. A defendant who wishes to avoid trial but does not wish to enter a guilty plea can enter a plea of **no contest**. A judge must permit the defendant to enter this type of plea and it can help the defendant in defending future civil lawsuits, as no admission or finding of wrongdoing exists as a result of this type of plea. A no contest plea asserts no admission of guilt but the defendant is admitting that the state has enough evidence to convict him. Sentencing would follow as with a guilty plea.

A **plea colloquy** is the process by which a defendant goes to court and tells the judge that he wishes to enter a guilty plea to certain charges. The specific description of the charge and a brief discussion of the facts surrounding the offense will be read to the defendant and she will be asked whether she enters a plea of guilty to that offense. The defendant will also be informed as to the maximum penalties that could be handed down at the time of sentencing. The judge will generally also ask the defendant a series of questions which assures him that the defendant is able to understand the consequences of his plea and to make sure that the defendant has not been coerced into entering the plea or promised anything in terms of his ultimate sentence. The judge will gauge whether the defendant seems to be under the influence of any substances that might make him unable to understand the entry of his plea. The defendant must also indicate that she is aware of her rights and especially her right to go to trial. In the federal court system, the court also makes a specific finding that there is a specific factual basis for the plea; in other words, the prosecution to some extent must prove to the court that it has good evidence to obtain a conviction. In addition, recently the Supreme Court has determined that although counsel does not have a duty to tell his client of every potential collateral consequence of entering a guilty plea, an attorney must inform his client if the defendant could face immigration consequences as a result of her plea.[16]

A **plea bargain**, like the decision as to whether to bring charges at all, is justified by the wide discretion that the prosecutor possesses. A defendant who is charged with several crimes might end up entering a guilty plea to only a few charges, and the prosecutor will in turn agree to drop others. This can be done as a result of a prosecutor's case being weak, witnesses being unwilling to

---

15. **Johnson v. Zerbst**, 304 U.S. 458 (1938).
16. **Padilla v. Kentucky**, 559 U.S. 356 (2010).

testify or being potentially poor witnesses, or just an attempt in the court system to move cases along more quickly. There is little constitutional law surrounding the area of plea bargains. A defendant does have the right to have counsel represent him throughout the plea bargaining process, and the attempt to negotiate a plea cannot be used against the defendant later if the defendant backs out of the plea and decides to take his case to trial. The Supreme Court has approved of and even encouraged plea bargaining, stating that the process is an essential component of our justice system.[17]

A prosecutor can agree to waive requesting that the court impose a mandatory minimum sentence or can suggest that he will not request that the judge enter a prison sentence if the defendant enters a plea, realizing that the judge has the ultimate sentencing decision. Further, a judge can deny any plea bargain that it wishes to and require the defendant to either take his case to trial or enter a **straight plea**, which would be to plead guilty to every charge that has been lodged against him. Although this sort of requirement is rare, occasionally a person will have such a long record or the crime will be so heinous that there is no way a plea bargain could be acceptable. Often cases charged under a state's death penalty statute can be pleaded down to a first-degree murder with a mandatory life imprisonment charge. This ensures that a defendant will be incapacitated while saving the public from the expenses of death penalty appeals and saving the victim's family from having the stress of dealing with the trial, appeal, and execution process. Occasionally a defendant will engage in what is called a **slow plea**. A defendant who pleads guilty might not be able to later appeal suppression and other evidentiary issues, so defendants who might otherwise have determined that they have no chance of prevailing at a jury trial might take their case to trial instead of entering a plea, in the hopes that they can have some evidence suppressed upon appeal and have their case returned to the lower court for further, more favorable, proceedings. Entering a guilty plea can result in a waiver of certain appellate issues.

Withdrawing a Guilty Plea

A defendant might decide that he wants to withdraw his guilty plea and proceed to trial. The defendant is more likely to be permitted to do this before he is sentenced, and he must have very specific reasons to be able to withdraw a plea after sentencing, such as a severe miscarriage of justice or extreme ineffectiveness of counsel. A defendant who wishes to withdraw his plea prior to sentencing must file a motion with the court, in writing, to request that the court allow him to withdraw it. Different states have different standards for the withdrawal, provided by state statute. In the case of **Kercheval v. United States**,[18] the Supreme Court ruled that a defendant can withdraw his plea of guilty prior to sentencing if the defendant shows "fair and just reasons" for

---

17. **Santobello v. New York,** 404 U.S. 257 (1971).
18. 274 U.S. 220 (1927).

wanting to withdraw it. Factors the court will consider when determining whether to permit the withdrawal of the plea include whether the defendant has asserted legal innocence, if there is a short period of time between the entry of the plea and the desire to withdraw the plea, and whether the defendant had the benefit of competent counsel when he entered his plea. Once a defendant has been sentenced, he will face difficulty in being permitted to withdraw his plea, and he will have to show very compelling grounds based on actual innocence. It is also possible for a defendant to be permitted to withdraw his plea if he can prove to the court that he did not enter his plea voluntarily and knowingly. If a defendant was unaware of the consequences of entering his plea, such as immigration consequences or the possible sentence he could receive, the court should permit the defendant to withdraw his plea. Ineffective assistance of counsel or an assertion of erroneous facts set forth by a the prosecution at the time of the plea are also reasons for the withdrawal of a plea.

Limitations on Entering a Plea

Although many factors influence whether a person will agree to enter a plea in his case as well as whether a prosecutor will agree to allow a defendant to enter a plea, it is very important that a defendant's plea be entered voluntarily in order to be valid. Sometimes a defendant can receive a lesser sentence based on a statute that permits leniency if a person enters a plea instead of taking his case to trial. In the case of **Corbitt v. New Jersey,**[19] the Supreme Court approved of a sentencing scheme that provided that a person who pleaded guilty could be sentenced to a term of either life imprisonment or 30 years of incarceration, as opposed to definitely receiving life in prison if the person went to a jury trial and was found guilty. The defendant argued that this penalized his right to a trial by jury, but the Supreme Court disagreed and permitted this sort of sentencing scheme.

Sentencing Following a Plea

Once a defendant has entered a plea, his case will generally move on to the sentencing phase. Sometimes sentencing can take place on the same day as the plea, especially if the offense is less serious and the defendant does not have a criminal record. However, when a more serious offense is involved or if the defendant has a history of criminal behavior, the courts are likely to schedule a sentencing for a month or two after the entry of the plea. This permits the court to order that a pre-sentence investigation be done and submitted to the judge. This permits the judge to consider the defendant's background and needs, including rehabilitation needs, when sentencing the defendant.

---

19. 439 U.S. 212 (1978).

Entering a plea is a major decision for a defendant, because he gives up his right to a trial, right to confront and cross-examine adverse witnesses, and the privilege against self-incrimination.

THE JURY TRIAL

A **jury** is a group of "ordinary citizens" whose job it is to decide which witnesses testifying in a trial are telling the truth; the jury is not supposed to make decisions about the law. Juries are used during a trial in which a person's guilt or innocence is decided. **Grand juries** are used in federal courts and in some state court systems to determine whether enough evidence exists to send a case to a jury or judge trial. Members of a grand jury are generally required to serve for a month, six months, or a year and hear any cases that are brought during that time. Trial jurors are usually chosen for just one case or a limited period of time and released when their duties regarding that case or short time period are fulfilled.

Jury Selection

The act of selecting a jury is an art and is not without controversy. In fact, jury consultants are often hired in high-profile cases to assist attorneys in determining which individuals would be more apt to find in their favor. Potential jurors are assembled based on state rules. They are generally called for jury duty based on a random selection from records such as voting records and records of those who have applied for driver's licenses. Potential jurors can be immediately excluded due to health or hardship, such as being unable to drive to the courthouse for jury duty or an inability to close one's business for a period of time to sit as a juror. In some states, persons who hold or have held certain occupations might be automatically excluded; for example, a police officer might be excluded from having to attend jury duty for a criminal case. Some states, however, do not allow exclusion for categories such as occupation and allow exclusion as a juror only if either the prosecution or defense **strike**, or eliminate, those people from the jury pool after reviewing all possible prospective jurors.

Managing the Jury

Jury members are always told that they should not discuss the case with anyone until it is completely over and their verdict has been rendered. They are instructed not to watch the news or read the newspaper so that their viewpoint of the evidence that is being presented during the trial is not swayed. Jury members are instructed not even to discuss the trial with other members of the jury until they have heard all of the evidence. Because of the problems with the media giving out information and, to some extent, assisting people in

A JURY HEARS A CASE

www.bigstock.com.

forming opinions about cases while they are in progress, jury members in high-profile cases are sometimes **sequestered**. This means that they are forced to stay in a hotel for the duration of the trial. Their contact with friends and family is generally monitored and limited and the court controls what they watch on television and what they read in order to make sure that none of the jurors receive outside information about the case. Jurors are accompanied by court officials when they eat their meals and even when they gather with each other for socialization, such as in a common area of the hotel. Sequestration is inconvenient and costly, but is necessary in some cases when the media is sure to report excessively on the case.

Jury nullification, mentioned previously in this book, refers to the fact that juries sometimes try to nullify or make a statement about the law by making a particular decision in a case, rather than just applying the law to the facts of a case. For example, consider a case brought in the State of Ohio in which a jury is charged with deciding whether a person is guilty of the possession of marijuana, which is an illegal act in that particular state. The defendant may sit on the stand and admit that he indeed possessed marijuana, but that he possessed it only because he was stricken with cancer and was using the marijuana for medicinal purposes. Although the Ohio state law does not provide that an exception to the law exists for the medical use of marijuana, jury members might believe that such a law should be in place. Thus, the jury would find the defendant not guilty based on its desire that the law be changed, and not because the jury really believes that the defendant is not guilty of the crime. Often, we do not know whether a jury has engaged in an act of nullification or has actually found a person not guilty, as the jury does not have to specifically declare that its decision was based on a nullification of the law. Speculation exists that the jury in the criminal case of O.J. Simpson, a professional football player who was accused of killing his former spouse and her friend, may have engaged in jury nullification. The Simpson trial was extremely long and the jury took a comparatively short amount of time making its decision to acquit Simpson. The trial included testimony that one of the police officers who was central to the investigation of the case was racist. (Simpson was African American and both of his victims were white.) It is possible that the jury was making a statement against prejudice police practices in rendering its verdict.

Jury nullification was even approved by the Supreme Court in the case of **United States v. Powell**.[20] In the **Powell** case, the defendant was charged with violating federal narcotics laws, including the possession of cocaine with the intent to distribute it. Some of the information used to convict her was obtained from tapped telephone conversations, and the defendant was thus also charged with using the telephone in committing conspiracy to sell the drugs. The jury acquitted the defendant on the possession with intent to sell charges but convicted her on some of the counts of using the telephone to facilitate the conspiracy to sell the drugs. These verdicts were inconsistent; if the jury felt that there was not enough evidence to support the charge of possession of drugs with the intent to sell them, it did not make sense that it felt she was conspiring to sell them through phone conversations. However, the Court stated that the jury verdicts need not be overturned, even if the verdicts made no sense. The Court stated that it is possible that the jury reached its verdict as a compromise (for example, attempting to appease two different groups in the jury room, one that wanted to convict on all charges and one that wanted to acquit on all charges) or that perhaps the jury even reached its decision based on a mistake. The Court stated that permitting courts to overturn jury verdicts that seemed "inconsistent" or erroneous would require the court to speculate as to what the jury was thinking or how it made its decision. The government argued that in this case the defendant was harmed by the acquittal, but the Court noted that incorrect jury decisions affect both the defendant and the government, and that each side takes its chances that the jury will make a poor decision. Finally, the Court stated that appeals and other post-trial actions are available for each side to challenge anything that they believe was illegal or unconstitutional in terms of jury decisions, but the Court would not second guess the jury merely because its verdict or verdicts seemed irrational or inconsistent.

---

20. 469 U.S. 57 (1984).

TRIAL PROCEDURES

Jury Selection Procedures

Obviously, one of the most important parts of a criminal case is the trial. Although many cases are resolved via a plea bargain, the small percentage of cases that do make it to trial can be won or lost based on a variety of factors. Some maintain that selecting the jury is very important, although others argue that the attorneys' personalities are very important. Every part of the trial is very important to the defendant's future.

Assuming a defendant does not choose to have a trial with a judge as fact finder, the first step of a trial is to select a jury. Prospective jurors come from all walks of life and arrive at the courthouse with many predisposed notions. Further, not all jurors are honest when answering questions that are posed to them by the court, for various reasons, including embarrassment, failing to remember certain things, or sometimes even an interest in either being on the jury or not being on the jury. Jurors are generally asked whether they have a bias toward a particular type of case or particular type of defendant. Although some are honest, others might not want to explain in front of a group of people that they are biased. Jurors are often also asked if they have any experience with the criminal justice system. Certainly if they had been a defendant they might not want to admit it. If they were victims, they might also have a difficult time answering certain questions or talking about their experience. For this reason, in some cases, judges will have an **in camera** proceeding in which jurors are questioned individually, rather than questioned as a group. Although this process takes longer, it allows each juror to be in a room with only the judge and the attorneys involved in the case, rather than having to discuss personal views and experiences in front of a large group of unfamiliar people. However, sometimes jurors are not interested in giving out personal information even in a small setting, as the judge and attorneys are still, in effect, strangers. Many times, potential jurists are given a list of questions to respond to in writing before the selection process begins so that attorneys have an idea of what type of information to ask each individual juror. Sometimes a defendant will waive the presence of a judge during the selection process but sometimes a judge is present. A judge can merely oversee the process or can take over the selection process, asking the majority of the questions rather than having the attorneys control the questioning.

Attorneys ask jurors for further information beyond that on the paper and then attempt to determine which jurors would be the most detrimental to their case. The jury selection process is not as much about selecting which jurors are wanted as it is eliminating the jurors who would be detrimental. Just one juror who refuses to convict, in the case of the prosecution, or refuses to acquit, in the case of the defense, could cause a hung jury (discussed later in this chapter). A juror with a strong personality could sway the rest of the jury members to vote his way. In addition to the information that prospective jurors volunteer about their occupations, family, and experience with the criminal justice system, attorneys can also consider a prospective juror's demeanor and facial expressions during the jury selection process.

The group of jurors that are assembled together for attorneys to consider is called a **venire**. Jurors receive very little pay and are required to attend jury duty or face sanctions by the court. Although many people look at jury duty as a chore, our system of justice would be entirely different if not for the people who do take time out of their schedule to serve as jurors. Juries generally consist of 12 members of the public and in a trial that is predicted to be longer, alternate jurors will also be chosen. These alternates will sit through the entire trial until it is time to **deliberate**, or make a decision on the case, and will thus be familiar with all of the facts of the case if another juror becomes ill or otherwise unable to serve throughout the trial. The number of alternate jurors selected will vary depending on the amount of time the trial is expected to last. A two-day trial might have one alternate juror while a trial that is expected to last three weeks may have three or four alternates. Alternate jurors are often somewhat disappointed when they sit and intently listen to the facts of the case throughout the entire trial but are unable to participate in the decision-making process once the trial is complete. However, because a defendant is permitted to have a jury of 12 render a verdict, the trial would need to be started again with a new jury if a juror became unable to continue to serve and no alternates had been selected.

Prospective jurors are usually given a form to fill out which includes general objective information about them that might be relevant in any case, such as their prior occupation, number of children, age, and whether they have ever been involved in the court system before as a juror or a victim, plaintiff, or defendant. The content of these questionnaires varies depending on whether the case is criminal or civil. See the sample jury questionnaire in Figure 8.3.

Jury consultants are professionals who are hired to assist attorneys in selecting jury members based on psychological factors. Attorneys also sometimes hire **shadow juries**, members of the community who somewhat mirror the backgrounds and beliefs of people on the actually jury. In a long trial, these "fake" jurors can provide feedback to an attorney in terms of what they believe is going well or not so well in a trial. Attorneys sometimes also hire members of the community to sit in on a trial run of the case before trial so that suggestions can be given as to how to tweak the testimony of the witnesses and other information for the actual trial. The issue of whether or not a jury's decision can be predicted is very controversial.

The answers set forth on a juror's questionnaire could immediately disqualify that individual, but most likely the attorneys or judge will request further information to clarify what was on the questionnaire. Once more information is gathered, the attorneys first will agree, sometimes with the help of the judge, on which jurors should be stricken **for cause**. Generally,

FIGURE 8.3. JUROR QUALIFICATION QUESTIONNAIRE

**JURY SELECTION COMMISSION
THIRTY-THIRD JUDICIAL DISTRICT
ARMSTRONG COUNTY, PENNSYLVANIA**

JUROR QUALIFICATION QUESTIONNAIRE

NOTICE TO SUMMONED JUROR:
You must answer all questions completely and truthfully. Failure to furnish complete and truthful information renders you subject to penalty for perjury. If you are unable, for any reason, to fill out this form yourself, you MUST have some OTHER PERSON do it for you. In that case, the OTHER PERSON filling out the form for you must complete the section set aside by heavy lines directly to the right of this notice.

PRINTED NAME OF OTHER PERSON COMPLETING FORM:
_____

STREET ADDRESS _____
CITY or TOWN

TELEPHONE No. _____
REASON OTHER PERSON IS COMPLETING FORM:
_____
_____

SIGNATURE OF OTHER PERSON COMPLETING FORM

1. JUROR'S NAME_____   Home Phone_____
   Address _____   _____
   _____   Work Phone _____
   _____

2. Occupation _____
   (If retired, student, housewife, so indicate)
   If retired or unemployed, state prior occupation _____

3. Have you served as a juror in our courts within the last three (3) years? _____
   If so, what year? _____ How many days did you serve? _____

4. Are you on Active Duty with the Armed Forces of The United States or of Pennsylvania? _____

5. Do you read, write and understand the English Language? _____

6. Do you have any mental or physical infirmity which you feel would interfere with performance of Jury Service? _____ If so, please specify_____

7. Have you been convicted of (or pleaded guilty to) any crime punishable by more than one year in prison? _____ If so, please specify _____
   If you answered YES, have you been granted a pardon? _____

8. Are you a citizen of the United States? _____

   JUROR'S SIGNATURE_____
   PRINTED or TYPEWRITTEN NAME _____

THIS FORM MUST BE COMPLETED AND RETURNED WITHIN FIVE (5) DAYS TO:
Armstrong County Jury Selection Commission
Courthouse
Kittanning, Pennsylvania 16201
See other side fo this sheet for important information.

It is the policy of the Commonwealth of Pennsylvania that all persons entitled to a jury trial in a civil or criminal action shall have the right to jurors selected at random from a representative cross-section of the eligible population of Armstrong County. It is further the policy of this Commonwealth that all qualified citizens shall have the opportunity to be considered for service as jurors in the Courts of this Commonwealth, and shall have an obligation to serve as juror when summoned for that purpose and no citizens shall be excluded from serve as a juror on the basis of race, color, religion, sex, national origin or economic status.

By law, NO PERSON SHALL BE EXEMPT OR EXCUSED FROM JURY DUTY EXCEPT THE FOLLOWING:

1. Persons in active service of the armed forces of the U.S. or Pennsylvania.
2. Persons who have served as jurors within the last three (3) years, except persons who served less than three (3) days, in which case they are exempt for only one year.
3. Persons who can demonstrate to the satisfaction of the Courts that jury service will involve undue hardship or extreme inconvenience.

Excuses from jury service will be granted by the Courts only in clearly eligible cases. If you wish to be excused from jury service, you MUST RETURN THE COMPLETED QUESTIONNAIRE TOGETHER WITH A FULL STATEMENT (below) OF YOUR REASONS FOR REQUESTING EXCUSAL. Please indicate in your statement whether you request permanent excusal or for a limited period of time. Requests for permanent excuse will be granted only in the most extreme cases. If your excuse is for health reasons, you must furnish a doctor's certificate.

REQUEST FOR EXCUSE

JUROR INFORMATION QUESTIONNAIRE
CONFIDENTIAL - NOT PUBLIC RECORD

TYPE OR PRINT USING INK

NAME: LAST	FIRST	MIDDLE INITAL
CITY/TOWNSHIP:	COMMUNITIES IN WHICH YOU RESIDED OVER THE PAST 10 YEARS:*	

MARITAL STATUS: □ MARRIED	□ SINGLE	□ SEPARATED	□ DIVORCED	□ WIDOWED

OCCUPATION	OCCUPATION(S) PAST 10 YEARS
OCCUPATION OF SPOUSE/OTHER	PAST 10 YEARS OCCUPATION OF SPOUSE/OTHER*

NUMBER OF CHILDREN	RACE: □ WHITE □ BLACK □ HISPANIC □ OTHER

LEVEL OF EDUCATION YOURS	SPOUSE/OTHER	CHILDREN*

	YES	NO
1. Do you have any physical or psychological disability or are you presently taking any medication?	□	□
2. Have you ever served as a juror before? If so, were you ever a hung jury?	□	□
3. Do you have any religious, moral or ethical beliefs that would prevent you from sitting in judgement in a criminal case and rendering a fair verdict?	□	□
4. Have you or anyone close to you ever been the victim of a crime?	□	□
5. Have you or anyone close to you ever been charged with or arrested for a crime, other than a traffic violation?	□	□
6. Have you or anyone close to you ever been an eyewitness to a crime, whether or not it ever came to trial?	□	□
7. Have you or anyone close to you ever worked in law enforcement of the justice system? This includes police, prosecutors, attorneys, detectives, security, or prison guards, and court related agencies?	□	□
8. Would you be more likely to believe the testimony of a police officer or any other law enforcement officer because of his or her job?	□	□
9. Would you be less likely to believe the testimony of a police officer or any other law enforcement officer because of his or her job?	□	□
10. Would you have any problem following the court's instruction that the defendant in a criminal case is presumed to be innocent unless and until proven guilty beyond a reasonable doubt?	□	□
11. Would you have any problem following the court's instruction that the defendant in a criminal case does not have to take the stand or present evidence, and it cannot be held against the defendant if he or she elects to remain silent or present no evidence?	□	□
12. Would you have any problem following the court's instruction in a criminal case that just because someone is arrested, it does not mean that person is guilty of anything?	□	□
13. In general, would you have any problem following and applying the judge's instruction on the law?	□	□
14. Would you have any problem during jury deliberation in a criminal case discussing the case fully but still making up your own mind?	□	□
15. Is there any other reason you could not be a fair juror in a criminal case?	□	□

I hereby certify that the answers on this form are true and correct. I understand that false answers provided herein subject me to penalties under 18 Pa.C.S. ss 4904 relating to unsworn falsification to authorities.

Signature_____   Date _____Page #

*Use additional sheets if needed

each side has an unlimited number of strikes for cause (also referred to as "challenge for cause" or "removal for cause"). There is no limit to the number of "for cause" strikes in a jury trial. A juror can be removed for cause in the following circumstances: (1) if he has a medical, physical, or mental condition that would prohibit him from being able to sit on the case or (2) if he has some sort of opinion or mindset that would prohibit him from being able to fairly decide the facts of a case. There is no specific list of what will qualify a juror for being stricken for cause. In a death penalty case, a juror who states that she is unable to render a death sentence for any person would be disqualified for cause. Conversely, anyone who states that a person who is guilty for murder must receive a death sentence could be stricken for cause. A person who is potentially a juror in a criminal case who states that he would always believe what a police officer says over what any other witness would say would most likely be stricken for cause, as would someone who says they would not believe or trust a police officer. Anyone who states that he cannot listen to the evidence and apply the law, as instructed by the judge, could be disqualified for cause. Any strike for cause must be accompanied by a specific reason and the trial judge must grant the strike and both attorneys must agree that cause is present.

Each side, prosecution and defense, will then engage in a series of strikes based on the form the person has filled out and other **voir dire** questions asked to the prospective jurors by either the attorneys or the judge. Voir dire means to "speak the truth." Attorneys can strike any juror they wish based on the juror's answers to these questions and potentially even based on what the juror is wearing or how they seem to "look at the defendant," as long as they are not striking jurors for a reason that the court considers discriminatory. Striking jurors based on race or gender is considered illegal, but it is often difficult to prove that a person was stricken by an opposing attorney for one of those reasons, especially if the attorney striking the juror can point to some other reason (occupation, age) that makes sense. Jurors may be asked voir dire questions in the presence of all other jurors, or in cases such as those involving the death penalty, the judge may bring each juror into his chambers and ask questions with only the attorneys present. One concern present in the selection of jurors is whether prospective jurors actually tell the truth. Consider some of the questions that jurors are asked, for example, in a case involving sexual assault. As you review these questions, consider whether you believe you, or other people you know, would want to answer these questions truthfully in front of either three people you do not know (in the case of a judge and two attorneys considering the questions privately) or in front of a group of, for example, 50 other prospective jurors, some of which you might know and most of whom you do not, while a judge, attorneys, the defendant, and the court reporter also observe and listen.

Questions:

1. Have you ever been the victim of a sexual assault?
2. Has anyone close to you, such as your mother, sister, significant other, or close friend, ever been the victim of a sexual assault?
3. Have you ever been convicted of a crime?
4. Have you ever been accused of a crime involving some form of sexual assault?
5. The defendant in this case is African American and the victim is white. Do you believe this difference in race would tend to influence your decision about whether the defendant committed a crime?

6. Have you ever had any interaction with a police officer? If so, was it a good or a bad interaction? Based on your interaction, do you believe that you would tend to believe a police officer more or less than some other citizen?
7. Do you believe that, because of religious reasons, you should not be passing judgment on the guilt or innocence of other individuals?

As you can see, many of these questions are very intrusive and personal, and they require that a person disclose very private facts. Although many judges try to have jurors answer this type of question in private, jurors are still required to give personal information to people they hardly know. Further, many people may not want to have to discuss their victimization or the victimization of family members or friends, and individuals sometimes cry during jury selection during these types of questions. Nonetheless, can you see how each question can assist either the prosecutor or the defense in attempting to determine whether that particular juror has a bias that might sway the decision he might make in the case? Another problem that could occur because of the types of questions that are asked is that individuals may avoid telling the truth about the issues. Certainly many juries are made up of individuals who claim not to have a prejudice but really do. Note that in death penalty cases, the jury is required to be "death qualified," meaning that no member of the jury can be so fundamentally opposed to the death penalty that he cannot sentence someone to death. A prospective juror can be excluded for cause if he is fundamentally opposed to the death penalty in a death penalty case.

As you can see, theoretically a jury will end up with a group of fairly neutral people, once each side has stricken the jurors it does not want to make a decision on its case. This theory only works, however, if an attorney really knows everything about the prospective jurors and if the jurors are truthful about their past, their views, and their prejudices.

The remaining jurors could be stricken under a limited number of **peremptory challenges** that the prosecution and defense each have. The number of peremptory strikes that each side has varies by state and depends often on whether the defendant is charged with misdemeanor offenses or felonies. Thus, more peremptory strikes will be available in a murder case than in a simple harassment case. Peremptory strikes do not need to be accompanied by a reason. Following are some examples of persons who might be removed from a jury under a peremptory challenge.

Prosecution:

a. A potential juror states that he has previously been arrested and that he has served time in jail, and that he believes he was wrongfully convicted.
b. A potential juror states that he has previously worked in a police agency and he believes that police officers are "out to get" citizens.

c. A potential juror who is being considered for a drug case states that he smokes marijuana and believes that laws that prohibit marijuana possession should be repealed.

d. A potential juror states that he does not believe that the state should be responsible for prosecuting people for crimes and that only God should be responsible for determining whether people have done something wrong.

e. A potential juror states that he watches a lot of crime shows and that he believes that no one can be found guilty unless forensic evidence, such as DNA evidence, is present, linking the defendant to the crime.

Defense:

a. A potential juror states that anyone who has been charged with a crime is most definitely guilty.

b. A potential juror states that he was the victim of a crime three years ago and that he does not believe the perpetrator received enough time in prison.

c. A potential juror states that his brother was murdered and that he has never forgiven the perpetrator and that he still has a difficult time coping with his brother's death.

d. A potential juror states that his cousin is a prison guard and that he believes his cousin when he states that all of the inmates are guilty.

e. A potential juror states that he does not trust Hispanic people; the defendant is Hispanic.

In most cases, a juror who makes statements such as the preceding statements, will be questioned further as to whether he believes he can set aside his bias and consider the case on its merits. However, even those who indicate they can do so might be stricken. Sometimes attorneys tend to strike people who hold a certain occupation, such as a teacher or a social worker, thinking that those people might be, for example, sympathetic to defendants. Once prospective jury members are stricken by each side, a certain number of the remaining jurors will make up the jury. A jury that has been selected is **impaneled**.

Because attorneys do not need to state any reason for exercising their peremptory challenges, generally these challenges cannot be argued against by the opposing side. However, occasionally a defendant can argue that a prosecutor struck a certain group of jurors in a discriminatory manner. These challenges are very narrowly defined by the Supreme Court. In **Batson v. Kentucky**,[21] the Supreme Court ruled that peremptory challenges that result in the exclusion of certain cognizable groups can be challenged. This is known as a **Batson** challenge and is normally argued by the defense to challenge peremptory challenges asserted by the prosecution.

---

21. 476 U.S. 79 (1986).

The specific group that the **Batson** case refers to is that of race. Batson was an African-American man charged with burglary and receiving stolen goods. His jury was composed entirely of white jurors. The prosecutor had peremptorily challenged six jurors, including all four African-American jurors who had initially been on the jury panel. The defendant argued that his right to have a jury drawn from a cross section of the community and his equal protection rights had been violated by the prosecution striking all of the potential black jurors. The Supreme Court stated that a prosecutor cannot strike all black jurors merely because they are black. Although the prosecutor argued that he had stricken the potential black jurors because they were young and might thus sympathize with the defendant, the Supreme Court nevertheless remanded the case for a new trial. However, the defense would need to prove that the race of the jurors was the sole reason they had been stricken in his case. The Court specifically stated as follows:

> The defendant initially must show that he is a member of a racial group capable of being singled out for differential treatment . . . In combination with that evidence, a defendant may then make a prima facie case by proving that in the particular jurisdiction members of his race have not been summoned for jury service over an extended period of time.[22]

The **Batson** decision has been expanded to apply to civil cases and has further been expanded to sex-based peremptory challenges, prohibiting the striking of female jurors in a sexual assault case involving a female victim. Realistically, it is difficult to prove that a potential juror is being stricken based solely on race or sex. As long as the prosecutor argues that there is some other reason for striking the person, including anything that is disclosed on the jury questionnaire or orally during the voir dire process, a defendant's challenge to that person being stricken will probably not succeed.

The issue of race was a major point of discussion following the 1995 acquittal of O.J. Simpson of charges of killing his wife and her friend. O.J. Simpson was black and his wife and her friend were white. The jury was composed of nine blacks, one Hispanic, and one white. Many opine that the acquittal verdict was a result of the race of the jury. In contrast, in 1992, a jury composed of mostly whites acquitted police officers who were caught on videotape beating a man named Rodney King, who was pulled over following a high-speed car chase in 1991. Even the officers who were not beating King did nothing to stop what many consider to be an excessive beating by the other officers. The acquittals of the officers are blamed for triggering riots in Los Angeles in which 53 people were killed and over 2,000 were injured. Of course, even if jurors are questioned

---

22. **Id.** at 86.

as to why they rendered a certain verdict in a case, it is unlikely that they would admit if their decision was based solely on racial grounds. Further, a juror could subconsciously include the race of a defendant in his final decision without consciously realizing that race influenced his decision.

Note that a person does not have the right to a jury if she is charged with a crime that is considered "petty." In **Baldwin v. New York**,[23] the Supreme Court acknowledged that disadvantages certainly exist when defendants are denied the right to have a jury trial. However, the advantage to the system of denying a jury trial is that adjudications can be speedier and spare expense in the court system. The most difficult part of this rule is that it is impossible to determine exactly what is considered "petty," but generally lower level offenses, including summary offenses and sometimes third-degree misdemeanors, are considered petty.

Although jury members are normally selected from the community in which the trial will take place, sometimes community members are biased if there has been excessive media coverage of the crime or if many community members were directly affected by the crime. For example, when terrorists hijacked and flew airplanes into the World Trade Center in New York City on September 11, 2001, everyone in the United States was deeply affected, but especially those individuals who resided in New York City. The trial of some of the conspiring terrorists was moved from New York City so that jury members would not be those who were closest to the situation. Similarly, when the Oklahoma City Federal Building was bombed in 1995 by Timothy McVeigh, McVeigh's trial was moved out of Oklahoma City due to the fact that many people in Oklahoma City knew someone who was affected by the many lives that were taken in that act of domestic terrorism. When a trial is moved so that a jury from outside the area hears the case, a **change of venue** occurs. Sometimes rather than moving the trial itself, which is rather expensive and inconvenient due to the fact that the judge, court staff, and all of the witnesses and attorneys also have to go to a different location, the court brings in jurors from another area. This is referred to as a **change of venire**. A change in venire also brings about expense due to the fact that jury members will need to be housed during the course of the trial and their travel expenses and meals will need to be provided by the court. Jury members who have to travel to a different jurisdiction will also generally have to take more days off work and spend time away from their families in the evenings if the trial takes more than one day. Unfortunately, jurors are not compensated for this sort of expense and receive only a very small stipend each day for serving as a juror.

---

23. 399 U.S. 66 (1970).

YOU BE THE JUDGE

In this case, assume you are an attorney, either prosecuting the case or defending the accused. Assume that you are conducting jury selection based on the following case and that you are selecting nine jurors. What type of jurors would you want?

The defendant in this case is Johnny Rodriguez, a 35-year-old Hispanic male. He is on trial for first-degree murder. Rodriguez was driving his 2001 Toyota Camry north on Interstate 79 about 5 miles south of Meadville, Pennsylvania, when he was pulled over by a Pennsylvania state police officer for speeding and a broken tail light. The Officer, Trooper Joseph Swanson, asked to see Rodriguez's driver's license, registration, and proof of insurance; Rodriguez indicated that he had none of those documents. Rodriguez was also acting very nervous; he was looking around constantly and his hands were shaking. Trooper Swanson asked Rodriguez if he could search Rodriguez's car; Rodriguez agreed to the search. Trooper Swanson looked in the back seat of the car and noticed a substance that appeared to be spatters of blood on the seat. He then asked Rodriguez to open the trunk; Rodriguez did and Trooper Swanson was shocked to find the corpse of a woman who was later identified as Charlene Brown, a 30-year-old prostitute from Conneaut Lake, Pennsylvania. Rodriguez denied having anything to do with Brown's death and indicated to Trooper Swanson that the vehicle he was driving belonged to a friend of his by the name of Tyrone Jones. Jones indicates that the vehicle does belong to him but that Rodriguez had borrowed it from him two days prior to the Trooper's discovery of the body and that Jones knew nothing about Brown or her death.

Prospective jurors are the following persons:

JURORS

NAME	AGE	GENDER	RACE
1. Jeremy Crocket	26	Male	White

—Truck mechanic whose sister was sexually assaulted by a Hispanic male

2. Shirley Johanson	25	Female	White

—Thinks that if a person is on trial he must be guilty

3. Jose Martinez	45	Male	Hispanic

—Devout Catholic whose mother was killed by a drunk driver

4. Jackson Vandemer	8	Male	White

—Truck driver whose brother was murdered while being carjacked

5. Dequan Waynewright   31   Male   Black
    —Works in construction and is very devoted to his wife and three children

6. Shaquisha Thomas   43   Female   Black
    —Full-time nursing student who also works at a local restaurant as a hostess

7. Jimmy Jordon   25   Male   White
    —Unemployed and is on disability due to an on-the-job injury

8. Roberta Swaggart   58   Female   Black
    —Divorced and works three jobs to help put her son through law school

9. Tom Smith   21   Male   White
    —College student majoring in engineering

10. Sue Gistlinger   30   Female   White
    —Waitress at a local restaurant who is attending college at night, majoring in
       criminal justice

11. Ray Sieklucki   70   Male   White
    —Retired from a local manufacturing shop; once received a speeding ticket from
       a police officer who he felt "roughed him up" a bit

12. Sarah Molino   32   Female   White
    —Was sexually assaulted by three fraternity brothers when she was in college

Which of the preceding persons do you want to be on your jury? Who do you strike based on the fact that you believe that person would be advantageous for the opposing side to have on the jury? Which of the prospective jurors who you would want on your side do you believe your opponent would most want to strike? Why?

Right to Compulsory Process

The Sixth Amendment provides that a defendant can utilize the power of a **subpoena** to obtain witnesses, documents, and other evidence that could assist him in presenting his case. A subpoena is a writ issued by a government agency that requires a person to either attend a hearing and testify, produce documents or records, or both. The word comes from the Latin term *subpoena*, meaning "under penalty." Subpoenas were used at common law and are now called "witness summons" in England. A subpoena can be necessary for many reasons. First, there are circumstances in which

FIGURE 8.4. SAMPLE SUBPOENA TO ATTEND AND TESTIFY

COMMONWEALTH OF PENNSYLVANIA
COUNTY OF ERIE

:
:
:
v.   :   NO.
:
:
:

SUBPOENA TO ATTEND AND TESTIFY

TO:

1.   You are ordered by the Court to come to:

(Specify Courtroom or other place)

at   , Pennsylvania, on
at   o'clock,   M., to testify on behalf of _____
_____in the above case, and to remain until excused.

2. And bring with you the following:

If you fail to attend or to produce the documents or things required by this subpoena, you may be subject to the sanctions authorized by Rule 234.5 of the Pennsylvania Rules of Civil Procedure, including but not limited to costs, attorney fees and imprisonment.

REQUESTED BY A PARTY/ATTORNEY IN COMPLIANCE WITH Pa.R.C.P. No. 234.2(a):

NAME: _____
ADDRESS:_____
_____

TELEPHONE: _____
SUPREME COURT ID #_____

BY THE COURT:

_____
Prothonotary

_____
Date: _____   Deputy
Seal of the Court

OFFICIAL NOTE: This form of subpoena shall be used whenever a subpoena is issuable, including hearings in connection with depositions and before arbitrators, masters, commissioners, etc. in compliance with Pa.R.C.P. No. 234.1. If a subpoena for production of documents, records or things is desired, complete paragraph 2.

Return of Service (Reverse Side of Subpoena)

On the _____ day of _____, _____, I, _____
served _____ (name of person served) with the
foregoing subpoena by : (Describe method of service)

_____

_____

I verify that the statements in this return of service are true and correct. I
understand that false statements herein are made subject to the penalties of 18 Pa.C.S.A.
Sect. 4904 relating to unsworn falsification to authorities.

Date: _____

_____
(signature)

witnesses, including victims, do not wish to attend a hearing and testify.
This could be because they feel intimidated, because it is too emotional
for them, or just because they do not wish to take the time to come to
the hearing. Once a court has issued a subpoena and served it on a person,
however, that person is required to come to court on the appointed date
and time or suffer the possibility of being held in contempt of a court
order and potentially being put in prison. Of course, a person who
issues a subpoena to another person must decide whether she actually
wants that person to attend a hearing and testify if the person does not
wish to attend and testify. However, the fact remains that a person is supposed to take an oath of veracity and tell the truth regarding any questions
that are posed of him. Subpoenas to produce documents or records are
often served on organizations such as a phone service provider to obtain
phone records relating to a case or a hospital relating to hospital records for
an individual.

A subpoena must generally be served in person and some states
require that a person who is going to issue a subpoena on an entity or
person first advise the other side of its intent so the other side can object
if any objections are appropriate. The most common objection would be
based on the argument that the information to be received through the
subpoena or the testimony to be given by a subpoenaed witness is not relevant to the case at hand. See Figure 8.4 for a sample of a subpoena to
attend and testify.

A landmark case in the area of compulsory process was that of
Washington v. Texas.[24]

---

24. 388 U.S. 14 (1967).

WASHINGTON V. TEXAS

FACTS: A Texas law restricted the ability of a defendant to call witnesses to speak on his behalf by prohibiting co-defendants (or, as stated in the statute, "co-participants") from testifying for each other. The rationale behind the law was that the co-defendants would be very likely to lie for each other. Jackie Washington was convicted of first-degree murder and sentenced to 50 years in prison. Washington testified on his own behalf at trial and blamed his accomplice, Charles Fuller, for the majority of the crime. He indicated that Fuller had been carrying the murder weapon at the scene of the crime and he requested that Fuller be able to testify on his behalf. The Court did not permit Fuller to testify because of the Texas statute, which, interestingly, did not prohibit the state from calling witnesses who were co-participants, if it wished to do so. Washington's conviction was upheld by the Texas Court of Criminal Appeals and it was then appealed to the Supreme Court.

ISSUE: Does the due process clause of the Fourteenth Amendment require states to follow the compulsory process rule of the Sixth Amendment?

HOLDING: States must follow the compulsory process rule, and prohibiting co-defendants from testifying at one another's trial violates the rule.

RATIONALE: The right to offer the testimony of witnesses is critical to a defendant's ability to present a defense by setting forth his version of the facts. The Court did not appreciate the disparity in the law that permitted the co-defendant's testimony to be used if it would help the prosecution but not if it would favor the defense. Thus, the law was arbitrary. Juries evaluate the truth of a witness's testimony and can do so in the case of a co-defendant. A court can determine whether a co-defendant's testimony is **material**, or significant to the matter at hand, and could deny the testimony for that reason, but not merely because the witness is a co-defendant.

A court must balance the defendant's right to compulsory process against other factors such as courtroom efficiency and costs. In fact, in the case of **Taylor v. Illinois**,[25] the Supreme Court determined that the testimony of a "surprise witness" presented by the defendant can be stricken, despite the compulsory process clause. A defendant has to cooperate with rules of evidence when presenting witnesses. The opinion of the Court stated that although "few rights are more fundamental than that of an accused to present witnesses in his own defense," the clause cannot be used irresponsibly by a client who refuses to or fails to follow the basic rules of the Court.

---

25. 484 U.S. 400 (1988).

YOU BE THE JUDGE

Defendant Valenzuela-Bernal is accused of transporting narcotics. The defendant was arrested with three other people who happened to be immigrants who were illegally in the country. Immigration officials want to deport the immigrants and take the position that the potential testimony of two of the three individuals would not be necessary for the prosecution of the case. Those two individuals are then deported. The defendant argues that he had a right to have those two individuals testify if he so desired and that an inability to do so would be a violation of his right to compulsory process. Does the government's interest in deporting the aliens so that the United States was no longer paying for their living and housing expenses outweigh the argument that the testimony of the two men was necessary for the defendant's case? Would it make a difference what type of testimony the two men were planning on offering?

THE TRIAL

Opening Statements

Trials always begin and end the same, with the prosecutor's words. (See Figure 8.5 for an overview of the course of a typical trial.) The prosecutor has the burden of proof and thus is able to present the first word and the last word to the jury. Following a few introductory words by the judge, the prosecutor opens the trial with his **opening statement** and the defense follows with its own in some states and waits until the prosecution has entered all of its evidence in others. Some states permit the defense to choose when it will present its opening statement. The purpose of an opening statement is to provide an overview of the case to the jury so its members can follow the evidence that the prosecutor expects to present. Evidence is only presented in a trial through the use of testimony of witnesses and is often disjointed and cannot always be presented in a manner that is easy to follow. If the jury knows the story behind the case and the general theory of the prosecutor's and defendant's case prior to hearing the evidence of the case, it will be able to better understand why certain evidence is being presented in the case. For example, in a case in which a defendant is being accused of robbing a gas station and the victim of the robbery who identified the robber describes him as having a bushy mustache and beard, it might be important to call as witnesses people who have worked with the defendant and can testify that he had a beard and mustache until the week before trial, when he shaved it off. However, if these witnesses present their testimony before the victim does, the jury might not understand why the witnesses are discussing the defendant's facial hair. An opening statement by the prosecutor that states

FIGURE 8.5. MOVEMENT OF CASE THROUGH CRIMINAL JUSTICE SYSTEM, PART 2

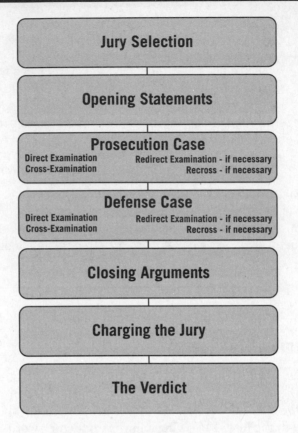

that it is believed that the defendant shaved his facial hair before trial because he would be claiming he was not the robber would assist the jury in determining the importance of this testimony. Anything either the prosecuting or defense attorney states in an opening statement involves what she predicts the evidence at trial will show and the jury will be told that the statements are not to be considered evidence. Occasionally a witness says something totally different from what an attorney believes that person is going to say and thus the jury must be informed that it should consider the witness's testimony as evidence and not the attorney's interpretation or prediction of it.

Presentation of Witnesses

Following opening statements by the prosecution and, sometimes, by the defense, the prosecution will present all of its witnesses. Although the presentation of the case generally begins with the police officer who investigated the case or the witness testifying, occasionally a witness who is an expert, for example, in firearms or DNA evidence, will begin the testimony. All evidence that is presented must come into the record through a witness. Pictures that are to be used must be authenticated by the person who took the photographs or at least by someone who can testify that the photographs accurately represent the scene as it appeared at or near the time of the crime. Occasionally the prosecution and defense will agree that certain pieces of evidence, including reports of experts, can be utilized as evidence through a **stipulation**, or agreement of both sides, without a person having to testify about the evidence. However, most evidence is not stipulated to and must be presented by the side that hopes to utilize the evidence in support of its case.

The prosecution will ask questions of each witness that it calls through **direct examination** and the defense will then ask questions of the witness via **cross-examination**. This cycle can repeat indefinitely, although eventually a trial judge could determine that all relevant questions have been asked and answered and can cut off the questioning. Cross-examination is used to try to show that a witness is biased or is lying, or that he is not telling the entire story. Any questions that can place doubt in the minds of jurors can be effective. Some attorneys believe, however, in the theory that you should never ask a question you do not know the answer to—if a witness has a good answer to a question asked on cross-examination, that question can actually bolster that witness's veracity in front of the jury. Occasionally a witness will be recalled to testify again if a subsequently testifying witness states a fact the first witness could verify or rebut in some way.

Motions by the Defense

Because the prosecution is required to meet the burden of proof beyond a reasonable doubt when prosecuting a case, it is possible that following the prosecution's presentation of all of its witnesses, the defense will request that the court grant a **motion for acquittal**. If the prosecution has not presented sufficient evidence to establish the crimes for which it is prosecuting the defendant, the court will grant this motion. Although it is rare for such motions to be granted, sometimes witnesses do not testify the way the prosecution believes they will or witnesses fail to show up for trial and thus sufficient evidence is not presented to sustain some or all of the charges.

Assuming the motion for acquittal is not granted by the judge, the defense will present its case. In some cases, the defense has no witnesses and the defendant chooses not to testify; then, the defense will rest without presenting evidence. Because the prosecution has the burden of proof, it is possible that this tactic could work. The jury would then base its decision on whether or not it believes that the prosecution's witnesses are indeed telling the truth. Following the presentation of any witnesses and the testimony of the defendant, if he chooses to testify, the defense will rest its case. Each side can then call rebuttal witnesses if necessary, to offer evidence that contradicts what a prior witness stated. The defense attorney might at this point make a motion for a **directed verdict**, arguing that when all evidence from both sides was considered, there is no way a jury could rule in the favor of the prosecution. Rarely are these types of motions sustained, as the judge would have to rule that the evidence that was presented could not possibly sustain the verdict. A reviewing court does not have the right to decide which witnesses are lying and which are telling the truth. The jury's decision as to the honesty of witnesses will always stand.

A third possible motion that could be made during a trial that would end the trial is a **motion for a mistrial**. Any time the jury hears information that is forbidden to it during a trial, a mistrial can be declared. The trial would end, and the prosecutor would have to determine whether to retry the defendant. (Double jeopardy generally does not apply in the case of a mistrial.) Normally, the defendant would request a mistrial, as evidence that generally results in a mistrial is most often something that could cause prejudice against the defendant. For example, a judge may have ruled that a defendant's prior criminal record should not be mentioned at trial. A witness might be testifying as to his knowledge about the defendant and might "accidentally" state that he knew that the defendant had a prior criminal record. This could be so prejudicial in the minds of the members of the jury that the judge will determine that the trial cannot go on.

Closing Arguments

Assuming the trial continues with no mistrial and no motion for directed verdict or acquittal being granted, closing arguments will be presented. This allows each side to summarize the evidence that was presented during trial and point out flaws or weaknesses in the other side's case. Again, information stated in the closing arguments is not considered evidence and if an attorney states that certain evidence was presented that was not, the opposing side can object to that statement. Attorneys also should not state their own beliefs about whether or not the defendant is guilty or any other improper remarks that would or could prejudice the jury.

Jury Deliberations

Once a jury is seated and has heard all evidence and arguments, the jury will receive **jury instructions** from the judge. These instructions include information about the law in general, the burden of proof which is required to be met in the case, and the specific law that applies to the case. States usually have standard jury instructions that are used by the courts, and attorneys will also prepare jury instructions to present to the court. In some states, jury instructions are given prior to the closing arguments. Jury instructions can be very long and, frankly, fairly boring and confusing to jury members. After sitting through days and potentially weeks of testimony and opening and closing arguments, it is sometimes difficult for jury members to concentrate on a long soliloquy by the judge in which rules and laws that relate to the case are set forth. Think about how many days you might have spent in an introductory criminal justice class discussing different types of crimes that are committed and the elements of each of those crimes. It may take you a few readings to understand the law. Now imagine you are a juror with no knowledge of the criminal justice system and that you are being asked to listen to the definitions of several crimes read to you by a judge and then apply the facts to those definitions. In some states, jurors are not even allowed to take notes. It can be very difficult to remember all of the important parts of the testimony that was given by witnesses plus all of the judge's instructions. Jurors may ask questions of the judge while deliberating but the questions must be asked in open court with all attorneys and the defendant present. Often jurors ask that the court reporter who sat in on the proceedings and kept a record of every word that was said during the trial read back the testimony, verbatim, from a certain witness, or that the judge further explain a point of law. Jurors are requested to pick one of the members as the "foreperson," who is responsible for communicating with the judge if questions are necessary and for keeping order and control in the jury room.

A jury deliberates alone, in a separate room off the courtroom, so that no outside forces can influence its decision. Thus, we generally know little about what has happened within the jury room or why a jury decided a case in a certain way. Jurors can talk about their deliberations after the trial has ended and they are dismissed, but they do not have to, and often jurors are reluctant to talk about the case when it is over. Jurors generally take their job very seriously and realize that their decision will affect a person's life for years to come. After the jury has made its decision, the jury members will again enter the courtroom and will be seated. Some judges or other court personnel announce the verdict, and in some cases, the jury foreperson will announce the verdict. The defendant may request that the jury be polled, especially in a case when the jury has declared that the defendant is guilty. **Polling the jury** is a request, generally made by a defense attorney in the case of a "guilty" verdict, to have each jury member publically state how he personally voted. Although generally each member does state the way he voted, occasionally if a juror feels as though he was pressured into voting a certain way, he might change his verdict once he has to stand in front of the defendant and state his verdict.

Occasionally, a jury is unable to come to a decision in a case. Criminal verdicts in many states must be unanimous and occasionally jurors may not all be able to agree on the outcome of a case. In this type of situation, a judge will normally speak to the jury and encourage the group to try again and to listen to each other and consider each other's points of view. However, if the jury is absolutely unable to make a determination as to the outcome of the case, a **hung jury** will result. When a jury is hung, its members do not believe that a decision will ever be reached. The jury is dismissed and the prosecutor will have to retry the defendant. The jurors do not have to, but can, speak to the prosecutor and defense attorney and their insights may assist the attorneys in prosecuting or defending the case if it is retried. A retrial of a case after a hung jury does not give rise to a double jeopardy issue. Occasionally a prosecutor will decide not to retry a case in which a hung jury resulted or will enter into a plea bargain with the defendant rather than risking the possibility of a subsequent jury finding the defendant not guilty.

The Supreme Court has approved of verdicts that are not unanimous if a state's law permits, for example, a 10-2 verdict. In **Apodaca v. Oregon,**[26] the Supreme Court permitted states to allow a less than unanimous verdict. The **Apodaca** case involved two different defendants, one convicted by a 11-1 verdict and the other convicted by a 10-2 verdict. The majority opinion of the Court held that a defendant does not have a constitutional right to a unanimous verdict. A concurring opinion of the Court stated that although the Sixth Amendment requires a unanimous verdict, the Fourteenth Amendment does not require incorporating that requirement to the states. The Court pointed out that when the Sixth Amendment was being proposed, it originally contained a unanimity requirement but that requirement was deleted as the amendment moved through various committees and the two branches of Congress. The Court stated that a jury trial is important as neutral jurists safeguard against corrupt judges, but that unanimity does not necessarily contribute to that common sense element. The defendants argued that to allow less than unanimous verdicts permits verdicts that are not based on a "cross-section of the community," which is a requirement for jurists. In other words, perhaps there are two minority members of a jury and those two members are the ones who vote not guilty, while the jurists who represent the majority of the community vote guilty. Such a verdict would be allowing the majority members to rule with no consideration of the voice of the minority members. The Court stated that as long as the minority members are not systematically excluded from the jury, the process is fair.

The Supreme Court also discussed the required size of juries in the case of **Ballew v. Georgia.**[27] Ballew was found guilty of a misdemeanor for exhibiting an obscene film. His conviction was handed down by a jury that consisted only of five members. The Supreme Court found that a trial by jury of only five members violated Ballew's right to a trial by jury as protected by the Sixth and Fourteenth Amendments. States did have to provide a certain number of jurists as that provision of the Sixth Amendment was important enough to be incorporated to the states. The Court stated that a jury must comprise a minimum of six people. The Court's reasoning was based on its belief that small juries cannot foster appropriate group deliberation. Jurists must remember the details that were presented to them in the trial, and this is difficult with fewer members. Further, the more jurors there are, the less likely one is to compromise her true beliefs about the case, and the jurors are less likely to be "self-critical and reflective" as jury size shrinks. The Court also considered statistics that supported the fact that the verdicts of smaller juries tended to be erroneous.

26. 406 U.S. 404 (1972).
27. 435 U.S. 223 (1978).

SENTENCING

A defendant has certain constitutional rights when he is being sentenced. Although a judge must obviously sentence within any statutory requirements that exist in a state or in the federal system, there are some general constitutional provisions that a judge must abide by as well, and sentencing statute schemes can be stricken down as being unconstitutional. The punishment a defendant receives should reflect the seriousness of the crime. Many states have passed laws that mandate certain sentences for certain crimes or enhance the regular sentence with more time if, for example, the crime is committed with a weapon. States have also passed laws referred to as **three strikes** laws, which mandate that a person who is convicted of three or more serious criminal offenses (generally felonies) receive a sentence of 25 years in prison to life. These laws were passed under the assumption that a person who has committed three serious crimes is likely to offend again and that he must be incapacitated by being in prison. The Supreme Court has upheld these laws as being constitutional. Although defendants argued that the laws were unconstitutional under the "cruel and unusual" provisions of the Eighth Amendment, the Supreme Court rejected that claim in **Ewing v. California**.[28] The facts of the case were interesting in that the crimes the defendant, Gary Ewing, committed did not seem particularly serious. Ewing had committed a theft in 1984, felony grand theft auto in 1988, petty theft in 1990, battery in 1992, burglary and several other crimes in 1993, and robbery, along with some other offenses, also in 1993. In 1999, he was paroled from prison and while on parole, in 2000, Ewing stole three golf clubs worth $399.00 each from a pro golf shop. He was convicted of felony grand theft of personal property and the judge chose to imprison Ewing to 25 years to life under California's three strikes statute. Ewing argued that the sentence was disproportionate to the crime; the court stated that Ewing's criminal history made the sentence appropriate.

The Supreme Court considered the case and compared it to prior cases in which it had upheld fairly long sentences for seemingly minor crimes. The Court's opinion focused on the current "trends" in criminal sentencing. The Court stated that three strikes laws "respond to widespread public concerns about crime by targeting the class of offenders who pose the greatest threat to public safety: career criminals." The Supreme Court stated that it would not second guess policy choices made in sentencing laws in various states. As long as the State of California had a reasonable basis for believing that dramatically enhanced sentences assisted the state in advancing the goals of its criminal justice system, the laws would be upheld. Regarding the fact that the current crime was fairly minor, the Court stated, "[i]n weighing the gravity of Ewing's offense, we must place on the scales not only his current felony, but also his

---

28. 538 U.S. 11 (2003). The Supreme Court decided another case on the same day which also upheld these types of laws in the case of **Lockyer v. Andrade**, 538 U.S. 63 (2003).

long history of felony recidivism. Any other approach would fail to accord proper deference to the policy judgments that find expression in the legislature's choice of sanctions."[29] Although Ewing's sentence was long, it reflected a rational judgment, which the court said it would defer to, that offenders who have committed serious felony offenses must be incapacitated so they do not commit further crimes. The issue of the Eighth Amendment cruel and unusual clause as it relates to the death penalty will be discussed later in this chapter.

The Supreme Court rendered a decision in 2012 that struck down a common sentencing scheme as it related to juveniles who committed murders. Many states' sentencing codes permitted a judge to sentence a juvenile who was tried as an adult and convicted of murder to be sentenced to life in prison without the possibility of parole. The Supreme Court ruled that these sentencing statutes were unconstitutional and violated the cruel and unusual provision of the Eighth Amendment. The Court ruled that judges must consider a defendant's youth and the nature of the crime he committed before issuing such a sentence. Previously, in the case of **Graham v. Florida**,[30] decided in 2010, the Court had determined that juvenile life without parole sentences are unconstitutional for cases in which the juvenile did not commit murder. In **Miller v. Alabama**, the Court extended this ruling to murder cases, stating that "[m]andatory life without parole for a juvenile precludes consideration of his chronological age and its hallmark features—among them, immaturity, impetuosity, and failure to appreciate risks and consequences."[31] Further, such a sentence "prevents taking into account the family and home environment that surrounds him—and from which he cannot usually extricate himself—no matter how brutal or dysfunctional."[32] The Court's ruling did not say that a judge can never sentence a juvenile to a life without the possibility of parole, but rather mandated that a judge should consider all facts and circumstances before handing down a sentence, rather than blindly following a sentencing code.

Another right a defendant has at the time of sentencing is the right to have an attorney present during the sentencing process[33] and to have that attorney be effective. Defendant's counsel should make an investigation into the defendant's background and personal history and should review the pre-sentence investigation report prior to the sentencing proceeding and bring any errors to the court's attention. As with any other effectiveness of counsel claim, a defendant arguing that her counsel was ineffective at the sentencing hearing must show not only that counsel failed to act as any other attorney in the same situation would act; she must also prove that the attorney's failure to act in a certain way prejudiced her case.

---

29. **Id**. at 29.
30. 560 U.S. ___ (decided May 17, 2010).
31. **Id**. at ___.
32. **Id**. at ___.
33. **Mempa v. Rhay**, 389 U.S. 128 (1967).

Finally, in many states a defendant has the right to speak on his own behalf at a sentencing hearing. Although this has not been mandated by the United States Constitution, many states have specifically included this right in their criminal code, as has the federal government. A defendant generally will apologize to the court and potentially to the victim for her actions and will bring information to the court which might sway the court to be more lenient in passing its sentence. States often provide this same right to victims who might wish to address the court at the time of sentencing and explain the impact the crime has had on them and their family. Although often victims request that the court be harsh with the defendant, sometimes victims request that the court be more lenient with the defendant.

YOU BE THE JUDGE

You are going to sentence a defendant, Antonio Barney, following a guilty plea that he entered. He pleaded to possession of a firearm without a license. He was frisked by police while standing outside a store in a high crime area of town. He did not threaten to use the weapon and he did not give the police any problems when he was arrested. The sentencing guidelines that govern the case provide that he can receive 12 to 24 months in prison for the crime or that he can receive a sentence of probation for up to 3 years. Barney is 22 years old and has a 2-year-old son who he cares for. His record includes one prior criminal act that he committed when he was 16 years old. At that time, he was in a fight in school with another boy who had threatened to rape Barney's sister. Barney is currently attending a local trade school to become an electrician. Barney's attorney states that due to his young age, his responsibility for his son, and the fact that he was not causing any problems at the store and just happened to be "at the wrong place at the wrong time," Barney should be sentenced in the lower range of the guidelines. The prosecutor argues that Barney is a menace to society. He questions why Barney would have had a gun near the store if he didn't intend to use it and points to Barney's juvenile record as an indication that Barney has a temper. How will you sentence Barney? Why?

THE EIGHTH AMENDMENT

Cruel and Unusual Punishment

The issue of what constitutes cruel and unusual punishment and whether capital punishment is cruel and unusual has been debated in our country since its inception and will, most likely, continue to be debated unless or until it is abolished. Although many have moral concerns about the imposition of death as a sentence for crime, the Supreme Court has considered the question in relation to whether or not it is actually unconstitutional for the state to put someone to death. The Eighth Amendment forbids punishments that are cruel and unusual. Why did the framers put this provision into the Constitution?

The British Magna Carta of 1215 suggested that punishments should fit the crime and that a small crime deserved a small punishment, including fines levied. (The Eighth Amendment also provides that fines should not be excessive.) The English Bill of Rights, written by Parliament in 1689, included the same language as that of the Eighth Amendment to the Constitution, regarding no excessive bail, excessive fines, or cruel and unusual punishment. The provision was placed in the English Bill of Rights as a reaction to the case of Titus Oates, who was convicted of lying in court. Several people had been executed as a result of the untrue statements that Oates had made. Oates then received imprisonment as a punishment but also received a further punishment, to be carried out annually, which included being confined in a pillory (stocks) for two days and then being whipped while tied to a moving cart for the third day. This case, and especially the fact that the punishment was to be carried out year after year, was a concern discussed by parliament when deciding to prohibit cruel and unusual punishment.

In terms of sentencing (other than capital punishment, which will be discussed later), the Supreme Court has looked at three strikes laws. California was the first state to pass a three strikes law, which provides for automatic high sentences once a defendant has committed three crimes. The Court has ruled that these types of sentencing schemes do not constitute cruel and unusual punishment. In 1978 in **Ingraham v. Wright**,[34] the Supreme Court ruled that the state can impose corporal punishment (such as paddling) in public schools, but that schools differ from prisons in that the public is involved enough in schools to be able to monitor any inappropriate punishment that takes place. So far, the Supreme Court has not changed its opinion on this topic, although most schools do not inflict corporal punishment today for fear of civil lawsuits and community outrage.

One issue regarding cruel and unusual punishment is that of prison conditions. Poor prison conditions can be unconstitutional, as long as an inmate can prove that conditions are objectively cruel and unusual and that they exist because of officials' deliberate indifference. These conditions can include ignoring an inmate's medical needs, exposure to second-hand cigarette smoke, and some forms of physical punishment, including certain types of restraining chairs and handcuffing an inmate to a post. The current use of chain gangs has been argued to be cruel and unusual, but so far the Supreme Court has not ruled that this form of punishment is cruel and unusual.

---

34. 430 U.S. 651 (1977).

Capital Punishment

The issue of handing down death as a sentence was not a concern when the Eight Amendment was written. The Supreme Court considered the issue of cruel and unusual punishment as it related to a death sentence as early as 1879 in the case of **Wilkerson v. Utah**.[35] The State of Utah had passed a law that permitted anyone convicted of a capital offense to be executed by being shot, hanged, or beheaded, with the defendant having the option of choosing the method. Wilkerson was found guilty by a jury trial of committing murder in the first degree and chose to be publicly shot. The Supreme Court upheld the sentence, referring to the English laws, which also permitted death as a sentence. However, the Court indicated that other types of capital punishment that had been used previously, including drawing and quartering a person, burning someone alive, disemboweling a person, or publically dissecting a person, would be considered cruel and unusual. Thus, although capital punishment was not cruel and unusual, certain methods of carrying it out could be, according to the Court.

In 1958, the Court again considered the issue of capital punishment, ruling that the Court should focus on the evolving standards of decency in society when considering the issue. In **Trop v. Dulles**,[36] the Court considered the case of a soldier whose citizenship had been taken away due to his being found guilty of desertion of the army. The Court stated that the penalty was too high for that crime. Although the case was not a death penalty case, the idea of evolving standards of justice has guided the Court's decisions since that case, including both death penalty case and other punishment issues.

Arguably, the most important case decided by the Supreme Court regarding capital punishment was **Furman v. Georgia**,[37] decided in 1972. Furman had robbed a person's house in the middle of the night, and he stated that when he was attempting to leave the house, he tripped and the weapon he was carrying accidentally discharged, killing one of the homeowners. He had previously told the police that he had fired a shot blindly while leaving. Regardless, under the **felony murder rule**, which states that anyone who commits a murder while committing another felony is guilty of a crime punishable by death, Furman was convicted of murder and sentenced to death. He appealed his case and it made its way up to the Supreme Court. Two other cases were consolidated with Furman's and both involved rape and not murder.

The Court's ruling was a 5-4 decision, with each justice writing his own opinion and very few judges agreeing with each other. The Court's overall ruling was that the automatic imposition of the death penalty in felony murder cases was unconstitutional. Some of the opinions focused on the unconstitutionality in general of the death penalty in terms of cruel and unusual punishment; others involved the arbitrary nature with which states had imposed

---

35. 99 U.S. 130 (1879).
36. 356 U.S. 86 (1958).
37. 408 U.S. 238 (1972).

the death penalty, discussing the racial bias against black defendants in particular that seemed to be present. None of the justices agreed completely on the rationale behind their decision but the 5-4 decision did abolish the death penalty as it was currently administered.

A writer of one of the majority opinions, Justice Potter Stewart, stated as follows:

> These death sentences are cruel and unusual in the same way that being struck by lightning is cruel and unusual. For, of all the people convicted of rapes and murders in 1967 and 1968, many just as reprehensible as these, the petitioners are among a capriciously selected random handful upon whom the sentence of death has in fact been imposed. My concurring Brothers have demonstrated that, if any basis can be discerned for the selection of these few to be sentenced to death, it is the constitutionally impermissible basis of race. . . . But racial discrimination has not been proved, and I put it to one side. I simply conclude that the Eighth and Fourteenth Amendments cannot tolerate the infliction of a sentence of death under legal systems that permit this unique penalty to be so wantonly and so freakishly imposed.[38]

The dissenting justices argued that capital punishment had always been accepted in the English and American legal system and that thus, it was supported by the American public. Further, the Fourteenth Amendment's language that no one should be deprived of life, liberty, or property without due process of law would imply that it is appropriate to take someone's life as a punishment.

The result of the **Furman** case was that a moratorium was placed on the death penalty until states could determine how better to implement it. This moratorium lasted until 1976 and although many expected that the death penalty would be abolished because of the Court's ruling, instead, 37 states enacted new death penalty statutes that they believed would comply with the Court's ruling. Some states passed statutes that permitted the death penalty to be imposed automatically for certain crimes. This type of statute was prohibited later by the Supreme Court.[39]

Other states proposed **bifurcated** trial and sentencing procedures. Bifurcating murder trials in which the death penalty could be imposed would allow juries to consider the offense the person committed separately from whether the person received the death penalty. Thus, the jury would first determine whether or not the defendant committed, for example, first-degree murder. If the jury determined that the defendant was guilty of first-degree murder and the law permitted the death penalty to be imposed for first-degree murder, the jury would then hear more information about the defendant and the crime that would help the jury make a decision as to whether the death penalty should be imposed. This type of decision making was upheld by the Supreme

---

38. **Id.** at 309.
39. *See* **Roberts v. Louisiana**, 428 U.S. 325 (1976).

Court in the Court's second landmark death penalty decision, **Gregg v. Georgia**,[40] decided in 1976. The Supreme Court reinstated Georgia's death penalty, agreeing with its revised penalties and bifurcated trial system. Interestingly, the Court stated in a 7-2 decision that the death penalty does not violate the evolving levels of decency that define a civilized society and that "capital punishment is an express of society's moral outrage at particularly offensive conduct. This function may be unappealing to many, but it is essential in an ordered society that asks its citizens to rely on legal processes rather than self-help to vindicate their wrongs."[41]

Another landmark case regarding punishment was that of **Coker v. Georgia**,[42] in which the Supreme Court decided whether certain offenses could be punishable by death.

COKER V. GEORGIA

FACTS: Ehrlich Anthony Coker escaped from prison while serving sentences for rape, kidnapping, first-degree murder, and aggravated assault. He broke into Allen and Elnita Carver's home and raped Elnita Carver before stealing the family vehicle. He was eventually located and tried and was convicted of rape, armed robbery, and other offenses. The jury found that aggravating factors were present in the rape, and thus he was sentenced to death on that charge. The Supreme Court of Georgia upheld the sentence and Coker appealed his case to the Supreme Court of the United States.

ISSUE: Is imposing the penalty of death for a rape conviction cruel and unusual punishment?

HOLDING: It is cruel and unusual punishment to impose death for a rape conviction.

RATIONALE: Rape does not cause the death of or serious injury to another person. Punishing a rape with death is excessive because it makes no measurable contribution to acceptable goals of punishment and thus is nothing more than the purposeless imposition of pain on the defendant. Further, death is grossly disproportionate and excessive for the crime of rape. The Court considered the fact that Georgia was the only state that still permitted the death penalty to be imposed in the case of a rape of an adult, and only two other states permitted it in the case of a rape of a child. Further, few juries in Georgia have voted to impose the death sentence in rape cases. Because a person who deliberately kills someone cannot receive the death penalty in Georgia unless aggravating circumstances are

---

40. 428 U.S. 153 (1976).
41. **Id.** at 183.
42. 433 U.S. 584 (1977).

found, it does not make sense that someone who did not commit murder could receive that penalty. In this particular case, the judges pointed out, the victim did not receive any serious or "lasting" injuries and it was not committed with excessive brutality.

Two justices dissented and one justice dissented in part. The crux of the dissent was that the Supreme Court was overstepping the bounds of its power by substituting its "policy judgment" for the state legislature's judgment. Rape is not a minor crime so the Georgian legislature can impose a severe penalty for it. A dissenting justice also argued that rape is "inherently one of the most egregiously brutal acts one human being can inflict upon another" and that the fact that the defendant had previously committed crimes could be considered an aggravating factor justifying the imposition of the death penalty. Rape is a "life endangering" crime and thus can be punished by death, which will ensure that the defendant does not commit further crimes.

Following these landmark decisions by the Supreme Court, other cases were brought in front of the Court to determine whether specific types of defendants could be subjected to the death penalty. These cases include the following decisions:

Roper v. Simmons[43] A person under the age of 18 cannot be executed; doing so would extinguish a juvenile's "potential to attain a mature understanding of his own humanity."

McCleskey v. Kemp[44] There is no proof that the death penalty is related to racial discrimination, so no constitutional race-related issue exists.

Atkins v. Virginia[45] It is unconstitutional to execute someone who is mentally retarded.

Ford v. Wainwright[46] An inmate who becomes mentally ill while in prison cannot be executed.

Singleton v. Norris[47] Officials can force a convicted murderer to take drugs for his mental condition so that he is sane enough to be executed.

APPEALS

If a defendant is unhappy with the outcome of his case at the trial court level, he can file an appeal to his state's intermediate level court, or in the case of a federal conviction, to the federal appeals court. The reviewing court will consider the

---

43. 543 U.S. 551 (2005).

44. 482 U.S. 920 (1987).

45. 536 U.S. 304 (2002).

46. 477 U.S. 399 (1986).

47. 267 F.3d 859 (8th Cir. 2001). This case was not granted allocatur by the Supreme Court; rather, the Supreme Court refused to hear the case, thus leaving the federal court's ruling intact.

record that has been made in the lower court and will base its ruling on that record. No new evidence or testimony can be presented to the appellate court. Any documents that have been filed in the case and any exhibits entered at trial can be considered, as can the **transcripts** from the lower court hearing, including the preliminary hearing, pre-trial hearings, the trial, the sentencing, and any post-sentence hearings. The transcripts that are prepared in a case include a word-for-word rendition of everything that was said by anyone during a court proceeding. A court stenographer sits in on proceedings and types everything that is being said, using a machine that in effect uses shorthand codes. Technology has also advanced to the point in which some jurisdictions are using transcription equipment that does not require a live stenographer but instead records the voices in the courtroom. The difference, however, between a reviewing court reading a transcript and actually being present in the courtroom during the proceeding is that the court is unable to watch the demeanor of the person speaking or hear the inflection in the person's voice. Thus, the reviewing court is unable to detect whether the person is telling the truth or not based on body language, eye contact, or the inflection of the person's voice. The court is also unable to sense things like humor or sarcasm when reading a written transcript. For these reasons and others, the reviewing court cannot determine who was telling the truth and who was lying while reading the transcripts. The jury or the judge at the trial court level act as the finders of fact, and the appellate court will not overturn those decisions unless they are determined to "shock its conscience." This would only happen if the reviewing court determined that there was absolutely no way that a rational jury or a rational judge would decide the case in the manner that it was decided at the trial court level. This type of determination by a reviewing court is very rare. Transcripts are expensive to obtain, but the Supreme Court ruled that an indigent client has the right to have trial transcripts produced at no cost, because they are so important to the reviewing court's ability to determine whether the lower court proceeding was free from error.[48] See Figure 8.6 for a sample page from a trial transcript.[49]

In most jurisdictions, a defendant has a right to appeal his case to the next level. The reviewing court must hear the case. After the initial appeal, in many states, the defendant does not have an absolute right to have his case heard. Defendants who wish to appeal their cases to the state's supreme court or the Supreme Court of the United States must request that the Court hear its case, through a request for allocatur, as discussed in Chapter 1. In fact, the Supreme Court ruled in 1894 that a defendant does not have to be afforded the right to appeal his case, although defendants argued that it was required under the concept of due process. In **McKane v. Durston**,[50] the Supreme Court decided that this was the case regardless of how grave the defendant's offense

---

48. **Griffin v. Illinois**, 351 U.S. 12 (1956).
49. Transcript taken from http://www.innocenceproject.org/Content/Cameron_Todd_Willingham_Trial_Transcripts.php.
50. 153 U.S. 684 (1894).

FIGURE 8.6. A PAGE FROM A TRIAL TRANSCRIPT

1	Q. Where did you go that evening and who were you with?
2	A. I went to Robin's Tavern, and I went with Frank Hagan and Peter
3	Benekos.
4	Q. How did you get there?
5	A. I drove my car.
6	Q. What type of car do you have?
7	A. A 2012 MINI-Cooper.
8	Q. What time did you arrive at the tavern?
9	A. I think I was around 11:00. Approximately after 11:00, I think.
10	Q. Who was at the tavern when you got there?
11	A. Anthony Hugar, Mike Sulkowski, and Pedro Rodriguez. I didn't know
12	anyone else at the tavern that night.
13	Q. How much did you drink at the tavern?
14	A. I don't know. A few beers I think. I started drinking beer and then I
16	blacked out and fell down.
17	Q. Did you go to the hospital?
18	A. Someone called an ambulance and the ambulance took me to the
19	hospital, yes.
20	Q. When did you realize you had fallen?
21	A. I woke up and realized I was in a hospital. My wife was there and she
22	told me that I had fallen down. I don't remember anything about falling,
23	and she said that the bartender, Brian Ripley, had called her and told her
24	that I had fallen and an ambulance was on its way.
25	Q. Did your wife ever tell you whether the bartender had mentioned
26	how many beers you had that night?
27	A. No, and frankly I never asked her. It wasn't something I wanted to
28	talk about with her, because she always told me I drank too much.
29	Q. Have you ever gone to drug and alcohol counseling, participated in
30	any inpatient program for alcohol abuse, or attended any meetings such
31	as Alcoholics Anonymous?

Page 28

was. The prosecution can also appeal a case, although such an appeal is generally rare. Because of the double jeopardy clause, a prosecutor can rarely appeal a case in which a defendant receives an acquittal. In fact, the Supreme Court stated that appeals by the prosecution "in criminal cases are something unusual, exceptional, not favored. The history shows resistance of the Court to the opening of an appellate route for the government until it was plainly provided by the Congress, and after that a close restriction of its uses to those authorized by statute."[51] States and the federal government can mandate narrow circumstances under which the prosecution can file an appeal.

However, a prosecutor can appeal a defendant's sentence, arguing that it was too lenient, or a prosecutor can appeal pre-trial rulings which might have excluded evidence that the prosecutor desired to present at the time of trial. The latter type of appeal might take place prior to the defendant's trial, plea, or sentencing, and is referred to as an **interlocutory appeal**. The general rule is that a case should only be appealed after it has gone through the entire process, all the way to sentencing and post-trial motions. However, certain matters require an appellate court to consider the issue before a trial can take place, as the result of the reviewing court's decision would greatly affect the trial. The Supreme Court has set forth the following three times that interlocutory appeals can be filed:[52] (1) the outcome of the case would be conclusively determined by the issue; (2) the matter appealed was collateral to the merits of the case, and (3) the matter would be unable to be reviewed by the reviewing court if the trial or other proceedings were permitted to proceed. **Stack v. Boyle**[53] is an example of a case in which the Supreme Court determined that a reviewing court must immediately make a decision on the defendant's argument, rather than waiting. In that case, the defendant wanted to appeal the amount of bail set by the trial court; he argued that the amount of bail required for him was too high and thus violated the Eighth Amendment guarantee against excessive bail. If the appellate court had waited until the defendant was tried and sentenced, the issue of the bail amount would have been moot. Following trial or a plea and sentencing, the defendant would have either been (1) sentenced and thus bail would have been moot or (2) acquitted and thus bail would have been moot. However, issues involving the suppression of evidence are not considered an appealable issue. The Supreme Court considers such issues to be related to an individual's trial, so they are not appealable until the outcome of the trial takes place. Many other issues are appealed following a defendant's sentence, including (1) the sentence itself, (2) whether the evidence presented at trial was sufficient to convict the defendant of the crime, (3) whether the judge erred in making any ruling during the trial, (4) whether a violation of the rules regarding disclosure of evidence took place, (5) whether a trial was speedy, and (6) whether jury selection was done properly.

---

51. **Carroll v. United States**, 354 U.S. 394 (1957).
52. **Lauro Lines s.r.l. v. Chasser**, 490 U.S. 495 (1989).
53. 342 U.S. 1 (1951).

An appellate court could determine that an error occurred at the trial court level, but could nevertheless fail to order a new trial or other new proceedings based on the use of the **harmless error** doctrine, discussed previously. This doctrine dictates that an error that occurred at the trial court level will only merit a remand back to the trial court if the error clearly changed the outcome of the proceedings. If enough evidence exists that could, and probably would, have resulted in the defendant's conviction other than the evidence that will be excluded from trial, the court will not reverse or remand the case. Consider the following scenario and decide whether the trial court's decision would or could have been different if the evidence the defendant wants excluded actually was.

QUESTIONS TO CONSIDER

1. Assume you are a defense attorney defending a Hispanic man who sexually assaulted a black teenager. What types of questions would you ask prospective jurors, and what answers would you desire for jurors? What answers would make you want to eliminate potential jurors? What questions do you believe prospective jurors would answer truthfully, and what questions do you believe jurors would not answer truthfully?

2. Read the cases of **Trop v. Dulles** and **Coker v. Georgia**. Research how many countries currently permit the imposition of a death sentence for murder. Can the Supreme Court's language in the **Trop** and **Coker** cases be used to argue that the death penalty should not be permitted in the United States today?

3. Compare the following factual scenario to that in the Sparky example in the "You Be the Judge" on page 33. A defendant is known to many people as "Killa." That is his nickname, and many people who have grown up with him and known him for a while do not know him by any other name. The defendant is being tried for murder. Some witnesses on the stand refer to him as "Killa" in their testimony, as they do not know of any other name for him. The defendant's attorney argues that the witness's use of his nickname is prejudicial to his case. How is this case the same or different than the Sparky example?

4. Read **In re Gault** and **McKeiver v. Pennsylvania**. Compare and contrast them. Why do the Court's arguments in **In re Gault** that allow juveniles to have certain procedural safeguards not apply to the issue of jury trial, according to **McKeiver v. Pennsylvania**? Can you reconcile the decisions of the two cases?

KEY TERMS

bench warrant

This type of arrest warrant can be issued when a defendant does not show up for a hearing, and the court has held that person in contempt of court.

booking

This process involves gathering information about a person, such as birth date, address, and so on, to properly admit them to the prison system.

change of venire

A change to a new panel of jurors (venire) who are brought in from outside the area to hear a case.

change of venue

A change of location (venue) for a trial so that a jury from outside the area hears a case.

discovery

The process of obtaining information from the other side regarding the specific evidence that each side holds, as well as the identities of any witnesses that will be used by either party. The prosecution does not have as much right to receive information from the defendant as the defendant does from the prosecution, because the burden of proof lies with the prosecution.

Federal Bail Reform Act of 1984

This act provided that in the federal system, judges could revoke pre-trial release for firearms possession, failure to comply with curfew, and failure to comply with other conditions. Further, any person who might be at risk of fleeing or posing a danger to any person in the community could be held for ten days and the act also provides for indefinite detention of certain persons, following a hearing.

hung jury

If the jury is absolutely unable to reach a decision in the case, a hung jury will result. When a jury is hung, it is indicating that it does not believe that a decision will ever be reached. The jury is dismissed, and the prosecutor will have to decide whether or not to retry the defendant. A hung jury is not a case of double jeopardy.

jury nullification

In this process the jury can actually choose, through their actions, to nullify a law that they believe to be unfair when they acquit a defendant whom they believe to be guilty of breaking that law.

peremptory challenges

Each side in a voir dire is given a certain number of challenges to use in selecting (or removing) potential jurors from the pool. Peremptory challenges are those which can remove a potential juror without giving a particular reason or cause for removal.

preliminary arraignment

At this stage of the proceedings, an individual is notified as to why he is being detained and may be given information regarding his right to counsel.

release of recognizance

In some cases, the Court may decide to release a defendant with no monetary bond, but on his own standing in the community, known as an ROR, or release on recognizance, bond. The defendant pledges to appear for any court proceedings scheduled for the future.

sequestered

A sequestered jury is kept in a hotel, isolated from the press and outside world, for the duration of the trial, to avoid any bias from forming in the minds of the jurors regarding the case.

statute of limitations

This doctrine determines the amount of time a prosecuting agency has to prosecute a particular crime.

voir dire

This is the process of jury selection, including the interviewing of members of the jury pool, and the right to peremptory challenges and challenges "for cause" to remove certain jurors from the pool.

KEY COURT CASES

Atkins v. Virginia

In this case, the Court ruled that it is unconstitutional to execute someone who is mentally retarded.

Batson v. Kentucky

In this case, the Court held that peremptory challenges that result in the exclusion of certain cognizant groups can be challenged as unconstitutional. This is known as a **Batson** challenge and is normally argued by the defense to challenge peremptory challenges asserted by the prosecution.

Coker v. Georgia

In this case, the Supreme Court ruled that it is cruel and unusual punishment to impose the death penalty for a rape conviction. It was ruled to be an excessive punishment for a crime that did not cause the death or serious injury of another person.

Furman v. Georgia

The most important capital case decided by the Supreme Court, this case saw a 5-4 ruling, with each justice writing his own opinion and very few judges agreeing with each other. The Court's overall ruling was that the automatic imposition of the death penalty in a felony murder case was unconstitutional. The result was that a moratorium was placed on the death penalty until states could determine how better to implement it.

Graham v. Florida

In this 2010 case, the Court determined that juvenile sentences of life without parole are unconstitutional for cases in which the juvenile did not commit murder.

Gregg v. Georgia

In this case, the Court reinstated Georgia's death penalty, agreeing with its revised penalties and the bifurcated trial system. Interestingly, the Court stated in a 7-2 decision that the death penalty does not violate the evolving levels of decency that define as civilized society.

Miller v. Alabama

In this case, the Court extended the **Graham v. Florida** ruling to murder cases stating that mandatory life without parole sentences preclude consideration of the chronological age and accompanying features of immaturity, impetuosity, and inability to discern risks and consequences. The Court's ruling did not say that a judge can never sentence a juvenile to a life without parole, but rather mandated that the judge should consider all the facts and circumstances before handing down such a sentence.

Roper v. Simmons

In this case, the Court ruled that a person under the age of 18 cannot be executed; doing so would extinguish a juvenile's "potential to attain a mature understanding of his own humanity."

Stack v. Boyle

This was a case in which the Supreme Court determined that a reviewing court must immediately make a decision on the defendant's argument, rather than waiting. In this case, the defendant was appealing the amount of bail as excessive. If the appellate court had waited until the defendant was tried and sentenced, the issue of the bail amount would have been moot.

THE FIRST AND SECOND AMENDMENTS: FREEDOM OF SPEECH, ASSEMBLY, RELIGION, AND THE RIGHT TO BEAR ARMS

9

LEARNING OBJECTIVES: Students will

1. Understand the freedom of speech clause and its limitations
2. Understand the terms defamation, libel, and slander, and distinguish between them
3. Understand the concept of flag desecration and know its parameters
4. Know the law surrounding obscenity and pornography
5. Understand the freedom of religion clause, the establishment clause, and the free exercise clause

The First and Second Amendments are peripherally related to the issue of the rights of criminal defendants in that they have been used to both justify and argue against the passage of certain laws that result in behavior being considered a crime. These amendments permit certain behaviors, but it has been left to the courts to determine how much protection to give those rights when they begin to affect the right of other citizens to live in a safe society. The right of individuals to speak freely, which naturally encompasses the right to protest freely, affected many of the major historical events in our country, such as the Vietnam War and, most recently, presidential elections. Consider how different our political process would be if individuals did not have the right to state their views to others. Even online social network applications such as Facebook and Twitter abound with comments focusing on political issues, including criticism of religion, the laws, and the president. These comments can legally be posted only because of the broad right to free speech, religion, and even press that has been permitted by the Supreme Court upon interpretation of the First Amendment. The Supreme Court considered the meaning of these clauses very early in its history and the provisions of the First Amendment were some of the first provisions to be incorporated to the states as being fundamental to the freedoms we experience in our country. As you consider the following analyses of the First and Second Amendments, consider whether you believe the framers of the Constitution were trying to make a statement by placing those amendments at the beginning of the Bill of Rights.

THE FIRST AMENDMENT

Congress shall make no law respecting an establishment of religion, or prohibiting the free exercise thereof; or abridging the freedom of speech, or of the press; or the right of the people peaceably to assemble, and to petition the Government for a redress of grievances.

—U.S. Constitution, Amendment I

The part of the First Amendment most relevant to the practice of criminal justice states that "Congress shall make no law . . . abridging the freedom of speech, or of the press; of the right of the people peaceably to assemble, and to petition the Government for a redress of grievances." The First Amendment was specifically adopted in response to censorship that was handed down from the British Crown to the colonists. Great Britain's censorship initially focused on banning certain forms of religious expression and was expanded to include political expression as well. The Crown even went so far as to prohibit books from being printed unless they were first reviewed by the Crown and to prohibit a person laughing at something that was considered "libelous." Great Britain had licensing laws (which were passed to prevent "unorthodox" religious thoughts and criticism of public officials) and seditious libel laws, which criminalized such criticism. Even laughing at "libelous" statements relating to the government could cause a person to be criminally punished.

Even though some of the ideas within our Constitution were inspired by rules and ideas that existed in Great Britain, in the area of freedom of speech, the ideas were all original to the United States. The framers of the United States Constitution considered this history when drafting the Constitution, and thus the very first constitutional amendment gives citizens the freedom of speech, religion, and expression. The First Amendment bans any governmental prohibition of religion, bans any governmental regulation of the content of speech, and provides for freedom of the press. Our political system is unique regarding our ability to state our views of current and future political figures. Our system is also unique in our ability as citizens to obtain government documents and other information freely. The fact that we can write a letter to the editor or give a public speech in which we criticize the policies of the current president is due to the framers' passage of the First Amendment. The First Amendment was

THE CAPITOL BUILDING IN WASHINGTON, D.C.

www.bigstock.com.

incorporated to the states via the Fourteenth Amendment's language that no state shall deprive any person of liberty.

Freedom of Speech

The First Amendment is used by almost every citizen of the United States every single day. The media in the United States is very powerful today because of the First Amendment. The Internet has added a whole new layer to the issue of freedom of speech, as our ideas can be disseminated quickly, in writing, to others. Freedom of speech also affects our criminal justice system, both in terms of our ability to obtain information about criminal proceedings and regarding issues of when something a person says can result in criminal charges. The First Amendment has provided an outlet for concerned citizens and citizens who are upset at our government to voice their concerns in an orderly manner without having to riot in the streets. The central word in the amendment seems to be that of "abridging," along with the definitions of speech and the press. What did the framers mean by the word abridging? Certainly laws have been passed by Congress and other legislative bodies that prohibit certain types of speech and limit the freedom of the press. "Abridge" must have a specific meaning that does not completely prohibit such laws when they are in the best interest of the citizens of the United States. Accordingly, as you will see, the Court has limited certain types of speech, rather than ruling that the amendment permits every possible word or phrase that anyone could utter to anyone else.

Speech involves much more than spoken words, and also goes beyond the concept of written words. Speech can include art, theater, movies, dance, singing, and any other expression that humans make. Displaying political yard signs, participating in and organizing marches and demonstrations, making speeches, distributing literature, soliciting membership in organizations, and even sending information of any type across the Internet are all considered "speech," and generally speaking, people can participate in these activities freely. Speech also includes silent demonstrations and displaying flags and other symbols. The original purpose of the First Amendment was to prohibit the government from controlling or limiting the free exchange of ideas. Further, through the passage of the First Amendment, the framers hoped to allow citizens to criticize the government, as this had been prohibited in England.

The First Amendment was originally meant to forbid the government from controlling the ideas of citizens, not to allow speech from one person to infringe on the right of others to live in a comfortable society. Thus, the government in the United States has been able to pass laws that prohibit people from threatening others, disturbing others by loud speech or actions, or offending society's sense of morals (such as child pornography). These laws punish people's conduct, rather than just the content of the speech itself, and thus the laws are determined to be constitutional.

The framers intended that the First Amendment would apply to Congress only, rather than to other forms of governments such as state governments, but in 1925 this concept was changed when the Supreme Court decided the case of **Gitlow v. New York**.[1] In **Gitlow**, the Supreme Court incorporated the First Amendment to all state and local governments through the Fourteenth Amendment due process clause. The **Gitlow** case involved a law passed by the State of New York that criminalized advocating overthrowing government by force or violence. Gitlow was convicted under the law when he disseminated Communist pamphlets that advocated the violent overthrow of the government. There was no evidence that Gitlow's actions actually caused anyone to attempt to overthrow the government. Thus, the Supreme Court had to grapple with the issue of whether the government would need proof of some "effect" of the language the government wished to stop, or at least a likelihood of some sort of result. The Supreme Court upheld New York's law, citing the due process clause and indicating that the right of free speech is included in the concept of due process. The **Gitlow** case was very politically charged when it was decided, as its decision followed the period of the "Red Scare" in the United States when members of the Communist and Socialist Parties were being prosecuted for "criminal anarchy." Gitlow's words, according to the Court, were

---

1. 268 U.S. 652 (1925).

words of "direct incitement." The state can use its police power to penalize such speech because it goes against the general welfare of the public. If the state has determined that the utterances in question involve likelihood of harm, they must be discouraged and it is appropriate for the state to do so. The dissenting opinion in that case, written by Justice Holmes, stated that Gitlow's words were "indefinite and ineffective" and thus did not constitute a present danger. Holmes stated that every idea is an incitement and may move the recipient of those words to some sort of action, depending on the context of the words and to other outside issues surrounding the receipt of the words by the listener. Thus, Holmes reasoned, for the majority opinion to state that Gitlow's words could be outlawed because they were an incitement proves nothing, as all words could be considered an incitement.

Freedom of speech also guarantees a citizen's right not to have to say anything. In **West Virginia State Board of Education v. Barnette**,[2] the Supreme Court ruled that it was unconstitutional for the State of West Virginia to pass a statute that required schoolchildren to recite the Pledge of Allegiance while saluting the American flag. The salute required by the board of education was a stiff, one-armed salute of the right hand; the hand was to remain raised while the pledge was recited. (Many opposed this particular salute as they likened it to the salute required to be given to Hitler.) Failure to salute and recite the pledge was considered to be insubordination on the part of the child, who would be expelled from school. In addition, the student's parents could be fined as much as $50 and jailed up to 30 days. The children who failed to salute the flag in the **Barnette** case were Jehovah's Witnesses, and their religion forbade them from saluting or pledging to symbols. Specifically, the Barnettes considered the flag a "graven image," and thus violated the Bible's command against making a graven image and bowing before it.

The Supreme Court's decision in the **Barnette** case did not focus as much on the religious aspects of the case as it did on the fact that states do not have the power to compel anyone's speech. The Court ruled that the type of salute required by the Virginia state board of education was a form of "utterance" and thus a means of communicating ideas, a concept that is protected under the First Amendment. The counterargument set forth by the board of education was that forcing the pledge was a good way to foster "school unity" and that local officials should be able to discipline their schoolchildren as they wished. The Court rejected both of these arguments, stating that "freedom to differ is not limited to things that do not matter much" and that no official should be able to prescribe what should be orthodox in politics or religion, with no exceptions. The concurring opinion stated that "[l]ove of country must spring from willing hearts and free minds, inspired by a fair administration of wise laws enacted by the people's elected representatives within the bound of express constitutional prohibitions."[3]

---

2. 319 U.S. 624 (1943).
3. Id. at 644.

An interesting case involved the Court's determination that speech cannot be regulated even if someone argues that regulating it is in the best interest of the community. In **Linmark Associates, Inc. v. Township of Willingboro**,[4] the community attempted to ban the posting of "for sale" and "sold" signs on real estate. How could this possibly help the community? Racial tensions were high in the community as the proportion of its nonwhite population had increased dramatically in the past several years. The township was concerned that "white flight" might occur and enacted an ordinance that prohibited its residents from having a "for sale" or "sold" sign on real estate. Township officials believed that if signs were posted, white neighbors would realize that other white members of the community were moving and would also place their houses up for sale. The township officials stated that they wished to prevent people panicking and selling their homes. The Supreme Court held that truthful information could not be withheld from the public for this type of reason, as the preference under the First Amendment is to risk some misuse of evidence that is freely available even if problems would arise if that information is suppressed and withheld from the public. The Court stated that the ordinance was an attempt to "enforce silence," which the Supreme Court did not agree with.

Vulgar and Crude Speech. Vulgar or crude speech has been referred to as speech that does not contribute to the exchange of ideas. However, as with pornography, discussed later, it is difficult to clearly define what language is considered vulgar and crude, as different people find different speech to be vulgar or crude. Additionally, is it appropriate for the courts to prohibit this category of speech? The Supreme Court first considered this issue in the case of **Cohen v. California**.[5] In this rather famous case, Cohen was arrested for appearing in a Los Angeles courtroom with a jacket that had lettering on it that read "F*** the draft." He was convicted under a California statute that prohibited "maliciously and willfully disturb[ing] the peace or quiet of any neighborhood or person [by] offensive conduct." The Supreme Court over-turned Cohen's conviction, ruling that the "simple" public display of the four-letter word could not be made a crime. Justice Harlan, writer of the majority opinion, wrote that "one man's vulgarity is another's lyric." The Court ruled that a state cannot attempt to censor its citizens' speech in order to make society more "civil." Further, it is difficult to separate heightened emotion from vulgarity in some cases, and the free exchange of ideas, which our society depends on, is often emotionally charged. The dissent in the **Cohen** case stated that Cohen's actions were what had been criminalized, not his speech, and that his conduct was "absurd and immature." However, the **Cohen** case preceded other cases in which the Supreme Court did limit "vulgar" speech, such as when the speech was being used in front of minors.[6]

---

4. 431 U.S. 85 (1977).
5. 403 U.S. 15 (1971).
6. E.g., **Bethel School District v. Fraser**, 478 U.S. 675 (1986).

Hate Speech. Speech that denigrates another, especially based on protected categories such as religion, race, or sexual orientation, remains a controversial issue despite being considered by the Supreme Court. After all, we cannot prosecute people for being mean or even for being bigoted or small minded. However, we should each also have the right not to have someone harassing us for something we believe in or some other characteristic that we might have. The Supreme Court has permitted hate speech as a protected category under the First Amendment. The Court grappled with this issue in the case of **R.A.V. v. City of St. Paul,**[7] in which the Court scrutinized the Bias-Motivated Crime Ordinance that had been passed in St. Paul, Minnesota. The Ordinance was clearly an attempt to criminalize behavior in which bias or hate was the focus. R.A.V. (referred to as such in the case because he was a juvenile at the time he was charged with the crime) was convicted of assembling a cross out of broken chair legs, then erecting the cross and burning it on the lawn of a neighboring African-American family. The ordinance stated as follows: "Whoever places on public or private property, a symbol, object, appellation, characterization or graffiti, including, but not limited to, a burning cross or Nazi swastika, which one knows or has reasonable grounds to know arouses anger, alarm or resentment in others on the basis of race, color, creed, religion or gender commits disorderly conduct and shall be guilty of a misdemeanor."[8] The defendant argued that the statute was overbroad.

The Supreme Court's decision in **R.A.V.** had no dissenting opinions. The members of the Court all agreed that the statute was indeed overbroad and "content based." The Court stated that the First Amendment prevents the government from prohibiting speech because of the ideas contained within the speech. Speech can only be restrained by the government when the benefits can be stated to be outweighed by the social interest citizens have in order and morality. The Court discussed that certain "time place and manner" restrictions could be placed on actions. For example, in the case of flag burning, although flag burning itself cannot be prohibited because that would restrict certain political expressions, local burning laws can prohibit the burning in certain areas or at certain times of the day. Similarly, burning laws can prohibit the burning of a cross at certain times and in certain places, but a law cannot be passed that always prohibits such a burning based on the underlying attempt to make a political statement. The members of the Court admitted that the burning of a cross on someone's front yard was "reprehensible" but that other statutes unrelated to speech or conduct could prohibit such behavior in a way that did not focus on the reasoning behind the burning. Time, place, and manner restrictions are not reasonable if those restrictions constitute a blanket ban, for example, on all yard signs in a city or on the dissemination of any written political materials whatsoever. Such bans must have a

---

7. 505 U.S. 377 (1992).
8. Id at 380.

YOU BE THE JUDGE

You are a councilmember for a small city. Citizens have been complaining that various religious and political groups have been canvassing the neighborhood at all hours, approaching houses in the attempt to pass out materials related to their beliefs. The individuals approach the house, ring the doorbell, and if the owner of the house comes to the door, the individuals hand them a tract which describes their religious or political views. Unless the homeowner engages the individual in conversation, the individuals then leave.

The neighbors attend a council meeting and request that your council pass an ordinance that states that no person may ring the doorbell of a home or knock on the door of the home if the intent is to discuss with the homeowner the individual's religious or political views.

Do you believe you can pass such an ordinance legally? What are the pros and cons to such an ordinance? What do you believe the Supreme Court of the United States would say about such an ordinance?

purpose in furthering the good of the community and must not be a complete ban on expression.

Actions that include hate can be criminalized. For example, an assault or a threat made to someone can result in criminal charges. Further, the Supreme Court has upheld statutes that enhance penalties for crimes that are carried out because of a race- or gender-based hate. In **Wisconsin v. Mitchell,**[9] the Supreme Court was faced with deciding whether a statute could allow sentencing courts to increase a sentence based on a revelation that a defendant intentionally selected the person against whom the crime was committed based on the victim's "race, religion, color, disability, sexual orientation, national origin or ancestry." The defendant, Mitchell, was with a group of individuals who watched the racially charged movie *Mississippi Burning* and decided to go, in their words, "move on some white people." The group saw a white 14–year–old walking across the street and decided to "get him." Ten members of the group ran toward the victim, kicked him, and knocked him to the ground, pummeling him for over five minutes. The victim was in a coma for four days. At trial, a jury convicted Mitchell of aggravated battery, and the court imposed a seven-year sentence. The lengthy sentence resulted from a state law enhancing the penalty for race crimes, and there was no disagreement at trial that indeed the motivation for the assault was the victim's race.

---

9. 508 U.S. 476 (1993).

The Supreme Court issued a unanimous decision in this case. The Court stated that the statute was directed at violence and conduct and not at expression, and thus was constitutional. The Court further reasoned that the State of Wisconsin had a compelling interest in preventing the effects of bias-motivated crimes. Bias-motivated crimes invoke unrest in the community and most certainly invoke extreme emotional distress on the victim. The Court also indicated that because the courts already consider statements made along with actions to determine motive in a criminal case, there is no problem with using those statements and motives to enhance an individual's sentence.

The most recent landmark Supreme Court case in the area of free speech is that of **Snyder v. Phelps**,[10] decided by the Court in 2011. The case involved the congregation of the Westboro Baptist Church, which for 20 years had picketed the funerals of members of the military. The purpose of the picketing was to make a statement that God hates the United States for its tolerance of homosexuality, especially in the military. The church was also protesting the clergy scandals that had taken place in the Catholic church. When members of the church went to Maryland to picket the funeral of a Marine who had been killed in Iraq in the line of duty, they quietly and peacefully displayed signs on public land that was approximately 1,000 feet from the church in which the funeral took place. The signs made statements such as "Thank God for Dead Soldiers," "Fags Doom Nations," "America Is Doomed," "Priests Rape Boys," and "You're Going to Hell." The protestors displayed the signs until approximately 30 minutes before the funeral began.

The Marine's father filed a diversity action against the church, the founder of the church, who had traveled to Maryland, and the founder's daughters who had also participated in the picketing. The suit included claims of intentional infliction of emotional distress, intrusion upon seclusion, and civil conspiracy. A jury found Westboro liable and entered a judgment of millions of dollars against the church. Westboro challenged the verdict, arguing that the First Amendment protected his speech. The case made its way to the Supreme Court. The Court ruled for the defendants, agreeing that their free speech had been violated. The Court stated that speech is considered to be of public concern when it can "be fairly considered as relating to any matter of political, social, or other concern to the community" or when it "is a subject of general interest and of value and concern to the public." The statement's controversial or arguable inappropriate nature should not be considered. The Court ruled that the speech in this case did relate to public, not private, matters, because it directly spoke to the morality of the United States and its citizens. Even if Westboro's speech was hurtful to the Marine's father and his grieving relatives, it was still protected. The jury had found that the picketing was "outrageous," as required in the state tort statute defining intentional infliction of emotional distress, but the First Amendment trumps the jury's finding. The Supreme Court reiterated that it would protect even

---

10. No. 09-751.

hurtful speech if it related to public issues, so as not to stifle public debate. One justice dissented, arguing that the Marine's father wanted only to bury his son in peace and that, because the picketers had chosen that particular funeral because the deceased practiced the Catholic faith and because he was in the military, the picketers were in fact trying to target Matthew Snyder, a private individual.

Criminalizing Speech Based on Attendant Actions.   Although our speech is well protected, our actions that attend that speech may not be, and the Court has indicated there is a difference between the two. The Supreme Court generally permitted the use of laws that prohibit certain types of "speech-related" conduct in the case of **United States v. O'Brien.**[11] Such laws are constitutional when they further a substantial government interest that is unrelated to suppressing the message that accompanies the conduct. In the **O'Brien** case, O'Brien burned his draft card during an antiwar demonstration. A federal statute made burning a draft card illegal. The Court stated that the government had a legitimate reason for preserving draft cards that was unrelated to prohibiting antiwar statements. As long as the real concern of the government is not on the message, but on the behavior, the statute will stand. The majority opinion of the Court set forth factors to be used by courts to determine when a regulation that combines both speech and nonspeech elements can be upheld:

1. The regulation must be within the constitutional power of the government to enact.
2. The regulation must further an important or substantial government interest.
3. The government interest that is furthered must be unrelated to the suppression of speech (otherwise described as being "content neutral").
4. The regulation must only prohibit the speech that is essential to further that interest.

The Supreme Court's rationale in **O'Brien** has been used to allow municipal officials to prohibit people from blocking entrances, obstructing traffic, and otherwise disturbing the peace by their actions through the use of noise ordinances and other state ordinances. It has also been utilized to support, for example, the wearing of black armbands in protest and the burning of flags by individuals in protest, as discussed further later in this chapter. A later Supreme Court decision, **Clark v. Community for Creative Non-Violence**,[12] slightly altered the factors set forth in the **O'Brien** decision. That case involved a group of people that was conducting demonstrations in the National Parks in Washington, D.C. The individuals involved in the

---

11. 391 367 (1968).
12. 468 U.S. 288 (1984).

demonstration were trying to bring attention to the plight of the homeless and erected "tent cities." However, the demonstrators were prohibited by the National Park Service from sleeping in the park. The Supreme Court stated that the National Park Service's prohibition did not violate the First Amendment because the prohibition was based on reasonable time, place, and manner restrictions. The restriction left open the group's ability to still state its message. The governmental interest here was "reasonable," which the court found was enough, as opposed to having to be "important or substantial."

Fighting Words. Fighting words are specifically excluded from First Amendment protection. Fighting words are any words that are used purely for purposes of inflicting injury. The Supreme Court has not compiled a specific list of words that will be considered fighting words; the context in which the words are used must always also be considered. The Supreme Court has stated that each of us must tolerate words that are insulting and outrageous.[13] Even police officers must tolerate citizens swearing at them, and in fact, the Supreme Court has said that police officers should expect that rude terminology will be directed toward them. Only when the words are accompanied by aggressive and belligerent physical gestures or motions will the police officer be able to arrest a rude citizen.

The Supreme Court has adopted two different approaches to consider whether words are, indeed, fighting words. In **Chaplinsky v. New Hampshire,**[14] the Supreme Court forbade certain types of words, including fighting words, bribery, perjury, and criminal solicitation. Chaplinsky had called a city official a "damned Fascist" and a "God-damned racketeer." The Court stated that these words would be likely to cause the person to whom they were addressed to fight. Because specific statutes could be overbroad in prohibiting too many different kinds of speech, the Supreme Court has also suggested that a balancing approach could be used, leaving the issue of what words are to be banned to individual courts to determine. This would result in much discretion in each case and the Court has allowed statutes such as the one utilized in the **Chaplinsky** case as long as the statutes are specific and can be narrowly construed. The Supreme Court has stated that it will only uphold a statute that involves prohibiting words that "have a direct tendency to cause acts of violence by the person to whom, individually, the remark is addressed."[15] For example, the Supreme Court decided that a statute that stated, "Any person who shall, without provocation, use to or of another, and in his presence . . . opprobrious words or abusive language, tending to cause a breach of the peace . . . shall be guilty of a misdemeanor" was unconstitutional. The Court indicated that this statute was too vague and that the

13. **Boos v. Barry**, 485 U.S. 312 (1988).
14. 315 U.S. 568 (1942).
15. Id. at 573.
16. **Gooding v. Wilson**, 405 U.S. 518 (1972).

terminology "opprobrious words or abusive language" did not involve words that rose to the level of a potential fight or "breach of the peace."[16]

The Supreme Court more recently considered the issue of fighting words in **City of Houston v. Hill**.[17] Hill had shouted at police officers in an attempt to divert their attention from his friend and was arrested under a municipal ordinance that made it unlawful for a person to "oppose, molest, abuse or interrupt any policeman in the execution of his duty." Hill challenged the ordinance's constitutionality and the Texas Federal Court of Appeals found that the ordinance was "overbroad" because its literal wording punished and could actually deter a significant range of speech. The Supreme Court agreed, stating that the statute was indeed overbroad, as it was not narrowly tailored to prohibit only disorderly conduct or fighting words, but could be utilized by police officers to criminalize behavior that involves words that are merely "annoying" or "offensive" as opposed to words that actually incite violence.

Defamation. **Defamation** is that act of making a statement in some form that presents a negative image of that person. **Libel** involves written words that defame someone and **slander** is the act of defaming someone through the spoken word. Libel and slander are prohibited criminally and civilly by state law. In the United States, truth is a defense to a defamation claim; the statement must make a claim that gives someone or something a negative image and be false. Further, privilege provides a complete bar to a defamation suit. At common law, two types of privileges exist: absolute and qualified. An **absolute privilege** is a statement that will not be considered defamation, even if it was made maliciously. This includes statements made in court and as part of the legislative process. A **qualified privilege** is often used by journalists who have written an article and believed that certain facts should be known in the public interest. Statements made in a public meeting or information relating to a public agency, such as a police department or a fire department, are important for the public to know and journalists should be able to repeat such statements in their work. As long as the statement by the journalist has not been made with malicious intent, it will be privileged and thus the journalist will be immune from suit.

Statements made against public figures, as opposed to private citizens, must be made with "actual malice" in order to be actionable. The reasoning behind this is that public figures place themselves in the spotlight and assume the risk that they will be criticized. The prohibition of libel and slander was viewed by early courts as being necessary to preserve peace and order in society. However, courts have also acknowledged that the government's act of limiting statements about others could result in limiting free speech, a right also guaranteed by the Constitution.

---

17. 482 U.S. 451 (1987).
18. 376 U.S. 254 (1964).

The landmark case in the area of free speech was **New York Times v. Sullivan**.[18] The New York Times had published an advertisement that asserted that officials in Montgomery, Alabama had acted violently in suppressing the protests of certain African Americans. The Montgomery County Police Commissioner sued the New York Times for libel, claiming that the content of the advertisement was dangerous to his reputation. The Supreme Court ruled that a public official wishing to prevail in a libel action must prove that the statements in question were made with "actual malice," which was defined as "knowledge that the statements were false or with reckless disregard of whether it was false or not." However, the standard for private individuals filing lawsuits remained lower, with no requirement of a showing of actual malice. Thus, although state law for libel suits varies, generally private individuals bringing a lawsuit need only prove that a person was negligent in making a statement. However, the expression of an opinion will not be considered defamatory; only a statement that purports to set forth a fact is considered defamatory. This allows citizens to state their opinions regarding a politician's stance on an issue.

Public Versus Private Persons. When considering cases of defamation, the Supreme Court has had to sort through the distinction between a false or damaging statement against a private individual and a similar statement made against a person who has somehow thrust himself into the limelight by running for public office or otherwise becoming a publicly known person. The Supreme Court considered this issue in the landmark case of **Gertz v. Robert Welch, Inc.**[19] The **Gertz** case was based on a scenario in which a police officer killed a young person and the deceased's family was represented by Gertz in a civil action against the officer. During the trial, Robert Welch, Inc., published an article about Gertz that referred to him as a "Communist" and as a member of a Marxist organization. The crux of the article was that the murder trial of the officer was part of a Communist conspiracy to discredit the local police department. The article implied that Mr. Gertz had a criminal record. The information contained in the article was inaccurate, so Gertz filed an action against Robert Welch, Inc.

Gertz sued Welch for libel and won at the trial court level. The trial court then reconsidered the suit, stating that Welch was protected by application of the **New York Times rule**. That rule states that discussion of any public issue in the media is protected, regardless of whether a person is an individual or a public figure. The trial court stated that because Gertz was unable to prove that Welch acted with "actual malice," the action against Welch could not stand. The Court considered the fact that Gertz was neither a public official nor a public figure, but that he was involved in a public issue. However, the Court stated that there was a need to balance the media's right to publish

19. 418 U.S. 323 (1974).

information against the legitimate interest of citizens in receiving compensation for harm that results to them from false statements that are disseminated about them. Thus, the **New York Times rule** does not apply to individuals and thus, mere involvement in a public issue does not bring a person to the level of a class of people who have less of an ability to sue for defamation. The **Gertz** case established that states can establish their own standards of liability for defamatory words made about private individuals. "Actual malice" must be present in order for someone who makes a defamatory statement about an individual to be liable for damages suffered by that person, such as the loss of a job or job opportunity based on the statement. The Supreme Court later determined that even a source that was not media related, such as the Dun & Bradstreet credit reporting agency, could be sued if a private person suffered damages as the result of poor reporting of that agency. A plaintiff might not need to prove damages; the court, instead, can presume damages. Further, the court can punish the defendant for his actions by giving damages to the plaintiff.

A statement must be proved to be false before it can be considered defamatory.[20] The case of **Milkovich v. Lorain Journal Co. et al.**[21] established the often stated phrase "truth is an absolute defense." The **Milkovich** case involved a high school wrestling match between rival schools in Cleveland, Ohio: Maple Heights High School and Mentor High School. A fight ensued following the match in which many people were injured and Milkovich, the wrestling coach for the Maple Heights team, was accused of causing the fight by publicly criticizing decisions made by the referee during the match and thus inciting the crowd to begin the fights. The Ohio High School Athletic Association (OHSAA) held a hearing the next day and put the Maple Heights High School wrestling program on probation for the following school year. Several wrestlers and their parents filed an appeal to that ruling and another hearing was held.

A sportswriter who attended the first, but not the second, hearing wrote about the second decision in the newspaper and made some statements in his published article which implied that Milkovich and another individual who testified at the hearing had lied while under oath (committed **perjury**) during the proceedings. Even the headlines for the articles implied that Milkovich lied, stating "Maple beat the law with the 'big lie'" and "Diadiun says Maple told a lie." The body of the article contained the following phrases, among others: "[I]f you're successful enough, and powerful enough, and can sound sincere enough, you stand an excellent chance of making the lie stand up, regardless of what really happened" and "Anyone who attended the meet, whether he be from Maple Heights, Mentor, or impartial observer, knows in his heart that Milkovich and Scott lied at the hearing after each having given his solemn oath to tell the truth." Milkovich filed suit against the

---

20. 497 U.S. 1 (1990).
21. 497 U.S. 1 (1990).

reporter, arguing that the statements of the reporter had harmed him because perjury is a criminal offense in Ohio. The Supreme Court ruled that the reporter's statements were "opinions" and that expressions of opinion often imply an assertion of objective fact. The Court stated that others could read the transcripts from the hearing themselves and make their own determination as to whether Milkovich and the other man lied and thus did not hold Milkovich liable because the truth could be ascertained from other sources and the reporter's statements reflected his opinion. The Court further stated that if a speaker states as follows: "In my opinion John Jones is a liar," he is implying knowledge of facts that lead him to this conclusion. Stating something as an opinion does not automatically allow the speaker to avoid being liable for that statement.

Finally, the Supreme Court has clearly stated that public officials and figures have little protection when it comes to statements made about them. In **Curtis Publishing Co. v. Butts**,[22] Wally Butts was the former director of athletics for the University of Georgia. He sought damages for an article that was published in a magazine and accused him of conspiring to "fix" a football game between the University of Georgia and the University of Alabama. Butts argued that the article was incorrect and that the writers should have spent more time investigating the facts to be included in the article and ascertaining their claims. The Supreme Court stated that different considerations apply to defamation actions brought by "public figures" like Mr. Butts, when official conduct is criticized. The Court stated that a person is not a public figure merely because he is wealthy or interesting to the public; however, in this case, Butts, by virtue of his position as athletic director for a major university would be a public figure (as opposed to a public official, who holds a position in government). A public official should expect public interest in him but can recover damages for defamatory falsehood only if that falsehood might result in substantial danger to his reputation. In Butts's case, the Court decided that the publisher of the article did act recklessly and Butts could collect money for the damages he sustained due to the publishing of the article.

Private individuals possess less of an expectation that they will be defamed. Further, private individuals do not usually have a direct route to the media to be able to counteract false statements that might be made about them. Thus, states may impose their own standards of defamation liability for private individuals. Most require that there be some negligence in publishing the misstatement and that the private individual receive only actual damages, and rarely punitive damages, from the defendant. Thus, a plaintiff would have to be able to prove to the court that the statement caused him, for example, to lose employment or face some other monetary damages directly because of the statement. This is, in most cases, very difficult to prove.

---

22. 388 U.S. 130 (1967).
23. 485 U.S. 46 (1988).

Public people, however, have been given protection by the Supreme Court. In **Hustler Magazine v. Falwell**,[23] Hustler Magazine published as part of an advertisement a parody of Jerry Falwell, a well-known minister, having a drunken, incestuous encounter with his mother in an outhouse. The ad contained a disclosure at the bottom, but Falwell nonetheless sued the magazine for invasion of privacy, libel, and intentional infliction of emotional distress. The Supreme Court stated that the advertisement could not have been considered by anyone to state actual facts, and thus Falwell could not recover any damages. The advertisement, according to the Court, was not made with knowledge that it was false or with reckless disregard of its falsity; here, the publisher acknowledged that it was false and should not have assumed that anyone would believe it was true. The Court further stated that speech cannot be suppressed merely for being "offensive."

Speech Criticizing the Government. The first case in which the Supreme Court prohibited speech was in 1919 in the case of **Schenck v. United States**.[24] Schenck was convicted under the Espionage Act of 1917, which made it a crime and authorized a sentence for anyone to cause or attempt to cause "insubordination, disloyalty, mutiny, or refusal of duty in the military or naval forces of the United States." Schenck had printed, distributed, and mailed 15,000 leaflets to men who were eligible for the draft, advocating that the men "dodge" the draft and encouraging them to assert their rights not to participate in the draft.

Schenck argued that the Espionage Act violated the freedom of speech clause. The Supreme Court affirmed Schenck's conviction, and Justice Oliver Wendell Holmes, writing the majority opinion, stated that Congress has the right to prohibit situations in which "the words used are used in such circumstances and are of such a nature as to create a clear and present danger that they will bring about the substantive evils that Congress has a right to prevent." The Court set forth the example that the danger of an individual falsely shouting the word "fire" in a crowded theater could lead to panic and thus poses a clear and present danger of people being harmed and that therefore such behavior is not protected under the First Amendment. The **Schenck** court also established various degrees of political speech. It gave low protection to speech that would tend to have the effect of force and would not appeal to reason or logic. It gave high protection to speech that was politically related and had a high degree of ideological content in order to protect political debate that would not seem to lead to some sort of violent action.

The prior test regarding words had been the "bad tendency" test set forth in the Supreme Court's decision in **Whitney v. California**.[25] The **Whitney** court permitted the state to outlaw membership in an organization that existed only to advocate, teach, and aid criminal syndicalism as defined by the Criminal

---

24. 249 U.S. 47 (1919).
25. 274 U.S. 357 (1927).

Syndicalism Act of California. The member, in that case, stated that she did not intend that the party be an instrument of terrorism or violence. Despite the intent of the group, the stated purpose of the organization was criminal. A concurring opinion authored in the **Whitney** case stated that freedom of expression is a "safety valve" for frustration and assists us in finding the truth through the competition of ideas. Thus, the Court can justify suppressing free speech only if reasonable grounds exist to fear that serious evil would result from the speech and that there is imminent danger that the serious evil will occur. The "clear and present danger" test, as this became known, was further referred to by the Supreme Court in dissenting opinions after the **Whitney** case until it was finally adopted by the Supreme Court.

The Supreme Court determined in its decision in **Frohwerk v. United States**[26] that in addition to spoken words, written words, such as those in a newspaper article, could be considered to present a clear and present danger. Frohwerk published articles in a newspaper attacking the position and recruitment efforts of the United States in World War I. The newspaper in which he published his articles was the "Missouri Staats Zeitung," a newspaper which focused on Germany. Specifically, the articles argued that the government made a "monumental and inexcusable mistake" sending soldiers to France and further stated that the German nation was full of strength and an "unconquerable spirit." The articles also focused on the argument that the United States entered into World War I to protect Wall Street. He then stated that the United States should "cease firing." Frohwerk was convicted under the Espionage Act and appealed his case to the Supreme Court. The Supreme Court determined that the articles could lead to an endangerment of the war effort and thus could be considered to create a clear and present danger. Justice Holmes's opinion stated that although it is possible these types of words could have been written without being criminal, in this case, the circulation of the paper was found to be "in quarters where a little breath would be enough to kindle a flame and that . . . fact was known and relied upon by those who sent the paper out."[27] The Court's decision was short but was relied on for the proposition that indeed a newspaper publication could incite people to action.

The companion case to the **Frohwerk** case was the case of **Debs v. United States**.[28] Debs made two public speeches in which he supported socialism and criticized capitalism and World War I. Like Frohwerk, Debs was convicted under the Espionage Act. The Supreme Court stated that political speech that denounced public policy and advocated an alternative could be made a criminal act. Debs was addressing potential military draftees and encouraging them to oppose the war by resisting the recruiting service. The Supreme Court ruled that Debs's speech created a clear and present danger as the

---

26. 249 U.S. 204 (1919).
27. **id.** at 209.
28. 249 U.S. 211 (1919).

Court believed that those who listened to Debs's speech would actually resist the draft, and resisting the draft was an illegal activity.

The **Schenck** "clear and present danger" rule was utilized until the Court changed it in 1969 in **Brandenburg v. Ohio,**[29] when the Supreme Court stated that the test should be whether the speech "is directed to inciting or producing imminent lawless action and is likely to incite or cause such action." Clarence Brandenburg was a Ku Klux Klan (KKK) leader in rural Ohio and invited a reporter from a Cincinnati television station to attend a KKK rally in 1964. The reporter filmed portions of the rally, which displayed men in robes and hoods carrying firearms, burning a cross, and making speeches which discussed "revengeance" against "Niggers" and "Jews." The speeches also announced a march planned to be held in Washington, D.C., on the Fourth of July.

Brandenburg was charged with "advocating violence," which was prohibited under Ohio's criminal statute that had been enacted in 1919 during the "Red Scare" regarding communism. The statute prohibited "voluntarily assembling with any society, group, or assemblage of persons formed to teach or advocate the doctrines of criminal syndicalism."[30] Brandenburg was fined $1,000 and sentenced to one to ten years in prison. He argued that the statute violated his First and Fourteenth Amendment rights to freedom of speech. The Supreme Court reversed his conviction. The issue considered by the Court in the **Brandenburg** case was whether a state law had to distinguish between mere advocacy and incitement to imminent lawless action. The Court ruled that three requirements must be met in order for speech to be prohibited: (1) intention to incite lawless action, (2) the imminence of that possibility, and (3) the likelihood that lawless action will follow. Thus, Ohio's law failed as it did not distinguish between actions that merely advocated a stance and actions that are likely to incite or produce action. Few cases in this area have been brought to the Supreme Court since it decided **Brandenburg**, so the Court has not had the occasion to further clarify the meaning of these three requirements.

The issue of free speech restrictions surfaced recently when lawmakers and politicians began to question whether they could restrict the availability of bomb making instructions on the Internet. Following the Oklahoma City bombing in 1995, Internet posts criticized the construction of the bomb used and made suggestions for making a bomb that would do more damage. In 1996, the full text of the "Terrorist Handbook" was published online, and included instructions on building a similar type of bomb that would do more damage. These Internet posts and other similar posts created controversy and resulted in legislation being introduced in the United States Senate. The legislation was an amendment to the Senate antiterrorism bill and made it illegal to distribute bomb-making information "if the disseminator knows

---

29. 395 U.S. 444 (1969).
30. Ohio Rev. Code §2923.13.

or intends the bomb will be used in a criminal act," punishing any such action by a $250,000 fine and 20 years of imprisonment. The bill was passed in 1997 by the Senate by a vote of 94–0. It was further passed in the House and the bill became law. However, the books can still be found on sale in print. Questions exist as to how this type of information can be prohibited online when it is not prohibited otherwise. The justification given by the government is that dissemination of such material on the Internet is a more rapid way to disseminate the material and can reach a larger audience.

The Supreme Court even forbids any ability by a legislature to curtail political expression by a person who was employed by the government. (It is common and legal for government employees to be prohibited from engaging in other types of political actions, such as openly supporting candidates.) In **Bond v. Floyd**,[31] the Supreme Court forbade a state legislature from refusing to seat an elected representative because he had given speeches that were critical of the Vietnam War. Bond argued that he was a pacifist, that he was not required to support the war, and that he believed he could still take the oath of office. Opposers argued that by speaking out against the war, Bond was discrediting the legislature, aiding enemies of the United States, violating Selective Service laws, and was in direct conflict to Bond's oath of office. The Supreme Court stated in support of its decision that a legislator cannot be held to a higher standard under the First Amendment than an ordinary private citizen can. Further, senators should not be limited in their ability to express their views; in fact, "[d]ebate on public issues should be uninhibited, robust, and wide-open."[32]

Public Versus Nonpublic Forums. Another distinction the Supreme Court has made in terms of the ability of people to express free speech is whether the property on which they are attempting to do so is public or not. Although the government cannot restrict speech on government property, it would be very difficult for government agencies to accomplish their day-to-day duties with protestors, picketers, and the like being constantly present. The Supreme Court has decided that in a public form, speech can only be restricted for important reasons. In a nonpublic forum, more restrictions can be placed on speech.

So how does the Court determine whether a forum is private or not? First, a forum can be public if it has historically been used for public assembly and the exchange of free ideas. Thus, streets and sidewalks, along with public parks, can be considered public. These are areas where typically protests, picketing, and other speeches have taken place. Further, public meeting halls would be considered a public forum. Private forums, then, include such locations that are owned by the government but are used to conduct

---

31. 385 U.S. 116 (1966).
32. This statement was a quote cited by the Court from the case of **New York Times v. Sullivan**, 376 U.S. 254 (1964).

daily business, such as post offices, courtrooms, offices, and the like. The Supreme Court has determined that it is appropriate and reasonable to restrict speech in public forums as long as the speech is neutral as to viewpoint and "reasonable" considering the type of function the forum serves. The Court has upheld restrictions such as a public bus prohibiting any political messages from being advertised on the side of the bus.[33] As long as no political signs are permitted and the authority is not picking and choosing who is able to advertise, the ban can be justified.

Flag Desecration. The first case involving flag desecration was decided by the Supreme Court in 1969 in **Street v. New York**.[34] Individuals had been burning flags in protest demonstrations and state statutes made it a crime to deface or defile the flag. The defendant in this case, Sydney Street, had burned a flag after hearing a news report regarding the murder of a man named James Meredith. Street was questioned by the police about his act of burning the flag, during which he set forth as his reason for burning the flag that "[i]f they let that happen to Meredith, we don't need an American flag." Street was charged with malicious mischief and was convicted.

The Supreme Court agreed to hear Street's case, but its decision was vague and the Court narrowly based its decision on the facts of that particular case without determining the larger issue of the constitutionality of whether flag burning could be banned. The Supreme Court stated that because the state had based its charges not only on the act of burning the flag but also on the words uttered by the defendant setting forth his reasoning for the burning, the Court would have to consider as part of its decision whether statutes can justify laws prohibiting the utterance of words against the flag. The Court stated that the state had not demonstrated that it had a sufficient interest in prohibiting such words. Thus, the Court did not rule on the constitutionality of a prohibition on burning the flag that does not also prohibit words that accompany that burning.

The flag burning issue was finally decided by the Supreme Court in **Texas v. Johnson**,[35] when Gregory Lee Johnson burned a flag during a protest at the Republican National Convention in Dallas, Texas. Witnesses to the act said they were not hurt but were offended. A Texas law prohibited vandalizing respected objects and Johnson was prosecuted, convicted, and sentenced to one year in prison and a $2,000 fine as a result of his actions. At that time, 48 out of 50 states had statutes in place that banned flag burning. In 1989, the Supreme Court ruled that Texas laws making flag burning a criminal act were unconstitutional, stating that "government may not prohibit the expression of an idea simply because society finds the idea offensive or disagreeable."

33. **Lehman v. City of Shaker Heights**, 418 U.S. 298 (1974).
34. 394 U.S. 576 (1969).
35. 491 U.S. 397 (1989).

The **Johnson** decision was a close decision, with five judges joining in the majority opinion and four justices dissenting. The Court spent a considerable amount of time discussing the fact that flag burning would be considered "speech," because speech is not restricted just to the spoken or written word. The Court also indicated that the First Amendment might apply to such cases depending on whether the person conveying the information in question intended to convey a particular message and also depending on whether those who viewed or heard the information would understand the intended message. The Court then stated that Johnson did intend that his actions convey a certain message to others. The Court declared that burning a flag does not always lead to "imminent lawless action," although such behavior could allow a prohibition of such actions. The concurring opinion actually stated that the flag protects "those who hold it in contempt." The dissenters indicated that the flag is such an important and unique symbol to our country that burning it in protest should be specifically banned and that the burning of the flag does nothing other than antagonize others. The dissenting opinion further implied that there are myriad other ways that persons who disagree with the government can get that point across to others.

Congress reacted to the **Johnson** case by passing a federal statute banning flag burning, but that law was struck down by the Supreme Court in 1990 in the case of **United States v. Eichman**.[36] The act challenged in **Eichman** was the 1989 **Flag Protection Act**, which forbade burning or otherwise desecrating the American flag and permitted burning only for proper disposal of worn-out flags. The defendants in the **Eichman** case were individuals who had burned American flags on the steps of the Capitol in Washington, D.C., in a protest of American policy. The **United States v. Haggerty** case, decided along with the **Eichman** case, involved individuals who burned a flag in Seattle, Washington, in protest on the date that the Flag Protection Act went into effect. The Flag Protection Act required that the Supreme Court hear cases involving the act, with no ability to turn down the case, and that the Court decide such cases in an expedited manner. Thus, the Supreme Court decided the case after hearing oral argument outside its regular session of court. In striking down the law, the Court stated that "[p]unishing desecration of the flag dilutes the very freedom that makes this emblem so revered, and worth revering."

Since the Court's decision in **Eichman**, the House of Representatives has passed sufficient votes to enact the **Flag Desecration Amendment**, although the amendment has failed in the Senate. The proposed amendment, also referred to as the "flag burning amendment" would amend the United States Constitution to allow Congress to pass laws prohibiting expression of political views through the physical desecration of the flag. The amendment simply stated that "The Congress shall have power to prohibit the physical desecration of the flag of the United States." In 2006, the amendment failed in the Senate by only one vote. The amendment was also voted on in 1995, 1997,

---

36 496 U.S. 310 (1990).

1999, 2000, 2001, 2003, and 2006 and passed in the House of Representatives on all occasions, although with fewer "yes" votes being cast in favor of it in the House as time has gone on. The language of the Flag Desecration Amendment is so broad that it could potentially result in the prohibition of all forms of flag desecration, including burning, but perhaps also including using the flag for some other purpose, such as clothing or a tablecloth. Civil liberty groups and defenders of the First Amendment argue that flag desecration is uncommon in the United States and that it will be difficult to determine what constitutes a "flag" under the amendment, because flags, for example, can be drawn by children on paper and take many other forms on t-shirts and other paper holiday decorations. Must all of these items be disposed of in a particular way or perhaps not disposed of at all? Those who support the passage of the Flag Desecration Amendment state that the flag is the most visible symbol that embodies our nation and is uniquely important to our society, viewed by citizens with "mystical reverence."

Commercial Speech. Commercial speech is speech that is used to advertise for or further the interests of a company or individual for the purposes of making profit. The Supreme Court has placed more restrictions on commercial speech than some other types of speech. For example, commercial transactions have always been highly regulated by the government. The Supreme Court has proposed a balancing test to determine the appropriate regulation of commercial speech. This test involves considering the interest of the government in prohibiting certain statements by the commercial entity and the interest of the organization in promoting itself. The following considerations are applicable to a determination of whether commercial speech is appropriate or can be banned:

1. Is the expression lawful, misleading, or fraudulent?
2. Is the asserted government interest substantial?
3. Does the regulation directly advance the governmental interest asserted?
4. Is the regulation more extensive than necessary to serve that interest?[37]

An example of a case in which the Court considered a ban against commercial speech was **Virginia Pharmacy Board v. Virginia Consumer Council, Inc.**[38] The Virginia Pharmacy Board had prohibited the advertisement of the retail prices of prescription drugs by pharmacists. The board argued that because the purpose of advertising prices would be purely economic, there was no problem in regulating the communication of them. The board stated that it wished to protect citizens from "unscrupulous" pharmacists who would use the advertising of their prices to the detriment of citizens. However, the Supreme Court disagreed, stating that consumers have an

---

37. **Central Hudson Gas & Electric Corp. v. Public Service Commission**, 447 U.S. 557 (1980).
38. 425 U.S. 748 (1976).

interest in the free flow of commercial information, and the flow of that information is important to the proper functioning of our economic system. The Court acknowledged that commercial speech does remain subject to proper restrictions in terms of time and place and considerations of false advertising; however, the First Amendment does protect most commercial speech. The concurring opinion indicated that certain professionals, such as lawyers, are regulated by ethical rules regarding proper advertising and that the Court was not trying to make any statement that those regulations would not be upheld.

Obscenity and Pornography. Obscene and pornographic materials are also regulated by the First Amendment. An obscene publication is not protected by the guarantee of freedom of speech and press, and both federal and state courts can ban obscene materials. However, courts face difficulties in defining what is considered "obscene." The theory of the Court is that speech must have some sort of "value" to society and that obscene speech has no such value. Of course, what has value to one person might not have value to another and therein lies the difficulty in defining such speech.

At common law, any material that tended to deprave and corrupt someone was considered obscene. Courts considered only the small portion of any text that was being considered obscene, rather than considering the portion in the context of the entire work in which it appears. This included works by many famous authors that were determined to potentially have an immoral effect on children. Federal and state governments have always been permitted to regulate these types of material, which generally are given no First Amendment protection, assuming they are obscene. The most controversial issue in this area that the Supreme Court has had to grapple with has been exactly how to define obscenity and pornography.

The initial definition of obscenity was set forth by the Court in 1947 in its decision in **Rosen v. United States**.[39] The definition was similar to that set forth in a case decided previously by the British courts. The standard was whether the material intended to "deprave or corrupt those whose minds are open to such immoral influences, and into whose hands a publication of this sort may fall." Later, in 1957, the Supreme Court established a different test in **Roth v. United States**,[40] determining that material was obscene if "the dominant theme of the material, taken as a whole, appeals to the prurient interest." The defendants in the **Roth** case argued that their material did not create a clear and present danger to society, and that it only "incited impure sexual thoughts." The Supreme Court stated that obscenity does not equate to sex; rather, obscenity deals with sex that appeals to "prurient interests." The concurring opinion in the **Roth** case asserted that the legislature has no power over sexual morality and each item that would be challenged as being obscene must be considered separately by the Court.

---

39. 161 U.S. 29 (1896).
40. 354 U.S. 476 (1957).

The dissent focused on the argument that all speech should be protected and that by failing to give obscenity the protection of the First Amendment, the Supreme Court is weighing the values of speech against silence.

The Supreme Court continues to wrestle with the exact definition of obscenity and how it should be applied. This is evidenced by the famous words of Justice Potter Stewart in the case of **Jacobellis v. Ohio,**[41] "I know it when I see it." Potter's words were uttered after the justices had viewed a French film that was claimed to be obscene, and Stewart and the other judges stated that the movie was not obscene, but failed to set forth specific factors that would assist other courts in determining when something is obscene.

A further test set forth by the Court in 1973 stated that an item is obscene if the following factors exist: (1) "the average person, applying contemporary community standards, would find the work, as a whole, appeals to the prurient interest," (2) "the work depicts or describes, in a patently offensive way, sexual conduct specifically defined by the applicable state law," and (3) "the work, taken as a whole, lacks serious literary, artistic, political, or scientific value."[42] The **Miller** case involved the owner of a mail order business who advertised the sale of "adult" material by sending flyers through the mail to people who had not even requested them; Miller was charged and found guilty of having violated a California law that prohibited the knowing distribution of obscene material. The lawsuit was brought by a person who had not requested the mailed materials and was offended upon opening them when they came through the mail.

The materials consisted of explicit pictures and drawings of men and women, often depicted in groups, and engaged in sexual acts, with their genitals exposed. The Supreme Court's three-part test, set forth previously, acknowledged that the government and courts should not undertake to regulate expression and any statute that regulated obscene materials had to be carefully limited. Following the decision in the **Miller** case, numerous people were prosecuted under obscenity statutes, because the Supreme Court had finally provided a specific definition of obscenity for lower courts to use. Many of the local statutes and zoning rules that regulate the placement of adult bookstores and theaters were developed by local and state governmental bodies following the Court's decision in **Miller**. The dissent in the **Miller** case, interestingly, suggested that the people should decide what is and is not obscene through the passage by popular vote of a constitutional amendment. Consider what you believe would be deemed obscene if a popular vote of our citizens was utilized to make this determination!

If a court decides that, using the **Miller** test, something is obscene, that obscene material cannot even be shown to consenting adults. In **Paris Adult Theatre I v. Slaton,**[43] a theater was showing films that claimed to be obscene,

41. 378 U.S. 184 (1964).
42. **Miller v. California**, 413 U.S. 15 (1973).
43. 413 U.S. 49 (1973).

and argued that because it was only showing it to consenting adults who chose to attend the viewings, there should be no restriction. The Supreme Court stated that the states have the power to make a "morally neutral" judgment about whether something is obscene and might have a tendency to injure the community as a whole, even if it is exposed to a limited number of willing persons. The Court acknowledged that the right of privacy might preclude regulation of certain obscene materials in the home; however, commercial use such as that of the Paris Adult Theatre is not considered "private." Note that some states use juries to determine whether something is obscene or not. However, a jury must also keep its determination within the confines of the standards set forth in the **Miller** case. A jury in the case of **Jenkins v. Georgia**[44] considered whether a film entitled *Carnal Knowledge* was obscene or not. The Supreme Court viewed the film and stated that the film does not "depict sexual conduct in a patently offensive way . . . While the subject matter of the picture is, in a broader sense, sex, and there are scenes in which sexual conduct including 'ultimate sexual acts' is to be understood to be taking place, the camera does not focus on the bodies of the actors at such times. There is no exhibition whatever of the actors' genitals, lewd or otherwise, during these scenes. There are occasional scenes of nudity, but nudity alone is not enough to make material legally obscene." The Court stated that it would ban "public portrayal of hard core sexual conduct for its own sake, and for the ensuing commercial gain," but that it would not ban the film *Carnal Knowledge*.

Pornography and the Internet. The Internet has added a whole new world in terms of the ability to distribute pornography, and Congress and state legislatures have attempted to respond accordingly. The Communications Decency Act of 1996 was passed by Congress in an attempt to remove pornography from the Internet. The Federal Communications Commission had already limited the use of obscenity in television and radio broadcasting, attempting to limit it to hours when minors would not be exposed to it. The Internet had no such regulation and Congress desired to regulate it. The Communications Decency Act[45] made it a criminal act for anyone to send someone under 18 years of age any "comment, request, suggestion, proposal, image, or other communication that, in context, depicts or describes, in terms patently offensive as measured by contemporary community standards, sexual or excretory activities or organs." It also criminalized any transmission of "obscene or indecent" materials to anyone under the age of 18. Opponents attacked the bill in many ways, including how it would affect medical records posted online and speech that was protected under the First Amendment, such as "indecent" words that might normally be used in daily speech.

---

44. 418 U.S. 153 (1974).
45. P.L. 104-104, 110 Stat. 133.
46. 521 U.S. 844 (1997).

In 1997, the United States Supreme Court considered the constitutionality of the Communications Decency Act in the case of **Reno v. American Civil Liberties Union**.[46] The Court held that certain provisions of the Communications Decency Law were unconstitutional and thus unenforceable except for the provisions that criminalized child pornography and obscenity. The Court determined that the Internet is entitled to the full protection that the media has and that unless the provisions were preventing obscenity as it had been previously defined by the Court or child pornography, the provisions were too broad. The decision was a unanimous one, with all nine judges agreeing that the law suppressed a large amount of speech that adults have a constitutional right to receive and address to each other. The Court opined that less restrictive alternatives would result in appropriate limitations on speech and thus those less restrictive provisions should be used. The Court reasoned that parents could decide for themselves what material their children could be exposed to. The Court did uphold the portion of the law stating that Internet service providers would not be held liable for anything that users would happen to place on Internet sites. Two former Supreme Court justices, Rehnquist and O'Connor, suggested that they would like to see an "adult zone" on the Internet that was not accessible to minors.

Child Pornography. The obscenity standard set forth in the **Miller** case does not apply to child pornography, as the Supreme Court has determined that the government has a paramount interest in protecting children from abuse. The Supreme Court first upheld the outlawing of the distribution of child pornography in **New York v. Ferber**.[47] The **Ferber** case involved two men who owned an adult bookstore in Manhattan, New York. Ferber sold to an undercover police officer two films depicting boys masturbating. He was charged with violating a New York law that prohibited the sale of anything that would depict any child under the age of 16 engaging in sexual conduct. Ferber argued that his actions were protected by the First Amendment. He was convicted, but his conviction was reversed by the New York Court of Appeals. The United States Supreme Court ruled that child pornography could be considered obscene and could thus be outlawed because the government has a compelling interest in preventing the sexual exploitation of children, and distributing anything that would depict sexual acts of children is related to the sexual abuse of children. Further, the Court indicated that visual images of children engaging in sexual activity have "negligible artistic value."

The Court again upheld the illegality of possession of child pornography in the later decided case of **Osborne v. Ohio**.[48] That case involved an Ohio statute which banned the possession of materials depicting child pornography, in

47. 458 U.S. 747 (1982).
48. 495 U.S. 103 (1990).

addition to the sale of such items. The Court reiterated its stance from the **Ferber** case, stating that permitting the possession of child pornography encourages its sale and manufacture, which, in turn, encourages the abuse of children. Further, the Supreme Court saw no problem with how the Ohio statute had been interpreted by the Ohio courts, because it was narrowly interpreted to ban nudity that constituted a lewd exhibition or involves "graphic focus on the genitals."

The Supreme Court had previously decided the case of **Stanley v. Georgia**,[49] in which the Court struck down a Georgia law which forbade adults to have any pornography in their home. The **Stanley** court likened such a restriction to the government trying to control someone's thoughts or morals. The **Osborne** Court distinguished the two cases by indicating that the Ohio statute was attempting to protect child victims, while the Georgia statute attempted to regulate the minds of adults.

The Supreme Court struck down the **Child Pornography Prevention Act of 1996**, which prohibited pornography that does not depict an actual child, if it "conveyed the impression" that it depicts a minor engaging in sexually explicit conduct. The Court determined that law was "overly broad" and thus unconstitutional under the First Amendment. However, most recently, the Supreme Court upheld the **PROTECT Act of 2003**, which prohibits offers to provide child pornography and requests by individuals to obtain child pornography, in the case of **United States v. Williams**.[50] The **Williams** case involved a special agent who, posing as a girl named "Lisa," entered an Internet chat room. The agent happened to come upon a public message posted by the defendant that stated that he had "good" pictures of his toddler to swap, or that he would even transfer images through a live webcam. The agent and the defendant exchanged nonpornographic pictures and then the defendant provided to the agent a picture of a three-year-old girl lying on a couch in her bathing suit. The defendant also provided five photographs of a one- to two-year-old female in nonsexual poses, one of which involved the child topless with her pants below her waistline. The defendant offered to provide further photographs, which were to include his four-year-old daughter in sexual poses and the defendant also shared in a hyperlink image of minors engaged in sexual conduct.

Based on this information, the agent obtained a search warrant and the defendant's home was searched and two computer hard drives were seized, which contained images of minors in sexual positions or displaying their genitalia. The defendant was charged with "pandering" (offering) pornographic material that leads people to believe it involves children, along with possession of child pornography. The defendant argued that the statute outlawing "pandering" was unconstitutionally overbroad. The Supreme Court upheld the statute, declaring that the statute was not overbroad in prohibiting the

---

49. 394 U.S. 557 (1969).
50. 553 U.S. 285 (2008).

offering of child pornography, again resting on the argument that offering such material leads to its dissemination and thus to the abuse of children. However, the Court cautioned that offering child pornography that is "virtual" (in other words, generated by computers or animated) would not be considered illegal and that an offer to request or receive child pornography was not prohibited if real children are not depicted. The defendant's pornography in this case was real and thus his conviction was upheld.

Search and Seizure of Literary Items. Because literary items are subject to First Amendment protection, search and seizure rules vary when literary items are to be seized. A warrant is always required to seize these items.[51] Also, an affidavit requesting a magistrate to approve the seizure of materials based on their obscenity must be very specific. The officer must either show the materials to the magistrate, when possible, or specifically describe them in detail. Further, the items to be seized must be very specifically stated—it is not enough to state that all "obscene materials" are to be seized. If there are numerous copies of the items, such as in a store or other distribution center, only one or two copies shall be seized, and the other copies should remain in the store until a court has made a final decision on whether or not the items are obscene.[52]

Memoirs. A publishing house signed an agreement with an author who had contracted with organized crime figure Henry Hill to produce a book about Hill's life. At that time, New York's **Son of Sam** law provided that if a person convicted of a crime published his memoir for profit, that for at least five years thereafter, all proceeds obtained from such works should be turned over to the Crime Victims Board. The publishing house which had signed the agreement brought suit, arguing that the Son of Sam law violated the First Amendment right to freedom of speech. The Supreme Court held that the Son of Sam law did in fact violate the First Amendment, as it singled out a certain type of speech to regulate, that of convicted criminals.

The Son of Sam law was passed after serial killer David Berkowitz (referred to as the "Son of Sam murders") was offered large amounts of money by various publishers who wished to publish his story and sell it for profit. The law was used 11 times in New York between the years of 1977 and 1990 to seize money from criminals whose stories were published for profit. The law was revised many times and in 2001 the law was revised to reflect that a victim of crime would be notified when the perpetrator receives more than $10,000 from any source. The victim would then be permitted to sue the perpetrator in civil court to attempt to reclaim some of the funds. This New York law, being narrower than the original Son of Sam law, has been upheld by the Supreme Court thus far. Some Son of Sam type laws in other

---

51. **Roaden v. Kentucky**, 413 U.S. 496 (1973).
52. **Heller v. New York**, 413 U.S. 483 (1973).

states have been declared unconstitutional. In high-profile cases, defendants will sometimes agree to Son of Sam type provisions as part of their plea bargain, which leaves them unable to argue that such provisions would violate their First Amendment rights, because the regulation was agreed to as part of the plea.

YOU BE THE JUDGE

A federal statute prohibits the wearing of military uniforms in dramatic productions when those productions tend to discredit the armed forces. Joe James participated in a skit which was performed several times in front of an armed forces induction center which demonstrated opposition to American involvement in the Vietnam conflict. The production was a part of a nationally coordinated peaceful antiwar movement which was to take place contemporaneously at several places throughout the country. Is the federal statute unconstitutional due to the freedom of speech clause?

Freedom of Conduct and Peaceable Assembly

An issue closely related to that of prohibited and regulated speech and included in the First Amendment under the right to peaceably assemble is the issue of conduct other than speech that might be disturbing to others, such as protests where a group of people block others from entering a building. Municipalities have attempted to pass ordinances that prohibit persons from assembling *en masse*, such as the ordinance passed in 1956 in Cincinnati, Ohio, that made it unlawful for "three or more persons to assemble, except at a public meeting of citizens, on any of the sidewalks, street corners, vacant lots or mouths of alleys, and there conduct themselves in a manner annoying to persons passing by, or occupants of adjacent buildings."[53] The punishment for violating the ordinance was a fine of up to $50 and/or imprisonment of up to 30 days. Coates, a student, was convicted of violating the ordinance after participating in a demonstration. Coates argued that the ordinance was vague and thus violated the due process clause.

In **Coates v. Cincinnati**[54] the United States Supreme Court determined that the ordinance was unconstitutional due to the fact that a police officer enforcing it would have to subjectively make a determination as to whether others were actually offended by the actions. The Court stated that it is impossible to determine what conduct is "annoying," as different conduct

---

53. Section 901 L6, Code of Ordinances of the City of Cincinnati (1956).
54. 402 U.S. 611 (1971).

is annoying to different people; thus, men of "common intelligence" must guess at the meaning of the ordinance. The justices determined that the language of the ordinance was too broad; it could, in effect, give too much power to police officers to regulate behavior, and it was unconstitutional. Similarly, in **Smith v. Goguen**,[55] the Supreme Court held that a statute that makes it a crime to treat the United States flag "contemptuously" was invalid because it gave police too much discretion in terms of whom to arrest. The case arose from a situation in which a person in Massachusetts was charged with violating the statute because he had a likeness of the flag affixed to his rear. The Court stated that it was not a fact that such behavior was "contemptuous" and that determination would have to be made by the individual police officer attempting to make the arrest and would depend on how that particular officer would believe the flag should be treated.

Another type of statute that has generally been struck down by courts are loitering statutes. For example, in **City of Chicago v. Morales**,[56] the Supreme Court struck down an ordinance passed by Chicago and referred to as "Chicago's Gang Congregation Ordinance." The ordinance prohibited "criminal street gang members" from loitering in public places. The ordinance also provided that if a police officer saw a person who he "reasonably believed" was a gang member loitering in a public place with one or more people, the officer must order the persons to disperse. Morales was ordered to disperse under such an ordinance and when he did not he was arrested. He argued that the ordinance was unconstitutional and the United States Supreme Court agreed. The Court stated that the law was so vague that "a person of ordinary intelligence" could not figure out what constituted innocent activity and what activity was legal and illegal. The Court stated that it was impossible for citizens to figure out, based on the ordinance's language, what conduct was being prohibited. Loitering statutes and ordinances that have been upheld are those which also specifically require proof of some criminal intent by the person who is charged with loitering. Thus, loitering in an area with the intent to commit a crime is illegal, but an officer must have proof that the person is intending to commit a crime, such as the sale of an illegal substance, or prostitution, before an arrest can be effectuated in accordance with the ordinance.

Freedom of Religion

The First Amendment presents two different concepts concerning religion. The first is the establishment clause, which prohibits Congress from passing laws to establish a national religion or require a person to practice a certain religion. The second is the free exercise clause, which permits a person to

---

55. 415 U.S. 566 (1974).
56. 527 U.S. 41 (1999).

believe in and practice any religion she wishes. As discussed in Chapter 1 of this text, one of the reasons the colonists left England was to secure religious freedom. The colonists brought a wealth of different religious traditions with them and as the United States has become even more of a "melting pot," many more religious traditions have been added to the mix. Even as the colonists settled, religions included Protestant, Catholic, and even Quakers. Now, our country boasts the inclusion of many religions, including Muslim, Buddhist, Hindu, and many others. The concept of "separation of church and state" comes from the religious clause of the First Amendment.

The Establishment Clause. The United States government is prohibited from dictating to its citizens what religion they should practice. This clause has also been interpreted as prohibiting the government from favoring any one religion over another.

The **establishment clause** was incorporated to the states by the Supreme Court in its decision in **Everson v. Board of Education**.[57] In the **Everson** case, taxpayers protested against the use of state funding to reimburse parents for transportation costs incurred on the public bus system in sending their children to parochial schools. The question brought before the Court was whether this use of state money actually established religion. The Court stated that religion was not established by this type of reimbursement, because the reimbursement for transportation was also offered to parents whose children were enrolled in public schools.

One of the most sweeping decisions made by the Supreme Court in the area of religion was in the case of **Wallace v. Jaffree**.[58] In that case, the Court determined that allowing a moment for students in public schools to meditate or have silent prayer, even if no particular religion was focused on, was used to encourage religious values and was thus unconstitutional.

In **Lemon v. Kurtzman**[59] the Supreme Court set forth a three-part test that it would use to judge whether a law violates the establishment clause. First, the law must clearly have primarily a secular purpose. Second, the law must have a principal effect that neither advances nor inhibits religion. Third, the law must not generate excessive entanglement between government and religion.

Although many of the Supreme Court cases in this area were decided in favor of restricting religion in various institutions, the Equal Access Law passed by Congress in 1984 actually permitted students to hold religious meetings in public school buildings when school was not in session.

The Free Exercise Clause. The Supreme Court considered the meaning of the **free exercise clause** of the First Amendment in 1890 in the case of **Davis v. Beason**.[60] The Court stated that intent of the First Amendment was to allow a

---

57. 330 U.S. 1 (1947).
58. 472 U.S. 38 (1985).
59. 403 U.S. 602 (1971).
60. 133 U.S. 333 (1890).

person to "entertain such notions respecting his relations to his Maker and the duties they impose as may be approved by his judgment and conscience, and to exhibit his sentiments in such form of worship, as he may think proper, not injurious to the rights of others."

The free exercise clause was incorporated to the states in 1940 in the case of **Cantwell v. Connecticut**.[61] The **Cantwell** case resulted from a group of Jehovah's Witnesses who solicited funds in a neighborhood populated primarily by Catholics. During their solicitations, the Jehovah's Witnesses played a recording entitled "Enemies" that criticized the Christian religion and, particularly, the Catholic Church. An altercation ensued between the two groups and the Jehovah's Witnesses were charged with breach of the peace. A statute that supported their conviction required groups to obtain a permit to solicit donations from people outside their organization. The Supreme Court ruled that the statute denied the defendants their due process rights and was considered an unconstitutional "prior restraint," as it gave the state excessive power in determining which groups must obtain a license to solicit. The Court also stated that the defendants did not pose a threat to public order by spreading a message regarding their religious beliefs. The Court considered the statute a censorship of religion and stated that the defendants were merely sharing their ideas with others. Further, when a person became very upset about the message, one of the Jehovah's Witnesses actually left the scene so as not to cause further problems. The Court stated that "[T]o condition the solicitation of aid for the perpetuation of religious views or systems upon a license, the grant of which rests in the exercise of a determination by state authority as to what is a religious cause, is to lay a forbidden burden upon the exercise of liberty protected by the Constitution."[62]

THE SECOND AMENDMENT: THE RIGHT TO BEAR ARMS

A well regulated militia, being necessary to the security of a free state, the right of the people to keep and bear arms, shall not be infringed.

—**U.S. Constitution, Amendment II**

In comparison to many other provisions of the Constitution, such as the First and Fourth Amendments, the Second Amendment has been somewhat absent from the Supreme Court decisions and most lower court decisions. Until 2008, the Supreme Court had not made a definitive decision regarding the meaning of the phrase "right to bear arms." Further, there was no decision regarding what an individual's remedy would be if the government in fact violated that right.

---

61. 310 U.S. 296 (1940).
62. **Id**. at 307.

When you read the Second Amendment, do you consider the first clause, which provides that a well-regulated militia must exist, to be the most important idea of the phrase, or do you consider the idea that people should be able to keep and bear arms to be the most important phrase? This question provides much controversy for people and organizations who advocate the right to bear arms and those who advocate that gun control is necessary in order for our society to be ordered and safe.

When you consider both the "militia" and the "keep and bear arms" phrases in the context of the period during which the framers lived, you will note that many customs have changed in our society since then. The colonists who settled our country needed to have an organized militia in order to fend off Native Americans as well as to fight Great Britain in their war for freedom. It is unclear what type of weapons the framers would have desired people to be permitted to possess, because many types of weapons are produced now that were not in existence at the time of the framers' drafting of the Second Amendment.

However, we also know that the framers desired that the government not take away the rights of people to possess the property they desired, and this might include weapons. The term "arms" is also unclear. What is considered an "arm" for purposes of the Constitution? Does this mean all firearms or only certain firearms that would not be commonly used by a militia? Because the language of the amendment is vague, because our culture has changed so much since the amendment was drafted, and because of the concern of how guns can be weapons of destruction, the controversy regarding gun control is a never-ending topic.

Historical Basis of the Second Amendment

The English Bill of Rights includes language regarding the right to bear arms. However, our Supreme Court has pointed out in its opinions relating to gun control that the English Bill of Rights was an individual right that was not related to serving in the militia, and that the focus of the right was that the English government was not permitted to disarm an individual. In other words, the right referred to in the English Bill of Rights was to protect those who already possessed firearms, not to ensure that those who did not already have arms would be able to have them. In fact, the provision also refers to "protestants," as the previous king of England (James II) had removed protestants' right to keep their weapons. The British government has often increased restrictions on firearms in that country, while recent United States Supreme Court decisions have moved toward prohibiting the passage of laws that would restrict the ownership of weapons, except for a few narrow exceptions, as will be discussed later.

Our Constitution garnered debate while it was being drafted because by establishing a federal government, the power to arm state militias was transferred from the states to the federal government. This did not bode well with the concern the colonists already had about the federal government's powers;

colonists worried that by transferring this power, the federal government could actually declare war against the states. Further, the colonists were concerned that their right to possess firearms could also be taken away by the federal government, and they felt that their right to bear arms provided a check against the tyranny of the government. The Federalist Papers include an assertion that the new government should be set up differently from that of England, where the government was afraid to trust citizens with arms. The first few drafts of the Second Amendment included a statement that no citizen would be required to bear arms if their religion prohibited it; however, a concern arose that this language would permit the government to do away with the militia based on religious reasons, so that phrase was eventually excluded.

Possible Interpretations of the Amendment

Grammatically, there are three ways the Second Amendment can be interpreted. First, it can be argued that the Second Amendment consists of an opening justification phrase followed by a declarative clause. Under this interpretation, the opening phrase is essential to the main clause, and this interpretation would result in a protection of the right to bear arms if a person is serving in the militia.

The second possible interpretation views the first phrase as one nonexclusive example of one instance in which individuals have the right to bear arms. Using this interpretation, the Second Amendment would protect the individual right to bear arms for more reasons than just military purposes.

The third possible interpretation views the first clause as explanatory; that militia service is the reason that we allow people to keep and bear arms, but that there are no other restrictions. Thus, the fact that the second part of the amendment guarantees the right to bear arms to "the people" means that all citizens can bear arms, not just those involved in the militia.

With these three possible interpretations in mind, the Supreme Court has ruled as follows when interpreting the Second Amendment.

Early Supreme Court Cases

The very first case considered by the Supreme Court which touched on the issue of the Second Amendment was **United States v. Cruikshank**,[63] a racially charged case in which the defendants were white and had killed more than 60 blacks in the Colfax massacre and had attempted to prohibit the black men from having weapons. The Court stated that the Bill of Rights only applied to the national government and not to private individuals. The next case to mention the amendment was **Presser v. Illinois**,[64] in which Presser, who headed a German-American paramilitary shooting organization, was arrested for leading a group of 400 armed men through the streets of Chicago in a

---

63. 92 U.S. 542 (1875).
64. 116 U.S. 252 (1886).

SECOND AMENDMENT COURT DECISIONS

MAJOR SECOND AMENDMENT SUPREME COURT CASES

1875   1886   1939   2008   2010

United States v. Cruikshank (1875)

The Bill of Rights only applies to the government, and not to individuals

Presser v. Illinois (1886)

The Second Amendment does not bar the states from enacting laws that bar private militias

United States v. Miller (1939)

No conflict exists between the National Firearms Act of 1934 and the Second Amendment

District of Columbia v. Heller (2008)

Citizens have a right to possess firearms even if they are not a member of the militia, for purposes of self defense within their homes. However, citizens do not have an unlimited right to possess firearms.

McDonald v. Chicago (2010)

The Second Amendment is applicable to the States; however, certain groups, such as felons and the mentally ill, should be banned from possessing firearms. Further, firearms can be banned from certain locations, such as schools.

military drill exercise. An Illinois law prohibited such behavior, and Presser was charged. At his trial, Presser argued that his Second Amendment rights were violated. The Supreme Court dismissed his case, stating that the Second Amendment does not bar the states from enacting laws that bar private militias and that the states have the authority to regulate the militia.

The first case in which the Supreme Court discussed the issue of the Second Amendment at length was in **United States v. Miller**,[65] which, interestingly, has been interpreted by opposing groups as supporting both sides of the issue. The **National Firearms Act of 1934** (NFA) was passed as a reaction to the "St. Valentine's Day Massacre," a shoot-out in Chicago that resulted in the deaths of seven people. The massacre was prompted by fighting between two powerful gangs, the "South Side Italian" gang, headed by Al Capone, and the "North Side Irish Gang," which was headed by Bugs Moran. The National Firearms Act required certain types of firearms, namely fully automatic firearms and short-barreled rifles and shotguns, to be registered with the agency, which later became the Bureau of Alcohol, Tobacco, Firearms, and Explosives, or ATF. Registration required payment of a $200 tax and the tax was to be paid again upon any later sale of the firearm.

The legislation was challenged in the Supreme Court by two individuals who had been prosecuted under the NFA. The individuals argued that the act

---

65. 307 U.S. 174 (1939).

was unconstitutional under the provisions of the Second Amendment because the amendment protects individuals' right to keep and bear arms. The government argued that the Second Amendment only protected military style weapons that were useful to an organized militia and that the prohibited weapons had never been used by militia. The Supreme Court voted unanimously and ruled that there was no conflict between the NFA and the Second Amendment, resting on the government's argument and thus focusing on the language in the Second Amendment that refers to the militia. The Court further stated that the "Militia," according to historical documents, involved "a body of citizens enrolled for military discipline" and that those citizens were required to report for duty, when called, with arms in hand.

Although the government saw this case as supporting its position, supporters of the defense and of gun control in general also argued that the Court's decision upheld their argument. First, the attorneys representing the defense in this case did not appear at the oral arguments in front of the Supreme Court owing to a lack of funding to physically travel there. Proponents of gun ownership stated that short-barreled shotguns had been utilized in warfare, and that the Supreme Court's reasoning that this type of weapon had not been used in military proceedings was incorrect and that no one had presented that fact to the court due to the defense's nonparticipation at oral argument. Second, the Court's final order in the case was to remand the proceedings to the federal district court for further findings and a decision based on the Court's discussion in the case. This decision never took place, as Miller, the person bringing the case to begin with, ironically had been shot and died prior to any remand of the case. Additionally, the other defendant involved in the case made a plea bargain after the issue had been taken in front of the Supreme Court, thus waiving his ability to make any further arguments regarding the constitutionality of the statute.

District of Columbia v. Heller.

District of Columbia v. Heller. In 2008, the Supreme Court finally decided a landmark case involving gun control, and the ability of individuals to keep and bear arms for self defense, in **District of Columbia v. Heller**.[66] Two federal district court cases had been decided regarding the issue, but one protected an individual's right to bear arms, while the other oppressed the right. The **Heller** case was actually planned by an individual named Robert A. Levy, who had never owned a gun but was interested in the constitutional issue of gun control and was willing to personally finance such a lawsuit. As such, Levy selected six plaintiffs to become the subjects of the lawsuit. The individuals ranged between the ages of 20 and 70, included three men and three women, and included four white individuals and two black individuals. Washington, D.C., had very strict firearms provisions, set forth in the **Firearms Control Regulations Act of 1975**. These provisions restricted residents of Washington, D.C., from owning handguns, except those citizens who were grandfathered in

---

66. 554 U.S. 570 (2008).

under the act by having their guns registered before 1975, along with those possessed by active and retired law enforcement officers. The act also required that all firearms be "unloaded and disassembled or bound by a trigger lock." The plaintiffs to the lawsuit argued that the law was unconstitutional under the Second Amendment.

The federal district court in which the lawsuit was brought dismissed the lawsuit and the plaintiffs appealed to the United States Court of Appeals for the Washington, D.C., circuit. The Court of Appeals reversed the dismissal and, after addressing some preliminary issues, held that the Second Amendment was "premised on the private use of arms for activities such as hunting and self-defense, the latter being understood as resistance to either private lawlessness or the depredations of a tyrannical government (or a threat from abroad)." The court determined that handguns are "arms" and thus may not be banned, although it did find that Second Amendment rights should be subject to what the court referred to as "reasonable" restrictions. These restrictions include limiting access of handguns to people who are mentally ill or have been convicted of certain crimes. The dissent in the **Heller** case indicated that the citizens of the District of Columbia could not receive the benefit of the Constitution, as the Constitution protects the states, and the District of Columbia was not a state.

The Supreme Court then considered the issue and heard the case on November 20, 2007. The Court received numerous *amicus curiae* briefs, with 47 briefs supporting the circuit court's decision and 20 urging the court to overturn the circuit court. States become involved, along with the Vice President of the United States, who supported overturning the ban on handguns, a position contrary to then President George W. Bush's administration's official position. The Supreme Court heard arguments in the case and considered the issue so important that it even permitted the attorneys to speak beyond the normal allotted time for argument.

The Supreme Court ruled that the Second Amendment protects an individual's right to possess a firearm regardless of whether or not that person had a connection to the militia, and further ruled that possession was authorized for self-defense purposes within the home. However, the Court stated that the Second Amendment right is not unlimited and does not provide the right to keep and carry any weapon, in any manner, and for any purpose. The Court agreed with banning the right to possess arms to certain groups, such as the mentally ill or felons, along with rules that prohibit carrying weapons in schools and government buildings. The Court stated that historically, dangerous and unusual weapons have been prohibited from being carried. Ultimately, the Court found that the handgun ban and trigger lock requirement was unconstitutional, as it applied to self-defense. These rules, according to the Court, made it impossible for citizens to use arms for the "core" purpose of self-defense. The dissent reasoned that the founders would have made the individual right aspect of the Second Amendment "express" if that was the purpose of the amendment and believed that the amendment instead was supposed to focus on issues of military arms, which is why the military language was placed in the beginning of the amendment. However, the Supreme Court's decision in **Heller** only ruled on the Second Amendment in terms of its application to the federal government, not to state and local governments.

Guy Montag Doe v. San Francisco Housing Authority. Following the **Heller** decision, the National Rifle Association (NRA) filed related lawsuits and sought to have the Second Amendment incorporated to the states through the Fourteenth Amendment, thus making it applicable to state and local governments, as well as the federal government. Most importantly, the NRA filed the **Guy Montag Doe v. San Francisco Housing Authority**[67] case the day after the Supreme Court issued the **Heller** decision. The complaint challenged the city's ban of guns from public housing. A settlement between the San Francisco Housing Authority and the NRA allowed residents to possess legal firearms in San Francisco Housing Authority apartment buildings, and as a result, the case never went to the Supreme Court.

McDonald v. Chicago. The most recent case to be considered by the United States Supreme Court in the area of the Second Amendment was **McDonald v. Chicago**.[68] The Federal District Court of Appeals in that case had upheld a Chicago ordinance banning the possession of handguns and other regulations that affected people's ability to possess rifles and shotguns. Specifically, the ordinance (1) prohibited the registration of handguns (which, in effect, resulted in a handgun ban), (2) required that guns be registered prior to any acquisition by Chicago residents, (3) mandated that guns be re-registered annually, with a repayment of the registration fee each year, and (4) rendered any gun to be unable to be re-registered if its registration lapsed.

The primary concern of the plaintiffs in the **McDonald** case was that handguns were unable to be re-registered. In its decision in **Heller**, the Court had recognized a distinction between weapons that were commonly used and those that were "dangerous" or "unusual," and the NRA's argument in **McDonald** was that handguns were neither dangerous nor unusual. The plaintiff also argued that the Second Amendment should be applicable to the states through the process of incorporation, and that the Supreme Court should overturn previous cases in which the Supreme Court had rejected incorporating all of the amendments to the states. Such a determination would have caused quite the commotion in both the civil and criminal realms of law, as many provisions which had previously not been followed by the states

---

67. Case No. 08-03112 TEH, California Northern District Court, filed June 27, 2008.
68. 561 U.S. 3025 (2010).

would be required to be followed, including, for example, the right to a grand jury indictment in state court. Although the majority opinion did not require the incorporation of all amendments, Justice Thomas's concurring opinion did propose such an incorporation.

Thirty-three *amicus curiae* briefs were filed in the **McDonald** case. The Court's decision overturned Chicago's gun restrictions, although it agreed with the **Heller** court that certain groups, such as felons and the mentally ill, should be banned from possessing firearms and that firearms could be banned in certain locations, such as public school property. The Court's decision, however, was limited to the issue of bans on handguns that were possessed for purposes of self-protection. The Court did not address whether other types of bans would also be unconstitutional.

Other state cases that have been decided in the area of gun control included a decision that upheld a state ban on Nunchaku sticks (a weapon used in martial arts),[69] and a case in which a court decided that certain Massachusetts gun lock regulations were not unconstitutional.[70] In the Massachusetts case, the gun lock restrictions only required a gun owner to secure a firearm when it is stored or outside the owner's immediate control. The Supreme Court of Massachusetts ruled that this did not prohibit ownership of a gun or the ability of someone to use the gun for self-defense purposes.

YOU BE THE JUDGE

A police officer is called to a domestic violence situation. The defendant/suspect has locked himself in a bedroom and the police officer approaches the bedroom and says, "I'm not here to arrest you—I just want to get your side of the story." The suspect tells the police officer to "go f*** himself" and says that he's going to "pick him off" and that if he has to go to jail, he will bring the police officer down with him. The officer waits outside the bedroom door, allows the suspect to calm down, and eventually arrests him. The suspect is ultimately charged with obstruction of justice, which prohibits a person from "using threats or force to knowingly attempt to intimidate or impede a law-enforcement officer lawfully engaged in the performance of his duties." The defendant argues that he cannot be charged with this crime, because he was simply exercising his right to free speech. Would you rule for or against the defendant?

---

69. **Maloney v. Rice**, 554 F.3d 56 (2d Cir. 2009).
70. **The Commonwealth v. Runyan**, 456 Mass. 230 (2010).

QUESTIONS TO CONSIDER

1. Read the United States Flag Code, Chapter 1 of Title 4 of the United States Code. What actions do you believe these rules should apply to? Are there any actions that could be taken against a flag that you believe the Supreme Court would say do not fall under these rules?

2. On the Internet, find arguments from advocates of gun control and from advocates of the right to bear arms. Look at the statistics cited by each group to support its argument. Which side do you believe has an argument that better comports with the language of the Second Amendment?

KEY TERMS

absolute privilege
This right is granted to allow statements without the risk of incurring punishment or legal action, such as defamation, even if they were made maliciously, including statements made in court and as part of the legislative process.

defamation
The action of making a statement in a form that damages a person's good reputation; libel or slander.

establishment clause
This clause of the First Amendment prohibits Congress from passing laws that establish a national religion or require a person to practice a certain religion.

free exercise clause
This clause of the First Amendment permits a person to believe and practice any religion she wishes.

libel
Publishing written words that defame someone.

qualified privilege
This defense permits persons in positions of authority or trust to make statements that would be considered slander and libel if made by anyone else. Such immunity is often used by journalists who have written an article and believe that certain facts should be known in the public interest, and as long as the statement by the journalist has not been made with malicious intent, the journalist will be immune from suit.

slander
False spoken statements that defame someone.

Son of Sam law
This New York State law required that any proceeds from a criminal's book should be turned over to the Crime Victims' Board for five years after publication. It was struck down by the Court as unconstitutional.

KEY COURT CASES

Brandenburg v. Ohio

In this case, the Supreme Court replaced the "clear and present danger" rule with a new standard for speech. The Court stated that the test should be whether the speech is "directed to inciting or producing imminent lawless action and is likely to incite or cause such action."

Everson v. Board of Education

The establishment clause was incorporated to the states by the Supreme Court in its decision in this case. The Court stated that religion was not established by the use of public funds to bus students to parochial schools, because the reimbursement for transportation was also offered to parents whose children were enrolled in public schools.

Gitlow v. New York

In this 1925 case, the Court incorporated the First Amendment to all state and local governments through the Fourteenth Amendment due process clause.

McDonald v. Chicago

This most recent case to deal with the Second Amendment involved a Chicago ordinance banning the possession of handguns and other regulations that affected people's ability to possess rifles and shotguns. The Court decision overturned Chicago's gun restrictions, although it agreed with the **Heller** court that certain groups, such as felons and the mentally ill, should be banned from possessing firearms and that firearms could be banned in certain locations, such as public school property. The Court's decision, however, was limited to the issue of bans on handguns for self-protection, and did not address whether other types of bans would also be unconstitutional.

Presser v. Illinois

This case involved a German-American paramilitary shooting group whose leader was arrested for leading them through Chicago in a military drill type exercise. The Court dismissed the case, saying that the Second Amendment does not bar the states from enacting laws that bar private militias and that the states have the authority to regulate the militia.

West Virginia State Board of Education v. Barnette

This case involved a citizen's right not to have to say anything. The Court ruled that it was unconstitutional for the State of West Virginia to pass a statute that required schoolchildren to recite the Pledge of Allegiance while saluting the American flag. The decision focused not on the religious aspects of the case, but on the fact that states do not have the power to compel anyone's speech.

APPENDIX A:
AMENDMENTS TO THE CONSTITUTION

Congress of the United States
begun and held at the City of New-York, on
Wednesday the fourth of March, one thousand
seven hundred and eighty nine.

THE Conventions of a number of the States, having at the time of their adopting the Constitution, expressed a desire, in order to prevent misconstruction or abuse of its powers, that further declaratory and restrictive clauses should be added: And as extending the ground of public confidence in the Government, will best ensure the beneficent ends of its institution.

RESOLVED by the Senate and House of Representatives of the United States of America, in Congress assembled, two thirds of both Houses concurring, that the following Articles be proposed to the Legislatures of the several States, as amendments to the Constitution of the United States, all, or any of which Articles, when ratified by three fourths of the said Legislatures, to be valid to all intents and purposes, as part of the said Constitution; viz.

ARTICLES in addition to, and Amendment of the Constitution of the United States of America, proposed by Congress, and ratified by the Legislatures of the several States, pursuant to the fifth Article of the original Constitution.

Note: The following text is a transcription of the first ten amendments to the Constitution in their original form. These amendments were ratified December 15, 1791, and form what is known as the "Bill of Rights."

Amendment I

Congress shall make no law respecting an establishment of religion, or prohibiting the free exercise thereof; or abridging the freedom of speech, or of the press; or the right of the people peaceably to assemble, and to petition the Government for a redress of grievances.

Amendment II

A well regulated Militia, being necessary to the security of a free State, the right of the people to keep and bear Arms, shall not be infringed.

Amendment III

No Soldier shall, in time of peace be quartered in any house, without the consent of the Owner, nor in time of war, but in a manner to be prescribed by law.

Amendment IV

The right of the people to be secure in their persons, houses, papers, and effects, against unreasonable searches and seizures, shall not be violated, and no Warrants shall issue, but upon probable cause, supported by Oath or affirmation, and particularly describing the place to be searched, and the persons or things to be seized.

Amendment V

No person shall be held to answer for a capital, or otherwise infamous crime, unless on a presentment or indictment of a Grand Jury, except in cases arising in the land or naval forces, or in the Militia, when in actual service in time of War or public danger; nor shall any person be subject for the same offence to be twice put in jeopardy of life or limb; nor shall be compelled in any criminal case to be a witness against himself, nor be deprived of life, liberty, or property, without due process of law; nor shall private property be taken for public use, without just compensation.

Amendment VI

In all criminal prosecutions, the accused shall enjoy the right to a speedy and public trial, by an impartial jury of the State and district wherein the crime shall have been committed, which district shall have been previously ascertained by law, and to be informed of the nature and cause of the accusation; to be confronted with the witnesses against him; to have compulsory process for obtaining witnesses in his favor, and to have the Assistance of Counsel for his defence.

Amendment VII

In Suits at common law, where the value in controversy shall exceed twenty dollars, the right of trial by jury shall be preserved, and no fact tried by a jury, shall be otherwise re-examined in any Court of the United States, than according to the rules of the common law.

Amendment VIII

Excessive bail shall not be required, nor excessive fines imposed, nor cruel and unusual punishments inflicted.

Amendment IX

The enumeration in the Constitution, of certain rights, shall not be construed to deny or disparage others retained by the people.

Amendment X

The powers not delegated to the United States by the Constitution, nor prohibited by it to the States, are reserved to the States respectively, or to the people.

Amendment XI

Passed by Congress March 4, 1794. Ratified February 7, 1795.

Note: Article III, section 2, of the Constitution was modified by amendment 11.

The Judicial power of the United States shall not be construed to extend to any suit in law or equity, commenced or prosecuted against one of the United States by Citizens of another State, or by Citizens or Subjects of any Foreign State.

Amendment XII

Passed by Congress December 9, 1803. Ratified June 15, 1804.

Note: A portion of Article II, section 1, of the Constitution was superseded by the 12th amendment.

The Electors shall meet in their respective states and vote by ballot for President and Vice-President, one of whom, at least, shall not be an inhabitant of the same state with themselves; they shall name in their ballots the person voted for as President, and in distinct ballots the person voted for as Vice-President, and they shall make distinct lists of all persons voted for as President, and of all persons voted for as Vice-President, and of the number of votes for each, which lists they shall sign and certify, and transmit sealed to the seat of the government of the United States, directed to the President of the Senate; — the President of the Senate shall, in the presence of the Senate and House of Representatives, open all the certificates and the votes shall then be counted; — The person having the greatest number of votes for President, shall be the President, if such number be a majority of the whole number of Electors appointed; and if no person have such majority, then from the persons having the highest numbers not exceeding three on the list of those voted for as President, the House of Representatives shall choose immediately, by ballot, the President. But in choosing the President, the votes shall be taken by states, the representation from each state having one vote; a quorum for this purpose shall consist of a member or members from two-thirds of the states, and a majority of all the states shall be necessary to a choice. [And if the House of Representatives shall not choose a President whenever the right of choice shall devolve upon them, before the fourth day of March next following, then the Vice-President shall act as President, as in case of the death or other constitutional disability of the President. –]* The person having the greatest number of votes as Vice-President, shall be the Vice-President, if such number be a majority of the whole number of Electors appointed, and if no person have a majority, then from the two highest numbers on the list, the Senate shall choose the Vice-President; a quorum for the purpose shall consist of two-thirds of the whole number of Senators, and a majority of the whole number shall be necessary to a choice. But no person constitutionally ineligible to the office of President shall be eligible to that of Vice-President of the United States.

*Superseded by section 3 of the 20th amendment.

Amendment XIII

Passed by Congress January 31, 1865. Ratified December 6, 1865.

Note: A portion of Article IV, section 2, of the Constitution was superseded by the 13th amendment.

Section 1. Neither slavery nor involuntary servitude, except as a punishment for crime whereof the party shall have been duly convicted, shall exist within the United States, or any place subject to their jurisdiction.

Section 2. Congress shall have power to enforce this article by appropriate legislation.

Amendment XIV

Passed by Congress June 13, 1866. Ratified July 9, 1868.

Note: Article I, section 2, of the Constitution was modified by section 2 of the 14th amendment.

Section 1. All persons born or naturalized in the United States, and subject to the jurisdiction thereof, are citizens of the United States and of the State wherein they reside. No State shall make or enforce any law which shall abridge the privileges or immunities of citizens of the United States; nor shall any State deprive any person of life, liberty, or property, without due process of law; nor deny to any person within its jurisdiction the equal protection of the laws.

Section 2. Representatives shall be apportioned among the several States according to their respective numbers, counting the whole number of persons in each State, excluding Indians not taxed. But when the right to vote at any election for the choice of electors for President and Vice-President of the United States, Representatives in Congress, the Executive and Judicial officers of a State, or the members of the Legislature thereof, is denied to any of the male inhabitants of such State, being twenty-one years of age,* and citizens of the United States, or in any way abridged, except for participation in rebellion, or other crime, the basis of representation therein shall be reduced in the proportion which the number of such male citizens shall bear to the whole number of male citizens twenty-one years of age in such State.

Section 3. No person shall be a Senator or Representative in Congress, or elector of President and Vice-President, or hold any office, civil or military, under the United States, or under any State, who, having previously taken an oath, as a member of Congress, or as an officer of the United States, or as a member of any State legislature, or as an executive or judicial officer of any State, to support the Constitution of the United States, shall have engaged in insurrection or rebellion against the same, or given aid or comfort to the enemies thereof. But Congress may by a vote of two-thirds of each House, remove such disability.

Section 4. The validity of the public debt of the United States, authorized by law, including debts incurred for payment of pensions and bounties for services in suppressing insurrection or rebellion, shall not be questioned. But neither the United States nor any State shall assume or pay any debt or obligation incurred in aid of insurrection or rebellion against the United States, or any claim for the loss or emancipation of any slave; but all such debts, obligations and claims shall be held illegal and void.

Section 5. The Congress shall have the power to enforce, by appropriate legislation, the provisions of this article.

*Changed by section 1 of the 26th amendment.

Amendment XV

Passed by Congress February 26, 1869. Ratified February 3, 1870.

Section 1. The right of citizens of the United States to vote shall not be denied or abridged by the United States or by any State on account of race, color, or previous condition of servitude—

Section 2. The Congress shall have the power to enforce this article by appropriate legislation.

Amendment XVI

Passed by Congress July 2, 1909. Ratified February 3, 1913.

Note: Article I, section 9, of the Constitution was modified by amendment 16.

The Congress shall have power to lay and collect taxes on incomes, from whatever source derived, without apportionment among the several States, and without regard to any census or enumeration.

Amendment XVII

Passed by Congress May 13, 1912. Ratified April 8, 1913.

Note: Article I, section 3, of the Constitution was modified by the 17th amendment.

The Senate of the United States shall be composed of two Senators from each State, elected by the people thereof, for six years; and each Senator shall have one vote. The electors in each State shall have the qualifications requisite for electors of the most numerous branch of the State legislatures.

When vacancies happen in the representation of any State in the Senate, the executive authority of such State shall issue writs of election to fill such vacancies: Provided, That the legislature of any State may empower the executive thereof to make temporary appointments until the people fill the vacancies by election as the legislature may direct.

This amendment shall not be so construed as to affect the election or term of any Senator chosen before it becomes valid as part of the Constitution.

Amendment XVIII

Passed by Congress December 18, 1917. Ratified January 16, 1919. Repealed by amendment 21.

Section 1. After one year from the ratification of this article the manufacture, sale, or transportation of intoxicating liquors within, the importation thereof into, or the exportation thereof from the United States and all territory subject to the jurisdiction thereof for beverage purposes is hereby prohibited.

Section 2. The Congress and the several States shall have concurrent power to enforce this article by appropriate legislation.

Section 3. This article shall be inoperative unless it shall have been ratified as an amendment to the Constitution by the legislatures of the several States, as provided in the Constitution, within seven years from the date of the submission hereof to the States by the Congress.

Amendment XIX

Passed by Congress June 4, 1919. Ratified August 18, 1920.

The right of citizens of the United States to vote shall not be denied or abridged by the United States or by any State on account of sex.

Congress shall have power to enforce this article by appropriate legislation.

Amendment XX

Passed by Congress March 2, 1932. Ratified January 23, 1933.

Note: Article I, section 4, of the Constitution was modified by section 2 of this amendment. In addition, a portion of the 12th amendment was superseded by section 3.

Section 1. The terms of the President and the Vice President shall end at noon on the 20th day of January, and the terms of Senators and Representatives at noon on the 3d day of January, of the years in which such terms would have ended if this article had not been ratified; and the terms of their successors shall then begin.

Section 2. The Congress shall assemble at least once in every year, and such meeting shall begin at noon on the 3d day of January, unless they shall by law appoint a different day.

Section 3. If, at the time fixed for the beginning of the term of the President, the President elect shall have died, the Vice President elect shall become President. If a President shall not have been chosen before the time fixed for the beginning of his term, or if the President elect shall have failed to qualify, then the Vice President elect shall act as President until a President shall have qualified; and the Congress may by law provide for the case wherein neither a President elect nor a Vice President shall have qualified, declaring who shall then act as President, or the manner in which one who is to act shall be selected, and such person shall act accordingly until a President or Vice President shall have qualified.

Section 4. The Congress may by law provide for the case of the death of any of the persons from whom the House of Representatives may choose a President whenever the right of choice shall have devolved upon them, and for the case of the death of any of the persons from whom the Senate may choose a Vice President whenever the right of choice shall have devolved upon them.

Section 5. Sections 1 and 2 shall take effect on the 15th day of October following the ratification of this article.

Section 6. This article shall be inoperative unless it shall have been ratified as an amendment to the Constitution by the legislatures of three-fourths of the several States within seven years from the date of its submission.

Amendment XXI

Passed by Congress February 20, 1933. Ratified December 5, 1933.

Section 1. The eighteenth article of amendment to the Constitution of the United States is hereby repealed.

Section 2. The transportation or importation into any State, Territory, or Possession of the United States for delivery or use therein of intoxicating liquors, in violation of the laws thereof, is hereby prohibited.

Section 3. This article shall be inoperative unless it shall have been ratified as an amendment to the Constitution by conventions in the several States, as provided in the Constitution, within seven years from the date of the submission hereof to the States by the Congress.

Amendment XXII

Passed by Congress March 21, 1947. Ratified February 27, 1951.

Section 1. No person shall be elected to the office of the President more than twice, and no person who has held the office of President, or acted as President, for more than two years of a term to which some other person was elected President shall be elected to the office of President more than once. But this Article shall not apply to any person holding the office of President when this Article was proposed by Congress, and shall not prevent any person who may be holding the office of President, or acting as President, during the term within which this Article becomes operative from holding the office of President or acting as President during the remainder of such term.

Section 2. This article shall be inoperative unless it shall have been ratified as an amendment to the Constitution by the legislatures of three-fourths of the several States within seven years from the date of its submission to the States by the Congress.

Amendment XXIII

Passed by Congress June 16, 1960. Ratified March 29, 1961.

Section 1. The District constituting the seat of Government of the United States shall appoint in such manner as Congress may direct:

A number of electors of President and Vice President equal to the whole number of Senators and Representatives in Congress to which the District would be entitled if it were a State, but in no event more than the least populous State; they shall be in addition to those appointed by the States, but they shall be considered, for the purposes of the election of President and Vice President, to be electors appointed by a State; and they shall meet in the District and perform such duties as provided by the twelfth article of amendment.

Section 2. The Congress shall have power to enforce this article by appropriate legislation.

Amendment XXIV

Passed by Congress August 27, 1962. Ratified January 23, 1964.

Section 1. The right of citizens of the United States to vote in any primary or other election for President or Vice President, for electors for President or Vice President, or for Senator or Representative in Congress, shall not be denied or abridged by the United States or any State by reason of failure to pay poll tax or other tax.

Section 2. The Congress shall have power to enforce this article by appropriate legislation.

Amendment XXV

Passed by Congress July 6, 1965. Ratified February 10, 1967.

Note: Article II, section 1, of the Constitution was affected by the 25th amendment.

Section 1. In case of the removal of the President from office or of his death or resignation, the Vice President shall become President.

Section 2. Whenever there is a vacancy in the office of the Vice President, the President shall nominate a Vice President who shall take office upon confirmation by a majority vote of both Houses of Congress.

Section 3. Whenever the President transmits to the President pro tempore of the Senate and the Speaker of the House of Representatives his written declaration that he is unable to discharge the powers and duties of his office, and until he transmits to them a written declaration to the contrary, such powers and duties shall be discharged by the Vice President as Acting President.

Section 4. Whenever the Vice President and a majority of either the principal officers of the executive departments or of such other body as Congress may by law provide, transmit to the President pro tempore of the Senate and the Speaker of the House of Representatives their written declaration that the President is unable to discharge the powers and duties of his office, the Vice President shall immediately assume the powers and duties of the office as Acting President.

Thereafter, when the President transmits to the President pro tempore of the Senate and the Speaker of the House of Representatives his written declaration that no inability exists, he shall resume the powers and duties of his office unless the Vice President and a majority of either the principal officers of the executive department or of such other body as Congress may by law provide, transmit within four days to the President pro tempore of the Senate and the Speaker of the House of Representatives their written declaration that the President is unable to discharge the powers and duties of his office. Thereupon Congress shall decide the issue, assembling within forty-eight hours for that purpose if not in session. If the Congress, within twenty-one days after receipt of the latter written declaration, or, if Congress is not in session, within twenty-one days after Congress is required to assemble, determines by two-thirds vote of both Houses that the President is unable to discharge the powers and duties of his office, the Vice President shall continue to discharge the same as Acting President; otherwise, the President shall resume the powers and duties of his office.

Amendment XXVI

Passed by Congress March 23, 1971. Ratified July 1, 1971.

Note: Amendment 14, section 2, of the Constitution was modified by section 1 of the 26th amendment.

Section 1. The right of citizens of the United States, who are eighteen years of age or older, to vote shall not be denied or abridged by the United States or by any State on account of age.

Section 2. The Congress shall have power to enforce this article by appropriate legislation.

Amendment XXVII

Originally proposed Sept. 25, 1789. Ratified May 7, 1992.

No law, varying the compensation for the services of the Senators and Representatives, shall take effect, until an election of representatives shall have intervened.

APPENDIX B:
HOW TO READ AND BRIEF A COURT CASE

At first, reading a court case might be difficult, but if you read the case with an idea of the important points that you need to discern from the case, reading cases can be much easier. Briefing a court case means that you are pulling out the important points of a case and categorizing them. A brief is really an organized outline of a case. When you are reading a case, you want to consider the following points:

1. What are the **FACTS** of the case? (What happened in this case? What people were involved? What actions did the police take in the case? What actions did the courts take?) The fact section can also include a recitation of what happened in each lower court.
2. What is the **LEGAL ISSUE** or **LEGAL QUESTION** presented in the case? (What question did the court have to decide? What law does a police officer or other person working in the criminal justice system have to follow based on the outcome of this case?)
3. What is the **HOLDING** or **ANSWER** in this case? (How did the court answer the legal issue or question posed in this case? How did this change the way a police officer or other court official does his job?)
4. What was the court's **REASONING** or **RATIONALE** regarding this case? (Why did the court rule the way it did? Was it based on prior cases the Supreme Court or other courts had decided? Was it based on an interpretation of the Constitution?)
5. If there was a concurring or dissenting opinion in the case, how did the rule or rationale of that opinion differ from that of the majority?

Following is an edited version of the Supreme Court's opinion in the case of **Terry v. Ohio**, a landmark Supreme Court case that permitted officers to conduct what has been known as a stop and frisk. Read the case with the preceding questions in mind.

TERRY v. OHIO

SUPREME COURT OF THE UNITED STATES

392 U.S. 1; 88 S. Ct. 1868; 20 L. Ed. 2d 889;
1968 U.S. LEXIS 1345; 44 Ohio Op. 2d 383

December 12, 1967, Argued

June 10, 1968, Decided

JUDGES: Warren, Black, Douglas, Harlan, Brennan, Stewart, White, Fortas, Marshall

OPINION BY: WARREN

OPINION

MR. CHIEF JUSTICE WARREN delivered the opinion of the Court.

This case presents serious questions concerning the role of the Fourth Amendment in the confrontation on the street between the citizen and the policeman investigating suspicious circumstances.

Petitioner Terry was convicted of carrying a concealed weapon and sentenced to the statutorily prescribed term of one to three years in the penitentiary. Following the denial of a pretrial motion to suppress, the prosecution introduced in evidence two revolvers and a number of bullets seized from Terry and a codefendant, Richard Chilton, by Cleveland Police Detective Martin McFadden. At the hearing on the motion to suppress this evidence, Officer McFadden testified that while he was patrolling in plain clothes in downtown Cleveland at approximately 2:30 in the afternoon of October 31, 1963, his attention was attracted by two men, Chilton and Terry, standing on the corner of Huron Road and Euclid Avenue. He had never seen the two men before, and he was unable to say precisely what first drew his eye to them. However, he testified that he had been a policeman for 39 years and a detective for 35 and that he had been assigned to patrol this vicinity of downtown Cleveland for shoplifters and pickpockets for 30 years. He explained that he had developed routine habits of observation over the years and that he would "stand and watch people or walk and watch people at many intervals of the day." He added: "Now, in this case when I looked over they didn't look right to me at the time."

His interest aroused, Officer McFadden took up a post of observation in the entrance to a store 300 to 400 feet away from the two men. "I get more purpose to watch them when I seen their movements," he testified. He saw one of the men leave the other one and walk southwest on Huron Road, past some stores. The man paused for a moment and looked in a store window, then walked on a short distance, turned around and walked back toward the corner, pausing once again to look in the same store window. He rejoined his companion at the corner, and the two conferred briefly. Then the second man went through the same series of motions, strolling down Huron Road, looking in the same window, walking on a short distance, turning back, peering in the store window again, and returning to confer with the first man at the corner. The two men repeated this ritual alternately between five and six times apiece—in all, roughly a dozen trips. At one point, while the two were standing together on the corner, a third man approached them and engaged them briefly in conversation. This man then left the two others and walked west on Euclid Avenue. Chilton and Terry resumed their measured pacing, peering, and conferring. After this had gone on for 10 to 12 minutes, the two men walked off together, heading west on Euclid Avenue, following the path taken earlier by the third man.

By this time Officer McFadden had become thoroughly suspicious. He testified that after observing their elaborately casual and oft-repeated reconnaissance of the store window on Huron Road, he suspected the two men of "casing a job, a stick-up," and that he considered it his duty as a police officer to investigate further. He added that he feared "they may have a gun." Thus, Officer McFadden followed Chilton and Terry and saw them stop in front of Zucker's store to talk to the same man who had conferred with them earlier on the street corner. Deciding that the situation was ripe for direct action, Officer McFadden approached the three men, identified himself as a police officer and asked for their names. At this point his knowledge was confined to what he had observed. He was not acquainted with any of the three men by name or by sight, and he had received no information concerning them from any other source. When the men "mumbled something" in response to his inquiries, Officer McFadden grabbed petitioner Terry, spun him around so that they were facing the other two, with Terry between McFadden and the others, and patted down the outside of his clothing. In the left breast pocket of Terry's overcoat Officer McFadden felt a pistol. He reached inside the overcoat pocket, but was unable to remove the gun. At this point, keeping Terry between himself and the others, the officer ordered all three men to enter Zucker's store. As they went in, he removed Terry's overcoat completely, removed a .38-caliber revolver from the pocket and ordered all three men to face the wall with their hands raised. Officer McFadden proceeded to pat down the outer clothing of Chilton and the third man, Katz. He discovered another revolver in the outer pocket of Chilton's overcoat, but no weapons were found on Katz. The officer testified that he only patted the men down to see whether they had weapons, and that he did not put his hands beneath the outer garments of either Terry or Chilton until he felt their guns. So far as appears from the record, he never placed his hands beneath Katz' outer garments. Officer McFadden seized Chilton's gun, asked the proprietor of the store to call a police wagon, and took all three men to the station, where Chilton and Terry were formally charged with carrying concealed weapons.

On the motion to suppress the guns the prosecution took the position that they had been seized following a search incident to a lawful arrest. The trial court rejected this theory, stating that it "would be stretching the facts beyond reasonable comprehension" to find that Officer McFadden had had probable cause to arrest the men before he patted them down for weapons. However, the court denied the defendants' motion on the ground that Officer McFadden, on the basis of his experience, "had reasonable cause to believe . . . that the defendants were conducting themselves suspiciously, and some interrogation should be made of their action." Purely for his own protection, the court held, the officer had the right to pat down the outer clothing of these men, who he had reasonable cause to believe might be armed. The court distinguished between an investigatory "stop" and an arrest, and between a "frisk" of the outer clothing for weapons and a full-blown search for evidence of crime. The frisk, it held, was essential to the proper performance of the officer's investigatory duties, for without it "the answer to the police officer may be a bullet, and a loaded pistol discovered during the frisk is admissible."

After the court denied their motion to suppress, Chilton and Terry waived jury trial and pleaded not guilty. The court adjudged them guilty, and the Court of Appeals for the Eighth Judicial District, Cuyahoga County, affirmed. State v. Terry, 5 Ohio App. 2d 122, 214 N. E. 2d 114 (1966). The Supreme Court of Ohio dismissed their appeal on the ground that no "substantial constitutional question" was involved. We granted certiorari, 387 U.S. 929 (1967), to determine whether the admission of the revolvers in evidence violated petitioner's rights under the Fourth Amendment made applicable to the States by the Fourteenth. Mapp v. Ohio, 367 U.S. 643 (1961). We affirm the conviction.

I.

The Fourth Amendment provides that "the right of the people to be secure in their persons, houses, papers, and effects, against unreasonable searches and seizures, shall not be violated. . . . " This inestimable right of personal security belongs as much to the citizen on the streets of our cities as to the homeowner closeted in his study to dispose of his secret affairs. For, as this Court has always recognized, "No right is held more sacred, or is more carefully guarded, by the common law, than the right of every individual to the possession and control of his own person, free from all restraint or interference of others, unless by clear and unquestionable authority of law." Union Pac. R. Co. v. Botsford, 141 U.S. 250, 251 (1891). We have recently held that "the Fourth Amendment protects people, not places," Katz v. United States, 389 U.S. 347, 351 (1967), and wherever an individual may harbor a reasonable "expectation of privacy," id., at 361 (MR. JUSTICE HARLAN, concurring), he is entitled to be free from unreasonable governmental intrusion. Of course, the specific content and incidents of this right must be shaped by the context in which it is asserted. For "what the Constitution forbids is not all searches and seizures, but unreasonable searches and seizures." Elkins v. United States, 364 U.S. 206, 222 (1960). Unquestionably petitioner was entitled to the protection of the Fourth Amendment as he walked down the street in Cleveland. Beck v. Ohio, 379 U.S. 89 (1964); Rios v. United States, 364 U.S. 253 (1960); Henry v. United States, 361 U.S. 98 (1959); United States v. Di Re, 332 U.S. 581 (1948); Carroll v. United States, 267 U.S. 132 (1925). The question is whether in all the circumstances of this on-the-street encounter, his right to personal security was violated by an unreasonable search and seizure.

We would be less than candid if we did not acknowledge that this question thrusts to the fore difficult and troublesome issues regarding a sensitive area of police activity—issues which have never before been squarely presented to this Court. Reflective of the tensions involved are the practical and constitutional arguments pressed with great vigor on both sides of the public debate over the power of the police to "stop and frisk"—as it is sometimes euphemistically termed—suspicious persons.

On the one hand, it is frequently argued that in dealing with the rapidly unfolding and often dangerous situations on city streets the police are in need of an escalating set of flexible responses, graduated in relation to the amount of information they possess. For this purpose it is urged that distinctions should be made between a "stop" and an "arrest" (or a "seizure" of a person), and between a "frisk" and a "search." Thus, it is argued, the police should be allowed to "stop" a person and detain him briefly for questioning upon suspicion that he may be connected with criminal activity. Upon suspicion that the person may be armed, the police should have the power to "frisk" him for weapons. If the "stop" and the "frisk" give rise to probable cause to believe that the suspect has committed a crime, then the police should be empowered to make a formal "arrest," and a full incident "search" of the person. This scheme is justified in part upon the notion that a "stop" and a "frisk" amount to a mere "minor inconvenience and petty indignity," which can properly be imposed upon the citizen in the interest of effective law enforcement on the basis of a police officer's suspicion.

On the other side the argument is made that the authority of the police must be strictly circumscribed by the law of arrest and search as it has developed to date in the traditional jurisprudence of the Fourth Amendment. It is contended with some force that there is not—and cannot be—a variety of police activity which does not depend solely upon the voluntary cooperation of the citizen and yet which stops short of an arrest based upon probable cause to make such an arrest. The heart of the Fourth Amendment, the argument runs, is a severe requirement of specific justification for any intrusion upon protected personal security, coupled with a highly developed system of judicial controls to enforce upon the agents of the State the commands of the Constitution. Acquiescence by the courts in the compulsion inherent in the field interrogation practices at issue here, it is urged, would constitute an abdication of judicial control over, and indeed an encouragement of, substantial interference with liberty and personal security by police officers whose judgment is necessarily colored by their primary involvement in "the often competitive enterprise of ferreting out crime." Johnson v. United States, 333 U.S. 10, 14 (1948). This, it is argued, can only serve to exacerbate police-community tensions in the crowded centers of our Nation's cities.

In this context we approach the issues in this case mindful of the limitations of the judicial function in controlling the myriad daily situations in which police-men and citizens confront each other on the street. The State has characterized the issue here as "the right of a police officer . . . to make an on-the-street stop, interrogate and pat down for weapons (known in street vernacular as 'stop and frisk')." But this is only partly accurate. For the issue is not the abstract propriety of the police conduct, but the admissibility against petitioner of the evidence uncovered by the search and seizure. Ever since its inception, the rule excluding evidence seized in violation of the Fourth Amendment has been recognized as a principal mode of discouraging lawless police conduct. See Weeks v. United States, 232 U.S. 383, 391-393 (1914). Thus its major thrust is a deterrent one, see Linkletter v. Walker, 381 U.S. 618, 629-635 (1965), and experience has taught that it is the only effective deterrent to police misconduct in the criminal context, and that without it the constitutional guarantee against unrea-sonable searches and seizures would be a mere "form of words." Mapp v. Ohio, 367 U.S. 643, 655 (1961). The rule also serves another vital function—"the imperative of judicial integrity." Elkins v. United States, 364 U.S. 206, 222 (1960). Courts which sit under our Constitution cannot and will not be made party to lawless invasions of the constitutional rights of citizens by permitting unhindered governmental use of the fruits of such invasions. Thus in our system evidentiary rulings provide the context in which the judicial process of inclusion and exclusion approves some conduct as comporting with constitutional guar-antees and disapproves other actions by state agents. A ruling admitting evidence in a criminal trial, we recognize, has the necessary effect of legitimizing the conduct which produced the evidence, while an application of the exclusionary rule withholds the constitutional imprimatur.

The exclusionary rule has its limitations, however, as a tool of judicial control. It cannot properly be invoked to exclude the products of legitimate police inves-tigative techniques on the ground that much conduct which is closely similar involves unwarranted intrusions upon constitutional protections. Moreover, in some contexts the rule is ineffective as a deterrent. Street encounters between citizens and police officers are incredibly rich in diversity. They range from wholly friendly exchanges of pleasantries or mutually useful information to hostile confrontations of armed men involving arrests, or injuries, or loss of life. Moreover, hostile confrontations are not all of a piece. Some of them begin in a friendly enough manner, only to take a different turn upon the injection of some unexpected element into the conversation. Encounters are initiated by the police for a wide variety of purposes, some of which are wholly unrelated to a desire to prosecute for crime. Doubtless some police "field interrogation" conduct violates the Fourth Amendment. But a stern refusal by this Court to condone such activity does not necessarily render it responsive to the exclusionary rule. Regardless of how effective the rule may be where obtaining convictions is an important objective of the police, it is powerless to deter invasions of constitutionally guaranteed rights where the police either have no interest in prosecuting or are willing to forgo successful prosecution in the interest of serving some other goal.

Proper adjudication of cases in which the exclusionary rule is invoked demands a constant awareness of these limitations. The wholesale harassment by certain elements of the police community, of which minority groups, particularly Negroes, frequently complain, will not be stopped by the exclusion of any evidence from any criminal trial. Yet a rigid and unthinking application of the exclusionary rule, in futile protest against practices which it can never be used effectively to control, may exact a high toll in human injury and frustration of efforts to prevent crime. No judicial opinion can comprehend the protean variety of the street encounter, and we can only judge the facts of the case before us. Nothing we say today is to be taken as indicating approval of police conduct outside the legitimate investigative sphere. Under our decision, courts still retain their traditional responsibility to guard against police conduct which is overbearing or harassing, or which trenches upon personal security without the objective evidentiary justification which the Constitution requires. When such conduct is identified, it must be condemned by the judiciary and its fruits must be excluded from evidence in criminal trials. And, of course, our approval of legitimate and restrained investigative conduct undertaken on the basis of ample factual justification should in no way discourage the employment of other remedies than the exclusionary rule to curtail abuses for which that sanction may prove inappropriate.

Having thus roughly sketched the perimeters of the constitutional debate over the limits on police investigative conduct in general and the background against which this case presents itself, we turn our attention to the quite narrow question posed by the facts before us: whether it is always unreasonable for a policeman to seize a person and subject him to a limited search for weapons unless there is probable cause for an arrest. Given the narrowness of this question, we have no occasion to canvass in detail the constitutional limitations upon the scope of a policeman's power when he confronts a citizen without probable cause to arrest him.

Our first task is to establish at what point in this encounter the Fourth Amendment becomes relevant. That is, we must decide whether and when Officer McFadden "seized" Terry and whether and when he conducted a "search." There is some suggestion in the use of such terms as "stop" and "frisk" that such police conduct is outside the purview of the Fourth Amendment because neither action rises to the level of a "search" or "seizure" within the meaning of the Constitution. We emphatically reject this notion. It is quite plain that the Fourth Amendment governs "seizures" of the person which do not eventuate in a trip to the station house and prosecution for crime—"arrests" in traditional terminology. It must be recognized that whenever a police officer accosts an individual and restrains his freedom to walk away, he has "seized" that person. And it is nothing less than sheer torture of the English language to suggest that a careful exploration of the outer surfaces of a person's clothing all over his or her body in an attempt to find weapons is not a "search." Moreover, it is simply fantastic to urge that such a procedure performed in public by a policeman while the citizen stands helpless, perhaps facing a wall with his hands raised, is a "petty indignity." It is a serious intrusion upon the sanctity of the person, which may inflict great indignity and arouse strong resentment, and it is not to be undertaken lightly.

We have noted that the abusive practices which play a major, though by no means exclusive, role in creating this friction are not susceptible of control by means of the exclusionary rule, and cannot properly dictate our decision with respect to the powers of the police in genuine investigative and preventive situations. However, the degree of community resentment aroused by particular practices is clearly relevant to an assessment of the quality of the intrusion upon reasonable expectations of personal security caused by those practices.

The danger in the logic which proceeds upon distinctions between a "stop" and an "arrest," or "seizure" of the person, and between a "frisk" and a "search" is twofold. It seeks to isolate from constitutional scrutiny the initial stages of the contact between the policeman and the citizen. And by suggesting a rigid all-or-nothing model of justification and regulation under the Amendment, it obscures the utility of limitations upon the scope, as well as the initiation, of police action as a means of constitutional regulation. This Court has held in the past that a search which is reasonable at its inception may violate the Fourth Amendment by virtue of its intolerable intensity and scope. Kremen v. United States, 353 U.S. 346 (1957); Go-Bart Importing Co. v. United States, 282 U.S. 344, 356-358 (1931); see United States v. Di Re, 332 U.S. 581, 586-587 (1948). The scope of the search must be "strictly tied to and justified by" the circumstances which rendered its initiation permissible. Warden v. Hayden, 387 U.S. 294, 310 (1967)

(MR. JUSTICE FORTAS, concurring); see, e. g., <u>Preston v. United States, 376 U.S. 364, 367–368 (1964)</u>; <u>Agnello v. United States, 269 U.S. 20, 30–31 (1925)</u>.

The distinctions of classical "stop-and-frisk" theory thus serve to divert attention from the central inquiry under the Fourth Amendment—the reasonableness in all the circumstances of the particular governmental invasion of a citizen's personal security. "Search" and "seizure" are not talismans. We therefore reject the notions that the Fourth Amendment does not come into play at all as a limitation upon police conduct if the officers stop short of something called a "technical arrest" or a "full-blown search."

In this case there can be no question, then, that Officer McFadden "seized" petitioner and subjected him to a "search" when he took hold of him and patted down the outer surfaces of his clothing. We must decide whether at that point it was reasonable for Officer McFadden to have interfered with petitioner's personal security as he did. And in determining whether the seizure and search were "unreasonable" our inquiry is a dual one—whether the officer's action was justified at its inception, and whether it was reasonably related in scope to the circumstances which justified the interference in the first place.

If this case involved police conduct subject to the Warrant Clause of the Fourth Amendment, we would have to ascertain whether "probable cause" existed to justify the search and seizure which took place. However, that is not the case. We do not retreat from our holdings that the police must, whenever practicable, obtain advance judicial approval of searches and seizures through the warrant procedure, see, e. g., <u>Katz v. United States, 389 U.S. 347 (1967)</u>; <u>Beck v. Ohio, 379 U.S. 89, 96 (1964)</u>; <u>Chapman v. United States, 365 U.S. 610 (1961)</u>, or that in most instances failure to comply with the warrant requirement can only be excused by exigent circumstances, sec, e. g., <u>Warden v. Hayden, 387 U.S. 294 (1967)</u> (hot pursuit); cf. <u>Preston v. United States, 376 U.S. 364, 367–368 (1964)</u>. But we deal here with an entire rubric of police conduct—necessarily swift action predicated upon the on-the-spot observations of the officer on the beat—which historically has not been, and as a practical matter could not be, subjected to the warrant procedure. Instead, the conduct involved in this case must be tested by the Fourth Amendment's general proscription against unreasonable searches and seizures.

Nonetheless, the notions which underlie both the warrant procedure and the requirement of probable cause remain fully relevant in this context. In order to assess the reasonableness of Officer McFadden's conduct as a general proposition, it is necessary "first to focus upon the governmental interest which allegedly justifies official intrusion upon the constitutionally protected interests of the private citizen," for there is "no ready test for determining reasonableness other than by balancing the need to search [or seize] against the invasion which the search [or seizure] entails." Camara v. Municipal Court, 387 U.S. 523, 534–535, 536–537 (1967). And in justifying the particular intrusion the police officer must be able to point to specific and articulable facts which, taken together with rational inferences from those facts, reasonably warrant that intrusion. The scheme of the Fourth Amendment becomes meaningful only when it is assured that at some point the conduct of those charged with enforcing the laws can be subjected to the more detached, neutral scrutiny of a judge who must evaluate the reasonableness of a particular search or seizure in light of the particular circumstances. And in making that assessment it is imperative that the facts be judged against an objective standard: would the facts available to the officer at the moment of the seizure or the search "warrant a man of reasonable caution in the belief" that the action taken was appropriate? Cf. Carroll v. United States, 267 U.S. 132 (1925); Beck v. Ohio, 379 U.S. 89, 96–97 (1964). Anything less would invite intrusions upon constitutionally guaranteed rights based on nothing more substantial than inarticulate hunches, a result this Court has consistently refused to sanction. See, e. g., Beck v. Ohio, supra; Rios v. United States, 364 U.S. 253 (1960); Henry v. United States, 361 U.S. 98 (1959). And simple "'good faith on the part of the arresting officer is not enough.' . . . If subjective good faith alone were the test, the protections of the Fourth Amendment would evaporate, and the people would be 'secure in their persons, houses, papers, and effects,' only in the discretion of the police." Beck v. Ohio, supra, at 97.

Applying these principles to this case, we consider first the nature and extent of the governmental interests involved. One general interest is of course that of effective crime prevention and detection; it is this interest which underlies the recognition that a police officer may in appropriate circumstances and in an appropriate manner approach a person for purposes of investigating possibly criminal behavior even though there is no probable cause to make an arrest. It was this legitimate investigative function Officer McFadden was discharging when he decided to approach petitioner and his companions. He had observed Terry, Chilton, and Katz go through a series of acts, each of them perhaps innocent in itself, but which taken together warranted further investigation. There is nothing unusual in two men standing together on a street corner, perhaps waiting for someone. Nor is there anything suspicious about people in such circumstances strolling up and down the street, singly or in pairs. Store windows, moreover, are made to be looked in. But the story is quite different where, as here, two men hover about a street corner for an extended period of time, at the end of which it becomes apparent that they are not waiting for anyone or anything; where these men pace alternately along an identical route, pausing to stare in the same store window roughly 24 times; where each completion of this route is followed immediately by a conference between the two men on the corner; where they are joined in one of these conferences by a third man who leaves swiftly; and where the two men finally follow the third and rejoin him a couple of blocks away. It would have been poor police work indeed for an officer of 30 years' experience in the detection of thievery from stores in this same neighborhood to have failed to investigate this behavior further.

The crux of this case, however, is not the propriety of Officer McFadden's taking steps to investigate petitioner's suspicious behavior, but rather, whether there was justification for McFadden's invasion of Terry's personal security by searching him for weapons in the course of that investigation. We are now concerned with more than the governmental interest in investigating crime; in addition, there is the more immediate interest of the police officer in taking steps to assure himself that the person with whom he is dealing is not armed with a weapon that could unexpectedly and fatally be used against him. Certainly it would be unreasonable to require that police officers take unnecessary risks in the performance of their duties. American criminals have a long tradition of armed violence, and every year in this country many law enforcement officers are killed in the line of duty, and thousands more are wounded. Virtually all of these deaths and a substantial portion of the injuries are inflicted with guns and knives.

The easy availability of firearms to potential criminals in this country is well known and has provoked much debate. See, e. g., President's Commission on Law Enforcement and Administration of Justice, The Challenge of Crime in a Free Society 239-243 (1967). Whatever the merits of gun-control proposals, this fact is relevant to an assessment of the need for some form of self-protective search power.

When an officer is justified in believing that the individual whose suspicious behavior he is investigating at close range is armed and presently dangerous to the officer or to others, it would appear to be clearly unreasonable to deny the officer the power to take necessary measures to determine whether the person is in fact carrying a weapon and to neutralize the threat of physical harm.

We must still consider, however, the nature and quality of the intrusion on individual rights which must be accepted if police officers are to be conceded the right to search for weapons in situations where probable cause to arrest for crime is lacking. Even a limited search of the outer clothing for weapons constitutes a severe, though brief, intrusion upon cherished personal security, and it must surely be an annoying, frightening, and perhaps humiliating experience. Petitioner contends that such an intrusion is permissible only incident to a lawful arrest, either for a crime involving the possession of weapons or for a crime the commission of which led the officer to investigate in the first place. However, this argument must be closely examined.

Petitioner does not argue that a police officer should refrain from making any investigation of suspicious circumstances until such time as he has probable cause to make an arrest; nor does he deny that police officers in properly discharging their investigative function may find themselves confronting persons who might well be armed and dangerous. Moreover, he does not say that an officer is always unjustified in searching a suspect to discover weapons. Rather, he says it is unreasonable for the policeman to take that step until such time as the situation evolves to a point where there is probable cause to make an arrest. When that point has been reached, petitioner would concede the officer's right to conduct a search of the suspect for weapons, fruits or instrumentalities of the crime, or "mere" evidence, incident to the arrest. There are two weaknesses in this line of reasoning, however. First, it fails to take account of traditional limitations upon the scope of searches, and thus recognizes no distinction in purpose, character, and extent between a search incident to an arrest and a limited search for weapons. The former, although justified in part by the acknowledged necessity to protect the arresting officer from assault with a concealed weapon, Preston v. United States, 376 U.S. 364, 367 (1964), is also justified on other grounds, ibid., and can therefore involve a relatively extensive exploration of the person. A search for weapons in the absence of probable cause to arrest, however, must, like any other search, be strictly circumscribed by the exigencies which justify its initiation. Warden v. Hayden, 387 U.S. 294, 310 (1967) (MR. JUSTICE FORTAS, concurring). Thus it must be limited to that which is necessary for the discovery of weapons which might be used to harm the officer or others nearby, and may realistically be characterized as something less than a "full" search, even though it remains a serious intrusion.

A second, and related, objection to petitioner's argument is that it assumes that the law of arrest has already worked out the balance between the particular interests involved here—the neutralization of danger to the policeman in the investigative circumstance and the sanctity of the individual. But this is not so. An arrest is a wholly different kind of intrusion upon individual freedom from a limited search for weapons, and the interests each is designed to serve are likewise quite different. An arrest is the initial stage of a criminal prosecution. It is intended to vindicate society's interest in having its laws obeyed, and it is inevitably accompanied by future interference with the individual's freedom of movement, whether or not trial or conviction ultimately follows. The protective search for weapons, on the other hand, constitutes a brief, though far from inconsiderable, intrusion upon the sanctity of the person. It does not follow that because an officer may lawfully arrest a person only when he is apprised of facts sufficient to warrant a belief that the person has committed or is committing a crime, the officer is equally unjustified, absent that kind of evidence, in making any intrusions short of an arrest. Moreover, a perfectly reasonable apprehension of danger may arise long before the officer is possessed of adequate information to justify taking a person into custody for the purpose of prosecuting him for a crime. Petitioner's reliance on cases which have worked out standards of reasonableness with regard to "seizures" constituting arrests and searches incident thereto is thus misplaced. It assumes that the interests sought to be vindicated and the invasions of personal security may be equated in the two cases, and thereby ignores a vital aspect of the analysis of the reasonableness of particular types of conduct under the Fourth Amendment. See Camara v. Municipal Court, supra.

Our evaluation of the proper balance that has to be struck in this type of case leads us to conclude that there must be a narrowly drawn authority to permit a reasonable search for weapons for the protection of the police officer, where he has reason to believe that he is dealing with an armed and dangerous individual, regardless of whether he has probable cause to arrest the individual for a crime. The officer need not be absolutely certain that the individual is armed; the issue is whether a reasonably prudent man in the circumstances would be warranted in the belief that his safety or that of others was in danger. Cf. Beck v. Ohio, 379 U.S. 89, 91 (1964); Brinegar v. United States, 338 U.S. 160, 174-176 (1949); Stacey v. Emery, 97 U.S. 642, 645 (1878). And in determining whether the officer acted reasonably in such circumstances, due weight must be given, not to his inchoate and unparticularized suspicion or "hunch," but to the specific reasonable inferences which he is entitled to draw from the facts in light of his experience. Cf. Brinegar v. United States supra.

We must now examine the conduct of Officer McFadden in this case to determine whether his search and seizure of petitioner were reasonable, both at their inception and as conducted. He had observed Terry, together with Chilton and another man, acting in a manner he took to be preface to a "stick-up." We think on the facts and circumstances Officer McFadden detailed before the trial judge a reasonably prudent man would have been warranted in believing petitioner was armed and thus presented a threat to the officer's safety while he was investigating his suspicious behavior. The actions of Terry and Chilton were consistent with McFadden's hypothesis that these men were contemplating a daylight robbery— which, it is reasonable to assume, would be likely to involve the use of weapons—and nothing in their conduct from the time he first noticed them until the time he confronted them and identified himself as a police officer gave him sufficient reason to negate that hypothesis. Although the trio had departed the original scene, there was nothing to indicate abandonment of an intent to commit a robbery at some point. Thus, when Officer McFadden approached the three men gathered before the display window at Zucker's store he had observed enough to make it quite reasonable to fear that they were armed; and nothing in their response to his hailing them, identifying himself as a police officer, and asking their names served to dispel that reasonable belief. We cannot say his decision at that point to seize Terry and pat his clothing for weapons was the product of a volatile or inventive imagination, or was undertaken simply as an act of harassment; the record evidences the tempered act of a policeman who in the course of an investigation had to make a quick decision as to how to protect himself and others from possible danger, and took limited steps to do so. The manner in which the seizure and search were conducted is, of course, as vital a part of the inquiry as whether they were warranted at all. The Fourth Amendment proceeds as much by limitations upon the scope of governmental action as by imposing preconditions upon its initiation. Compare Katz v. United States, 389 U.S. 347, 354-356 (1967). The entire deterrent purpose of the rule excluding evidence seized in violation of the Fourth Amendment rests on the assumption that "limitations upon the fruit to be gathered tend to limit the quest itself." United States v. Poller, 43 F.2d 911, 914 (C. A. 2d Cir. 1930); see, e. g., Linkletter v. Walker, 381 U.S. 618, 629-635 (1965); Mapp v. Ohio, 367 U.S. 643 (1961); Elkins v. United States, 364 U.S. 206, 216-221 (1960). Thus, evidence may not be introduced if it was discovered by means of a seizure and search which were not reasonably related in scope to the justification for their initiation. Warden v. Hayden, 387 U.S. 294, 310 (1967) (MR. JUSTICE FORTAS, concurring). We need not develop at length in this case, however, the limitations which the Fourth Amendment places upon a protective seizure and search for weapons. These limitations will have to be developed in the concrete factual circumstances of individual cases. See Sibron v. New York, post, p. 40, decided today. Suffice it to note that such a search, unlike a search without a warrant incident to a lawful arrest, is not justified by any need to prevent the disappearance or destruction of evidence of crime. See Preston v. United States, 376 U.S. 364, 367 (1964). The sole justification of the search in the present situation is the protection of the police officer and others nearby, and it must therefore be confined in scope to an intrusion reasonably designed to discover guns, knives, clubs, or other hidden instruments for the assault of the police officer.

The scope of the search in this case presents no serious problem in light of these standards. Officer McFadden patted down the outer clothing of petitioner and his two companions. He did not place his hands in their pockets or under the outer surface of their garments until he had felt weapons, and then he merely reached for and removed the guns. He never did invade Katz' person beyond the outer surfaces of his clothes, since he discovered nothing in his pat-down which might have been a weapon. Officer McFadden confined his search strictly to what was minimally necessary to learn whether the men were armed and to disarm them once he discovered the weapons. He did not conduct a general exploratory search for whatever evidence of criminal activity he might find.

We conclude that the revolver seized from Terry was properly admitted in evidence against him. At the time he seized petitioner and searched him for weapons, Officer McFadden had reasonable grounds to believe that petitioner was armed and dangerous, and it was necessary for the protection of himself and others to take swift measures to discover the true facts and neutralize the threat of harm if it materialized. The policeman carefully restricted his search to what was appropriate to the discovery of the particular items which he sought. Each case of this sort will, of course, have to be decided on its own facts. We merely hold today that where a police officer observes unusual conduct which leads him reasonably to conclude in light of his experience that criminal activity may be afoot and that the persons with whom he is dealing may be armed and presently dangerous, where in the course of investigating this behavior he identifies himself as a policeman and makes reasonable inquiries, and where nothing in the initial stages of the encounter serves to dispel his reasonable fear for his own or others' safety, he is entitled for the protection of himself and others in the area to conduct a carefully limited search of the outer clothing of such persons in an attempt to discover weapons which might be used to assault him. Such a search is a reasonable search under the Fourth Amendment, and any weapons seized may properly be introduced in evidence against the person from whom they were taken.

Affirmed.

MR. JUSTICE BLACK concurs in the judgment and the opinion except where the opinion quotes from and relies upon this Court's opinion in Katz v. United States and the concurring opinion in Warden v. Hayden.

CONCUR BY: HARLAN; WHITE

CONCUR

MR. JUSTICE HARLAN, concurring.

While I unreservedly agree with the Court's ultimate holding in this case, I am constrained to fill in a few gaps, as I see them, in its opinion. I do this because what is said by this Court today will serve as initial guidelines for law enforcement authorities and courts throughout the land as this important new field of law develops.

A police officer's right to make an on-the-street "stop" and an accompanying "frisk" for weapons is of course bounded by the protections afforded by the Fourth and Fourteenth Amendments. The Court holds, and I agree, that while the right does not depend upon possession by the officer of a valid warrant, nor upon the existence of probable cause, such activities must be reasonable under the circumstances as the officer credibly relates them in court. Since the question in this and most cases is whether evidence produced by a frisk is admissible, the problem is to determine what makes a frisk reasonable.

If the State of Ohio were to provide that police officers could, on articulable suspicion less than probable cause, forcibly frisk and disarm persons thought to be carrying concealed weapons, I would have little doubt that action taken pursuant to such authority could be constitutionally reasonable. Concealed weapons create an immediate and severe danger to the public, and though that danger might not warrant routine general weapons checks, it could well warrant action on less than a "probability." I mention this line of analysis because I think it vital to point out that it cannot be applied in this case. On the record before us Ohio has not clothed its policemen with routine authority to frisk and disarm on suspicion; in the absence of state authority, policemen have no more right to "pat down" the outer clothing of passers-by, or of persons to whom they address casual questions, than does any other citizen. Consequently, the Ohio courts did not rest the constitutionality of this frisk upon any general authority in Officer McFadden to take reasonable steps to protect the citizenry, including himself, from dangerous weapons.

The state courts held, instead, that when an officer is lawfully confronting a possibly hostile person in the line of duty he has a right, springing only from the necessity of the situation and not from any broader right to disarm, to frisk for his own protection. This holding, with which I agree and with which I think the Court agrees, offers the only satisfactory basis I can think of for affirming this conviction. The holding has, however, two logical corollaries that I do not think the Court has fully expressed.

In the first place, if the frisk is justified in order to protect the officer during an encounter with a citizen, the officer must first have constitutional grounds to insist on an encounter, to make a forcible stop. Any person, including a policeman, is at liberty to avoid a person he considers dangerous. If and when a policeman has a right instead to disarm such a person for his own protection, he must first have a right not to avoid him but to be in his presence. That right must be more than the liberty (again, possessed by every citizen) to address questions to other persons, for ordinarily the person addressed has an equal right to ignore his interrogator and walk away; he certainly need not submit to a frisk for the questioner's protection. I would make it perfectly clear that the right to frisk in this case depends upon the reasonableness of a forcible stop to investigate a suspected crime.

Where such a stop is reasonable, however, the right to frisk must be immediate and automatic if the reason for the stop is, as here, an articulable suspicion of a crime of violence. Just as a full search incident to a lawful arrest requires no additional justification, a limited frisk incident to a lawful stop must often be rapid and routine. There is no reason why an officer, rightfully but forcibly confronting a person suspected of a serious crime, should have to ask one question and take the risk that the answer might be a bullet.

The facts of this case are illustrative of a proper stop and an incident frisk. Officer McFadden had no probable cause to arrest Terry for anything, but he had observed circumstances that would reasonably lead an experienced, prudent policeman to suspect that Terry was about to engage in burglary or robbery.

His justifiable suspicion afforded a proper constitutional basis for accosting Terry, restraining his liberty of movement briefly, and addressing questions to him, and Officer McFadden did so. When he did, he had no reason whatever to suppose that Terry might be armed, apart from the fact that he suspected him of planning a violent crime. McFadden asked Terry his name, to which Terry "mumbled something." Whereupon McFadden, without asking Terry to speak louder and without giving him any chance to explain his presence or his actions, forcibly frisked him.

I would affirm this conviction for what I believe to be the same reasons the Court relies on. I would, however, make explicit what I think is implicit in affirmance on the present facts. Officer McFadden's right to interrupt Terry's freedom of movement and invade his privacy arose only because circumstances warranted forcing an encounter with Terry in an effort to prevent or investigate a crime. Once that forced encounter was justified, however, the officer's right to take suitable measures for his own safety followed automatically.

Upon the foregoing premises, I join the opinion of the Court.

MR. JUSTICE WHITE, concurring.

I join the opinion of the Court, reserving judgment, however, on some of the Court's general remarks about the scope and purpose of the exclusionary rule which the Court has fashioned in the process of enforcing the Fourth Amendment.

Also, although the Court puts the matter aside in the context of this case, I think an additional word is in order concerning the matter of interrogation during an investigative stop. There is nothing in the Constitution which prevents a policeman from addressing questions to anyone on the streets. Absent special circumstances, the person approached may not be detained or frisked but may refuse to cooperate and go on his way. However, given the proper circumstances, such as those in this case, it seems to me the person may be briefly detained against his will while pertinent questions are directed to him. Of course, the person stopped is not obliged to answer, answers may not be compelled, and refusal to answer furnishes no basis for an arrest, although it may alert the officer to the need for continued observation. In my view, it is temporary detention, warranted by the circumstances, which chiefly justifies the protective frisk for weapons. Perhaps the frisk itself, where proper, will have beneficial results whether questions are asked or not. If weapons are found, an arrest will follow. If none are found, the frisk may nevertheless serve preventive ends because of its unmistakable message that suspicion has been aroused. But if the investigative stop is sustainable at all, constitutional rights are not necessarily violated if pertinent questions are asked and the person is restrained briefly in the process.

DISSENT BY: DOUGLAS

DISSENT

MR. JUSTICE DOUGLAS, dissenting.

I agree that petitioner was "seized" within the meaning of the Fourth Amendment. I also agree that frisking petitioner and his companions for guns was a "search." But it is a mystery how that "search" and that "seizure" can be constitutional by Fourth Amendment standards, unless there was "probable cause" to believe that (1) a crime had been committed or (2) a crime was in the process of being committed or (3) a crime was about to be committed.

The opinion of the Court disclaims the existence of "probable cause." If loitering were in issue and that was the offense charged, there would be "probable cause" shown. But the crime here is carrying concealed weapons; and there is no basis for concluding that the officer had "probable cause" for believing that that crime was being committed. Had a warrant been sought, a magistrate would, therefore, have been unauthorized to issue one, for he can act only if there is a showing of "probable cause." We hold today that the police have greater authority to make a "seizure" and conduct a "search" than a judge has to authorize such action. We have said precisely the opposite over and over again.

In other words, police officers up to today have been permitted to effect arrests or searches without warrants only when the facts within their personal knowledge would satisfy the constitutional standard of probable cause. At the time of their "seizure" without a warrant they must possess facts concerning the person arrested that would have satisfied a magistrate that "probable cause" was indeed present. The term "probable cause" rings a bell of certainty that is not sounded by phrases such as "reasonable suspicion." Moreover, the meaning of "probable cause" is deeply imbedded in our constitutional history. As we stated in Henry v. United States, 361 U.S. 98, 100–102:

"The requirement of probable cause has roots that are deep in our history. The general warrant, in which the name of the person to be arrested was left blank, and the writs of assistance, against which James Otis inveighed, both perpetuated the oppressive practice of allowing the police to arrest and search on suspicion. Police control took the place of judicial control, since no showing of 'probable cause' before a magistrate was required.

"That philosophy [rebelling against these practices] later was reflected in the Fourth Amendment. And as the early American decisions both before and immediately after its adoption show, common rumor or report, suspicion, or even 'strong reason to suspect' was not adequate to support a warrant for arrest. And that principle has survived to this day. . . .

". . . It is important, we think, that this requirement [of probable cause] be strictly enforced, for the standard set by the Constitution protects both the officer and the citizen. If the officer acts with probable cause, he is protected even though it turns out that the citizen is innocent. . . . And while a search without a warrant is, within limits, permissible if incident to a lawful arrest, if an arrest without a warrant is to support an incidental search, it must be made with probable cause. . . . This immunity of officers cannot fairly be enlarged without jeopardizing the privacy or security of the citizen."

The infringement on personal liberty of any "seizure" of a person can only be "reasonable" under the Fourth Amendment if we require the police to possess "probable cause" before they seize him. Only that line draws a meaningful distinction between an officer's mere inkling and the presence of facts within the officer's personal knowledge which would convince a reasonable man that the person seized has committed, is committing, or is about to commit a particular crime. "In dealing with probable cause, . . . as the very name implies, we deal with probabilities. These are not technical; they are the factual and practical considerations of everyday life on which reasonable and prudent men, not legal technicians, act." Brinegar v. United States, 338 U.S. 160, 175.

To give the police greater power than a magistrate is to take a long step down the totalitarian path. Perhaps such a step is desirable to cope with modern forms of lawlessness. But if it is taken, it should be the deliberate choice of the people through a constitutional amendment. Until the Fourth Amendment which is closely allied with the Fifth, is rewritten, the person and the effects of the individual are beyond the reach of all government agencies until there are reasonable grounds to believe (probable cause) that a criminal venture has been launched or is about to be launched.

There have been powerful hydraulic pressures throughout our history that bear heavily on the Court to water down constitutional guarantees and give the police the upper hand. That hydraulic pressure has probably never been greater than it is today.

Yet if the individual is no longer to be sovereign, if the police can pick him up whenever they do not like the cut of his jib, if they can "seize" and "search" him in their discretion, we enter a new regime. The decision to enter it should be made only after a full debate by the people of this country.

Following is a sample brief of this case.

FACTS: An Ohio police officer noticed two men standing on a street corner in a high-crime area of town. The men were engaged in suspicious behavior. One man would walk up to a store window, look inside, and return to his companion; this happened about a dozen times. The men also spoke with a third man and then walked with him on the street. The officers suspected that the men were casing the store with the intent to rob it. The officer approached the men and asked them for their names; the men only mumbled a response. The officer then patted one of the men down and found a pistol. He charged the man with carrying a concealed weapon. The man moved to suppress the pistol as being seized illegally. The trial judge denied the motion to suppress, the Ohio Court of Appeals affirmed the trial court's ruling, and the Ohio State Supreme Court dismissed the appeal. The case was then considered by the United States Supreme Court.

ISSUE: Can a police officer conduct a limited pat down of a person, searching for weapons, when the person is acting suspiciously in a high crime area but when no probable cause exists for arrest?

HOLDING: An officer may conduct a carefully limited search of a person for weapons if has "reasonable suspicion" that the person is armed and dangerous.

RATIONALE: The government's interest in preventing harm to the public must be balanced against a person's right not to be searched. However, if a police officer can point to specific and articulable facts that justify the intrusion, a search can be conducted. The government has a legitimate interest in preventing and detecting potential crime. Police officers need to protect themselves and others in situations in which they do not have probable cause but they believe that danger might be present owing to a person being armed. In this case, nothing that the defendant or his comrades did dispelled the officer's belief that the defendant was not on the street for a legitimate purpose.

Concurring opinions stated that a police officer has a right to frisk a suspect if he suspects a crime of violence is about to ensue.

A dissenting opinion stated that the majority decision gave a policeman more authority to make a seizure and conduct a search than a judge has and that it is appropriate to infringe upon a person's personal liberty only if probable cause is present.

GLOSSARY

absolute privilege This right is granted to allow statements without the risk of incurring punishment or legal action, such as defamation, even if they were made maliciously, including statements made in court and as part of the legislative process.

affidavit of probable cause This document is a statement of all the information that the officer knows either from personal observation or from the investigation she has conducted in connection with a particular crime that leads her to believe that it is necessary to search a particular place for certain items.

allocatur When the state supreme court agrees to hear and make a ruling on an appeal; it is the state equivalent of a petition for certiorari.

anticipatory search warrant This is an exception that permits a person to obtain a search warrant when the establishment of probable cause is not actual, but anticipated.

Articles of Confederation Approved in 1781, they set forth the structure for the new government, allowing the states to retain some power while also delegating power to what has become the federal government, which in turn allowed the government to be centralized while maintaining the individual governments established in the colonies, which later became states.

bail This device is used by courts to allow persons charged with a crime to be released by posting financial security or agreeing to certain terms of release.

basis of knowledge prong This prong considers how the individual who is providing the hearsay information obtained his information. This prong can also be satisfied with the "self-verifying" detail.

bench warrant This type of arrest warrant can be issued when a defendant does not show up for a hearing, and the court has held that person in contempt of court.

beyond a reasonable doubt The burden of proof needed for conviction in a criminal trial, based on the evidence presented at trial.

Bill of Rights The first ten amendments to the Constitution, guaranteeing certain basic civil liberties.

Blockburger rule This rule states that a person cannot be convicted of a charge that has the same elements as another charge; however, a defendant can be tried for two charges that seem similar as long as each charge has one element that the other does not.

booking This process involves gathering information about a person, such as birth date, address, and so on, to properly admit them to the prison system.

burden of proof This term refers to how much evidence a jury needs in order to find a person liable, and is different from criminal and civil cases.

change of venire A change to a new panel of jurors (venire) who are brought in from outside the area to hear a case.

change of venue A change of location (venue) for a trial so that a jury from outside the area hears a case.

common law Law made by the court in an area in which the legislature has not passed a law.

concurring opinion Written opinion issued by a Supreme Court justice when a justice agrees on the result, but not the reasoning, of a Court ruling.

consent decrees Agreements between an agency and the courts in which an agency agrees to abide by certain rules; they require agencies to provide certain training for their police officers along with the promise that the department would consider racial profiling issues in establishing policies.

crime control model This model is based on the concept that crime control is of the utmost importance and should be the focus of the Court in making decisions in cases in which criminal procedure is an issue; advocates of this model are concerned with moving cases efficiently and quickly through the criminal justice system, and believe that the accused party must be guilty, and thus their cases should not be particularly concerned with procedure and process.

curtilage The area connected to a home where the intimate activities of life take place.

defamation The action of making a statement in a form that damages a person's good reputation; libel or slander.

direct information This type of evidence includes a person's prior criminal record, an observation of furtive conduct, admissions made to a police officer, associations with other known criminals, and physical evidence.

discovery The process of obtaining information from the other side regarding the specific evidence that each side holds, as well as the identities of any witnesses that will be used by either party. The prosecution does not have as much right to receive information from the defendant as the defendant does from the prosecution, because the burden of proof lies with the prosecution.

dissenting opinion Written opinion of the Supreme Court justices who oppose the majority ruling.

due process This practice assures that certain procedures are followed before a court can take away someone's right or impose penalties upon that person, and consists of substantive and procedural due process.

due process model This model focuses on human rights and freedoms, and assumes that all individuals are innocent until proven guilty. Advocates of this model argue that the most important characteristic of our justice system is the right of all people to be free from governmental interference, and that this consideration should be the focus at all levels.

Electronic Communications Act This act supplemented the wiretap act, and provides similar rules for the interception of electronic communications such as those from computers when they are being transferred. It does not affect the seizure of electronic communications that have already been sent and are being stored, for example, on the hard drive of a computer.

establishment clause This clause of the First Amendment prohibits Congress from passing laws that establish a national religion or require a person to practice a certain religion.

evanescent evidence Evidence such as a suspect's blood alcohol level or other quick-to-be-destroyed evidence.

exclusionary rule This rule, which provides for the exclusion of evidence that was obtained by law enforcement agencies in violation of the Fourth Amendment, was adopted by the Supreme Court for federal cases in 1886 and later extended to the state level with the **Mapp v. Ohio** case in 1961. It protects against the use of illegally seized evidence in trial, protecting Fourth Amendment rights of those who are charged with crimes.

exculpatory evidence Any evidence held by the prosecution that might be helpful to the defense; the prosecution has an obligation to turn over all exculpatory evidence to the defense.

executive branch Branch of government developed in Article II of the Constitution, referring to the office of the president.

exigent circumstances Circumstances under which law enforcement personnel may enter a building or other structure without a search warrant, acting on the basis that people are in imminent danger, evidence is about to be destroyed, or that a suspect is going to escape.

expectation of privacy This ruling was the extension of the right to privacy in specific places, such as houses, and recognizes that individuals should have a reasonable expectation of privacy in certain situations and locales.

Federal Bail Reform Act of 1984 This act provided that in the federal system, judges could revoke pretrial release for firearms possession, failure to comply with curfew, and failure to comply with other conditions. Further, any person who might be at risk of fleeing or posing a danger to any person in the community could be held for ten days; the act also provides for indefinite detention of certain persons, following a hearing.

free exercise clause This clause of the First Amendment permits a person to believe and practice any religion she wishes.

fruit of the poisonous tree doctrine This doctrine provides that evidence that is obtained as a result of evidence discovered in an illegal initial search will also be excluded from court.

general deterrence If evidence is excluded in a case and all officers become concerned enough to change their actions so that the same thing does not happen in any of their cases, this process would be considered general deterrence.

general warrants These documents allowed local law enforcement to enter and search the homes of colonists in order to look for books and papers that were being used to criticize the government.

Great Compromise This agreement allowed both types of representation—based on population but also equal votes per state—with the House of Representatives being selected based on population and the Senate based on equal representation; it also adopted a system based on shared power between legislative, executive, and judicial branches.

habeas corpus Literally meaning "to have the body," this term refers to the wrongful imprisonment of an individual.

harmless error An error, such as the introduction of inadmissible evidence into a trial, that does not have an adverse effect on the outcome of the trial.

harmless error rule This doctrine mandates that even if the prosecutor makes a statement that is inappropriate or unethical, or if there is an erroneous ruling regarding evidence entered into trial, the case will be reversed only if the court finds that the evidence actually changed the outcome of the trial.

hearsay information Information provided by witnesses and not known first hand by the officer in charge of a case.

hung jury If the jury is absolutely unable to reach a decision in the case, a hung jury will result. When a jury is hung, it is indicating that it does not believe that a decision will ever be reached. The jury is dismissed, and the prosecutor will have to decide whether or not to retry the defendant. A hung jury is not a case of double jeopardy.

implied acquittal Under this doctrine, a conviction of one charge constitutes an acquittal of all other charges based upon the same facts, thus preventing the defendant from being retried on the other charges.

independent source doctrine An exception to the exclusionary rule, this doctrine applies when a prosecutor can prove to the court that the evidence challenged by the defendant was not obtained as a result of the initial illegal search.

indictment This is the actual piece of paper that a prosecutor gives to the grand jury that charges a person with a crime.

inevitable discovery This rule states that if police were sure to have discovered the evidence in some other manner notwithstanding the illegal seizure, the evidence can be admitted.

inventory searches Searches that occur when the police examine the contents of a vehicle designated to be stored on the police impound lot, or examine the personal items of a defendant upon arrest.

investigatory stops These stops are made when an officer suspects criminal behavior. The Court has ruled that the whole picture must be taken into account, and that based on that picture, the detaining officers must have a particularized and objective basis for suspecting the person of criminal activity.

judicial branch Branch of government responsible for legal actions, established in Article III of the Constitution, which specifically created the Supreme Court as the highest court in the United States.

jury nullification In this process the jury can choose, through their actions, to nullify a law that they believe to be unfair, when they acquit a defendant whom they believe to be guilty of breaking that law.

legislative branch Law-making branch of government developed in Article I of the Constitution that is Congress, including the House of Representatives and the Senate.

libel Publishing written words that defame someone.

lineup This process of identification uses a group of possible suspects, often similar in physical characteristics to the described perpetrator, presented side by side for the witness or victim to identify.

majority opinion The written decision of at least five of the nine Supreme Court justices.

mere encounter Police interaction with the public in which a police officer has the authority to ask someone questions in order to conduct an investigation.

Miranda rights These rights include the right to remain silent, the consequences of giving up that right, and the right to counsel.

Miranda warnings Also known as **Miranda** rights, this statement must be issued by officers to suspects, when they are placed under arrest, to inform them of their Fifth Amendment rights not to incriminate themselves. ("You have the right to remain silent. . . .")

New Jersey Plan Resolution proposed at the Constitutional Convention calling for a similar government structure to the Articles of Confederation, and supported by many of the smaller states.

open fields Any place beyond the area of a home where the intimate activities of life take place.

peremptory challenges Each side in a voir dire is given a certain number of challenges to use in selecting (or removing) potential jurors from the pool. Peremptory challenges can remove a potential juror without giving a particular reason or cause for their removal.

petition for certiorari This petition is filed when a defendant or the commonwealth/government loses a case and either party wishes to appeal the decision; it is a request for an appellate court to agree to consider and make a ruling on the case.

photographic array A series of photographs that are shown to a victim or witness for the purpose of identifying the perpetrator of a criminal act.

plain feel rule This doctrine allows an officer to identify an object as being contraband based simply on touching the item, as in a pat-down search, without visual confirmation of the object.

plain view This doctrine states that an officer may seize anything that is clearly in her field of vision, regardless of probable cause or permission to search by owner.

plurality opinion An opinion for which the rationales clearly differ but the justices reached the same result.

preliminary arraignment At this stage of the proceedings, an individual is notified as to why he is being detained, and he may be given information regarding his right to counsel.

preponderance of the evidence The burden of proof needed in a civil trial to convince the jury that the accused did in fact perpetrate the actions attributed to him, based on the evidence presented at trial.

procedural law Any legal rules that tell courts and attorneys how to proceed with a case, including the "rules of evidence."

protective sweep A search of the area of the person's arm span, the area under their control when they are being arrested, and the area surrounding the arrestee.

qualified immunity This defense can be used by officials to protect them from being sued; it applies whenever an official acts with a mistaken belief, as long as that belief is reasonable.

qualified privilege This defense permits persons in positions of authority or trust to make statements that would be considered slander and libel if made by anyone else. Such immunity is often used by journalists who have written an article and believe that certain facts should be known in the public interest, and as long as the statement by the journalist has not been made with malicious intent, the journalist will be immune from suit.

release on recognizance (ROR) The release of a defendant without monetary bond, based on his standing in the community. The defendant pledges to appear for any court proceedings scheduled for the future.

roving wiretaps These surveillance orders do not specify all of the carriers and third parties that are involved in the surveillance, but rather they are attached to the individual the law enforcement agency wishes to eavesdrop upon.

seizure When a person or property is taken into custody. Two things may be seized: people and property. Property is seized when there is some meaningful interference with an individual's possessory interest in that property. A person is seized when a police officer accosts an individual and restrains his freedom to walk away.

sequestered When a jury is kept in a hotel, isolated from the press and outside world, for the duration of the trial, to avoid any bias from forming in the minds of the jurors regarding the case.

showup This process is similar to a lineup, but with only one person, the suspect, being presented to the victim or witness for identification.

silver platter doctrine This doctrine referred to the fact that defendants in federal court had the benefit of exclusionary rule while those in state courts did not.

slander False spoken statements that defame someone.

Son of Sam law This New York State law required that any proceeds from a criminal's book should be turned over to the Crime Victims' Board for five years after publication. It was struck down by the Court as unconstitutional.

specific deterrence If a particular officer violates the Constitution and the evidence obtained by him is excluded, and he decides not to violate the law in the future, this process would be considered specific deterrence.

standby counsel When a defendant wants to represent himself, but the court is not convinced that he can do so effectively, the Court may appoint a standby counsel, who is an attorney who sits with the defendant in court and aids in the raising of objections and questioning of witnesses, if necessary.

standing The ability of an individual or other entity to bring an action or challenge evidence in court.

statute of limitations This doctrine determines the amount of time a prosecuting agency has to prosecute a particular crime.

statutory law Law passed by legislature.

stop and seizure It is sometimes difficult to determine when a stop becomes a seizure, but the determining factor is whether a reasonable person would feel free to leave. Probable cause must exist to execute a seizure. A seizure may take place in one of two ways, through physical force by the officer, or by an officer's show of authority. Generally, a seizure take place while a person is in motion, either on foot or in a vehicle, but an officer can also seize a person when the person is sitting or standing still.

Strickland test This two–part test was set forth by the Court to determine the effectiveness of counsel. First, the Court must determine whether the counsel's actions were actually deficient. If so, then the defendant must show that it was the counsel's deficient actions that altered the outcome of the trial in a negative manner.

substantive law Guarantees that citizens' liberty will be protected, according to the Fourteenth Amendment.

totality of the circumstances This test for probable cause states that both the veracity and basis of knowledge prongs of the hearsay evidence test need not be satisfied to prove probable cause if the rest of the available evidence suggests that there is sufficient reason to suspect criminal activity.

USA Patriot Act The Uniting and Strengthening America by Providing Appropriate Tools Required to Intercept and Obstruct Terrorism Act, passed in 2001, reduced restrictions placed on the ability of law enforcement agencies to search telephone and email communications and medical, financial, and other records, and eased prior restrictions on foreign intelligence gathering.

veracity prong This prong means that the magistrate must determine why she should believe a person, based on the credibility of the witness and the information being provided.

Virginia Resolution Resolution proposed at the Constitutional Convention calling for a national government with a legislature, executive branch, and judicial branch.

voir dire This is the process of jury selection, including the interviewing of members of the jury pool, along with the right to peremptory challenges and challenges "for cause" to remove certain jurors from the pool.

waiver of right to counsel A defendant has the right to choose not to have counsel represent him at any point of the proceedings; however, judges prefer that defendants be represented by counsel, and a defendant will have to prove that he is knowingly and intelligently waiving his right to counsel.

warrantless searches The scope of a warrantless search allows the officers to search beyond the individual being taken into custody, and usually includes the person's arm span or grabbing area.

writs of assistance These documents allowed individuals to enter and search the homes of colonists, generally for no reason at all, to assist the British government in searching for smuggled goods.